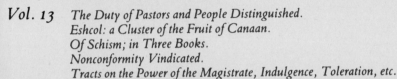

The Works of John Owen

VOLUME XX

The Works of
JOHN OWEN

EDITED BY
William H. Goold

VOLUME XX

The Banner of Truth Trust

THE BANNER OF TRUTH TRUST

Head Office
3 Murrayfield Road
Edinburgh
EH12 6EL
UK

North America Sales
PO Box 621
Carlisle
PA 17013
USA

bonneroftruth.org

This edition of *The Works Of John Owen* first published by
Johnstone & Hunter, 1854-55

Reprinted by the Banner of Truth Trust, 1991
Reprinted 2010, 2018, 2023

VOLUME XX

*

ISBN
This volume (HEBREWS 4): 978 0 85151 615 8
7-volume set: 978 0 85151 619 6

*

Printed in the USA by
Versa Press Inc.,
East Peoria, IL.

AN

EXPOSITION

OF THE

EPISTLE TO THE HEBREWS.

WITH

PRELIMINARY EXERCITATIONS.

BY JOHN OWEN, D.D.

EDITED BY W. H. GOOLD, D.D.

VOL. IV.

QVÆRAMVS

SVPERNA

EDINBURGH:

JOHNSTONE AND HUNTER.

M.DCCC.LIV.

AN EXPOSITION

OF THE

EPISTLE TO THE HEBREWS.

CHAPTER III.

VERSES 7–11.

HAVING demonstrated the pre-eminence of the Lord Christ above Moses in their respective ministries about the house of God, the apostle, according unto his design and method, proceeds unto the application of the truth he had evinced, in an exhortation unto stability and constancy in faith and obedience. And this he doth in a way that adds a double force to his inference and exhortation; —first, in that he presseth them with the *words*, testimonies, and examples recorded in the Old Testament, unto which they owned an especial reverence and subjection; and then the nature of the *examples* which he insists upon is such as supplies him with a new argument unto his purpose. Now this is taken from the dealing of God with them who were disobedient under the ministry and rule of Moses; which he further explains, verses 15–19. For if God dealt in severity with them who were unbelieving and disobedient with respect unto him and his work who was but a servant in the house, they might easily understand what his dispensation towards them would be who should be so with respect unto the Son and his work, who is Lord over the whole house, and "whose house are we."

Ver. 7–11.—Διὸ, καθὼς λέγει τὸ Πνεῦμα τὸ ἅγιον· Σήμερον, ἐὰν τῆς φωνῆς αὐτοῦ ἀκούσητε, μὴ σκληρύνητε τὰς καρδίας ὑμῶν, ὡς ἐν τῷ παραπικρασμῷ, κατὰ τὴν ἡμέραν τοῦ πειρασμοῦ ἐν τῇ ἐρήμῳ, οὗ ἐπείρασάν με οἱ πατέρες ὑμῶν, ἐδοκίμασάν με, καὶ εἶδον τὰ ἔργα μου, τεσσαράκοντα ἔτη. Διὸ προσώχθισα τῇ γενεᾷ ἐκείνῃ, καὶ εἶπον· Ἀεὶ πλανῶνται τῇ καρδίᾳ· αὐτοὶ δὲ οὐκ ἔγνωσαν τὰς ὁδούς μου. Ὡς ὤμοσα ἐν τῇ ὀργῇ μου· Εἰ εἰσελεύσονται εἰς τὴν κατάπαυσίν μου.

There are some little varieties in some words and letters observed in some old manuscripts, but of no importance or use, and for the most part mere mistakes; as ἐνδοκίμασαν for ἐδοκίμασαν, ταύτῃ for ἐκείνῃ, εἶπα for εἶπον; as many such differences occur, where some have tampered to make the apostle's words and the translation of the LXX. in all things to agree.

Καθώς, "sicut;" the Syriac and Arabic translations omit this word. "Wherefore the Holy Ghost saith." Ὡς ἐν τῷ παραπικρασμῷ. So the LXX. in the psalm, "sicut in exacerbatione," "in irritatione,"—"in the provocation." Syr., "ut ad iram eum provocetis tanquam exacerbatores," both in the psalm and here also, departing both from the Hebrew text and the apostolical version,—"that you stir him not up to anger as provokers." Κατὰ τὴν ἡμέραν τοῦ πειρασμοῦ. So the LXX. in the psalm. Vulg., "secundum diem tentationis,"—"according to the day of temptation;" that is, as those others, the fathers of the people, did in the day of temptation: so also in this place following the LXX. in the psalm, though not only the original but that version also might more properly be rendered, "sicut in die tentationis," "as in the day of temptation." Οὗ ἐπείρασαν. The translator of the Syriac version in the psalm, "qua tentarunt," that is, "qua die;" referring it unto the time of the temptation, "the day wherein." Here "quum," "when," to the same purpose. Neither was there any need of the variety of expression, the word used by that translator in both places being the same, referring unto time, not place,—the day of temptation, not the wilderness wherein it was. Vulg., "ubi," properly "where;" as the Arabic, "in quo," "in which,"—"desert," the next antecedent. Ethiop , "Eo quod tentarunt eum patres vestri, tentarunt me,"—"Whereas your fathers tempted him, they tempted me." For it was Christ who was tempted in the wilderness, 1 Cor. x. 9.

"Saw my works τεσσαράκοντα ἔτη,"—"forty years." Here the apostle completes the sense; for although sundry editions of the New Testament, as one by Stephen, and one by Plantin, out of one especial copy, place the period at ἔργα μου, "my works," yet the insertion of διό after τεσσαράκοντα ἔτη by the apostle, proves the sense by him there to be concluded. So is it likewise by the Syriac in the psalm, and by all translations in this place. However, the Ethiopic, omitting διό, seems to intend another sense. The LXX. and Vulgar Latin in the psalm follow the original; though some copies of the LXX. have been tampered withal, to bring them to conformity with the apostle here, as usually it hath fallen out. And there is no doubt but that the order of the words in the Syriac version on the psalm came from this place.

Προσώχθισα, "offensus fui," "incensus fui;" Arab., "exsecratus sum,"—"I cursed this generation."

Ἀεὶ πλανῶνται. The original in the psalm, עַם זֶה,[1] "this people," which in the psalm is followed by the Syriac; and, contrary to the apostle, the same expression is retained in that version on this place. The LXX. in the psalm have taken in these words of the apostle, and left out those of the original; wherein they are (as almost constantly in the Psalms) followed by the Vulgar Latin.

Διό, "wherefore." It expresseth an inference from what was spoken before, manifesting the ensuing exhortation to be deduced from thence. And it hath respect unto the exhortation itself which the apostle directly enters upon, verse 12, "Take heed, brethren,"—'Wherefore take heed, brethren.' There is therefore a hyperbaton in the discourse, the words that agree in sense being separated by an interposition of other things; and there is between them a digression to an example or argument for the better enforcement of the exhortation itself.

Καθὼς λέγει τὸ Πνεῦμα τὸ ἅγιον, "as the Holy Ghost saith;" or, 'that I may use the words of the Holy Ghost.' There is an emphasis in the manner of the expression,—τὸ Πνεῦμα τὸ ἅγιον, "that Holy Spirit;" so called κατ᾽ ἐξοχήν, by

---

[1] The Hebrew in the psalm is in reality עַם לֵבָב.—ED.

way of eminency, the third person in the Trinity, who in an especial manner spake in the penmen of the Scripture. Those holy men of God spake ὑπὸ Πνεύματος ἁγίου Φερόμενοι, "moved," "acted," "inspired by the Holy Ghost," 2 Pet. i. 21.

Καθὼς λέγει, "as he saith." This may intend either his first immediate speaking in his inspiration of the psalmist, as it is expressed, chap. iv. 7, ἐν Δαβὶδ λέγων, "saying in David," where these words are again repeated; or his continuing still to speak these words to us all in the Scripture. Being given out by inspiration from him, and his authority always accompanying them, he still speaketh them.

The words reported by the apostle are taken from Ps. xcv. 7-11. He mentions not the especial place, as speaking unto them who either were, or whom he would have to be exercised in the word, 2 Tim. iii. 15. Besides, though such particular citations of places may be needful for us, for a present help unto them that hear or read, it was not so to the holy penmen of the New Testament, whose writings are continually to be searched and meditated upon all our lives, John v. 39. Whereas ours are transient and for the present occasion, every thing in their writings (which makes us attentive and industrious in our search) is to our advantage. The leaving, therefore, of an uncertainty whence particular quotations are taken is useful to make us more sedulous in our inquiries.

This psalm the apostle makes use of both in this chapter and the next. In this, he manifests it to contain a useful and instructive example, in what happened unto the people of God of old. In the next, he shows that not only a moral example may be taken from what so fell out, but also that there was a type in the things mentioned in it (and that according unto God's appointment) of our state and condition; and moreover, a prophecy of the gospel state of the church under the Messiah, and the blessed rest therein to be obtained. Here we have the consideration of it as historical and exemplary; in the next we shall treat of it as prophetical.

The Jews had a tradition that this psalm belonged unto the Messiah. Hence the Targum renders these words of the first verse, לְצוּר יִשְׁעֵנוּ, "to the rock of our salvation," קֳדָם תְּקִיף פּוּרְקָנָא, "before the mighty one of our redemption;" with respect unto the redemption to be wrought by the Messiah, whom they looked for as the Redeemer, Luke xxiv. 21. So ver. 7, יוֹמָא דֵין, "in that day," seems to refer unto the same season. And the ancient Jews do frequently apply these words, "To-day, if ye will hear his voice," unto the Messiah. For from these words they have framed a principle, that if all Israel would repent but one day the Messiah would come, because it is said, "To-day, if ye will hear his voice." So in the Talmud. Tract. Taanith., distinc. Mamarai Maskirin. And the same words they used in Midrash Shirhashirim, cap. v. ver. 2. And this is no small witness against them as to the person of the Messiah; for he is God undoubtedly concerning whom the psalmist speaks, as is evident from verses 2–7. He whose voice they are to hear, whom they acknowledge to be the Messiah, is "Jehovah, the great God," verse 3; "who made the sea, and formed the dry land," verse 5; "the LORD our maker," verse 6. And indeed this psalm, with those that follow unto the 104th, is evidently of those new songs which belong unto the kingdom of the Messiah. And this is among the Jews the שִׁיר חָדָשׁ, or principal "new song," expressing that renovation of all things which under it they expect. The next psalm expresseth it: "Sing unto the LORD שִׁיר חָדָשׁ," "a new song." מִזְמוֹר זֶה עַל הֶעָתִיד, saith Rashi, "This psalm is for the time to come;" that is, the days of the Messiah. Σήμερον, הַיּוֹם, "hodie," "to-day," "this day." A certain day or space of time is limited or determined, as the apostle speaks in the next chapter. And the psalm being in part, as was showed, prophetical, it must have a various application; for it both expresseth what was then done and spoken in the type, with regard to what was before as the foundation of all, and intimateth what should afterwards be accomplished in the time prefigured, in what the words have respect unto as past.

The general foundation of all lies in this, that a certain limited present space of time is expressed in the words. This is the moral sense of them :—limited, because a day; present, because to-day. And this space may denote in general the continuance of men's lives in this world. הַיּוֹם; that is, saith Rashi, בעולם הזה, "in this world," in this life: afterwards there will be neither time nor place for this duty. But yet the measure of such a day is not merely our continuance in a capacity to enjoy it, but the will of God to continue it. It is God's day that is intended, and not ours, which we may outlive, and lose the benefit of it, as will afterwards appear.

Again, the general sense of the word is limited to a special season, both then present when the words were spoken, and intimated in prophecy to come afterwards. For the present, or David's time, that refers, saith Aben Ezra, to בֹּאוּ נִשְׁתַּחֲוֶה, "come, let us fall down and worship," verse 6; as if he had said, ' If you will hear his voice, come and worship before him this day.' And in this sense, it is probable that some especial feast of Moses' institution, when the people assembled themselves unto the solemn worship of God, was intended. Many think that this psalm was peculiarly appointed to be sung at the feast of tabernacles. Neither is it unlikely, that feast being a great type and representation of the Son of God coming to pitch his tabernacle amongst us, John i. 14. Let this, then, pass for David's typical day. But that a farther day is intended herein the apostle declares in the next chapter. Here the proper time and season of any duty, of the great duty exhorted unto, is firstly intended, as is evident from the application that the apostle makes of this instance, verse 13, "Exhort one another daily, while it is called הַיּוֹם," σήμερον, "to-day;" that is, 'whilst the season of the duty is continued unto you.' So was it also originally used by the psalmist, and applied unto the duties of the feast of tabernacles, or some other season of the performance of God's solemn worship.

Ἐάν, "si," "if;" a mere conditional, as commonly used. But it is otherwise applied in the New Testament, as Matt. viii. 19, "I will follow thee ὅπου ἐάν ἀπέρχῃ,"—" whithersoever thou goest." And chap. xii. 36, "Every idle word ὃ ἐὰν λαλήσωσιν οἱ ἄνθρωποι,"—" which men shall speak." There is no condition or supposition included in these places, but the signification is indefinite, " whosoever," " whatsoever," " whensoever." Such may be the sense of it in this place; which would, as some suppose, remove a difficulty which is cast on the text; for make it to be merely a conditional, and this and the following clause seem to be coincident, " If ye will hear," that is, obey his voice, "harden not your hearts;" for to hear the voice of God, and the not hardening of our hearts, are the same. But there is no necessity, as we shall see, to betake ourselves unto this unusual sense of the word.

Τῆς φωνῆς αὐτοῦ ἀκούσητε,—" Ye will hear his voice :" בְּקֹלוֹ תִשְׁמָעוּ . Wherever this construction of the words doth occur in the Hebrew,—that שָׁמַע is joined with בְּקֹל, whether it be spoken of God in reference unto the voice of man, or of man in reference unto the voice of God,—the effectual doing and accomplishment of the thing spoken of is intended. So Num. xiv. 22, " They have tempted me these ten times, וְלֹא שָׁמְעוּ בְּקוֹלִי," " and have not heard my voice;" that is, ' have not yielded obedience to my command.' So of God with reference unto men: Josh. x. 14, "There was no day like that, before nor after it, לִשְׁמֹעַ יְהֹוָה בְּקוֹל אִישׁ," that " the LORD should hearken to the voice of a man;" that is, effectually to do so great a thing as to cause the sun and moon to stand still in heaven. So between man and man, Deut. xxi. 18, 19. See Matt. xviii. 15–17. It is frequently observed, that to "hear," to "hearken," in the Scripture, signifies to "obey," or to "yield obedience to the things heard ;" as to "see" doth to "understand" or

" believe," and to " taste" denotes " spiritual experience ;" words of outward sense being used to express the inward spiritual acts of the mind. Sometimes I say it is so, but this phrase is always so used. The Holy Ghost, therefore, herein lays down the duty which we owe to the word, to the voice of God, when we hear it in the way of his appointment,—that is, to yield sincere obedience unto it ; and the hinderance thereof is expressed in the next words. Now, as this command is translated over into the gospel, as it is by our apostle in the next chapter, it hath respect unto the great precept of hearing and obeying the voice of Christ, as the great prophet of the church ; given originally, Deut. xviii. 19, " Whosoever will not hearken unto my words, which he shall speak in my name" (for the Father speaketh in the Son, Heb. i. 1, 2). "I will require it of him," Acts iii. 22, 23 ; which was again solemnly renewed upon his actual exhibition : Matt. xvii. 5, " This is my beloved Son, in whom I am well pleased; hear ye him." See 2 Pet. i. 17. And he is thereon, as we have seen, compared with Moses in his prophetical office, and preferred above him, John i. 17, 18.

בְּקֹלוֹ , τῆς φωνῆς αὐτοῦ. קֹל יְהֹוָה , " the voice of the LORD," is sometimes taken for his *power*, inasmuch as by his word, as an intimation and signification of the power which he puts forth therein, he created and disposeth of all things. See Ps. xxix. 3–5, 7–9, where the mighty works of God's power and providence are assigned unto his voice. See also Mic. vi. 9. Sometimes it is used for the *revelation of his will* in his commands and promises. This is the λόγος προφορικός of God, the word of his will and pleasure. But it is withal certain that קֹל and φωνή are used principally, if not solely, for a sudden, transient voice or speaking. For the word of God as delivered in the Scripture is דָּבָר and λόγος, sometimes ῥῆμα, not קֹל or φωνή. So the lifting up of the voice amongst men, is to make some sudden outcry ; as, " They lifted up their voice and wept." These words, then, do ordinarily signify a sudden, marvellous speaking of God from heaven, testifying unto any thing. So doth φωνή, Mark i. 11, Καὶ φωνὴ ἐγένετο ἐκ τῶν οὐρανῶν,—"And there was a voice from heaven." So Matt. xvii. 5; Luke iii. 22; John xii. 28,᾽Ηλθεν οὖν φωνὴ ἐκ τοῦ οὐρανοῦ,—" There came therefore a voice from heaven:" which when the multitude heard, they said βροντὴν γεγονέναι, " that it thundered ;" for thunder was called קֹל אֱלֹהִים , " the voice of God." So the קֹלֹת , " the voices," Exod. xix. 16, that accompanied the בְּרָקִים or " lightnings," that is, the thunders that were at the giving of the law, are rendered by our apostle φωνὴ ῥημάτων, Heb. xii. 19; that is, the thunders from heaven which accompanied the words that were spoken. So is φωνή used Acts x. 13, 15, xxvi. 14. Hence came the בת קול , " Bath Kol" among the ancient Jews: or, as in the Chaldee, ברת קלא , Gen. xxxviii. 26. " There came filia vocis" (" the daughter of the voice") " from heaven." And so the Syriac version in this place : אן ברת קלה תשמעון , " if you will hear the daughter of the voice." They called it so, as being an effect or product of the power of God, to cause his mind and will to be heard and understood by it. They thought it was not the voice of God himself immediately, but as it were the echo of it,—a secondary voice, the offspring of another. And whereas they acknowledge, that after the building of the second temple the רוח נבואה, or רוח הקדוש , the " Spirit of prophecy and of inspiration," ceased in their church, they contend that revelations were made by the בת קול , or immediate voice from heaven, though they can instance in none but those which concerned our Saviour, which the apostles declared and made famous, 2 Pet. i. 17. But it may be there is that in this tradition which they understand not. Elias in his Tishbi tells us, בעלי הקבלה אומרים שהוא קול של מדה אחת מדות הנקראת קול אולי קול הוא כן הוא,—" The Cabbalists say that it is the voice of a property in God which is called Kol; and it may be it is so." They have no other way to express a person in the divine nature but by מדה , a special property. And one of these, they say, is called " Kol," that is, " the Word," the eternal Word or Son of God. His especial speaking is intended in this expression; which is true. So his speaking is called his "speaking from heaven," Heb. xii. 25; although I deny not but that the immediate speaking of the Father in reference unto the Son is sometimes so expressed, Matt. xvii. 5, 2 Pet. i. 17. But an especial, extraordinary word is usually so intended. So our Saviour tells the Pharisees, that they had not heard τὴν φωνήν, the voice of God at any time, nor seen his εἶδος, his shape, John v. 37. They had heard the voice of God in the reading and preaching of the word, but that was ὁ λόγος, "his word." His φωνήν they had not heard. Notwithstanding all their pretences and boastings, they had not at any time extraordinary revelations of God made unto them. For there is an allusion to the revelation of the will of God at Horeb, when his קֹול, or φωνή, or "voice," was heard, and his מַרְאֶה or εἶδος, his "shape," appeared, or a miraculous appearance of his presence was made; both now being accomplished in himself in a more eminent manner, as the apostle declares, John i. 16–18. It is true the Lord Christ calls his ordinary preaching, as we say, "viva voce," τὴν φωνήν, his "voice," John x. 3, 16; but this he doth because it was extraordinary, his person, work, and call being so. Wherefore the psalmist in these words, as to the historic and typical intendment of them, recalls the people unto the remembrance and consideration of God's speaking unto them in the giving of the law at Horeb, and exhorts them unto obedience unto it formally upon that consideration,—namely, that the will of God was uttered unto them in a marvellous and extraordinary manner. And as to the prophetical intendment of it, he intimates another extraordinary revelation of it, to be made by the Messiah, the Son of God.

Μὴ σκληρύνητε τὰς καρδίας ὑμῶν, אַל־תַּקְשׁוּ לְבַבְכֶם;—" Harden not your hearts." This expression is sacred; it occurs not in other authors. To harden the heart, is a thing peculiarly regarding the obedience that God requireth of us. Σκληρότης, "hardness," is indeed sometimes used in heathen writers for stubbornness of mind and manners. So Aristotle says of some that they are ὀνομαστότατοι ἐπὶ σκληρότητι, "famous for stubbornness." Such as Homer describes Achilles to have been, who had περισκελεῖς φρένας, "a hard, stubborn, inflexible mind." So is σκληροτράχηλος sometimes used, "duricervicus," "hard-necked" or "stiff-necked," "curvicervicum pecus," "a crook-necked, perverse beast." But σκληρύνω, "to harden," is scarcely used unless it be in the New Testament and in the translation of the Old by the LXX. Three times it occurs in the New Testament,— Acts xix. 9, Rom. ix. 18, and in this chapter; everywhere by Paul, so that it is a word peculiar unto him. Σκληρύνειν τὴν καρδίαν, therefore, "to harden the heart," in a moral sense, is peculiar to holy writ; and it is ascribed both to God and man, but in different senses, as we shall see afterwards. By this word the apostle expresseth קָשָׁה out of the original; that is, "to be hard, heavy, and also difficult." In Hiphil it is "to harden and make obdurate," and is used only in a moral sense. The LXX. render it constantly by σκληρύνω, "induro;" or βαρύνω, "gravo," 1 Kings xii. 4; to "harden," or to "burden." Sometimes it is used absolutely: Job ix. 4, הִקְשָׁה אֵלָיו, "hardened against him," that is, himself;— "hardened himself against him." Ofttimes it hath עֹרֶף, the "neck," added unto it: מַקְשֶׁה עֹרֶף, Prov. xxix. 1, that "stiffeneth," or "hardeneth his neck;" as one that goes on resolvedly, as will not so much as turn aside or look back towards any one that calls him. Sometimes it hath רוּחַ, the "spirit" joined to it: Deut. ii. 30, הִקְשָׁה אֶת־רוּחוֹ, "he hardened his spirit." But most commonly it hath לֵב the "heart," as here. And it still in man denotes a voluntary perverseness of mind, in not taking notice of, or not applying the soul unto the will of God as revealed, to do and observe it.

Ὡς ἐν τῷ παραπικρασμῷ, "as in the provocation;" כִּמְרִיבָה. The LXX. render this word, where it is first used, by λοιδόρησις, "convitium," "a reproach," Exod. xvii. 7; afterwards constantly by ἀντιλογία, "contradiction," or contention by words, as Num. xx. 13, xxvii. 14, Deut. xxxiii. 8; and nowhere by παρα-πικρασμός, as in this place of the psalm. Hence some suppose it is evident that the present Greek translation is not the work or endeavour of the same persons, but a cento of many essays. I rather think that we have hence a new evidence of the insertion of the apostle's words into that version; for, as I will not deny but that the writers of the New Testament might make use of that Greek version of the Old which was then extant, so that many words and expressions are taken from them, and inserted in that which we now enjoy, is too evident for any man of modesty or sobriety to deny. And this word, as here compounded, is scarce used in any other author. Πικρός is "bitter," in opposition to γλυκύς, "sweet," "pleasant;" that is the proper, natural sense of the word. So also of πικρόω and πικραίνω, "to make bitter to the taste" or sense. But the metaphorical use of these words in a moral sense is frequent for "exacerbo," "provoco." The Hebrew כָּעַס, is "to stir up to anger," "to vex," "imbitter," "provoke," as 1 Sam. i. 6. So παραπι-κρασμός must be "exacerbatio," "provocatio," an imbittering, a provocation to anger by contention: מְרִיבָה, which here is so rendered, is "jurgium," a strife agitated in words. We render it "chiding." The story which this principally refers unto is recorded, Exod. xvii. 1-7, "And they pitched in Rephidim: and there was no water for the people to drink. Wherefore the people did chide with Moses, and said, Give us water that we may drink. And Moses said unto them, Why chide ye with me? wherefore do ye tempt the LORD? And the people thirsted there for water; and the people murmured against Moses, and said, Wherefore is this that thou hast brought us up out of Egypt, to kill us and our children, and our cattle, with thirst? And Moses cried unto the LORD, saying, What shall I do unto this people? they be almost ready to stone me. And the LORD said unto Moses, Go on before the people, and take with thee of the elders of Israel; and thy rod, wherewith thou smotest the river, take in thine hand, and go. Behold, I will stand before thee there upon the rock in Horeb; and thou shalt smite the rock, and there shall come water out of it, that the people may drink. And Moses did so in the sight of the elders of Israel. And he called the name of the place Massah, and Meribah, because of the chiding of the children of Israel, and because they tempted the LORD, saying, Is the LORD among us, or not?" Another story to the like purpose we have of what befell the people in the wilderness of Zin nearly forty years afterwards, when, in their murmuring for water, another rock was smitten to bring it forth, whereon it is added, "This is the water of Meribah; because the children of Israel strove with the LORD," Num. xx. 13. It is also said on the same occasion that they "chode with Moses," verse 3.

Κατὰ τὴν ἡμέραν τοῦ πειρασμοῦ, כְּיוֹם מַסָּה;—" as in the day of Massah," or " temptation;" מַסָּה, from נָסָה, "to tempt;" the other name given to the place before mentioned in Exodus: for thence it is that the apostle takes his example, where both the names are mentioned, and where the place is said to be called Massah and Meribah; whereas in that of Numbers it is only said, "This is the water of Meribah," or strife. And yet it may be not without respect to the latter also. The first instance was at the beginning, the latter at the close of their provocations. As they began so they ended. This was a remarkable passage between God and that people; for, first, a double name is given to the place where it fell out: "He called the name of the place Massah, and Meribah," Exod. xvii. 7. Meribah, which the apostle renders παραπικρασμός, seems principally or firstly to respect Moses as the object of it : verse 2, וַיָּרֶב הָעָם עִם מֹשֶׁה, "and the people chode with Moses." Thence had the place the name of Chiding, "Meribah," from " jareb." And God was the immediate object of their temptation. So in the text there is made a distribution of these things distinctly, whence these several names arose. "And Moses said unto the people, מַה־תְּרִיבוּן עִמָּדִי מַה־תְּנַסּוּן אֶת־יְהוֹה," " Why do ye chide with me" (Meribah)? " and wherefore do ye tempt the LORD "

(Massah)? For in the same things and words wherein they chode with Moses
they tempted the Lord. And hence the same word, of chiding, striving, contending, or provoking, is used in this matter towards the Lord also: Num. xx. 13,
רָבוּ אֶת־יְהֹוָה, " they strove" (or " chode") " with the LORD."

Secondly, This matter, as a thing exceedingly remarkable, is often called over
and remembered again in the Scripture. Sometimes on the part of the people;
and that, 1. To reproach and burden them with their sins, as Deut. ix. 22, " And
at Massah ye provoked the LORD to wrath;" and sometimes, 2. To warn them of
the like miscarriages, chap. vi. 16, " Ye shall not tempt the LORD your God, as
ye tempted him in Massah." So also in the 95th Psalm, from whence the apostle
takes these words. Again, it is remembered as an instance of the faithfulness of
Levi, who clave to God in those trials: Deut. xxxiii. 8, " And of Levi he said,
Let thy Thummim and thy Urim be with thy Holy One, whom thou didst prove at
Massah, and with whom thou didst strive at the waters of Meribah."

The mercy likewise that ensued in giving them waters from the rock is frequently celebrated, Deut. viii. 15, Ps. lxxviii. 15, 16, cv. 41, Neh. ix. 15. Moreover, in this rock of Horeb lay hid a spiritual Rock, as our apostle tells us, 1 Cor.
x. 4, even Christ, the Son of God, who, being smitten with the rod of Moses, or
the stroke and curse of the law administered by him, gave out waters of life freely
to all that thirst and come unto him. In this matter, therefore, is comprehended
a great instance of providence and a great mystery of grace. But yet notwithstanding all this, although the especial denomination of the sin of the people be
taken from that instance of Exod. xvii., yet the expressions are not to be confined
or appropriated only thereunto. For the particular provocation on which God
sware against them that they should not enter into his rest fell out afterwards,
Num. xiv., as we shall see in our progress. But this is eminently referred unto,
—1. Because it was upon the very entrance of that course of provoking which
they constantly persisted in until they were consumed; 2. Because of the signal
and significant miracles and works which God wrought thereon.

Ἐν ἐρήμῳ, בַּמִּדְבָּר;—"in the desert," or "wilderness," namely, of Midian, whereinto that people entered upon their coming through the sea. In their way towards Horeb, their fourth station was at Rephidim, where the things fell out
before recounted. So they received refreshment in a type, from the spiritual
Rock, some days before the giving of the fiery law.

Οὗ ἐπείρασάν με, אֲשֶׁר נִסּוּנִי. אֲשֶׁר is referred both to time and place as well as
persons. We render οὗ here, " when,"—" when your fathers tempted me;" and
so אֲשֶׁר in the psalm; referring what is spoken to the time mentioned, or the day
of temptation. So the Syriac, "in which day." The Vulg. Lat., " ubi," " where,"
that is in the desert, at Meribah or Massah. And this is the proper signification
of the word. Nor is either οὗ or ποῦ, the interrogative, ever used in any good
authors to denote time, but place only. " Where," that is בַּמִּדְבָּר, in the wilderness, where they tempted God and saw his works forty years.

Οἱ πατέρες ὑμῶν, אֲבוֹתֵיכֶם;—" your fathers," or "forefathers;" πρόγονοι, " progenitors," 2 Tim. i. 3. So is πατέρες often used, and אָבוֹת most frequently; although in one place רִאשֹׁנִים be added : אֲבוֹתָם הָרִאשֹׁנִים, Jer. xi. 10;—the first
springs and heads of any nation or family,—the whole congregation in the wilderness, whose posterity they were.

Ἐδοκίμασάν με, בְּחָנוּנִי;—" proved me." This word is seldom used in an ill
sense, as the former is almost continually. בָּחַן is to have experience, upon search,
investigation, and trial, Ps. cxxxix. 23. The experience, therefore, that they had
of the power of God upon their temptations, is that which by this word is intended. ' They " proved me," and found by trial that I was in the midst of them.'

Καὶ εἶδον τὰ ἔργα μου, גַּם־רָאוּ פָעֳלִי;—" and saw my works." "And saw my
work," in the psalm. גַּם is rendered by καί. It signifies "also," " moreover,"

somewhat above a mere conjunction; and so doth *καί*, most frequently "quinetiam." Some suppose it may be here taken for "etsi," "etiamsi," "although." 'They tempted me, and proved me, "although they saw my works."' And so these words are placed as an aggravation of their sin in tempting of God, distrusting of him, after they had had such experience of his power and goodness, in those mighty works of his which they saw. But the order of things also seems to be intended. First they tempted God,—"They tempted me." Then they had an experience of his power,—"They proved me;" and that by the production of his mighty works which they saw. For generally all the works of God in the wilderness, whether of mercy or judgment, were consequents of, or ensued upon the people's tempting of him. Such was his bringing water out of the rock, and sending of quails and manna. The people murmured, chode, strove, tempted; then the power of God was manifested and the works were wrought which they saw. So were the judgments that he wrought and executed on Korah, Dathan, and Abiram; and on the spies that brought up an evil report on the land, with those that adhered unto them. This order and method of things is here expressed. They tempted God by their complaints, repinings, murmurings, seditions, unbelief, weariness of their condition, with impatient desires and wishings after other things. Hereupon they had frequent trials of the power, care, and faithfulness of God; as also of his holiness, and indignation against their sins. All these were made manifest in the mighty works of providence, in mercies and judgments which he wrought amongst them, and which they saw. They had them not by report or tradition, but saw them with their own eyes, which was a great aggravation of their unbelief. Jarchi refers this to the works of God in Egypt only; but this is contrary to our apostle, although they are not to be excluded: Num. xiv. 22, "They have seen my glory, and my miracles" (my glorious works), "which I did in Egypt, and in the wilderness."

Τεσσαράκοντα ἔτη,—"forty years." Here the apostle finisheth the sense of the words, referring them to what goes before: 'They saw my works forty years.' The psalmist, as was before observed, placeth these words in the beginning of the next verse, and makes them to respect the season of God's indignation against them for their sins; אַרְבָּעִים שָׁנָה,—"forty years was I grieved." By the apostle, the space of time mentioned is applied unto the people's seeing of the works of God; by the psalmist, to God's indignation against them. And these things being absolutely commensurate in their duration, it is altogether indifferent to which of them the limitation of time specified is formally applied; and the apostle shows it to be indifferent, in that in the 17th verse of this chapter he applies the space of time unto God's being grieved with them, as here unto the people's sin: "With whom was he grieved forty years?" Only, it may be, the apostle made this distinction of the words to intimate, that the oath of God against the entering of that people into his rest was not made after the end of forty years, as the order of the words in the psalm seems to import: "Forty years long was I grieved with this generation, and said, It is a people that do err in their heart, and they have not known my ways: unto whom I sware in my wrath, that they should not enter into my rest." They seem to intimate, that God thus sware in his wrath after he had been grieved with them forty years. But they do but seem so: really they only declare that it was the same people with whom he was grieved concerning whom he sware; for the oath of God here intended is that mentioned, Num. xiv. 20–23. The people falling into a high sedition and murmuring, upon the report of the spies that were sent to search the land, the Lord sware by himself that that whole generation should wander forty years in that wilderness, until they were all consumed. Now, this was upon the next year after their coming up out of Egypt, and after which the forty years of their provocations and God's indignation ensued. But these things, as to time, were of

the same duration. The people came out of Egypt, and entered into the wilderness in the first month of the year. At the end of the fortieth year from their
coming out of Egypt, the eleventh month of it, is issued the history of three of
the books of Moses,—Exodus, Leviticus, Numbers. In the last month of that
year Moses reviewed and repeated the whole law, the dealings of God, and sins of
the people, as recorded in the book of Deuteronomy. About the end of that
month, as is probable, he died, and was lamented thirty days, or all the first
month of the forty-first year. After which, about three or four days, the people
prepared to pass over Jordan, under the conduct of Joshua, chap. i. 11. This
was the space of time mentioned, containing as wonderful issues and successes of
things as ever befell the church of God in the like space of time. Every year in
the whole forty was full of instances of the people's sins, provocations, temptations,
and unbelief; and every year also was filled with tokens of God's displeasure and
indignation, until the close of the whole dispensation came, wherein that generation
that came out of Egypt under Moses was consumed, and the indignation of God
rested in their consumption. And it is not unlikely but that the apostle minds
the Hebrews of this space of time granted unto their forefathers in the wilderness
after their coming up out of Egypt, with their abuse of it, because an alike space
of time was now, in the patience of God, allotted unto the whole church and
people of the Jews, between the preaching of Christ and that wasting destruction that was to come upon them. And according to this type it fell out with
them; for, as after their forefathers, who came up under Moses out of Egypt
were consumed in forty years in the wilderness, a new church, a new generation,
under the conduct of Joshua, entered into the rest of God; so within forty years
after the preaching of spiritual deliverance unto them, which was rejected by them,
that whole generation was cut off in the wrath of God, and a new church of Jews
and Gentiles, under the conduct of the true Joshua, enters into the rest of God.

Διὸ προσώχθισα,—" Wherefore I was grieved." The apostle here alters the
tenor of the discourse in the psalmist, by interposing a reference unto the cause
of God's being grieved with the people, in the word διό, " wherefore;" that is,
because of their manifold temptations and provocations, not cured, not healed,
although for so long a season they beheld his works. They continued in the
same kind of sins on the account whereof God was first provoked, and sware
against their entering into the land. For, as we have before observed, the oath
of God passed against them at the beginning of the forty years; but they abiding
obstinately in the same sins, the execution of that oath had respect unto all their
provocations during the whole forty years. Προσώχθισα, " I was grieved." This
word is supposed peculiar unto the Hellenistical Jews, nor doth it occur in any
other author, but only in the Greek version of the Old Testament. Nor is it used
by the LXX. in any place to express קוץ, the word here used in the original, but they render it by κάμνω, ἐκτήκω, and κοπέω. In the New Testament it is
only in this place, and thence transferred into the psalm. It is generally thought
to be derived from ὄχθη or ὄχθος, " the bank of a river, a rising hill or ridge by the
water's side." Thence is ὀχθέω, " to be offended," to bear a thing difficultly, with
tediousness and vexation, so as to rise up with indignation against it, like the
ground that riseth against the waters. Προσοχθίζω is the same, with an addition
of sense, " to be greatly grieved." And this word, " to be grieved," is ambiguous
even in our language: for it either is as much as " dolore affici," to be affected
with sorrow and grief, or a being wearied, accompanied with indignation; as we
say, such or such a thing is grievous,—that is, " grave," " molestum," or " troublesome." And so is the word here used, " grieved," that is burdened, and provoked,
offended. So Jerome: "Displicuit mihi generatio ista," "displeased me." "Pertuli
eam, sed non sine tædio,"—" I bare them, but not without wearisomeness." Sym-
machus and Aquila render the original word by δυσαρεστέομαι, " to be displeased."

קוֹט. אָקוֹט is a word often used, and of an ambiguous signification,—" to cut off," " to contend," " to abominate," (hence by the Arabic it is rendered " cursed them,") to be " divided with trouble, offence, weariness, and grief." It is commonly in the feminine gender, and joined with נַפְשִׁי, " my soul," or חַיָּי, " my life." This is the intendment of it: The appointed time of God's patience was worn out with their continued provocations, so that he was wearied with them, and weary of them,—he could bear them no longer.

The Vulgar Latin in some copies reads, " Proximus fui huic generationi,"—" I was near to this generation." And so are the words still in some of the Roman offices. Some think that countenance is given hereto by the sense of the word προσώχθισα, which may signify " accedere" or " proximare ad ripam animo hostili,"—" to draw near to a shore, a bank, with a hostile mind."

Now, it doth not denote only that particular provocation, when God in an especial manner entered his caveat against them that they should not enter into his rest, seeing not only the psalmist in this place, but also our apostle, verse 17, directly refers it to the frame of his mind towards them during the whole forty years. He was *wearied by them,* and grew *weary of them.*

Τῇ γενεᾷ ἐκείνῃ, " that generation ;" בְּדוֹר, " in the generation,"—that is, " with that generation." דוֹר is an age of man, or rather the men of one age: Eccles. i. 4, " One generation passeth away, and another generation cometh,"—that is, the men of one age. See Deut. xxxii. 7. So is γενεή, as in Homer's Iliad, vi. 146:—

Οἵη περ φύλλων γενεὴ, τοιήδε καὶ ἀνδρῶν.

And when it is taken for " ætas" or " seculum," it doth not primarily intend a duration of time, but the persons living in that time. Herodotus, in Euterpe, reckons thirty years to a γενεά, a " generation." So doth Plutarch also in De Defect. Oraculorum. The generation here denotes no limited season, but compriseth all the persons that came up out of Egypt above twenty years of age, who all died within the space of forty years afterwards.

Ἀεὶ πλανῶνται τῇ καρδίᾳ, " They always err in heart;" עַם תֹּעֵי לֵבָב הֵם, " They are a people erring in heart." The words of the psalmist are somewhat changed by the apostle, but the sense is absolutely the same, for, taking the people to be sufficiently signified, he adds a word to denote the constant course of their provocations,—" always," on all occasions, in every trial. Not in any one condition did they give glory to God, neither in their straits nor in their deliverances, neither in their wants nor in their fulness, but continually tempted and provoked him with their murmurings and unbelief. עַם תֹּעֵי לֵבָב הֵם, " Populus errantes corde," or " errantium corde;" that is, " populus vecors,"—" a foolish, unteachable people." תָּעָה is most usually " so to err as to wander out of the way :" Isa. liii. 6; Gen. xxxvii. 15; Prov. vii. 25. And in Hiphil, it is " to cause to err or wander," " to seduce," " to draw aside :" Hos. iv. 12; Isa. xix. 13. And it is properly rendered by πλανάω and πλανάομαι, which have both a neuter and active signification,—" to err," " to wander," and " to seduce" or " draw aside :" whence πλάνος is " erro," " vagabundus," " a wanderer," " a vagabond;" and also " deceptor," " seductor," " impostor," " a seducer," " a deceiver," or " impostor." In both which senses the Jews blasphemously applied it unto our Lord Jesus Christ, Matt. xxvii. 63. The words, then, denote not a speculative error of the mind, a mistake or misapprehension of what was proposed unto them,—in which sense the terms of error and erring are most commonly used,—but a practical aberration or wandering by choice from the way of obedience made known unto them; and therefore they are said " to err in their heart," τῇ καρδίᾳ. For though that be commonly taken in the Scripture for the entire principle of moral operations, and so compriseth the mind and understanding, yet when an immediate respect is had unto duties and sins, it hath an especial regard to the affections and desires of the heart; so that to " err in heart," is, " through the seductions and impulsions of corrupt affections, to have the mind and judgment corrupted, and then to depart from the ways of obedience."

Αὐτοὶ δὲ οὐκ ἔγνωσαν τὰς ὁδούς μου,—" and they have not known my ways; " וְהֵם לֹא יָדְעוּ דְרָכָי. The apostle renders וְ by δέ, an adversative, " but;" which is frequently used for καί, " and," as it is rendered by ours. Yet an opposition may also be intimated, " They have not known." It is said before that they " saw the works of God," which were parts of his " ways ;" and his laws were made known unto them. Of these two parts do his ways consist,—the ways of his providence, and the ways of his commands; or the ways wherein he walketh towards us, and the ways wherein he would have us walk towards him. And yet it is said of this people, that " they knew not his ways." As we said, therefore, before concerning their error, so we must now say concerning their ignorance, that it is not a simple nescience that is intended, but rather an affected dislike of what they did see and know. It seems to be made up of two parts:—First, They did not so spiritually and practically know the mind, will, and intention of God in them, as thereon to believe in him, to trust him, and to honour him. This is the knowledge of God which is required in the law and promised in the covenant. Secondly, In that light and knowledge which they had of the ways of God, they liked them not, they approved them not, they delighted not in them. And this is the constant intention of that word to " know," where the object of it is God, his ways, or his will.

' Ὡς ὤμοσα ἐν τῇ ὀργῇ μου,—" so I sware in my wrath;" אֲשֶׁר־נִשְׁבַּעְתִּי. The use of the word אֲשֶׁר is so various, as that it may denote either the persons spoken unto or the reason of the things spoken. The Vulgar Latin in some copies reads in this place, " quibus," " to whom," as though it had taken ὡς for οἷς, but commonly, " sicut ;" ὡς is often put for ὥστε, " quapropter," " so that." So Beza, " whereupon," " for which cause" or " reason,"—the consideration of the state, condition, and multiplied miscarriages of that people that came out of Egypt.

" I sware." Of the oath of God and his swearing we must deal afterwards expressly. The declared unalterable purpose of God about the dying of that people in the wilderness, expressed in the way of an oath, is that which is intended. And God is said to swear in his wrath, because he declared that purpose of his under a particular provocation. The whole matter is recorded, Num. xiv. 21–23, and verses 28–35, " But as truly as I live, all the earth shall be filled with the glory of the LORD. Because all those men which have seen my glory, and my miracles, which I did in Egypt, and in the wilderness, have tempted me now these ten times, and have not hearkened to my voice; surely they shall not see the land which I sware unto their fathers, neither shall any of them that provoked me see it. . . . . . Say unto them, As truly as I live, saith the LORD, as ye have spoken in mine ears, so will I do to you : your carcasses shall fall in this wilderness ; and all that were numbered of you, according to your whole number, from twenty years old and upward, which have murmured against me, doubtless ye shall not come into the land concerning which I sware to make you dwell therein, save Caleb the son of Jephunneh, and Joshua the son of Nun. But your little ones, which ye said should be a prey, them will I bring in, and they shall know the land which ye have despised. But as for you, your carcasses, they shall fall in this wilderness. And your children shall wander in the wilderness forty years, and bear your whoredoms, until your carcasses be wasted in the wilderness. After the number of the days in which ye searched the land, even forty days, (each day for a year,) shall ye bear your iniquities, even forty years; and ye shall know my breach of promise. I the LORD have said, I will surely do it unto all this evil congregation, that are gathered together against me: in this wilderness they shall be consumed, and there they shall die."

We have here the especial occasion of this swearing of God. The whole fabric of the ark and tabernacle being finished, the worship of God established, the law and rules of their polity being given unto them, and a blessed frame of government in things sacred and civil set up amongst them, their military camp, charge, and order in marching, to avoid emulation and confusion, being disposed, all things seemed to be in a great readiness for the entrance of the people into the promised land. Whereas they were but a confused multitude when they came out of Egypt, God had now formed them into a beautiful order both in church and state. This he insists on in his dealings with them, Ezek. xvi. Why should they now stay any longer in that wilderness, which was neither meet to entertain them nor designed for their habitation? Wherefore, to prepare a way for their entrance into Canaan, spies are sent by God's direction, with excellent instructions, to search out the land, Num. xiii. 17-20. Upon their return, the peevish, cowardly, unbelieving multitude, terrified with a false report which they made, fall into an outrageous repining against God and sedition against their ruler.

Hereupon the Lord, wearied as it were with their continued provocations, and especially displeased with their last, whereby they had, what lay in them, frustrated his intentions towards them, threatened to consume the people as one man, chap. xiv. 12; but Moses, pleading with him the interest of his own name and glory, prevailed to divert the execution of that commination. And yet so great was this provocation, and so absolutely had the people of that generation discovered themselves to be every way unfit to follow the Lord in that great work, that, to show the greatness of their sin, and the irrevocableness of his purpose, he sware with great indignation concerning them, in manner and form above declared.

Εἰ εἰσελεύσονται,—" if they shall enter." So in the Hebrew, אִם־יְבֹאוּן,—"if they shall enter." So, frequently in the place of Numbers from whence the story is taken. The expression is imperfect, and relates to the oath of God wherein he sware by himself. As if he had said, 'Let me not live,' or 'not be God, if they enter;' which is the greatest and highest asseveration that so they should not do. And the concealment of the engagement is not, as some suppose, from a πάθος, causing an abruptness of speech, but from the reverence of the person spoken of. The expression is perfectly and absolutely negative. So Mark viii. 12, with Matt. xvi. 4; 1 Sam. xiv. 44; 1 Kings xx. 10.

Εἰς τὴν κατάπαυσίν μου,—" into my rest." The pronoun "my" is taken either *efficiently* or *subjectively*. If in the first way, the rest that God would give this people is intended;—'They shall not enter into the land which I promised to give unto Abraham and his seed, as a state of rest, after all their wanderings and peregrinations upon my call and command.' Or it may be expounded subjectively, for the rest of God himself; that is, the place wherein he would fix his worship and therein rest. And this seems to be the proper meaning of the word " my rest;" that is, 'the place where I will rest, by establishing my worship therein.' Hence this was the solemn word of blessing at the moving of the ark of God, "Arise, O LORD, into thy rest;" so Ps. cxxxii. 8, 2 Chron. vi. 41. "A place for the LORD, an habitation for the mighty God of Jacob," Ps. cxxxii. 5. So he calls his worship his rest and the place of his rest, Isa. xi. 10, and lxvi. 1. And the Targumist renders these words, "Into the rest of the house of my sanctuary:" as he speaks elsewhere, "This is my rest for ever;" which place is cited by Rashi on these words.[1]

---

[1] VARIOUS READINGS.—Instead of the clause, οὗ ἐπείρασάν . . . . . ἐδοκίμασάν με, as it stands above, Tischendorf reads οὗ ἐπείρασαν οἱ πατέρες ὑμῶν ἐν δοκιμασίᾳ. Lachmann concurs with him; and the manuscripts quoted in support of this

Ver. 7–11.—Wherefore, as the Holy Ghost saith, To-day,
if ye will hear his voice, harden not your hearts, as in
the provocation, in the day of temptation, in the wilderness: where your fathers tempted me, proved me,
and saw my works. Wherefore I was grieved with
that generation, and said, They do always err in their
hearts; but my ways they have not known. So I
sware in my wrath, If they shall enter into my rest.

The exhortation is here pursued which was engaged into at the
beginning of the chapter, and which after some diversion is returned
unto at the close of the sixth verse. The argument whereby it is
confirmed and carried on in these words is taken "ab eventu per-
nicioso," from the pernicious event of the alike disobedience in
others, which the Hebrews are dehorted from. And this the apostle
shows by an eminent instance, or the induction of an example to
that purpose. And this was such as those to whom he wrote knew
to be so as it was by him reported; which they had especial reason
to attend unto and consider, which had formerly been recommended
to them, and which was purposely designed to be monitory unto
them in their present condition : which things render an example
cogent and effectual. Known it was to them, as being recorded in
the Scripture, wherewith they were acquainted; and it was likewise
of near concernment unto them, so deserving their consideration,
inasmuch as it was their own progenitors or forefathers who so miscarried as to be therein proposed unto them for an example of an
evil to be avoided. It had also, after the first recording of it in the
history of the times wherein it fell out, Num. xiv., been resumed
and recommended unto their most diligent consideration, Ps. xcv.
And, as he afterwards informs them, there was a prophecy infolded,
or a typical representation made of their present state and condition, with directions for their wise and safe deportment under it.
All these things render the example proper, and the exhortation
from it cogent.

Now, whereas the example had been twice recorded,—once *materially*, where the fact is first expressed, and then *formally*, as an
example, where it is resumed and improved by the psalmist,—our
apostle takes it together with its improvement out of the latter

reading are such as A B C D E, C D E inserting με after ἐπείρασαν. Both of these
critics, moreover, read ταύτῃ instead of ἐκείνῃ.
EXPOSITION.—Erasmus, Calvin, Grotius, Bengel, Wetstein, Carpzov, Ernesti,
Bleek, etc., connect all the quotations, verses 7–11, under the government of
καθώς, as the *protasis*, of which verse 12 is the *apodosis*. Schlichting, Cappellus, Heinrichs, Kuinoel, Klee, and Ebrard, understand καθώς . . . . . ἅγιον as a
parenthesis, and the citations as dependent upon the preceding διό.
TRANSLATION.—Καὶ εἶδον, "although they saw."—*De Wette.*—ED.

place. It lies therefore before us under both considerations,—as a fact recorded by Moses, as an example pressed by the psalmist.

FIRST, We may consider in the words,—

First, The note of inference wherein the apostle engageth the whole unto his purpose, " Wherefore."

Secondly, The manner of his introduction of this persuasive example, both as to the fact and its former improvement, "As the Holy Ghost saith."

Thirdly, The manner of its proposition, in way of exhortation; wherein we have,—

First, The *general matter of it,* which is obedience unto God; expressed,—1. By a supposition, including a positive assertion of the duty especially intended, "If ye will hear his voice." 2. By a prohibition or removal of the contrary, "Harden not your hearts."

Secondly, The *time* or season of its due performance, "To-day."

SECONDLY, There is in the words the *example itself* on which the exhortation is built or founded: and this consists of two parts or branches;—First, The sin; and, Secondly, The punishment of the persons spoken of.

First, The *sin:* on the account whereof there are mentioned,—

1. The *persons sinning;* they were the "fathers," the fathers or progenitors of them to whom he wrote; "your fathers," illustrated by their multitude,—they were a whole "generation."

2. The *quality* or nature of their sin, which consisted in two things;—(1.) Provocation, "As in the provocation;" (2.) Temptation of God, "And in the day of temptation . . . . . . they tempted me and proved me."

3. The *aggravation* of their sin;—(1.) From the place where it was committed,—it was "in the wilderness;" (2.) From the means of the contrary which they had to have preserved them from it,—they saw the works of God, "And saw my works;" (3.) From the duration and continuance of their sinning, and the means of the contrary, "Forty years."

Secondly, The *punishment* of their sin is expressed in the pernicious event that ensued, whence the exhortation is taken; and therein is expressed,—

1. The "causa procatarctica," or procuring cause, in the sense that God had of their sin: it grieved him, "Wherefore I was grieved with that generation."

2. The expression that he gave of it, containing a double aggravation of their sin,—(1.) In its principle, "They did err in their hearts;" (2.) In their continuance in it, they did so always, "And said, They do always err in their hearts;" (3.) In its effects, "They did not know his ways."

3. There is the " causa proegoumena," or " producing cause" of the punishment mentioned, in the resolution that God took and expressed concerning the persons sinning: which also hath a double aggravation:—(1.) From the manner of his declaring this resolution; he did it by an oath, " Unto whom I sware:" (2.) From the frame of his spirit; it was in his wrath, " Unto whom I sware in my wrath." (3.) The punishment of the sin itself, expressed negatively, " If they shall enter into my rest;" that is, they shall not do so. And this also hath a double aggravation:—[1.] From the act denied; they should not " enter,"—not so much as enter: [2.] From the object; that was the rest of God,—" They shall not enter into my rest."

We have so particularly insisted on the opening of the words of this paragraph, that we may be the more brief in the ensuing exposition of the design and sense of them; wherein also we shall interpose the observations that are to be improved in our own practice.

FIRST, The illative, " wherefore," as was first observed, denotes both the deduction of the ensuing exhortation from the
Διό. preceding discourse, and the application of' it unto the particular duty which he enters upon, verse 12. " Wherefore;" that is, ' Seeing the Lord Christ, who is the author of the gospel, is in his legatine or prophetical office preferred far above Moses in the work of the house of God, as being the son and lord over that house as his own, wherein Moses was a servant only, let us consider what duty is incumbent on us, especially how careful and watchful we ought to be that we be not by any means diverted or turned aside from that obedience which he requires, and which on all accounts is due unto him.' This he pursues unto verse 11, where the hyperbaton that is in these words is issued.

Obs. I. No divine truth ought in its delivery to be passed by, without manifesting its use, and endeavouring its improvement unto holiness and obedience.

So soon as the apostle had evinced his proposition concerning the excellency of Christ in his prophetical office, he turns himself unto the application of it unto them that are concerned in it. Divine knowledge is like a practical science; the end of all whose principles and theorems is in their practice; take that away and it is of no use. It is our wisdom and understanding how to live unto God; to that purpose are all the principles, truths, and doctrines of it to be improved. If this be not done in the teaching and learning of it, we fight uncertainly, as men beating the air.

Obs. II. In times of temptations and trials, arguments and exhortations unto watchfulness against sin and constancy in obedience are to be multiplied in number, and pressed with wisdom, earnestness, and diligence.

Such was the season now with these Hebrews. They were exposed to great trials and temptations: seduction on the one hand by false teachers, and persecution on the other hand by wrathful adversaries, closely beset them. The apostle, therefore, in his dealing with them adds one argument unto another, and pursues them all with pathetical exhortations. Men are often almost unwilling to be under this advantage, or they quickly grow weary of it. Hence our apostle closeth this hortatory epistle with that entreaty, chap. xiii. 22: "Suffer the word of exhortation." He was afraid they might have thought themselves overburdened with exhortations. And this befalls men on three accounts:—

1. When they are grieved by their multiplication, as if they proceeded from a jealousy concerning their sincerity and integrity; so was it with Peter, John xxi. 17.

2. On a confidence of their own strength, which they would not have suspected; as with the same Peter, Matt. xxvi. 33.

3. From a secret inclination lying against the thing exhorted unto, or to the thing dehorted from.

But these are the ordinances of God for our preservation in such a condition; and these our necessities in it do call for. And pregnant instances hereof are given by our apostle, especially in this epistle and in that unto the Galatians, whose condition was the same with that of these Hebrews. Both of them were in danger to be seduced from the simplicity of the gospel by inveterate prejudices and the subtilty of false teachers; both of them were encompassed with dangers, and exposed unto persecutions. He understood their temptations and saw their dangers. And with what wisdom, variety of arguments, expostulations, exhortations, and awakening reproofs, doth he deal with them! what care, tenderness, compassion, and love, do appear in them all! In nothing did the excellency of his spirit more evidence itself, than in his jealousy concerning and tender care for them that were in such a condition. And herein the Lord Christ set him forth for an example unto all those to whom the work of the ministry and dispensation of the gospel should afterwards be committed. In this care and watchfulness lie the very life and soul of their ministry. Where this is wanting, whatever else be done, there is but the carcass, the shadow of it.

This, then, is of excellent use, provided,—1. That the arguments in it proceeded on be solid and firm (such as in this case are everywhere laid down by our apostle), that our foundation fail us not in our work. Earnest exhortations on feeble principles have more of noise than weight; when there is an aim of reaching men's *affec-*

tions, without possessing their *minds* with the due reasons of the things treated about, it proves mostly evanid, and that justly.

2. That the exhortation itself be grave and weighty, *duty* ought to be clothed with words of wisdom, such as may not, by their weakness, unfitness, uncomeliness, betray the matter intended, and expose it unto contempt or scorn. Hence the apostle requires a singular ability unto the duty of admonition, Rom. xv. 14, " Filled with all knowledge, able also to admonish one another."

3. That the love, care, and compassion of them who manage such exhortations and admonitions be in them made to appear. Prejudices are the bane and ruin of mutual warnings. And these nothing can remove but a demonstration of love, tenderness, and compassion, acting themselves in them. Morose, peevish, wrathful admonitions, as they bring guilt upon the admonisher, so they seldom free the admonished from any. This course, therefore, the condition of them that are tempted,—who are never in more danger than when they find not a necessity of frequent warnings and exhortations,—and the duty of those who watch for the good of the souls of men, require to be diligently attended unto.

Secondly, The manner of the introduction of the persuasive example proposed is to be considered, " As saith the Holy Ghost." The words are the words of the psalmist, but are here ascribed unto the Holy Ghost. Our apostle, as other divine writers of the New Testament, useth his liberty in this matter. Sometimes they ascribe the words they cite out of the Old Testament unto the penmen of them; as to Moses, David, Isaiah, Jeremiah, and the like,—Luke xxiv. 27; Matt. ii. 17, iv. 14; John xii. 41; Acts ii. 25: sometimes to the books wherein they are written; as, "It is written in the book of Psalms," Acts i. 20: and sometimes they ascribe them unto the principal author, namely, the Holy Ghost, as in this place. Now, as they used their liberty therein, so it is not to be supposed that they fixed on any particular expression without some especial reason for it. And the ascribing of the words of the psalmist in this place immediately unto the Holy Ghost, by whom he was inspired and acted, seems to have been to mind the Hebrews directly of his authority. His intention from the words was, to press a practical duty upon them. In reference unto such duties the mind ought to be immediately inflamed by the authority of him that requires it. ' Consider,' saith he, ' that these are the words of the Holy Ghost' (that is, of God himself), ' so that you may submit yourselves to his authority.' Besides, the apostle intends to manifest that those words have respect unto the times of the gospel, and in an especial manner unto that season of it which was then passing over the Hebrews. He therefore minds them that they were given out by the Spirit of prophecy, so that the concernment of the church in all ages must lie in them. "The Holy Ghost saith;" that is, as he spake to them of old in and by David (as it is expressed, chap. iv. 7), so he continues to speak them unto us in the Scripture, which is not only his word, but his voice, his speaking, living, and powerful voice; for so we may comprise both senses before mentioned.

Obs. III. Exhortations unto duty ought to be well founded, to be built on a stable foundation, and to be resolved into an authority which may influence the consciences of them to whom they do belong.

Without this they will be weak and enervous, especially if the duties exhorted unto be difficult, burdensome, or any way grievous. Authority is the formal reason of duty. When God gave out his law of commandments, he prefaced it with a signification of his sovereign authority over the people, " I am the LORD thy God." And this is our duty in giving our exhortations and commands from him. The engagement of his authority in them is to be manifested. " Teach men," saith our Saviour, " to do and observe whatsoever I have commanded," Matt. xxviii. 20. His commands are to be proposed to them, and his authority in them to be applied unto their souls and consciences. To exhort men in the things of God, and to say, ' This or that man saith so,' be he the pope or who he will, is of no use or efficacy. That which you are to attend unto is what the Holy Ghost saith, whose authority the souls of men are every way obnoxious unto.

Obs. IV. Whatever was given by inspiration from the Holy Ghost, and is recorded in the Scripture for the use of the church, he continues therein to speak it to us unto this day.

As he lives for ever, so he continues to speak for ever; that is, whilst his voice or word shall be of use to the church. "As the Holy Ghost saith;" that is, speaks now unto us. And where doth he speak it? In the 95th Psalm; there he says it, or speaks it unto us. Many men have invented several ways to lessen the authority of the Scripture, and few are willing to acknowledge an *immediate speaking of God* unto them therein. Various pretences are used to subduct the consciences of men from a sense of his authority in it. But whatever authority, efficacy, or power the word of God was accompanied withal, whether to evidence itself so to be, or otherwise to affect the minds of men unto obedience, when it was first spoken by the Holy Ghost, the same it retains now it is recorded in Scripture, seeing the same Holy Ghost yet continues to speak therein.

Thirdly, There is in the words, *first*, The matter of the exhortation intended, that which it aims at and intends. This in general is obedience unto God, answerable unto the revelation which he makes of himself and his will unto us. And this is,—1. Expressed in a supposition, including a positive assertion of it, "If ye will hear his voice;"—'It is your duty so to do; and this is that which you are exhorted unto.'

(1.) The voice of God is ordinarily the word of his command, the voice or signification of his will; which is the rule of all our duty or obedience. (2.) In this place, as commonly elsewhere, not the word of command in general is intended, but an especial call or voice of God in reference unto some especial duty at some especial season. Such was the voice of God to the people in the wilderness at the giving of the law, which the people heard, and saw the effects of. Hence is the *command* translated into the *voice* of God, in giving out the gospel by the ministry of his Son Jesus Christ. From the former is the occasion of the words taken in the psalm; and to the latter is the application of it made by the apostle. (3.) The psalmist speaks to the people as if the voice of God were then sounding in their ears. For that which was once the voice of God unto the church (being recorded in the Scripture) continues still to be so; that is, it is not only materially his revealed will and command, but it is accompanied with that special *impression of his authority* which it was at first attested withal. And on this ground all the miracles wherewith the word of old was confirmed are of the same validity and efficacy towards us as they were towards them that saw them; namely, because of the sacredness of the means whereby they are communicated to us.

This, then, is the object of the duty exhorted unto, the voice of God: which, as it is used by the apostle, is extended virtually and consequentially to the whole doctrine of the gospel, but with especial respect to the revelation of it by Christ Jesus; as in the psalm it regards the whole doctrine of the law, but with especial regard unto the delivery of it to Moses on mount Sinai. The act exercised about it is hearing, " If ye will hear his voice." The meaning of this word hath been before explained. It is an act of the whole soul, in understanding, choosing, and resolving to do, the will of God declared by his voice, that is intended. And this further appears from the ensuing charge: "If ye will hear, harden not your hearts;" that is, ' If you think meet to obey the voice of God, if you will choose so to do, take heed of that which would certainly be a hinderance thereof.' Thus dealeth the apostle with the Hebrews; and herein teacheth us that,—

Obs. V. The formal reason of all our obedience consists in its relation to the voice or authority of God.

So, therefore, doth the apostle express it, so is it declared in the whole Scripture. If we do the things that are commanded, but not with respect to the authority of God by whom they are commanded, what we so do is not obedience properly so called. It hath the *matter of obedience* in it, but the *formal reason* of it, that which

should render it properly so, which is the life and soul of it, it hath
not: what is so done is but the carcass of duty, no way acceptable
unto God. God is to be regarded as our sovereign Lord and only
lawgiver in all that we have to do with him. Hereby are our souls
to be influenced unto duty in general, and unto every especial duty
in particular. This reason are we to render to ourselves and others
of all the acts of our obedience. If it be asked why we do such or
such a thing, we answer, Because we must obey the voice of God.
And many advantages we have by a constant attendance unto the
authority of God in all that we do in his worship and service; for,—
(1.) This will keep us unto the *due rule and compass of duty*, whilst
we are steered in all that we do hereby. We cannot undertake or
perform any thing as a duty towards God which is not so, and which,
therefore, is rejected by him, where he saith, " Who hath required
these things at your hand?" This is no small advantage in the
course of our obedience. We see many taking a great deal of pains
in the performance of such duties as, being not appointed of God,
are neither accepted with him, nor will ever turn unto any good
account unto their own souls. Had they kept upon their consciences
a due sense of the authority of God, so as to do nothing but with
respect thereunto, they might have been freed from their labouring
in the fire, where all must perish, Mic. vi. 6–9. Such are most of
the works wherein the Papists boast. (2.) This, also, will not suffer
us to *omit any thing* that God requires of us. Men are apt to divide
and choose in the commands of God, to take and leave as it seems
good unto them, or as serves their present occasion and condition.
But this also is inconsistent with the nature of obedience, allowing
the formal reason of it to consist in a due respect unto the voice of
God; for this extends to all that is so, and only to what is so. So
James informs us that all our obedience respects the authority of
the Lawgiver, whence a universality of obedience unto all his commands doth necessarily ensue. Nor doth the nature of any particular sin consist so much in respect to this or that particular precept
of the law which is transgressed or violated by it, as in a contempt
of the Lawgiver himself, whence every sin becomes a transgression
of the law, James ii. 9–11. (3.) This will strengthen and fortify the
soul against all dangers, difficulties, and temptations that oppose it in
the way of its obedience. The mind that is duly affected with a
sense of the authority of God in what it is to do will not be " territa
monstris." It will not be frightened or deterred by any thing that
lies in its way. It will have in readiness wherewith to answer all objections, and oppose all contradictions. And this sense of the authority of God requiring our obedience is no less a gracious effect of the
Spirit, than are that freedom, and cheerfulness, and alacrity of mind
which in these things we receive from him.

Obs. VI. Every thing in the commands of God, relating unto the manner of their giving out and communicating unto us, is to be retained in our minds and considered as present unto us.

The psalmist, "after so long a season," as the apostle speaks, calls the people to hear the voice of God, as it sounded on mount Sinai at the giving of the law.   Not only the law itself, and the authority of God therein, but the manner also of its delivery, by the great and terrible voice of God, is to be regarded, as if God did still continue so to speak unto us.   So also is it in respect of the gospel.   In the first revelation of it God spake immediately "*in the Son;*" and a reverence of that speaking of God in Christ, of his voice in and by him, are we continually to maintain in our hearts.   So in the dispensation of the gospel he continues yet to speak from heaven, Heb. xii. 25.   It is his voice and word unto us no less than it was when in his own person he spake on the earth.   And God being thus, both in his commands and the manner of his giving them out, rendered present unto us by faith, we shall receive a great incitation unto obedience thereby.

Obs. VII. Consideration and choice are a stable and permanent foundation of obedience.

The command of God is here proposed unto the people, to their understanding to consider it, to their wills to choose and embrace it: "If ye will hear his voice."   'Consider all things, all concerns of this matter; *whose* command it is, in what *manner* given, what is the *matter* of it, and what are its *ends,* and what is our own concernment in all this.'   Men that are engaged into some course of obedience or profession as it were by chance, or by their minds being merely pre-occupied with education or custom, will leave it by chance or a powerful diversion at any time.   Those who are only compelled unto it by some pungent, galling convictions, so that they yield ¦obedience not because they like it or choose it, but because they dare not do otherwise, do assuredly lose all respect unto it as their convictions do by any means wear off or decay.

A deliberate choice of the ways of God, upon a due consideration of all their concernments, is that which unchangeably fixeth the soul unto obedience.   For the strongest obligations that are unto it ought to be in our own wills.   And it is the most eminent effect of the grace of Christ, to make his people willing in the day of his power; nor is any other obedience acceptable with God, Rom. xii. 1.

2. The apostle carries on and enforceth his exhortation unto obedience, in the words of the psalmist, by a caution against or prohibition of the contrary, or that which would utterly prevent it, as having done so formerly in others: "Harden not your hearts."   To clear his intention herein, we must inquire,—(1.) What is intended by "heart;" and, (2.) What by the "hardening" of it.

(1.) The heart in the Scripture, spoken of in reference unto moral obedience, doth not constantly denote any one especial faculty of the soul; but sometimes one, sometimes another, is intended and expressed thereby. What is peculiarly designed, the subject-matter treated of and the adjuncts of the word will discover. Thus, sometimes the heart is said to be "wise," "understanding," to "devise," to be "filled with counsel;" and, on the other side, to be "ignorant," "dark," "foolish," and the like;—in all which places it is evident that the mind, the τὸ ἡγεμονικόν, the guiding, conducting, reasoning faculty is intended. Sometimes it is said to be "soft," "tender," "humble," "melting;" and, on the other side, "hard," "stubborn," "obstinate," and the like;—wherein principal regard is had to the will and affections. The word, therefore, is that whereby the principle of all our moral actions, and the respective influence of all the faculties of our souls into them, are expressed.

(2.) By the sense of the object is the meaning of the *act* prohibited to be regulated: "Harden not." The expression is metaphorical, and it signifies the unfitness and resistency of any thing to receive a due impression from that which is applied unto it; as wax when it is hard will not receive an impression from the seal that is set unto it, nor mortar from the trowel. The application that is made in the matter of obedience unto the souls of men is by the Spirit of God, in his commands, promises, and threatenings; that is, his voice, the whole revelation of his mind and will. And when a due impression is not made hereby on the soul, to work it to an answerableness in its principles and operations thereunto, men are said to resist the Spirit, Acts vii. 51; that is, to disappoint the end of those means which he makes use of in his application to them. By what ways or means soever this is done, men are thereby said to harden their hearts. Prejudices, false principles, ignorance, darkness and deceit in the mind, obstinacy and stubbornness in the will, corruption and cleaving unto earthly and sensual objects in the affections, all concur in this evil. Hence in the application of this example, verse 13, the apostle exhorts the Hebrews to take heed that they be not "hardened through the deceitfulness of sin." Now, deceit firstly and principally respects the mind, and therein consists the beginning and entrance into the sin of hardening the heart. A brief consideration of the condition of the people in the wilderness upon whom this evil is charged, will give much light into the nature of the sin that here comes under prohibition. What were the dealings of God with them is generally known, and we have elsewhere declared. As he gave them instruction from heaven, in the revelation and delivery of the law, and intrusted them with the singular benefit of the erection of his worship amongst them, so he afforded them all sorts of mercies, protections, deliverances, provision, and guidance; as also made them sensible of his severity and holiness, in great and terrible judgments. All these, at least the most part of them, were also given out unto them in a marvellous and amazing manner. The end of all these dispensations was to teach them his will, to bring them to hearken to his voice, to obey his commands, that it might be well with them and theirs. In this state and condition sundry things are recorded of them; as,—(1.) That they were dull, stupid, and slow of heart in considering the ways, kindness, and works of God. They set not their hearts to them to weigh and ponder them, Deut. xxxii. 28, 29. (2.) What they did observe and were moved at (as such was the astonishing greatness of some of the works of God amongst them, such the overpowering obligations of many of his dealings with them, that they could not but let in some present transient sense of them upon their minds), yet they soon forgot them and regarded them not, Ps. lxxviii. 11, 12. (3.) That their affections were so violently set upon earthly, sensual, perishing things, that in comparison of them they despised all the promises and threatenings of God, resolving to pursue their own hearts' lusts whatever might become of them in this world and to eternity, Ps. lxxviii. 18, 19. All which are manifest in the whole story of their ways and doings. By this means their minds and spirits were brought into such a frame and condition, that as they did not, so they could not hearken to the voice of God, or yield obedience unto him: they became "a stubborn and rebellious generation; a generation that set not their heart aright, and whose spirit was not steadfast with God," Ps. lxxviii. 8. For by these ways and degrees of sin, they contracted a habit of obstinacy, perverseness, and uncircumcision of heart,—neither did the Lord, in his sovereign pleasure, see good by his effectual grace to circumcise the hearts of the persons of that generation, that they might fear and serve him,—whereby they came to be hardened unto final unbelief and impenitency. It appears, then, that unto this sinful hardening of the heart, which the people in the wilderness were guilty of, and which the apostle here warns the Hebrews to avoid, there are three things that do concur:—(1.) The mind's sinful inadvertency and neglect, in not taking due notice of the ways and means whereby God calls any unto faith and obedience. (2.) A sinful forgetfulness and casting out of the heart and mind such convictions as God, by his word and works, his mercies and judgments, deliverances and afflictions, at any time is pleased to cast into them and fasten upon them. (3.) An obstinate cleaving of the affections unto carnal and sensual objects, practically preferring them above the motives unto obedience that God proposeth to us. Where these things are, the hearts of men are so hardened that in an ordinary way they cannot hearken unto the voice of God. We may hence also take some observations for our instruction.

Obs. VIII. Such is the nature, efficacy, and power of the voice or word of God, that men cannot withstand or resist it, without a sinful hardening of themselves against it.

There is a natural hardness in all men before they are dealt withal by the word, or this spiritual hardness is in them by nature. Hardness is an adjunct of that condition, or the corruption of nature, as is darkness, blindness, deadness, and the like; or it is a result or consequent of them. Men being dark and blind, and dead in trespasses and sins, have thence a natural hardness, an unfitness to receive impressions of a contrary kind, and a resistency thereunto. And this frame may be increased and corroborated in men by various vicious and prejudicate habits of mind, contracted by custom, example, education, and the practice of sin. All this may be in men antecedent unto the dispensation or preaching of the word unto them. Now unto the removal or taking away of this hardness, is the voice or the word of God in the dispensation of it designed. It is the instrument and means which God useth unto that end. It is not, I confess, of itself absolutely considered, without the influencing operation of the Spirit of grace, able to produce this effect. But it is able to do it in its own kind and place; and is thence said to be "able to save our souls," James i. 21; "able to build us up, and to give us an inheritance among all them which are sanctified," Acts xx. 32; being also that "immortal seed" whereby we are begotten unto God, 1 Pet. i. 23. By this means doth God take away that natural darkness or blindness of men; "opening the eyes of the blind, turning them from darkness to light," Acts xxvi. 18; "shining in their hearts, to give them the knowledge of his glory in the face of Jesus Christ," 2 Cor. iv. 6; as also "quickening them who were dead in trespasses and sins;" and thereby he removes that hardness which is a consequent of these things. And God doth not apply a means to any end which is unsuited to it or insufficient for it. There is therefore usually such a concomitancy of the Spirit with every dispensation of the word of God that is according to his mind and will, as is able and sufficient to remove that hardness which is naturally upon the hearts of men.

Every one, therefore, to whom the word is duly revealed, who is not converted unto God, doth *voluntarily* oppose his own obstinacy unto its efficacy and operation. Here lies the stop to the progress of the word in its work upon the souls of men. It stays not unless it meets with an actual obstinacy in their wills, refusing, rejecting, and resisting of it. And God, in sending of it, doth accompany his word with that power which is meet to help and save them in the state and condition wherein it finds them. If they will add new obstinacy and hardness to their minds and hearts, if they will fortify themselves against the word with prejudices and dislike, if they will resist its work through a love to their lusts and corrupt affections, God may justly leave them to perish, and to be filled with the fruit of their own ways. And this state of things is variously expressed in the Scripture. As,—(1.) By *God's willingness* for the salvation of those unto whom he grants his word as the means of their conversion, Ezek. xviii. 23, xxxiii. 11; 2 Pet. iii. 9; 1 Tim. ii. 4. (2.) By his *expostulations* with them that reject his word, casting all the cause of their destruction upon themselves, Matt. xxiii. 34. Now, as these things cannot denote an intention in God for their conversion which should be frustrated, which were to ascribe weakness and changeableness unto him; nor can they signify an exercise towards them of that effectual grace whereby the elect are really converted unto God, which would evert the whole nature of effectual grace, and subject it to the corrupt wills of men; so·they express more than a mere proposal of the outward means, which men are not able savingly to receive and improve. There is this also in them, that God gives such an efficacy unto these means as that their operation doth proceed on the minds and souls of men in their natural condition, until, by some new acts of their wills, they harden themselves against them. And, (3.) So the gospel is proposed to the *wills* of men, Isa. lv. 1, Rev. xxii. 17.

Hence it is that the miscarriage of men under the dispensation of the word, is still charged upon some *positive actings of their wills* in opposition unto it, Isa. xxx. 15, Matt. xxiii. 37, John iii. 19, v. 40. They perish not, they defeat not the end of the word towards themselves, by a mere abode and continuance in the state wherein the word finds them, but by rejecting the counsel of God made known to them for their healing and recovery, Luke vii. 30.

Obs. IX. Many previous sins make way for the great sin of finally rejecting the voice or word of God.

The not hearing the voice of God, which is here reproved, is that which is final, which absolutely cuts men off from entering into the rest of God. Unto this men come not without having their hearts hardened by depraved lusts and affections. And that it is their nature so to do shall be afterwards declared. Here we only respect the connection of the things spoken of. Hardening of the heart goes before final impenitency and infidelity, as the means and cause of it. Things do not ordinarily come to an *immediate issue* between God and them to whom the word is preached. I say *ordinarily*, because God may immediately cut off any person upon the first refused tender of the gospel; and it may be he deals so with many, but ordinarily he exerciseth much patience towards men in this condition. He finds them in a state of nature; that is, of enmity against him. In this state he offers them terms of peace, and waits thereon, during the season of his good pleasure, to see what the event will be.

Many in the meantime attend to their lusts and temptations, and so contract an obdurate senselessness upon their hearts and minds; which, fortifying them against the calls of God, prepares them for final impenitency. And this is the first thing that is considerable, in the general matter of the exhortation in hand.

Secondly, The time and season for the performance of the duty exhorted unto is expressed,—" To-day." " To-day if ye will hear his voice." The various respects of the limitation of the season of this duty have been spoken to in the opening of the words. The moral sense of it is no more but the present and proper season of any duty; which what is required unto, in this case of yielding obedience to the voice of God, shall be afterwards declared. And in this sense the word is generally used in all authors and languages. So is הַיּוֹם frequently in the Hebrew in other places, as in this. And a proper season they called יוֹם טוֹב, " a good day," ' a meet season,' 1 Sam. xxv. 8. It may be only a day of feast is there intended, which they called יוֹם טוֹב, " a good day," ' a day of mirth and refreshment,' Lev. xxiii. And so it is commonly used by the rabbins, especially for the feast which the high priest made his brethren after the day of expiation; for on that day they were obliged to many observations, under the penalty of excision. This begat fear and terror in them, and was part of their yoke of bondage. Wherefore when that service was over, and they found themselves safe, not smitten by the hand of God, they kept יוֹם טוֹב, " a good day," whereon they invited unto a feast all the priests that ministered. But most frequently they so express a present opportunity or season. So the Greeks use σήμερον, as in Anacreon,—

Σήμερον μέλει μοι· τὸ δὲ αὔριον τίς οἶδε;—

" My care is for to-day" (the present season); " who knows to-morrow" (or the time to come)?

To the same purpose are ἡμέρα and αὔριον, used in the gospel, Matt. vi. 34: Μὴ οὖν μεριμνήσητε εἰς τὴν αὔριον· ἡ γὰρ αὔριον μεριμνήσει τὰ ἑαυτῆς· ἀρκετὸν τῇ ἡμέρᾳ ἡ κακία αὐτῆς·—" Take no care for the morrow" (things future and unknown): " the morrow shall take care for the things of itself " (provision shall be made for things future according as they fall out). " Sufficient unto the day" (the present time and season) " is the evil thereof." To the same purpose do they use " hodie" in the Latin tongue, as in these common sayings,—

" Sera nimis vita est crastina, viv' hodie:"

And,—

" Qui non est hodie, cras minus aptus erit;"

with many other sayings of the like importance. This, then, is the sense and meaning of the word absolutely considered . The apostle exhorts the Hebrews, in the words of the psalmist, to make use of the present season, by the use of means, for the furtherance of their

faith and obedience, that they may be preserved from hardness of
heart and final unbelief. And what arguments unto duty are suggested from a present season shall afterwards be considered. To
enforce this exhortation, the apostle minds them that there is in the
words of the psalmist,—1. A retrospect unto a monitory example.
For others there were who had their day also, their season. This
they improved not, they answered it not, nor filled it up with the
duty that it was designed unto; and therefore the sad event befell
them mentioned in the text. Hence doth he enforce his exhortation:
'It is now to-day with you, it was once to-day with them of old;
but you see what a dark, sad evening befell them in the close of their
day. Take heed lest it be so with you also.' 2. A respect unto
the day enjoyed in the time of the psalmist, which completed the
type; of which before. And yet further;—there was, 3. More than
a mere example intended by the psalmist. A prophecy also of the
times of the gospel was included in the words, as our apostle declares
in the next chapter. Such a season as befell the Jews at the giving
of the law, is prefigured to happen to them at the giving of the gospel. The law being given on mount Sinai, the church of the Hebrews who came out of Egypt had their day, their time and season
for the expressing of their obedience thereunto, whereon their entrance into Canaan did depend. This was their day, wherein they
were tried whether they would hearken unto the voice of God or
no; namely, the space of thirty-eight or forty years in the wilderness.
The gospel was now delivered from mount Sion. And the church
of the Hebrews, to whom the word of it first came, had their *peculiar day*, prefigured in the day after the giving of the law enjoyed
by their forefathers. And it was to be but a day, but one *especial
season*, as theirs was. And a trying season it was to be,—whether
in the limited space of it they would obey the voice of God or no.
And this especial day continued for the space of thirty-eight or forty
years,—from the preaching of the gospel by our Lord Jesus Christ,
and his death, unto the destruction of Jerusalem by Titus; wherein
the greatest part of the people fell, after the same example of unbelief with their forefathers, and entered not into the rest of God.
This was the day and the season that was upon the Hebrews at this
time, which the apostle exhorts them to the use and improvement
of. Σήμερον, then, or "to-day," signifies in general a present season,
which men are not long to be intrusted with; and it hath a triple
respect, limitation, or application:—1. Unto the *season* enjoyed by
the people in the wilderness, who neglected it. 2. Unto the *persons* spoken unto in the psalmist typically, who were exhorted to
use it. 3. Unto the *present Hebrews*, whose gospel day was
therein foretold and prefigured. In all which we are instructed
unto the due use of a present season.

Obs. X. Old Testament examples are New Testament instructions.

Our apostle elsewhere, reckoning sundry instances of things that fell out amongst the people of old, affirms of them Ταῦτα δὲ πάντα τύποι συνέβαινον ἐκείνοις, 1 Cor. x. 11;—"All these things befell them as types." The Jews have a saying, כל מה שאירע אבות סימן לבנים;—"That which happeneth unto the father is a sign or example unto the children." In general, and in the order of all things, "Discipulus est prioris posterior dies;"—"The following day is to learn of the former." Experience is of the greatest advantage for wisdom. But there is more in this matter. The will and appointment of God are in it. From thence, that all the times of the old testament, and what fell out in them, are instructive of the times and days of the new, not only the words, doctrines, and prophecies that were then given out, but the actions, doings, and sufferings of the people which then fell out, are to the same purpose. There is more in it than the general use of old records and histories of times past, which yet are of excellent use unto a wise consideration in things moral and political. This many have made it their work to manifest and demonstrate. The sum of all is comprised in those excellent words of the great Roman historian concerning his own work, [Liv., Pref.] :—"Ad illa mihi acriter pro se quisque intendat animum, quæ vita, qui mores fuerint: per quos viros, quibusque artibus, domi militiæque, et partum et auctum imperium sit. Labente deinde paullatim disciplina, velut desidentes primo mores sequatur animo; deinde ut magis magisque lapsi sint; tum ire coeperint præcipites: donec ad hæc tempora, quibus nec vitia nostra, nec remedia pati possumus, perventum est. Hoc illud est præcipue in cognitione rerum salubre ac frugiferum; omnis te exempli documenta in illustri posita monumento intueri : inde tibi quod imitere capias; inde, fœdum inceptu, fœdum exitu, quod vites;"—"Hereunto" (in reading this history) "let every one diligently attend, to consider who were the men, what was their life and manners, by what means and arts this empire was both erected and increased. And then, moreover, how good discipline insensibly decaying was attended with manners also differing from the former; which in process of time increasing, rushed all things at length headlong into these times of ours, wherein we can endure neither our vices nor their remedies. This is that which, in the knowledge of past affairs, is both wholesome and fruitful,—that we have an illustrious monument of all sorts of examples, from whence you may take what you ought to imitate, and know also, by the consideration of actions dishonest in their undertaking and miserable in the event, what you ought to avoid." And if this use may be made of human stories, written by men wise and prudent, though in many things ignorant, partial, factious, as most historians have been, unable in

many things to judge of actions whether they were really good or
evil, praiseworthy or to be condemned, and in all things of the
intentions with which and the ends for which they were done; how
much more benefit may be obtained from the consideration of those
records of times past, which as they were delivered unto us by persons
divinely preserved from all error and mistake in their writings, so
they deliver the judgment of God himself, to whom all intentions
and ends are open and naked, concerning the actions which they do
report! Besides, the design of human story is but to direct the
minds of men in things just and honest with reference unto *political
society* and the good of community in this world, with respect
whereunto alone it judgeth of the *actions* of men and their *events;*
but all things in the Scriptures of the Old Testament are directed
unto a higher end, even the pleasing of God and the eternal
fruition of him. They are therefore, with the examples recorded
in them, of singular and peculiar use as materially considered. But
this is not all. The things contained in them were all of them designed of God for our instruction, and yet do continue as an especial
way of teaching. The things done of old were, as Justin Martyr
speaks, προκηρύγματα τῶν κατὰ Χριστοῦ,—"fore-declarations of the
things of Christ." And Tertullian, to the same purpose, "Scimus ut
vocibus, ita rebus prophetatum;"—"Prophecy or prediction consisted
in things as well as words." And Chrysostom, Serm. ii., de Jejun.,
distinguisheth between prophecy by speech or words, and prophecy
by examples or actions.

Our apostle expressly treateth of this subject, 1 Cor. x. Considering the state of the people, in their deliverance from Egypt
and abode in the wilderness, he refers the things relating unto them
to two heads;—1. God's *miraculous works* towards them, and
marvellous dealings with them; 2. Their *sins* and miscarriages,
with the punishments that befell them. Having mentioned those
of the first sort, he adds, Ταῦτα δὲ τύποι ἡμῶν ἐγενήθησαν,—"Now
these were all our examples," verse 6,—types representing God's
spiritual dealing with us. And having reckoned up the other, he
closeth his report of them with Ταῦτα δὲ πάντα τύποι συνέβαινον
ἐκείνοις,—'They befell them, that God in them might represent unto
us what we are to expect, if we sin and transgress in like manner.'
They and their actions were our types. Τύπος, "a type," hath many
significations. In this use of it, it signifies a rude and imperfect
expression of any thing, in order to a full, clear, and exact declaration of it. So Aristotle useth παχυλῶς καὶ ὡς ἐν τύπῳ in opposition
to ἀκριβῶς διορίζειν,—a general and imperfect description, to an exact
distinction. Thus they were our types, in that the matter of our
faith, obedience, rewards, and punishments, were delineated afore-
hand in them.

Now, these types or examples were of three sorts:—1. Such as were *directly instituted* and appointed for this end, that they should signify and represent something in particular in the Lord Christ and his kingdom. It is true that God did not institute any thing among the people of old but what had its present use and service amongst them; but their present use did not comprehend their principal end. And herein do types and sacraments differ. Our sacraments have no use but that with respect unto their spiritual end and signification. We do not baptize any to wash the body, nor give them the supper of the Lord to nourish it. But types had their *use* in *temporal* things, as well as their *signification* of things *spiritual.* So the sacrifices served for the freeing of the people from the sentence of the law as it was the rule of their polity or civil government, as well as to prefigure the sacrifice of the body of Christ.

Now those types which had a solemn, direct, stated institution, were materially either *persons,* as vested with some certain offices in the church, or *things.*

(1.) *Persons.* So the Lord raised up, designed, and appointed Moses, Aaron, Joshua, David, Solomon, and others, to typify and represent the Lord Christ unto the church. And they are to be considered in a threefold capacity:—[1.] Merely *personal,* as those individual men; unto which concernment all their moral good and evil did belong. In this sense what they did or acted had no respect unto Christ, nor is otherwise to be considered but as the examples of all other men recorded in the Scriptures. [2.] As to the *offices* they bare in the church and among the people, as they were prophets, captains, kings, or priests. In this respect they had their present use in the worship of God and government of that people according to the law. But herein, [3.] In the *discharge of their offices and present duties,* they were designed of God to represent in a way of prefiguration the Lord Christ and his offices, who was to come. They were a transcript out of the divine idea in the mind and will of God, concerning the all-fulness of power and grace that was to be in Christ, expressed by parcels and obscurely in them, so as by reason of their imperfection they were capable. (2.) These types consisted in *things,* such as were the sacrifices and other institutions of worship among the people. That this was the design and end of the whole Mosaical divine service we shall manifest in our progress. This, therefore, is not the place to insist particularly upon them.

2. There were such things and actions as had only a *providential ordination* to that purpose,—things that occasionally fell out, and so were not capable of a solemn institution, but were as to their events so guided by the providence of God as that they might prefigure and represent somewhat that was afterwards to come

to pass. For instance, Jeremiah, chap. xxxi. 15, sets out the lamentation of Rachel,—that is, the women of the tribe of Benjamin,
upon the captivity of the land: "A voice was heard in Ramah,
lamentation, and bitter weeping; Rachel weeping for her children,
refused to be comforted for her children, because they were not."
It is evident from chap. xl. 1, that after the destruction of Jerusalem
by the Babylonians, Nebuzar-adan gathered the people together
that were to go into captivity at Ramah.   There the women, considering how many of their children were slain, and the rest now to
be carried away, brake out into woful and unspeakable lamentation.
And this was ordered, in the providence of God, to prefigure the
sorrow of the women of Bethlehem upon the destruction of their
children by Herod, when he sought the life of our Saviour; as the
words are applied, Matt. ii. 17, 18.   And we may distinguish things
of this kind into two sorts,—

(1.) Such as have received a *particular application* unto the
things of the new testament, or unto spiritual things belonging to
the grace and kingdom of Christ, by the Holy Ghost himself in the
writings of the Gospel.   Thus, the whole business of Rebekah's conceiving Jacob and Esau, their birth, the oracle of God concerning
them, the preference of one above the other, is declared by our
apostle to have been ordained in the providence of God to teach his
sovereignty in choosing and rejecting whom he pleaseth, Rom. ix.
So he treateth at large concerning what befell that people in the
wilderness, making application of it to the churches of the gospel,
1 Cor. x.; and other instances of the like kind may be insisted on,
almost innumerable.

(2.) This *infallible application* of one thing and season unto another, extends not unto the least part of those teaching examples
which are recorded in the Old Testament.   Many other things
were ordained in the providence of God to be instructive unto
us, and may, by the example of the apostles, be in like manner
applied; for concerning them all we have this general rule, that
they were ordained and ordered in the providence of God for this
end, that they might be examples, documents, and means of instruction unto us.   Again, we are succeeded into the same place in the
covenant unto them who were originally concerned in them, and so
may expect answerable dispensations of God towards ourselves; and
they were all written for our sakes.

3. There are things that fell out of old which are meet to
illustrate present things, from a proportion or similitude between
them.   And thus where a place of Scripture directly treats of one
thing, it may, in the interpretation of it, be applied to illustrate
another which hath some likeness unto it.   These expositions the
Jews call מדרשים, and say they are made כדרך משל, "parabolical"

or "mystical;" wherein their masters abound. We call them allegories; so doth our apostle expressly, Gal. iv. 21–26. Having declared how the two covenants, the legal and evangelical, were represented by the two wives of Abraham, Hagar and Sarah; and the two sorts of people, even those that sought for righteousness by the law and believers, by their children, Ishmael and Isaac; he adds that these things are an allegory. Chrysostom supposeth that Paul useth that expression, of an allegory, in a large sense, for any type or figure, seeing the things he mentioneth were express types the one of the other. But the truth is, he doth not call the things themselves an allegory, for they had a reality, the story of them was true; but the exposition and application which he makes of the Scripture in that place is allegorical,—that is, what was spoken of one thing he expounds of another, because of their proportion one to another, or the similitude between them. Now this doth not arise hence, that the same place of Scripture, or the same words in any place, have a diverse sense, a *literal* sense and that which is *mystical* or allegorical; for the words which have not one determinate sense have no sense at all: but the things mentioned in any place holding a proportion unto other things, there being a likeness between them, the words whereby the one are expressed are applied unto the other.

Now, in the using of these allegorical expositions or applications of things in one place unto another, sundry things are wisely and diligently to be considered; as,—

1. That there be a *due proportion* in general between the things that are one of them as it were substituted in the room of another. Forced, strained allegories from the Scripture are a great abuse of the word. We have had some who have wrested the Scripture unto monstrous allegories, corrupting the whole truth of the literal sense. This was the way of Origen of old in many of his expositions; and some of late have taken much liberty in the like proceeding. Take an instance in that of the prophet Hosea, chap. xi. 1, "Out of Egypt have I called my son." The words are directly spoken of the people of Israel, as the passage foregoing evinceth: "When Israel was a child, then I loved him, and called my son out of Egypt." But these words are applied by the evangelist unto the Lord Christ, Matt. ii. 15; and that because of the just proportion that was between God's dealing with that people and with him, after he was carried into Egypt.

2. That there be a *designed signification* in them. That is, although the words are firstly and principally spoken of one thing, yet the Holy Ghost intended to signify and teach that whereunto they are applied. An intention of the application is included in them. Thus these words of the prophet, "Out of Egypt have I

called my son," did firstly and properly express God's dealing with
the people of Israel; but there was also an intention included in
them of shadowing out his future dealing with his only Son, Christ
Jesus. The discovery hereof is a matter of great skill and wisdom;
and great sobriety is to be used in such applications and allusions.

3. That the first, *original sense* of the words be sacredly observed.
Some will not allow the words of Scripture their first, natural sense,
but pretend that their allegories are directly intended in them; which
is to make their expositions poisonous and wicked.

I have added these things because I find many very ready to
allegorize upon the Scripture without any due consideration of the
analogy of faith, or the proportion of things compared one to another, or any regard to the first, genuine sense of the words which
they make use of. This is plainly to corrupt the word of God; and
however they who make use of such perverted allusions of things
may please the fancies of some persons, they render themselves
contemptible to the judicious.

But in general these things are so. All things in the Old Testament, both what was spoken and what was done, have an especial
intention towards the Lord Christ and the gospel; and therefore in
several ways we may receive instruction from them. As their institutions are our instructions more than theirs, we see more of the
mind of God in them than they did; so their *mercies* are our
encouragements, and their *punishments* our *examples*. And this
proceedeth,—

1. From the way that God, in infinite wisdom, had allotted
unto the *opening and unfolding of the mystery of his love*, and
the dispensation of the covenant of grace. The way, we know,
whereby God was pleased to manifest the counsels of his will in
this matter was gradual. The principal degrees and steps of his
procedure herein we have declared on the first verse of this epistle.
The light of it still increased, from its dawning in the first promise,
through all new revelations, prophecies, promises, institutions of
worship, until the fulness of time came and all things were completed in Christ; for God had from of old designed the perfection
of all his works towards his church to be in him. In him all the
treasures of wisdom and knowledge were to be laid up, Col. ii. 3;
and all things were to be gathered into a head in him, Eph. i. 10.
In him God designed to give out the express image of his wisdom,
love, and grace, yea, of all the glorious properties of his nature. For
as he is in himself, or his divine person, "the image of the invisible
God," Col. i. 15, "the brightness of glory, and the express image of
his person," Heb. i. 3, so he was to represent him unto the church;
for we have the "knowledge of the glory of God in the face of Jesus
Christ," 2 Cor. iv. 6. In him,—that is his person, his office, his work,

his church,—God perfectly expressed the eternal idea of his mind concerning the whole effect of his love and grace. From hence he copied out, in various parcels, by prophecies, promises, institutions of worship, actions, miracles, judgments, some partial and obscure representations of what should afterwards be accomplished in the person and kingdom of Christ. Hence these things became types, that is, transcripts from the great idea in the mind of God about Christ and his church, to be at several seasons, in divers instances, accomplished among the people of old, to represent what was afterwards to be completed in him. This the apostle Peter declares fully, 1 Epist. i. 9–12, "Receiving the end of your faith, the salvation of your souls. Of which salvation the prophets have inquired and searched diligently, who prophesied of the grace that should come unto you: searching what, or what manner of time, the Spirit of Christ which was in them did signify, when it testified beforehand the sufferings of Christ and the glory that should follow. Unto whom it was revealed, that not unto themselves, but unto us, they did minister the things which are now reported unto you by them that have preached the gospel." The prophets were those who revealed the mind and will of God to the church of old; but the things which they declared, although they had a present use in the church, yet principally they respected the Lord Christ, and the things that afterwards were to come to pass. And herein were they instructed by that Spirit of Christ wherewith they were inspired, namely, that the things they declared, and so the whole work of their prophecy wherein they ministered, did principally belong to the times of the gospel. And therefore are they all for our instruction.

2. This is part of that privilege which God had reserved for that church which was to be planted and erected immediately by his Son. Having reckoned up the faith of the saints under the old testament, what it effected, and what they obtained thereby, the apostle adds, that yet "God had provided some better thing for us, that they without us should not be made perfect," Heb. xi. 40. Neither themselves nor any thing that befell them was perfect without us. It had not in them its full end nor its full use, being ordained in the counsel of God for our benefit. This privilege did God reserve for the church of the new testament, that as it should enjoy that perfect revelation of his will in Christ which the church of the old testament received not, so what was then revealed had not its perfect end and use until it was brought over to this also.

See hence what use we are to make of the Scriptures of the Old Testament. They are all ours, with all things contained in them. The sins of the people are recorded in them for our warning, their obedience for our example, and God's dealing with them on the account of the one and the other for our direction and encouragement in believing. We are not to look on any parts of them as bare stories of things that are past, but as things directly and peculiarly ordered, in the wise and holy counsel of God, for our use and advantage. Especial instances we shall meet with many, towards the end of the epistle.

Consider also what is expected from us above them that lived under the old testament. Where much is given much is required. Now we have not only the superadded helps of gospel light, which they were not intrusted with, but also whatever means or advantages they had, they are made over unto us, yea, their very sins and punishments are our instructions. As God in his grace and wisdom hath granted unto us more light and advantage than unto them, so in his righteousness he expects from us more fruits of holiness, unto his praise and glory.

There is yet another observation which the words opened will afford unto us, arising from the season, which the apostle presseth upon their consideration in that word "to-day." And it is that,—

Obs. XI. Especial seasons of grace for obedience are in an especial manner to be observed and improved.

For this end are they given, and are made special, that they may be peculiarly improved. God doth nothing in vain, least of all in the things of grace, of the gospel of the kingdom of his Son. When he gives an especial day to the husbandman and vineyard, it is for especial work. "To-day, if ye will hear his voice." We may therefore inquire, first, what is necessary unto such an especial season; and then what is required unto a due observance and improvement of it. And I shall refer all, by a due analogy, unto those especial days respected in the text.

1. For the first, such a day or season consists in a concurrence of sundry things:—

(1.) In a *peculiar dispensation of the means of grace;* and hereunto two things are required:—

[1.] Some *especial effects of providence,* of divine wisdom and power making way for it, bringing of it in, or preserving of it in the world. There is, there ever was, a strong opposition at all times against the preaching and dispensation of the gospel. It is that which the gates of hell engage themselves in, although in a work wherein they shall never absolutely prevail, Matt. xvi. 18. As it was with Christ, so it is with his word. The world combined to *keep* him from it, or to *expel* him out of it, Acts iv. 25–27. So it dealeth with his gospel and all the concernments of it. By what ways and means, on what various pretences this is done, I need not here declare, as it is generally known. Now when God, by some especial and remarkable acts of his providence, shall powerfully remove, overcome, or any way divert that opposition, and thereby make way for the preaching or dispensation of it, he puts a speciality upon that season. And without this the gospel had never made an entrance upon the kingdom of Satan, nor been entertained in any nation of the world. The case before us gives us an instance. The day mentioned in the text was that which the people enjoyed in the wilderness, when the worship of God was first revealed unto them and established amongst them. By what means this was brought about is summed up in the prophet Isaiah, chap. li. 15, 16: " I am the LORD thy God, that divided the sea, whose waves roared: The LORD of hosts is his name. And I have put my words in thy mouth, and I have covered thee in the shadow of mine hand, that I may plant the heavens, and lay the foundations of the earth, and say unto Zion, Thou art my people." The work which God wrought when he brought the people out of Egypt was so great, that it seemed to be the creation of a new world, wherein the heavens were planted, and the foundations of the earth were laid. And what was the end of it, what was the design of God in it? It was all to put his words into the mouths of his people, to erect Zion or a church-state amongst them, to take them into a covenant-relation with himself for his worship. This made that time their special day and season. The like works, for the like purpose, at any time will constitute the like season. When God is pleased to make his arm bare in behalf of the gospel, when his power and wisdom are made conspicuous in various instances for the bringing it unto any place, or the continuance of its preaching against oppositions, contrivances, and attempts for its expulsion or oppression, then doth he give a special day, a season unto them who do enjoy it.

[2.] It consists in an *eminent communication of the gifts of the Holy Ghost* unto those by whom the mysteries of the gospel are to be dispensed, and that either as to the increase of their number or of their abilities, with readiness unto and diligence in their work. When God thus "gives the word, great is the army of them that publish it,"—הַמְבַשְּׂרוֹת צָבָא רָב, Ps. lxviii. 12. The word is of the feminine gender, and denotes the churches; which, verse 27 of that psalm, are called מַקְהֵלוֹת, which we render " congregations;" that is, churches, in the same gender: "Bless ye God in the congregations," —בְּמַקְהֵלוֹת, the churches or congregations publishing "the word" or "glad tidings," as the word signifies. And hereof there is צָבָא רָב, "a great army:" for the church in its work and order is כַּנִּדְגָּלוֹת, as " bannered ones;" that is, כַּנִּדְגָּלוֹת צְבָאוֹת, as " bannered armies," " armies with banners," Cant. vi. 10. When God "gave the word" (it is a prophecy of the times of the gospel), " great was the number of מַקְהֵלוֹת הַמְבַשְּׂרוֹת," that like armies with banners, not for weapons, but

for order and terror to the world, "preached" or "published it." Such
was the day that our apostle called the Hebrews to the consideration of. It was not long after the ascension of Christ when the
gifts of the Spirit were poured out on multitudes of all sorts, as was
foretold: Acts ii. 16–18, "This is that which was spoken by the
prophet Joel; And it shall come to pass in the last days (saith God),
I will pour out of my Spirit upon all flesh: and your sons and your
daughters shall prophesy, and your young men shall see visions, and
your old men shall dream dreams: and on my servants, and on my
handmaids, I will pour out in those days of my Spirit, and they shall
prophesy." The extent of the communication of the Spirit at that
season is emphatically expressed in these words, "I will pour out
my Spirit upon all flesh." As the act of *pouring* denotes abundance,
freedom, largeness, plenty, so the object, or "all flesh," signifies the
extent of it, unto all sorts of persons. And you know how great and
eminent were the gifts that were communicated unto many in those
days; so that this work was every way complete. By this means
the churches were many, whose work and duty it is to be στύλοι καὶ
ἑδραιώματα τῆς ἀληθείας, 1 Tim. iii. 15, "the pillars of the truth,"—
that is, to hold it up, and to hold it forth, Phil. ii. 16. When,
then, there is any such season wherein in any proportion or similitude unto this dispensation, or in a way or manner any thing extraordinary, God is pleased to give or pour out of the gifts of his Spirit
upon many, for the declaration and preaching of the word of truth,
then doth he constitute such an especial day or season as that we
are inquiring after.

(2.) When God is pleased to give out signal *providential warnings*,
to awaken and stir up men unto the consideration of and attendance
unto his word and ordinances, this makes such a season to become a
special day; for the end of extraordinary providences is to prepare
men for the receiving of the word, or to warn them of impendent
judgments for the contempt of it. This mark did God put upon the
season respected here by the apostle. For unto the mention of the
pouring out of the Spirit that of signs and judgments is adjoined:
Acts ii. 19, 20, "And I will shew wonders in heaven above, and
signs in the earth beneath; blood, and fire, and vapour of smoke:
the sun shall be turned into darkness, and the moon into blood, before that great and notable day of the Lord come." The things here
spoken of were those signs, prodigies, and judgments, which God
showed unto and exercised the people of the Jews withal before the
destruction of Jerusalem, even those foretold by our Lord Jesus
Christ, Matt. xxiv. And they were all wrought during the time
that they enjoyed the dispensation of the gospel before described.
And what was the end of them? It was evidently to put a signal
mark and note upon that day and season of grace which was then

granted unto that people; for so it is added, verse 21, " And it shall come to pass, that whosoever shall call on the name of the Lord shall be saved,"—that is, whosoever shall make use of these warnings by signs, and wonders, and dreadful representations of approaching indignation and wrath, so as to attend unto the word dispensed by virtue of the plentiful effusion of the Spirit before mentioned, and yield obedience thereunto (that is, make use of the day granted to them), they shall be saved, when others that are negligent, rebellious, and disobedient, shall utterly perish.

(3.) When it is a season of the accomplishment of prophecies and promises for the effecting of some great work of God in and upon the outward state of the church, as to its worship. The day the people had in the wilderness was the time when the great promise given unto Abraham four hundred and thirty years before was to have its typical accomplishment. Hereupon the outward state of the church was wholly to be altered; it was to be gathered from its dispersion in single families, into a national union, and to have new ordinances of worship erected in it. This made it a great day to the church. The day whereunto the application of these things is made by the apostle, was the season wherein God would make that great alteration in the whole worship of the church, by the last revelation of his mind and will in the Son. This was a great day and signal. So also when the time comes of the fulfilling of any especial prophecy or prediction for the reformation of the church, it constitutes such a season. Something of this nature seems to be expressed, Rev. xiv. 6–8 : " And I saw another angel fly in the midst of heaven, having the everlasting gospel to preach unto them that dwell on the earth, and to every nation, and kindred, and tongue, and people, saying with a loud voice, Fear God, and give glory to him, for the hour of his judgment is come. . . . . . And there followed another angel, saying, Babylon is fallen, is fallen, that great city, because she made all nations drink of the wine of the wrath of her fornication." The time approaching wherein Babylon is to be destroyed, and the church to be redeemed from under her tyranny, as also to be freed from her pollution, and from drinking any more of the cup of her fornication,—which is the greatest change or alteration that the outward state of it is left obnoxious unto in the world,—the everlasting gospel is to be preached with such glory, beauty, and efficacy, as if it were delivered from the midst of heaven; and men will have an especial day of repentance and turning unto God given unto them thereby. And thus is it also at sundry seasons, wherein the Lord Christ deals with his churches in one place or another in a way of " preludium," or preparation unto what shall ensue in his appointed time amongst them all.

These and the like things do constitute such a special season and day as that we inquire after; and whether such a day be not now in many places, needs no great travail of mind or eminency of understanding to determine.

2. It is declared in the proposition laid down, that such a day, such a season, is diligently to be attended unto and improved. And the reasons or grounds hereof are,—

(1.) Because *God expects it.* He expects that our applications unto him in a way of obedience should answer his unto us in a way of care and tenderness,—that when he is earnest in his dealings with us, we should be diligent in our observance of him. Every circumstance that he adds unto his ordinary dispensations is to have its weight with us; and in such a day they are many. See Isa. v. 1, etc.: " My well-beloved hath a vineyard בְּקֶרֶן בֶּן־שָׁמֶן," " in an horn of a son of oil" (" planted in a fat and fruitful soil;" that is, furnished with all possible means to render it fruitful): " and he fenced it" (protected it by his providence from the incursion of enemies), " and gathered out the stones thereof" (removed out of it whatever was noxious and hurtful,—it may be the gods of wood and stone in an especial manner out of the land); " and planted it with the choicest vine" (in its order, ordinances, and institutions of worship), " and built a tower in the midst of it" (that is, for its defence; namely, the strong city of Jerusalem, in the midst of the land, which was built "as a city that is compact together," all as one great tower, " whither the tribes went up, the tribes of the LORD, unto the testimony of Israel," Ps. cxxii. 3, 4), " and also made a wine-press therein" (the temple and altar, continually running with the blood of sacrifices): " and he looked that it should bring forth grapes." His expectations answer his care and dispensations towards his church. That is the meaning of the word וַיְקַו,—he "looked," he " expected." Expectation properly is of a thing future and uncertain,—so is nothing unto God; being therefore ascribed unto him, it only signifies what is just and equal, and what in such cases ought to be: such a vineyard ought to bring forth grapes answerable to all the acts of God's care and grace towards it; and we may see in that place what is the end of frustrating such an expectation. Such are the dealings of God with churches and persons in the day we have described, and an expectation of such fruit is it accompanied withal.

(2.) Such a day is the season that is allotted unto us for *especial work*, for *especial duty.* Some singular work is the end and design of such a singular season. So the apostle informs us, 2 Pet. iii. 11: " Seeing then that all these things shall be dissolved, what manner of persons ought ye to be in all holy conversation and godliness?" The supposition in the words, concerning the dissolution of all these things, is an intimation of such a day as we have described from one circumstance of it, namely, the impendent judgments of God then threatened to the church and state of the Jews, which was now expiring. And the inference that he makes from that supposition is unto a peculiar holiness and godliness. That this at such a time is intended, is a thing so evident, that he refers it to the judgment of them to whom he wrote. " What manner of persons ought ye to be?"—'Judge in yourselves, and act accordingly.' Great light, great holiness, great reformation, in hearts, houses, churches, are expected and required in such a day. All the advantages of this season are to have their use and improvement, or we lose the end of it. Every thing that concurs to the constitution of such a day hath advantages in it to promote special work in us; and if we answer them not our time for it is irrecoverably lost; which will be bitterness in the end.

(3.) Every such day is *a day of great trials.* The Lord Christ comes in it with his fan in his hand, to sift and try the corn; to what end is declared, Matt. iii. 12: " His fan is in his hand, and he will throughly purge his floor, and gather his wheat into the garner; but he will burn up the chaff with unquenchable fire." The " fan" of Christ is his word, in and by the preaching whereof he separates the precious from the vile, the " wheat" from the "chaff." He comes into his "floor," the church, where there is a mixture of corn and chaff; he sifts and winnows them by his word and Spirit, so discarding and casting off light, empty, and fruitless professors. Such a day is described by Daniel, chap. xii. 10: " Many shall be purified, and made white, and tried; but the wicked shall do wickedly: and none of the wicked shall understand; but the wise shall understand." " Many," that is, of the saints, " shall be purified,"— יִתְבָּרֲרוּ, " purged" (made clean from such spots, stains, or defilements, as in their affections or conversation they had contracted); " and made white,"—יִתְלַבְּנוּ, (shall be whitened in their profession,—it shall be rendered more eminent, conspicuous, and glorious); " and tried," —יִצָּרְפוּ (as in a furnace, that it may appear what metal they are of). Thus shall it be with believers, so shall they be exercised in their spirits, and so approved; but wicked and false professors shall be discovered, and so far hardened that they shall go on and grow high in their wickedness, unto their utter destruction. So it fell out on the day of his coming in the flesh, and so it was foretold, Mal. iii. 1–3. The whole people jointly desired his coming, but when he came few of them could abide it or stand before it. He came to try them and purify them; whereon many of them, being found mere dross, were cast off and rejected. Christ in such a day tries all sorts of persons, whereby some are approved, and some have an end put to their profession, their hypocrisy being discovered. And it therefore concerns us heedfully to regard such a season; for,—

(4.) *Unto whom such a day is lost, they also themselves are lost.* It is God's last dealing with them. If this be neglected, if this be despised, he hath done with them. He says unto them in it, "This is the acceptable time, this is the day of salvation." If this day pass over, night will come wherein men cannot work. So speaks our Saviour concerning Jerusalem, which then enjoyed that day, and was utterly losing it: Luke xix. 41, 42, "And when he was come near, he beheld the city, and wept over it, saying, If thou hadst known, even thou, at least in this thy day, the things which belong unto thy peace! but now they are hid from thine eyes." Both the things, and words, and manner of expression declare the greatness of the matter in hand. So doth the action of our Saviour, —" he wept;" which is but once more recorded of him in the gospel, John xi. 35. And the word here used, ἔκλαυσε, denotes a weeping with lamentation. The consideration of what he was speaking unto moved his holy, tender, merciful heart unto the deepest commiseration. He did it also for our example and imitation, that we might know how deplorable and miserable a thing it is for a people, a city, a person, to withstand or lose their day of grace. And the words here used also are of the like importance: " If thou hadst known, even thou." The reduplication is very emphatical, "Thou, even thou," —' thou ancient city, thou city of David, thou seat of the temple and all the worship of God, thou ancient habitation of the church;' " if thou hadst known." And there is a wish or a desire included in the supposition, which otherwise is elliptical, "If thou hadst known," —' O that thou hadst known!' Εἰ is sometimes well rendered by " utinam." And again it is added, " At least in this thy day." They had enjoyed many lesser days of grace, and many before in the messages and dealings of the prophets, as our Saviour minds them in that great parable, Matt. xxi. 33–36. These they despised, persecuted, and rejected, and so lost the season of their preaching; but they were lesser days, and not decretory of their state and condition. Another day they were to have, which he calls " This their day;" the day so long foretold, and determined by Daniel the prophet, wherein the Son of God was to come, who was now come amongst them. And what did he treat with them about? " The things which belonged unto their peace,"—of repentance and reconciliation unto God, the things which might have given them peace with God, and continued their peace in the world; but they refused these things, neglected their day, and suffered it to pass over them unimproved. What was the issue thereof? God would deal no more with them, the things of their peace shall now be hid from them, and themselves be left unto destruction. For when such a dispensation is lost, when the evening of such a day is come, and the work of it not accomplished,—

[1.] It may be God will bring a wasting *destruction* upon the persons, church, or people that have despised it. So he dealt with Jerusalem, as it was foretold by our Saviour in the place before insisted on, Luke xix. 43, 44: 'The things of thy peace are now over and hid from thee.' What then will follow or ensue? Why, "The days shall come upon thee, that thine enemies shall cast a trench about thee, and compass thee round, and keep thee in on every side, and shall lay thee even with the ground, and thy children within thee; and they shall not leave in thee one stone upon another; because thou knewest not the time of thy visitation;"—'Because thou hast not discerned thy day, nor regarded it, hast not answered the mind of God in it, all this shall speedily befall thee,'—as it did accordingly. The same hath been the issue of many famous Christian churches. The very places where they were planted are utterly consumed. Temporal judgments are ofttimes the issue of despised spiritual mercies. This is the language of those providential warnings by signs and prodigies, which ofttimes such a season is accompanied withal. They all proclaim the impendent wrath of God upon the neglect of his gracious call. And with examples hereof are all records, sacred and ecclesiastical, filled.

[2.] God may, and sometimes doth, leave such a people, church, or persons, as have withstood his dealings in a day of grace, in and unto their outward station in the world, and yet *hide the things of their peace* utterly from them, by a removal of the means of grace. He can leave unto men their kingdoms in this world, and yet take away the kingdom of heaven, and give that unto others. They may dwell still in their houses, but be in the dark, their candlestick and the light of it being consumed. And this hath been the most common issue of such dispensations, which the world groans under at this day. It is that which God threateneth, 2 Thess. ii. 11, 12. Because men would not receive the truth in the love thereof,—that is, because they would not improve the day of the gospel which they enjoyed,—"God sent them strong delusion, that they should believe a lie." And how came it to pass? By removing the sound and sincere preaching of the word, he gave advantage to seducers and false teachers to impose their superstition, idolatry, and heresies upon their credulity. So God punished the neglect and disobedience of the churches of Europe under the papal apostasy. And let us take heed lest this vial of wrath be not yet wholly emptied; or,—

[3.] God may leave unto such persons the outward dispensation of the means of grace, and yet *withhold that efficacy of his Spirit* which alone can render them useful to the souls of men. Hence the word comes to have a quite contrary effect unto what it hath under the influences of God's especial grace. God in it then speaks unto a people as is expressed Isa. vi. 9, 10: "Hear ye indeed, but understand not; and see ye indeed, but perceive not. Make the heart of this people fat, and make their ears heavy, and shut their eyes; lest they see with their eyes, and hear with their ears, and understand with their heart, and convert, and be healed." 'I have now done with them,' saith God; 'I have no design or purpose any more to deal with them about their conversion and healing. And therefore, although I will have the preaching of the word as yet continued unto them, yet it shall have no effect upon them, but, through their own unbelief, to blind them and harden them to their destruction.' And for these reasons, amongst others, ought such a day as we have described carefully to be attended unto.

This duty being of so great importance, it may be justly inquired, How may a man, how may a church know that it is such day, such a season of the gospel with them, so as to be suitably stirred up unto the performance of their duty? I answer, They may do so two ways:—

1. From the *outward signs* of it, as the day is known by the light and heat of the sun, which is the cause thereof. What concurs to such a day was before declared. And in all those things there are signs whereby it may be known. Neglect and ignorance hereof were charged by our Saviour on the Jews, and that frequently; so Matt. xvi. 3: "O ye hypocrites, ye can discern the face of the sky, but can ye not discern the signs of the times?" How they discerned "the face of the sky" he shows in verses 2, 3; namely, they judged by usual known prognostics what the weather would be in the evening or morning, that so they might accordingly apply themselves unto their occasions. 'But,' saith he, 'as God hath planted such signs in things natural, hath so ordered them that one should be a sign and discovery of another, so he hath appointed signs of this day of grace, of the coming of the Messiah, whereby it also may be known. But these,' saith he, 'ye cannot discern.' Οὐ δύνασθε, "Ye cannot." But withal he lets them know why they could not. That was because they were hypocrites, and either grossly neglected or despised the means and advantages they had to that purpose. The signs we have before mentioned are such, as being brought at any time to the rule of the word, they will reveal the season that they belong unto. And herein consisted the wisdom of those children of Issachar, who had "understanding of the times, to know what Israel ought to do," 1 Chron. xii. 32.

2. Such a day or season will manifest itself by its *efficacy*. When God applies such a concurrence of means, he will make men one way or other sensible of his design and end. The word in such a day will either refine and reform men, or provoke and enrage them. Thus when the witnesses preach,—which is a signal season of light and truth,—they "torment them that dwell on the earth," Rev. xi. 10. If they are not healed, they will be tormented. So it was at the first preaching of the gospel,—some were converted, and

the rest were hardened: a signal work passed on them all, and those who dispensed the word became a "sweet savour in them that are saved, and in them that perish." The consciences of men will discover their times. God will one way or other leave his witness within them. An especial day will make an especial approach unto their hearts. If it make them not better, they will be worse; and this they may find by the search of themselves. God in this dispensation effectually speaks these words unto an evident experience in the minds of men: "He that is unjust, let him be unjust still; and he which is filthy, let him be filthy still; and he that is righteous, let him be righteous still; and he that is holy, let him be holy still," Rev. xxii. 11.

The especial duty incumbent on men in such a day, is in all things to hearken to the voice of God.

We now proceed unto the SECOND part of the words under consideration, comprising the *example itself* insisted on, and whereon the exhortation itself is founded. And this consists of two general parts: first the *sin*, and secondly the *punishment* of the people of old.

First, The sin is contained in these words: "As in the provocation, in the day of temptation in the wilderness: where your fathers tempted me, proved me, and saw my works, forty years."

1. The first thing occurring in the words according unto our former distribution of them, relating to the sin mentioned, is the *persons* of the sinners. They were their "fathers," the progenitors of them to whom the apostle wrote. And they are in the next verse further described by their multitude,—they were a whole generation, " I was grieved with that generation."

Who these were was declared before in the exposition of the words, and it is plain from the story who are intended. It was the people that came up out of Egypt with Moses; all of whom that were above twenty years of age at their coming into the wilderness, because of their manifold sins and provocations, died there, Caleb and Joshua only excepted. So the Lord threatened, Num. xiv. 26–30, " And the LORD spake unto Moses and unto Aaron, saying, How long shall I bear with this evil congregation, which murmur against me? I have heard the murmurings of the children of Israel, which they murmur against me. Say unto them, As truly as I live, saith the LORD, as ye have spoken in mine ears, so will I do to you; your carcasses shall fall in this wilderness, and all that were numbered of you, according to your whole number, from twenty years old and upward, which have murmured against me, doubtless ye shall not come into the land concerning which I sware to make you dwell therein, save Caleb the son of Jephunneh, and Joshua the son of Nun." And so it came to pass; for when the people were numbered again in the plains of Moab, it is said, " Among these there was

not a man of them whom Moses and Aaron the priest numbered, when
they numbered the children of Israel in the wilderness of Sinai;"
that is, besides those two who were excepted by name, Num. xxvi.
64, 65. These were the fathers of the present Hebrews; that is, as it
is expressed, Jer. xi. 10, אֲבוֹתָם הָרִאשֹׁנִים,—their "forefathers," as we
render the words; rather their "first fathers," those whom God
first took into the express covenant with himself, for the place hath
respect unto that very sin which is here reported: "They are turned
back to the iniquity of their first fathers, which refused to hear my
words," who hearkened not unto the voice of God. And this limits
the term unto those in the wilderness, seeing the former patriarchs
did not refuse to hear the word of God. But they are generally
called אָבוֹת indefinitely, πατέρες, the "fathers," as others also that
followed in succeeding generations; once by our apostle they are
termed πρόγονοι,—" progenitors," 2 Tim. i. 3. Now the psalmist mentioning (and our apostle from him) the sin of the people in the wilderness, and proposing it with its consequents unto the present
Hebrews, calls them their "fathers,"—

(1.) Because that people were exceedingly apt to boast of their
fathers, and to raise a confidence in themselves that they must needs
receive mercy from God on their account. And they had, indeed,
no small privilege in being the posterity of some of those fathers.
Our apostle reckons it as one of their chief advantages, Rom. ix.
4, 5: "Who are Israelites, to whom pertaineth the adoption, and
the glory, and the covenants, and the giving of the law, and the
service of God, and the promises; whose are the fathers, and of
whom, as concerning the flesh, Christ came." It hath a place in
the great series of the privileges of that church. And when the
church-state is made over to the Gentiles, it is promised her, that
instead of these fathers she should have her children, Ps. xlv. 16,—
those that should succeed unto them in holiness and the favour of
God. But this people ran into a woful mistake, which their posterity are hardened in at this day. Their only privilege in this
matter was because God had freely and graciously given his promises unto their fathers, and taken them into covenant with himself; and the due consideration hereof tended only to the exaltation
oi the rich and free grace of God. So Moses expressly declares,
Deut. vii. 7, 8, and elsewhere. But forgetting or despising this,
they rested on the honour and righteousness of their fathers, and
expected I know not what as due unto them on that account. This
vain confidence our Saviour frequently rebuked in them, and so
did the apostle. And for this reason the psalmist and the apostle,
having occasion to mention the sins of the people of old, calls them
their "fathers;" minding them that many of them in whom they
gloried were sinful provokers of God.

(2.) It is done to mind them of their *near concernment in the example* proposed unto them.   It is not taken from amongst strangers, but it is what fell out amongst their own progenitors.

(3.) To warn them of *their danger.*   There is a propensity in children to follow the sins of their fathers.   Hence some sins prove eminently national in some countries for many generations.   The example of parents is apt to infect their children.   The Holy Ghost, then, here intimates unto them their proneness to fall into disobedience, by minding them of the miscarriage of their fathers in the same kind.   This intimates unto them both their duty and their danger.   Again, these fathers are further described by their number.   They were a whole "generation;" that is, all the people of that age wherein they were in the wilderness.   And this contains a secret aggravation of the sin mentioned, because there was in it a joint conspiracy as it were of all the persons of that age.   These are they who were guilty of the sin here reported.   And we may observe from this expression and remembrance of them,—

Obs. XII. That the examples of our forefathers are of use and concernment unto us, and objects of our deepest consideration.

God in his dealings with them laid in instruction for their posterity.   And when parents do well, when they walk with God, they beat the path of obedience plain for their children; and when they miscarry, God sets their sins as buoys to warn them who come after them of the shelves that they split upon.   " Be not as your fathers, a stiff-necked generation," is a warning that he oft repeats.   And it is in the Scripture an eminent part of the commendation or discommendation of any, that they walked in the way of their progenitors.   Where any of the good kings of Judah are testified unto for their integrity, this is still one part of the testimony given unto them, that they walked in the way of David their father, in the paths that he had trod before them.   And on the other side, it is a brand on many of the wicked kings of Israel, that they walked in the ways of Jeroboam the son of Nebat.   Their examples, therefore, are of concernment unto us,—

First, because ofttimes the same kind of temptations are continued unto the children that the fathers were exercised withal. Thus we find in experience that some temptations are peculiar to a nation, some to a family, for sundry generations; which produce peculiar national sins, and family sins, so that at least they are prevalent in them.   Hence the apostle chargeth national sins on the Cretians, from the testimony of Epimenides, who had observed them amongst them;—

Κρῆτες ἀεὶ ψεῦσται, κακὰ θηρία, γάστερις ἀργαί,

Tit. i. 12, "The Cretians are alway liars, evil beasts, slow bellies."

Lying, dissimulation, cruelty, and sloth, were the sins of that nation from one generation to another, children learning them from the example of their parents. So many families for a long season have been infamous for cruelty, or deceit, or the like. And these hereditary sins have proceeded in part from hereditary temptations: some are inlaid in their natural constitutions, and some are inseparably annexed unto some special course of life and conversation, wherein persons of the same family succeed one another. Now it is a great warning unto men, to consider what sad events have befallen them that went before them by yielding unto those temptations which they themselves are exercised withal.

Again, there is a blessing or a curse that lies secretly hid in the ways of progenitors. There is a revenge for the children of the disobedient unto the third and fourth generation; and a blessing on the posterity of the obedient for a longer continuance. The very heathen acknowledged this by the light of nature. Plato says expressly, Εἰς τετάρτην γενεὰν διαβιβάζει τὴν τιμωρίαν,—" Punishment falls on the fourth generation." And they had the substance of it from their oracle:—

> Ἀλλὰ κακῶς ῥέξασι δίκας τέλος οὐχὶ χρονιστὸν
> Ἠδὲ παραίτατον· εἰ καὶ διὸς ἔκγονοι εἶεν
> Κ' αὐτῆς γὰρ κεφαλῆσι, καὶ ἐν σφιτεροίσι τεκέσσιν
> Εἰλεῖται· καὶ πῆμα δόμοις, ἐπὶ πήμασι, βαίνει.

So is that saying common in the same case, Iliad. Γ′ 308:—

> Καὶ παίδων παῖδες, τοί κεν μετόπισθε γίνωνται.

The design is what we have asserted, of the traduction of punishment from wicked parents to their posterity. But there are conditions of the avoidance of the curse, and enjoyment of the blessing. When fathers have made themselves obnoxious to the displeasure of God by their sins, let their posterity know that there is an addition of punishment coming upon them, beyond what in an ordinary course of providence is due unto themselves, if they continue in the same sins. So God tells Moses, in the matter of the golden calf which Aaron had made, when he had prevailed with him not immediately to destroy the whole people: " Nevertheless," saith he, " in the day when I visit I will visit their sin upon them," Exod. xxxii. 34;—that is, ' If by their future sins and idolatry they shall provoke me to visit and punish them, I will add unto their punishment somewhat from the desert of this sin of their forefathers.' Whence is that proverb among the Jews, " That there is no evil befalls them but it hath in it some grain of the golden calf." ופקדתי עליהם מעט מן העון הזה עם שאר העונות, saith Rashi,—" He will mix a little somewhat of the guilt of this sin with the rest of their sins." And therefore the same word, of " visiting," is here used as in the threatening in the commandment, Exod. xx. 5. And when one generation after another shall persist in the same provoking sins, the weight of God's indignation grows so heavy, that ordinarily in one part or other it begins to fall within the third or fourth generation. And doth it not concern men to consider what have been the ways of their forefathers, lest there lie a secret, consuming curse against them in the guilt of their sins? Repentance and forsaking their ways wholly intercept the progress of the curse, and set a family at liberty from a great and ancient debt to the justice of God. So God stateth this matter at large, Ezek. xviii. Men know not what arrears may by this means be chargeable on their inheritances; much more, it may be, than all they are worth is able to answer. There is no avoidance of the writ for satisfaction that is gone out against them, but by turning out of the way wherein they are pursued. The same is the case of the blessing that is stored for the posterity of the obedient, provided they are found in the way of their forefathers. These things render them and their ways objects of our consideration. For moreover,—

Obs. XIII. It is a dangerous condition, for children to boast of the privilege of their fathers, and to imitate their sins.

This was almost continually the state of the Jews. They were still boasting of their progenitors, and constantly walking in their sins. This they are everywhere in the Scripture charged withal. See Num. xxxii. 14. This the Baptist reflected on in his first dealing with them: " Bring forth," saith he, " fruits meet for repentance; and think not to say within yourselves, We have Abraham to our father," Matt. iii. 8, 9. On every occasion they still cried out, " We have Abraham to our father,"—he who was so highly favoured of God, and first received the promises. For his sake and by his means they expected to be saved temporally and eternally. Hence they have a saying in their Talmud, שאברהם יושב על פתחי של גיהנם שלא להניח לירד פישעי ישראל בגיהנם;—"Abraham sits at the gates of hell, and will not permit that any transgressors of Israel shall go in thither,"—a great reserve against all their 'sins, but that it will deceive them when they are past relief. It is true they had on this account many privileges, as our apostle testifies in sundry places, Rom. iii. 1, 2, ix. 4, 5; and so he esteemed them to be as to his own personal interest in them, Phil. iii. 4, 5. But whilst they trusted unto them and continued in the sins of them who had abused them, it turned to their further ruin. See Matt. xxiii. 29–32. And let their example deter others from countenancing themselves in privileges of any kind whilst they come short of personal faith and obedience. Again,—

Obs. XIV. A multitude joining in any sin gives it thereby a great aggravation.

Those here that sinned were all the persons of one entire generation. This made it a formal, open rebellion, a conspiracy against
God, a design as it were to destroy his kingdom and to leave him
no subjects in the world. When many conspire in the same sin it
is a great inducement unto others to follow. Hence is that caution
in the law, Exod. xxiii. 2, " Thou shalt not follow a multitude to do
evil." The law, indeed, hath an especial respect unto judgment and
causes of differences among men. But there is a general direction
in the law for our whole course : לֹא־תִהְיֶה אַחֲרֵי־רַבִּים לְרָעֹת;—" Thou
shalt not be after many" (or "great men") "unto evils,"—'Take
heed of the inclination of a multitude unto evil, lest thou art also
carried away with their errors and sin;' and this aggravates the sin
of many. It doth so also, that the opposition unto God therein is
open and notorious, which tends greatly to his dishonour in the
world. And what resentment God hath of the provocation that lies
herein is fully expressed in Numbers, chap. xiv., from verse 20 unto
verse 35, speaking of the sin of the congregation in their unbelief and
murmuring against him. In the first place, he engageth himself by
his oath to vindicate his glory from the reproach which they had
cast upon it, verse 21, " As truly as I live," saith he, " all the earth
shall be filled with the glory of the LORD." Some take these words
to be only an asseveration of that which follows; as if God had said,
' As truly as I live, and as the earth is filled with my glory, all
these men shall perish;' but the words rather contain the principal
matter of the oath of God. He swears that as they, by their conjunct sin and rebellion, had dishonoured him in the world, so he, by
his works of power and vengeance on them, would fill the earth again
with his glory. And there is in the following words a representation of a great πάθος, or "commotion," with great indignation:
" They have," saith he, " seen my miracles, and have tempted me
now these ten times," verse 22. The Hebrew doctors do scrupu-
lously reckon up these temptations. The first, they say, is in Exod.
xiv. 11, when they said, " Because there were no graves in Egypt."
The second in Marah, Exod. xv. 24, " The people murmured against
Moses, saying, What shall we drink?" The third in the desert of
Sin, Exod. xvi. 2, 3, " The whole congregation of the children of
Israel murmured against Moses and Aaron, and said, Would to God
we had died by the hand of the LORD in Egypt, when we sat by the
flesh-pots." The fourth when they left manna until the morning,
Exod. xvi. 19, 20, " And Moses said, Let no man leave of it till
the morning. Notwithstanding they hearkened not unto Moses;
but some of them left of it until the morning, and it bred worms,
and stank." The fifth was when some of them went out to gather
manna on the Sabbath-day, Exod. xvi. 27, 28, which God called a
" refusing to keep his commandments and his laws." The sixth was

in Rephidim, at the waters of Meribah, Num. xx. 2–13. The seventh in Horeb, when they made the calf, Exod. xxxii. The eighth at Taberah, Num. xi. 1–3. The ninth at Kibroth-hattaavah, Num. xi. 31–34. The tenth upon the return of the spies, Num. xiv. Thus are the ten temptations reckoned up by some of the Jews, and by others of them they are enumerated with some little alteration. But whether the exact number of ten be intended in the expression is very uncertain; it seems rather to intend multiplied temptations, expressed with much indignation. So Jacob when he chode with Laban told him, "Thou hast changed my wages ten times," Gen. xxxi. 41; that is, frequently, which he so expressed in his anger and provocation. So doth God here,—"Ye have tempted me these ten times;" that is, 'So often, so far, that I neither can nor will bear with you any longer.' In the whole discourse (which sinners ought to read and tremble at) there is represented as it were such a rising of anger and indignation in the face of God, such a commotion of soul in displeasure (both made use of to declare an unchangeable will of punishing), as scarce appears again in the Scripture. Thus it is for a multitude to transgress against God, as it were by a joint conspiracy. Such issues will all national apostasies and provocations receive. And this is the first general part of the example proposed to consideration, namely, the persons sinning, with the observations that arise from thence.

2. The second is the matter or *quality of their sin*, which is referred unto two heads:—(1.) Their *provocation*, "In the provocation, in the day of temptation." (2.) Their *tempting* of him, "They tempted me, and proved me."

(1.) Their sin consisted in their provoking. It seems not to be any one particular sin, but the whole carriage of the people in the actions reflected on, that is intended; and that not at any one time, but in their whole course. The word in the original, as was declared, signifies "to chide," "to strive," "to contend," and that in words: Isa. xlv. 9, הוֹי רָב אֶת־יֹצְרוֹ,—"Woe unto him that striveth with his Maker!" And how doth or may he do it? "Shall the clay say to him that made it?" etc. It is by "saying," by speaking against him, that he may so strive with him. But the apostle hath expressed it by a word denoting the effect of that chiding, that is exacerbation or provocation. The expression of the actions here intended, in the places before mentioned, Exod. xvii. Num. xx. 13, the chiding of the people, as we observed before, is directly said to be with Moses, as their tempting afterwards is of the Lord. Thus Moses says unto them, "Why chide ye with me? wherefore do ye tempt the LORD?" Exod. xvii. 2. But it is also said expressly, "They strove" (the same word) "with the LORD," Num. xx. 13. The meaning is, that "striving" or "chiding" (מְרִיבָה, from רוּב) being properly an altercation with or in words, Moses, and not God, was the immediate object of their chiding; but because it was about and concerning the works of God, which Moses had no relation unto but as he was his minister, servant, and employed by him, the principal object of their chiding, as formally a sin, was also God himself. In striving with Moses they strove with him, and in chiding with Moses they chode with him. This expression, then, in general compriseth all the sinful actions of that people against God under the ministry of Moses.

There are two things to be considered in this matter of provocation;—[1.] The *sin* that is included in it; [2.] The *event* or consequent of it,—God was provoked. The former seems firstly intended in the Hebrew word, the latter in the Greek.

[1.] For the sin intended, it is evident from the story that it was unbelief acting itself by murmuring and complaints; the same for the substance of it by which also they tempted God. This the apostle declares to have been the great provoking sin, verse 19: "So we see that they could not enter in, by reason of unbelief." That was the sin which so provoked God as that "he sware in his wrath that they should not enter into his rest." Yet it is not their unbelief absolutely considered that is intended, but as it brought forth the effects of chiding with Moses and murmuring against God, which on all occasions they fell into. Though unbelief itself, especially in such a season, be a provoking sin, yet this murmuring and chiding so added unto its provocation that it is directly laid on their accounts. But they also, as the apostle says, are to be resolved into their spring or cause,—that is, unbelief. They are but an especial sign, circumstance, or effect of their unbelief.

[2.] The effect of this sin was the provocation or exacerbation of God. The Hebrew word which the apostle here expresseth by παρα-πικρασμός, is כַּמְּרִיבָה; which sometimes is taken actively, for "provoking," "inciting," "stimulating," "imbittering;" sometimes passively, for "indignation," "perturbation," "sorrow," "grief," "trouble." In the whole it includes the imbittering of the mind of its object, with an excitation unto anger, displeasure, and wrath. Now, these things are ascribed unto God only by an anthropopathy. Such effects being usually wrought in the minds of the best men when they are unjustly and ungratefully dealt withal, God, to show men the nature of their sins, ascribes them unto himself. His mind is not imbittered, moved, or changed; but men have deserved to be dealt withal as if it were so. See Jer. viii. 19; 2 Kings xxi. 15; Isa. lxv. 3; Jer. xxv. 7, xxxii. 29; 2 Chron. xxviii. 25.

Now, this provocation of God by their unbelief, acting itself in murmuring, chiding, and complaining, is further expressed from the season of it,—it was in the "day of temptation," the day of Massah. The denomination is taken from the name of the place where they first murmured for water, and tempted God by the discovery of their unbelief. As it was called Meribah from the contention, chiding, and provoking, so it was called Massah from the tempting of God there,—the " day of temptation." In this expression, not the addition of a new sin to that of provocation is intended, but only a description of the sin and season of that sin. It was in the " day of temptation" that God was so provoked by them. How also they tempted him we shall see afterwards. Now, as this day signally began upon the temptation at Meribah, so it continued through the whole course of the people's peregrination in the wilderness,—their multiplied tempting of God made this whole time a " day of temptation."

Now, let us consider hence some further observations :—

Obs. XV. The sinful actings of men against those who deal with them in the name of God, and about the works or will of God, are principally against God himself.

The people chode with Moses; but when God came to call it to an account, he says they strove with him and provoked him. So Moses told the people, to take them off from their vain pretences and coverings of their unbelief : Exod. xvi. 2, " The whole congregation murmured against Moses and Aaron." But saith he, verse 7, " The LORD heareth your murmurings against him : and what are we that ye murmur against us?" As if he had said, ' Mistake not yourselves, it is God, and not us, that you have to do withal in this matter. What you suppose you speak only against us, is indeed directly though not immediately spoken against God.' So God himself informs Samuel, upon the repining of the people against him : " They have not rejected thee, but they have rejected me, that I should not reign over them;" because he ruled them immediately in the name of God, 1 Sam. viii. 7. They pretended weariness of the government of Samuel, but were indeed weary of God and his rule. And so what was done against him, God took as done against himself. And under the new testament, our Saviour in particular applies this rule unto the dispensers of the gospel, Luke x. 16 : saith he, " He that heareth you heareth me; and he that despiseth you despiseth me; and he that despiseth me despiseth him that sent me." The preachers of the gospel are sent by Christ, and therefore their opposition and contempt do first reflect dishonour upon him, and through him upon God himself.

And the reason hereof is, because in their work they are representatives of God himself,—they act in his name and in his stead, as his ambassadors : 2 Cor. v. 20, " Now then," saith the apostle, " we are ambassadors for Christ, as though God did beseech you by us : we pray you in Christ's stead, be ye reconciled to God." They treat with men as sent of God, in his name, about the affairs of Christ. The violation of an ambassador amongst men is always esteemed to redound unto the dishonour of him by whom he is employed; for it is he unto whom the injury and affront are principally intended, especially if it be done unto him in discharge of his office Nor are kings or states ever more highly provoked than when an injury is offered or an affront done unto their ambassadors. The Romans of old utterly destroyed Tarentum in Italy, and Corinth in Greece, on that account; and occasions of the same nature have been like of late to fill the world with blood and tumult. And the reason is, because, according to the light of nature, what is done immediately against a representative as such, is done directly and intentionally against the person represented. So it is in this case. The enmity of men is against God himself, against his way, his works, his will, which his ambassadors do but declare. But these things absolutely are out of their reach. They cannot reach them nor hurt them; nor will they own directly an opposition unto them. Therefore are pretences invented by men against those who are employed by God, that under their covert they may execute their rage against God himself. So Amaziah, priest of Bethel, complained to Jeroboam the king, saying, "Amos hath conspired against thee in the midst of the house of Israel: the land is not able to bear all his words." It is not because he preached against his idolatry, or denounced the judgments of God against the sins of men, that Amaziah opposeth him; no, it is merely on the account of his sedition, and the danger of the king thereby, Amos vii. 10. And when, as it is likely, he could not prevail with the king for his destruction, he deals with him personally himself, to flee away, and so to render himself suspected, verses 12, 13. He had used an invidious expression concerning him to the king, קָשַׁר עָלֶיךָ,—" He hath conspired against thee;" that is, to take away thy life. The word is used concerning two kings of Judah, one after another, and the matter ended in their death, 2 Chron. xxiv. 25, xxv. 27. And it is mostly used for a conspiracy ending in death. And yet all this was from enmity against God, and from no affection to the king. Under the shade of such pretences do men act their opposition unto God upon his messengers. God sees that they are all but coverts for their lusts and obstinacy,—that himself is intended; and he esteems it so accordingly.

Instruction lies plain herein for them who, by vainly-invented pleas and pretences, do endeavour to give countenance to their own consciences in opposition unto those who speak in the name and treat about the things of God. Let them look to it; though they may so satisfy themselves, in and by their own prejudices, as to think they do God good service when they kill them, yet they will find things in the issue brought unto another account. This lies so clear from what hath been spoken that I shall not further insist on it. But let them principally consider this, and thence what is incumbent on them, who are called to deal with others in the name of God. And,—

[1.] Let them take heed that they neither do, nor act, nor speak any thing but what they have sufficient warrant from him for. It is a dangerous thing to entitle God or his name unto our own *imaginations*. God will not set his seal of approbation, he will not own a concernment in our lie, though we should think that it tends to his glory, Rom. iii. 7. Neither will he own what is done against us as done against himself, unless we stand in his counsels, and be found in the ways of his will. There is no object of a more sad consideration, than to see some men persecuting others for their errors. They that persecute,—suppose them in the right as to the matter in difference between them and those whom they do oppress,—yet do certainly act against God in what they pretend to act for him; for they usurp his authority over the souls and consciences of men. And they that are persecuted do sacrifice their concernments to the darkness of their own minds. God may concern himself in general to own their integrity towards himself, even in their mistakes; but in the particular wherein they suffer he will not own them. Whether, therefore, we are to do or to suffer any thing for God, it is of great concernment unto us to look well to our call or warrant. And then,

[2.] When men are secured by the word and Spirit of God that their message is not their own, but his that sent them,—that they seek not their own glory, but his,—they may have hence all desirable grounds of encouragement, supportment, and consolation, in all the straits and temptations they meet withal in this world. They can be no more utterly prevailed against (that is, their testimony cannot) than can God himself. So he speaks to Jeremiah: "I will make thee a fenced brazen wall; they shall fight against thee, but they shall not prevail against thee: for I am with thee to save thee, and to deliver thee, saith the LORD," Jer. xv. 20. And in what they suffer God is so far concerned, as to account all that is done against them to be done against himself. Christ is hungry with them, and thirsty with them, and in prison with them, Matt. xxv. 35–40. Again,—

Obs. XVI. Unbelief manifesting itself in a time of trial is a most provoking sin.

This, as we have showed, was the sin of the people in their provocation of God. And it is a great sin,—the great sin, the spring of all sins at all times; but it hath many aggravations attending of it in a time of trial. And this compriseth the first sense of the limitation of time in that word, " This day," before intimated, namely, an especial time and season wherein the guilt of this sin may be eminently contracted. For I speak not of unbelief in general with respect unto the covenant and the promises thereof, but of unbelief as working in a *distrust of God* with respect unto the *dispensations of his providence.* It is a disbelieving of God as to any concernment of our own when we have a sufficient warrant to believe and put our trust in him, when it is our duty so to do. And two things we may make a brief inquiry into:—

[1.] What is required that men may be in such a condition as wherein they may contract the guilt of this sin? And hereunto three things do belong:—

1st. That in general *they be found in the way of God.* God's promises of his presence, and of his protection unto men, are confined unto his own ways, which alone are theirs, or ought so to be: " He shall give his angels charge over thee, to keep thee in all thy ways," Ps. xci. 11;—that is, the ways that he hath appointed thee to walk in. The benefit of which promise the devil vainly attempted to deprive our Saviour of, by seducing him to ways that were not his, ways that God had not appointed. Men in ways of their own,—that is, in the crooked paths of sin,—are not obliged to trust in God for mercy and protection in them. So to do, or to pretend so to do, is to entitle God to their lusts. For men to say they trust in God in the pursuit of their covetousness, injustice, oppression, sensuality, or in ways wherein these things have a prevailing mixture, or to pray for the protecting, the blessing presence of God in them, is a high provocation. Every difficulty, every opposition that such men meet withal is raised by God to turn them out of their way. And to expect their removal by him, or strength and assistance against them, is to desire the greatest evil unto their own souls that in this world they are obnoxious unto. The Israelites here blamed were in the way of God, and no opposition ought to have discouraged them therein.

2dly. That in particular *they have a warrantable call to engage into that way wherein they are.* A way may be good and lawful in itself, but not lawful to a man that enters upon it without a sufficient call to engage in it. And this deprives men also of the grounds of expectation of God's presence, so as to that particular way wherein they cannot contract the guilt of this sin; though commonly it is distrust of God that casts men into such ways. It was the way and work of God that the Israelites should destroy the Amorites and possess their land; but when they would in a heat, without a sufficient warrant, go up into the hill and fight with them, Moses says unto them, " Go not up, for the LORD is not among you; . . . . . and they were discomfited unto Hormah," Num. xiv. 42–45. Unto a lawful way, then, in general, a lawful call in particular must be added, or we have not a sufficient foundation for the discharge of that duty whose defect is now charged by us.

3dly. They must have a sufficient warranty of the presence and protection of God. This is that which makes faith and trust a duty. And God gives it two ways,—1. In general, in the promise of the covenant, wherein he hath undertaken to be with us, to bless us, and to carry us through the course of our duty: Heb. xiii. 5, "He hath said, I will never leave thee, nor forsake thee." This alone is a sufficient ground and foundation for faith and trust in every condition. And this the Israelites had in the promise made unto Abraham and others of their forefathers. 2. By giving some signal instances of his power, wisdom, and care, in his presence with us, by protection, direction, preservation, or deliverance, in those ways of his wherein we are engaged. When by this means he hath given us experience of his goodness, faithfulness, and approbation of the ways wherein we are, this adds a specialty unto the general warrant for faith in the word of promise. And this they also had in all those works of God which they saw for forty years.

[2.] It must be inquired, what it is that makes any time or season to be a day of trial, seeing the miscarriage of men in such a season is expressed as a great aggravation of their sin. And they are the things that follow:—

1*st*. That there be a concernment of the glory of God in the performance of that duty wherein we are to act faith, or to trust in God. So God tried the faith of Abraham in a duty wherein his glory was greatly concerned. For by his obedience in faith, it appeared to all the world that Abraham respected God, and valued a compliance with his will above all things in this world whatever. So God himself expresseth it, Gen. xxii. 12: "Now I know that thou fearest God, seeing thou hast not withheld thy son, thine only son from me." This was the tenth and last trial that befell Abraham. Nine times he had been tried before:—1. In his departure out of his country; 2. By the famine which drove him into Egypt; 3. In the taking away of his wife there by Pharaoh; 4. In his war with the four kings; 5. In his hopelessness of issue by Sarah, whence he took Hagar; 6. In the law of circumcision; 7. His wife taken from him again by Abimelech; 8. His casting out of Hagar after she had conceived; 9. His expulsion of Ishmael. In some of these it is known how he failed, though in most of them he acquitted himself as became the father of the faithful. But now the " fluctus decumanus" came upon him, his last and utmost trial, wherein he was made a spectacle to men, angels, and devils. The Jews tell us great stories of the opposition made by Satan, in his arguing with Abraham and Isaac about and against their obedience in this thing; and no doubt but he employed himself unto that purpose. And it is endless to show how many eyes were upon him; all which gave a concernment of glory unto God. Here, therefore, Abraham in a most especial manner acquits himself; whence God gives him that testimony, "Now I know that thou fearest God;" that is, 'Now thou hast made

it known beyond all exception.' And this puts a blessed close unto
all his signal trials. When, therefore, God calls men forth unto the
performance and discharge of any duty wherein his glory and honour
in the world is concerned, then he makes it unto them a time of
trial.

2dly. Difficulties and opposition lying in the way of duty make
the season of it a time of trial. When men have wind and tide
with them in their sailing, neither their strength nor their skill is
tried at all; but when all is against them, then it is known what
they are. When the sun shines and fair weather continues, the
houses that are built on the sand continue as well as those that are
built on the rock; but when the rain, and the floods, and the wind
come, they make the trial. Whilst men have outward advantages
to encourage them in the ways of God, it is not known what principles they act from; but when their obedience and profession are attended with persecution, reproach, poverty, famine, nakedness, death,
then it is tried what men build upon, and what they trust unto,—
then it is to them a time of trial.

Further; to give light unto our proposition, we may inquire how
or by what means men do or may act and manifest their unbelief
at such a time or season. And this may be done several ways:—

[1.] By *dissatisfaction in and discontent at that condition of
difficulty whereinto they are brought by the providence of God
for their trial.* Herein principally did the Israelites offend in the
wilderness. Their condition pleased them not. This occasioned all
their murmurings and complaints whereby God was provoked. It
is true they were brought into many straits and difficulties; but
they were brought into them for their trial by God himself, against
whom they had no reason to repine or complain. And this is no
small fruit, effect, and evidence of unbelief in trials,—namely, when
we like not that condition we are brought into, of poverty, want,
danger, persecution. If we like it not, it is from our unbelief. God
expects other things from us. Our condition is the effect of his wisdom, his care and love, and as such by faith ought it to be acqui-
esced in.

[2.] By *the omission of any duty that is incumbent on us, because of the difficulties that attend it, and the opposition that is
made unto it.* The "fearful" and "unbelieving" go together, Rev.
xxi. 8. When our fear or any other affection, influenced or moved by
earthly things, prevails with us to forego our duty, either absolutely
or in the most special and eminent instances of its practice, then
unbelief prevails in the time of our trials. And this way also in
particular did the Israelites fail. When they heard of fenced cities
and sons of Anak, they gave up all endeavours of going into the
land of Canaan, and consulted of making a captain to lead them

back again into Egypt. And no otherwise is it with them who forego their profession because of the giant-like opposition which they find against it.

[3.] When *men turn aside and seek for unwarrantable assist-ances against their difficulties.* So did this people,—they made a calf to supply the absence of Moses; and were contriving a return into Egypt to deliver them out of their troubles. When men in any thing make flesh their arm, their hearts depart from the Lord, Jer. xvii. 5.

[4.] When *men disbelieve plain and direct promises merely on the account of the difficulties that lie against their accomplish-ment.* This reflects unspeakable dishonour on the veracity and power of God;—the common sin of this wilderness people, they limited God, and said, Can he do this or that? Seldom it was that they believed beyond what they enjoyed. Here lay the main cause of their sin and ruin. They had a promise of entering into the land. They believed it not; and, as our apostle says, they " could not enter in because of unbelief." The promise was to their nation, the pos-terity of Abraham; the accomplishment of it in their persons de-pended on their faith. Here was their trial. They believed not, but provoked God; and so perished.

Now, the reasons of the greatness of this sin, and its aggravations, are contained in the previous description of it. Every instance de-claring its nature manifests it also to be heinous. I shall take up and only mention three of them:—

[1.] There is, as was showed, an *especial concernment of the glory of God* in this matter. He calls men forth in such a season to make a trial of their obedience. He makes them therein, as the apostle speaks, a spectacle unto men and angels. And the hinge that the whole case turns upon is their faith. This all other actings hold a conformity unto. If here they discharge themselves aright, the glory of God, the manifestation whereof is committed unto them, is preserved entire. If herein they fail, they have done what lies in them to expose it to contempt. See Num. xiv. 21. So was the case in the trial of Job. God permitted Satan to try to the utter-most whether he believed in him and loved him sincerely or no. Had Job failed herein, how would Satan have vaunted and boasted, and that against God himself! And the same advantage do others put into his hands, when at any time they miscarry in point of faith in a time of trial.

[2.] The *good and welfare, the peace and prosperity* of the church in this world, depend on the deportment of men belonging to it in their trials; they may, at least as unto God's outward dispensations to-wards them, sin at a cheaper rate at other times. A time of trial is the turn of a church's peace or ruin. We see what their unbelief cost this whole generation in the wilderness; and these Hebrews, their posterity, were now upon the like trial. And the apostle by this instance plainly intimates unto them what would be the issue if they continued therein; which accordingly proved to be their utter rejection.

[3.] Add hereunto, that it is the design of God in such particular instances to try our *faith in general* as to the promises of the covenant and our interest therein. The promise that this people had principally to deal with God about, was that of the covenant made with Abraham, the which all pretended to believe. But God tried them by the particular instances mentioned; and failing therein, they failed as unto the whole covenant. And it is so still. Many pretend that they believe the promises of the covenant as to life and salvation by it firmly and immovably. God tries them by particular instances, of persecution, difficulty, straits, public or private. Here they abide not, but either complain and murmur, or desert their duty, or fall to sinful compliances, or are weary of God's dispensations. And this manifests their unsoundness in the general; nor can it be otherwise tried.

Again, observe that,—

Obs. XVII. There is commonly a day, a time, wherein unbelief ariseth to its height in provocation.

We showed before that there is a day, an especial season of God's dealing with the sons of men, by his word and other means of grace. The due observance and improvement hereof is of the greatest importance unto them. " To-day, if ye will hear his voice;"—that is, the day wherein God's dispensations of grace and patience come to their ἀχμή, "status rerum inter incrementum et decrementum,"— their height. After this, if not closed with, if not mixed with faith and obeyed, they either insensibly decline, in respect of their tender or efficacy, or are utterly removed and taken away. In like manner there is a day, a season wherein the unbelief of men in its provocation comes to its height and uttermost issue, beyond which God will bear with them no longer, but will break off all gracious intercourse between himself and such provokers. This was the direct case with these Israelites. They had by their unbelief and murmuring provoked God ten times, as was declared before; but the day of their provocation, the season wherein it arrived to its height, came not until this trial mentioned, Num. xiv., upon the return of the spies that went to search the land. Before that time God often reproved them, was angry with them, and variously punished them, but he still returned unto them in a way of mercy and compassion, and still proposed unto them an entrance into his rest, according to the promise; but when that day once came, when the provocation of their unbelief was come to its height, then he would bear with them no longer, but swears in his wrath that they should not enter into his rest. From that day he took hold of all occasions to exercise severity against them, flooding them away, Ps. xc. 5, until that whole evil generation was consumed. And so it was with their posterity as to their church and national state. God sent unto them, and dealt variously with them, by his prophets, in several generations. Some of them they persecuted, others they killed, and upon the matter rejected them all, as to the main end of their work and message. But yet all this while God spared them, and continued them a people and a church,—their provocation was not come unto its height, its last day was not yet come. At length, according to his promise, he sent his Son unto them. This gave them their last trial, this put them into the same condition with their forefathers in the wilderness, as our apostle plainly intimates in the use of this example. Again, they despised the promises,—as their fathers had done in the type and shadow, so did they when the substance of all promises was tendered and exhibited unto them. This was the day of their last provocation, after which God would bear with them no more in a way of patience; but enduring them for the space of near forty years, he utterly rejected them;—sending forth his servants, " he slew those murderers, and burned up their city." This is that which our Saviour at large declares in his parable of the householder and his husbandmen, Matt. xxi. 33–41.

And thus in God's dealing with the antichristian state, there is a season wherein the angel swears that " there shall be time no longer," Rev. x. 6; that God would no longer bear with men, or forbear them in their provocations and idolatries, but would thenceforth give them up unto all sorts of judgments spiritual and temporal, unto their utter confusion,—yea, " send them strong delusion, that they should believe a lie, that they all might be damned who believed not the truth, but had pleasure in unrighteousness," 2 Thess. ii. 11, 12. And concerning this day two things may be observed:— [1.] That it is *uncertain;* [2.] That it is *unalterable.*

[1.] It is *uncertain.* Men know not when their provocations do come or will come unto this height. Jerusalem knew not in the entrance of her day that her sin and unbelief were coming to their issue, and so was not awakened to their prevention; no more than the men of Sodom knew when the sun arose that there was a cloud of fire and brimstone hanging over their heads. Men in their sins think they will do as at other times, as Samson did when his locks were cut, and that things will be made up between God and them as formerly,—that they shall yet have space and time for their work and duty; but ere they are aware they have finished their course, and filled up the measure of their sins. " For man also knoweth not his time: as the fishes that are taken in an evil net, and as the birds that are caught in the snare; so are the sons of

men snared in an evil time, when it falleth suddenly upon them,"
Eccles. ix. 12. For the day of the Lord's indignation comes "as a
snare on them that dwell on the face of the earth," Luke xxi. 35.
And men are often crying, "Peace, peace," when sudden destruction
comes upon them, 1 Thess. v. 3. When Babylon shall say "she sits
as a queen, and is no widow" (her sons being again restored unto
her), "and shall see no sorrow; then shall her plagues come in one
day, death, and mourning, and famine, and she shall be utterly
burned with fire," Rev. xviii. 7, 8. Hence is Christ so often said
to come as a thief, to manifest how men will be surprised by him
in their sins and impenitency. And if the outward peace and the
lives of men in this condition be respited for a while, as ofttimes
they are, yet they are no longer under a dispensation of patience.
There is nothing between God and them but anger and wrath. If
men knew when would be their last trial, and which were it, we
think they would rouse up themselves to a deep consideration of it,
and a serious compliance with the call of God. But this, in the
holy will and wisdom of God, is always hid from them, until it be
too late to make use of it, until it can produce no effects but a few
despairing wishes. God will have none of his warnings, none of his
merciful dispensations put off or slighted with the hope and expectation of another season, by a foolish promising whereof unto themselves men ruin their souls every day.

[2.] It is *unalterable and irrecoverable.* When the provocation of unbelief comes to this height there is no space or room left
for repentance, either on the part of God or the sinner. For men,
for the most part, after this they have no thought of repenting.
Either they see themselves irrecoverable, and so grow desperate, or
become stupidly senseless and lie down in security. So those false
worshippers in the Revelation, after time was granted unto them no
longer, but the plagues of God began to come upon them, it is said
they repented not, but bit their tongues for anger, and blasphemed
God. Instead of repenting of their sins, they rage against their
punishment. And if they do change their mind in any thing, as
Esau did when he saw the blessing was gone, it is not by true repentance, nor shall it be unto any effect or purpose. So the Israelites finished their sin by murmuring against the Lord upon the
return of the spies, and said they would not go up into the land,
but would rather return into Egypt, Num. xiv. But after a while
they changed their minds, "and they rose up early in the morning,
and gat them up into the top of the mountain, saying, Lo, we be
here, and will go up unto the place which the LORD hath promised," verse 40. But what was the issue? Their time was past, the
Lord was not among them: "The Amalekites came down, and the
Canaanites which dwelt in that hill, and smote them, and discom-

fited them, even unto Hormah," verse 45. Their change of mind
was not repentance, but a new aggravation of their sin. Repentance also in this matter is hid from the eyes of God. When Saul
had finished his provocation, Samuel, denouncing the judgment of
God against him, adds, "And also the Strength of Israel will not
lie nor repent," 1 Sam. xv. 29. God firms his sentence, and makes
it irrevocable, by the engagement of his own immutability. There
is no change, no alteration, no reprieve, no place for mercy, when
this day is come and gone, Ezek. xxi. 25.

Let persons, let churches, let nations, take heed lest they fall
unawares into this evil day. I say unawares to themselves, because
they know not when they may be overtaken by it. It is true, all
the danger of it ariseth from their own negligence, security, and
stubbornness. If they will give ear to previous warnings, this day
will never come upon them. It may not, therefore, be unworthy
our inquiry to search what prognostics men may have into the
approach of such a day. And,—

[1.] When *persons, churches, or nations, have already contracted the guilt of various provocations*, they may justly fear that
their next shall be their last. 'You have,' saith God to the Israelites, 'provoked me these ten times,'—that is, frequently, as hath
been declared,—'and now your day is come. You might have considered before, that I would not always thus bear with you.' Hath
God, then, borne with you in one and another provocation, temptation, backsliding?—take heed lest the great sin lies at the door, and
be ready to enter upon the next occasion. As God told Cain, Gen.
iv. 7, "If thou dost not do well חַטָּאת לַפֶּתַח רֹבֵץ," "peccatum ad
ostium cubat,"—"sin lies down at the door," as a beast ready to enter
on the next occasion, the next opening of it. After former provocations so lieth that which shall fill the ephah, and have the talent of
lead laid upon it. Take heed, gray hairs are sprinkled upon you,
though you perceive it not. Death is at the door. Beware lest
your next provocation be your last. When your transgressions
come to three and four, the punishment of your iniquities will not
be turned away. When that is come, you may sin whilst you will
or while you can; God will have no more to do with you but in a
way of judgment.

[2.] When *repentance upon convictions of provocations lessens
or decays*, it is a sad symptom of an approaching day wherein iniquity will be completed. Useful repentance,—that is, that which is
of any use in this world for the deferring or retarding of judgment,
—is commensurate unto God's dispensations of patience. When
the fixed bounds of it (as it hath fixed bounds) are arrived at, all
springs of repentance are dried up. When, therefore, persons
fall into the guilt of many provocations, and God giving in a con-

viction of them by his word or providence, they are humbled for
them according to their light and principles; if they find their
humiliations, upon their renewed convictions, to grow weak, decay,
and lessen in their effects,—they do not so reflect upon themselves
with self-displicency as formerly, nor so stir up themselves unto
amendment as they have done upon former warnings or convictions,
nor have in such cases their accustomed sense of the displeasure
and terror of the Lord,—let them beware, evil is before them,
and the fatal season of their utmost provoking is at hand, if not
prevented.

[3.] When *various dispensations of God towards men have been
useless and fruitless*, when mercies, judgments, dangers, deliverances, signally stamped with respect unto the sins of men, but
especially the warnings of the word, have been multiplied towards
any persons, churches, or nations, and have passed over them without their reformation or recovery, no doubt but judgment is ready
to enter, yea, if it be into the house of God itself.

Is it thus with any, is this their estate and condition?—let them
please themselves while they please, they are like Jonah, asleep in
the ship, whilst it is ready to be cast away on their account.
Awake and tremble; you know not how soon a great, vigorous, prevalent temptation may hurry you into your last provocation. And
this is the first head of sin instanced in.

(2.) They are said also to have tempted God: " In the temptation; when your fathers tempted me." Wherein their provocation did consist, and what was the sin which is so expressed, we
have declared. We must now inquire what was their tempting
of God, of what nature was their sin therein, and wherein it did
consist. To tempt God is a thing frequently mentioned in the
Scripture, and condemned as a provoking sin. And it is generally
esteemed to consist in a venturing on or an engaging into any way,
work, or duty, without sufficient call, warrant, or rule, upon the
account of trusting God therein; or, in the neglect of the use of
ordinary means in any condition, desiring, expecting, or trusting
unto any extraordinary assistances or supplies from God. So when
men seem rashly to cast themselves into danger, out of a confidence
in the presence and protection of God, it is said that they tempt
God. And sundry texts of Scripture seem to give countenance to
this description of the sin of tempting of God. So Isa. vii. 11,
12: When the prophet bade Ahaz ask a sign of the Lord in the
depth or in the height above, he replied, " I will not ask, neither
will I tempt the LORD;"—that is, ' I will rest in what thou hast
said, and not tempt God by seeking any thing extraordinary.' And
so when Satan tempted our Saviour to show his power by casting
himself down from a pinnacle of the temple,—which was none of

his ways,—Matt. iv. 7, he answers him by that saying of Deut. vi. 16, "Thou shalt not tempt the LORD thy God." To venture, therefore, on any thing, unwarrantably trusting unto God for protection, is to tempt him. And this is usually and generally allowed as the nature of this sin and sense of this expression.

But yet I must needs say, that upon the consideration of all the places where mention is made of tempting the Lord, I am forced to embrace another sense of the meaning of this expression, which if it be not utterly exclusive of that already mentioned, yet it is doubtless more frequently intended, and doth more directly express the sin here condemned. Now, this is a distrust of God whilst we are in any of his ways, after we have received sufficient experiences and instances of his power and goodness to confirm us in the stability and certainty of his promises. Thus to do is to tempt God. And when this frame is found in any, they are said to tempt him; that is, to provoke him by their unbelief. It is not barely and nakedly to disbelieve the promises, it is not unbelief in general, but it is to disbelieve them under some peculiar attestation and experience obtained of the power and goodness of God in their pursuit and towards their accomplishment. When, therefore, men are engaged into any way of God according to their duty, and meeting with opposition and difficulty therein, if they give way to despondency and unbelief, if they have received any signal pledges of his faithfulness, in former effects of his wisdom, care, power, and goodness, they tempt God, and are guilty of the sin here branded and condemned. The most eminent instances of tempting God in the Scripture, and which are most frequently mentioned, are these of the Israelites in the wilderness. As they are here represented in the story, so they are called over again both in the Old Testament and the New: Ps. lxxviii. 41, "Yea, they turned back and tempted God, and limited the Holy One of Israel;" and 1 Cor. x. 9, they "tempted Christ." And wherein did this temptation consist? It was in this, and no other,—they would not believe or trust God when they were in his way, after they had received many experiences of his power and presence amongst them. And this is directly expressed, Exod. xvii. 7, "They tempted the LORD, saying, Is the LORD among us, or not?" They doubted of and questioned his presence, and also all the pledges and tokens which he had given them of it. And this sin of theirs the psalmist at large pursues, showing wherein it did consist, Ps. lxxviii. 22, 23, "They believed not in God, and trusted not in his salvation, though he had commanded the clouds from above, and opened the doors of heaven." Verse 32, "For all this they sinned still, and believed not for his wondrous works." Verses 41, 42, "They turned back and tempted God, and limited the Holy One of Israel. They remembered not

his hand, nor the day when he delivered them from the enemy."
Thus plain doth he make the nature of their sin in tempting of
God. It was their distrust and disobeying of him, after they had
received so many encouraging evidences of his power, goodness, and
wisdom amongst them. This, and this alone, is in the Scripture
called tempting of God. For that of our Saviour, Matt. iv. 7, " Thou
shalt not tempt the Lord thy God," it was taken, as was observed,
from Deut. vi. 16, where the following words are, " as ye tempted
him in Massah." Now this tempting of God at Massah was that which
we have declared, namely, the disbelieving of him after many evidences of his power and faithfulness. And this directly answers the
end for which our Saviour made use of these words; which was to
show that he was so far satisfied of God's presence with him, and of
his being the Son of God, that he would not tempt him by desiring
other experience of it, as though what he had already were not
sufficient. And the reason why Ahaz said he would not tempt the
Lord in asking a sign, was no other but because he believed not
either that he would give him a sign or that he would deliver: and
therefore he resolved to trust to himself, and with his money to
hire the Assyrians to help him; which he did accordingly, 2 Kings
xvi. 7–9.

And this sin is called tempting of God, from its *effect*, and not
from its *formal nature*. They "tempted God;" that is, by their unbelief they provoked him and stirred him up to anger and indignation. And from the discovery of the nature of this sin we may
observe, that,—

Obs. XVIII. To distrust God, to disbelieve his promises, whilst a
way of duty lies before us, after we have had experiences of his
goodness, power, and wisdom, in his dealing with us, is a tempting
of God, and a greatly provoking sin.

And a truth this is that hath ציד בפיו, " meat in his mouth," or
instruction ready for us, that we may know how to charge this aggravation of our unbelief upon our souls and consciences. Distrust of
God is a sin that we are apt, upon sundry perverse reasonings, to
indulge ourselves in, and yet is there nothing wherewith God is
more provoked. Now, it appears in the proposition laid down, that
sundry things are required that a person, a church, a people, may
render themselves formally guilty of this sin; as,—

[1.] That *they be called unto or engaged in some especial way of
God.* And this is no extraordinary thing. All believers who attend
unto their duty will find it to be their state and condition. So were
the Israelites in the wilderness. If we are out of the ways of God,
our sin may be great, but it is a sin of another nature. It is in his
ways that we have his promises, and therefore it is in them, and
with reference unto them, that we are bound to believe and trust in

him; and on the same account, in them alone can we tempt God by our unbelief.

[2.] That in this way *they meet with oppositions,* difficulties, hardships, temptations; and this, whilst Satan and the world continue in their power, they shall be sure to do. Yea, God himself is pleased ofttimes to exercise them with sundry things of this nature. Thus it befell the people in the wilderness. Sometimes they had no bread, and sometimes they had no water; sometimes enemies assaulted them, and sometimes serpents bit them. Those things which in God's design are trials of faith, and means to stir it up unto a diligent exercise, in their own natures are grievous and troublesome, and in the management of Satan tend to the producing of this sin, or tempting of God.

[3.] That *they have received former experiences of the goodness, power, and wisdom of God,* in his dealings with them. So had this people done; and this God chargeth them withal when he reproacheth them with this sin of tempting him. And this also all believers are or may be made partakers of. He who hath no experience of the especial goodness and power of God towards him, it hath been through his own negligence and want of observation, and not from any defect in God's dispensations. As he leaveth not himself without witness towards the world, in that " he doth them good, sending them rain from heaven, and fruitful seasons, filling their hearts with food and gladness;" no more is he wanting towards all believers, in giving them especial tokens of his love, care, and kindness towards them; for he is the " saviour of all men," but " specially of those that believe," 1 Tim. iv. 10. But as the most in the world take no notice of the effects of his care and goodness towards them, so many believers are negligent in treasuring up experiences of his especial care and love towards them. Yet this hinders not but that the ways and dealings of God are indeed such as have been declared.

Now, where these things concur, the distrust of God is a high provocation of him. It is unbelief, the worst of sins, expressing itself to the greatest disadvantage of God's glory, the height of aggravations; for what can God do more for us, and what can we do more against him? Surely, when he hath revealed his ways unto us, and made known unto us our duty; when he hath given us pledges of his presence with us, and of his owning of us, so as to seal and ascertain his promises unto us; then for us, upon the opposition of creatures, or worldly difficulties, about outward, temporary, perishing things (for their power and efficacy extends no farther), to disbelieve and distrust him, it must needs be a high provocation to the eyes of his glory. But, alas! how frequently do we contract the guilt of this sin, both in our personal, family, and more public concernments!

A due consideration hereof lays, without doubt, matter of deep humiliation before us.

And this is the second general head insisted on by the apostle in the example proposed,—namely, the nature of the sin or sins which the people fell into, and which he intends to dehort his Hebrews from.

3. The third general head of this discourse contains a triple aggravation of the sin of the people in their provoking and tempting of God:—(1.) From the *place* wherein they so sinned,—it was in the wilderness. (2.) From the *means* they had to the contrary,—they saw the works of God. (3.) From the *continuance* of the use of those means, and the duration of their sin under them,—it was thus for forty years: "They saw my works forty years." For these, as they are circumstances of the story, so they are aggravations of the sin mentioned in it.

(1.) They thus dealt with God in the wilderness: what wilderness is intended we showed before, in the exposition of the words. And however there may be a peculiar respect unto that part of the wilderness wherein the definitive sentence of their exclusion from the land of Canaan was given out against them,—which was in the wilderness of Paran, Num. xii. 16, at the very borders of the land that they were to possess, as appears chap. xiv. 40,—yet because the time of forty years is mentioned, which was the whole time of the people's peregrination in the deserts of Arabia, I take the word to comprehend the whole. Here, in this wilderness, they provoked and tempted God. And this contains a great aggravation of their sin; for,—

[1.] This was the place wherein they were brought into *liberty*, after they and their forefathers had been in sore bondage unto the Egyptians for sundry ages. This was a mercy promised unto them, and which they cried out for in the day of their oppression: "They cried; and their cry came up unto God, by reason of the bondage," Exod. ii. 23. Now, to handsel their liberty, to make an entrance into it by this rebellion against God, it was a provoking circumstance.

[2.] It was a place wherein they lived solely and visibly upon *God's daily extraordinary provision* for them. Should he have withheld a continual working of miracles in their behalf, both they and theirs must have utterly perished. This could not but have affected them with love and fear, great preservatives of obedience, had they not been extremely stupid and obdurate.

[3.] They were in a place where they had *none to tempt* them, to provoke them, to entice them unto sin, unless they wilfully sought them out unto that very end and purpose; as they did in the case of Midian. The people now "dwelt alone, and were not reckoned

among the nations." Afterwards, indeed, when they dwelt among
other nations, they learned their manners; but as that was no excuse
for their sin, so this was a great aggravation of it, that here it sprung
merely from themselves and their own evil heart of unbelief, continually prone to depart from the living God.

(2.) It was a place wherein they continually *saw the works of God;*
which is the second general head mentioned in the aggravation of
their sin: "They saw my works." And this did aggravate their sin
on many accounts:—

[1.] From the evidence that they had that such works were
wrought, and that they were wrought of God,—they saw them. This
Moses laid weight on, Deut. v. 3, 4, "The LORD made not this covenant with our fathers, but with us, even us, אִתָּנוּ אֲנַחְנוּ אֵלֶּה," "who are
all of us here alive this day. The LORD talked with you face to face
in the mount out of the midst of the fire." "Not with our fathers;"
that is, say some, ' our forefathers who died in Egypt, and heard not
the voice of God in Horeb:' or, "Not with our fathers;" that is, only,—
their fathers were alive at the giving of the law, 'but the covenant was
not made with them only, but with us also.' So Rashi on the place,
לא את אבותינו כלבד, "Not with our fathers only." And then כִּי אִתָּנוּ is
as much as כִּי גַּם אִתָּנוּ, as Aben Ezra observes, "with us also." And he
confirms this kind of speech from that of God to Jacob, "Thy name
shall be called no more Jacob, but Israel;"—that is, 'Thou shalt not
be called only so;' for he was frequently called Jacob afterwards.
Others suppose that by the "fathers," Abraham, and Isaac, and Jacob,
are intended, who were the especial fathers of the people. Now,
they received the promise, and therein had the covenant of grace
confirmed unto them, but had no share in the special covenant
which was made in, by, and at the giving of the law; and in this
sense the emphasis is on the word הַזֹּאת,—בְּרִית הַזֹּאת, "this covenant,"
this which is now made in the giving of the law. For my part, I
am apt to think that God doth in these words of Moses show his
indignation against all that provoking generation of their fathers in
that wilderness, and affirms his covenant was not made with them,
because they despised it, and received no benefit by it; for it had a
peculiar respect unto the land of Canaan, concerning which God
sware that they should not enter it. ' It was not with *them,*' saith
he, ' whom God despised and regarded not, but with you who are
now ready to enter into the promised land, that this covenant was
made.' See Heb. viii. 9. The ground why I produced this place,
is to show what weight is to be laid on immediate transactions with
God,—personal seeing of his works. Herein they had an advantage
above those who could only say with the psalmist, Ps. xliv. 1, "We
have heard with our ears, O God, our fathers have told us, what work
thou didst in their days, in the times of old." They saw with their

own eyes what was but told or reported unto others. And herein they had a double advantage,—

1*st.* In point of *evidence.* They had the highest and most unquestionable evidence that the works mentioned were wrought, and wrought of God,—they *saw* them. And this is clearly the most satisfactory evidence concerning miraculous works. Hence our Saviour chose those to be the witnesses of his miracles who had been αὐτόπται, "spectators," of them.

2*dly.* In point of *efficacy* for their end. Things seen and beheld have naturally a more effectual influence on the minds of men than those which they only hear of or are told them:—

> "Segnius irritant animos demissa per aures,
> Quam quæ sunt oculis subjecta fidelibus."—Hor. ad Pison., 180.

This, therefore, greatly aggravates their sin,—that they themselves saw these works of God, which were signal means of preserving them from it.

[2.] From the *nature of the works* themselves which they saw. They were such as were eminent effects of the properties of God, and means of their demonstration, and therein of the revelation of God unto them. Some of them were works of *power*, as his dividing of the sea, whose waves roared; some of *majesty* and *terror*, as the dreadful appearances, in thunders, lightnings, fire, smoke, and earthquake, at the giving of the law; some of *severity* and *indignation* against sin, as his drowning the Egyptians, the opening of the earth to swallow up Corah, Dathan, and Abiram, and the plagues that befell themselves; some of *privilege*, favour, love, and grace, as the giving of the law, intrusting them with his oracles, and forming them into a church and state, Isa. lvii. 16; some of *care* and *providence* for their continual supply, in giving water from the rock, and bread from heaven, and preserving their garments from waxing old; some of *direction* and *protection*, as in the cloud and pillar of fire, to guide, direct, and refresh them night and day in that waste howling wilderness;—in all which works God abundantly manifested his power, goodness, wisdom, grace, faithfulness, tendering them the highest security of his accomplishing his promises, if they rejected not their interest in them by their unbelief. And it is a matter well worthy consideration, how excellently and pathetically Moses pleads all these works of God with them in the Book of Deuteronomy. And all these works of God were excellent means to have wrought up the hearts of the people unto faith and obedience; and unto that end and purpose were they wrought all of them. This he frequently declared whilst they were under the accomplishment, and thereon afterwards reproacheth them with their unbelief. What could be more suited to beget in the minds of men a due apprehension of the greatness, goodness, and faithfulness of God, than they were? And what is a more effectual motive unto obedience than such apprehensions? The neglect of them, therefore, carries along with it a great aggravation of sin. To tempt God, to murmur against him, as though he could not or would not provide for them, or make good his word unto them, whilst they saw, as it were, every day, those great and marvellous works which had such an impression of his glorious image upon them, it made way for their irrecoverable destruction.

(3.) The third aggravation of the sin of this people is taken from the *time of their continuance in it,* under the use of the means to the contrary before insisted on,—it was "forty years." The patience of God was extended towards them, and his works were wrought before them, not for a week, or a month, or a year, but for forty years together! And this increaseth the greatness and strangeness of this dispensation, both on the part of God, and theirs also;—on the part of God, that he should bear with their manners so long, when they had so often deserved to be destroyed as one man, and which he had threatened often to do; and on their part, that so long a course of patience, accompanied with so many works of power and mercy, all of them for their instruction, most of them unto their present benefit and advantage, should have no effect upon them to prevent their continuance in their sin unto their ruin.

And these are the aggravations of their sin, which the psalmist collects from the circumstances of it, and which the apostle repeats for our warning and instruction; and this we shall draw out in the ensuing observations.

Obs. XIX. No place, no retiredness, no solitary wilderness, will secure men from sin or suffering, provocation or punishment.

These persons were in a wilderness, where they had many motives and encouragements unto obedience, and no means of seduction and outward temptation from others, yet there they sinned and there they suffered. They sinned in the wilderness, and their carcasses fell in the wilderness; they filled that desert with sins and graves. And the reason hereof is, because no place as such can of itself exclude the principles and causes either of sin or punishment. Men have the principle of their sins in themselves, in their own hearts, which they cannot leave behind them, or yet get off by shifting of places, or changing their stations. And the justice of God, which is the principal cause of punishment, is no less in the wilderness than in the most populous cities; the wilderness is no wilderness to him,— he can find his paths in all its intricacies. The Israelites came hither on necessity, and so they found it with them; and in after ages some have done so by choice,—they have retired into wildernesses for the furtherance of their obedience and devotion. In this very wilderness, on the top of Sinai, there is at this day a monastery of persons professing themselves to be religious, and they live there to increase religion in them. I once for some days conversed with their chief (they call him Archimandrite) here in England. For aught I could perceive, he might have learned as much elsewhere. And, indeed, what hath been the issue of that undertaking in general? For the most part, unto their old lusts men added new superstitions, until they made themselves an abomination unto the Lord, and utterly useless in the world, yea, burdensome unto human society. Such persons are like the men of Succoth whom Gideon taught with "the thorns and briers of the wilderness," Judges viii. 16. They learned nothing by it but the sharpness of the thorns and the greatness of their own folly. No more did they at best learn any thing from their wilderness retirements, but the sharpness of the place, which was a part of the punishment of their sin, and no means sanctified for the furtherance of their obedience. These two things, then, are evident:—

[1.] That the *principle* of men's unbelief and disobedience is *in themselves,* and in their own hearts, which leaves them not upon any change of their outward condition.

[2.] That no *outward state of things,* whether voluntarily chosen by ourselves, or we be brought into it by the providence of God, will either cure or conquer, or can restrain the inward principles of sin and unbelief. I remember old Jerome somewhere complains, that when he was in his horrid cave at Bethlehem, his mind was frequently among the delicacies of Rome. And this will teach us,—

1st. In every outward condition to look principally *to our own hearts.* We may expect great advantages from various conditions, but shall indeed meet with none of them, unless we fix and water the root of them in ourselves. One thinks he could serve God better in prosperity, if freed from the perplexities of poverty, sickness, or persecution; others, that they should serve him better if called unto afflictions and trials. Some think it would be better with them if retired and solitary; others, if they had more society and company. But the only way, indeed, to serve God better, is to abide in our station or condition, and therein to get better hearts. It is Solomon's advice, מִכָּל־מִשְׁמָר נְצֹר לִבֶּךָ, Prov. iv. 23, "Above or before every watch or keeping, keep thy heart." It is good to keep the *tongue,* and it is good to keep the *feet,* and it is good to keep the *way,* as he further declares in that place, but saith he, "Above all keepings, keep thy heart." And he adds a great reason for his caution: "For," saith he, " out of it are the issues of life." Life and death, in the means and causes of them, do come out of the heart. So our Saviour instructs us that in our hearts lie our treasures; what they are, that are we, and nothing else. Thence are all our actions drawn

forth, which not only smell of the cask, but receive thence principally their whole moral nature, whether they are good or bad.

2dly. Look for all relief and for help against sin *merely from
grace.* A *wilderness* will not help you, nor a *paradise.* In the one
Adam sinned, in whom we all sinned; in the other all Israel sinned,
who were an example unto us all. Men may to good purpose go
into a wilderness to exercise grace and principles of truth, when the
acting of them is denied elsewhere: but it is to no purpose to go
into a wilderness to seek for these things; their dwelling is in the
love and favour of God, and nowhere else can they be found. See
Job xxviii. 12–28. Do not expect that mercies of themselves will
do you good, or that afflictions will do you good, that the city or
the wilderness will do you good; it is grace alone that can do you
good. And if you find inward benefits by outward things, it is
merely from the grace that God is pleased to administer and dispense with them. And he can separate them when he pleaseth.
He can give mercies that shall be so *materially,* but not *eventually,*
—like the quails, which fed the bodies of the people whilst leanness
possessed their souls. And he can send affliction that shall have
nothing in it but affliction,—present troubles leading on to future
troubles. Learn, then, in all places, in every state and condition,
to live in the freedom, riches, and efficacy of grace; for other helps,
other advantages have we none.

3dly. Let us learn, *that whithersoever sin can enter punishment can follow.* " Culpam sequitur pœna pede claudo." Though
vengeance seems to have a lame foot, yet it will hunt sin until it
overtake the sinner: Ps. cxl. 11, " Evil shall hunt the violent man
to overtake him." Go where he will, the fruits of his own evil and
violence, the punishment due to them, shall hunt him and follow
him; and though it should sometimes appear to be out of sight, or
off from the scent, yet it will recover its view, and chase until it hath
brought him to destruction,—לְמִדְחֵפֹת, " to thrustings down," until he
be utterly thrust down. Saith the Targum, " The angel of death
shall hunt him until he thrust him down into hell." The heathen
owned this:—

> " Quo fugis, Encelade? quascunque accesseris oras,
>   Sub Jove semper eris."

Punishment will follow sin into the wilderness, where it is separated from all the world; and climb up after it to the top of the
tower of Babel, where all the world conspired to defend it. It
will follow it into the dark, the dark corners of their hearts and
lives, and overtake them in the light of the world. God hath ἔνδικον
ὄμμα, " an eye of revenge," that nothing can escape. " Can any
hide himself in secret places that I shall not see him? saith the
LORD. Do not I fill heaven and earth? saith the LORD," Jer. xxiii.

24. God declares whence it is that none can hide from his presence or escape his justice. It is from his omnipresence; he is everywhere, and all places are alike unto him. Adam when he had sinned went behind a tree; and others, they would go under rocks and mountains; but all is one, vengeance will find them out. This is that Δίκη which the barbarians thought would not let a murderer live, however he might escape for a season, Acts xxviii. 4.

Obs. XX. Great works of providence are a great means of instruction; and a neglect of them, as to their instructive end, is a great aggravation of the sin of those who live when and where they are performed.

" They saw my works," saith God, works great and wonderful, and yet continued in their sin and disobedience. This heightened their sin, and hastened their punishment. We shall take an instance in one of the works here intended, which will acquaint us with the design, end, and use of them all; and this shall be the appearance of the majesty of God on mount Sinai at the giving of the law. The works accompanying it consisted much in things miraculous, strange, and unusual,—as thunder, lightning, fire, smoke, earthquakes, the sound of a trumpet, and the like. The usual working of the minds of men towards these unusual effects of the power of God, is to gaze on them with admiration and astonishment. This God forbids in them: Exod. xix. 21, " Charge the people, lest they break through unto the LORD to gaze." This is not the end or design of God in these works of his power, in these appearances and evidences of his majesty, that men should gaze at them to satisfy their curiosity. What, then, was aimed at in and by them? It was to *instruct* them unto a due fear and awful reverence of God, whose holiness and majesty were represented unto them; that they might know him as " a consuming fire." And this was declared in the issue. For the people coming up unto a due fear of God for the present, and promising obedience thereon, God took it well of them, and approved it in them, as that which answered the design of his works: Deut. v. 23–29, " And it came to pass, when ye heard the voice out of the midst of the darkness, (for the mountain did burn with fire,) that ye came near unto me" (these are the words of Moses to the people), " even all the heads of your tribes, and your elders; and ye said, Behold, the LORD our God hath shewed us his glory and his greatness, and we have heard his voice out of the midst of the fire: . . . . . Now therefore why should we die? for this great fire will consume us. . . . . . Go thou near and hear all that the LORD our God shall say; and speak thou unto us all that the LORD our God shall speak unto thee; and we will hear it, and do it. And the LORD heard the voice of your words when ye spake unto me; and the LORD said unto me, I have heard the voice of the words of this people, which they have spoken unto thee: they have well said all that they have spoken. Oh that there were such an heart in them, that they would fear me, and keep all my commandments always, that it might be well with them, and with their children for ever!" God never casts " bruta fulmina;" all his works are vocal. They speak, or rather he speaks in them. Now, that they may be instructive unto us, sundry things are required:—

[1.] That we *take notice of them*, and notice of them to be *his*. Some are so stayed, or so obstinate, or so full of self and other things, that they will take no notice at all of any of the works of God. His hand is lifted up, and they will not see, they will not behold it. He passeth by them in his works on the right hand and on the left, but they perceive it not. Others, though they take notice of the works themselves, yet they will not take notice of them to be his; like the Philistines, they knew not whether the strange plague that consumed them and destroyed their cities were God's hand or a chance. But until we seriously consider them, and really own them to be the works of God, we can make no improvement of them.

[2.] We are to *inquire into the especial meaning* of them. This is wisdom, and that which God requireth at our hands: so Mic. vi. 9, " The voice of the LORD crieth unto the city, and the man of wisdom shall see thy name: hear ye the rod, and who hath appointed it." קוֹל יְהֹוָה, " The voice of the LORD," is often taken for the power of God manifesting itself in its effects and mighty works. In this sense it is repeated six or seven times in one psalm, Ps. xxix. 3–9. The voice of God here, then, is the works of God. And what do they do? They have a voice, they " cry to the city." The voice of God in his rod doth so; that is, his afflicting and correcting works, as in the end of the verse. It cries לָעִיר, "to the city;" that is, the city of God, Jerusalem, or the church: though some think that לָעִיר is put for לְהָעִיר " ad excitandum;" it cries to excite or stir up men,—that is, to repentance and amendment. And what is the issue? תּוּשִׁיָּה, " The man of wisdom," say we,—it is wisdom, or rather substance, that is, the substantial wise man, who gives no place to vanity and lightness,—he " shall see the name of God: " that is, he shall discern the power and wisdom of God in his works ; and not only so, but the mind of God also in them, which is often signified by his " name." See John xvii. 6. And so it follows, " Hear ye the rod;" they are works of the rod, or correction, that he speaks of. This he commands us to "hear;" that is, to understand. So שָׁמַע frequently signifies. So speak the servants of Hezekiah to Rabshakeh, Isa. xxxvi. 11, "Speak, we pray thee, unto thy servants in the Syrian language, כִּי שֹׁמְעִים אֲנַחְנוּ,"—" for we hear it;" that is, can understand it. So are we to "hear the rod;" that is, to learn and understand the mind of God in his works. This is required of us. And that we may do so, two things are necessary:—

1st. That we consider and be well acquainted with *our own condition*. If we are ignorant hereof we shall understand nothing of the mind of God in his dispensations. Security in sin will take away all understanding of judgments. Let God thunder from heaven in the revelation of his wrath against sin, yet such persons will be secure still. God doth not often utterly destroy men with great and tremendous destructions before he hath given them previous warnings of his indignation. But yet men that are secure in sin will know so little of the sense of them, that they will be crying " Peace and safety," when their final destruction is seizing upon them, 1 Thess. v. 3. God speaks out the curse of the law in his works of judgment; for thereby is " the wrath of God revealed from heaven against the ungodliness of men," Rom. i. 18. But yet when men hear the voice of the curse so spoken out, if they are secure, they will bless themselves, and say they shall have peace, though they add drunkenness to thirst, Deut. xxix. 19. And this for the most part blinds the eyes of the wise men of this world. They neither see nor understand any of the works of God, though never so full of dread or terror, because being secure in their sin, they know not that they have any concernment in them. If they do at any time attend unto them, it is as the people did to the voice that came from heaven unto our Saviour;—some said it thundered, others, that an angel spake. One says one thing of them, another, another thing, but they endeavour not to come unto any certainty about them. This is complained of, Isa. xxvi. 11, " LORD, when thy hand is lifted up, they will not see." The lifting up of the hand in general is to work or to effect any thing; in particular, to correct, to punish, it being the posture of one ready to strike, or redoubling his blows in striking; as God doth when his " judgments are in the earth," verse 9. In this state of things, saith the prophet, " They will not see;" they will neither consider nor endeavour to understand the mind of God in his works and judgments. And how doth God take this of them? Saith he, " The fire of thine enemies shall devour them;" that is, either their own fiery envy at the people of God, mentioned in the foregoing words, shall consume themselves,—they shall be eaten up and consumed with it, whilst they will not take notice of the mind of God in his judgments towards them; or, 'the fire wherewith at length thou wilt consume all thine adversaries shall fall upon them;' or, lastly, ' thou wilt turn in upon them a wicked, furious people, who shall destroy them,'—as it befell the Jews, to whom he speaks in particular. One way or other God will severely revenge this security, and neglect of his works thereon. But they who will wisely consider their own condition,—how it is between God and them,—wherein they have been faithful, wherein false or backsliding,—what controversy God hath, or may justly have with them,—what is the condition of the state, church, or nation whereunto they do belong,—will discern the voice of God in his great works of providence. So is the matter stated, Dan. xii. 10, " Many shall be purified, and made white, and tried; but the wicked shall do wickedly: and none of the wicked shall understand; but the wise shall understand." And when shall this be? When there is " a time of great trouble," verse 1,—when God's judgments are greatly in the world. The end of these troubles is to purify men, to cleanse them, by the removal of all " filth of flesh and spirit" that they may have contracted, as dross is taken away from silver in the furnace; and to make them white, by causing their sincerity, constancy, and perseverance in their holy profession to appear in their trials. But the wicked men, secure in their sins, shall yet continue in their wickedness, and thereby shall be so blinded that none of them shall understand the mind of God in his great works and tremendous dispensations. But הַמַּשְׂכִּילִים, "they that have an understanding" in their own state and condition, and in the state of things in the church of God (as it is said of the men of Issachar, that they were יוֹדְעֵי בִינָה לָעִתִּים, " knowing in the seasons"), "they shall understand," or come to the knowledge of the will of God and their duty in these things. And of a failure herein see how God complains, Deut. xxxii. 28, 29.

2dly. That we consider what *peculiar impressions* of his will God puts upon any of his works. Hereby we may know much of his mind and design in them. All the works of God, if duly considered, will be found to bear his image and superscription. They are all like him, were sent by him, and are becoming him. They have on them tokens and marks of infinite wisdom, power, and goodness. Those of providence which he intends to be instructive have a peculiar impression of the design of God upon them, and a wise man may see the eye of God in them. So he speaks in the psalmist, " I will guide thee with mine eye," Ps. xxxii. 8. He would make him see the way and paths that he was to walk in, by that respect which he would have unto them in the works of his providence. This, then, I say, we should inquire after and wisely consider; because,—

Obs. XXI. The greater evidence that God gives of his power and goodness in any of his works, the louder is his voice in them, and the greater is the sin of them that neglect them; which also is another proposition from the words.

God made then his works evident unto them, so that they saw them,—" They saw my works;" so they could not deny them to be his. But if men will shut their eyes against the light, they justly perish in their darkness. God sometimes hides his power, Hab. iii. 4, " That was the hiding of his power." That is, as the Targumist adds, it was laid open; his power, that before was hid from the people,

was now manifested. But sometimes he causeth it to shine forth; as
it is said in the same place, "He had horns coming out of his hand,"—
קַרְנַיִם מִיָּדוֹ לוֹ "Horns," or shining beams, rays of glory, arose from
his hand, or his power, in the manifestation of it in his works. He
caused his power to shine forth in them, as the sun gives out light
in its full strength and beauty. Then for men not to take notice of
them will be a signal aggravation of their sin and hastening of their
punishment. Now, we can never know what appears of God in his
works, unless by a due consideration of them we endeavour to understand them or his mind in them. Again,—

Obs. XXII. Because the end of all God's works, of his mighty
works of providence towards a person, a church, or nation, is to
bring them to faith and repentance; which is also another observation that the words afford us.

This end he still declared in all his dealings with this people.
And it is the principal design of the Book of Deuteronomy to improve the works of God which they had seen unto this end. And
"who is wise, and he shall understand these things? prudent, and
he shall know them? for the ways of the LORD are right, and the
just shall walk in them, but the transgressors shall fall therein,"
Hos. xiv. 9. And herein lies a great aggravation of the misery of
the days wherein we live,—the works, the great works of God, are
generally either despised or abused. Some account all that is spoken
of them ὡσεὶ λῆρος, as a mere fable, as some did of old the things
concerning the resurrection of Christ, upon the first report of it,
Luke xxiv. 11. And if they are not so in themselves, but that such
things as are spoken of are done in the world, yet as to their relation unto God they esteem it a fable. Chance, natural causes,
vulgar errors, popular esteem, were the originals with such persons
of all those great works of God which our eyes have seen or our ears
heard, or which our fathers have reported unto us. "Brutish persons
and unwise!" there is scarce a leaf in the book of God, or a day in
the course of his providence, that doth not judge and condemn the
folly and stupidity of their pride. The very heathen of old either
by reason scorned, or by experience were made afraid, to give countenance unto such atheism. Nor do I esteem such persons, who
live in an open rebellion against all that is within them and without
them, against all that God hath done or said, worthy any consideration. "Because they regard not the works of the LORD, nor the
operation of his hands, he shall destroy them, and not build them
up," Ps. xxviii. 5. Others will not deny God to be in his works, but
they make no use of them but to gaze, admire, and talk. There is
somewhat less evil in this than in the former atheism, but no good
at all. Yea, where God multiplies his calls by his works, men by
this slight consideration of them insensibly harden their hearts into

security. Others abuse them,—some by making them the rise of their vain and foolish prognostications: ' There is such a prodigy, such a strange work of God, such a blazing star,' or the like.   What then? 'Such or such a thing shall follow this or that year, this or that month.'   This is a specious way whereby atheism exalts itself; for nothing can give countenance to these presumptions but a supposition of such a concatenation of causes and effects as shall exclude the sovereign government of God over the world.   Others contend about them; some whose lives are profligate, and whose ways are wicked, are afraid lest they should be looked on as pointed against them and their sins, and therefore they contend that they have no determinate language, no signification in them.   Others are too forward to look upon them as sent or wrought to countenance them in their desires, ways, and aims.   Amongst most, by these and the like means, the true design of God in all his great and strange works is utterly lost, to the great provocation of the eyes of his glory.   This, as I have showed, is every man's faith, repentance, and obedience; which how they have been improved in us by them we may do well to consider.   Again, observe from the words that,—

Obs. XXIII. God is pleased ofttimes to grant great outward means unto those in whom he will not work effectually by his grace.

Who had more of the first than these Israelites in the wilderness?   As the works of God amongst them were the greatest and most stupendous that ever he had wrought from the foundation of the world, so the law was first vocally given unto them and promulgated amongst them; and not only so, but they had the gospel also preached unto their ears as we,—not so clearly, indeed, but no less truly, Heb. iv. 1, 2.   See their privileges and advantages as they are enumerated by our apostle, Rom. iii. 2, ix. 4, 5.   God might well say of them as he did afterwards of their posterity, " What could have been done more to my vineyard, that I have not done in it?" Isa. v. 4;—for fencing, and planting, and stoning, nothing more could have been done.   Outward means, ordinances, afflictions, mercies, they wanted not; and yet all this while God did not circumcise their hearts to love him with all their heart, and all their soul, that they might live, as he promiseth at other times to do, Deut. xxx. 6: yea, it is said expressly that he gave them not eyes to see, or ears to hear, that they might know him and fear him.   He did not put forth or exercise an effectual work of inward grace during their enjoyment of the outward means before mentioned.   And therefore, when God promiseth to make the covenant of grace under the gospel effectual unto the elect, by writing his law in their hearts, and putting his fear into their inward parts, he says expressly and emphatically that he will not make it as he made that with the people in the wilderness; and that for this reason, because they (that is, the generality of them) had only the outward administration of it, and did not enjoy this effectual communication of saving grace, which is there called a writing of the law in our hearts, and putting of the fear of God in our inward parts, Heb. viii. 8–12, from Jer. xxxi. 31–34. In like manner, when our Lord Jesus Christ preached the gospel unto all, yet it was to some only to whom it was given to know the mysteries of the kingdom of God, Matt. xiii. 11–16. I know some are displeased at this; but for the most part they are such as will be pleased with nothing that God either doeth or saith, or can do or say, unless he would give them a law or a gospel to save them *in and with their sins.* They are ready to dispute that God is unjust if he give not grace to every man, to use or abuse at his pleasure, whilst themselves hate grace and despise it, and think it not worth acceptance if laid at their doors. But thus God dealt with this people in the wilderness; yea, they had means of obedience granted them after he had sworn they should die for their disobedience. And who art thou, O man, that disputest against God? Nay, the righteousness of God in this matter is clear and conspicuous; for,—

[1.] God is not obliged to grant any *especial privilege, even as unto the outward means of grace, unto any of the sons of men.* And to show his sovereignty and absolute freedom herein, he always granted them with great variety in a distinguishing manner. So he did of old: "He shewed his word" (דְּבָרָיו, "his words," that is, his institutions) "unto Jacob, his statutes and his judgments unto Israel. He hath not dealt so with any nation; and as for his judgments, they have not known them," Ps. cxlvii. 19, 20. These outward means themselves were their peculiar privilege and enclosure. This was the advantage of the Jews, that "unto them," and unto them alone, "were committed the oracles of God," Rom. iii. 2. And God, as he gave and granted these outward means of grace to them alone, so he might have justly denied them unto them also; or else he might have granted them unto all others and withheld them from them. For he dealt not thus with them because they were in and of themselves in any thing better than those who were excluded from their privileges, Deut. vii. 6–9. And thus God dealeth still, even unto this day, with the nations of the world; some he intrusteth with the gospel, and some have not the sound of it approaching unto them. Man would not abide in the condition wherein God made him, Eccles. vii. 29; and God may justly leave him in the condition wherein by sin he hath cast himself. That he will afford outward means unto any is of mere grace, liberality, and bounty. And shall we say he is unjust if he give no more, when no rule or law of justice obligeth him unto what he doth? Men may by such means and apprehensions sooner provoke God to take away what they have than to add to them what they have not. A beggar's murmuring as though he had not his due, when any thing is given him, is the worst way of getting his alms increased.

[2.] Even *outward means* themselves, when *singly dispensed*, have many *blessed ends* which shall be effected by them; for they all tend variously to the glory of God. This, I acknowledge, is despised by men of profane and wicked principles, who have no concernment therein. Men whom nothing will satisfy but the making of all grace so common as that it should be prostituted unto the corrupt wills of men, to be used or abused at their pleasure, as indeed they utterly evert all effectual grace, so they must find another scripture to countenance them in their opinion. The Book of God will not do it. They measure things merely by their own advantage. But to those that know God and love him this is of great weight. That the wisdom, holiness, goodness, righteousness, and severity of God, be exalted and glorified, as they are in the dispensation of the outward means of grace, though eventually not effectual unto the salvation of some, is a matter of great rejoicing unto all that do believe. Again, they may redound unto the great advantage of men, and that both in this world and unto eternity. So saith our Saviour, Matt. xi. 23, "And thou, Capernaum, which art exalted unto heaven, shalt be brought down to hell: for if the mighty works, which have been done in thee, had been done in Sodom, it would have remained unto this day." The exaltation of Capernaum consisted in its enjoyment of the outward means of grace, in the preaching and miracles of our Saviour; and although the end of all was that she was to be brought down to hell for her obstinacy in unbelief, yet whilst she enjoyed these things she had a real privilege, and was much exalted thereby. And there might have been a use of these means, which although it would not have delivered Capernaum from hell at last, because not prevalent against final impenitency, yet it might have delivered it from that hell of temporal destruction which befell it not long after, as prevailing against their open and professed obstinacy. And so Sodom, had she been intrusted with the like means of instruction, might have continued in her outward state and condition by such a use of them unto that or unto this day. For there may be such a conviction of sin as may produce that repentance and humiliation which will avert *temporal judgments*, which will not produce repentance unto salvation and deliverance from *judgments eternal*. And this renders the gospel the greatest privilege and advantage of any kingdom or nation in the world, and their principal interest to maintain it. Whatever work God is pleased to do secretly and effectually on the hearts of any, to bring them to the eternal enjoyment of himself, the very outward dispensation of the gospel itself is suited to bring forth that profession and amendment of life in all which shall secure unto them the enjoyment of peace and tranquillity in this world. Besides, the taking off of men from their present sinful courses will tend to the mitigation of their future punishment or a diminution of their stripes. There are, then, many mercies in this one of the outward means of grace, considered absolutely and in itself.

[3.] Where God grants the use of the outward means of grace to any, ordinarily, if not always, *he hath a design to communicate by them especial saving grace unto some.* These means granted unto the people in the wilderness, where they seem to have had as sad an event as ever they had anywhere in the world, yet were not lost as to their end and use of the conveyance of especial grace towards some. Some, yea doubtless many, were converted unto God by them, and made obedient. That they died in the wilderness is no argument as unto individuals that they died in final unbelief,—no, though we should conclude that they died all penally; for they did so as they were members and parts of that people, that provoking generation, which God dealt withal according to the demerit of the community. And so, many men may fall and be cut off penally in national desolations, as those desolations are just punishments for the sins of that nation, though they themselves were not personally guilty of them. So the daughters of Zelophehad state the matter, Num. xxvii. 3, " Our father died in the wilderness, and he was not in the company of them that gathered themselves together against the LORD; but died in his own sin." He was a sinner as all men are, and so on his own personal account there was no reason to complain of his dying in the wilderness; but yet he had no hand in those especial provocations for which God was so displeased as that he cut them off signally in his wrath, and finally. But he, it may be, and many others of them doubtless, had the spiritually efficacious benefit of the means of grace which they enjoyed. The matter is plain in Caleb, Joshua, and others, and a great multitude of the new generation, who believed and entered into rest. Now, the *saving of one soul* is worth the preaching of the gospel to a *whole nation*, and that for many years. And whilst God carries on his work visibly, he will take care secretly that not one hidden grain of his Israel shall fall unto the ground.

To sum up this whole matter: These outward means are granted unto men in a way of grace, favour, and bounty. Their ends, singly considered, are good, holy, and righteous. Moreover, they are all of them properly effectual in that they always attain the end whereunto they are designed. And that men are not bettered by them, or more advantaged than they are, is merely from their own pravity and obstinacy. And those who approve not of this dispensation seem to have a great mind to contend with Him who is mightier than they.

Furthermore, from the exposition before premised we may observe, that,—

Obs. XXIV. No privilege, no outward means of grace, no other advantage whatever, will secure men in a course of sinning from the wrath and justice of God.

Who could be made partakers of more things of that kind than were this people at that time? Besides the great privilege derived unto them from their fathers, in that they were the posterity of Abraham, the friend of God, and had the token of his covenant in their flesh, they had newly erected amongst them a glorious church-state, wherein they were intrusted with all the ordinances of God's worship. These privileges the apostle sums up, Rom. ix. 4, 5, " Who are Israelites; to whom pertaineth the adoption, and the glory, and the covenants, and the giving of the law, and the service of God, and the promises; whose are the fathers." " The adoption" was theirs; God had no other children or family in the world but them,—they were his family when his curse was upon all other families of the earth. And " the glory" was theirs; it was unto them and amongst them that God so manifested his glory as that it became their glory, their glory above all the nations of the world. And " the covenants" were theirs; both the covenant that was made with Abraham, in all the benefits of it, and the especial covenant that God made with them at Sinai. There also was the law given unto them, and the solemn worship of God, in all the laws and ordinances thereof, made their peculiar. What works of providence God wrought amongst them we have declared. Doubtless they bare themselves high on these things. So when they contended with Moses and Aaron, their plea was, " that all the people was holy," so that they saw no reason for their peculiar pre-eminence. And who also amongst the sons of men is not ready on far less occasions so to do? Some cry they are the church, and some boast of other things; but be men what they will, their privileges and advantages what they can desire, if they are secure and obstinate sinners, the wrath of God at one time or other will overtake them. And some will one day find to their sorrow what their boasting will cost them. Laodicea hath done so long ago; and so in due time will she who says, " I sit as a queen, and shall see no sorrow." For although the *hand of church privilege* should join in with the *hand of secular advantage*, yet the guilty shall not go unpunished. And one reason hereof lies in another proposition that ariseth from the words, namely, that,—

Obs. XXV. There are determinate bounds fixed unto God's patience and forbearance towards obstinate sinners.

So here he assigned the space of forty years for the consumption of this provoking generation. And as in the point of promise it is observed, that the very same night wherein the time limited was accomplished the people were delivered out of Egypt; so in the point of threatening it is remembered, that at the end of forty years, wherein the people wandered in the wilderness, there was not one remaining of those who were first numbered in Horeb. However men may flatter and please themselves, nothing can secure sinners from punishment in the appointed season. See 2 Pet. iii. 8–10.

Secondly, We shall now proceed to the last thing contained in the example insisted on by the apostle; and that is, the *consequent of the sin of the people in their punishment*. And this is expressed,—

1. In the *procuring cause* of it,—that in the sense God had of their sin, it grieved him: " Wherefore I was grieved with that generation." The meaning of the words, both in the psalm and in this place, hath been before declared. It expresseth how God stood affected towards the people, as to the inward frame of his heart; for these affections doth God take upon himself for our instruction. He says that he will " rejoice over his people, assuredly with his whole heart and his whole soul," Jer. xxxii. 41; and upon the account of their sin it is said, that it " grieved him at his heart that he had made man on the earth," Gen. vi. 6. And these expressions, wherever they are used, are signs of great and signal actions. So in the last case mentioned, God said " it grieved him at his heart," because he was going to do that which could proceed from no principle that we can apprehend but great trouble and molestation. That, then, which is here intended is such a σχέσις, such a " frame" or " habit" of mind or heart in God, as had the people of that generation for its object. It is not, then, λύπη, " dolor," or " grief," properly so called, that is here intended; neither does either of the words here used, the one by the psalmist, the other by the apostle, express that passion: for although God ascribes it often unto himself, yet it is not here intended, but rather indignation and trouble. He was burdened, vexed, displeased beyond what patience or forbearance could extend unto. In brief, it includes these two things:—(1.) *The judgment or mind of God* concerning the greatness of their sin, with all its aggravations; and, (2.) *His determinate will of punishing them*. Hence we may observe that,—

Obs. XXVI. The heart of God is greatly concerned in the sins of men, especially of those who on any account are his people, and so esteemed.

Men live, and act, and speak, as if they thought God very little concerned in what they do, especially in their sins; that either he takes no notice of them, or if he do, that he is not much concerned in them. That he should be grieved at his heart,—that is, have such a deep sense of men's sinful provocations,—they have no mind to think or believe. They think that, as to thoughts about sin, God is altogether as themselves, Ps. l. 21. But it is otherwise; for God hath,—

(1.) A *concernment of honour* in what we do. He made us for his glory and honour; nothing whereof can we any way assign unto him but by our obedience; and whatever is contrary hereunto tends directly to his dishonour. And this God cannot but be deeply sensible of. He cannot deny himself. If men lose the rent which they expect from their tenants, and have obliged them to pay, and which they refuse upon mere will and stubbornness, they will find themselves to have a concernment therein; and shall God lose all the revenue that is due unto him, without expressing an indignation against the guilt of men who deal so unjustly and fraudulently with him? Nay, he is deeply concerned in this matter, as he is our sovereign Lord.

(2.) He is concerned in *point of justice* also, as he is the supreme ruler and governor of all the works of his own hands. He is God, to whom vengeance doth belong, who hath said, "Vengeance is mine, and I will recompense." And he needs no other reason to induce him to punish sin but himself, his holiness and his justice being his nature. And this he expresseth after the manner of men, affirming that he is grieved, or vexed and provoked to indignation, with the sins of men. How this provocation is heightened by this aggravation of sin, that it is committed by his own people, under peculiar, unspeakable, obligations unto obedience, hath been declared before.

2. Proceed we with the exposition of the words. There is in them the judgment that God made and gave concerning this people and their sin, which is expressed as the reason why he was grieved with them: " He said, They do always err in their hearts; and my ways they have not known."

"He said;"—not that God expressly used these words, but he made this judgment concerning them. This was the sense he had conceived of them. So the word is most frequently used for the conception of the mind. It is the λόγος ἐνδιάθετος, or "sense of the mind," not the λόγος προφορικός, or "outward expression," that is intended.

And in this judgment which God passed on that sinful generation he declares three things:—(1.) The principle of all their sins,—they did " err in their hearts." (2.) Their constancy in or obstinacy unto this principle,—they did so " always." (3.) The consequent, or rather *concomitant* evil unto or with these,—they knew not the ways of the Lord: "And they have not known my ways."

(1.) God placeth the original of all their miscarriages in their error,—*the error of their hearts*. An error of the heart in things moral, is a practical misjudging of what is good or evil unto men. So this people, through the power of their lusts and darkness, their temptations and obstinacy, did, in many instances wherein they were tried, judge that sin and rebellion were better for them than faith, submission, and obedience. They did not in general notionally and formally judge that sin, as sin, was better than obedience, which no creature is capable of doing; but practically and particularly they judged that it was better for them to do the things wherein their sin consisted than to omit or forego them: so they "erred in their hearts." There the seat of their error is fixed. Now, besides that the heart is here, as in sundry other places, taken for the practical understanding, or for the whole principle of all our moral actions, as it regards both the mind, will, and affections, the expression seems to intend a further discovery of the nature of their sin, with a further aggravation of it. They sinned from and with their hearts; and God lets them know that he doth not so much insist on their outward actions, as that he took notice that their hearts were not right with him. That was the principle of all their rebellions, for which he abhorred them. As he spake in another place of the same people, when their hearts went after their idols, " he regarded them not."

(2.) The adjunct of this their error is their *constancy* unto it, or persistency in it: "They do always err." Two things may be denoted hereby: [1.] That in all instances, whenever it came to a trial, they practically chose the wrong side. It may be they did not so universally, but they did so generally, which warrants the denomination. Or, [2.] It denotes the continuance in their error; ἀεί is, "not to cease" or "give over." Though God had exercised great patience and forbearance towards them for a long season, yet they would never change their minds or hearts at any time.

(3.) There is the consequent of this great principle of their sin, or rather, another concomitant principle of their miscarriages,— they knew not the ways of God: "And they have not known my ways." This may be exegetical of the former, and declare wherein their error consisted, namely, in this, that they knew not, they judged not aright of the ways of God. But, as I said, I shall rather look upon it as another principle of their miscarriages. As they erred in their hearts because they liked the ways of sin, so they disliked the ways of God because they knew them not, and from both rushed into all manner of miscarriages and provocations. We are hence instructed first, that,—

Obs. XXVII. In all the sins of men God principally regards the principle; that is, the heart, or what is in it.

"They do err," saith he, "in their hearts." The heart he principally requires in our obedience; and this he principally regards in men's disobedience. " My son," saith he, " give me thine heart;" and, "O that there were such an heart in them, that they would fear me!"

When the heart is upright, as to its general frame, design, and principle, God will bear with many failings, many miscarriages. And when it is false, and gone off from God, thousands of duties are of no esteem with him. We know little, yea, directly nothing, of the hearts of men; and a man would therefore think that we should little concern ourselves in them, or not at all, but merely rest satisfied in outward acts and effects, wherein our concernment lies. But yet even amongst us it is quite otherwise. If once a man begins justly to suspect that the hearts of them with whom he hath to do be not upright with him, but false and guileful, let them pretend what they will, and act what they please, all is utterly disregarded and despised. So saith he, Hom. Il. *i.* 312,—

’Εχθρὸς γάρ μοι κεῖνος, ὁμῶς ’Αΐδάο πύλησιν,
"Ος χ’ ἕτερον μὲν κεύθει, ἐνὶ φρεσὶν, ἄλλο δὲ βάζει·—

" I hate him like the gates of hell, who, pretending fairly to me, reserves other things in his mind."

And if it be thus with men, who judge of the hearts of others only by effects, and that with a judgment liable to be inflamed by groundless suspicions and corrupt imaginations, how much more must it be so with God, before whose eyes all the hearts of men lie open and naked, whose glory and property it is to be καρδιογνώστης,—the judge, searcher, knower of all hearts? Again,—

Obs. XXVIII. The error of the heart in the preferring the ways of sin before obedience, with its promises and rewards, is the root of all great provoking sins and rebellions against God.

Many sins are the effects of men's impetuous lusts and corruptions; many they are hurried into by the power and efficacy of their temptations; most are produced by both these in conjunction;—but as for great provocations, such as carry in them apostasy, or rebellion against God, they proceed from a deceiving and a deceived heart. There are many noisome and hurtful errors in the world, but this is the great soul-ruining error, when the heart is practically corrupted to ˉprefer sin and its wages before obedience and its reward. It seems, indeed, a hard and difficult thing to do this notionally, especially for such as admit of any sense of eternity. But yet the contrary hereunto, namely, to prefer obedience, with its promises and rewards, consisting in things future and invisible, unto sin and its present ways, is expressed as an act or fruit of faith, and which nothing else will enable us unto. This was the evidence of the faith of Moses, that he " chose rather to suffer affliction with the people of God, than to enjoy the pleasures of sin for a season; esteeming the reproach of Christ greater riches than the treasures in Egypt: for he had respect unto the recompence of the reward," Heb. xi. 25, 26. And so the apostle expresseth the working of faith in this matter: 2 Cor. iv. 18, " While we look not at the things which are seen, but at the things which are not seen: for the things which are seen are temporal; but the things which are not seen are eternal." It is the work of faith so to look into, so to see and discern invisible and eternal things, as on their account to prefer obedience unto God, with afflictions, temptations, and persecutions, unto sin, with all its present pleasures and wages. But, practically, this is frequently found amongst men. And how this is brought about or effected; how the mind is prejudiced and obstructed, as to its making a right judgment concerning its rules; how it is diverted from a due consideration of the things and reasons that should influence it, and lead it thereunto; how it is entangled and seduced unto a present approbation of appearing satisfactions; and how the will is thereby deceived into a consent unto sin, I have declared in a particular discourse to that purpose.[1] In brief, when the directive part of the mind is diverted from attending unto the reason of things proposed unto it; when it is corrupted by false pretences imposed on it by the outrage of corrupt lusts and affections, which have possessed the imagination with their objects and their present deceivableness; when the judging, accusing faculty of it is baffled, slighted, and at least partially silenced, as wearied with doing its work in vain, and accustomed to repulses; when in its reflective acts, whereby it should receive impressions from its own self-accusations and reproofs, it is made obtuse, hard, and senseless, not regarding what is spoken in it or to it; and when by these means carnal affections bear sway in the soul, impetuously inclining it to seek after their satisfaction, then is the heart under the power of the error we speak of,—that error which is the principle of all great provocations and apostasies from God.

For, [1.] This sets all the lusts of the soul at liberty to seek after their satisfaction in sin; [2.] Makes it slight and contemn all the promises annexed unto obedience; and, [3.] Disregard the threatenings that lie against sin, and so prepares it for the utmost rebellion.

And of all errors let us take heed of this *practical error* of the heart. It is not men's being orthodox, or sound in their opinions, that will relieve them if they are under the power of this great, fundamental error. And it is a matter to be lamented, to see how men will contest for their opinions under the *name of truth*, and cast all manner of severe reflections on those that oppose them, whilst themselves err in their hearts, and know not the ways of God. And this is a frame which of all others God most abhorreth; for when men pretend to be for him, and are really against him, as all such are, shall not the Searcher of hearts find it out? Orthodox liars, swearers,

---

[1] See the author's treatise on Temptation, vol. vi. of this edition of his works. —ED.

drunkards, adulterers, oppressors, persecutors, are an unspeakable burden unto the patience of God. Again,—

Obs. XXIX. A constant persistency in a course of sin is the utmost, highest, and last aggravation of sin.

"They do always err,"—in every instance of obedience, and that continually. This filled up their measure; for herein consists that finishing of sin which brings forth death, James i. 15. Sin may be conceived and brought forth, and yet death not ensue. But if it be finished, if men err in their hearts always, inevitable destruction will be the consequent of it. This, as was said, is the highest and last aggravation of sin ; for,—

[1.] It includes a *neglect and contempt of all times and seasons of amendment.* God gives unto men, especially those who live under the dispensation of the word, many peculiar times or seasons for their recovery. They have their day, their especial day, wherein they ought in an especial manner to look after the things of their peace, as hath been declared. It may be this day is often revived to the persons spoken of, and often returned upon them; but it is as often despised and neglected by them.

[2.] It includes a *rejection and disappointment of the means of repentance* which God is pleased graciously to afford unto them. During the season of his patience towards sinners, God is pleased to grant unto them sundry means and advantages for their amendment, and that in great variety; but they are all rejected and rendered fruitless in an unchanged course of sinning.

[3.] It includes a *contempt of the whole work of conscience from first to last.* Many assistances conscience doth receive in its work: convictions from the word, excitations by judgments, mercies, dangers, deliverances; but yet in this condition all its actings are baffled and despised. And what can be more done against God? what can add to the guilt of such sin and sinners?

And this may serve to justify God in his severity against persons that "always err in their hearts," that continue in a course of sinning. In the day when the secrets of all hearts shall be disclosed, and all transactions between God and the souls of men laid open, the holiness, righteousness, and just severity of God against impenitent sinners, will on these and other accounts be gloriously displayed.

Obs. XXX. None despise or desert the ways of God but those that know them not.

For whatever they may profess, yet indeed profligate sinners know neither God nor his ways: "They err in their hearts; and have not known my ways." Who would seem more fully to have known the ways of God than this people? The ways of his providence, wherein he walked towards them, and the ways of his law, wherein they were to walk towards him, were all before them. They saw the former

themselves, and that appearance of the power, wisdom, and greatness of God in them, as never had any generation of men from the
foundation of the world. And for the ways of his law and worship,
who should know them if they did not? They heard God himself pro-
claiming his own law on mount Sinai, and had it afterwards written
by him in tables of stone; and for the residue of his institutions,
they received them by fresh revelation, seeing them all exemplified
in the erection of the tabernacle and practice of the service of it.
And yet all this while, being unbelieving and obdurate, "they knew
not the ways of God;" nay, though they professed that they knew
them, and that they would observe them, yet in truth they knew
them not. And such were their posterity and successors in unbelief
and disobedience, of whom the apostle speaks, Tit. i. 16, "They profess
that they know God; but in works they deny him, being abominable,
and disobedient, and unto every good work reprobate." So was it
with this people; so it is with all that despise the ways of God.
Whatever they profess,—as some of them will be forward enough to
profess much,—yet indeed they know not God or his ways. So our
Saviour tells the Pharisees, that, notwithstanding all their boasting
of their wisdom, skill, and knowledge of the law, and of God himself, yet being, as they were, proud, hypocritical self-justiciaries, that
they had not indeed "heard his voice at any time, nor seen his
shape," John v. 37; that is, that they had no real acquaintance with
him or knowledge of him.

Whatever notion such persons have or may have of the ways of
God, whatever skill in the outward letter of his laws and institutions,
yet they know neither the righteousness, nor the holiness, nor the
efficacy, nor the usefulness, nor the beauty of any of them. These
things are spiritually discerned, and they are spiritually blind; these
are *spirit* and *life*, and they are *flesh*, and *dead*. And all this is
evident from men's despising of the ways of God or their dereliction
of them. This none can do but those that know them not; for,
"they that know the name of the Lord,"—that is, any of the ways
whereby he reveals himself,—" will put their trust in him," Ps. ix.
10. They will forsake neither him nor them. What Paul speaks
in a way of extenuation as to some of the Jews, " Had they known
it, they would not have crucified the Lord of life," we may apply by
way of exprobration unto some: ' Had they known the ways of God,
as once they professed they did, they would not have forsaken them.'
And this may support us against the offences and scandals that are
in the world upon the account of the apostasies of professors. Some
that have professed religion in its power turn sensual worldlings;
some who have professed it in its truth, as Protestants, turn Papists
and idolaters. Shall any reflection be taken from hence, or be cast
on the right ways of God, as though they were such as deserved to

be deserted? Whatever men, such men, have pretended or professed, the truth is, they never knew the ways of God in their light, power, efficacy, or beauty. Julian, that infamous apostate, was wont to boast concerning the Scriptures, "That he had read them, known them, and condemned them." Unto whom it was truly replied, "That if he had read them, yet he understood or knew them not;" of which there needed no other evidence but that he condemned them.

3. "Unto whom I sware in my wrath, that they should not enter into my rest."

This is the last thing that remaineth to be considered; and it is the issue or event of the sin before declared,—what it came to in the holiness and righteousness of God, and what was the punishment that was inflicted on the offenders. And in this decretory sentence of God concerning this people, after all their temptations and provocations, there is considerable,—

(1.) The *irrevocableness of the sentence denounced against them.* It is not any longer a mere threatening, but a sentence irreversibly passed, and enrolled in the court of heaven, and committed for execution unto the honour, power, and veracity of God; for he "sware" unto it, or confirmed it by his oath. All mere promises or threatenings whatever about temporal things have a tacit condition included in them. This, as occasion requires, is drawn forth, so as to alter and change the event promised or threatened. But when God interposeth with his oath, it is to exclude all reserves on such tacit conditions,—it is to show that the time wherein they might take place or be of use is elapsed. And the threatening so confirmed becomes an absolute sentence. And until it comes unto this, the state of sinners is not absolutely deplorable. But when the oath of God is gone out against them, all reserves for mercy, all former allowances of conditions are utterly cut off. And this is not the state only of them concerning whom it is recorded in an especial manner that he did so swear; but in such instances God shows what is the way of his holiness and severity with all sinners who fall into the like provocations with them. For hereon doth the apostle ground his exhortation and caution, Heb. iv. 11, "Let us labour therefore to enter into that rest, lest any man fall after the same example of unbelief;" but if the tenor of God's dealings with such unbelievers were not absolutely the same, if the oath of God extended only unto that generation, though they fell, yet others might stand under the same guilt with them, which the apostle hence demonstrates to be otherwise.

(2.) The *greatness of their sin, in the great offence that God took at it,* and the provocation which, as it were, befell him thereon: He "sware in his wrath;" that is, with great indignation. Let the place be read as before set down, where the frame of the heart of God towards them is expressed, and the greatness of his wrath and indignation will appear. Now, whereas the holy nature of God is not in itself capable of such commotions, of such smoking wrath and anger as are therein described and represented, the sole end of these expressions must needs be to show the heinousness of the sin that the people were guilty of. And herein lies an infinite condescension of God, in taking care to instruct some in and by his deserved wrath against others: for such weak and mean creatures are we, that we have need thus to be instructed in the holiness of God's nature and the severity of his justice against sin; for whatever we may ween concerning ourselves, we are not indeed capable of any perfect notions or direct apprehensions of them, but stand in need to have them represented unto us by such effects as we can take in the species of into [our] minds.

(3.) There is in the words the *punishment itself* denounced against this provoking people,—that they should not enter into the rest of God. And there is a double aggravation of the punishment in the manner of the expressing of it :—

[1.] In the *act* denied: "They shall not enter,"—no, not so much as enter into it. Doubtless many of the people during their wanderings in the wilderness had great desires that they might at least see the place promised for a habitation to their posterity, and wherein all their future interests were to be stated. So in particular had Moses. He prayed, saying, "I pray thee, let me go over, and see the good land that is beyond Jordan, that goodly mountain, and Lebanon," Deut. iii. 25. So, doubtless, did many others of them pray and desire. But the sentence is passed,—they shall not now so much as enter into it, nor set one foot within its borders.

[2.] In the *expression of the object* denied there lieth another aggravation. He doth not say that they shall not enter into the land of Canaan, no, nor yet into the promised land; but he describes it by such an adjunct as may let them see the greatness of their sin and their punishment, and of his displeasure. "They shall not," saith he, "enter into my rest;"—'It is my rest, the place where I will dwell, where I will fix my worship and make myself known: you shall not enter into my rest.'

And so have we passed through this passage of this chapter; on which though it may be we have seemed to dwell somewhat long, yet, as I suppose, not longer than the matter doth require, nor indeed so long as we should and would have done, but that sundry concerns of it will again occur unto us, both in this and the next chapter. Some few observations from the last clause of the words we may yet touch upon; as,—

Obs. XXXI. When God expresseth great indignation in himself against sin, it is to teach men the greatness of sin in themselves.

For that end is he said here to "swear in his wrath." There are expressions in Scripture about God's respect unto the sins of men that are strangely emphatical; as,—sometimes he is said to be "pressed under them as a cart is pressed that is laden with sheaves;" sometimes, that he is "made to serve with sin, and wearied with iniquity;" sometimes to be "broken" with the whorish heart of a people, and "grieved at the heart" that he had ever made such a creature as man; sometimes, that the sins of men are a "fume in his nostrils," that which his soul loatheth; commonly, to be "angry," "vexed," and "grieved," to be "wrathful," "stirred up to fury," and the like.

Now, all these things, taken properly, do include such alteration, and consequently imperfections and weaknesses, as the pure, holy, perfect nature of God can by no means admit of. What is it, then, that God intends by all these expressions, by these ascriptions of that unto himself which really is not in him, but might indeed justly befall that nature whereof we are partakers, on the supposition of the like occasions? As was said, it is all to express what indeed sin doth deserve, and that a recompence of revenge is to be expected, or that it is of so great a demerit as to excite all the perturbations mentioned in the nature of God, were it any way capable of them. So doth he make use of all ways and means to deter us from sin. And there is much of love, tenderness, and care in all these expressions of anger, wrath, and displeasure. So he is pleased to teach us, and such teachings do we stand in need of. Again,—

Obs. XXXII. God gives the same firmitude and stability unto his threatenings that he doth unto his promises.

He swears to them also, as he doth in this place. Men are apt secretly to harbour a supposition of a difference in this matter. The *promises* of God they think, indeed, are firm and stable; but as for his *threatenings*, they suppose one way or other they may be evaded. And this deceit hath greatly prevailed in and inflamed the minds of men ever since the first entrance of sin. By this deceit sin came into the world,—namely, that the threatenings of God either would not be accomplished, or that they were to be understood after another manner than was apprehended. 'Hath God said so, that you shall die if you eat? Mistake not; that is not the meaning of the threatening; or, if it be, God doth not intend to execute it; it will be otherwise, and God knows it will be otherwise.' This gave sin its first entrance into the world; and the same deceit still prevails in the minds of men. 'Hath God said that sinners shall die, shall be cursed, shall be cast into hell? Yea, but sure enough it will be otherwise; there will be one way or other of escape. It is good to affright men with these things, but God intends not so to deal with them. Whatever the threatenings be, many things may intervene to prevent their execution. What God promiseth, indeed, that shall come to pass; we may expect it and look for it; but as for these threatenings, they depend on so many conditions, and may so easily at any time be evaded, as that there is no great fear of their execution.' But what is the ground of this feigned difference between the promises and threatenings of God, as to their stability, certainty, and accomplishment? Where is the difference between the two clauses in that text, "He that believeth shall be saved, and he that believeth not shall be damned?" Are not the holiness of God and his faithfulness as much concerned in the comminatory part as in the promissory part of his word? Would not a failure in the one be as prejudicial to his glory as in the other? The principles from which his threatenings proceed are no less essential properties of his nature than those which are the springs of his promises; and his declaration of them is no less accompanied with the engagement of his veracity and faithfulness than that of the other; and the end aimed at in them is no less necessary to the demonstration of his glory than that which he designeth in his promises. And we see in this particular instance that they are also confirmed with the oath of God, even as his promises are. And let none think that this was an extraordinary case, and concerned only the men of that generation. This oath of God is part of his law, it abides for ever; and all that fall into the like sin with them, attended with the like circumstances, do fall under the same oath of God,—he swears concerning them, that they shall not enter into his rest. And we little know how many are even in this world overtaken in this condition, the oath of God lying against them for their punishment, and that eternal. Let men take heed of this great self-deceiving; and let not men be mockers in this matter, lest their bands be made strong; for,—

Obs. XXXIII. When men have provoked God by their impenitency to decree their punishment irrevocably, they will find severity in the execution.

"They shall not enter,"—no, not so much as enter. "Behold," saith our apostle, "the severity of God: on them which fell, severity," Rom. xi. 22. Men will find that there is severity in the execution who despised the threatening, and that "it is a fearful thing to fall into the hands of the living God." When sinners shall see the whole creation on fire about them, hell open under them, and the glorious, dreadful Judge of all over them, they will begin to have a due apprehension of his terror. But then cries, outcries, repentings, and wailings, will be of no use. This is the time and place for such considerations, not when the sentence is executed,—no, not when it is irrevocably confirmed.

Obs. XXXIV. It is the presence of God alone that renders any place or condition good or desirable.

"They shall not," saith God, "enter into my rest." This makes heaven to be heaven, and the church to be the church;—every thing answers the manner and measure of the presence of God. And without this, Moses expressly preferred the wilderness before Canaan.

VERSES 12–14.

In the close of this chapter the apostle makes application of the example which he had produced out of the psalmist unto his present purpose; namely, to dehort the Hebrews from that sin which in them would answer unto the unbelief and disobedience of their forefathers, from the pernicious and destructive event which befell them thereon. And it must be still remembered that he presseth on them the consideration of that season of trial which they were then under, and which directly answered unto that time of trial which their fathers had in the wilderness. And there are three parts of that discourse of the apostle which ensueth unto the end of this chapter:—First, An *exhortation*, built upon what he had before laid down and given evidence of, with confirmation unto it by the example produced out of the psalmist, verses 12–14. Secondly, An *especial consideration* and improvement, unto the end aimed at, of sundry parts of the example insisted on, verses 15–18; and therein many enforcements of the exhortation laid down are contained. Thirdly, A *general conclusion* is drawn out of his whole previous discourse, and laid down as the ground of his future progress, verse 19.

The first part of this discourse comes now under consideration in the ensuing words:—

Ver. 12–14.—Βλέπετε, ἀδελφοί, μή ποτε ἔσται ἔν τινι ὑμῶν καρδία πονηρὰ ἀπιστίας, ἐν τῷ ἀποστῆναι ἀπὸ Θεοῦ ζῶντος· Ἀλλὰ παρακαλεῖτε ἑαυτούς, καθ᾽ ἑκάστην ἡμέραν, ἄχρις οὗ τὸ σήμερον καλεῖται, ἵνα μὴ σκληρυνθῇ τις ἐξ ὑμῶν ἀπάτῃ τῆς ἁμαρτίας. Μέτοχοι γὰρ γεγόναμεν τοῦ Χριστοῦ, ἐάνπερ τὴν ἀρχὴν τῆς ὑποστάσεως μέχρι τέλους βεβαίαν κατάσχωμεν.

Μή ποτε. Ποτέ is omitted or neglected in many translations, as the Syriac, Arabic, Ethiopic; "ne sit," "that there be not," "let there not be." Vulg. Lat., "ne forte," "lest haply;" with respect unto the uncertainty of the event: some, "ne quando," "ne ullo tempore," "lest at any time," "that at no time," with respect unto the season of such event.

Ἔν τινι ὑμῶν, "in aliquo vestrum," so the Vulg. Lat. Ar.; "in ullo vestrum," Beza, more properly; so we, "in any of you." בְּאֱנָשׁ מִנְּכוֹן, "in homine ex vobis," "in a man," "in any man of you." Arab., "in corde ullius vestrum," "in the heart of any of you;' taking in the word "heart" out of the next clause, which there it supplies by adding "wickedness," "the wickedness of unbelief."

Καρδία πονηρὰ ἀπιστίας, "cor malum incredulitatis; so the Vulg. Lat.,— "an evil heart of unbelief." לִבָּא בִישָׁא דְלָא מְהֵימֵן, "cor malum quod non fidele sit," "an evil heart that is not faithful" or "believing." Others, "cor malum et incredulum," "an evil and unbelieving heart."

Ἐν τῷ ἀποστῆναι. Ar., "in discedere." Vulg. Lat., "discedendi." Beza, "ut desciscatis." Properly "descisco" is "to depart unlawfully," "to withdraw

wickedly;" that is, to apostatize from an engagement of duty. Syr., וְתִּפְרְקוּן,
" and you should withdraw," or " draw back."

Παρακαλεῖτε ἑαυτούς. Vulg. Lat., " adhortamini vosmetipsos," " exhort
yourselves." Eras., " vos invicem," to the same purpose. Beza, " exhortamini
alii alios," " exhort one another:" as we also. Syr., אֶלָּא בְעוֹ מֵן נַפְשְׁכוֹן, " sed postu-
late ab anima vestra," "but ask" (or " require") "it of your soul;" that is, of your-
self. Tremel., " sed examinate vos ipsos," " but examine yourselves;" that is,
by inquiry. This expresseth somewhat another duty as to the manner of its
performance, but to the same purpose.

Καθ᾽ ἑκάστην ἡμέραν. Arias, " per unumquemque diem." Vulg. Lat., "per
singulos dies," " every day;" that is, " sigillatim," " separately and distinctly
considered." Syr., כֻּלְּהוֹן יוֹמָתָא, " omnibus diebus," " always." Beza, " quoti-
die;" that is, as ours, " daily," " every day."

Ἄχρις οὗ τὸ σήμερον καλεῖται. Vulg. Lat., " donec hodie cognominatur;"
Arias, "usque quo;" Beza, "quoad dies appellatur hodiernus,"—" whilst it is called
the present day," " to-day." עַד מָא דְלְיוֹמָא דְמִתְקְרָא יוֹמָא, " until the day which
is called to-day," or, " this day." It is uncertain what day is intended by that
translator. It seems to be the day of death; which answers the " omnibus diebus" before; that is, " hujus vitae," " all the days of this life."

Ἵνα μὴ σκληρυνθῇ τις ἐξ ὑμῶν. Vulg. Lat., " ut non obduretur quis ex vobis;"
Beza, " nequis ex vobis;"—" lest any of you be hardened." The Ethiopic adds,
" that there be none that may say that any one of them is hardened in any sin."

Ἀπάτη is rendered by some " deceptio," by some " seductio,"—" a seducing
deceit." Rhemists, " that none of you be obdurate with the fallacy of sin;"
most darkly and corruptly.

Μέτοχοι γεγόναμεν τοῦ Χριστοῦ, " Christi participes facti, effecti sumus," Beza;
" consortes." Syr., אֶתְחַלַּטְן, " commixti sumus Christo,"—" we are immixed with
Christ;" that is, as I suppose, " united unto him." Ethiop., " we are as Christ."

Ἐάνπερ. Vulg. Lat., " si tamen;" but πέρ is not exceptive. Beza, " si
modo," " if so be." The Syriac takes no notice of it; nor we in our translation,
" if."

Ἀρχὴν τῆς ὑποστάσεως. Vulg. Lat., "initium substantiæ ejus;" adding " ejus"
to the text and corrupting the sense. Beza, " principium illud quo sustentamur,"
—" that beginning " (or " the beginning") " of that whereby we are supported."
We, " the beginning of our confidence." Rhemists, " yet so as if we keep the
beginning of his substance firm." Castalio, "hoc argumentum ab initio ad finem
usque,"—" this argument" (or " evidence") "from the beginning unto the end."
Syr., " if from the beginning unto the end we abide in this firm substance" or
"foundation." Ethiop, " if we persevere to keep this new testament." All to
the same purpose.

Ver. 12-14.—Take heed, brethren, lest there be in any
of you an evil heart of unbelief, in departing [*wickedly*]
from the living God. But exhort one another [*yourselves*] daily [*every day*], whilst it is called To-day;
lest any of you [*among you*] be hardened through the
[*seducing*] deceitfulness of sin. For we are made partakers of Christ, if so be we hold the beginning of our
confidence steadfast unto the end.

In these three verses there are three things in general proposed
by the apostle:—First, An *exhortation unto the avoidance of an*

evil, even that which it is his principal design to caution them
against, and to dissuade them from, verse 12. Secondly, A *proposal of one useful means* whereby they may be assisted in its
avoidance, verse 13. Thirdly, An *enforcement of the exhortation from that evil,* and unto the use of that means, from sundry
considerations, is added, verse 14.

In the FIRST of these we may consider what is included in it,
namely,—1. The dependence of this exhortation on the discourse foregoing. 2. The compellation used by the apostle in this renovation
of an especial address unto the Hebrews, " Brethren." 3. The duty
he exhorts them unto; and that, (1.) As to the act of it, "Take
heed;" (2.) " As to the persons concerned, " Lest there be in any of
you;" (3.) As to object of it, or the evil dehorted from, " An evil
heart of unbelief;" which is further described by its effects, " In departing from the living God."

SECONDLY, 1. The means of the prevention of the evil dehorted from
is presented, verse 13; and this in general is by exhortation against
it, " Exhort:" which hath a treble qualification,—(1.) As to the persons by whom it is to be performed or the means used, " One another;" (2.) The season of its performance, which also includes the
manner of it, " Every day;" (3.) With a limitation of that season,
" Whilst it is called To-day." 2. An especial enforcement of this
preventive duty from the danger of their condition, which would
be increased by a neglect thereof. And this is described,—(1.)
From the cause of it, " The deceitfulness of sin;" (2.) From its
tendency and effects, " Lest any be hardened through the deceitfulness of sin."

THIRDLY, There is a general enforcement of the whole, both as to
the evil to be avoided and the means to be used for that purpose;
and this is taken from their state and condition on supposition of
the avoidance of the one and observance of the other, verse 14.
And this is,—1. Expressed, " For we are partakers of Christ;" and,
2. Declared as to its dependence on the preceding exhortation,
" If so be we hold the beginning of our confidence steadfast unto the
end."

In the *exhortation* proposed, in the *first place,* there is included,
— 1. A dependence on the discourse foregoing. Some suppose a
hyperbaton in the words, and that this " take heed" depends immediately on the " wherefore" which is in the beginning of verse 7, as
was intimated on that place. So the following words are introduced only as an instance to enforce the exhortation by. In this
sense the reference here is to be taken immediately from the authority of Christ over his house, and the necessity of our perseverance
to the securing of our interest in that house, as verses 5, 6; " Wherefore, take heed, brethren." But the truth is, the matter of this

exhortation is educed so directly and immediately out of the foregoing example, that we must in it own a respect thereunto; for the
words are a plain inference from that discourse, though the note of
illation be omitted. As if the apostle had said, 'Seeing it is thus,
seeing our forefathers, who were our types, and are proposed for an
example unto us, did so miscarry under a dispensation of God representing that which he exerciseth now towards us, let us take heed.'
This is the dependence of the words.

2. The apostle returning unto the Hebrews with an especial
address and exhortation, renews his former *affectionate
compellation*, " Brethren." This hath been spoken unto,
verse 1 of this chapter, where the reader may find the reason of it,
and what is contained in it. Only the cause wherefore he repeats
it again seems to be, that it might appear that he had no commotion of spirit upon him in his pressing the severe instance and example insisted on. A minister must be ἐπιεικής, 1 Tim. iii. 3, "meek,"
" patient," not easily provoked; μὴ ὀργίλος, Tit. i. 7, " not soon
angry" with his flock, or any of them. And tenderness, gentleness,
demonstrations of love and care towards them with whom we have
to do, secretly soften them, and open their ears and hearts to let
in a word of instruction and exhortation. 'Ο ἥλιος τόν ἄνεμον ἐνίκησε.
Besides, he obviates any suspicion that might arise as though he
insinuated a fear of such an evil in them, and might make them think
that he had hard thoughts of them. By this appellation he removes all such jealousies, and lets them know that the best of
saints had need be cautioned sometimes against the worst of evils.

3. The *manner* of the performance of the duty exhorted unto, and,
(1.) The act of it, is expressed in the first word, Βλέπετε,
"Take heed." Βλέπω is firstly and properly "to see" and
"behold," as that is an act of sense; then "to take heed," or "beware,"
an act of the mind;—by an easy translation, first " video," then
" caveo." And when it is used for " to see" as an act of sense, it
commonly hath respect unto expectation, either of some good to be
received, or of some inconvenience to be watched against. And because men look out or about them to beware of dangers, the word is
used for "to take heed" or " beware." In this sense it is often used
in the New Testament, yea, so far as I have observed, it is peculiar
unto the sacred writers; especially it is frequently used by our apostle,
as 1 Cor. i. 26, x. 18; Phil. iii. 2; Eph. v. 15; Col. ii. 8. And sometimes it is used transitively affecting the object, merely for " to consider:" 1 Cor. i. 26, Βλέπετε τὴν κλῆσιν ὑμῶν,—" Consider your calling;" chap. x. 18, Βλέπετε τὸν 'Ισραὴλ κατὰ σάρκα,—" Consider Israel
according to the flesh." Sometimes it hath a reciprocal pronoun
joined with it, Βλέπετε ἑαυτούς, 2 John 8, " Consider" or "look well
to yourselves." Sometimes it is used absolutely, as here, and signifies

Ἀδελφοί.

Βλέπετε.

to beware of somewhat; but in this sense it hath often ἀπό joined with it; as Mark viii. 15, Βλέπετε ἀπὸ τῆς ζύμης τῶν Φαρισαίων: which in Matt. xvi. 6 is προσέχετε, " take heed of" (beware of) " the leaven of the Pharisees." And ἀπό is sometimes omitted, as Phil. iii. 2, Βλέπετε τοὺς κύνας, βλέπετε τοὺς κακοὺς ἐργάτας, βλέπετε τὴν κατατομήν,—that is, ἀπὸ τῶν κύνων, and so of the rest;—" Take heed of dogs, take heed of evil workers, take heed of the concision," ' that ye neither join with them nor be hurt by them.' This is here the use of the word; " care," " heedfulness," " circumspection with respect to danger and opposition, and those imminent or near," is that which the word imports: whence observe that,—

Obs. I. There is need of great care, heedfulness, watchfulness, and circumspection, for a due continuance in our profession, to the glory of God and advantage of our own souls.

A careless profession will issue in apostasy open or secret, or great distress, Matt. xiii. 5, 6, Cant. iii. 1, 5. Our course is a warfare; and those who take not heed, who are not circumspect in war, will assuredly be a prey to their enemies. Be their strength never so great, one time or other they will not avoid a fatal surprisal.

And there is a necessity of this heedful attendance in us, from the *manifold duties* that, in all things and at all times, are incumbent on us. Our whole life is a life of duty and obedience. God is in every thing to be regarded by us. So that we are to be attentive unto our duty on all occasions, Ps. xvi. 8; Gen. xvii. 1. If we fail in matter or manner, what lies in us we spoil the whole; for " bonum oritur ex integris, malum ex quolibet defectu." Any one defect is enough to denominate an action evil; but unto that which is good there must be a concurrence of all necessary circumstances. See Eph. v. 15, 16. And who is sufficient for these things? God alone by his Spirit and grace can enable us hereunto. But he works these things *by us* as well as *in us*, and gives heedful diligence where he gives success.

But it is with especial reference unto difficulties, oppositions, dangers, temptations, that this caution is here given us to be cautious. And who can reckon up the number or dispose into order these things, and that whether we consider those that constantly attend us or those that are occasional? Among oppositions, snares, and dangers, that we are constantly exposed unto, and which without heedfulness we cannot avoid, the apostle here instanceth in one, namely, that of " an evil heart of unbelief," which must be spoken unto. And he giveth an instance in those that are occasional, Eph. v. 15, 16, "Walk circumspectly,......because the days are evil." There is an especial evil in the days wherein we live, which we cannot avoid without great circumspection. Now this taking heed consisteth,—

[1.] In a due *consideration of our danger.* He that walks in

the midst of snares and serpents, and goes on confidently, without
consideration of his danger, as if his paths were all smooth and safe,
will one time or other be entangled or bitten. Blind confidence in
a course of profession, as if the whole of it were a dangerless road,
is a ruining principle, 1 Pet. i. 17; Prov. xxviii. 14; " A prudent man
foreseeth the evil, and hideth himself; but the simple pass on, and
are punished," Prov. xxii. 3. It is the highest folly not to look out
after dangers, and which usually ends in sorrow, trouble, and punishment. Fear is necessary in continual exercise; not a fear of distrust or diffidence, of anxious scrupulosity, but of care, duty, and
diligence. Continually to fear dangers in all things, brings a useless, perplexing scrupulosity, where men's principle of duty is only
a harassed, convinced conscience, and the rule of it is the doctrines
and traditions of men. But where the principle of it is the Spirit of
grace, with all this fear there is liberty; and where the rule of it is
the Word, there is safety, peace, and stability. Men at sea that are
in the midst of rocks and shelves, and consider it not, will hardly
avoid a shipwreck. Livy tells us that Philopœmen, that wary
Grecian commander, wherever he went, though he were alone, he
was still considering all places that he passed by, how an enemy
might possess them and lay ambushes in them to his disadvantage,
if he should command an army in those places. Hereby he became
the most wary and expert captain of his age. So should a Christian do: he should always consider how, where, by what means, his
spiritual adversaries may ensnare or engage him, and so either avoid
them or oppose them; and not be like the simple, pass on heedlessly
and be punished, Eph. vi. 11, 12, etc.

[2.] In a due *consideration of the especial nature of those snares
and dangers that we are exposed unto.* It is not enough that in
general we know and reckon on it that we are obnoxious unto
dangers, but we must learn what are the especial dangers, as things
are circumstanced in our lives, callings, ways, times, and seasons,
that are apt easily to beset us. To know and continually ponder
their nature and advantages, this is wisdom, the greatest wisdom
we can exercise in the whole course of our walking and profession,
1 Pet. v. 8. He that takes heed in this will not likely fail in any
other instance. But here custom, security, false-pleasing, confidence
of our own strength, negligence, and sloth, all put in to delude us.
And if we are here imposed on, that we weigh not aright the nature
and efficacy of our own peculiar snares and temptations, we shall
assuredly at one time or another fail and miscarry in the course of
our obedience. This was David's wisdom when " he kept himself
from his own iniquity," Ps. xviii. 23. God would have us cast all our
care about earthly things on him, but be watchful ourselves, through
his grace, about spiritual. But we are apt to fail on both hands.

[3.] It is *so* to heed them as to endeavour *to avoid them,* and that in all their occasions, causes, and advantages, in their whole work and efficacy. We are not only to consider them when they assault us, but to watch against all ways whereby they may so do. This is the duty of a man that stands armed on his guard. He is very regardless of his enemy who never seeks to avoid him but when he sees him or feels him. Men will consider the lion's walk, so as not without good means of defence to be found in it. The lion is in all the especial oppositions we are exercised with. We had need continually to be "fenced with iron and the staff of a spear," as 2 Sam. xxiii. 7, and yet to avoid them what we are able. God expresseth his great dislike of them that " walk contrary to him," as we have rendered the words, Lev. xxvi. 21, וְאִם תֵּלְכוּ עִמִּי קֶרִי;—' If you walk with me at a peradventure, or at all adventures, carelessly, negligently, without due consideration of your duty and your danger,'—this God will not bear.

[4.] *Consider them so as to oppose them.* And this consisteth in these things:—1*st.* In being always ready armed and standing on your guard, Eph. vi. 13; Mark xiii. 37; 2 Sam. xxiii. 7. 2*dly.* In calling in help and assistance, Heb. ii. 18, iv. 16. 3*dly.* In improving the supplies granted us with faith and diligence, Heb. xii. 1. And these are some of the things that belong unto this duty; and they are but some of them, for it is diffused through the whole course of our profession, and is indispensably required of us, if we would abide in the beauty and glory of it unto the end. And therefore the negligence and sloth of many professors can never enough be bewailed. They walk at all adventure, as if there were no devil to tempt them, no world to seduce, ensnare, or oppose them, no treachery in their own hearts to deceive them. And hence it is that many are sick, and many are weak, and some are fallen asleep in sin. But what our Saviour said to all of old, he says still to us all, " Watch," Mark xiii. 37.

(2.) There are the *persons* concerned in this duty, Μή ποτε ἔσται ἔν τινι ὑμῶν,—" Lest there be in any of you." Μή ποτε is somewhat more emphatical than the " lest," where- Μή ποτε. by alone we render it. " Ne forte," say some translations,—" Lest perchance," with respect unto a dubious event. Others, " Ne quando,"—" Lest there be at any time," " lest so, that there should be," ἔν τινι ὑμῶν, "in any of you." The apostle doth not seem in these words strictly to intend every indi- Ἔν τινι ὑμῶν. vidual person, as if he had said, ' Let every one of you look to him-self and his own heart, lest it be so with him;' but he speaks unto them collectively, to take care that there be none such amongst them,—that none be found amongst them with such a heart as he cautions them against. And this, consequently, falls on every individual; for where all are spoken unto, every one is concerned. The same kind of expression is used to the same purpose, chap. xii. 15, 16, Ἐπισκοποῦντες μή τις ὑστερῶν,—" Watching," overseeing mutually, "with diligence, lest any" among you "fail of the grace of God; lest any root of bitterness springing up trouble you, and thereby many be defiled; lest there be any fornicator, or profane person, as Esau." Here the caution is evidently given unto the whole church, and the duty of the whole is expressed thereon. So is it likewise in this place, as appears from the direction that he gives for the right performance of this duty, in and by mutual watchfulness and exhortation, in the next verse. This, then, is proposed, [1.] To the whole church, to the whole society, and consequentially to every member thereof; so that we may hence observe,—

Obs. II. Godly jealousy concerning, and watchfulness over the whole body, that no beginnings of backsliding from Christ and the gospel be found amongst them, is the duty of all churches of believers.

He that first put in an exception to this rule was the first apostate from God, who did it to cover a former sin. הֲשֹׁמֵר אָחִי אָנֹכִי, says Cain, Gen. iv. 9, "Am I my brother's keeper?"—'Is it my duty to look after him, to take care of him, or what becomes of him?' God proposed the question so unto him as it was apt in its own nature to lead him to confession and repentance. But he was now hardened in sin, and having quarrelled with God and slain his brother, he now casts off all the remaining dictates of the law of nature, accounting that one brother is not bound to take care of the welfare of another. Mutual watchfulness over one another by persons in any society is a prime dictate of the law of our creation, which was first rejected by this first murderer; and every neglect of it hath something of murder in it, 1 John iii. 11, 12, 15. In a church relation the obligation unto this duty is ratified by institution. Upon the officers of the church it is incumbent by the way of office; on all believers, as members of the church, in a way of love: Lev. xix. 17, "Thou shalt not hate thy brother in thine heart; thou shalt in any wise rebuke thy neighbour, and not suffer sin upon him." He that doth not watch over his brother to prevent his sin, or recover him from it, as much as lies in him, he hates him, and is so far a murderer. And the necessity of this duty is expressed in the word used to declare it, and the manner of its usage: הוֹכֵחַ תּוֹכִיחַ,—" rebuking thou shalt rebuke him;" that is, plainly and effectually, and that with such rebukes as consist in arguings, reasonings, and pleadings, to bring on a conviction. So the word signifies, and is used as to the pleadings or reasonings of men with God 'to prevail with him: Job xiii. 3, "Surely I would speak to the Almighty, I desire הוֹכֵחַ אֶל־אֵל," " to reason" (argue, plead) "with God, until I can prevail with him." And it is used of God's

pleading with men, to bring them to conviction, Isa. i. 18, לְכוּ־נָא,
וְנִוָּכְחָה,—"Go to" (or "come now"), "and let us plead together."
So that an effectual dealing with a brother about sin is included.
And this is enforced in the latter clause of the words, וְלֹא־תִשָּׂא עָלָיו
חֵטְא; which may well be rendered, "And thou shalt not bear iniquity
for him,"—that is, make thyself guilty of his sin, by not reproving
him. And for that jealousy which is to accompany this watchfulness, and the effects of it, our apostle gives in an example in himself,
2 Cor. xi. 2, 3, "I am jealous over you with godly jealousy: . . . . .
for I fear," (μή πως, as here μή ποτε) "lest by any means . . . . . your
minds should be corrupted from the simplicity that is in Christ." This
belongs to their watch, as they watch for the souls of their people, "as
they who must give account," Heb. xiii. 17. The discharge of this
duty will be required of them on the account of their office, and
that when, I fear, some will be hard put to it for an answer. For
the Scripture is full of threatenings and denunciations of sore judgments against those that shall be found neglective herein. But
doth this excuse other believers, members of churches, from a share
and interest in this duty? No, doubtless, unless it renders them
Cains,—that is, transgressors against the light of nature, and who, as
to the institutions of Christ, manifest themselves not to be members
of the same mystical body with them that really believe. For in
the observation of this and the like duties of their common interest
doth the preservation of that body consist. Christ is the head,
"from whom the whole body fitly joined together and compacted
by that which every joint supplieth, according to the effectual working in the measure of every part, maketh increase of the body, unto
the edifying of itself in love," Eph. iv. 16. Every joint, every part
in this mystical body that receives influences of life from Christ,
the head, and so holds of him, is to work effectually, and to give
out the supplies which it receives from Christ, unto the preservation,
increase, and edification of the whole.

There is, indeed, a causeless suspicion that some are apt to indulge
unto, instead of this watchful jealousy. But this is the bane of
churches and of love, as that is the preservation of them both. The
apostle placeth ὑπόνοιας πονηράς, "evil surmises," or "suspicions," among
the works of "men of corrupt minds," 1 Tim. vi. 4, and that deservedly; but this godly, watchful jealousy, is that which he commends
unto others in the example of himself. And whatever appearance
they may have one of the other, they may be easily distinguished.
Jealousy is a solicitous care, proceeding from love; suspicion, a vain
conjecturing, proceeding from curiosity, vanity, or envy. He that
hath the former, his heart is ruled by love towards them concerning whom he hath it. From thence he is afraid lest they should
miscarry, lest any evil should befall them; for love is the *willing*

of all good unto others, that they may prosper universally. Suspicion is an effect of curiosity and vanity of mind; whence commonly there is somewhat of envy, and secret self-pleasing in the miscarriages of others, mixed with it,—a fault too often found amongst professors. And this vice puts forth itself in vain babbling and unheedful defamations; whereas the other works by love, tenderness, prayer, and mutual exhortation, as in the next verse. Again, this jealous watchfulness hath for its end the glory of Christ and his gospel, with the good of the souls of others. This is that which the apostle aims to ingenerate and stir up in the Hebrews, as is evident from his discourse; when vain suspicion hath no end but the nourishing of the lusts from whence it doth proceed. The foundation whereon this duty is built is the common concernment of all believers in the same good or evil, which are the consequents of men's abiding in Christ or departing from him, in reference whereunto this jealous watch is to be ordered. "Take heed lest there be among you an evil heart of unbelief, in departing from the living God." The good that will ensue on the avoidance of this evil is twofold: the glory of Christ, and the salvation of the souls of them who make profession of his name. And have we not a concernment in these things? Is it not our concernment that Christ be glorified by the professed subjection of the souls of men unto him, and their perseverance therein? that his name, his grace, his power, be glorified, in the holiness, fruitfulness, and stability in profession, of all that are called by his name? If we are not concerned in these things, if we are not deeply concerned in them, we are none of his.

In like manner, are we not concerned that the members of the same body with us should be kept alive, kept from putrefying, from being cut off and burned before our eyes? Are we not concerned that an eye doth not go out, that an arm doth not wither, that a leg be not broken, yea, that a finger be not cut? If it be so, we are not ourselves members of the body. The like may be said of the evil that ensues on the sin of apostasy, which in this duty we labour to obviate and prevent. That which principally of this kind might be insisted on, is the troublesome, defiling infection wherewith apostasy in any is attended; which our apostle speaks unto, chap. xii. 15. The failing of one is commonly the infection and defiling of many. There is a filthy leaven in apostasy, which if not carefully heeded may leaven the whole lump. Ofttimes also it springs from or is accompanied with some word of error that eats like a gangrene. "Principiis obsta" is the great rule in these cases. And the duty spoken unto is one signal means of the prevention of this evil. And herein lies our concernment; as also in the preventing of that punishment that may befall the whole for the sins of some, Josh. xxii. 18, 20. And it is the defect which is in this and the like kind of duties which manifests and makes naked that miserable degeneracy which Christians in general, in these latter evil days, are fallen into. Who almost hath any regard unto them? Instead of these fruits of spiritual love, men for the most part follow "divers lusts and pleasures, living in malice and envy, hateful, and hating one another." The practical duties of Christianity are amongst many derided. To watch over one another, to warn, to exhort one another, are looked on as things, if possible, beneath contempt. And it is a shame to mention or report the ways and means of dealing with and about the sins of men, which by some are substituted in the room of those appointed in the gospel unto their utter exclusion. But the rule is stable, and will in due time, through the strength of Christ, prevail against the lusts of men.

Obs. III. [2.] It is the duty of every individual believer to be intent on all occasions, lest at any time, or by any means, there should be found in him " an evil heart of unbelief."

This, as was showed, follows on the former, and is a necessary consequence of it. But this so directly falls in with what will be offered from the next clause that thereunto we refer it.

(3.) The evil thus earnestly cautioned against is expressed, [1.] In the *principle* of it, and that is, Καρδία πονηρὰ τῆς ἀπιστίας: and, [2.] In the *work or effect of that principle*, in these words, Ἐν τῷ ἀποστῆναι ἀπὸ Θεοῦ ζῶντος.

[1.] The principle of the evil is "an evil heart of unbelief." What is meant by καρδία, "the heart," in the sense wherein it is here used, was declared on the verses preceding; what is meant by πονηρά, " evil," shall be showed in its proper place. In special, it is said to be " an evil heart τῆς ἀπιστίας,"—" of unbelief;" that is, say most, ἄπιστος, " cor malum et incredulum," " an evil heart, and incredulous," or " unbelieving,"—an evil and unbelieving heart. So the genitive case of the substantive is put for the adjective,—ἀπιστίας for ἄπιστος, by a Hebraism not unusual. In this sense "unbelieving" is either exegetical, declaring what is meant by the " evil heart" in this place, even an unbelieving heart; or it is additious, and so a heart is signified which in general is evil, and in particular unbelieving. But there seems to me to be more in this expression; and that ἀπιστίας here is " genitivus efficientis,"—denoting the principal efficient cause rendering the heart so evil as that it should " depart from the living God." Καρδία ἀπιστίας, then, "a heart of unbelief," is more than καρδία ἄπιστος, " an unbelieving heart;" for this latter word is sometimes used to express a defect in believing, and not unbelief absolutely. So John xx. 27, Μὴ γίνου ἄπιστος, ἀλλὰ πιστός,— " Be not unbelieving, but believing." They are the words of Christ unto Thomas, who, though he failed in his faith, yet was not absolutely without faith. I confess the word is generally used in Scrip-

ture to express a negative unbeliever, or an infidel; but there is
something peculiar in this expression, "A heart of unbelief,"—that
is, under the power of it, principled by it in its actings. What this
unbelief is, and how the heart is rendered πονηρά, "evil," thereby,
we must now inquire.

As for unbelief, it is usually distinguished into that which is negative and that which is privative.

1st. *Negative* unbelief is whenever any man or men believe not,
or have not faith, although they never had the means of believing
granted unto them. For when men believe not, they are unbelievers, whether they have had any means of believing or no, or
whether their unbelief be culpable or no, whatever may be the nature or degree of its demerit. So the apostle calls him an unbeliever who comes in accidentally to the assembly of the church,
who never heard the word preached before, 1 Cor. xiv. 23, 24. In
this sense, all those persons and nations who have never had as yet
the gospel preached unto them are infidels, or unbelievers; that is,
they are so negatively,—they believe not, but yet cannot be said to
have in them "an evil heart of unbelief."

2dly. It is *privative*, when men believe not, although they enjoy the
means of faith or believing. And herein consists the highest acting
of the depraved nature of man. And it is on many accounts the
greatest provocation of God that a creature can make himself guilty
of. For it is, as might be manifested, an opposition unto God in
all the properties of his nature, and in the whole revelation of his
will. Hence the gospel, which is a declaration of grace, mercy, and
pardon, though it condemns all sin, yet it denounceth the final condemnation of persons only against this sin: "He that believeth
shall be saved; but he that believeth not shall be damned," Mark
xvi. 16.

Now this privative unbelief is twofold:—(1st.) In *refusing to believe* when it is required; (2dly.) In *rejecting the faith* after it hath
been received. (1st.) The first is, when the object of faith, or that
which is to be believed, is according unto the mind of God, and in
the way of his appointment proposed unto men; when sufficient evidence is given unto the truth and goodness of what is so proposed;
and when the authority is made known on which faith is required;
yet they refuse to believe. For these three things,—a revelation of
the things to be believed made known in the way of God, sufficient
evidence given unto the truth proposed, and a just assertion of the
authority of God requiring faith and obedience,—do render the unbelief of men privative. Now, as this hath its root in the natural
darkness, blindness, and depravedness of the minds of men, so it is
educed and acted not without new sinful prejudices, and stubbornness of the will, refusing to attend unto and consider the evidences

that are given unto the truth proposed, or the goodness and excellency of the things themselves contained in the propositions of truth; nor without signal effects of hardness of heart, love of sin and pleasure, keeping men off from the obedience required. Some instances may clear these particulars:—

[1st.] The root of this unbelief is in the original depravation of our natures, with that spiritual impotency and enmity to God wherein it doth consist. There is such an impotency in us by nature, that no man of himself, by his own strength, can believe, can come to Christ. So himself informs us, John vi. 44: "No man," saith he, "can come to me, except the Father draw him;"—that is, none can believe unless they are in an especial manner "taught of God," as he explains himself, verse 45. Again, by nature that "carnal mind" is in all men, which is "enmity against God," which is "not subject unto his law, neither indeed can be," Rom. viii. 7. Hereunto may be referred all that is spoken about the death of men in sin, their blindness and distrust, their alienation from God and obstinacy therein. This is the root and remote cause of all unbelief. Men in the state of nature neither can nor will believe the gospel; but,—

[2dly.] Besides this general cause of unbelief, when it comes unto particular instances, and the gospel is proposed unto this or that man for his assent and submission unto it, there is always some especial corruption of mind or will, voluntarily acted, if the soul be kept off from believing; and on the account thereof principally and not merely of original impotency and enmity against God, is the guilt of unbelief reflected upon the souls of the sinners. There is the same fundamental remote cause of unbelief in all that refuse the gospel; but the next immediate proper cause of it is peculiar to every individual unbeliever:—

First, Some are kept off from believing the gospel by *inveterate prejudices in their minds*, which they have taken in upon corrupt principles and interests. This shut up of old most of the Jews under their unbelief. They had received many prejudices against the person of Christ, which on all occasions they expressed; and so were offended at him and believed not. That he was poor, that he came out of Galilee, that the rulers and teachers of the church rejected him, were their pleas against him. So also they had against his doctrine, and that principally on two false principles;—one of justification by the works of the law, as our apostle directly declares, Rom. ix. 31, 32, x. 3; the other, of the perpetuity or unchangeableness of the institutions of Moses, with which the apostle deals in this epistle. And these prejudices arose partly from their pride in seeking after righteousness by the works of the law, and partly from a corrupt desire of earthly things, riches, dominion, and wealth, which they expected with and by their Messiah, whereof I have treated elsewhere at large. These were in many the immediate causes of their unbelief, as is everywhere manifest in the gospel. And so is it with many at all times. Prejudices against the preachers of the gospel on sundry accounts, and against their doctrine, as either useless, or false, or unintelligible, or somewhat they know not what, which they do not like, keep them off from attending to the word and believing. See John v. 44.

Secondly, An *especial obstinacy of will* from those prejudices offereth itself in this matter. So our Saviour tells the Pharisees, John v. 40, "Ye will not come to me, that ye might have life." It is not the perverseness and obstinacy that is in the wills of all men by nature that our Saviour here intendeth, but an especial perverseness in them, arising out of an especial envy unto and hatred of him and his doctrine. Hence they did not only not receive him,—which might be charged on their natural impotency,—but they put forth a positive act of their wills in refusing and rejecting him. And on this account the guilt of men's unbelief is absolutely resolved into their own wills. And whether it be discovered or no, this is the condition with many in all times and seasons.

Thirdly, *Love of sin* is with some the immediate cause of their actual unbelief: John iii. 19, "This is the condemnation, that light is come into the world, and men loved darkness rather than light, because their deeds were evil." The light of the gospel is brought unto a place or people; they come so near it as to discover its end and tendency; but so soon as they find that it aims to part them and their sins, they will have no more to do with it. And on this account doth condemnation follow the preaching of the gospel, though its own proper end be salvation and that only. And this is the common way of the ruin of souls: they like not the terms of the gospel, because of their love of sin; and so perish in and for their iniquities.

Fourthly, *Stupid ignorance*, arising from the possessing of the minds of men with other things, inconsistent with the faith and obedience of the gospel, through the craft and subtilty of Satan, is another cause hereof. So our apostle tells us, 2 Cor. iv. 4, that "the god of this world hath blinded the minds of them which believe not, lest the light of the glorious gospel of Christ, who is the image of God, should shine unto them." It is when the minds of men are beamed into with the light of the gospel that they do believe; for by that light is faith produced. How is this hindered, how is it obstructed? It is by the *darkness and blindness* of their minds. What darkness is this,—that which is natural and common unto all? No, but that which is in a peculiar manner brought and reflected on the minds of some men by the craft and deceits of the god of this world; that is, through his temptations and suggestions, he so fills and possesses their minds with the things of this world (whence he is here peculiarly called "the god of this world"), that they are kept in a stupid and brutish ignorance of spiritual things. And this keeps them off from believing. These are a few of the many instances that might be given of the immediate causes of their privative unbelief, which consists in the rejecting or not receiving the truths of the gospel, when they are proposed in a due manner unto the minds of men.

And this fully clears the holiness and righteousness of God in his judgments against final and impenitent unbelievers to whom the gospel is preached; for as that *impotency* which is in them naturally is culpable,—and it is no excuse for them for not believing because of themselves they could not so do, seeing it is by their own default that they are brought into that condition,—so every one in his own person who believeth not doth, by a voluntary act of his will, reject the gospel, and that on such corrupt principles as none can deny to be his sin.

(2*dly.*) There is an unbelief that consists in a *rejection of the truth of the gospel after that it hath been admitted, acknowledged, and professed.* Some, after they have been convinced of the truth, and made profession of it, yet, through the temptations of the world, the corruption of their own hearts, love of sin, or fear of persecution, do suffer their convictions to wear off, or do cast them out, and reject the faith they have owned. Hereof is frequent mention made in the gospel, and no less frequent caution given against it. And this in general is the highest aggravation of this sin. For although the former kind of privative unbelief will certainly prove destructive to them that continue in it, and it may be said that this can do no more, yet this hath two great evils attending it that the other hath no concernment in.

The first is, the *difficulty that there is in being recovered out of this condition.* He who hath already withstood the efficacy of the only remedy for his distempers, who hath rejected and despised it, what can cure him? This he who never received the gospel, be he never so bad or sinful, is not obnoxious unto. He hath not as yet, as it were, made a trial of what it is; and is free from that contempt cast upon it which is done by the other, who declares that he hath made trial of it, and valueth it not. This, on many reasons, renders his recovery difficult, almost impossible.

Again, There is a degree of this unbelief which puts a soul *absolutely into an irrecoverable condition in this world.* For whereinsoever the formality of the sin against the Holy Ghost that shall not be pardoned doth consist, yet this is the matter of it, and without which it is impossible that any one should be guilty of that sin. There must be a renunciation of truth known and professed, or the

guilt of that sin cannot be contracted. Now this, be they never so
wicked, they are free from who never received, admitted, or professed the truth. The sin against the Holy Ghost is a sin peculiar
unto them who have made profession. And from this ariseth an
especial aggravation of their punishment at the last day. So the
apostle Peter determines this matter: "It had been better for them
not to have known the way of righteousness, than, after they have
known it, to turn from the holy commandment delivered unto
them," 2 Epist. ii. 21.

Again, This unbelief in rejecting the gospel is either *notional* and
practical, or *practical* only. [1st.] If it be notional it will also be
practical. If men once reject their profession of the truth of the
gospel, quenching their light into it and understanding of it, their
practice of sin will be answerable thereunto. Renegadoes from the
gospel are the greatest villains in the world. Neither do men voluntarily renounce the light, but to give themselves up to the deeds
of darkness.

[2dly.] It may be practical only. So is it in them who "profess
that they know God, but in works deny him, being abominable,
and disobedient, and unto every good work reprobate," Tit. i. 16,—
men who walk in some kind of profession, yet "their end is destruction," and that because "their god is their belly, and their glory is
their shame, who mind earthly things," Phil. iii. 19. The corruptions of such men do absolutely prevail over their convictions, and
the power of sin in their wills and affections casts off all influencing
light from their minds or understandings. Such men as these, although they do not in words deny the truth of the gospel, yet they
yield no obedience unto it. They neither expect any good from its
promises, nor fear any great evil from its threatenings, which formerly had made some more effectual impressions upon them. And
this is the condition of unspeakable multitudes in the world.

Now, the unbelief here intended by the apostle is this privative
unbelief, consisting in the rejection of the truth of the gospel after
it hath been received and professed. And this also may be considered two ways:—[1st.] *Initially*, as to some degrees of it;
[2dly.] As it may be *finished and completed*. Of these our apostle
treateth severally and distinctly. Of the former in this place, and
Heb. iv. 11–13, chap. xii. 15, 16; of the latter, chap. vi. 4–6, chap.
x. 26, 27. The first consists in any declension of heart from Christ
and the gospel. This may be in various degrees and on several
accounts. The latter is a total renunciation of the gospel, of which
we spake before. It is the former that the apostle here intends,
and therein a prevention of the latter: and therefore concerning it
we must consider two things:—[1st.] Wherein it consists, or what are
the ways of its entrance into and prevailing upon the minds of men.

[*2dly.*] By what means it renders the heart evil when it is brought under the power thereof.

[*1st.*] It consists in *the soul's receiving impressions from arguments and reasonings against profession,* in the whole or any degrees of it. Satan is and will be casting " fiery darts" at the soul, but when the "shield of faith" is held up constantly and steadfastly, they are immediately quenched, Eph. vi. 16; yea, it is the work of faith to arm the soul on all hands, that assaults make no impression upon it. If that fail, if that faint, more or less they will take place. And when or wherein the soul is brought but to parley with an objection, then and therein unbelief is at work, whether it be as unto a particular fact or as unto our state. It was so with our first parents in the very entry of their treaty with Satan, in giving a considering audience unto that one question, " Hath God said so ?" Our great Pattern hath showed us what our deportment ought to be in all suggestions and temptations. When the devil showed him " all the kingdoms of the world and the glory of them," to tempt him withal, he did not stand and look upon them, viewing their glory, and pondering their empire, though he was fully assured that after all he could despise and trample upon the offer, and him that made it; but instantly, without stay, he cries, " Get thee hence, Satan," and further strengthens his own authority with a word of truth, which was his rule, Matt. iv. 10. Innumerable are the inclinations, objections, temptations, that lie against the profession of the gospel, especially in times of difficulty, particularly against steadfastness and preciseness in profession. That the whole of it be laid aside, or the degrees of it be remitted, is the great design of Satan, the world, and the flesh. To hearken unto what Satan suggests, though but under a pretence of seeing what is in it, to reason with the world, to consult with flesh and blood, contains the first actings of unbelief towards corrupting the heart in order unto a departure from God.

[*2dly.*] It consists in or acts itself by *a secret dislike of something, notionally or practically, in the gospel.* This was a common thing in the hearers of our Saviour. They disliked this or that in his doctrine or teaching, and that sometimes in things concerning faith, sometimes in things concerning obedience. So did those with whom he treated, John vi. Whilst he taught them in general of the " bread of God that came down from heaven," they were pleased with it, and cried, " Lord, evermore give us this bread," verse 34; but when he began to acquaint them in particular that he himself was that bread, that his flesh was meat, and his blood was drink,— that is, that they were the spiritual nourishment of the souls of men, especially as given for them in his death,—they began to be offended and to murmur, they disliked it, crying, " This is an hard saying;

who can hear it?" verses 60, 61. And what was the effect of this
dislike? Plain and open apostasy: verse 66, "From that time many
of his disciples went back, and walked no more with him." And
whence did this dislike and murmuring arise? It was merely the
acting of their unbelief, as our Lord declared, verses 63, 64, 'My
words, which you so dislike, are spirit and life, "but there are some
of you that believe not." You pretend exceptions against my words,
apprehended in your gross and carnal manner, but the true reason
of the dislike of them is your own unbelief. God,' saith he, 'hath
not as yet given faith unto you; for I told you before, that "no man
can come unto me" (that is, believe in me and the gospel) "except
it were given unto him of my Father" (verse 65); and in this doth
your unbelief act itself.' This was in matter of faith; and we have
an instance unto the same purpose in the matter of obedience. The
young man mentioned, Matt. xix., had a great respect unto the
teaching of the Lord Christ, for he comes unto him to be instructed
in the way to eternal life. And this he did with so much zeal and
sincerity, according to his present light, that our Saviour approved
them in him; for it is said he looked on him and "loved him," Mark
x. 21. And he likes his first lesson or instruction, according to his
understanding of it, very well; but when the Lord Jesus proceeded
to make a particular trial of him in an especial instance, bidding
him sell what he had and give it to the poor, and follow him, this
he liked not, but went away sorrowful, verses 21, 22.

Now, there are three things in the gospel and the profession of
it about which unbelief is apt to act itself by this dislike; which
if not obviated, will prove a beginning of turning away from the
whole:—First, The purity and spirituality of its worship; secondly,
The strictness and universality of its holiness or obedience; and,
thirdly, The grace and mystery of its doctrine.

First, It acts itself in dislike against *the purity, simplicity, and
spirituality of its worship.* This was that wherein our apostle had
principally to do with the Jews. They were apt, all of them, to
admire the old, glorious, pompous worship of the temple, and so to
dislike the naked simplicity of gospel institutions. And in like
manner was he jealous over the Corinthians, "lest they should be
corrupted from the simplicity that is in Christ," 2 Cor. xi. 3; that
is, in the worship of God as instituted and appointed by him. This
was always a great offence unto all unbelievers. Hence the Pagans
of old objected unto the Christians, that they had a religion, or a
worship of God, without temples, altars, images, or pompous ceremonies; whence they looked on them as mere atheists. And this
dislike of the purity and simplicity of the gospel worship is that
which was the rise of, and gave increase or progress unto the whole
Roman apostasy. And this is that which, through the unbelief of

men, keeps the gospel in other nations under so much reproach, contempt, and persecution at this day. Men like not the plain, unspotted institutions of Christ, but are pleased with the meretricious Roman paint, wherewith so great a part of the world hath been beguiled and infatuated.

Secondly, *The severity and universality of obedience* which it requireth is another thing that unbelief prevails to put forth dislike against. It makes use of the flesh to this purpose. Something or other it would be gratified in, within doors or without, or at least be spared, and not in all things pursued as the gospel requires. To be always, and in all things, private and public, personal and in all relations, mortified, crucified, and denied, to have no rest given unto it, the flesh likes it not; and unbelief makes use of its aversation to bring the whole soul into a dislike of that doctrine whereby all this is required. Thus Peter tells us of some that "turn from the holy commandment delivered unto them," 2 Epist. ii. 21. He gives us not only the nature of the sin of them whom he blames,—that they turn away from the commands of Christ in the gospel; but he gives us also the reason why they do so,—it is because of their holiness. They turn aside from the " holy commandment." Many professors have been wearied out with an observance of that holiness which this profession doth require. Hence commonly there are most apostates from the strictest ways of profession. The more universally holiness is pressed, the more weary will prevailing unbelief make men of their ways.

Thirdly, It worketh accordingly with respect unto *the grace and mystery of the gospel.* Of old time it prevailed with many to look upon the whole of it as folly. The " preaching of the cross" was " foolishness" unto them that believed not; that is, the saving of sinners by the substitution of Christ in their room, and the atonement he made by his death and blood-shedding, was so. Now, this being a matter of great importance, I shall crave a little to digress from our immediate work and design, whilst I demonstrate that a secret dislike of the principal mysteries of the gospel is the original and cause of most of the degeneracies, backslidings, and apostasies that are found amongst professors in these latter days.

Our apostle tells us that the " preaching of the cross" was " foolishness to them that perished," 1 Cor. i. 18; and they perished merely on that account,—it was foolishness unto them, they liked not the mystery of it, they saw no wisdom in it. And this he said with respect unto Jews and Gentiles, as is manifest in that place. To confirm this, I shall instance in some of the principal heads of the doctrine of the gospel, and show how unbelief prevails with men to dislike them, to reject them, and to look on them as folly.

(First,) And the first is this,—That Jesus of Nazareth, poor and

contemptible as he was in the world, generally esteemed by the men
of those days wherein he lived to be a seducer, a glutton, a blas-
phemer, a turbulent person, hated of God and man, being taken as
a thief, and hanged upon a tree, and so slain by the consent of the
world, Jews and Gentiles, as a malefactor, was the Son of God, the
Saviour of the world, and is both Lord and Christ.

This is the beginning of the gospel, which the apostle preached
to the Jews and Gentiles, Acts ii. 22–24, " Ye men of Israel, hear
these words; Jesus of Nazareth, a man approved of God among you
by miracles, and wonders, and signs, which God did by him in the
midst of you, as ye yourselves also know: him, being delivered by
the determinate counsel and foreknowledge of God, ye have taken,
and by wicked hands have crucified and slain: whom God hath
raised up." That is, ' This Jesus of Nazareth which we preach,—
him whom you remember well enough, he was among you but the
other day, and preached unto you, and wrought signs and miracles
among you; and you may further remember him by an infallible
token, for with wicked hands you crucified and slew him.' ' Well,
and what of this Jesus whom we slew and crucified ?' ' Why,' saith
the apostle, ' ἀσφαλῶς γινωσκέτω, " Let all the house of Israel know
assuredly that God hath made him both Lord and Christ,"' verse
36. ' Him ! who is that ? an appearance of the eternal Word ? a
dispensation of grace appearing in him ? the Light of God in man ?'
'No, no; but τοῦτον τὸν Ἰησοῦν, ὃν ὑμεῖς ἐσταυρώσατε,—" that same Jesus
whom ye crucified." That same man whom about eight weeks ago
you crucified, him hath he made " both Lord and Christ;" or in
his resurrection and exaltation declared so to be.' And this the Holy
Ghost lays a sure foundation of in his expression of his incarnation
and birth. The angel tells Mary his mother, Συλλήψῃ ἐν γαστρί, καὶ
τέξῃ υἱόν, Luke i. 31, " Thou shalt conceive in thy womb, and bring
forth a son,"—conceive him by the power of the Most High, and
bear him after the manner of women. And then, verse 35, Τὸ γεννώ-
μενον ἅγιον, etc., "That holy thing, that shall be born of thee, shall be
called the Son of God." That " holy thing" was the child which
she conceived, afterwards called Jesus of Nazareth. And it was
termed a "holy thing," because it was ἀνυπόστατον, not a person of
itself, as conceived by her, had not a personal subsistence in, by, and
of itself, but subsisted in the person of the Son of God; on which
account it was called " The Son of God." And when he was born,
the angel tells the shepherds, that that day was born "a Saviour,
Christ the Lord," Luke ii. 11; who, he tells them in the next verse,
was βρέφος ἐσπαργανωμένον, κείμενον ἐν τῇ φάτνῃ, " the infant that was
wrapped in swaddling-clothes, and placed in the manger." To
this purpose do the apostles declare themselves again: Acts iii.
13–15, " The God of Abraham, and of Isaac, and of Jacob, the God

of our fathers, hath glorified his Son Jesus; whom ye delivered up, and denied him in the presence of Pilate, when he was determined to let him go. But ye denied the Holy One and the Just, and desired a murderer to be granted unto you, and killed the Prince of life, whom God hath raised from the dead." Still they direct them to the man whom they saw, and knew, and dealt wickedly and injuriously withal. And this man, he tells them, this Christ, must be received in the heavens " until the restitution of all things," when he shall come again, verses 19–21. So himself lays this as the foundation of all his preaching, John viii. 24, "If," saith he, " ye believe not that I am he, ye shall die in your sins,"—'That I, Jesus of Nazareth, that speak unto you, and converse with you, am the Messiah, the Saviour of the world, you shall die and perish for evermore.' This, I say, is one, and one of the first fundamental principles of the gospel; and I shall a little manifest how *unbelief dislikes* this principle, and by that dislike prevails with men unto an apostasy from the gospel itself.

I might insist upon the great instance hereof in the nation of the Jews, unto whom he was sent first and in an especial manner; but I have done this at large in the first part of our Prolegomena unto this work, whereunto I refer the reader. Only we may mind him how this was fore-expressed concerning them by the prophet Isaiah, chap. liii. 2, " He hath no form nor comeliness; and when we shall see him, there is no beauty that we should desire him." They could not see or discern any thing in him for which they should receive him, or believe in him, as to the end for which he was sent of God. As Hiram, king of Tyre, when he saw the cities which Solomon had given him, they displeased him, and he called them " Cabul," and so he rejected them, 1 Kings ix. 13; so did the Jews, when they came to see the Lord Christ, they were displeased with him, and reproaching him with many opprobrious terms, utterly rejected him; under the power of which unbelief they yet reject him. I might also insist on the pagans of old, who derided the crucified God of the Christians; but I will leave them under the conquest which the gospel obtained against them. Mention also might be made of the Gnostics, and other ancient heretics, with their endless genealogies and fables, making him to be only an appearance of a man; and though himself said he was a man, and his friends said he was a man, and God himself said he was a man, and that he " sent forth his Son, made of a woman, made under the law," though he lived and died a man, yet they would not acknowledge him so to be. But these are long since gone off the stage, although we have yet to do with their offspring under several forms and shapes. The popish figment also of transubstantiation, springing from the same root, utterly overthrowing the human nature of Christ, and our salvation wrought therein,

might be on this account remarked.   And so also might the imagination of the Mennonites, who will not grant that the man of whom
we speak took flesh of the substance of the virgin, but that his flesh
was spiritual, as they speak, brought from heaven, and only passing
through the womb of the Virgin, that he might appear to be a man.
And so said some of old; concerning whom Tertullian says, that according to their opinion, " Maria non filium gestabat in utero, sed
hospitem,"—"Mary bare not her son in her womb, but a guest." For
they utterly dislike it, that one partaker of flesh and blood like ourselves should be this Son of God.   And therefore this figment, which
overthrows the covenant of God with Abraham, and all the promises
of the Messiah, that he should be of his seed, and of the seed of
David, at once rejecting the whole Old Testament, and turning the
stories of the genealogy of Christ, recorded to manifest the faithfulness of God in his promises, into fables, must be exalted in the room
and place of that truth which is so fully, so frequently asserted in
the gospel, and which is the prime foundation of all our profession.
All these oppositions unto and apostasies from the gospel sprang from
this especial cause, or the dislike of unbelief against this principle of
the mystery of its doctrine.   But I shall particularly instance in two
sorts of persons, that are of nearer concernment unto us than any of
these:—

And the first is of them whom they call Quakers.   It is strange
to think into how many forms and shapes they have turned themselves to darken the counsel of God in this matter, and to hide their
own apprehension from the light.   At their beginning in the world
they made (many of them) no scruple plainly to affirm, that all that
is spoken concerning Christ was a mere dispensation of God, and an
appearance of the Light; but as for such a man as we have described,
they had no regard of him.   This at first served their turns, and
they intended no more by Christ but that which they call the *Light
of God* within them.   But what shall we say unto these things? If
all the testimonies that we have given unto " the man Christ Jesus,"
if all that is spoken of him in the gospel, all that he did, all that he
suffered, what he now doth in heaven by intercession, what he shall
do at the day of judgment, all that is required of us towards him, in
faith, love, and obedience, be not enough to prove him a real individual man, we may certainly be all of us in a mistake as to what
we ourselves are in this world,—we may be all dispensations, who
have hitherto taken ourselves to be the sons and daughters of men.
But it is some while since they seem to have forsaken this imagination, being driven from it by the common expostulations of every
ordinary Christian, " What do you think of Jesus that died at Jerusalem?"   They have begun in words to acknowledge his person, but
yet continue strangely to obscure their thoughts concerning him, and

to confound it, or the presence of God in and with him, with their own pretended light. And whence doth this arise? It is merely from the secret dislike that unbelief hath of this mystery of God. Hence they cannot see that "form and comeliness" in him for which he should be desired.

Again, others there are who grant that all we have spoken concerning the human nature of Christ is true,—that he was so born, that he so died, and he was so a man, as we have declared. And this man, say they, was justly called, and is so, the Son of God, because God employed and exalted him unto all power in heaven and earth. But that he should be the eternal Son of God, that the eternal Word should be made flesh, that a divine person should receive the human nature into subsistence with itself, this they utterly reject. This is the way of the Socinians. The testimonies being so many, so plain, so uncontrollable, that are given in the Scripture unto this truth, what is it that can carry men to advance a contradiction unto them to their own ruin? Why, unbelief doth not like this mystery of " God manifested in the flesh." This insensibly alienates the soul from it; and what men pretend to receive by the conduct of reason and argument, is indeed nothing but prejudices imposed on their minds by the power of unbelief.

(Secondly,) Another main fundamental principle of the gospel is, that by the obedience unto God, death, and blood-shedding of this same Jesus, who was crucified and slain, are redemption, forgiveness of sins, deliverance from the wrath to come, righteousness, and acceptation with God, to be obtained, and by him only.

The other proposition respected the *person* of Christ, this doth his *mediation*. And this, in the second place, was insisted on in the first preaching of the gospel. That this is the sum of the doctrine of the Scriptures concerning him, himself taught his disciples, Luke xxiv. 45–47, "Then opened he their understanding, that they might understand the scriptures, and said unto them, Thus it is written, and thus it behoved Christ to suffer, and to rise from the dead the third day: and that repentance and remission of sins should be preached in his name." And this the apostles jointly express, exclusively unto all other mediums as to the end proposed, Acts iv. 12, " Neither is there salvation in any other: for there is none other name under heaven given among men, whereby we must be saved."

The great inquiry of men in the world, convinced of an immortal condition, is that which we have expressed, Acts xvi. 30, " What must we do to be saved?" This lies in their thoughts more or less all their days, and is rolled in their hearts under that severe notion, Isa. xxxiii. 14, " Who among us shall dwell with the devouring fire? who among us shall dwell with everlasting burnings?" And of this inquiry there are two parts:—

[First,] How they may obtain *forgiveness of sin:* Mic. vi. 6, "Wherewith shall I come before the LORD, and bow myself before the high God? shall I come before him with burnt-offerings, with calves of a year old? will the LORD be pleased with thousands of rams, or with ten thousands of rivers of oil? shall I give my first-born for my transgression, the fruit of my body for the sin of my soul?" When a real sense of the guilt of sin is by any means brought upon the soul, it is vehement and urgent, and will give them in whom it is no rest, until they can fix on some way of relief.

[Secondly,] What they shall do for a *righteousness,* upon the account whereof they may obtain acceptance with God. For it is not enough that men may be one way or other acquitted from sin, but they must be made righteous also. In this case, the Jews sought for righteousness "as it were by the works of the law," Rom. ix. 32; for a righteousness they knew they must have, and "being ignorant of God's righteousness, they went about to establish their own righteousness," Rom. x. 3.

Now, this head of the gospel that we have mentioned is a direct answer unto these two questions. For in answer unto the first it declares, that by this Jesus Christ alone is forgiveness and remission of sins to be obtained. "In him we have redemption through his blood, the forgiveness of sins," Eph. i. 7. See Heb. ix. 12–14. This was, as the gospel declares, the design of God the Father, Rom. iii. 24, 25; and of his own love and good-will, Rev. i. 5. And this the apostles preached ἐν πρώτοις, "amongst the chiefest things" of their message to the world, 1 Cor. xv. 3. And to the second it answers, that by the obedience and suffering of Christ alone is the righteousness inquired after to be obtained: for by his obedience, "the obedience of one," are "many made righteous," Rom. v. 19. For not only "by him is preached unto us the forgiveness of sins," but "by him all that believe are justified," Acts xiii. 38, 39. See Phil. iii. 8, 9; 1 Cor. i. 30.

This is another important part of the mystery of the gospel, and that which unbelief greatly dislikes; that is, it is apt to beget in the soul a dislike of it. And a great instance we have in the world of its power and efficacy to draw men off from the gospel; for unbelief in this matter is the real foundation of the whole Papacy. They cannot rest in Christ alone for righteousness and forgiveness of sins. Hence hath sprung their sacrifice of the mass for the quick and dead; hence their indulgences from the treasures of the church; hence their penances and works satisfactory for sin; hence their purgatory, religious houses, pilgrimages, intercession of saints and angels, confessions and absolutions, with the remainder of their abominations. All these things spring from no other root but this, —namely, that from the power of their unbelief, men think it a

foolish thing to look for pardon and righteousness solely from another, and not to trust to themselves in any thing. And the reason
why they have multiplied instances to the same purpose is, because they can indeed find rest and satisfaction in none, and do
therefore please and deceive their souls with this variety. And
what is it that hath driven a company of poor deluded souls amongst
ourselves to trust unto a fancied light within them, and a feigned
perfection in their ways? They cannot think it wise, prudent, safe,
they like it not, to rest, to trust for their all upon one who lived
and died so long ago. Men make sundry pretences, use divers
arguings and pleas, for their turning aside unto their crooked paths,
—endeavour by all means possible to justify themselves; but the
bottom of all lies here, that this doctrine of the cross is foolishness
unto them, and they are under the power of their unbelief, which
dislikes the mysteries of it.

(Thirdly,) Another principle of the same mystery is, That the way
and means whereby forgiveness of sin, righteousness, and acceptance
with God for sinners, are attained by this Jesus Christ, is, that by the
sacrifice of himself, his death, and blood-shedding, with the punishment for sin which he voluntarily underwent, God was atoned,
his justice satisfied, and his law fulfilled; and that because he had
ordered, in his infinite wisdom and sovereignty, with the will and
consent of Christ himself, to charge all the sins of all the elect upon
him, and to accept of his obedience for them, he undertaking to be
their Surety and Redeemer. To clear this principle the gospel
teacheth,—

[First,] That notwithstanding all that was visibly done unto Jesus
by the Jews and others, yet the *hand and counsel of God* were in
the whole business, designing him thereunto. See Acts ii. 22, 23;
Rom. iii. 25.

[Secondly,] That his own *merciful and gracious goodness* concurred herein. However the Jews seemed to hale him up and down
as a malefactor, and violently to slay him, yet if his own will had not
been in the work, unto another end than what they had in design,
they had had no power over him, John x. 18. But he came on set
purpose to lay down his life a ransom, Matt. xx. 28, and to offer himself a sacrifice for sinners; which he performed accordingly, Eph.
v. 2; Gal. ii. 20; Rev. i. 5; Heb. i. 3.

[Thirdly,] That the *end* of all this was that which we before laid
down, namely, that he might be " made sin for us, that we might be
made the righteousness of God in him," 2 Cor. v. 21. So also, Gal.
iii. 13; Isa. liii. 4–6, 11; 1 Pet. i. 18, 19.

And against this principle also unbelief riseth up with great power
and efficacy in many, and that on sundry accounts; for,—

[First,] That God should comply as it were, and have a hand in that work, for any end of his, wherein Satan, and men as wicked as ever the sun shone upon, did execute the fulness of their rage and villany, and for which he afterwards utterly and miserably destroyed those murderers, is folly to some. Hence were a thousand fables raised of old about the passion of Christ: some turned the whole story into an allegory; some said it was acted only in show and appearance, and not in reality and truth; some, that he was conveyed away, and Barabbas crucified in his stead, with sundry other such foolish abominations.

[Secondly,] Some of late, refusing to see the wisdom, holiness, and righteousness of God in this matter, in bringing about his own counsels, and doing his own work, notwithstanding the interposition of the sins of the worst of men, deny that God determined any thing herein, but left it wholly unto the liberty of the Jews, on the determination of whose wills the whole work of salvation was suspended.

[Thirdly,] Some reject the whole matter itself. That the just should suffer for the unjust, the innocent undergo the punishment due to the guilty, that one should sin and another suffer,—that he whom God loved above all should undergo his wrath for them and their deliverance whom he had grounds of righteousness to hate and destroy, is a foolish thing unto them. This all the Socinians in the world despise. And it is rejected by the Quakers amongst ourselves, and variously corrupted by the Papists and others. And there is none of all these but will plead reasons and arguments for their opinions. But this that we insist on is the true and real ground of their miscarriages. They are under the power of that unbelief which acts itself by a dislike of the mysteries of the gospel. Pretend what they will, it is unbelief alone that is the cause of their apostasy. I might instance in other principles of the like nature and importance, but I should dwell too long on this digression.

[3dly.] It works by and consists in a *growing diffidence of the promises and threatenings of the gospel.* The great work and duty of faith is to influence the soul unto universal obedience and an abstinence from all sin, out of a regard unto the promises and threatenings of God. So our apostle directs in 2 Cor. vii. 1. And when the efficacy of this influence begins to wear off and decay, it is from the prevalency of unbelief. And there are many ways whereby it works and produceth this effect, to take off the soul from a due regard to the promises and threatenings of the gospel. A sense, liking, love of, and satisfaction in present things, with carnal wisdom, arising from an observation of strange promiscuous events in the world, give a principal contribution hereunto; but these things are not here to be insisted on.

And these things have been spoken to discover the nature and the work of that unbelief, which the apostle here warns and cautions all professors concerning; and we have especially considered it as to its entrance towards a departure from God. And hence we may observe that,—

Obs. IV. The root of all backsliding, of all apostasy, whether it be notional or practical, gradual or total, lies in unbelief.

I have dwelt long already on this matter of unbelief; and I had reason so to do, for this is the hinge on which the discourses of the apostle in this chapter and the next do turn. The nature of it, with its causes, ways and means of prevalency, with its danger and means of prevention, are the things which he lays before them. But I shall confine my discourse within due bounds, and therefore speak unto this proposition only with reference unto that influence which unbelief hath on the heart to render it evil : " Take heed, lest there be in you an evil heart of unbelief,"—καρδία πονηρά, " cor malum." This is the only place in the New Testament where a disapproved heart hath this adjunct of " evil," " an evil heart." It is in other places termed σκληρός, "hard," and ἀμετανόητος, " impenitent," Rom. ii. 5, but here only " evil." In the Old Testament it is sometimes said to be רע, " evil," as Jer. iii. 17, vii. 24, xi. 8, xvi. 12, xviii. 12. This the LXX. renders by πονηρός,—that is, " malus," " perversus," " scelestus," " improbus;" one that is " wicked" and " flagitious." The original of the word would denote one that is industriously wicked; for it is from πένω, by πονέω, "to labour diligently and with industry, though conflicting with difficulties." Hence the devil, because he is industriously and maliciously wicked, is called ὁ πονηρός, " the wicked one:" " When any one heareth the word of the kingdom, and understandeth it not, then cometh ὁ πονηρός,"—" the wicked one," Matt. xiii. 19. So are we taught to pray, 'Ρῦσαι ἡμᾶς ἀπὸ τοῦ πονηροῦ, Matt. vi. 13, " Deliver" (or " rescue") " us from that evil one." And it is said, that " the whole world lieth ἐν τῷ πονηρῷ," 1 John v. 19,—" under the power of that wicked one." When, therefore, any heart is said to be πονηρά, an evil, wicked, flagitious frame is intended.

Our present inquiry is only how the heart is gradually brought under this denomination by the power and efficacy of unbelief, and that with especial respect unto that particular sin of departing from God. And this is done several ways:—

[*1st.*] Unbelief sets all the corrupt lusts and affections of the heart at liberty to act according to their own perverse nature and inclination. The heart of man is by nature evil; all the thoughts and imaginations of it are " only evil continually," Gen. vi. 5. It is full of all " corrupt affections," which act themselves and influence men in all they do. The gospel cometh in a direct opposition unto these lusts and corrupt affections, both in the root and in the fruit of them; for " the grace of God that bringeth salvation hath appeared unto us, teaching us that, denying ungodliness and worldly lusts, we should live soberly, righteously, and godly, in this present world," Tit. ii. 11, 12. There is no greater duty that it chargeth our souls withal than the mortification, crucifying, and destruction of them, and this indispensably, if we intend to be made partakers of the promises of it, Col. iii. 5–8; Rom. viii. 13. Moreover, it is the first proper work of that faith whereby we believe the gospel, in and upon our own souls, to cleanse them from these lusts and affections. It is the work of faith to purify the heart, being the great means or instrument whereby God is pleased to effect it: " Purifying our hearts by faith," Acts xv. 9. For, receiving the promises, it teacheth, persuadeth, and enableth us to " cleanse ourselves from all unclean- nesses of the flesh and spirit, perfecting holiness in the fear of God," 2 Cor. vii. 1. Now, these two, faith and the gospel, make up our profession,—the one being that wherewith or whereby we profess, the other that which we do profess. And they both concur in this design, namely, the purifying of the heart. So far as these prevail upon us or in us, that work is successful. And where there is no weakening of the lusts of the heart, no restraint laid upon them, no resistance made unto them, there is no profession at all, there is nothing of faith or gospel that takes place; for "they that are Christ's have crucified the flesh with the affections and lusts," Gal. v. 24. They have done so actually in some measure or degree. All, then, who have taken upon them the profession of the gospel in reality, although it be only upon the account of light and convic- tion, have restrained and have curbed them, and taken upon themselves a *law of resistance* unto them. Hence all of them pro- ceed so far at least as to " escape the pollutions of the world, through the knowledge of the Lord and Saviour Jesus Christ," 2 Pet. ii. 20. Those who attain not hereunto are in no sense to be esteemed such as profess the gospel. But now whenever unbelief be- ginneth to influence the heart towards the frame described, it sets in the first place these corrupt lusts and affections at liberty to act them- selves according to their own nature. And this it doth two ways:—

First, With respect unto the *gospel* and its efficacy for the mor- tification of them; for it takes off, weakens, and disarms those con- siderations which the gospel tenders unto the souls of men for that end. The way and means whereby the gospel of itself worketh towards the mortification of the lusts of the heart is by the proposi- tion of its promises and threatenings unto the minds of men. These work *morally* upon them; for the consideration of them causeth men to set themselves against all those things which may cause them to come short of the one, or make them obnoxious unto the other, 2 Cor. vii. 1   Now all influence upon the soul unto this end from hence is intercepted by unbelief. Its proper nature and work lies in begetting a disregard of gospel promises and threatenings through a diffidence of them. And hereof we have examples every day. Men are in a constant way wrought upon by the preaching of the word ; that is, their minds are influenced by a taste of the good things proposed and promised in it, and are brought under a sense of the terror of the Lord in its threatenings. The first proper effect hereof in themselves, is the resistance of their lusts and the reformation of their lives thereon. But we see that many of these, losing, through unbelief, a sense of that impression that was on them from the word, have all their lusts let loose unto rage and violence; and so return again like "the dog to his vomit, and the sow that was washed to her wallowing in the mire," as 2 Pet. ii. 22.

Secondly, With respect unto *faith* itself. This is evident from the nature of the thing; for where unbelief thrives or grows, there faith must decay and wax weak. But especially it impedes and hinders faith in the work before described, by depriving it of the means and instruments whereby it works, which are care, watchfulness, or vigilancy against sin; for its great design lies in making the soul negligent, careless, and slothful in the opposition of sin. Where this is attained, the whole work of faith is defeated, and lust is set at liberty. And where this is so, it immediately returns to act according to its own corrupt and perverse nature; which, as we have elsewhere at large declared, is "enmity against God." And this consists both in an aversation from God and an opposition unto him. Look, then, whatever approaches a man in his profession hath made towards God, the work of these lusts and corruptions, now at liberty, is to incline him to withdraw and depart from them. This renders the heart evil, and disposeth it unto an utter departure from the living God.

[2*dly*.] It renders the heart evil by debasing it, and casting all good, honest, ingenuous, and noble principles out of it. The gospel furnisheth the mind of man with the best and highest principles towards God and man that in this world it is receptive of. This might easily be evinced against all the false and foolish pretences of the old philosophy or present atheism of the world. Whatever there is of faith, love, submission, or conformity unto God, that may ingenerate a return into that image and likeness of him which we fell from by sin and apostasy; whatever is of innocency, righteousness, truth, patience, forbearance, that may render us fruitful, and useful in or needful unto the community of mankind; whatever is pure, lovely, peaceable, praiseworthy, in a man's own soul and the retirements of his mind, is all proposed, taught, and exhibited by the word of the gospel. Now, principles of this nature do lively ennoble the soul, and render it good and honourable. But the work of unbelief is to cast them all out, at least as to their especial nature communicated unto them by the gospel, which alone brings with it an impress of the image and likeness of God. And when this is separated from any of the things before mentioned, they are of no value. This, then, renders the heart base and evil, and gives it an utter dislike of communion or intercourse with God.

[3dly.] It accumulates the heart with a dreadful guilt of *ingratitude against God*, which before profession it was incapable of. When a person hath been brought unto the knowledge of the gospel, and thereby vindicated out of darkness, and delivered from the sensuality of the world; and hath moreover, it may be, "tasted of the good word of God, and of the powers of the world to come;" for such a one to draw back, to forsake the Lord and his ways, through the power of unbelief, there is a great aggravation attending his sin, 2 Pet. ii. 20, 21. And when once the heart is deflowered by this horrible sin of ingratitude, it will prostitute itself of its own accord unto all manner of abominations. And for us, it is good to have this spring of all our danger in the course of our profession continually in our eye. Here it lies, the root of it is here laid open; and if it be not continually watched against, all our other endeavours to persevere blameless unto the end are and will be in vain.

[2.] The next thing in the words is that *especial evil* which the apostle cautions the Hebrews against, as that which a heart made evil by the prevalency of unbelief would tend unto, and which is like to ensue if not prevented in the causes of it; and that is, "departing from the living God:" Ἐν τῷ ἀποστῆναι ἀπὸ Θεοῦ ζῶντος.

Ἐν τῷ: that is, say some, εἰς τό,—the sense whereof would be, "so that you should depart." But ἐν τῷ is more significant

'Ἐν τῷ.   and no less proper in this language. And the article thus varied with the infinitive mood denotes a continued act,— "that it should be departing;"—"that the evil heart should work and operate in a course of departing from God."

Ἐν τῷ ἀποστῆναι. Ἀφίστημι is a word ἐκ τῶν μέσων, of an indifferent

'Ἀποστῆναι.   signification in itself, and is used to express any kind of departure, physical or moral, from a person or thing, a place or a principle. Sometimes it is expressive of a duty: 2 Tim. ii. 19, "Whosoever nameth the name of Christ, ἀποστήτω ἀπὸ ἀδικίας,"—"let him depart from iniquity." So also 1 Tim. vi. 5. Sometimes it denotes the highest sin: 1 Tim. iv. 1, "The Spirit speaketh expressly, that in the latter season ἀποστήσονταί τινες τῆς πίστεως," —"some shall depart from the faith." And the departure here prophesied of is signally termed ἡ ἀποστασία, "the departure," or "apostasy," 2 Thess. ii. 3. So that the word is to be expounded from the subject-matter treated of, and the especial object of it. And it is a word in its moral sense oftener used by our apostle than by all the other sacred writers besides. Once in the gospel it is used absolutely for a sinful falling away, Luke viii. 13: "They believe for a season, καὶ ἐν καιρῷ πειρασμοῦ ἀφίστανται,"—"in the time of persecution they fall away," they turn apostates.   And from this word are the common names of apostates and apostasy taken; that is, the great sin of forsaking or departing from the profession of the gospel. "In discedendo," say interpreters; Beza, "in desciscendo," properly. It is, in an evil sense, a revolting, a treacherous defection from truth and duty.   It answers unto סוּר, which is used in an indifferent sense, to depart from any thing, good or evil, and sometimes is applied unto a perverse departure from God; as Hos. vii. 14.   And in this especial sense it expresseth סָרַר, which is to be perverse, stubborn, and contumacious in turning away from God, or that which is good and right in any kind, so as to include a rebellion in it, as the departure here intended doth; that is, to revolt.

The *object of this departure* is by our apostle in this place particularly expressed, ἀπὸ Θεοῦ ζῶντος,—"from the living God."   It is plain that it is apostasy from the profession of the gospel which is intended; and we must inquire into the reasons why the apostle doth thus peculiarly express it, by a *departure from the living God.*   I shall propose those which to me seem most natural:—

1st.   It may be that these Hebrews thought nothing less than that their departure from the profession of the gospel was a departure from the living God.   Probably they ᾽Απὸ Θεοῦ ζῶντος.
rather pretended and pleaded that they were returning to him; for they did not fall off unto idols or idolatry, but returned to observe, as they thought, the institutions of the living God, and for a relinquishment whereof the blaspheming and persecuting part of them traduced our apostle himself as an apostate, Acts xxi. 28. To obviate this apprehension in them, and that they might not thereby countenance themselves in their defection, which men are apt to do with various pretences, the apostle lets them know that after the revelation of Christ and profession of him, there is no departure from him and his institutions but that men do withal depart from the living God.   So John positively declares on the one hand and the other, 2 Epist. 9, " Whosoever transgresseth, and abideth not in the doctrine of Christ, hath not God.   He that abideth in the doctrine of Christ, he hath both the Father and the Son."   In a recession from the gospel or doctrine of Christ, God himself is forsaken.   He that hath not the Son, he hath not the Father; as, on the other side, continuance in the doctrine of the gospel secureth us an interest not in the Son only, but in the Father also.   He, then, that rejects Christ in the gospel, let him pretend what he will of adhering unto one God, he hath forsaken the living God, and cleaves unto an idol of his own heart; for neither is the Father without the Son, nor is he a God unto us but in and by him.

2*dly.* It may be he would mind them of the person and nature of him from whom he would prevent their departure, namely,
that however in respect of his office, and as he was incarnate, he was
our mediator, our apostle, and high priest, yet in his own divine person
he was one with his Father and the blessed Spirit, the living God.

3*dly.* (which either alone or in concurrence with these other
reasons is certainly in the words), That he might deter them from
the sin he cautions them against by the pernicious event and consequent of it; and this is, that therein they would depart from him
who is the great, terrible, and dreadful God, the living God, who is
able to punish and avenge their sin, and that to all eternity. And
this appears to be in the words, in that he again insists on the same
argument afterwards; for to the same purpose he tells them that
" it is a fearful thing to fall into the hands of the living God," chap.
x. 31. And as this property of life, as it is in God essentially and
causally, whence he is called " The living God," is exceedingly and
eminently accommodated to encourage us unto faith, trust, confidence,
and affiance in him, in all straits and difficulties, whilst we are in
the way of our duty,—as our apostle declares, 1 Tim. iv. 10, " For
therefore we both labour and suffer reproach, because we trust in
the living God;" or, ' This is that which encourageth us unto and
supporteth us in all our labourings and sufferings, namely, because
he whom we trust in, whom we expect assistance from here, and a
reward hereafter, is the living God:' so it is that which deservedly
casts the greatest awe and terror upon the minds of men in their
sins and rebellion against him. For as this life of God includes in
it the notion and consideration of all those properties which hold
out encouragements unto us in things present and to come; so it doth
also that of those dreadful attributes of his power, holiness, and
eternity, which sinners have reason to bethink themselves of in their
provocations of him. Thus he frequently prefaceth expressions of
his severity against stubborn sinners with אָנִי חַי, " I live, saith the
LORD ;" as it were bidding of them to consider what thence they were
to expect. And this seems to me the principal reason why the
apostle thus states the sin of their apostasy, that it is a departure
from the living God.

4*thly.* He may also so express it, at once to intimate unto them
the greatness and folly of their sin. They thought, it may be,
it was but the leaving of these or those observances of the gospel;
but, saith he, it is a departure, a flagitious defection and revolt, from
the living God. And who knows not this to be the greatest sin and
highest folly imaginable? To depart from him who will be so great
a reward unto them that obey him, and so severe a judge of them
that forsake him, what greater guilt or folly is the nature of man
capable of?

And this is the evil which the apostle here cautions professors against, which I have insisted on the longer, because it is directly opposite unto that great duty which it is the general design of the epistle to press them unto. And we shall take such observations from this last clause of the verse as the words and the reasons of using them do present unto us; and the first is, that,—

Obs. V. The malignity and venom of sin is apt to hide itself under many, under any shades and pretences.

I speak not of the evasions and pretexts wherewith men endeavour to cover or countenance themselves in their miscarriages in the world, and unto others, but of those pleas and pretences which they will admit of in their minds, partly to induce their wills and affections unto sin, and partly to relieve and countenance their consciences under sin. Amongst those reasonings which these Hebrews had in themselves about a relinquishment of the gospel and its institutions, they never considered it as an apostasy from the living God. They looked upon it as a peculiar way of worship, attended with difficulties and persecutions, which perhaps they might please God as well in the omission of. By this means did they hide from themselves that mortal malignity and poison that was in their sin. And so it is in every sin. The subtlety and deceit of lust doth still strive to conceal the true and proper nature of sin whereunto it enticeth or is enticed. When Naaman the Syrian would, notwithstanding his conviction, abide in his idol-worship, because of his secular advantage, it is but a going with his master into the house of Rimmon, and bowing there, not that he intended to have any other God but the God of Israel, 2 Kings v. 18;—so long ago had he practically learned that principle which men had not until of late the impudence doctrinally to advance in the world, namely, that an *arbitrary rectifying of men's intentions* alters the nature of their moral and spiritual actions. Hence they say, that if one man kill another, not with an intention to kill him, but to vindicate his own honour by his so doing, it is no sin, or at least no great sin, or much to be regarded. And what is this but directly to comply with the deceitfulness of sin, which we have laid down? for none sure is so flagitiously wicked as to make the formal nature of sin their object and end; nor, it may be, is human nature capable of such an excess and exorbitancy, from itself and its concreated principles, but still some other end is proposed by a corrupt design and incitation of the mind, which is a blind unto its wickedness. But of this deceit of sin I have treated at large in another discourse.[1] Therefore,—

Obs. VI. The best way to antidote the soul against sin, is to represent it unto the mind in its true nature and tendency.

---

[1] On Indwelling Sin in Believers, vol. vi. of this edition of the author's works. —ED.

The hiding of these was the way and means whereby sin first entered into the world. Thereby did Satan draw our first parents into their transgression. Hiding from them the nature and end of their sin, he ensnared and seduced them. In the same way and method doth he still proceed. This caused our apostle here to rend off the covering and vain pretences which the Hebrews were ready to put upon their relinquishment of the gospel. He presents it here naked unto them, as a fatal *defection and apostasy from the living God;* and therein gives them also to understand its end, which was no other but the casting of themselves into his revenging hand unto eternity. So dealt Samuel with Saul in the matter of Amalek. Saul pretended that he had only brought fat cattle for sacrifice; but Samuel lets him know that there was rebellion in his disobedience, abhorred of God like the sin of witchcraft. Indeed, if not all, yet the principal efficacy of temptation consists in hiding the nature and tendency of sin, whilst the mind is exercised with it; and therefore the discovery and due consideration of them must needs be an effectual means to counterwork it and to obviate its prevalency. And this is the principal design of the Scripture, in all that it treats about sin. It establisheth the command against it, by showing what it is, the iniquity, folly, and perversity of it; as also what is its end, or what in the righteousness of God it will bring the sinner unto. Hence the great contest that is in the mind, when it is hurried up and down with any temptation, is, whether it shall fix itself on these right considerations of sin, or suffer itself at the present to be carried away with the vain pleas of its temptation in its attempt to palliate and cover it.

And on this contest depends the final issue of the matter. If the mind keep up itself unto the true notion of the nature and end of sin, through the strength of grace, its temptation will probably be evaded and disappointed. So it was with Joseph. Various suggestions he had made to him, but he keeps his mind fixed on that, "How can I do this great wickedness, and sin against God?" which preserved him and delivered him, Gen. xxxix. 9. But if the mind be prevailed with to admit of those representations of sin which are made unto it in its temptations, sin in the perpetration of it will ensue. And this is the principal part of our wisdom about sin and temptations, namely, that we always keep our minds possessed with that notion and sense of the nature and end of sin which God in his word represents unto us, with a complete watchfulness against that which the deceit of lust and the craft of Satan would suggest. Again,—

Obs. VII. Whoever departs from the observation of the gospel and the institutions thereof, doth in so doing depart from the living God; or, an apostate from the gospel is an absolute apostate from God.

This the apostle expressly teacheth the Hebrews in this place.

Men think it almost a matter of nothing to play with gospel institutions at their pleasure. They can observe them or omit them as
seems good unto themselves. Nay, some suppose they may utterly
relinquish any regard unto them, without the least forfeiture of the
favour of God. But this will appear to be otherwise; for,—

1st. In their so doing, *the authority of God over their souls and
consciences is utterly rejected*, and so consequently is God himself;
for where his authority is not owned, his being is despised. Now,
there are various ways whereby God puts forth and manifests his
authority over men. He doth it in and by his works, his law, by
the consciences or inbred notions of the minds of men. Every way
whereby he reveals himself, he also makes known his sovereign
authority over us; for sovereign power or authority is the very first
notion that a creature can have of its Creator. Now, all these ways
of revealing the authority of God are recapitulated in the gospel,
God having brought all things unto a head in Christ Jesus, Eph. i.
10. " All power in heaven and in earth,"—that is, as to the actual
administration of it,—is given into his hand, Matt. xxviii. 18; and he
is " given" or " appointed to be head over all things," Eph. i. 20–22,
as we have at large declared on the third verse of the first chapter:
God, therefore, doth not put forth or exercise the least of his power
but in and by Christ; for "the Father judgeth no man, but hath
committed all judgment unto the Son," John v. 22. Now, the
Lord Christ exerciseth this power and authority principally by the
gospel, which is the " rod of his power," Ps. cx. 2. Hereunto, then,
are reduced all other ways whatever whereby the authority of God
is exerted over the souls and consciences of men. And if this be
rejected, the whole authority of God is utterly cast off. This, therefore, is done by all who reject, relinquish, or despise the gospel;
they forsake God himself, the living God, and that absolutely and
utterly. God is not owned where his monarchy is not owned. Let
men deal so with their rulers, and try how it will be interpreted.
Let them pretend they acknowledge them, but reject the only way,
all the ways they have, for the exercise of their authority, and it
will doubtless be esteemed a revolt from them.

2dly. There is no other way or means whereby men may yield
any obedience or worship unto God but *only by the gospel*, and
so no other way whereby men may express their subjection unto
him or dependence upon him; and where this is not done, he is
necessarily forsaken. Whatever men may say, or do, or pretend, as
to the worship of God, if it be not in and by the name of Christ, if
it be not appointed and revealed in the gospel, it is not performed
unto the living God, but to an idol of their own hearts; for the only
true God is the God and Father of our Lord Jesus Christ, and
therefore by what act or acts soever men may design to give honour

unto God, and to own their dependence on him, if it be not done in Christ, according to the gospel, it is all an abomination unto him. He says of all such worship, as he did of the sacrifices of the Israelites, when their hearts went after their idols, Amos v. 26, it is all to Moloch and Chiun, and not to him. Such, I say, is all the worship that men design to offer unto the living God, when not according to the gospel; such was the worship of the Samaritans of old, as our Saviour testified; and such is the worship of the Jews and Mohammedans at present. Their pretence of owning one God will not free them from offering their sacred services to Moloch and Chiun, images and stars of gods which they have framed unto themselves. When, therefore, any depart from the gospel, they depart from the living God; because they have no way left unto them whereby they may glorify him as God, and he that doth not so renounceth him. And therefore our apostle, speaking of those heathens who had those notions of one God which some boast of at this day and choose to rest in, affirms plainly that they were ἄθεοι ἐν τῷ κόσμῳ, Eph. ii. 12,—" atheists whilst they were in the world." They knew not how to glorify God by any acceptable worship: and as good not to own God at all as not to glorify him as God; for after God in the first precept hath required that we should have him for our God, and none else, that we may do so, and know how to do so, he required in the second, with the same authority, that we worship and glorify him according unto his own mind and prescription.

3dly. There is no other way whereby we may obtain the least encouraging *intimation of the favour or good-will of God* towards us, no way whereby his grace or his acceptance of us may be firmed and assured unto us, but this only; and where there is not a sufficient ground hereof, no man can abide with God in a due manner. If men have not a stable foundation to apprehend God to be good, and gracious, and willing to receive them, they will no otherwise respect or esteem him but as the poor Indians do the devil, whom they worship that he may do them no harm. I do know that men have strange presumptions concerning the goodness and inclination of God unto sinners; and according unto them they pretend highly to love God and delight in him, without respect unto the Lord Christ or the gospel: but it were an easy thing to divest their notions of all those swelling words of vanity wherewith they dress them, and manifest them to be mere presumptions, inconsistent with the nature of God and all the revelation that he hath made of himself. Whatever may be apprehended in God of this nature or to this purpose is either his χρηστότης, his natural goodness, kindness, benignity, and love; or his φιλανθρωπία, which includes all the free acts of his will towards mankind for good. And our apostle affirms that the ἐπιφανεία, the revelation, declaration, and appearance of both these, is merely from and by the gospel, or the grace of God by Jesus Christ, Tit. iii. 4–7; and without this it is impossible but that men will abide in their apostasy from God, or return unto it.

4thly. There is no other way wherein we may look for a reward from God, or hope to come unto the *enjoyment of him*, but only by the gospel. And this also is necessary, that we may honour him as God, as the living God. This is the end whereunto we were made: and if we leave the pursuit hereof, we cast off all regard unto God; for if God be not considered as " a rewarder of them that diligently seek him," as in himself an " exceeding great reward," he is not considered as God. And whoever doth not pursue a design of coming to the enjoyment of God, he hath forsaken him. Now, there is no direction herein or hereunto but the gospel, as Acts iv. 12.

And this will discover the great multitude of practical atheists that are in the world. Many there are who have been educated in some observance of the gospel, and some who have been brought under great conviction by the word of it, who do yet, by the power of their lusts and temptations in the world, come to renounce and despise all the institutions, ordinances, and worship of the gospel, and consequently the author of it himself; for it is a vain thing to pretend love or honour unto Christ, and not to keep his commandments. However, they would not be reckoned among atheists, for they still acknowledge one, or the one God. But they do herein but industriously deceive their own souls. Then they forsake the living God, when they forsake the gospel of his Son.

And let us all know what care and reverence becomes us in the things of the gospel. God is in them, even the living God. Otherwise he will be neither known nor worshipped. His name, his authority, his grace, are enstamped on them all.

Obs. VIII. When a heart is made evil by unbelief, it is engaged in a course of sinful defection or revolt from the living God. So that word imports, ἐν τῷ ἀποστῆναι, the sense whereof was explained before.

Ver. 13.—" But exhort one another daily [*every day*], whilst it is called To-day, lest any of you [*among you*] be hardened by the deceitfulness of sin."

Here lies one means of preventing the evil mentioned in the verse foregoing. And we have in it, as was showed, the duty itself, and the persons concerned in it, the manner and season of its performance, with a limitation of that season, and an especial enforcement from the danger of its neglect, as we shall see in our opening of the words.

First, the duty intended is expressed in the first word, παρακαλεῖτε. Παρακαλέω is "to exhort," "entreat," "beseech;" and also "to comfort," "to refresh," "to relieve:" and παρακαλέομαι is constantly "to receive comfort" or "consolation," "to be comforted." Παράκλησις is used in the same variety, sometimes for "comfort" or "consolation," as Luke ii. 25; Acts ix. 31, xv. 31; Rom. xv. 5; 2 Cor. i. 3–5;—sometimes for "exhortation," Acts xiii. 15; Rom. xii. 8; 1 Tim. iv. 13; 2 Cor. viii. 4, 17. Sometimes interpreters are in doubt whether to render it by "exhortation" or "consolation," as Acts xv. 31; 1 Thess. iv. 18. In this very epistle it is used in both these senses: for "consolation," chap. vi. 18; for "exhortation," chap xii. 5, xiii. 22. Hence the Holy Ghost, in the writings of John the apostle, is called ὁ παράκλητος in the Gospel, chap. xiv. 16, 26, xv. 26, xvi. 7; and the Lord Christ himself, 1 John ii. 1; and this, from the ambiguity of the application of the word, we render in the first place "a comforter," in the latter "an advocate."

The first and principal signification of παρακαλέω is "to exhort," "to desire," "to call in," and so it is constantly used in Greek authors, and scarce otherwise; and it is secondarily only "to comfort." But there is a near affinity between these things; for the way of administering consolation is by exhortation: 1 Thess. iv. 18, "Comfort one another with these words,"—παρακαλεῖτε ἀλλήλους. That is, 'Exhorting and persuading with one another, by these words administer unto each other mutual consolation. And all exhortation ought to be only by consolatory words and ways, to render it acceptable, and so effectual. So it is observed of Barnabas, who was "a son of consolation," that he had a great excellency in exhorting men also: Acts xi. 23, 24, "When Barnabas came, and had seen the grace of God, he was glad, and exhorted them all, that with purpose of heart they would cleave unto the Lord. For he was a good man, and full of the Holy Ghost and of faith." The word intimates a very prevalent way of exhorting in Barnabas: and that because he was ἀνὴρ ἀγαθός, "a good man;" not in the ordinary sense, a holy, just man; but one that was benign, kind, condescending, apt to comfort and refresh them with whom he had to do. In this sense is ἀνὴρ ἀγαθός used, Rom. v. 7. Παρακαλεῖν, therefore, "to exhort," is to persuade with good, meek, and comfortable words, upon grounds of consolation, and unto that end that men may be comforted. This is incumbent on some by virtue of office, Rom. xii. 8, "He that exhorteth, on exhortation;" and on all believers as occasion doth require, as the next words manifest, declaring the persons concerned in this duty.

Ἑαυτούς, "vosmetipsos," Vulg. Lat., and the Rhemists,—"yourselves;" improperly, for the apostle doth not require of every one to exhort himself, nor will the word bear that sense. But ἑαυτούς "yourselves," is put for ἀλλήλους, that is, "one another," as also it is

Col. iii. 16; Eph. iv. 32; 1 Thess. v. 13;—"vos invicem," "alii alios." This is incumbent on all believers, mutually to exhort, and to bear the word of exhortation.

The *season* of the performarᴄe of this duty is adjoined, which includeth also the manner of it: Καθ' ἑκάστην ἡμέραν. "Daily," say we, or "every day." A day is often taken for a season; so that to do a thing daily is to do it in its season. To do it sedulously, heedfully, in every proper season, is to do it daily; for although the expression denotes every day distinctly and separately, yet the sense is not that no natural day be omitted wherein we do not actually discharge this duty towards one another. But plainly two things are intended;—1. A constant readiness of mind, inclining, inducing, and preparing any one for the discharge of this duty; 2. An *actual discharge* of it on all just occasions, which are to be watched for and willingly embraced. So we are commanded to "pray ἀδια-λείπτως," 1 Thess. v. 17, "indesinenter;" that is, without remitting the habitual inclination of the mind unto prayer, or omitting any meet occasion or opportunity for it. So also it is said that we ought πάντοτε προσεύχεσθαι, Luke xviii. 1,—"to pray always;" which is interpreted, Col. iv. 2, by τῇ προσευχῇ προσκαρτερεῖτε,—"abide" (or "persevere") "in prayer against all opposition." In Hebrew, תָּמִיד בָּל־הַיּוֹם, as Isa. li. 13,—"continually every day." Καθ' ἑκάστην ἡμέραν, is "sedulously and constantly," both as to the frame of our hearts and opportunities of actual performance of this duty. And this these Hebrews now stood in an especial need of, because of the manifold temptations and seductions wherewith they were exercised.

Hereunto is added a limitation of the season of this duty as to its continuance: Ἄχρις οὗ τὸ σήμερον καλεῖται,—"Whilst it is called To-day;" that is, 'Be sedulous in the discharge of this duty whilst the season of it doth continue.' The occasion of this expression is taken from what was before discoursed of. There was a day proposed unto the people of old, a season that was called הַיּוֹם, or σήμερον, "to-day." And two things are included in it;—1. An *opportunity* as to advantage; 2. A *limitation* of that opportunity as to duration or continuance. 1. A day of opportunity is intended. The word in the psalm, הַיּוֹם, had, as was judged on good ground, respect unto some solemn feast wherein the people assembled themselves to celebrate the worship of God; it may be the feast of tabernacles, which was a great representation of the dwelling of the Lord Christ amongst us, John i. 14. This was a season which they were to improve whilst they did enjoy it. But it was typical only. The apostle now declares to these Hebrews that the great day, the great season, of old shadowed out unto their forefathers, was now really and actually come upon them. It was justly called "To-day" with them whilst they enjoyed the gospel.

2. There is a limitation of this day of opportunity included in the words, "Whilst it is called To-day;"—'whilst the time wherein you live is such a season as to be called a day, that is, a day of grace;'— whilst that season was continued unto them which was prefigured in the day before mentioned. The apostle saw that the day or season of these Hebrews was almost ready to expire. It continued but a few years after the writing of this epistle. This he secretly minds them of, and withal exhorts them to improve their present advantages, and that especially in and unto the discharge of the great duty of mutual exhortation; that so they might prevent among them the great evil of departing from the living God, and that which tends thereunto, in the hardening of their hearts through the deceitfulness of sin. For herein lies the enforcement of the exhortation unto the duty insisted on, namely, from the pernicious consequent of its neglect; wherein first occurs,—

Τίς ἐξ ὑμῶν.   The persons concerned: Τίς ἐξ ὑμῶν, "Any of you," "any among you;"—'any one that is of your society, that is engaged in the same profession with you, and partaker of the same privileges;' 'any of you believing Hebrews.' And herein the apostle extends his direction unto mutual watchfulness and exhortation unto all, even the meanest of the church.

Ἀμαρτίας.   Secondly, The spring or cause of the evil that is to be feared in the neglect intimated, and that is sin: Ἁμαρτία, הַטָּאת,—a general name for all or any sin. Our apostle constantly useth it to express original sin, the sin of our nature, the root on which all other sins do grow. And this is the sin here intended; the sin that by nature dwelleth in us, that is present with us when we would do good, to hinder us, and is continually working to put forth its venomous nature in actual sins or transgressions. This he calls elsewhere a "root of bitterness," which springs up unto defilement, chap. xii. 15.

Ἀπάτη.   Thirdly, There is the way or means whereby this sin worketh to produce the effect expressed, and that is by deceit: Ἀπάτη τῆς ἁμαρτίας. Vulg. Lat., "fallacia peccati;" and the Rhemists thence, "the fallacy of sin,"—somewhat improperly, considering the ordinary use of that word, being taken only for a caption or deceit in words. But yet there is a fallacy in every sin; it imposeth paralogisms or false arguings on the mind, to seduce it. Ἀπάτη is " deceit," and signifies both the faculty of deceiving, the artifice used in deceiving, and actual deceit, or deceiving itself. The derivation of the word gives some light unto the nature of the thing itself. Ἀπατάω is from ἀ privative, and πάτος, as Eustathius and the Etymologist agree. Πάτος is "via trita," "a beaten way," "a path." So that ἀπατάω is to " draw any one out of the right way," the proper beaten path. And it is well rendered by "seduco," that is, "seorsum duco," "to lead aside," "to seduce." But it is of a larger sense, or "by any ways or means to deceive." And ἀπάτη principally denotes an innate faculty of deceiving rather than deceit itself. Ἀπάτη τοῦ πλούτου, Matt. xiii. 22, "the deceitfulness of riches;" and ἀπάτη τῆς ἀδικίας, 2 Thess. ii. 10, "the deceitfulness of unrighteousness;" is that aptitude that is in riches and unrighteousness, considering the state and condition of men in this world, and their temptations, to deceive them with vain hopes, and to seduce them into crooked paths. Once it is put for sin itself: Eph. iv. 22, Κατὰ τὰς ἐπιθυμίας τῆς ἀπάτης,—"According to the lusts of deceit:" that is, of sin, which is deceitful; unless it may be rendered by the adjective, ἀπατηλοῦς, or ἀπατήτους, as it is done by ours, "deceiving" (or "deceitful") "lusts." See 2 Pet. ii. 13. Here, as it is joined with "sin," as an adjunct of it, it denotes not its acting primarily, but that habitual deceit that is in indwelling sin, whereby it seduceth men and draweth them off from God.

Lastly, The evil itself particularly cautioned against is expressed in that word σκληρυνθῇ, "should be hardened;" of the sense and importance whereof we have spoken fully on the foregoing verses. *Σκληρυνθῇ.* The design, then, of this verse is to prescribe a duty unto the Hebrews, with the manner of its performance, and the season they had for it, which might prevent their departure from God through an evil heart of unbelief, by preserving it from being hardened by the deceitfulness of sin; our concernment wherein will be manifest in the ensuing deductions from it:—

Obs. I. Sedulous mutual exhortation is an eminent means to obviate and prevent the design of the deceitfulness of sin.

The apostle having declared the pernicious consequence of departing from God through the deceitfulness of sin, and the danger that professors are in of so doing, singles out this duty as a signal means of its prevention. And hereby, as great weight is laid upon it, so great honour is done unto it. We may, therefore, do well to consider both the nature of it and the manner of its performance; for its efficacy unto the end proposed depends merely on its institution. There are many practical duties that are neglected because they are not understood; and they are not understood because they are supposed to have no difficulty in them, but to be exposed to every lazy and careless inquiry. High notions, curious speculations, with knotty controversies, are thought to deserve men's utmost diligence in their search and examination; but for these practical duties, it is generally supposed that they are known sufficiently at a word's speaking, if they were but practised accordingly. Yet it will be found that the great wisdom of faith consists in a spiritual acquaintance with the true nature of these duties; which indeed are therefore practically neglected because they are not doctrinally understood. I shall

therefore offer somewhat here briefly towards the right understanding of the nature of this duty and the manner of its performance;
and to this purpose some things we are to observe with respect unto
the persons that are to perform it, and some things with respect
unto the duty itself:—

First, For the *persons* concerned, this duty of exhortation is incumbent on some by virtue of especial office, and on others by virtue
of especial love.

1. Some it is expected from upon the account of *their office;* so it
is of all ministers of the gospel. The duty of constant exhortation,—
that is, of persuading the souls of men unto constancy and growth
in faith and obedience, unto watchfulness and diligence against the
deceitfulness of sin, and that from the word of truth, in the name
and authority of Christ,—is the most important part of their ministerial office. This are they diligently to attend unto: Ὁ παρακαλῶν, ἐν
τῇ παρακλήσει, Rom. xii. 8;—"Let him that exhorteth" (his office
taketh name from this part of his work) "attend unto" (or "abide
in") "exhortation." This is it which is required of him, and will be
expected from him. So our apostle distributes the whole ministerial work into three parts, enjoining their observance unto his son
Timothy: 1 Tim. iv. 13, "Diligently attend," saith he, τῇ ἀναγνώσει,
"to reading;" that is, studying and meditating on the holy Scriptures, for his own information and growth,—which ministers ought to
do all their days, and not to sit down lazily with a pretence of their
attainments: and secondly, τῇ παρακλήσει, "to consolatory exhortation,"—the duty before us; and lastly, τῇ διδασκαλίᾳ, "to doctrinal
instruction," for the enlightening and informing of the minds of his
disciples. These are the principal duties of an evangelical minister.
So he again conjoins teaching and exhortation, as the two main parts
of preaching, 1 Tim. vi. 2. And these he would have a minister to
be instant in, or insist upon, εὐκαίρως, ἀκαίρως, "in and out of season," 2 Tim. iv. 2,—a proverbial expression denoting frequency and
diligence. Where this is neglected by any of them, they deal
treacherously with God and the souls of men. But this ministerial
work is not that which is here intended. But, 2. There is that
which is mutual among believers, founded in their common interest,
and proceeding from especial love. And this especial love is that
which distinguisheth it from another duty of the same nature in
general with this, which we owe unto all mankind; for the eternal
law of nature binds us to love our neighbour as ourselves. Now, we
neither do nor can love any without endeavouring of their good, and
effecting of it according to our power. And herein is comprised a
persuading of men unto what is good for them, and a dehorting
them from that which is morally evil and pernicious, as occasions
and opportunities are offered. Thus dealt Lot with the Sodomites;

whom the Holy Ghost therefore commends, though they reviled him as a pragmatical intruder into their concernments. So God and the world have very different measures and touchstones of moral duties. But there is somewhat special in the duty here intended; for it is confined unto them who are brethren in the same fellowship of professing the gospel, verse 1, and proceeds from that mutual love which is wrought in them by the Spirit of Christ, and required of them by the law of Christ. And this differs from that philanthropy, or love to mankind in general, which ought to be in us; for they have different principles, different motives, different effects, and different ways of expression. The one is an inbred principle of the law of nature, the other an implanted grace of the Holy Ghost; the one required from a common interest in the same nature, the other from an especial interest in the same new nature. In brief, the one is a general duty of the law, the other an especial duty of the gospel. I say, this especial love is the spring of this mutual exhortation.

Secondly, And to the *right performance* of it the things ensuing do appertain:—

1. That they who perform it find in themselves an *especial concernment* in the *persons and things* with whom and about which they treat in their exhortations. It will not admit of any pragmatical curiosity, leading men to interpose themselves in matters wherein they are no way concerned. " Knowing," saith the apostle, τὸν φόβον τοῦ Κυρίου, ἀνθρώπους πείθομεν, 2 Cor. v. 11;—' The reason why we exhort men, or persuade them to their duty, is because of our compassion towards them, inasmuch as we know the terror or dread of God, with whom in this matter they have to do, and that it is φοβερόν, a very fearful thing to fall into his hands when he is provoked,' Heb. x. 31. If men find not themselves really concerned in the glory of God, and their hearts moved with compassion towards the souls of men, whether they are in office in the church or not, it will be their wisdom to abstain from this duty, as that which they are no way fitted to discharge.

2. An *especial warranty* for the particular exercise of this duty is required of us. Our duty it is in general to exhort one another, by virtue of this and the like commands; but as unto the especial instances of it, for them we must look for especial warranty. Those who shall engage into this or any other duty at adventures will but expose themselves and it to contempt. Now this especial warranty ariseth from a due coincidence of rule and circumstances. There are sundry particular cases wherein direct and express rule requires the discharge of this duty; as (1.) In case of sin; Lev. xix. 17, " Thou shalt not hate thy brother in thine heart: thou shalt in any wise rebuke thy neighbour, and not suffer sin upon him." For even rebukes belong to this general head of exhortation, nor are they ever to be

without it. (2.) Of ignorance in the truth: so dealt Priscilla and Aquila with Apollos when they instructed him in the way of God, Acts xviii. 24–26. And many the like cases are instanced in. Add unto such rules a due consideration of circumstances, relating unto times, seasons, persons, and occasions, and it will form the warranty intended.

3. *Especial wisdom, understanding, and ability,* are hereunto required. It is an easy thing to spoil the best duty in the manner of its performance: and as other things may spoil a duty, so a defect in spiritual skill for the performance of it can never suffer it to be right. If men, then, have not a sound judgment and understanding of the matter about which this mutual exhortation is to be exercised, and of the way whereby it is to be managed, they may do well to leave it unto them who are better furnished with "the tongue of the learned to know how to speak a word in season;"—I mean as to the solemn discharge of it; otherwise occasional mutual encouragements unto faith and obedience are the common and constant duties of all believers. And the apostle speaks of the generality of Christians in those primitive times, that they were so "filled with all knowledge" as that they were "able to admonish one another," Rom. xv. 14; wherein as he requires an ability for it, so he ascribes it unto them. And unto them it belongs to see,—(1.) That it be *done with words of truth.* It is truth alone that in things of this nature is accompanied with *authority,* and attended with *efficacy.* If there be any failure in this foundation, the whole superstructure will sink of itself. Those, then, who undertake this duty must be sure to have a word of truth for their warrant, that those who are exhorted may hear Christ speaking in it; for whatever influence other words or reasonings may have on their affections, their consciences will be unconcerned in them. And this should not only be virtually included in what is spoken, but also formally expressed, that it may put forth its authority immediately and directly. As exhortations that fail in truth materially (as they may, for men may exhort and persuade one another to error and false worship) are pernicious, so those which are not formally spirited or enlivened by an express word of Scripture are languid, weak, and vain. (2.) That it may be managed, unless especial circumstances require some variation, with *words good and comfortable,* words of consolation and encouragement. The word here used, as hath been shown, signifies to comfort as well as to exhort. Morose, severe expressions become not this duty, but such as wisdom will draw out from love, care, tenderness, compassion, and the like compliant affections. These open and soften the heart, and make the entrance of the things insisted on smooth and easy into it. (3.) That it be accompanied with care and diligence for a suitable example in the practice and walking of the *persons exhorting.* An observation of the contrary will quickly frustrate the weightiest words

that look another way. Exhortation is nothing but an encouragement given unto others to walk with us or after us in the ways of
God and the gospel. " Be followers of me," saith our apostle, " as I
am of Christ." And these are some of the heads on which we might
discourse of this duty; which in that great degeneracy of Christianity
whereinto the world is fallen, were not unnecessary to do, but I must
not too much enlarge upon particulars:—

Obs. II. Gospel duties have an especial efficacy attending them
in their especial seasons: " While it is called To-day." Every thing
hath its beauty, order, and efficacy from its proper season. Again,—

Obs. III. We have but an uncertain season for the due performance of most certain duties. How long it will be called " To-day,"
we know not. The day of our lives is uncertain. So is the day of
the gospel, as also of our opportunities therein. The present season
alone is ours; and, for the most part, we need no other reason to
prove any time to be a season for duty but because it is present.

Obs. IV. The deceit which is in sin, and which is inseparable
from it, tends continually to the hardening of the heart. This is
that which is principally taught us in these words; and it is a truth
of great importance unto us, which might here be properly handled,
but having at large discoursed of the whole of the deceitfulness of sin
in another treatise,[1] I shall not here resume the discussion of it.

Ver. 14.—" For we are made partakers of Christ, if we hold the
beginning of our confidence firm unto the end."

This is the last part of this fourth περιοχή, or section of this chapter. As to its coherence with the verses foregoing, it containeth an
enforcement of the general exhortation unto perseverance, and the
avoidance of backsliding or apostasy in all the causes and tendencies
unto it, as also of the particular duties which the apostle had now
proposed as effectual means unto those ends: for he lets them know
that all their interest in Christ, and all the benefits they did expect
or might be made partakers of by him, did depend upon their
answering his exhortation unto constancy and perseverance in their
profession; and, moreover, that whereas men are apt to wax weary
and faint, or to grow slothful in the course of their profession, sometimes so soon almost as they are entered into it, unless they continue
the same diligence and earnestness of endeavours as at the first, so
as to abide steadfast unto the end, they would have no benefit either
by Christ or the gospel, but rather fall assuredly under that indignation of God which he had newly warned them of. This in general
is the design of the words.

In the particulars there are:—1. A state and condition expressed
from whence the force of the argument is taken: " We are made
partakers of Christ." 2. An application of that condition unto our-

---

[1] On Indwelling Sin, vol. vi. of the author's works.—ED.

selves, as to the way whereby it may be declared and evidenced: "If
we hold fast the beginning of our confidence steadfast unto the end."

Γάρ. The causal connection, γάρ, "for," shows the respect
of these words unto those foregoing, according as we
have declared it; and it manifests that the apostle induceth an enforcement of his preceding exhortation.

The state and condition intimated is expressed in these words,

Γεγόναμεν. Μέτοχοι γεγόναμεν τοῦ Χριστοῦ. Γεγόναμεν denotes some
time past, "We have been made:" which excludes one
application of the words, namely, unto a future participation of Christ
in glory, which here should be promised, but suspended upon the
condition of our holding steadfast the beginning of our confidence
unto the end; as if it were said, 'We are made partakers of Christ,'
that is, we shall be so hereafter, 'in case we continue constant and
persevere;' which sense (if it be so) is embraced by those who are
ready to lay hold on all appearing advantages of opposing the assurance and perseverance of believers. But a present state is here declared, and that which is already wrought and partaken of. And,
indeed, the consideration of this word doth rightly state the relation
of the several parts of the words mentioned: "We are made partakers of Christ, if we hold fast the beginning of our confidence;"
that is, we are so thereby, either *causally* and *formally*, or *interpre-
tatively* and *declaratively*. If in the first sense, then our participation of Christ depends on our perseverance unto the end, nor can
we come unto the one until we have attained the other. But this
is contrary to the text, which supposeth us actually instated in that
participation, as the words necessarily require. If it be in the latter
sense, then our perseverance is enjoined as an evidence of our participation of Christ, that whereby it may be tried whether it be true
and genuine,—which if it be, it will be producing this effect; as
James requires that we should try or evidence and manifest our faith
by our works, of what sort it is.

We are made μέτοχοι τοῦ Χριστοῦ, "partakers of Christ." This

Μέτοχοι τοῦ Χριστοῦ. expression is nowhere used but only in this place. The
word μέτοχος itself is but once used in the New Testa-
ment, but only by our apostle; and μετέχω, from whence
it comes, not at all but by him. And he interprets it by κοινωνία,
"communion," or "participation:" for affirming that "the bread which
we break is κοινωνία τοῦ σώματος τοῦ Χριστοῦ," "the communion of the
body of Christ," 1 Cor. x. 16, he adds, Πάντες ἐκ τοῦ ἑνὸς ἄρτου μετέχομεν, verse 17, "We all partake of that one bread;" which is a
sacramental expression of the same thing here intended. Most expositors suppose the name Christ to be here taken metonymically
for the benefits of his mediation, in grace here, and right to future
blessedness. Some suppose it to be only an expression of being a

disciple of Christ, and so really to belong unto him. But the true and precise importance of the words may be learned from the apostle in his use of those of an alike signification with reference unto Christ himself, Heb. ii. 14: "Because the children are partakers of flesh and blood,"—that is, because those whom he was to redeem were men, partakers of human nature,—καὶ αὐτὸς παραπλησίως μετέσχε τῶν αὐτῶν, "He himself in like manner took part of the same." He was partaker of us, partook of us. How? By taking flesh and blood,— that is, entire human nature, synecdochically so expressed, to be his own, as he expresseth it, verse 16, "He took not on him the nature of angels, but he took on the seed of Abraham;" that is, the nature of man derived from the loins of Abraham, according to the promise made unto him. How, then, are we partakers of him, partakers of Christ? It is by our having an interest in his nature, by the communication of his Spirit, as he had in ours by the assumption of our flesh. It is, then, our union with Christ that is intended, whereby we are made "members of his body, of his flesh, and of his bones," Eph. v. 30. A participation of the benefits of the mediation of Christ is included in these words, but not firstly intended, only as a consequent of our intimate union with him. And this the Syriac translation seems to have understood, reading the words by אֶתְחַלַּטְן גֵּיר עַם מְשִׁיחָא,—"We are mingled" (or "mixed") "with Christ;" that is, joined with him, united unto him. And this is that which the apostle puts to the trial, as the hinge on which their present privileges and future happiness did entirely depend. And this is the sense which Chrysostom and the Greeks that follow him do fix upon. Saith he, Τί ἐστι μέτοχοι γεγόναμεν τοῦ Χριστοῦ; μετέχομεν αὐτοῦ, φησίν· ἕν ἐγενόμεθα ἡμεῖς καὶ αὐτὸς, εἴπερ αὐτὸς μὲν κεφαλή, σῶμα δὲ ἡμεῖς, συγκληρονόμοι καὶ σύσσωμοι. Ἐν σῶμά ἐσμεν, ἐκ τῆς σαρκὸς αὐτοῦ, φησι, καὶ ἐκ τῶν ὀστέων αὐτοῦ·—"What is it to be 'partakers of Christ?'" He and we are made one; he the head, we the body, co-heirs and incorporated with him. We are one body with him, as he speaks, of his flesh and bones." So he. The trial and evidence hereof is declared in the last words, Ἐάνπερ τὴν ἀρχὴν τῆς ὑποστάσεως μέχρι τέλους βεβαίαν κατάσχωμεν·—"If so be that we hold fast" (or "steadfast") "the beginning of our confidence unto the end." So we. It is by all agreed, that, for the substance of it, the same matter is here intended as in verse 6; and that that which is there called καύχημα τῆς ἐλπίδος, "the glorying of hope," is here termed ἀρχὴ τῆς ὑποστάσεως, "the beginning of confidence;" because it is said of   Ἀρχὴ τῆς ὑποστάσεως. each of them that they are to be "kept steadfast unto the end." But the expression here used is singular, and hath left an impression of its difficulty on most translations and expositions. Hence hath arisen that great variety that is amongst them in rendering and expounding of these words. "Initium substantiæ ejus," saith the Vulgar; and the Rhemists from thence, "The beginning of his substance," adding "his" to the text. Arias Montan. and Erasmus, "Principium substantiæ;"—"The beginning of substance." Beza, "Principium illud quo sustentamur;"—"That beginning" (or "principle") "whereby we are sustained." Castalio, "Hoc argumentum ab initio ad finem usque;"—"This argument from the beginning to the end." Syriac, "From the beginning unto the end, if we abide in this substance," or "foundation." Ethiopic, "If we persevere to keep this new testament." We, "The beginning of our confidence." By which variety it appears that some know not how to express the words, as not well understanding of them, and that others were not satisfied with the conjectures of their predecessors. Neither are expositors more agreed about the meaning of the words. Some by ἀρχὴ τῆς ὑποστάσεως understand the gospel, some faith, some hope, some confidence, some Christ himself. Most fix on faith to be intended, which they say is termed ὑπόστασις, or "substance," because it is that which supports us, causeth us to subsist in Christ, as the just do live by faith. But it may not be amiss to inquire a little more exactly into the proper emphasis and importance of this expression.

Ὑπόστασις properly signifies "substance." It is applied unto somewhat distinct in the *being of the Deity*, Heb. i. 3, where it is said that the Son is the "express image of the Father's hypostasis;" and there it can signify nothing but an especial manner of existence or subsistence in the divine nature,—that is, a person; whence the eastern church first, and after the western, agreed in three hypostases in the divine nature,—that is, as we speak, three persons, or three different manners of the subsistence of the same individual being. In things human it denotes *acts*, and not *substances*. And as it is used *only* by our apostle, so it is used by him *variously;* as for confidence, 2 Cor. ix. 4, Ἐν τῇ ὑποστάσει ταύτῃ τῆς καυχήσεως,—"In this confidence of boasting;" whence ours have translated it in this place "confidence." And it may be the rather, because as it is there joined with καύχησις, so he maketh use of καύχημα in the same subject with this, verse 6. But the ὑπόστασις of the apostle in that place was not a confidence of boldness, but that infallible certainty which he had of his apostleship wherein he gloried. That was it which he stood firmly on. Chap. xi. 1 of this epistle, the apostle maketh use of it in the description he gives of faith; yet so as to denote an *effect* of it, and not its *nature:* Ἔστι δὲ πίστις, ἐλπιζομένων ὑπόστασις,—"Faith is the hypostasis of things hoped for;" "Illud quo extant quæ sperantur,"—"That whereby the things that are hoped for do exist." Things that are absolutely in themselves future, absent, unseen, are, as unto their efficacy, use, benefit, fruits, and effects, made by faith present

*Τῆς ὑποστά-
σιως.*

unto the soul, and have a subsistence given them therein. It is not, then, faith itself, but an effect of it, that is there described by the apostle.

If, then, by "the beginning of our substance," "subsistence," or "confidence," faith is intended, it is because it is that which gives us all these things by our interest in Christ and the benefits of his mediation. But I confess the expression is abstruse in this sense, and difficult to be understood.

It may therefore be understood of the gospel itself, which is called "the beginning of our confidence," because it is the means of begetting faith in us, and producing that profession wherein we are to persevere; and this sense is embraced by some expositors.

There seems yet to me that there is another more genuine sense of the word, suited to the scope of the place and design of the apostle, without wresting it from its native signification. We have showed that our partaking of Christ is our being *united* unto him; and the ὑπόστασις, "hypostasis," which on that union we are bound to preserve and maintain, is our subsistence in Christ, our abiding in him, as the branches in the vine. So the word signifies, and so it is here used. And although Chrysostom supposes that it is faith which is intended, yet it is on the account of this effect of our subsistence in those things that he so judgeth: Τί ἐστιν ἀρχὴ τῆς ὑποστάσεως; τὴν πίστιν λέγει, δ᾽ ἧς ὑπέστημεν, καὶ γεγενήμεθα καὶ συνουσιώθημεν, ὡς ἄν τις εἴπο᾽—"He speaks of faith, by which we subsist" (in Christ), "and are begotten, and, as I may so say, consubstantiated with him;" that is, solidly, substantially united unto him. Now, our subsistence in Christ is twofold:—1. By *profession* only, which is the condition of the branches in the vine that bear no fruit, but are at length cut off and cast into the fire; 2. By *real union*. And the trial of which of these it is that we are partakers of, depends on our perseverance.

Τὴν ἀρχὴν τῆς ὑποστάσεως. Beza, "Principium illud quo sustentamur,"—"That principle" (or "beginning") *"whereby we are sustained."* But this I do not understand; for it Τὴν ἀρχήν. makes ἀρχή, "the beginning," to denote the thing itself recommended unto us, and which we are to preserve, whereof the hypostasis mentioned is only an effect, or that whereby the work of the beginning is expressed. But ἀρχή is nowhere used in any such sense, nor doth it appear what should be intended by it. Besides, it is plainly here an adjunct of our subsistence in Christ;—the beginning of it. And this may be considered two ways;—1. Absolutely, it is begun in profession or reality, and it is to be continued; 2. Emphatically, for the usual attendancies of our faith and profession at their beginning. The beginning of our engagement unto Christ is for the most part accompanied with much love, and other choice affections, resolution, and courage; which without great care and watchfulness we are very ready to decay in and fall from.   And in this sense it is here used.

The remainder of the words, μέχρι τέλους βεβαίαν κατάσχωμεν, " Hold steadfast unto the end," have been opened on verse 6, and we need not again insist upon them.

I shall only add, that the apostle joining himself here with the Hebrews in this matter, " We are partakers, if we hold fast," he shows that this is a general and perpetual rule for professors to attend unto, and the touchstone of their profession, by which it may be tried at the last day.   And hence are the ensuing observations:—

Obs. I. Union with Christ is the principle and measure of all spiritual enjoyments and expectations.

The apostle sums up all, both what we do enjoy by the gospel at present, and what right unto or expectation we have of future blessedness and happiness, in this one expression, " We are partakers of Christ."   That our union with him is thereby intended hath been declared in the exposition of the words.   The nature of this union, and wherein it doth consist, I have elsewhere manifested and vindicated;[1] I shall therefore here only confirm the proposition laid down.   It is *the principle and measure* of all spiritual enjoyments. For as Christ is unto us " all, and in all," Col. iii. 11, so " without him we can do nothing," we are nothing, John xv. 5; for whereas we live, "it is not we, but Christ liveth in us," Gal. ii. 20.   And the truth hereof appears,—

First, Because it is itself, in the order of nature, the first truly saving spiritual mercy, the first *vital grace* that we are made partakers of; and that which is the first of any kind is the measure and rule of all that ensues in that kind.   As is the root, so are the branches and the fruit.   They do not only follow the nature of it, but live upon its supplies.   All our grace is but a participation of the root, and therein of the fatness of the olive tree; and we bear not the root, but the root bears us, Rom. xi. 17, 18.   Whatever precedes this is not true saving grace; and whatever follows it proceeds from it:—1. Whatever work of excision or cutting off there may be of a branch from the wild olive, it is its incision into the true olive which communicates unto it life and fruit-bearing; for after it is cut off from the wild olive and dressed, it may either be cast away or left to wither.   Whatever work of *conviction* by the word of the law, or of *illumination* by the word of the gospel, or of *humiliation* from both by the efficacy of the Spirit in all, there may be wrought in the minds and souls of men, yet there is nothing truly saving, vital, and quickening in them, until they be implanted into Christ.   Under any other preceding or preparatory work, however it

---

[1] See On Communion with God, vol. ii. of this edition of the author's works. —ED.

be called, or whatever may be the effects of it, they may wither, die, and perish. Men may be so cut off from the old stock of nature as not to have sin grow or flourish in them, not to bear its blossoms, nor visible fruit, and yet have no principle of grace to bring forth fruit unto holiness. And, 2. That whatever grace follows it proceeds from it, is evident from the nature of the thing itself. For our uniting unto Christ consisteth in or immediately ariseth from the *communication* of his Spirit unto us; for "he that is joined to the Lord is one Spirit," 1 Cor. vi. 17. Our conjunction unto him consists in our participation of the same Spirit with him. And by this Spirit is Christ himself, or the nature of Christ, formed in us, 2 Pet. i. 4. And if all the grace that we are or can be made partakers of in this world be but that nature, in the several parts and acts of it, that from whence it proceeds, whereby it is formed in us, must needs in order of nature be antecedent unto it. No grace we have, or can have, but what is wrought in us by the Spirit of Christ. Whence else should we have it? Doth it grow naturally in our own gardens? or can other men plant and water it, and give it life and increase? Nay, but all grace is the fruit and effect of the Spirit, as the Scripture everywhere declares. See Gal. v. 22, 23. It implies, then, a contradiction, that any one should have any lively saving grace, and not antecedently in order of nature receive the Spirit of grace from Christ: for he is the cause, and grace is the effect; or, as he is savingly bestowed, according to the promise of the covenant, he is the spring and fountain, or efficient cause, of all grace whatever. Now, our union with Christ, our participation of him, consists in the inhabitation of the same Spirit in him and us; and the first work of this Spirit given unto us, bestowed upon us, is to form Christ in us, whereby our union is completed. But it will be asked, whether the Spirit of Christ doth come into a soul that hath no grace?—if so, then he may be in a graceless person. I answer, that although this in order of nature is consequent unto the communication of the Spirit unto us, as the effect is and must be to the cause, as light and heat in the beam are unto the sun, yet it hath a simulty of time with it; as Austin speaks well of the original of the soul, "Creando infunditur, et infundendo creatur." God doth not first create a soul, giving it an existence of its own, without union with the body, but creates it in and by its infusion. So the Spirit doth not come unto us, and afterward quicken or sanctify us; but he doth this by his coming unto us, and possessing our hearts for and with Christ. This the apostle calls the forming of Christ in us, Gal. iv. 19, Ἄχρις οὗ μορφωθῇ Χριστὸς ἐν ὑμῖν, "Until Christ be formed" (or "fashioned") "in you,"—as a child is fashioned or formed in the womb; that is, 'until the whole image and likeness of Christ be imparted unto and implanted upon your souls.' This is the new creature that is wrought in every one that is in Christ;

that every one is who is in Christ: for the introduction of this new
spiritual form gives denomination unto the person. He that is "in
Christ Jesus is a new creature," 2 Cor. v. 17. And this is "Christ
in us, the hope of glory," Col. i. 27.

1. It is " Christ in us:" for, (1.) It is from him, he is the author
of it, and thence he is said to be "our life," Col. iii. 4. (2.) It is like
him, it is his image, and by and through him the image of God,
2 Cor. iii. 18; Eph. iv. 23, 24. (3.) It is that which gives us a spiritual continuity unto Christ; for being united unto him as members unto the head, there must be a constant communicative motion
of blood and spirit between him and us, which is hereby, Eph. iv. 16;
Col. ii. 19. And without this we are without Christ, or so separated
from him as that we can do nothing, John xv. 5; for suppose a
believer to stand " seorsum," alone by himself, χωρὶς Χριστοῦ, at a
distance from Christ, without a course and recourse of spiritual supplies from him, and he can do nothing but die. Cut off a member
from the body, dissolve its natural continuity to the head, and all
the world cannot fetch life into it. Take a member, suppose a
hand, lay it as near the head as you will, bind it to it, yet if it hath
not a natural continuity with the head, it will not live. It is so
here. A member separated from Christ hath no life. Let it seem
to lie near the Head by profession and many engagements, if it
have not this spiritual continuity unto Christ, it hath no life in it.
2. It is the " hope of glory,"—(1.) as the kernel is the hope of
fruit; (2.) as a pledge or earnest is the hope of the whole contract.
In this forming of Christ in us are we made partakers of all grace
and holiness in the principle and root of them, for therein doth this
image of God in Christ consist. Now, this proceeding from our
union, the latter is, and must be, before it in order of nature, and so
be the rule, measure, and cause of all that ensues.

Secondly, It is the *first in dignity;* it is the greatest, most
honourable, and glorious of all graces that we are made partakers
of. It is called "glory," 2 Cor. iii. 18. The greatest humiliation
of the Son of God consisted in his taking upon him of our nature,
Heb. ii. 8, 9. And this was "the grace of our Lord Jesus Christ,
that, though he was rich,"—rich in the eternal glory, the glory that
he had with the Father before the world was, John xvii. 5, as being
in himself "God over all, blessed for ever," Rom. ix. 5,—"for our
sakes he became poor," 2 Cor. viii. 9, by taking on him that nature
which is poor in itself, infinitely distanced from him, and exposed
unto all misery; which our apostle fully expresseth, Phil. ii. 5–7,
" Let this mind be in you, which was also in Christ Jesus: who,
being in the form of God, thought it not robbery to be equal with
God: but made himself of no reputation, and took upon him the
form of a servant, and was made in the likeness of men." There

was indeed great grace and condescension in all that he did and
humbled himself unto in that nature, as it follows in that place,
" And being found in fashion as a man, he humbled himself, and
became obedient unto death, even the death of the cross," verse 8;
but his assumption of the nature itself was that whereby most signally ἑαυτὸν ἐκένωσε, he " emptied" and " humbled himself, and made
himself of no reputation." On this all that followed did ensue, and
on this it did depend. From hence all his actings and sufferings
in that nature received their dignity and efficacy. All, I say, that
Christ, as our mediator, did and underwent in our nature, had its
worth, merit, use, and prevalency from his first condescension in
taking our nature upon him; for from thence it was that whatever he so did or suffered, it was the doing and suffering of the Son
of God. And, on the contrary, our grace of union with Christ, our
participation of him and his nature, is our highest exaltation, the
greatest and most glorious grace that we can be made partakers of
in this world. He became poor for our sakes, by a participation of
our nature, that we through his poverty may be rich in a participation of his, 2 Cor. viii. 9. And this is that which gives worth and
excellency unto all that we may be afterwards intrusted with. The
grace and privileges of believers are very great and excellent, but
yet they are such as do belong unto them that are made partakers
of Christ, such as are due to the quickening and adorning of all the
members of his body; as all privileges of marriage, after marriage
contracted, arise from and follow that contract. For being once
made co-heirs with Christ, we are made heirs of God, and have a
right to the whole inheritance. And, indeed, what greater glory
or dignity can a poor sinner be exalted unto, than to be thus intimately and indissolubly united unto the Son of God, the perfection
whereof is the glory which we hope and wait for, John xvii. 22, 23.
Saith David, in an earthly, temporary concern, " What am I, and
what is my father's family, that I should be son-in-law unto the
king, being a poor man, and lightly esteemed?" How much more
may a sinner say, ' What am I, poor, sinful dust and ashes, one that
deserves to be lightly esteemed by the whole creation of God, that
I should be thus *united unto the Son of God,* and thereby become
his son by adoption!' This is honour and glory unparalleled. And
all the grace that ensues receives its worth, its dignity, and use from
hence. Therefore are the graces and the works of believers excellent, because they are the graces and works of them that are united
unto Christ. And as without this men can have no inward, effectual, saving grace; so whatever outward privileges they may lay hold
of or possess, they are but stolen ornaments, which God will one day
strip them naked of, unto their shame and confusion.

Thirdly, It is the first and principal grace, in respect of *causality and efficacy.* It is the cause of all other graces that we are made partakers of; they are all communicated unto us by virtue of our union with Christ. Hence is our adoption, our justification, our sanctification, our fruitfulness, our perseverance, our resurrection, our glory. Hence is our *adoption;* for it is upon our receiving of him that this right and privilege is granted unto us of becoming the sons of God, John i. 12. No man can be made the adopted son of God but by an implantation into him who is the natural Son of God, John xv. 1–6, xx. 17. And thence also are the consequent privileges that attend that estate; for " because we are sons, God sends forth the Spirit of his Son into our hearts, crying, Abba, Father," Gal. iv. 6,—that is, to own God, and address ourselves unto him under the consideration of the authority and love of a father. And hence is our *justification:* for,—1. Being united unto Christ, we are interested in that *acquitment* from the condemning sentence of the law which was granted unto himself when he satisfied it to the utmost, Rom. i. 3, 4; Isa. l. 8, 9. For he was acquitted as the head and surety of the church, and not on his own personal account, for whereas he did no sin, he owed no suffering nor satisfaction to the law; but as " he suffered for us, the just for the unjust," so he was acquitted as the representative of his whole church. By our union, therefore, unto him, we fall under the sentence of acquitment, which was given out towards whole Christ mystical, head and members. 2. Our union with him is the ground of the *actual imputation* of his righteousness unto us; for he covers only the members of his own body with his own garments, nor will cast a skirt over any who is not " bone of his bones, and flesh of his flesh." And so he is " of God made unto us righteousness," 1 Cor. i. 30. Hence also is our *sanctification,* and that both as to its *principle* in a new spiritual nature, and as unto its *progress* in fruitfulness and holiness. The principle of it is the Spirit itself of life, holiness, and power. This God sheds on us through Jesus Christ, Tit. iii. 6, or on the account of our interest in him, according to his promise, John vii. 38, 39. And for this cause is he said to be " our life," Col. iii. 4, because in him lie the springs of our spiritual life, which in and by our regeneration, renovation, and sanctification is communicated unto us. And its progress in fruitfulness is from thence alone. To teach this, is the design of the parable used by our Saviour concerning the vine and its branches, John xv.; for as he showeth our abiding in him to be as necessary unto us, that we may bear fruit, as it is unto a branch to abide in the vine to the same purpose; so without our so doing we are of no more use, in the ways of God, than a branch that is cut off and withered, and cast aside to burn. And men do but labour in the fire, who, in the pursuit of their convictions, endeavour after holiness or the due performance of good works, without deriving strength for them from their relation unto Christ; for all that they do is either nothing in itself, or nothing as unto acceptation with God. "We are the workmanship of God, created in Christ Jesus unto good works," Eph. ii. 10. Becoming new creatures by our *inbeing* in him, 2 Cor. v. 17, we are thereby enabled unto those good works, or fruits of holiness, which God hath ordained that we should walk and abound in. And hence on many accounts is our *perseverance;* for, 1. By virtue hereof we are interested in the covenant, which is the great means of our preservation, God having engaged therein so to write his law in our hearts as that we shall not depart from him, Jer. xxxi. 33. Now, this covenant is made with us under this formal consideration, that we are the children and seed of Abraham, which we are not but by our union with Christ, the one seed, to whom the promises of it were originally made, as our apostle declares, Gal. iii. 16. 2. His care is peculiar for the members of his body: for as "no man hateth his own flesh, but loveth and cherisheth it," nor will suffer any of his members to perish, if by any means he can prevent it; so is the heart of Christ towards those that are united to him, and therein are "members of his body, of his flesh, and of his bones," Eph. v. 29, 30. And therefore, 3. The care of giving out supplies unto us for assistance against opposition and strength for duties, which is the grace of perseverance, is incumbent on him. Our *resurrection* also depends on this union,—I mean, a blessed resurrection in joy and glory unto light and life eternal; for this resurrection is nothing but the entire gathering up together of the whole body of Christ unto himself, whereof he gave us a pledge, example, and assurance, in his own person. So the apostle assures us, Rom. viii. 11, "If the Spirit of him that raised up Jesus from the dead dwell in you" (which, as hath been showed, is the means of our union with him), "he that raised up Christ from the dead shall also quicken your mortal bodies by his Spirit that dwelleth in you." And this he expressly proveth at large, 1 Cor. xv. And this lands us in eternal glory; which, as was observed before, is nothing but the consummation and perfection of this union with Christ. And hence it appears on how many accounts it is the principle and measure of all other graces and privileges whatever.

And we may see hence how great our concernment is to inquire diligently into this *foundation of all grace, mercy, and glory.* If we fail here, as too many seem to do, we do but run in vain, and build in vain, and boast in vain, for all will be lost and perish. We may do well to remember what became of the house that was built on the sand, when its trial came: it fell, and its fall was great and irreparable. Such will be the end of the *profession of men* that doth not spring and arise from *union with Christ.* Many ways there are whereby this may be put to the trial, on which all our peace, satisfaction, and assurance of spirit in the things of God, do depend. I shall only consider that which our apostle here proposeth, and that in the ensuing observation:—

Obs. II. Constancy and steadfastness in believing is the great touchstone, trial, and evidence of union with Christ, or a participation of him.

So it is here proposed by the apostle. We are "partakers of Christ,"—that is, declared, manifested, and evidenced so to be,—"if we hold fast the beginning of our subsistence in him firm unto the end." So our Saviour, describing the great trials of men's faith that shall befall them, adds that in the close, as the certain note of discrimination: "He that endureth to the end shall be saved," Matt. x. 22. It is enduring faith that is *true faith*, and which evidenceth us indeed to be partakers of Christ. And he gives it as a mark of a false profession, that it "but dureth for a while," Matt. xiii. 21. Further to explain, evince, and improve this truth, it may be observed,—

First, That there are many appearing evidences of union with Christ that may and do fail. The blade is an appearing evidence of well-rooted corn, but it often fails, and that for want of root, Matt. xiii. 21. Now, by such an appearance I do not intend a pretence, or that there is therein a show made of what is not; only there is something which appears to be that which it is not; or it is somewhat, but not what it appears to be. And so it is a failing sign, not a τεχμήριον, or assured, infallible token. Things of this nature may be such as to satisfy them in whom they are that they are really united unto Christ; but this through their own darkness and mistakes. And they may be such as others may, nay ought to be satisfied in, to the same purpose concerning them, as not being able to evince them to be otherwise by any rule or word of truth. So was it with many that are mentioned in the gospel. They professed themselves to belong unto Christ. This they did on some grounds that were satisfactory to themselves. They were also accepted by others as such, and that judging according to rule and as they ought. And yet, after all, they were either discovered to be hypocrites, or declared themselves apostates. Now, these kinds of signs must extend so far, as [that] there is nothing whereby union with Christ may be evidenced, nothing that is required according to rule thereunto, but there must be something in those who are thus deceived and do deceive that shall make an appearance and resemblance thereof. They must have μόρφωσιν τῆς εὐσεβείας, 2 Tim. iii. 5, a complete "delineation of holiness" upon them, or they can have no pretence unto any such plea. They must be able to give an account of a work of conviction, humiliation, illumination, conversion, and of closing with Christ; as also of affections someway suitable unto such a work. If they utterly fail herein, however any out of darkness and self-love may flatter and deceive themselves, yet others have a rule to judge them by. But this now we have in daily experience, as there was the same also from the first preaching of the gospel,—men may give such an account of the work of the grace of God in them as themselves may believe to be saving, and such as others who have reason to be concerned in them may rest in and approve; in this apprehension they may walk in a course of profession many days, it may be all their days, and yet at last be found utter strangers from Christ. But yet this happens not from the nature of the thing itself, as though our union with Christ in this life were absolutely indiscernible, or at least attended with such darkness and inextricable difficulties, as that it is impossible to make a true and undeceiving judgment thereof; but mistakes herein proceed from the blindness of the minds of men, and the deceitfulness of sin, with some secret inclination to rest in self or sin, that is in them. And these are such effectual causes of self-deceivings in this matter, that the Scripture abounds in commands and cautions for our utmost diligence in our search and inquiry, whether we are made partakers of Christ or no, or whether his Spirit dwell in us or no: which argue both the difficulty of attaining an assured confidence herein, as also the danger of our being mistaken, and yet the certainty of a good issue upon the diligent and regular use of means unto that purpose; for,—

Secondly, There may be certain and undeceiving evidences of a present participation of Christ; or, which is all one, men may have a certainty sufficient at present to support and comfort them in their obedience, and which in the issue will neither fail them nor make them ashamed, that they are " partakers of Christ." And this in our passage must necessarily be briefly confirmed. We speak of them who are really believers, who have received saving faith as a gift from God. " Now faith is ἐλπιζομένων ὑπόστασις, πραγμάτων ἔλεγχος οὐ βλεπομένων," Heb. xi. 1. It is that which gives subsistence unto the things believed in our minds, and is such an argument of them as will not deceive. There is nothing can possibly give the mind a more undeceiving assurance than that which causeth its object to subsist in it, which unites the mind and the truth believed in one subsistence. This faith doth in spiritual things. Hence our apostle ascribes unto it, as its effect, παῤῥησίαν καὶ προσαγωγὴν ἐν πεποιθήσει, Eph. iii. 12,—a " grounded boldness," with a " confident trust;" which are the highest expressions of the mind's assurance. And if this be not enough, he asserts a πληροφορία, as that which it may be regularly improved into, Heb. vi. 11, x. 22; that is, such a persuasion as fills the mind with all the assurance that the nature of it is capable of. For as a ship can have no impression from the wind further than it is able to receive in its sails, no more are we capable of any impression of the certainty of divine truths or things believed other than the nature of our minds can admit of; which is, that there must still be an allowance of some doubts and fears, by reason of its own imperfection. But if the expressions before used may fail us, it is certain that we can be certain of nothing,—no, not of this that we are certain of nothing; for they are expressions of the highest certainty and assurance that the mind of man is capable of. It is, then, in the nature of faith itself, rightly exercised and improved, to evidence this matter unto our souls.

Again, The Holy Ghost himself, who neither can deceive nor be deceived, gives peculiar testimony to our sonship or adoption, which is a consequent of our union with Christ; for none have any power to become the sons of God but such as are united unto him, John i. 12. This testimony is asserted, Rom. viii. 15, 16, " Ye have received the Spirit of adoption, whereby we cry, Abba, Father. The Spirit itself beareth witness with our spirits, that we are the children of God." And wherein soever this testimony doth consist, or by what means soever it be granted unto us,—concerning which I shall not here dispute,—it is a testimony sure and infallible in itself, and bringing assurance to the mind to which it is granted, sealing unto it its sonship, adoption, and union. And when the Holy Spirit giveth this " new name," of a son of God, unto any believer, he knows it, though others understand it not, Rev. ii. 17; for he makes his own testimony evident unto us, without which his care and love towards us would be lost, and the end of our peace and comfort be frustrated. Hence we are said to " receive the Spirit which is of God, that we may know the things that are freely given to us of God," 1 Cor. ii. 12. It is the Spirit of God whereby the good things mentioned are bestowed on us and wrought in us; but this is but part of his work and office towards us,—he doth moreover distinctly satisfy and assure us that we are indeed made partakers of those good things.

Moreover, we have in this matter the examples of those who have gone before us in the faith, proposed unto our imitation and for our consolation. They had that evidence and assurance of an interest in Christ which we insist upon. So our apostle declares in the name of all believers, Rom. viii. 38, 39: " I am persuaded," saith he, " that nothing shall separate us from the love of God, which is in Christ Jesus our Lord." And the rejoicing, yea, triumphant manner wherein he expresseth this his persuasion manifests his full satisfaction in the truth which he proposed. And so the apostle John tells us, that we both " perceive the love of God" towards us, and that "we know that we have passed from death unto life," 1 Epist. iii. 14, 16; both which depend on our union with Christ, and which by them is made evident and sure unto us. See Ps. xxiii. 6. Hereon is founded that great command, that we should "give diligence to make our calling and election sure," 2 Pet. i. 10; that is, unto our own souls, for in themselves they are unalterable. And if this, in the use of means, may not be effected, there were no room left for this precept or exhortation.

This is also confirmed unto us from the nature and *use of the sacraments;* which I know not what they think of who deny this truth. In the one of them God sets his seal unto our initiation into Christ: for it is, as circumcision was of old, the "seal of the righteousness of faith," Rom. iv. 11; which, as I have showed, we obtain not but by a *participation of Christ* and initiation into him. And therefore is there required in us the *restipulation of a good conscience,* to answer the testimony of God therein, 1 Pet. iii. 21. The other expressly confirms our participation of Christ, and our interest in the pardon of sins through his blood; being appointed of God as the way whereby mutually is testified his grace unto us and our faith in him. See 1 Cor. x. 16, 17. And if we may not, if we ought not, to rest assured of what God testifies unto us and sets his seal unto, it cannot but be our duty sometimes to make God a liar; for so we do when we believe not his testimony, 1 John v. 10. But to prevent any hesitation in this matter, he hath not left this under a bare testimony, but hath also confirmed it by his oath; and that to this end, that we might have "strong consolation,"—which, without an undeceiving assurance, we cannot obtain, Heb. vi. 17. 18. It is therefore certain that there may be, and there are, infallible evidences of a present participation of Christ. But yet observe further, that,—

Thirdly, No grace, no sign or mark, will any longer or any further be an evidence or testimony in this matter, but only as the soul is effectually influenced unto perseverance thereby. If any grace whatever once lose its *efficacy* in or upon the soul, unto all such acts of obedience as are required unto constancy and persistency in our profession, it loseth all its *evidencing power* as to our present state and condition. For instance, faith, as unto the nature of it, and as unto its main effect, of our adherence unto Christ, may abide in us, when yet, by reason of the power of temptation or prevalency of corruptions, it may not act effectually unto spiritual experience for the constant performance of all such duties as are required unto our persistency in Christ in a due manner, nor as unto such an abstinence from all sin as is required thereunto. But when it doth so fail, it can no longer evidence our union with Christ, but the soul wherein it is will be left unto many disquietments and uncertainties. It is faith only that is effectual, by love and in universal obedience, and only as it is so, will give in this evidence. Although, therefore, perseverance is not of the essence of faith, but is a grace superadded thereunto, yet the evidencing power of faith in this case is taken from its efficacy towards that end, namely, as it is experimentally subservient unto the power of God to preserve us unto salvation. Hence, before the completing of our perseverance, which is not to be before the full end of our course, it is the principal evidence of our union with Christ, in the ways and means whereby itself is continued and preserved.

Fourthly, It is an evidence of union, in that it is an effect of it; and there is a good demonstration of a cause from its proper and peculiar effect. Where an effect is produced that cannot be wrought but by such a cause, it is declared and manifested thereby; as even the magicians concluded from the miracles of Moses, that "the finger of God" was in them. Now, our constancy and perseverance, as I have showed, are an effect of our union with Christ, and from no other original can they be educed. And this doth most eminently appear in the time and case of trials and oppositions, such as was the season and condition that the Hebrews were under at present. When a believer shall consider what difficulties, distresses, and spiritual dangers he hath passed through, and been delivered from, or hath prevailed against; and withal that he hath in himself no power, strength, or wisdom, that should procure for him such a success, but rather that on the contrary he hath been often ready to faint, and to let go the "beginning of his confidence;" it will lead him to a discovery of those secret springs of supplies that he hath been made partaker of; which are nothing but this union with Christ, and participation of him. Besides, this perseverance is the due issue and exsurgency of grace constantly exercised, with an improvement and growth thereby. And all growth in grace, in what kind soever it be, is an emanation from this one foundation of our union with Christ, which is therefore manifested thereby.

Fifthly, This also may be added,—Whatever profession hath by any been made, whatever fruits of it have been brought forth, whatever continuance in it there hath been, if it fail totally, it is a sufficient evidence that those who have made it were never "partakers of Christ." So our apostle, having declared that some of great name and note were apostatized and fallen off from the gospel, adds that yet "the foundation of God standeth sure," that "the Lord knoweth them that are his," 2 Tim. ii. 17–19; manifesting that those who did so, notwithstanding their profession and eminency therein, were never yet owned of God as his in Christ. And another apostle tells us, that those who went out from them, by a defection from the faith, were in truth none of them, or really united unto Christ with them, 1 John ii. 19. And where there are partial decays in faith and profession, it gives great ground of suspicion and jealousy that the "root of bitterness" is yet remaining in the heart, and that Christ was never formed in it. Let not men, therefore, please themselves in their present attainments and condition, unless they find that they are thriving, growing, passing on towards perfection; which is the best evidence of their union with Christ.

Obs. III. Persistency in our subsistence in Christ unto the end is a matter of great endeavour and diligence, and that unto all believers. This is plainly included in the expression here used by the apostle, Ἐάνπερ τὴν ὑπόστασιν βεβαίαν κατάσχωμεν. The words denote our utmost endeavour to hold it fast, and to keep it firm and steadfast. Shaken it will be, opposed it will be; kept it will not, it cannot be, without our utmost diligence and endeavour. It is true our persistency in Christ doth not, as to the issue and event, depend absolutely on our own diligence. The *unalterableness of our union with Christ*, on the account of the faithfulness of the covenant of grace, is that which doth and shall eventually secure it. But yet our own diligent endeavour is such an indispensable means for that end, as that without it it will not be brought about; for it is necessary to the continuance of our subsistency in Christ, both " necessitate præcepti," as that which God hath commanded us to make use of for that end, and " necessitate medii," as it is in the order and relation of spiritual things one to another ordained of God to effect it. For our persistence in our subsistence in Christ is the emergency and effect of our acting grace unto that purpose. Diligence and endeavours in this matter are like Paul's mariners, when he was shipwrecked at Melita. God had beforehand given him the lives of all that sailed with him in the ship, Acts xxvii. 24; and he believed that it should be even as God had told him, verse 25. So now the preservation of their lives depended absolutely on *the faithfulness and power* of God. But yet when the mariners began to flee out of the ship, Paul tells the centurion and the soldiers that unless those men stayed they could not be saved, verse 31. But what need he think of shipmen, when God had promised and taken upon himself the preservation of them all? He knew full well that he would preserve them, but yet that he would do so in and by the use of means. If we are in Christ, God hath given us the lives of our souls, and hath taken upon himself in his covenant the preservation of them; but yet we may say with reference unto the means that he hath appointed, when storms and trials arise, unless we use our own diligent endeavours, " we cannot be saved." Hence are the many cautions that are given us, not only in this epistle wherein they abound, but in other places of Scripture also, that we should take heed of apostasy and falling away; as, " Let him that thinketh he standeth take heed lest he fall;" and, " Take heed that we lose not those things which we have wrought;" and, "Hold fast that thou hast, lest another take thy crown," with the like innumerable.

These warnings are not given merely to professors in general, whose condition is dubious whether they are true believers or no; nor unto those that are entering only on the ways of Christ, lest they should recoil and desert them; but they are given unto all true believers, those of the greatest growth and attainments, Phil. iii. 11-13, that they may know how indispensably necessary, from the appointment of God and the nature of the thing itself, our watchful diligence and endeavours are unto our abiding in Christ. And they are thus necessary,—

First, Upon the account of the *opposition* that is made thereunto. In this one thing, namely, to *separate us from Christ*, is laid out all the skill, power, and craft of our *spiritual adversaries*. For this end are the " gates of hell"—that is, the power, counsel, and strength of Satan—peculiarly engaged. His great design is to cast them down and prevail against them who are built upon the Rock; that is, who are united unto Christ. Our Saviour, indeed, hath promised that he shall not prosper, Matt. xvi. 18; but it is that he shall not " prevail;" which argues a disappointment in a fight or contest. So the "gates of hell shall not prevail;" but we are to watch and contend that they may not. This also is the principal design of the world upon us and against us. It sets all its engines on work to separate us from Christ. Our apostle reckons them up, or at least gives a catalogue of the principal of them, Rom. viii. 35, 36; and gives us assurance that they shall never be able to attain their end, or to dissolve the union between Christ and us. But yet he lets us know that our success is a conquest, a victory, which is not to be won without great care and watchfulness, undergoing many difficulties, and going through many hazards, verse 37. And, which is worst of all, we fight against ourselves; we have lusts in us that "fight against our souls," 1 Pet. ii. 11, and that in good earnest. Yea, these are the worst enemies we have, and the most dangerous, as I have elsewhere declared. This opposition to our persistency in Christ makes our diligence for the continuance and preservation of it necessary.

Again, It is necessary upon the account of our *peace, consolation*, and *fruitfulness* in this world. And these belong to our subsistence in Christ. Without the two former we have no satisfaction in ourselves, and without the latter we are of no use to the glory of God or good of others. Now, as our eternal happiness depends on this diligence as the *means* of it, so do these things as their *condition;* which if we fail in, they also will fail and that utterly. It is altogether in vain to expect true peace, solid consolation, or a thriving in fruitfulness, in a slothful profession. These things depend wholly on our spiritual industry. Men complain of the fruit, but will not be persuaded to dig up the root. For all our spiritual troubles, darkness, disconsolations, fears, doubts, barrenness, they all proceed from this bitter root of negligence, which springs up and defiles us. Those, then, that know how to value these things may do well to consider how the loss of them may be obviated. Now this spiritual diligence and industry consisteth,—

1. In a *watchful fighting* and contending against the whole work of sin, in its deceit and power, with all the contribution of advantage and efficacy that it hath from Satan and the world. This the apostle peculiarly applies it unto, in the cautions and exhortations given us, to "take heed" of it, that we be not "hardened" by it, seeing its whole design is to impair or destroy our interest and persistency in Christ, and so to draw us off "from the living God."

2. In a *daily, constant cherishing* and labouring to improve and strengthen every grace by which we abide in Christ. Neglected grace will wither, and be "ready to die," Rev. iii. 2; yea, as to some degrees of it, and as to its work in evidencing the love of God unto us, or our union with Christ, it will utterly decay. Some of the churches mentioned in the Revelation had lost their "first love," as well as left their "first works." Hence is that command that we should "grow in grace;" and we do so when grace grows and thrives in us. And this is done two ways:—(1.) When any individual grace is improved: when that faith which was weak becomes strong, and that love which was faint and cold becomes fervent and is inflamed; which is not to be done but in and by the sedulous exercise of these graces themselves, and a constant application of our souls by them to the Lord Christ, as hath been before declared. (2.) By adding one grace unto another: 2 Pet. i. 5, "And besides this, giving all diligence, add to your faith, virtue; and to virtue, knowledge." This is the proper work of spiritual diligence, namely, to add one grace unto another. This is the nature of gospel graces, because of their concatenation in Christ, and as they are wrought in us by one and the self-same Spirit, that the exercise of one leads us to the stirring up and bringing in the exercise of another into the soul. And the graces that in order of practice lie as it were behind, will not be taken notice of or known, but by the due improvement of those whose practice is antecedaneous unto them. Hence some good men live all their days and never come to the actual exercise of some graces, although they have them in their root and principle. And the reason is, because way is not made unto them by the constant improvement of those other graces from out of whose exercise they do spring.

And is it any wonder if we see so many either decaying or unthrifty professors, and so many that are utterly turned off from their first engagements? For consider what it is to abide in Christ;—what watchfulness, what diligence, what endeavours are required thereunto! Men would have it to be a plant that needs neither watering, manuring, nor pruning, but that which will thrive alone of itself;

but what do they then think of the opposition that is continually made unto it, the endeavours that are used utterly to root it out? Certainly, if these be not watched against with our utmost industry, decays, if not ruin, will ensue. We may also add here, that,—

Obs. IV. Not only our profession and existence in Christ, but the gracious beginnings of it also, are to be secured with great spiritual care and industry. The substance whereof may be spoken unto in another place.

VERSES 15–19.

There is some difficulty about these verses, namely, whether they appertain unto and depend upon the discourse foregoing, or whether they are the beginning of another, on which the exhortation in the first verse of the next chapter doth depend. Chrysostom, with the Greeks that follow him, as Theophylact and Œcumenius, asserts the latter. And therefore they suppose a hyperbaton in the words, and that all that discourse which is between the 15th verse of this chapter and the 1st of the next is an occasional digression; as if the sense of the apostle ran to this purpose: ' Seeing it is said, To-day, if ye will hear his voice, harden not your hearts, as in the pro-vocation; let us therefore fear, lest, a promise being left us of entering into his rest, any of you should seem to come short of it.' But there is no necessity of such a long trajection of the sense, nor of feigning the hyperbaton intimated. The genuine sense and proper contex-ture of the apostle's discourse requires their connection with what went before. And the exhortation in the first verse of the next chapter is taken from what he immediately after argueth and proveth. And I shall not insist upon the division of the chapters, which is arbitrary and of no authority. I shall therefore, in the first place, rightly state the coherence of these discourses, and then pro-ceed to the exposition of the words.

Three things the apostle hath stated in his preceding arguing and exhortation:—First, The *evil* which he would have the He-brews carefully to avoid under the preaching of the gospel unto them, or their hearing of the voice of God; and that is the "hard-ening of their hearts." Secondly, The *cause* hereof, which he per-suades them diligently to obviate; which is the "deceitfulness of sin." Thirdly, The *effect* and *consequent* of that evil; which is apostasy, or a "departing from the living God." Hereunto he sub-joins one special means for the prevention of this evil in its causes and consequents; and that is mutual exhortation. Now, whereas he had drawn all the parts of his discourse from an example re-corded in Moses, and resumed by David in the Psalms, with an intimation that it was by the Holy Ghost in him put over unto the use of the church under the gospel, and therein in an especial manner of the present Hebrews, he returns to show, that his discourse was fully warranted from that example as recorded originally by Moses, and repeated by the Holy Ghost in the Psalms. Moreover, there were yet remaining some circumstances of the example insisted on, which the Holy Ghost would have us observe for our instruction, which lay not in the way of his former discourse to collect and observe. These here he gathereth up, and in them gives a great confirmation to the grounds and reasons of his exhortation. This is his general design. The parts of his discourse are as followeth:—

1. He calls over the example and his own improvement of it summarily again, to lay it as a foundation of what he had further to infer from it, verse 15.

2. He makes a tacit comparison between them who came out of Egypt under the conduct of Moses, which part of it is expressed, and those who were then called to the profession of the gospel, which is implied, verse 16.

3. The former sort he expressly distributes into two kinds. The first whereof he describes, (1.) By their *sin:*—[1.] In general, they hardened their hearts and provoked God, verse 16. [2.] In particular, this their sin was their unbelief, verses 18, 19. (2.) By the *respect that God had towards them*, which also is twofold:— [1.] That he was "grieved" with them. [2.] That he "sware in his wrath" against them, verses 17, 18. (3.) By their *punishment*, which in like manner is expressed two ways:—[1.] Positively, that "their carcasses fell in the wilderness," verse 17. [2.] Negatively, that "they did not enter into God's rest," verses 18, 19. By all which instances the apostle manifests that his exhortation of them from this example was well founded therein, especially seeing the psalmist had in a spirit of prophecy prepared it for the use of those days and these; for justly ought they to be jealous over themselves, lest any of them should fall into the like sin, and fall by the same punishment.

4. He manifests that he doth not insist only on the danger of the sin dehorted from, and the penalty annexed unto it, as though the nature of this example were merely comminatory or threatening; but he declares also, partly expressly and partly by just consequence, the blessed success which they obtained who fell not into the sins of infidelity and apostasy from God; and so strengthens his exhortation from the promises of God and his faithfulness in them. This he doth in these words, "Howbeit not all that came out of Egypt," verse 16; that is, [all] did not provoke God; which is but one head of the antithesis between the two several sorts mentioned, which is to be understood and preserved in all the other instances. As if he should have said, 'Some on the other side "hardened not

their hearts," "provoked not God," but believed and obeyed his voice; hence God was "not angry with them," "sware not against them," their "carcasses fell not in the wilderness," but they "entered into the rest of God." And thus will it be with them who shall continue to believe and obey the gospel.'

5. He adds a general conclusion, as the sum of what he had evinced out of the words of the psalm; which also he intended further to improve, as he doth in the next chapter, verse 19.

Ver. 15–19.—Ἐν τῷ λέγεσθαι· Σήμερον, ἐὰν τῆς φωνῆς αὐτοῦ ἀκούσητε· μὴ σκληρύνητε τὰς καρδίας ὑμῶν, ὡς ἐν τῷ παραπικρασμῷ. Τινὲς γὰρ ἀκούσαντες παρεπίκραναν, ἀλλ᾽ οὐ πάντες οἱ ἐξελθόντες ἐξ Αἰγύπτου διὰ Μωυσέως. Τίσι δὲ προσώχθισε τεσσαράκοντα ἔτη; οὐχὶ τοῖς ἁμαρτήσασιν, ὧν τὰ κῶλα ἔπεσον ἐν τῇ ἐρήμῳ; Τίσι δὲ ὤμοσε μὴ εἰσελεύσεσθαι εἰς τὴν κατάπαυσιν αὐτοῦ, εἰ μὴ τοῖς ἀπειθήσασι; Καὶ βλέπομεν, ὅτι οὐκ ἠδυνήθησαν εἰσελθεῖν δι᾽ ἀπιστίαν.

Some few differences there are amongst translations; such as may, some of them, give light into the sense of the words may be remarked.

Ver. 15.—Ἐν τῷ λέγεσθαι. Beza, "interim dum dicitur,"—"in the mean-time, while it is said." "Interim dum," are not amiss supplied, if that be the sense of the words, which generally is supposed so to be. Erasmus, "in hoc quod dicitur,"—"in this that is said," or, "whereas it is said;" which is suited unto the trajection of the words supposed by the Greeks before mentioned. Syriac, אֶרְכָּא דַאֲמִיר, "sicut dictum est,"—"as it is said," respecting a repetition of the testimony, "again." Arias, "in dici," that is, "in dicendo,"—"in saying;" so the Arabic, Vulgar Lat., "dum dicitur;" and so we, "while it is said." I had rather, for reasons after to be mentioned, render the words, "whereas it is said;" which also is the proper sense of ἐν τῷ λέγεσθαι,—the infinitive with a preposition being often to be construed by the subjunctive mood.

Ἐν τῷ παραπικρασμῷ. Beza and the Vulg. Lat., "quemadmodum in illa exacerbatione,"—"as in that provocation;" expressing the article, which Erasmus and most translators omit: neither is it needful to be expressed, it being a mere repetition of the words, and not a reference unto them, that the apostle hath in hand. Syriac, "harden not your hearts, to provoke him," or "that you should provoke him," "to anger," "exasperate him;" respecting the sin feared in them, when it is the past sin of their forefathers that is intended. Ethiopic, "Because he saith, To-day, if ye will hear his voice, harden not your hearts, for they provoked him who heard."

Ver. 16.—Τινὲς γὰρ ἀκούσαντες παρεπίκραναν. The Syriac begins here the interrogatory part of this discourse: "For who are they that when they have heard provoked him?" But τινές is indefinite, and not interrogative, as the following words manifest, for the process is not by a redditive pronoun, but an exceptive adverb.

Διὰ Μωυσέως, בְּיַד מֹשֶׁה,—"By the hands of Moses;" a frequent Hebraism for guidance or conduct.

Ver. 17.—Τίσι δὲ προσώχθισε; Beza, "quibus infensus fuit?"—"with whom was he angry," or "provoked?" Vulg. Lat., "infensus est," in the present tense; which is blamed by Erasmus, and corrected by Vatablus and Arias, as that which regards what was long since past. Arabic, as before, "whom did he curse?" Syr., "who were a weariness to him?" Of the ground of which variety we spake before, on verse 10.

᾽Ὧν τὰ κῶλα ἔπεσον. Beza, "quorum artus conciderant,"—"whose members fell;" Vulg. Lat., "quorum cadavera prostrata sunt,"—"whose carcasses were cast down;" Erasmus, "quorum membra;" Syr., וְגַרְמֵיהוּן,—"and their bones:" whose members, bodies, bones, carcasses, fell in the wilderness. Of the proper signification of the word I shall speak afterwards.

Ver. 18.—Εἰ μὴ τοῖς ἀπειθήσασι. Beza and Erasmus, "nisi iis qui non obedierunt,"—"but unto them who obeyed not." Arias, "si non incredulis,"—"if not unto the unbelievers." Vulg. Lat., "iis cui increduli fuerunt;" which our Rhemists render, "but unto them which were incredulous." Syr., דְּלָא אֶתְטְפִּיסוּ, "qui non acquieverunt," "qui assensum non præbuerunt,"—"who gave not assent," that is, to the word or voice of God which they heard.[1]

Ver. 15.—Whereas it is said, To-day, if ye will hear his voice, harden not your hearts, as in the provocation.

The introduction unto the ensuing discourse is in these first words, ᾽Ἐν τῷ λέγεσθαι, "Whilst it is said;" so we, after the Vulgar Latin, and sundry other interpreters, "dum dicitur," or ᾽Ἐν τῷ λέγεσθαι. to that purpose, as was observed. Thus these words are a reintroduction of the former exhortation; and therefore some supply ὑμῖν or ἡμῖν unto them, "to you," or "to us,"—"Whilst it is said to you" (or "us"), "To-day, if ye will hear his voice, harden not your hearts:" and so this exhortation is enforced, with new considerations, unto the end of the chapter. But this seems not to be the meaning of the apostle, and so not the due connection or construction of the words. For the same exhortation being before laid down from the psalmist, and applied unto the Hebrews, verses 7, 8, with a full improvement of it in the verses following, it is not reasonable to think that he should immediately again repeat it, and that in the same words, only somewhat more obscurely expressed. For in this way the meaning of the words must be, 'While it is day with you, while you enjoy the season that is so called, harden not your hearts.' But this is far more clearly expressed, verse 13,—"Exhort one another DAILY, while it is called To-day," with respect to what was before spoken, verses 7, 8. Others, therefore, as Erasmus, render the words by "In hoc quod dicitur,"—"In this that,"

[1] VARIOUS READINGS.—It is evident, even from the train of thought, that the true reading is τίνες, τίσι, and not, with Œcum., Theoph., Luther, Calvin, Grotius, etc., τινὲς, τισί, "only some." The author could infer only from the universality of sin in the time of Moses that the Israelites entered not into their rest, and therefore that the promise still awaited its fulfilment; he could not have inferred this from the fact that "only some had sinned at that time, and had been punished." So far Ebrard; in which view he agrees with Griesbach and Tischendorf, who both point these clauses interrogatively.

EXPOSITION.—᾽Ἀλλά, in a series of questions, and standing at the head of a question, means *vero, porro.* It serves to connect and give intensity to the interrogation. So here; ἀλλά, *truly, indeed, certè.* The meaning is, 'Might I not ask, Did not all who came out of Egypt rebel?'—*Stuart.*

TRANSLATIONS.—᾽Ἀπειθ. Disobedient.—*Conybeare and Howson.* Καὶ βλέπομεν. We see then, or, thus we see.—*Stuart, Turner.*—ED.

or, "Whereas it is said." And so a new exhortation should be intended, whose application, after a digression in a long hyperbaton
unto the end of this chapter, is laid down in the first verses of the
next. But this sense also we rejected in opening the general design
of these verses. The words, therefore, are to be taken simply and
absolutely, so as to indicate a repetition of the former testimony,
and its improvement unto some further ends and purposes. Ἐν τῷ
λέγεσθαι, רֶאֱמֹר, "Whereas it is said,"—'Whereas these words are used
in the psalmist, and are recorded for our instruction.' And herein
the apostle intends,—1. Not only the repetition of the precise words
here mentioned, but by them calls over again the whole story that
depends upon them, which is usual in such quotations. Out of the
whole he intends now to take new observations unto his purpose in
hand; for there are yet remaining some particular circumstances of
the matter of fact insisted on of great importance, and much conducing unto his design, and to the establishment of the conclusion
that he lays down, verse 19, which the apostle, in his first view of
the words, had not yet considered or improved, as not lying in the
way of his discourse then in hand. For their sakes doth he give
this review unto the whole. 2. As of the story, so of his own exhortation upon it, the apostle lays down these words as a recapitulation,
which gives influence unto the process of his discourse,—"For some,"
saith he, "when they had heard, did provoke," verse 16. As if he
had said, 'Consider what hath been spoken, that the same befall not
you as did them who provoked and perished.' And we may see
hence,—

Obs. I. That every circumstance of the Scripture is instructive.

The apostle having before urged the authority of the psalm,
and the example recorded in it unto his purpose, here he again
resumes the words before insisted on, and from sundry circumstances of them, with the matter contained in them, further
argues, reasons, and carrieth on his exhortation. For he considers,
—1. Who they were that sinned and provoked God; wherein he
observes that it was "some" of them, and not absolutely all who
came out of Egypt: which how useful it was unto his purpose we
shall afterwards declare. 2. What became of them who so sinned.
"Their carcasses," saith he, "fell in the wilderness;" which circumstance doth not a little set forth the indignation of God against their
sin, and his severity against their persons. 3. He presseth in particular the consideration of the oath of God, and manifests its exact
accomplishment, that none who shall fall under the same condition
may ever expect or hope for an escape. Lastly, From the consideration of the whole, he collects what was evidently the direct and
especial sin that procured so great a destruction, and peremptorily
excluded that people out of that rest of God, namely, their "unbe-

lief." These are the παραλειπόμενα that the apostle gathers up in these verses, which, belonging unto the subject he insisted on, fell not before orderly under his consideration.

Obs. II. God hath filled the Scripture with truth.

Whence one said well, " Adoro plenitudinem Scripturarum,"— " I reverence the fulness of the Scriptures." Ps. cxxxviii. 2, " He hath magnified his word above all his name;" or made it more instructive than any other way or means whereby he hath revealed himself. For not only doth the whole Scripture contain the whole counsel of God, concerning his own glory and worship, our faith, obedience, and salvation, but also every parcel of it hath in it such a depth of truth as cannot by us be perfectly searched into. Ps. cxix. 18, " Open thou mine eyes," saith the psalmist, " that I may behold wondrous things out of thy law." There are wonderful things in the word, if God be pleased to give us light to see it. It is like a cabinet of jewels, that when you pull out one box or drawer and search into it, you find it full; pull out another, it is full; and when you think you have pulled out all, yet still there are some secret recesses in the cabinet, so that if you search further you will find more. Our apostle seems to have drawn out all the boxes of this cabinet, but making a second search into the words, he finds all these things treasured up, which he had not before intimated nor touched upon. It was said by some of old, that the " Scripture hath fords where a lamb may wade, and depths where an elephant may swim." And it is true in respect of the perspicuity of some places, and the difficulty of others. But the truth is also, that God hath in his grace and wisdom so ordered its concernments, that,—1. What from the nature of the things themselves, which are suited unto the various states, conditions, and apprehensions of the minds of men ; 2. What from the manner of their expression, on which a character of divine wisdom is impressed ; 3. What from the authority of God putting itself forth in the whole and every particular ; 4. What from its being not only " propositio veritatis," but " vehiculum gratiæ;" many, most, yea, all the particular places of it and passages in it, are such as through which a lamb may wade safely, and an elephant swim without danger of striking against the bottom. Let any lamb of Christ come, in that order, with that reverence unto the reading or hearing the word of God (the Scripture itself I mean) which is required, and he will find no place so dark or difficult but that it will yield him that refreshment which is suited unto him and safe for him, and something of God he will obtain; for either he will find his graces excited, or his mind enlightened, or his conscience peculiarly brought into a reverence of God. And let the wisest, the most learned and experienced person, that seems like an elephant in spiritual skill and strength amongst the flock, come to the plainest

place, to search out the mind and will of God in it, if he be humble
as well as learned,—which if he be not he is not wise,—he will scarce
boast that he hath been at the bottom of it, and hath perfectly comprehended all that is in it, seeing whatever we know, " we know but
in part." And they may all of them, elephants and lambs, meet at
the same passages of this river that makes glad the city of God,
these waters of rest and quietness, Ps. xxiii. 2, where the lambs may
wade safely, and the elephants swim together. The poorest of the
flock, in the right use of means, may take enough for themselves,
even suitable direction and refreshment, from those very places of
Scripture whose depths the learnedest guides of the church are not
able to sound or fathom. Not only in several places, but in the
same place, text, or testimony of Scripture, there is food meet for
the several ages of Christians, whether babes and children or strong
men; with light and direction for all sorts of believers, according to
the degrees of their own inward light and grace. It is like manna,
which, though men gathered variously according to their strength
and appetite, yet every one had that proportion which suited his
own eating. When a learned man, and one mighty in the Scriptures, undertakes the consideration of a place of Scripture, and
finds, it may be, in the issue, that with all his skill and industry, with
all his helps and advantages, though attended in the use of them
with fervent prayer and holy meditation, he is not able to search it
out unto perfection, let him not suppose that such a place will be of
no advantage unto them who are not sharers in his advantages, but
rather are mean and unlearned; for they may obtain a useful portion for themselves where he cannot take down all. If any one look
on this river of God like behemoth on Jordan, " trusting that he
can draw it up into his mouth," or take up the whole sense of God
in it, he of all others seems to know nothing of its worth and excellency. And this ariseth, as was observed, principally from the
things themselves treated of in the Scripture. For, divine and spiritual truths having God not only as their immediate fountain and
spring, but also as their proper and adequate object, there is still
somewhat in them that cannot be searched out unto perfection.
As he said, " Canst thou by searching find out God? canst thou
find out the Almighty unto perfection?" Job xi. 7, עַד־תַּכְלִית שַׁדַּי
תִּמְצָא,—"find him out to a perfect comprehension," or "to a consummation of knowledge," that it should be perfect. This neither the
nature of God nor our condition will admit of. We do at best but
" follow after," that we may in our measure " apprehend that for
which we also are apprehended of Christ Jesus," Phil. iii. 12. And
these things are so tempered by divine wisdom unto the faith and
light of believers, and therein unto the uses of their consolation and
obedience, that something hereof is plainly exhibited to every spi-

ritual eye: always provided that their search and inquiry be regulated according to the will of God, in a due use of the means; for to this purpose not only the private endeavours of men are required, but the use also of the public ministry, which is ordained of God to lead men gradually into continual further acquaintance with the will of God in the Scripture.

Some think that it belongs unto the *fulness of the Scripture* that each place in it should have various senses,—some say three, some four. But this, indeed, is to empty it of all fulness; for if it have not everywhere one proper determinate sense, it hath none at all. This it hath; but the things which the words of it are signs of and are expressed by, are so great, deep, and mysterious, and have such various respects unto our light, faith, and obedience, as that it is unsearchably instructive unto us. " The commandment is exceeding broad," Ps. cxix. 96, רְחָבָה מְאֹד;—the word used to express the wideness of the sea, Ps. civ. 25, הַיָּם גָּדוֹל וּרְחַב יָדַיִם,—" The great sea," that hath " wide and large arms," which it stretcheth out to comprehend the whole earth. So doth the command widen and stretch out its arms, to comprehend the whole church of God, to water it and to make it fruitful. God having enstamped his authority and wisdom upon it, every concernment of it, every consequence from it, every circumstance reported in it, hath its authority in and upon the consciences of men for the end whereunto it is designed. Hence we may observe, that in the quotations of testimonies out of the Old Testament in the New, it is very seldom that the principal aim and intendment of any place is insisted on, but rather some peculiar specialty that is either *truly included* in the words or *duly educed* by just consequence from them.

And this may teach men what diligence they ought to use in searching and studying of the Scripture. Slight, inadvertent considerations will be of little use in this matter. Especially is this incumbent on them whose duty and office it is to declare and expound them unto others. And there is amongst many a great miscarriage in these things, and that both in some that *teach*, and some that only privately read or *meditate* on the word. Some men preach with very little regard to the Scripture, either as to the *treasury* and promptuary of all the truth they are to dispense, or as to the *rule* whereby they are to proceed. And some are ready to coin notions in their own minds, or to learn them from others, and then attempt to put them upon the Scripture. or obtain countenance from thence unto them: and this is the way of men who invent and vent false opinions and groundless curiosities, which a previous due reverential observance of the word might have delivered them from. And some again, and those too many, super-

ficially take up with that sense of the words which obviously presents itself unto their first consideration, which they improve to their
own purpose as they see cause. Such persons as these see little of
the wisdom of God in the word; they enter not into those mines of
gold; they are but *passengers*, they do not " stand in the counsel of
God, to hear his word," Jer. xxiii. 22. It is certain that the diligent search into the Scriptures which is commended unto us, which
the worth of them and the things contained in them requires, and
which that fulness and comprehension of truth that is in them doth
make necessary, is by most neglected. And the same may be observed in multitudes of commentators and expositors. They express things otherwise one than another, but for the most part
directly the same. Seldom any one ventures into the deep one
step beyond what he sees his way beat before him, and, as he supposes, his ground secure; though a diligent inquirer may often find
the most beaten path either to turn away from the fountain, or at
least to end and fail before it comes there. I would not speak any
thing to encourage men in bold adventures, groundless conjectures,
and curious pryings into things hidden, secret, and marvellous;
but it is humble diligence, joined with prayer, meditation, and
waiting on God for the revelation of his will, in the study of the
Scripture, upon the account of the fulness of its treasury, and the
guiding, instructive virtue wherewithal its concerns are accompanied,
that I would press after. And hence I am persuaded that the
church of God hath, through his care and faithfulness, had great
advantage from their opposition unto the truth who, to countenance
their own errors, have searched curiously into all the concernments
of the words of many testimonies given unto the truth. For though
they have done this to their own destruction, yet " out of this eater
there hath come forth meat;" for they have not only given an occasion unto, but imposed a necessity upon us to search with all diligence into every concernment of some most material passages in
the Scripture, and that to the clearing of the truth and the stablish-
ing of the minds of many. That which I would press from these
considerations, grounded on the precedent before us, wherein the
apostle, from sundry latent circumstances of the text, draws out singular useful observations in reference unto our faith and obedience,
is, that our utmost diligence, especially in them who are called unto
the instruction of others, is required in this neglected, yea despised
work of searching the Scriptures. And as a consequent of the
neglect hereof, I cannot but say that I have observed a threefold
defect amongst sundry teachers, that was in general intimated before; as, first, When men scarce at any time make use of the
Scripture in their preaching any further than to make remarks and
observations on the obvious sense of any place, neither entering

themselves, nor endeavouring to lead their hearers into the secret and rich recesses of them. And secondly, which is worse, When men without the Scripture design their subjects, and project the handling of them, and occasionally only take in the words of the Scripture, and that guided more by the sound than the sense of them. And thirdly, which is worst of all, When men by their own notions, opinions, curiosities, and allegories, rather draw men from the Scripture than endeavour to lead them unto it. The example of our great apostle will guide us unto other ways of proceeding in our work.

Ver. 16.—For some, when they heard [*the word*], provoked; howbeit not all who came out of Egypt by Moses.

The intention of the apostle in this and the ensuing verses, as hath been observed, is to confirm his preceding exhortation from the example proposed unto them, and that on the consideration of the various events that befell their forefathers in the wilderness, with respect, on the one hand, unto the promises and threatenings of God, and on the other, to their faith and disobedience. To this end, in this verse he makes a distribution of the persons who came forth of Egypt under the conduct of Moses, and heard the voice of God in the wilderness:—They all "came out of Egypt," they all "heard" the voice of God; howbeit all did not "provoke," but only "some." Two things, then, are affirmed of them all in general;—First, That they "all came out of Egypt by Moses;" Secondly, That they all "heard" the voice of God. And the limitation respects one instance only,—some of these all "provoked," and some did not. The first thing in general ascribed unto them is, that they "came out of Egypt by Moses." A few words, but comprehensive of a great story; a work wherein God was exceedingly glorified, and that people made partakers of greater mercies and privileges than ever any before them from the foundation of the world: the pressing whereof upon the minds and consciences of the people is one main end of the Book of Deuteronomy. Moses sums up much of it, chap. iv. 34: "Did ever God assay to go and take him a nation from the midst of another nation, by temptations, by signs, and by wonders, and by war, and by a mighty hand, and by a stretched-out arm, and by great terrors, according to all that the LORD your God hath done for you?"

"Tantæ molis erat *Judæam* condere gentem."

And besides the other circumstances that the apostle expressly insists upon, this is mentioned here to intimate what obligation was on this people to attend unto the voice of God, in that he brought them up out of Egypt; and therefore it pleased God to preface the whole

law of their obedience with the expression of it, "I am the LORD
thy God, which have brought thee out of the land of Egypt," Exod.
xx. 2. Διὰ Μωυσέως, "By Moses." "By the hand of
Διὰ Μωυσίως.
Moses," saith the Syriac. That is, either under his conduct and guidance, or through the prevalency of the miraculous
works which God wrought by him. Both these senses the prophet
expresseth, Isa. lxiii. 11, 12: "Then he remembered the days of old,
Moses, and his people, saying, Where is he that brought them up
out of the sea with the shepherd of his flock? where is he that put
his Holy Spirit within him? that led them by the right hand of
Moses with his glorious arm, dividing the water before them, to make
himself an everlasting name?" Both the conduct of Moses, and the
miracles that God wrought by him, are comprised in their coming
up "by Moses." And, by the way, it may be observed, that in this
preparation and consultation, as it were, about new mercies to be
bestowed on that people, there are several persons in the Deity introduced treating about it, and calling to remembrance their former
actings towards them. He that speaks is the person of the Father,
whose love and compassion are celebrated, verses 7–9, as they are
everywhere peculiarly ascribed unto that person. And he that is
spoken of, and as it were inquired after to appear again in the work
of their salvation, which peculiarly belongs unto him, he is called
the "Angel of his presence," verse 9, and the LORD himself, verse 14;
that is, the person of the Son, unto whom the actual deliverance of
the church in every strait doth belong, and he is therefore here, as
it were, inquired after. And with reference unto this work by Moses
it is said, "And by a prophet the LORD brought Israel out of Egypt,
and by a prophet was he preserved," Hos. xii. 13. And this belongeth unto the whole people, none excepted.

Secondly, This also is ascribed to them, that they "heard:" for
whereas it is said, "Some, when they heard, provoked," it is not
meant that some only heard, and provoked; but of them that
heard, some only provoked. What they heard was declared before,
—the voice of God, as it is said, "To-day, if ye will hear his voice."
And this may be taken either strictly, for the hearing of the voice of
God at the giving of the law on mount Sinai, when the whole congregation heard קֹלֹת, those voices of God in thundering and dreadful agitations of the mount wherewith it was accompanied, and the
voice of God himself whereby the law was pronounced,—that is, an
audible voice framed for that purpose by the ministry of angels; or
it may be taken more largely, for a participation in all those instructions which God granted unto them in the wilderness. There seems,
indeed, to be an especial respect unto the giving of the law, though
not merely the promulgation of the ten words on Sinai, but the
whole system of precepts and ordinances of worship that attended;

for therein "they were evangelized, even as we," Heb. iv. 2. And also, their hearing is spoken of as that which was past (" When they had heard") before their provoking, which yet signally happened in the second year after their coming out of Egypt. This, then, was the voice of God which they heard.

The sin which is appropriated unto some of them who thus "came out of Egypt," and " heard," is that παρεπίκραναν, they "provoked,"—that is, God, whose voice, or word, or law they heard. The meaning of this word, and the nature of the sin expressed by it, have been spoken to before. I shall add one place that explains it: Hos. xii. 15, הִכְעִים אֶפְרַיִם תַּמְרוּרִים, " Ephraim hath provoked bitternesses;" that is, very bitterly. Great provocations have a " bitterness" in them, as the word here denotes, which causeth God to loathe the provokers.

By these considerations doth the apostle enforce his exhortation before insisted on, and show the necessity of it. This is, that they would diligently attend unto the word of the gospel, and steadfastly continue in the profession thereof. 'For,' saith he, ' when the people of old heard the voice of God in that dispensation of his law and grace which was suited unto their condition, some of them provoked him; whereas they may do so also who hear his voice in the dispensation of the gospel, therefore doth it highly concern them to take care that this be not the event of their mercy therein.'

Lastly, The apostle adds expressly a limitation, with respect to the persons who heard and provoked: " Howbeit not all." In his preceding discourse he had expressed the sin and punishment of the people indefinitely, so as at first view to include the *whole generation* in the wilderness, without exception of any. Here, out of the story, he puts in an exception of some even of them who came up out of Egypt under the conduct of Moses. And there are three sorts of persons who lay claim to an interest in the privilege:—1. Those who, being under *twenty years of age*, were not numbered in the wilderness of Sinai, in the second year after their coming up out of Egypt, Num. i. 1–3; for of those that were then numbered there was not a man left, save Caleb and Joshua, when the people was numbered again in the plains of Moab by Moses and Eleazar, chap. xxvi. 63, 64. These are they who died because of their provocation; those who before were under twenty years old being now the body of the people that was numbered. 2. The *tribe of Levi:* for the threatening and oath of God were against all of them that were numbered in the wilderness of Sinai, Num. xiv. 29, and the account is accordingly given in of the death of the numbered ones only, chap. xxvi. 63, 64; but in the taking of that first muster-roll Moses was expressly commanded not to take the number of the Levites, chap. i. 47-49. However, I much fear, by the course

of the story, that the generality of this tribe fell also. 3. *Caleb
and Joshua;* and it is certain that these are principally, if not
solely intended. Now, the reason why the apostle expresseth this
limitation of his former general assertion is, that he might enforce
his exhortation with the example of them who believed and obeyed
the voice of God, and who thereon both enjoyed the promises and
entered into the rest of God; so that he takes his argument not only
from the severity of God,—which at first view seems only to be represented in his instance and example,—but also from his faithfulness
and grace, which are included therein. And we may now a little further consider what is contained in these words for our instruction;
as,—

Obs. I. Many hear the word or voice of God to no advantage, but
only to aggravate their sin.

Their hearing renders their sin provoking unto God, and destructive to their own souls. " Some, when they heard, provoked."
Daily experience is a sufficient confirmation of this assertion. The
word of God is preached unto us, the voice of God sounds amongst
us. As our apostle speaks, Heb. iv. 2, " Unto us was the gospel
preached, as well as unto them;" and that with many advantages on
our part. They heard the gospel indeed, but obscurely, and in law
language, hard to be understood; we have it plainly, openly, and
without parables, declared unto us. They heard the voice of him
that spake on earth; we, his who speaks from heaven. But what is
the issue of God's thus dealing with us? Plainly, some neglect the
word, some corrupt it, some despise it,—few mix it with faith, or yield
obedience unto it. The dispensers of it may for the most part take
up the complaint of the prophet, " Who hath believed our report?
and to whom is the arm of the LORD revealed?" Isa. liii. 1. And
unto many, after their most serious and sedulous dealing with them
in the name of God, they may take up the apostle's close with the
unbelieving Jews, Acts xiii. 41, " Behold, ye despisers, and wonder,
and perish." Most of them unto whom our Saviour preached perished. They got nothing by hearing his doctrine, through their
unbelief, but an aggravation of their sin and the hastening of their
ruin. So he told Capernaum and the rest of the towns wherein he
had wrought his miracles, and to whom he preached the gospel. His
presence and preaching for a while brought them into a condition
above that of Jerusalem,—they were " lifted up unto heaven;" but
their unbelief under it brought them into a condition worse than
that of Sodom,—they were " brought down to hell," Matt. xi. 21–24.
It is, I confess, a great privilege, for men to have the word preached
unto them and to hear it, Ps. cxlvii. 19, 20; but privileges are as
men use them. In themselves they are of worth and to be prized;
but unto us they are as they are used. Hence the gospel becomes

unto some "a savour of death unto death," 2 Cor. ii. 16. Yea, Christ himself, in his whole ministry, was "a stone of stumbling and rock of offence to both the houses of Israel, a gin and a snare to the inhabitants of Jerusalem," Isa. viii. 14, Luke ii. 34. And the enjoyment of any part of the means of grace is but a trial. And when any rest therein they do but boast in the putting on of their harness, not knowing what will be the end of the battle. And let none mistake unto whom the word of God comes, as it did unto this people in the wilderness. They are engaged; and there is no coming off but conquerors, or ruined. If they receive it not, it will be the aggravation of their sins, the eternal destruction of their souls. The reasons why it will do so I have insisted on in the exposition of chap. ii. 1–3.

Obs. II. In the most general and visible apostasies of the church, God still preserves a remnant unto himself, to bear witness unto him and for him by their faith and obedience: "They provoked; howbeit not all."

They were indeed many who provoked, but not all. A few they were, but yet some there were who inherited the promise. The professing church in the world was never nearer ruin than at this time. Once, had Moses stood out of the way, had he not with all his might of faith and zeal abode in the breach, God had disinherited them all, and utterly destroyed them, and reserved him only for a new stock or spring, Exod. xxxii. 9–14; Ps. cvi. 23. God had indeed at this time a great secret people, in the children of that generation; but the visible professing church consisted principally in the men that were numbered,—and it is not to be supposed that their wives were much behind their husbands in their murmurings, being more naturally than they, in straits and difficulties, prone to such miscarriages, by reason of their fears. And, "quantillum abfuit," how near was this whole church to destruction! how near to apostasy! How many soever retained their faith, only Caleb and Joshua retained their profession. When God of old brought a flood upon the world for their wickedness, the professing church, that had been very great and large in the posterity of Seth, was reduced to *eight persons,* and one of them a *cursed hypocrite.* And once Elijah could see no more in Israel but himself. There were indeed then seven thousand *latent believers,* but scarce another *visible professor.* And it is not hard to imagine how little true faith, regularly professed, there was in the world when Christ was in the grave. And under the fatal apostasy foretold in the Revelation, those that "kept the testimony of Jesus" are reduced to so small a number as that they are spoken of under the name of "two witnesses." But yet in all these hazardous trials and reductions of the number of professors, God always hath maintained, and ever will, a remnant, true, faithful, pure, and undefiled, unto himself. This he hath done, and this he will do,—

1. To *maintain his own kingdom* in the world. Satan, by his temptations and the entrance of sin, had greatly defaced the beauty, glory, and order of that kingdom which God first erected in the world, to be governed by the law of creation. But God still retains his sovereignty and authority in it and over it, in all its disorder, by his all-disposing providence; but that he might lose nothing by this attempt of his adversary, as not in power or interest, so neither in honour or glory, he erected in the first promise a new kingdom of grace. Unto this kingdom he gives his Son to be the head,— "the head over all things to the church," Eph. i. 22; and it unto him, to have therein an "everlasting dominion," enduring through all ages, so that of the increase of his rule and government therein there should be no end, Isa. ix. 7. Now, this kingdom cannot be thus preserved, unless some be always, by real saving grace, and the profession of it, kept and maintained as subjects thereof. The kingdom of providence, indeed, under all its alterations, is natural unto God, and necessary. It implies a contradiction that there should be a creature, and God not the sovereign Lord of it. But this kingdom of grace depends on the purpose and faithfulness of God. He hath taken upon himself the continuance and preservation of it unto the end. Should it at any time totally fail, Christ would be a king without a kingdom, a head without a body, or cease to be the one and the other. Wherefore God will secure some, that neither by the abuse of their own liberty, nor by the endeavours of the gates of hell, shall ever be drawn off from their obedience. And this God, in his grace, power, and faithfulness, will effect, to make good his promises unto Christ, which he multiplied unto that purpose from the foundation of the world.

2. Should all faith *utterly fail in the earth*, should all professors provoke God and apostatize from him, all gracious intercourse between the Holy Spirit and mankind in this world would be at an end. The work of the Spirit is to convert the souls of men unto God, to sanctify them to be temples for himself to dwell in, to guide, teach, lead, and comfort them, by supplies of his grace. Suppose, then, that no saving grace or obedience should be left in the earth, this work of the Spirit of God must utterly fail and cease. But this consisteth not with his glorious immutability and power: he hath undertaken a work, and he will not faint in it, or give it over one moment, until it be accomplished, and all the elect brought unto God. If, therefore, the natural children of Abraham fail, he will out of the stones and rubbish of the Gentiles raise up a living temple unto God, wherein he may dwell, and provide a remnant for him on the earth.

3. God will do this *for the work that he hath for some of his in all ages* and seasons to do in the world. And this is great and various. He will have some always to conflict with his adversaries and overcome them, and therein give testimony to the power of his grace and truth. Could sin and Satan drive all true grace, faith, and obedience out of the world, they would complete their victory; but so long as they have any to conflict withal, against whom they cannot prevail, themselves are conquered. The victory is on the other side, and Satan is sensible that he is under the curse. Wherever true faith is, there is a victory, 1 John v. 4. By this doth God make his remnant as a "brazen wall," that his enemies shall fight against in vain, Jer. xv. 20. Be they, therefore, never so few, they shall do the work of God, in conquering Satan and the world through the "blood of the Lamb."

4. God will always have a *testimony given to his goodness, grace, and mercy.* As in the ways of his providence he never "left himself without witness," Acts xiv. 17, no more will he in the ways of his grace. Some he will have to give testimony to his goodness, in the calling, pardoning, and sanctifying of sinners; which who shall do if there be none on earth made partakers of that grace? They are proper witnesses who testify what they know and have experience of.

And lastly, God will always have a *revenue of especial glory out of the world* in and by his worship. And this also must necessarily cease and fail, should not God preserve to himself a remnant of them that truly fear him.

And if this be the way of God's dealing, we may see what becomes sometimes of that which the Papists make a note of the church,—namely, number and visibility. He that would choose his party by tale would scarce have joined himself with Caleb and Joshua, against the consent of about six hundred thousand men, who cried out to stone them because they were not of their mind. God's way, indeed, is always to preserve some; but sometimes his way is to reserve but a few,—as we have seen in sundry instances before mentioned.

Again, It is evident from whence it is that the church of God hath passed through so many trials, hazards, and dangers, and yet hath not to this day at any time utterly been prevailed against. It escaped of old when Cain slew Abel; when "all flesh had corrupted its ways," and God brought the flood upon ungodly men, it escaped then in the family of Noah; as it did afterwards in that of Abraham; so it did in the wilderness by the fidelity of Moses, Caleb, and Joshua. Since the establishment of the Christian church, it is known what dreadful opposition it hath been exercised withal. Once the world groaned, admiring to see itself surprised into Arianism; afterwards all "wondered after the beast," and none were suffered to live that received not his mark,—a high renunciation of the authority of Jesus Christ. Yet from the jaws of all these hazards, these deaths, hath the church been preserved, and triumphed against all oppositions. God hath undertaken its preservation, and he will make it good to the uttermost. He hath given the Lord Christ power and authority to secure his own interest and concerns in the earth. And he sends the Spirit to convert and sanctify his elect, and will so do until the consummation of all things. A thread of infinite wisdom, care, and faithfulness, hath run along in this matter from the beginning hitherto, and it shall not be cut off or broken. And this may also give us satisfaction and security for the future as to that remnant of Jacob which lies in the midst, in the bowels of many nations,—it shall be preserved. He spake proudly who encouraged the pilot in a storm with " Cæsaris fortunam vehis,"— " Fear not, thou carriest the fortune of Cæsar;" which, though not then, yet soon after failed him. Believers are engaged in a bottom that hath Christ in it, and his interest, and the faithfulness of God, to secure its safe arrival in the harbour of eternal rest and peace. There is at this day a dreadful appearance of an opposition to the city of God. Paganism, Mohammedanism, Popery, Atheism, with sundry gross heresies, are in combination, as it were, against it. The contribution also of strength and craft which they have from the lusts and worldly interests of men is incredible. But yet we see that in the midst of all these storms and fears the Lord is pleased to preserve a remnant to himself, neither themselves nor their adversaries knowing how; and upon the grounds mentioned he will assuredly continue to do so to the end.

Obs. III. God lays a few, a very few ofttimes, of his secret ones in the balance against the greatest multitude of rebels and transgressors.

They that provoked God were about six hundred thousand men, and upon the matter two only opposed them. But, in the language of the Holy Ghost, all that great multitude were but "some,"— some, not "all;" the principal part was preserved in those who were obedient. They were his portion, his inheritance, his jewels, dear to him as the apple of his eye, and deservedly preferred unto the greatest heap of chaff and rubbish.

In the two next verses the apostle proceedeth to evince the necessity and enforce the use of his preceding exhortation, from the *circumstances* of the example insisted on; and this he doth by way of interrogation. He proposeth in them questions on the matter of fact, and answers them from what is either directly expressed, or undeniably included in the words insisted on.

Ver. 17, 18.—But with whom was he grieved forty years? was it not with them that had sinned, whose carcasses fell in the wilderness? And to whom sware he that they should not enter into his rest, but to them that believed not?

The kind of arguing here used by the apostle is not simply interrogatory, but it is that which is said to be by interrogation and subjection; that is, when a question is drawn, and an answer substituted out of the same matter; which hath such an efficacy for conviction and persuasion, that the great Roman orator seldom omits it in any of his orations. And it is so especially when the question proposed is "interrogatio rei," an inquiry into a matter of fact; and the answer returned is "interrogatio λέξεως," in form of speech an interrogation, but really an answer. Such is the apostle's manner of arguing here. The interrogation, verse 17, "With whom was he grieved forty years?" is "interrogatio rei;" and the answer returned is in an interrogatory form of speech,—"Was it not with them that had sinned, whose carcasses fell in the wilderness?"

The words of the interrogation were explained on verse 10, whereunto the reader is referred. In this repetition of them, the design of the apostle is to fix on the minds of the Hebrews the consideration of the people's sin, and God's dealing with them thereon.

The answer unto this first inquiry consists in a double description of them with whom God was so long grieved or displeased,—First, By their sin, "Was it not with them that sinned?" Secondly, By their punishment, "Whose carcasses fell in the wilderness."

And we may consider first what is *included,* and then what is *expressed* in this answer. For the first, It is plainly included that God was not thus displeased with them *all.* Let not any apprehend that God took a causeless distaste at that whole generation, and so cast them off and destroyed them promiscuously, without distinction. As they were some only, and not all, that provoked; so it was with some only, and not all, that God was displeased. And two things do thence necessarily ensue to his purpose and advantage:— First, That his exhortation is enforced by showing that it was not an ordinary promiscuous event that befell their fathers in the wilderness, but that they passed under a distinguishing dispensation of God towards them, according to their deportment, as they also were like to do. Secondly, That they might also consider that with those who sinned not, who provoked not, God was not displeased, but according to his promise they entered into his rest; which promise in a more excellent sense still remains for their benefit, if they were not disobedient.

The first thing expressed in the words, or the first part of the
description of them with whom God was displeased, is
their *sin:* "Was it not with them that sinned?" Their
sin is first mentioned in general, and then the particular
nature of it is afterwards declared. There were three sorts of sins
that the people were guilty of in the wilderness:—1. They were
universally guilty of *personal sins* in their distinct capacities. And
these may justly be supposed to be great and many. But these are
not they which are here intended; for if in this sense God should
mark iniquity, none could stand, Ps. cxxx. 3. Neither were they
free from sins of this nature who are here exempted from being
objects of God's displeasure. 2. *Especial provocations,* wherein great
numbers of the people were engaged, but not the whole congregation. Such was the rebellion of Korah, Dathan, and Abiram, with
their accomplices, who were many and great, even "two hundred
and fifty princes, famous in the congregation, men of renown," Num.
xvi. 2; the idolatry and adulteries of Peor, which infected many of
the princes and people, with the like instances. 3. *General sins* of
the whole congregation; which consisted in their frequent murmurings and rebellions, which came to a head as it were in that great
provocation upon the return of the spies, Num. xiv., when they not
only provoked God by their own unbelief, but encouraged one another to destroy those two persons, Joshua and Caleb, who would
not concur in their disobedience: "All the congregation bade stone
them with stones," verse 10. This distinction was observed by the
daughters of Zelophehad in their address for an inheritance among
their brethren: " Our father," say they, " died in the wilderness,
and he was not in the company of them that gathered themselves
together against the Lord in the company of Korah; but died in
his own sin," Num. xxvii. 3. They acknowledge him guilty of
personal sins, and deny not but that he joined in the general provocation of the whole congregation, but only that he had a hand
in those especial provocations which God fixed an eminent mark of
his displeasure upon, by cutting off the provokers with fearful,
sudden, and signal judgments; whereas others were gradually consumed by death in a natural way. But it is this last kind of sin,
in the guilt whereof the whole congregation was equally involved,
that the apostle intends in this expression, " Was it not with them
that sinned ?" Observe,—

Obs. I. God is not displeased with any thing in his people but
sin; or, sin is the only proper object of God's displeasure, and the
sinner for sin's sake: 'With whom was he displeased, but with them
that sinned ?'

I need not set up my candle in the sun of this truth. I wish it
were as seriously considered practically as it is confessed and ac-

knowledged notionally. Every revelation of God, by his word or works, bears witness hereunto; and every man hath that witness hereof in himself as will not admit him to doubt of it. The nature of God, the law of God, the light of conscience, the sense that is in all of a judgment, at present fixed, and certainly future, testify unto it. And doubtless great is the power of sin and the craft of Satan, which prevail with most to continue in sin, notwithstanding this uncontrollable conviction.

Obs. II. Public sins, sins in societies, are great provocations of God.

It was not for their private and personal sins that God was thus provoked with this people, but for their conspiracy, as it were, in sin. The reasons hereof are manifest, and I shall not insist upon them. God help cities and nations, especially such as hear the voice of God, well to consider it, and all of us, to take heed of national prevailing sins!

Secondly, The apostle describes these persons by their punishment: "Whose carcasses fell in the wilderness." Κῶλα, —how variously this word is rendered by translators I   Κῶλα.
have showed before. That which the apostle intendeth to express, is the words of God unto the people, Num. xiv. 29: בַּמִּדְבָּר הַזֶּה יִפְּלוּ פִגְרֵיכֶם;—"In this wilderness shall your carcasses fall." Which is emphatically repeated, verse 32, פִגְרֵיכֶם אַתֶּם יִפְּלוּ בַמִּדְבָּר הַזֶּה;—"Your carcasses, you, shall fall in this wilderness." אַתֶּם, "you," is emphatically added, as to apply the threatening to their persons immediately, so to show them it should be their lot and not their children's, as they murmured; as also to express a πάθος and indignation in the delivery. פֶּגֶר is from פָּגַר, to be "weary," "faint," "cold," "frigore enecari" (whence is that word), "slothful." Thence is פֶּגֶר, "peger," "a dead carcass," a thing cold, without life, heat, or motion. It is used sometimes for the carcass of a beast, commonly called נְבֵלָה, "That which is fallen," so Gen. xv. 11; most frequently for the carcasses of men. Elias Levita supposeth that it denotes only the carcasses of wicked men. And indeed it is most commonly, if not always, so used. See Amos viii. 3; Isa. xiv. 19, xxxiv. 3, lxvi. 24; Jer. xxxiii. 5; Ezek. xliii. 9. There seems to be an exception unto this observation of Elias, from Jer. xli. 9: "And the pit whereinto Ishmael cast אֵת כָּל־פִּגְרֵי הָאֲנָשִׁים,"—"all the carcasses of the men whom he slew." But whether this be of force against the observation of Elias I know not. Those men might be wicked for aught that appears in the text. Now, this word the LXX. render sometimes by σῶμα, "a body," Gen. xv. 11; σῶμα νεκρόν, "a dead body," Isa. xxxvii. 36;—sometimes by νεκρός, "a dead person," 2 Chron. xx. 24, Jer. xxxiii. 5; πτῶμα, "cadaver," "a carcass," Ezek. vi. 5;—but most frequently by κῶλον, the word here used by the apostle, as

Num. xiv. 29, 32, 33, the place here referred unto. Κῶλον is a "member," "membrum," or "artus;" which words are of the same importance and signification; and the whole compages of them is the same with the body. As Tydeus in Statius, Theb. viii. 739:—

> "—— Odi artus, fragilemque hunc corporis usum."

And the same author again, of Agylleus, ibid. vi. 841:—

> "Luxuriant artus, effusaque sanguine laxo
> Membra natant."

Hence interpreters promiscuously render the word here by "membra" or "artus." Κῶλα are principally "crura" and "lacerti;" the greater members of the body, arms, legs, and thighs, whose bones are greatest and of longest duration. In the singular number, therefore, it signifies not the whole body, but some distinct member of it; and thence it is translated into the use of speech, and denotes a part of a sentence, a sub-distinction. But κῶλα, in the plural number, may denote the whole carcass. I suppose the פְגָרִים, or "carcasses" of the people, may here be called their κῶλα, their "members" or their "bones," as Suidas renders the word; because probably in those great plagues and destructions that befell them, their rebellious carcasses were many of them left on the ground in the wilderness, where consuming, their greater bones lay scattered up and down. So the psalmist complains that it befell them at another season: Ps. clxvii. 7, "Our bones are scattered at the grave's mouth, as when one cutteth and cleaveth wood upon the earth." In such a work, pieces of the hewed or cleft wood will lie scattered up and down, here and there, in some places covering the earth,—so did their bones; and said to be at the mouth of the grave, because the opening of the earth is that which gives a grave to the carcasses of men. The appearance and spectacle hereof the Roman historian represents in the carcasses, or bones rather, of the legions cut off by Herminius in Germany with Quintilius Varus, and left in the open field, when six years after Germanicus brought his army to the same place:—" In medio campi albentia ossa (κῶλα) ut fugerant, ut restiterant, disjecta vel aggerata; adjacebant fragmina telorum, equorumque artus," Tacit. Ann., lib. i.;—"In the midst of the field, bones grown white, scattered or heaped, as they had fled, or resisted; by them lay pieces of broken weapons, with the members of horses." A great and sore destruction or judgment this is accounted amongst men, and therefore is it made a representation of hell, Isa. lxvi. 24, "They shall go forth, and look upon the carcasses of the men that have transgressed against me; for their worm shall not die, neither shall their fire be quenched; and they shall be an abhorring unto all flesh." Some of the Jews refer these words to the victory they fancy that they shall have against Gog and Magog, when they come to fight against their Messiah. It is literally much more true concerning the believing Gentiles, whose calling is expressly foretold and prophesied of in the foregoing verses, who saw the severe judgment of God on the unbelieving Jews, when, in the fatal destruction of their city and temple, their carcasses were truly cast out on the earth, and were " an abhorring unto all flesh." But here is also a representation of the final judgment of the last day, and everlasting punishment of the wicked; whereunto some of the words are applied, Mark ix. 44; which the Targum on the place also applies them unto. The casting out, therefore, of carcasses to be beheld and abhorred is a sore judgment. And the Jews suppose that all those who died under God's displeasure in the wilderness were shut out of heaven or the world to come, Tractat. Sanhed. Perek. x. They inquire expressly who shall and who shall not be saved; and at once they deal pretty liberally with themselves: כל ישראל יש להם חלק לעולם הבא,—" All Israel shall have a part in the world to come:" which they prove out of these words of the prophet, " Thy people shall be all righteous," Isa. lx. 21; which indeed would do it to the purpose, could they prove themselves all to be the people there intended. But afterwards they lay in many exceptions to this rule, and among the rest דור המדבר אין להם חלק לעולם הבא;—" The generation in the wilderness have no portion in the world to come." And they add their reason: שנא במדבר הזה יתמו ושם ימותו;—" Because it is said, ' In the wilderness shall ye be consumed, and there shall ye die.'" The redoubling of the expression, " ye shall be consumed," " ye shall die," they would have to signify first temporal death, then eternal.

Their carcasses ἔπεσον; " prostrata sunt," say some,—" were cast down;" properly "ceciderunt," "fell," that is, penally,—an aggravation of their destruction. He doth not say, they " died," but their carcasses "fell;" which intimates contempt and indignation; and so do the words denote in the story itself. And this is the second part of the description that is given of those with whom God was displeased for their sin, "Their carcasses fell in the wilderness;" the use whereof to the apostle's purpose hath been declared. And we may see that,—

Obs. III. God sometimes will make men who have been wickedly exemplary in sin righteously exemplary in their punishment.

" They sinned," saith the apostle, " and provoked God; and their carcasses fell in the wilderness." To what end is this reported? It is that we might take heed that we " fall not after the same example of unbelief," Heb. iv. 11. There is an example in unbelief, and there is an example in the fall and punishment of unbelievers. This subject our apostle handles at large, 1 Cor. x. 5, 8–11. The substance of his discourse in that place is, that God made the people in the wilderness, upon their sinful provocations, examples of his severity unto them that should afterwards live ungodly. And the

apostle Peter declares the same truth in the instances of the angels
that sinned, the old world, and Sodom and Gomorrah, 2 Epist. ii. 4–6.
God made them ὑπόδειγμα, an express "example" and "representation" of what should be done in others. And in the law of old, the
reason why punishment was to be indispensably inflicted on presumptuous sinners, was that others might "hear and fear, and do so
no more." Besides, in that government of the world by his providence which God is pleased to continue, all ages and stories are full
of instances of exemplary judgments and punishments, befalling and
inflicted on such as have been notorious in their provocations; he
thereby "revealing his wrath from heaven against the ungodliness
of men," Rom. i. 18. And oftentimes those judgments have had in
them a direct testimony against and discovery of the nature of the
sins revenged by them. Our Saviour, indeed, hath taught us that
we are not to fix particular demerits and sins, by our own surmises,
on persons that may be overtaken with dismal providences in the
world, merely because they were so overtaken. Such was the condition of the "Galileans whose blood Pilate mingled with their sacrifices," and the "eighteen upon whom the tower in Siloam fell, and
slew them;" of whom he denies that, from what befell them, we have
any ground to judge that they were "greater sinners" than others,
Luke xiii. 1–5. This only in such cases may be concluded, namely,
that such persons were sinners as all are, and therefore righteously
obnoxious at any time unto any severe judgment of God.

And the reason of God's singling them out in such a manner is
that mentioned in the same place by our Saviour, namely, to declare and proclaim unto others in the like condition with themselves,
that "unless they repented, they should all likewise perish." And
so it befell this people, who neglected these instructive examples.
Within a few years, thousands and tens of thousands of them had
their blood, as it were, mingled with their sacrifices, being slain by
multitudes in the temple, the place of their offerings; and no less
number of them perishing in the fall and ruin of their walls and build-
ings, battered down by the Romans. But in such cases God takes out
men to be instructive in their sufferings unto others in a way of sovereignty, as he caused the man to be born blind, without any respect
unto particular demerit in himself or his parents, John ix. 2, 3.
But yet this hinders not but that when men's sins are visible, they
are, as the apostle speaks, "open beforehand, going before to judgment," 1 Tim. v. 24. They are πρόδηλοι, "manifest" to the judgment of all men, before they come to be laid open at the last day.
And they "go to judgment" before the sinners themselves are
brought thither. And with respect unto such as these, God may
and doth oftentimes, so connect provoking sins and extraordinary
judgments or punishments, that men cannot but see and own the

relation that is between them. Such were the sins of the old world and the flood, of Sodom and the fire, of Dathan and the earth opening its mouth to receive him, with the rest of the instances frequently enumerated in the Scripture. Such are all stories and reports of time in the world filled withal; and our own days have abounded with pregnant instances to the same purpose. And God will do thus,—

First, To *bear witness to his own holiness and severity.* In the ordinary course of the dispensation of his providence, God gives constant testimony unto his goodness and patience. " He maketh his sun to rise on the evil and on the good, and sendeth rain on the just and on the unjust," Matt. v. 45. He " never left himself without witness, in that he did men good, and gave them rain from heaven, and fruitful seasons, filling their hearts with food and gladness," Acts xiv. 17. This constant testimony doth God give unto his goodness and patience amongst men; and his design therein is to bring them to an acknowledgment of him, or to leave them in their wickedness utterly without excuse. For under the enjoyment of these things he leaves the generality of mankind; by whom for the most part they are abused, and God in them is despised. But things will not end so. He hath appointed a day wherein he will call them over again; and will require his corn, and wine, and oil, his health, his peace, his plenty, his prosperity, at the hands of men. Yet, though this be his ordinary way of proceeding, he doth not absolutely commit over his severity and indignation against sin to be manifested and asserted by his written threatenings and comminations of things future. He will sometimes " rise up to his work, his strange work; his act, his strange act," Isa. xxviii. 21;—that is, to execute great and fearful present judgments on sinners; which though it be and seem a " strange work," seldom coming to pass or effected, yet it is " his work," a work that becomes him, and whereby he will manifest his holiness and severity. He reveals his judgments from heaven against the ungodliness of men, Rom. i. 18; and this he doth by *exemplary punishments* on *exemplary sinners.*

Secondly, God doth thus to *check and control the atheism* that is in the hearts of men. Many, whilst they see wicked men, especially open and profligate sinners, prospering in a constant course, are ready to say in their hearts that there is no God, or that he hath forsaken the earth; or with Job, chap. ix. 24, "The earth is given into the hand of the wicked: . . . . . if not, where, and who is he?" —' Where is he, or who is he, that should punish them in or for all their enormous provocations?' or, as they, Mal. ii. 17, " Where is the God of judgment?" And this encourageth men in their wickedness, as the wise man expressly tells us: " Because sentence against an evil work is not executed speedily, therefore the heart of the sons of men is fully set in them to do evil," Eccles. viii. 11. The consideration hereof makes them cast off all regard of God, and to pursue the lusts of their hearts according to the power of their hand. To stay men in this course, God sometimes hurls a thunderbolt amongst them,—casts out an amazing judgment in a way of vengeance on some notable transgressors. When men have long travelled, or have been long upon a voyage at sea, if they meet with nothing but smiles of sun and wind, they are apt to grow careless and negligent, as though all must needs be smooth to their journey's end. But if at any time they are surprised with an unexpected clap of thunder, they begin to fear lest there be a storm yet behind. The language of nature upon such judgments as we speak of is, " Est profecto Deus, qui hæc videt et gubernat;" or as the psalmist expresseth it, " Verily there is a reward for the righteous: verily there is a God that judgeth in the earth." And were it not that God doth sometimes awe the world with his "strange work" of vengeance, which he executes at his pleasure, so that great sinners can never be secure one moment from them, it is to be feared that the atheism that is in the hearts of men would bring them everywhere to the condition of things before the flood, when the " whole earth was filled with violence," and " all flesh had corrupted its ways." But these judgments do secretly influence them with that dread and terror which prescribe some bounds to the lusts of the worst of men.

Thirdly, God will do thus for the *encouragement of them whom he hath designed to bear witness to himself* in the world against the wickedness of men. The principal work of the servants of God in the world is to bear witness unto God, his being, his holiness, his righteousness, his goodness, his hatred of sin. For this cause are they for the most part mocked, despised, and persecuted in the world. So saith our apostle: " For therefore we both labour and suffer reproach, because we trust in the living God," 1 Tim. iv. 10. And sometimes they are ready to faint in their trials. It is unto them like " a sword in their bones," while their enemies say unto them, " Where is your God?" Ps. xlii. 10. They have, indeed, a sure word of promise to trust unto and to rest upon, and that which is able to carry them safely and quietly through all temptations and oppositions; but yet God is pleased sometimes to relieve and refresh their spirits by confirming their testimony from heaven, bearing witness to himself and his holiness by his visible, tremendous judgments upon openly notorious provokers. So saith the psalmist: " God shall take them away as with a whirlwind, both living, and in his wrath;"—in the midst of their days he shall bring judgment and destruction upon them, fearfully, suddenly, unexpectedly, unavoidably, like a whirlwind. And what then? " The righteous shall rejoice when he seeth the vengeance; he shall wash his feet in the blood of the wicked," Ps. lviii. 9, 10;—that is, God's executing of dreadful judgments on wicked men to their destruction, shall justify them in their testimony and profession, and wash off all aspersions cast upon them; which shall cause them to "rejoice," or cleanse their own ways upon the example set before them, and the mouth of iniquity shall at least for a season be stopped.

The use hereof is,—1. That which Hannah proposeth, 1 Sam. ii. 3, "Talk no more so exceeding proudly; let not arrogancy come out of your mouth; for the LORD is a God of knowledge, and by him actions are weighed." Let men take heed how they arrogantly boast themselves in their sin and wickedness,—which is too common with provoking sinners; for God is a God of knowledge and judgment. If they regard not the judgment that is for to come, but put the evil day far away from them, yet let them take heed lest God single them out unto some signal vengeance in this world, to make them examples unto those that shall afterwards live ungodly. It is to me strange, that some men, considering their course and ways, should be so stupidly secure as not to fear every moment lest the earth should open and swallow them up, as it did Dathan and Abiram, or that thunder or lightning from heaven should consume them as it did Sodom, or that one judgment or other should overtake them as they are acting their villanies. But they are secure, and will cry "peace," until they are surprised with "sudden destruction."

2. Let us learn to glorify God because of his righteous judgments. The saints in heaven go before us in this work and duty, Rev. xi. 15–18, xv. 3, 4, xix. 1, 2. So they did of old in the earth; as in that signal instance of the song of Moses upon the destruction of the Egyptians in the Red Sea, Exod. xv. 1–19. And God requires it at our hands. Not that we should rejoice in the misery of men, but we should do so in the vindication of the glory of God, which is infinitely to be preferred before the impunity of profligate sinners.

Obs. IV. Great destructions, in a way of judgment and vengeance, are instituted representations of the judgment and vengeance to come.

I dare not say, with the Jews, that all this provoking generation perished eternally, and that none of them shall have a blessed lot or portion in the world to come. They might repent of their sins and provocations. The oath of God was as to their temporal punishment, not their eternal ruin. There is a repentance which may prevail for the removal, or at least deferring, of a temporal judgment threatened and denounced, if not confirmed by oath, which yet is not prevalent to free the sinner from eternal ruin. Such was the repentance of Ahab, and probably that of Nineveh. And there is a repentance and humiliation that may free the soul from eternal ruin, and yet not take off a temporal judgment threatened against it. Such was the repentance of David upon his adultery. The Lord put away the guilt of his sin, and told him that he should not die penally, but would not be entreated to spare the life of the child, nor him in those other sore afflictions which afterwards befell him on the same account. And thus might it be with some, yea, with many of those Israelites. God might give them repentance to make way for the pardon and forgiveness of their persons; nevertheless he would so far take vengeance on their inventions as to cause their carcasses to fall in the wilderness. But yet this must be acknowledged, that their punishment was a great representation of the future judgment, wherein ungodly unbelievers shall be cast off for ever; for, as they fell visibly under the wrath and displeasure of God, and their carcasses were cast out in the wilderness as a loathsome abomination, so their judgment overtook them under this formal consideration, that they were excluded out of the rest of God. And these things together give an evident resemblance of the judgment to come, when sinners shall perish eternally under the wrath of God, and be for ever excluded out of his rest. So Jude affirms the same of the destruction of Sodom and Gomorrah, verse 7. And hence many of God's great judgments in this world are set out under such expressions, as that the teaching of the dread of the final judgment at the last day seems principally to be intended in them. See Isa. xxxiv. 1–5; Dan. vii. 9–11; Matt. xxiv. 29; Heb. x. 26, 27; 2 Pet. iii. 5–7; Rev. vi. 12–17.

Ver. 18.—The apostle pursues his design yet further, in making application of the example laid down and insisted on unto the Hebrews, by way of interrogation, as to one circumstance more. And hereunto an answer is returned by him, and that such as is evidently supplied out of the story itself. Here also he discovers what was that particular sin which was the ground of all their other transgressions and miscarriages, the declaration of the danger and guilt whereof he principally intends: " And to whom sware he that they should not enter into his rest, but to them that believed not?"

The question proposed is annexed unto that foregoing, and declared to be designed unto the same purpose, by the respective copulative δέ, which we render "and," "And to whom." The words Δί.   of this question have been explained before on verse 11. Only here is one thing added. For whereas it is there said only that "God sware in his wrath that they should not enter into his rest," —that is, he sware so *concerning them*,—it is here intimated, that for their greater terror, and the manifestation of his wrath and indigna-

tion, he sware so *to them:* Τίσι ὤμοσε, "To whom did he swear." And
so it appears to have been from the story. For though
the words of the Lord were repeated unto the people by   Τίσι ὤμοσι.
Moses and Aaron, yet the people themselves are proposed as they
unto whom he spake and sware: "As ye have spoken in mine ears,
so will I do to you: your carcasses shall fall in this wilderness," Num.
xiv. 28, 29. This inquiry the apostle makes upon that typical example wherein the present condition of the church of the Hebrews
was represented.

The answer which he returns hereunto, which is evidently collected from the whole matter, contains the instruction
intended by him: Εἰ μὴ τοῖς ἀπειθήσασι; The word, as I   Τοῖς ἀπειθήσασι.
have showed, is variously rendered;—by some, "obeyed
not;" by some, " believed not;" by some, " assented not," " acqui-
esced not." Πείθω is " to persuade," by words, or any other means.
And ἀπειθέω is properly, " not to be persuaded," so as to do the thing
that the persuasion leads unto. And if that persuasion be with
authority, that dissent is "to be disobedient or contumacious." And
these are varied according as the proposal of the persuasion which
they respect hath been. For it may sometimes be by an exhortation in general, and sometimes it may be attended with commands,
promises, and threatenings, which vary, if not the kind, yet the degree
of the sin intended. 'Απείθεια is usually " inobedientia," " contu-
macia," and sometimes "rebellio;"—"disobedience," "stubbornness,"
or " rebellion." But the same words are often in the New Testament rendered by "unbelief," "infidelity," "incredulity," "not to believe;"—as indeed the word πίστις itself, or "faith," is from πείθω, "to
persuade;" and in other authors is nothing but that persuasion of
mind which is begotten in any man by the arguments and reasons
that are proposed unto him for that purpose. But the promiscuous
rendering of that word by " disobedience" or " unbelief," seeing
these things formally differ, is not so safe, and ought to be reduced
unto some certain rule. This, for aught I can perceive, interpreters
have not done, but have indifferently rendered it by the one word
or the other. 'Απείθεια, we render " unbelief," Rom. xi. 30, 32, Heb.
iv. 11; and by " disobedience," Eph. ii. 2, v. 6, Col. iii. 6; but for
the most part we place the other word in the margin: ἀπειθέω,
commonly, by " believe not," Rom. xi. 30, 31, xv. 31, Acts xiv. 2,
xvii. 5, xix. 9; sometimes by " obey not," Rom. ii. 8, x. 21, 1 Pet.
ii. 7, 8, iii. 20, iv. 17: and ἀπειθής everywhere by " disobedient,"
Luke i. 17, Acts xxvi. 19, Rom. i. 30, 2 Tim. iii. 2, Tit. i. 16, iii. 3.
And the like variety may be observed in other interpreters. I suppose, as was said, that the translation of this word may be reduced
unto some certain rule. 'Απείθεια and ἀπειθέω do certainly denote a
denial of the proper effect of πείθω: the effect of persuasion is not

produced. Now, this persuasion is not merely and solely an exhortation by words, but whatever it is that hath, or ought to have, a moral power to prevail with the mind of a man to do or not to do any thing, it hath the virtue of a persuasion. Thus in commands, in promises, in threatenings, there is a persuasion. This is common to them all, that they are fitted and suited to prevail with the minds of men to do or not to do the things which they do respect. But there is some peculiar adjunct whereby they are distinguished as to their persuasive efficacy,—as *authority* in commands, *faithfulness* in promises, *severity* in threatenings, *power* and *holiness* in all. That which is persuasive in commands, as formally such, is authority and power; that which is so in promises, is faithfulness and power; and so of threatenings. Look, then, in any place what is the formal reason of the persuasion whose disappointment is expressed by ἀπειθέω and ἀπείθεια, and we shall understand what it is that firstly and directly is intended by them. That whereby we answer a command is obedience, because of the authority wherewith it is attended, and our not being persuaded or prevailed on thereby is disobedience; that whereby we answer a promise is faith, or trust, or believing, and our failing herein is unbelief. Not that these things can be separated from one another, as though we could obey and not believe, or believe and not obey, but that they are thus distinguished one from another. Wherever, then, these expressions occur, we must consider whether they directly express the neglect of the command of God or of his promise. If it be of the former, they are duly rendered by " disobeying" and " disobedience;" if the latter, by "unbelief," " incredulity," and the like. Now, because these things are of a near alliance and cannot be separated, wherever one is expressed, the conjunction of the other is also understood; as in this place. Their ἀπείθεια did principally respect the *promise* of God to give them the land of Canaan, and his power to effect it, so that *unbelief* is firstly and principally intended,—they would *not believe* that he would or could bring them into that land ; but yet because they were also under the command of God to go up and possess it, their unbelief was accompanied with disobedience and rebellion. This, then, is the meaning of these words in this place, '"To whom did he swear that they should not enter into his rest?" It was unto them to whom the promise of it being made, and a command given that they should be ready to go up and possess it, they would not, they did not acquiesce in the faithfulness and power of God, believed not his word, and thereupon yielded not obedience unto his command.' And this was sufficient both to provoke and justify the severity of God against them in his oath, and the execution of it.

Obs. I. All unbelief is accompanied with contumacy and rebellion.

It is ἀπείθεια, and those in whom it is are not persuaded to comply with the mind and will of God. I intend that *privative unbelief* which hath been before explained. When the object or thing to be believed is sufficiently proposed and made known unto any person, which renders it his duty actually to believe, especially when it is proposed in the way and manner prescribed by God in the gospel,— that is, with the highest reasons, motives, and persuasive induce ments conceivable,—if such a person mix not the word spoken with faith, his unbelief is privative, and ruinous to his soul; and that because it hath contumacy and rebellion accompanying of it. Now, two things concur in disobedience, contumacy, and rebellion (for I use them in the same general sense, as those which agree in the same general nature, for they denote only distinct aggravations of the same sin): First, An *unpersuadableness of mind*, and that against evident convincing reasons. When a man is persuaded by such as have right, or whose duty it is so to deal with him unto the doing of any thing, or the belief of any truth, with and by the use of such arguments as are suited in such cases to work and prevail with the minds of men, and he have nothing to object to what is proposed unto him, and yet complieth not in a way of obedience or assent, we say such an one is obstinate and perverse, one not persuaded by reason; he is " *contumax.*" See Prov. i. 23–25. Secondly, A *positive act of the will* in opposition unto and in rejection of the things proposed unto it, as those which it likes not, it approves not of, but rather despiseth, Isa. xxx. 15. Now, if among the arguments used to prevail with the mind, that of supreme authority be one, then *rebellion* is added unto *disobedience* and stubbornness, Rom. x. 21. And both these concur in unbelief. Unbelievers 'may pretend, may plead other things, why they do not believe, or they may profess that they do believe when they are utter strangers from it; but the true reason of this abode in their state and condition is the unpersuadableness of their minds, and the disobedience of their wills, both attended with contumacy and rebellion against God. To evince this we may consider,—

1. That the gospel requiring faith in the promises, doth obviate or take away all objections that can be made against it on any account whatever. Objections against believing may arise either,— (1.) On the part of him who is the *author* of the things proposed to be believed;—and that either, [1.] as unto his *power* and faithfulness; or, [2.] as unto his *will*, goodness, and grace. Or, (2.) They may arise on the part of the *things themselves* proposed to be believed ;—as that they are either, [1.] not *good* and desirable in themselves; or, [2.] not *needful;* or, [3.] not *adequate* or suited unto the end for which they are proposed. Or, (3.) On the part of the *persons themselves* required to believe;—as that they are not

things for them, but that they are either [1.] too hard and difficult
for them to attain; or [2.] tòo good for them to expect; or [3.] too
far above them to understand. But now all these objections are
obviated and prevented in the gospel. And no ground is left unto
any sinner whereon he may manage any of them against the exhortations and commands of it to believe. This hath been so well evidenced in particular by sundry holy and learned persons, that I shall
not need to insist thereon.

2. The gospel makes it appear that its commands and exhortations to believe are most *reasonable in themselves*, and most reasonably to be accepted by sinners; and that on all accounts of reason
whatever: as, (1.) Upon the account of *righteousness* in him that
requires faith or belief of men. He that doth so may do so, and
that justly. He requires no more but what is due unto him, and
which cannot be denied him without the highest sin, folly, and disorder. This the gospel fully declares. It is God who requires faith
in us; and it is so far from being unrighteous that he should so do,
that it is of infinite grace and love that he will. (2.) On the account
of *necessity* on the part of them who are required to believe. This
also the gospel lays open and naked before the eyes of men. It doth
not leave them to flatter themselves with vain hopes, as though
they might do well enough without answering the command of God
in this matter, or might find out some other way for their help and
relief; but it plainly and frequently declares that without the due
performance of this duty they must perish, and lie under the wrath
of God to eternity. (3.) On the account of the *goodness, grace, and
condescension* that are in the proposal of the object of faith, and the
command of beliêving. The things themselves are excellent and
precious, and our advantage by an interest in them so great and
unspeakable, as that they are everywhere in the gospel manifested
to be the effects of infinite grace and love. (4.) Of *safety:* an end
is proposed to be aimed at, and that deliverance from sin, death,
hell, and vengeance everlasting; with the attainment of rest, peace,
and blessedness, in the enjoyment of God. This end all convinced
persons aim at; and there is a secret preparation in the seeds of
natural light to incline the minds of men to seek after this end.
Now, the gospel proposeth the things which it requires to be believed as the only way and means for the attaining this end; and that
this way is safe and secure, that never any one miscarried in it, or
shall do so for ever, it gives all the assurance that the word, promise, covenant, and oath of God can yield or afford. On all which
it follows that it is a reasonable thing that we should believe.

3. Consider the *manner* how the gospel proposeth unto us the
object of faith, or the things which it requireth us to believe. It doth
not do this by a mere naked revelation or declaration of them unto

us, attended with a severe command. It adds entreaties, exhortations, reasonings, encouragements, promises, threatenings; every way it proceedeth that is meet and suited to prevail on the minds of rational creatures. All the things of our own eternal concernment are proposed unto us with that gentleness, tenderness, condescension, that love, that earnestness, that evidence of a high concern in us and our good, that patheticalness and compassionate affection, as will assuredly aggravate the guilt of rejecting the tender which it makes.

4. All these things the gospel proposeth, urgeth, presseth upon us in the *name and authority of God.* It requireth, exacteth, and commandeth faith in men, in a way of obedience unto the supreme authority of God.

Now, if these things, and sundry others of the like consideration, do concur in the proposals and commands of the gospel, it is evident that sinners' unbelief must have disobedience, contumacy, and rebellion accompanying of it. For can a man refuse that which is so proposed unto him, upon such reasons and considerations, in the way and manner intimated, all enforced with the authority of God, but that he must contract the guilt of the highest rebellion against him? And hence it is that the Scripture everywhere layeth the cause of men's unbelief on their wills, their love of sin, their obstinacy and hardness of heart, as hath been before declared. And hence it will follow, that,—

Obs. II. Unbelief not only justifies but glorifies the greatest severities of God against them in whom it prevails.

The apostle having declared the severity of God towards the people in the wilderness, adds this as the reason of it,—it was because of their "unbelief." They provoked him by their unbelief, and therefore were so severely destroyed as he had declared. And besides, his principal intention is to manifest that those who follow them in the same sin, now under the gospel, would in like manner perish, and that eternally; and that in their destruction God will glorify himself. The truth of this proposition is sufficiently evinced from what hath been discoursed on that foregoing; for if there be that contumacy and rebellion attending unbelief which we have manifested, it will undeniably follow that God is exceeding righteous and glorious in his greatest severities against them who abide in the guilt of it; in this, that "he that believeth not the Son shall not see life, but the wrath of God abideth on him," John iii. 36. I shall add only one consideration more for the further evidencing of this truth: The design of God in the gospel, in and by the things proposed unto our faith, is to glorify himself and all the holy attributes of his nature. And this is the effect of his counsel and wisdom, after that many of them were, as it were, obscured by sin, unto the eternal ruin of sinners: God, I say, in the gospel, through the mediation of Christ, the principal subject of all the promises and immediate object of our faith, designeth to manifest and glorify his righteousness and holiness, Rom. iii. 24–26; his power and wisdom, 1 Cor. i. 18, 23, 24; his mercy, grace, and goodness, Eph. i. 6; his patience and forbearance, 2 Pet. iii. 9; his faithfulness and bounty in rewarding believers with eternal life, Rom. vi. 23. In sum, by this way and means he hath designed that manifestation of himself, his nature, his will, his goodness, his wisdom and counsel, wherein he will be admired, adored, and glorified by angels and men unto eternity, 2 Thess. i. 10. This is the design of God in and by the gospel. And it is that which becomes him, because it is natural and necessary unto him in all things to will his own glory. Now, unbelief is nothing but the attempt of sin and Satan to frustrate the whole design of God, to make him a liar, 1 John v. 10, to keep him from being owned, acknowledged, and worshipped, as God only wise, infinitely righteous, holy, faithful, gracious, and bountiful. And this upon the matter is to oppose the being of God. It is to deny that he was righteous and holy in requiring the punishment due to sin of our Sponsor or Mediator,—that is, in punishing sin; to deny that he was infinitely wise and gracious in sending his Son to save that which was lost; to deny that the way which he hath provided for the salvation of sinners is good, sufficient, and safe; to deny his faithfulness in the accomplishment of his promises, and his truth and veracity about what he hath affirmed concerning the salvation of sinners by Jesus Christ. And where, then, is the glory of God? or what is left unto him for which he should be glorified or worshipped? And can this atheistical, rebellious attempt be too severely revenged? Is not God not only justified in that decretory sentence, " He that believeth not shall be damned," but doth it not in the hearts of all the creation cry aloud for the vindication of his glory from this great contempt cast upon it, and horrible attempt to frustrate his design for the advancement of it? As sure as God is God, unbelief shall not go unpunished. Yea, from the gracious salvation of believers, and righteous condemnation of them who will not believe, doth arise that great and triumphant glory wherein God will be admired and adored by the whole rational creation unto eternity. And this further appears; for,—

Obs. III. The oath of God is engaged against no sin but unbelief.

As God hath given his oath for the confirmation and consolation of believers, both as to the things which they are to believe and as to their assured safety on their believing, and to nothing else directly in a way of *grace*, for it is annexed unto his covenant; so he hath in a way of *justice* engaged his oath against no sin but that of unbelief, and to the exclusion of unbelievers from eternal rest. "To whom sware he that they should not enter into his rest, but to them that believed not?" Other sins there are that have great provocations in them,—so had the murmurings of the people in the wilderness; but it is their relation unto unbelief, their growing upon that stock or root, that gives them such a height of provocation, as that God at any time enters a caveat against them by his oath. And in this sense it is not said amiss, that *unbelief* is the only damning sin; because as there is no other sin but may be, but shall be, remitted or pardoned unto men upon believing, so the formal consideration on which other sins fall under judgment, in them to whom the gospel is preached, is unbelief.

These things I shall put together, to represent the apostle's exhortation, with the grounds and reasons of it, as unto our own concernment therein. For these things belong unto us, and they may be improved unto the use of all sorts of persons; as,—

1. Unto them who have never *much considered* their duty or concernment in this matter. I intend not open and profligate sinners, though the terror hereof will one day reach them in particular. "This is their condemnation, that light is come into the world, and they love darkness more than light, because their deeds are evil." But it is them whom I aim at, whose consciences are so far awakened as that they would abstain from sin, and do good, with respect unto their latter end. They would be saved from "the wrath to come," but as to believing, or mixing the promise of the gospel with faith, they have not endeavoured after it, or do not at all understand it. But this is the hinge on which their eternal condition doth turn. They may do well, therefore, to consider what hath been said from the apostle in this matter, and what is their concern therein, to examine their hearts what hath passed between God and them. For with whom is God provoked? concerning whom doth he thus swear that they shall not enter into his rest? Is it not against you, and such as you are, who believe not, whilst you continue in that state and condition?

2. Unto those who are *in doubt* whether they should believe or no; not *notionally* and *indefinitely*, but *practically* and in particular. This is the state of many in their minds and consciences, which causeth them to fluctuate all their days. But what is it that they doubt of in this matter? Is it whether it be their duty to believe or no?—it is indispensably required of them, by the command of God; so that not to do so is the greatest height of disobedience that they can make themselves guilty of. Is it whether they may do so or no, and whether they shall find acceptance with God in their so doing?—this calls the righteousness and faithfulness of God in question; it is no otherwise, where to believe is our duty by vir-

tue of his command, to question our acceptance in the performance
of that duty. Is it because of the many objections which they find
arising up in themselves against themselves, which leave them no
hope of a personal participation of the good things promised?—but
what are all their objections before those evidences that are tendered in the gospel unto the contrary, which we have touched upon?
The truth is, if men will not believe, it is out of love to sin, and a
dislike of the design of God to glorify himself by Jesus Christ; and
what will be the issue thereof hath been declared. If, then, it be a
question with you whether you shall believe or not, consider what
will be the event if you do not. The demerit of your sin is such as
that it will justify, yea, and glorify God, in his greatest severity
against you; and his *oath* is engaged that you shall never enter into
his rest. What like this can you fear on the other hand? and why
do you doubt what course to take?

3. Unto *believers*. Meat may be taken for them out of this eater.
All this terror and dread of God's severity speaks peace and consolation unto their souls; for as the oath of God is engaged against the
entrance of unbelievers into rest, so also is it for the eternal security
of them that do believe.

Ver. 19.—So we see that they could not enter in, because
of unbelief.

This verse contains, in a *summary conclusion*, what the apostle
had evinced by all his former arguings from the example of their
forefathers as recorded by Moses, and the renewed representation of
it for their use by David. And he lays it down as the especial
foundation of that exhortation which he intends to pursue in the
next chapter.

Καὶ βλίπομιν. "And we see;" that is, 'It is evident from what hath
been laid down and proved;' or, 'This we have evinced,
given an ocular demonstration of it.'

"Now we see;"and this evident conclusion consists of two parts:—
1. An assertion, "That they could not enter in." 2. The reason of
it, "Because of unbelief." 1. In the first the apostle doth not only
declare the "factum" and event,—they did not enter, they died in
the wilderness, there their carcasses fell; but the "jus" also, in a
negation, οὐκ ἠδυνήθησαν,—"they could not enter;" that
Οὐκ ἠδυνή- is, they lost all right unto an entrance by virtue of any
θησαν. promise of God. Whatever desire they had so to do,
as they manifested their desires by their mourning at the heavy
tidings brought them by Moses concerning their exclusion, Num.
xiv. 39; whatever attempts they made for that end, as they got
themselves up and fell upon the Canaanites and Amalekites that were
next them, so to begin their conquest, by whom they were defeated,

verses 40, 44, 45; having lost all right unto the promise, "they could not enter." "Illud possumus, quod jure possumus;"—" In things moral our ability is commensurate unto our right." This being lost, " they could not enter." The expression is elliptical, and "God's rest" is to be supplied from the foregoing verse. "He sware they should not enter into his rest." And his determination is the rule of our right. *Εἰσελθεῖν.*

2. The reason and cause hereof is expressed in the last words, " Because of unbelief." They that shall look over the whole story of the sins of the people, and of God's deal- *Δι᾽ ἀπιστίαν.* ing with them, would perhaps of themselves fix upon other causes of their exclusion from the rest of God, as the Jews their posterity do to this day. Might not they say, 'It was because of their idolatry in making the golden calf, which became a reproach unto them in all ages?' So great a sin this was, that when God passed it by, as to their present destruction, he reserved, as it were, liberty to himself to remember it in after-visitations. Exod. xxxii. 34: " Go," saith he, " lead the people unto the place of which I have spoken unto thee. .....Nevertheless, in the day when I visit, I will visit their sin upon them." Hence the Jews have a saying, that "no trouble be-falleth Israel but there is in it an ounce of the golden calf." Or, they might think the cause of it was their abominable mixture of all sorts of sins, in their conjunction with the Midianites and Moabites, worshipping Baal-peor, eating the sacrifices of the dead, and giving themselves up unto uncleanness. Their frequent murmurings also would occur unto their minds. But our apostle lays it here abso-lutely and wholly on their unbelief, and evidently proves it so to have been. A sin this is that men are very unapt to charge themselves withal; but that which above all others will be charged on them by God. And this is here charged on this people most righteously,—

(1.) Because the name which God was then designing to glorify among them, and himself thereby, was that of JEHOVAH: Exod. vi. 3, 'I will now be known by my name JEHOVAH.' And his purpose, by the renewed revelation and engagement of that name, was to teach them that he would now manifest the stability of his promises in their accomplishment. By their unbelief, therefore, did they rebel against God, and oppose his design in the especial revela-tion of himself whereby he would be glorified.

(2.) Because their unbelief was the spring and cause of all their other sins. Hence were their idolatries, and adulteries, and mur-murings, and all their other provocations.

(3.) Because they had herein often broken with God from under great convictions; for oftentimes, upon his mighty works, their minds had been conquered to the profession of faith and confidence: "The people feared the LORD, and believed the LORD, and his servant Moses,"

Exod. xiv. 31. But immediately on the next trial they met withal they renounced their own experiences, and despised the faithfulness and power of God, which before they acknowledged, chap. xv. 24.

(4.) Because their last provocation was with direct respect unto the promise, which we have at large insisted on from Num. xiv., "So we see that they could not enter in, because of unbelief."

There are sundry things that these words present unto us for our instruction; but as this verse is but a recapitulation of, and conclusion from what was before disputed and confirmed, so the practical truths contained in it have formerly occurred unto us as to the substance or main design of them; and some of them we shall be again minded of in the beginning of the next chapter. Here, therefore, I shall only briefly propose them; and they are these that follow:—

Obs. I. Whatever we consider in sin, God principally considers the root and spring of it in unbelief, as that which maketh the most direct and immediate opposition unto himself.

The people in the wilderness were guilty of many provoking sins before God entered the caution mentioned against their entrance into his rest; yet the Holy Ghost sums up all here in their unbelief. This was that which God regarded, and which he would not pass by without a severe animadversion upon it; for indeed,—

Obs. II. Unbelief is the immediate root and cause of all provoking sins.

As faith is the spring and cause of all obedience (for "without faith it is impossible to please God," and the obedience that is accepted with him is "the obedience of faith"), so is unbelief of all sin. All sins of flesh and spirit have no other root. Did men believe either the promises or threatenings of God, they would not by their sins so despise him and neglect him as they do. And as this is so with respect unto the *total prevalency of unbelief,* so it is as to its partial efficacy. As our obedience follows in proportion to the operation of our faith, so do all our sins and irregularities answer the working and prevalency of unbelief in us.

Obs. III. To disbelieve God with respect unto any especial design of glorifying himself, is the greatest and highest provocation.

Thus was it with this wilderness generation. God in his dealings with them had a great design in hand. He was now about to glorify himself, by his faithfulness in his promise and oath unto Abraham, his power in the deliverance of the people, and his grace in bringing of them into a typical rest. This design of God did they, as much as lay in them, endeavour to frustrate by their unbelief. This, therefore, God will not bear withal in them. The especial design of God under the gospel, is to glorify himself in Jesus Christ, by the deliverance of his elect, according to his promise and covenant, from death and hell, and the bringing of them unto eternal rest. Unbelief in this matter lies against this great and glorious design of God; and it is evident what will be the end thereof: for,—

Obs. IV. Unbelief deprives men of all interest in or right unto the promises of God.

There was a promise given unto this people of their being brought into the land of Canaan; but yet they entered not into it,—they died in the wilderness. How came this to pass? The apostle here declares that they disinherited themselves, and lost all their interest in the promise, by their unbelief. And let not others entertain better hopes of their condition hereafter, whilst here they follow their example; for,—

Obs. V. No unbeliever shall ever enter into the rest of God; which, ἐὰν ὁ Κύριος ϑελήσῃ, καὶ ζήσωμεν, shall be confirmed in our considerations on the next chapter.

Μόνῳ τῷ Θεῷ δόξα.

CHAPTER IV.

THIS chapter is of the same nature and carrieth on the same design with that foregoing. That contained an exhortation unto faith, obedience, and perseverance, enforced by an instance in the pernicious event or punishment which befell them who were guilty of sin contrary unto those duties. And this was done by the exposition and application of a *prophetical testimony,* suggesting an example of God's dealing with unbelievers formerly. Now, whereas in the words of the psalmist there is not only a *moral example* proposed unto us, but a prophecy also is interwoven therein concerning the rest of God in Christ by the gospel, and our duty thereon, the apostle proceeds to expound, improve, and confirm his exhortation from the scope, design, and words of that prophecy. Wherefore, in the beginning of this chapter he resumes his exhortation, in an immediate coherence with and dependence upon what he had before discoursed. Hence some think that the first verse of this chapter is unduly cut off and separated from that foregoing, whereunto it doth belong; yea, some, as we intimated before, that this discourse of the apostle doth immediately succeed unto the 14th verse of the preceding chapter, that which ensueth being a digression to be included in a parenthesis. But, as was said, the words of the psalmist containing a representation of a moral example from things past in the church, and a prophetical description of the future state and condition of the church, the apostle having made use of the former or moral example, in the preceding discourses, arguings, expostulations, and exhortations, here entereth upon the exposition and improvement of the latter, or the words of the psalmist, with reference unto their prophetical prospect towards the times of the gospel, and the instruction which was laid up for the use of those times in the example that he had insisted on. Herein,—

1. He proposeth the *duty* which he aimeth to press upon those Hebrews, as that which is required in the words of the psalmist, from the example represented in them; with an especial enforcement of it, from the consideration of the *sin and punishment* of them whose example is proposed, which followeth thereon, verses 1, 2.

2. He vindicates the foundation of his *exhortation*, by showing that the "rest" which the psalmist speaks of, and which he persuades them to endeavour an entrance into, and to take heed that they fail not, or come not short of, was yet remaining to be enjoyed, verse 3; as being neither the rest of God from the works of creation, with the sabbatical rest which ensued thereon, verses 4–6 ; nor yet the rest of Canaan, which Joshua brought the people into, verses 7, 8; but a spiritual rest, which remained for believers to enjoy, verses 8–10.

3. Hence he resumes his *exhortation* with respect unto his explication and vindication of the prophetical testimony by him produced, verse 11.

4. This he again strengtheneth by a *double argument* or consideration:—(1.) In a way of caution, by proposing unto them the nature of the word of God wherein they were concerned, verses 12, 13. (2.) In a way of encouragement from the priesthood of Christ, whereby this rest was procured for believers; and therein makes a transition to the declaration and exposition of that priesthood, with the effects and consequents of it, in the six ensuing chapters.

VERSES 1, 2.

Φοβηθῶμεν οὖν, μή ποτε, καταλειπομένης ἐπαγγελίας εἰσελθεῖν εἰς τὴν κατάπαυσιν αὐτοῦ, δοκῇ τις ἐξ ὑμῶν ὑστερηκέναι. Καὶ γάρ ἐσμεν εὐηγγελισμένοι, καθάπερ κἀκεῖνοι· ἀλλ᾽ οὐκ ὠφέλησεν ὁ λόγος τῆς ἀκοῆς ἐκείνους, μὴ συγκεκραμένος τῇ πίστει τοῖς ἀκούσασιν.

Ver. 1.—Φοβηθῶμεν οὖν, "timeamus ergo," "metuamus igitur,"—more properly, "let us fear, therefore."

Μή ποτε. Vulg. Lat., "ne forte." Rhem., "lest perhaps,"—as though it intended the uncertainty of the event. Beza and Eras., "ne quando," "lest at any time." Ours omit the force of ποτέ, "lest." If it have an especial signification, it respects the several seasons or occasions which in the "fear" enjoined we ought to have regard unto.

Καταλειπομένης ἐπαγγελίας. Vulg. Lat., "relicta pollicitatione:" "pollicitatio" being an improper word in this matter, all modern translators have changed it into "promissio." Rhem., "forsaking the promise." But the words in the V. L. are capable of another sense,—namely, "a promise being left." Beza and Eras., "derelicta promissione;" which determines the sense, "the promise being left," " forsaken," " neglected:" accordingly the Ethiopic, " let us not reject his command." The Syriac otherwise, with respect to the continuance of a promise, דְּלְמָא כָּד קָים מוּלְכָנָא,—" ne forte stante promissione," " ne forte dum stat promissio,"—" lest whilst the promise standeth," "continueth," or " is firm," namely, of entering into rest. This is followed by the Arabic, " whereas a certain promise remaineth." Of this difference in sense we must treat in our exposition of the words.

Εἰσελθεῖν εἰς τὴν κατάπαυσιν αὐτοῦ. See chap. iii. 11, 18.

Δοκῇ τις ἐξ ὑμῶν ὑστερηκέναι. Vulg. Lat., "existimetur aliquis è vobis deesse." Rhem., " some of you be thought to be wanting." " Deesse" neither expresseth the meaning of the original word nor hath any proper sense in this place, as both Erasmus and Beza observe. Arias, " defici," " fail." Δοκῇ: Eras., Bez., "videatur," "should seem " or " appear;" more properly than "existimetur," it referring to the persons spoken unto, and their deportment, not the opinion or judgment of others concerning them. Ὑστερηκέναι: Eras., " frustratus fuisse," " to have been frustrated;" that is, in his hopes, expectations, profession, or of entering. Men will be deceived, if they hope to enter into God's rest and yet neglect his promise; which is the sense he takes the words in. Beza, " fuisse per tarditatem exclusus;" endeavouring to express the precise signification of the word he somewhat obscures the sense,— to have been excluded from it by keeping behind," by slowness, in not going forward. Δοκῇ τις ἐξ ὑμῶν: The Syriac, נשתכח אֱנָשׁ מִנְכוּן, " a man should be found amongst you;" omitting that sense of the word δοκῇ which many expositors insist on, as we shall see. Arab., " any one of you should think." Ὑστερηκέναι: Syr. fills up the sense, דְּפָאֵשׁ מֶן דַלְמֶעַל, " that should cease from entering," or " fail of entering." Ours, " seem to come short of it," properly.

Ver. 2.—Καὶ γάρ ἐσμεν εὐηγγελισμένοι. Vulg. Lat., " etenim et nobis nunciatum est." Erasmus, " annunciatum est." Rhem., " for unto us it was denounced." Improperly all of them, nor is " denounce" any way significant in this matter. Beza, " etenim nobis evangelizatum est." Ours, " for unto us was the gospel preached," and so the word signifies: " etenim sumus evangelizati," " for we are evangelized;" of which construction afterwards. Syr., אסתברין, " nunciatum est;" more properly, " evangelizatum est," " the gospel is," or " was preached."

Ὁ λόγος τῆς ἀκοῆς. Vulg. Lat., " sermo auditus." Rhem., " the word of hearing;" taking " auditus" for a substantive and not a participle, which also the original requireth. Eras., " non profuit illis audisse sermonem," " it profited them not to have heard the word." Ours, " the word preached." Syr., מלתא דשמעו, " the word which they heard." Of the meaning of the phrase of speech used in the original we shall treat afterwards.

Μὴ συγκεκραμένος. The Complutensian copy, which is followed by sundry vulgar editions, reads συγκεκραμένους, making this word agree with ἐκείνους, " those that heard," and not with λόγος, " the word" that was heard. And this reading is followed by the Arabic and Ethiopic translations. Συγκεκραμένος: Vulg. Lat., " admistus;" Eras., " cum fide conjunctus;" Beza, " contemperatus;"—all to the same purpose, " mixed," " joined," " tempered," with faith.

Τῇ πίστει. " Fide," " cum fide," " fidei,"—" with faith," " unto the faith."

Τοῖς ἀκούσασιν. Vulg. Lat., " fidei ex iis quæ audiverant." Rhem., " with faith of those things which they heard;" referring τοῖς to the things heard, and not to the persons hearing; but that ἀκούσασιν will not bear.[1]

---

[1] VARIOUS READINGS.—Συγκεκραμέν. Instead of the Attic form, some codices have συγκεκερασμένος, which Ebrard deems the true reading. Συγκεκερασμένους is the reading of codices A B C D, as also of several important versions. Recent commentators, with the exception of Ebrard, prefer the latter; in which case the sense would be, "because they were not united in the faith with those who obeyed."

Ver. 1, 2.—Let us therefore fear, lest, a promise being
left of entering into his rest, any of you should seem at
any time to come short [*to fail*]. For unto us was the
gospel preached, even as unto them [*we were evangelized
even as they*]; but the word of hearing did not profit
them, being not mixed with faith in them that heard.

These two verses, as they may and do contain an improvement of
the example and inferences made from it, as expressed in the preceding chapter, so withal and principally the apostle gives the Hebrews a further demonstration that what he had insisted on was of
near concernment unto them, and that their condition was therein
represented. For they might be apt to say, ' What have we to do
with the people in the wilderness, with the promise of entering into
Canaan, or with what the psalmist from thence exhorted our fathers
unto of old, who were still held under the same dispensation?' But
saith the apostle, ' These things belong unto you in an especial manner; for besides that you may in the example proposed see evidently
what you are to look for and expect from God, if you fall into the
same sin which he therein expresseth his severity against, so the
things treated of in the psalm are a prophetical direction designed
for your especial use in your present condition.'

The way in particular which the apostle insists on to press these
things upon them is,—1. By *exhorting* them to that duty and those
considerations which are the just consequents of the things by him
proposed unto them; 2. By *manifesting* that their concernment in
those things did afford him a just foundation of his exhortation.
The exhortation is contained in the first verse, and the confirmation
of it in the second.

Ver. 1.—And there is, verse 1,—1. The frame of spirit expressed
which the apostle exhorts the Hebrews unto, on the consideration
of what he had minded them of, and of their interest therein,—
" Let us therefore fear." 2. A supposition on which the exhortation
to this duty and frame is founded,—" A promise being left of entering into rest." 3. The evil to be prevented by attendance unto the
duty proposed,—" Lest any of you should seem to come short of it."
Whether this be an evil of sin or of punishment shall be afterwards
inquired into.

Ver. 2.—There ensues in the second verse a confirmation of what
is in the first proposed, and that,—1 On the account of a parity in

TRANSLATIONS.—Καταλ. ἰπαγγ. The *promise being contemned.—Erasmus,*
Luther, Calvin, Gerhard. That no one appear to remain behind *the promise
which is still left.—Cramer, Ernesti.* That no one show himself as too late, *seeing
that a promise is still with us.—Bleek, Olshausen, Stuart.* Lest *while there is a
promise to be fulfilled,* any of you imagine that he has come too late.—*Schöttgen,
Baumgarten, Schulz, Wahl, Bretschneider, Ebrard.*—ED.

condition between us and those from whom the example is taken,
—" Unto us was the gospel preached, even as unto them." 2. On
the account of the evil success of them in that condition, with the
reason thereof,—" But the word preached did not profit them, because it was not mixed with faith in them that heard."

Our way being thus prepared, we may open the words in particular as they lie in the context.

Φοζηθῶμεν οὖν. Οὖν, "therefore." An illative, manifesting the deduction of the present exhortation from the preceding
discourse and example. We have now several times
observed that the apostle is constant unto this method, namely, of
educing new exhortations immediately out of arguments doctrinally
proposed and confirmed. This makes his discourse nervous, and his
exhortation efficacious; shutting up the minds of them with whom
he deals, leaving them no place unto evasion or tergiversation. And
herein, unto the weight and authority of his words, he adds the
reasonableness of his inferences, and from both concludes the necessity of the duty which he proposeth.

Φοζηθῶμεν,—"Let us fear." The noun φόζος, and the verb φοζέομαι,
are used in the New Testament to express all sorts of
"fears" and "fearing;" such are natural, civil, sinful,
and religious fear. They are therefore of a larger extent, and more
various use, than any one radical word in the Old Testament.

The fear here intended is religious, relating to God, his worship,
and our obedience. And this is fourfold:—First, Of *terror.*
Secondly, Of *diffidence.* Thirdly, Of *reverence.* Fourthly, Of *care,*
solicitousness, and watchfulness. And concerning these, I shall first
show what they are, or wherein they consist, and then inquire which
of them it is that is here intended:—

First, There is a *fear of dread and terror;* and this respecteth
either, 1. God; or, 2. Other things, wherein we may be concerned
in his worship:—

1. Of God. And this is either expressive of, (1.) The object, the
thing feared, or God himself; or, (2.) The subject, or person fearing,
the frame of heart in him that feareth:—

(1.) Fear respects the object of fear, that which we do fear:
"Knowing therefore τὸν φόζον τοῦ Κυρίου," 2 Cor. v. 11,—"the fear of
the Lord," or the "terror," as we render it; that is, how great,
dreadful, holy, and terrible he is. Hence Jacob calls God, פַּחַד יִצְחָק,
Gen. xxxi. 42, 53,—the "Fear of Isaac," or him whom Isaac served,
worshipped, feared. And פַּחַד, when it respects the subject, denotes that kind of fear which hath greatness, dread, and terror for
an object; whereas they express a reverential fear by יְרָאָה. This
fear the apostle hath respect unto, Heb. xii. 28, 29: "Let us serve
God acceptably with reverence and godly fear; for our God is a

consuming fire." The fear of dread and terror in God, requires the fear of reverence in us, in all that we have to do with him. A respect hereunto is expressed by sinners, Isa. xxxiii. 14, and Mic. vi. 6, 7.

(2.) Fear expresseth that frame of heart and spirit which is in men towards an object apprehended dreadful and fearful. And this also is twofold:—

[1.] A consternation and dread of spirit, on the apprehension of *God as an enemy*, as one that will punish and avenge sin. This is עַד, which is joined with פַּלָּצוּת, Ps. lv. 6, "a trembling horror." This befell Adam upon his sin, and that inquisition that God made about it, Gen. iii. 10; and Cain, Gen. iv. 13. Such a consideration of God as would beget this frame in him Job often deprecates, chap. ix. 34, xxiii. 6. And the same is intended in the places above cited, Isa. xxxiii. 14; Mic. vi. 6, 7. Something hereof befell them of old who, upon the apprehension that they had seen God, concluded that they should die. They had a dread which fell on them from an apprehension of his excellency and holiness, and terrified them with thoughts that they should be consumed. And this fear, in its latitude, is a consternation of spirit, on an apprehension of God's greatness and majesty, with respect unto present or future judgments,—when the mind is not relieved by faith in the reconciliation made by Jesus Christ,— weakening, disheartening, and alienating the heart from God.

[2.] An awful fear of *God's greatness and holiness*, with respect unto deserved and impendent judgments in this world. This fear may befall believers, and be at some seasons their especial duty. This David expresseth, Ps. cxix. 120, "My flesh trembleth for fear of thee; and I am afraid of thy judgments." And elsewhere on the same account he declares that "fearfulness and trembling laid hold on him," Ps. lv. 5. So Habakkuk expresseth his condition under the like apprehension, chap. iii. 16, "When I heard, my belly trembled; my lips quivered at the voice: rottenness entered into my bones, and I trembled in myself." And this fear of dread and terror, thus qualified, is both good and useful in its kind. And this is that which Joshua labours to ingenerate in the minds of the people, chap. xxiv. 19, 20. And of great use it is to the souls of men, both before and after their conversion unto God. Of a fear of awe and reverence in general, with respect unto the greatness and holiness of God, we shall treat afterwards.

2. There may be a fear of dread and terror in our way of obedience, which may respect *other things*. Such are the oppositions and difficulties which we do or may meet withal, either from within or without, in our course, which may incline us to despondency and despair. This in particular befell David, when, notwithstanding the promise of God to the contrary, he concluded that "he should one day perish by the hand of Saul," 1 Sam. xxvii. 1. This the Scripture

expresseth by חָתַת, which we render "to be dismayed," Josh. i. 9, "Be not terrified, nor be thou dismayed." The word signifies "to be broken;" and when applied unto the mind, it denotes "to be sore terrified, so as to sink in courage and resolution;" which we well express by being "dismayed,"—to be broken and weakened in mind, through a terror arising from the apprehension of oppositions, difficulties, and dangers. It is ascribed unto men when God strikes a terror into them, or when they are terrified with their own fears, Isa. xxx. 31, Jer. x. 2,—a consternation and horror of mind; and עָרַץ, a word of the same signification, is often joined with it. This fear, therefore, arising from a discouraging, terrifying apprehension of dangers and oppositions, weakening and disenabling the soul to make use of due means vigorously in the discharge of its duty, can have no place here; yea, it is directly contrary to and inconsistent with the end aimed at by the apostle. And this is the first sort of fear that any way respects our religious obedience unto God. See Isa. viii. 12, 13, li. 12, 13; Matt. x. 28.

Secondly, There is a *fear of distrust* and diffidence, or a fear arising from or accompanied with a distrust of the accomplishment of God's promises, at least as to our interest in them. This is a defect in faith, and opposite unto it. This was the fear which ruined the Israelites in the wilderness. Being discouraged through their difficulties, "They believed not in God, and trusted not in his salvation," Ps. lxxviii. 22. And this cannot be here charged on us as our duty. A fluctuation and hesitation of mind about the promises of God, or the event of our condition in a course of sincere obedience, is not required of us, nor accepted from us. For no duty is acceptable with God but what is not only consistent with faith, but also proceedeth from it. The same faith that works by love, works also by delight; and it casts out this fear of distrust and diffidence. And no fear can be our duty but what is a fruit and effect of it. Believers do not receive "the spirit of bondage again to fear," Rom. viii. 15; nay, it is that which Christ died to deliver us from, Heb. ii. 14, 15. But it may be considered two ways;—1. As it partakes of the nature of diffidence, in opposition to faith and liberty, and so it is utterly to be rejected; 2. As it partakes of the nature of godly jealousy, and is opposed to security, and so it may be cherished, though it be not here intended.

Thirdly, There is a *fear of reverence*,—a reverential fear of God. This is that which most commonly is intended by the name of the "fear of God," both in the Old Testament and the New. And it is not an especial duty, suited unto some seasons and occasions, but that which concerns us in our whole course, in all our ways and actings. Sometimes it is taken subjectively, for the internal reverential frame of our hearts in all wherein we have to do with God; and sometimes objectively, for the worship of God itself. So is the nature of it expressed, Deut. xxviii. 58, "Observe the words of this law, that are written in this book, that thou mayest fear this glorious and fearful name, THE LORD THY GOD." The glorious and dreadful majesty of God is the object of it and motive unto it, which gives it the nature of reverence. And the way whereby it is exercised and expressed is a due observation of the worship of God according to the law. But neither is this that which is peculiarly intended, as not being more incumbent on us in one season than another, on one account than another.

Fourthly, There is a *fear of circumspection*, care, and diligence, with respect unto the due use of the means, that we may attain the end proposed unto us. This some would confound with a fear of diffidence, dread, and terror, with respect unto the uncertainty of the end; but it is quite of another nature. And as that is everywhere condemned in us, so this is no less frequently commended unto us: Rom. xi. 20, "Be not high-minded, but fear." Phil. ii. 12, "Work out your own salvation with fear and trembling." 1 Pet. i. 17, "Pass the time of your sojourning here in fear." Prov. xxviii. 14, " Happy is the man that feareth alway;" that is, with this fear of watchfulness, diligence, and spiritual care. But as to the other it is affirmed, that " God hath not given us the spirit of fear," 2 Tim. i. 7, or of bondage, through diffidence and uncertainty of the event of our obedience. Now, the acting of the soul in and about the use of means is ascribed unto fear, when the mind is influenced by a due apprehension of the threatenings and severity of God against sin, they being the way whereby we are delivered from being obnoxious unto them. Thus Noah, when God had denounced his judgments against the old world, although they were not yet seen, did not appear in any preparation made for them, yet believing that they would be inflicted accordingly, εὐλαϐηθείς, "being moved with fear, he prepared an ark," Heb. xi. 7. Apprehending the severity of God, believing his threatenings, his mind was influenced into that fear which put him with diligence on the use of those means whereby he and his family might be saved and preserved.

It will, from these considerations, be plainly evidenced what that fear is which is here enjoined and prescribed unto us. An instance and example of God's severity against unbelievers is laid down and proposed unto our consideration by the apostle in his preceding discourse. In this example of God's dealing with them of old, he declares also that there is included a commination of dealing with all others in the same manner, who shall fall into the same sin of unbelief with them. None may flatter themselves with vain hopes of any privilege or exemption in this matter. Unbelievers shall never enter into the rest of God. This he further confirms in these two verses, though his present exhortation be an immediate infer- ence from what went before: "Wherefore let us fear." How must we do this? with what kind of fear? Not with a fear of diffidence, of doubting, of wavering, of uncertainty as to the event of our obe- dience. This indeed may, this doth, befall many, but it is enjoined unto none; it is a fruit of unbelief, and so cannot be our duty. Neither can it be that which was intimated in the second place under the first head, namely, a dread and dismayedness of mind upon a prospect of difficulties, oppositions, and dangers in the way. This is the sluggard's fear, who cries, " There is a lion without, I shall be slain in the streets." To expel and cast out this fear, as that which weakens and disheartens men in their profession, is one of the espe- cial designs of the apostle in this epistle. Nor is it that general fear of reverence which ought to accompany us, in all wherein we have to do with God. For this is not particularly influenced by threatenings and the severity of God, seeing we are bound always so to "fear the LORD and his goodness;" nor is this fear required of us, as was said, more at one season than another. It remains, there- fore, that the fear here intended is mixed of the first and the last of those before mentioned. And so two things are included in it:— First, An awful apprehension of the holiness and greatness of God, with his severity against sin, balancing the soul against temptation. Secondly, A careful diligence in the use of means, to avoid the evil threatened unto unbelief and disobedience. And the right stating of these things being of great moment in our practice, it must be further cleared in the ensuing observations. As,—

Obs. I. The gospel, in the dispensation thereof, is not only at- tended with promises and rewards, but also with threatenings and punishments. This, for the substance of it, hath been already spoken unto, on chap. ii. 2, 3.

Obs. II. Gospel comminations ought to be managed towards all sorts of professors promiscuously, be they true believers, temporary, or hypocrites. So they are here proposed by the apostle unto the Hebrews without exception or limitation, and amongst them were persons of all the sorts mentioned. But this also will be comprised under the third proposition; namely, that,—

Obs. III. Fear is the proper object of gospel comminations, which ought to be answerable to our several conditions and grounds of ob- noxiousness unto those threatenings.

This is that which the apostle presseth us unto, on the consider- ation of the severity of God against unbelievers, peremptorily ex- cluding them out of his rest, after they had rejected the promise. "Let us," saith he, "therefore fear." What fear it is that in re- spect unto believers is here intended hath been declared. We shall now inquire how far and wherein the minds of men ought to be influenced with fear from gospel threatenings, and of what use that is in our walking with God. For there is, as was said, a threatening included in the example of God's severity towards unbelievers, before insisted on. And unto that the apostle hath a retrospect in this exhortation; as well as he hath also a regard to the present promise, whose consideration ought to have the same influence on the minds of men, as shall be declared.

Gospel threatenings are distinguished first with respect to their *objects*, or those against whom they are denounced or to whom they are declared, and also with respect to their own nature or the *subject-matter* of them. Of the persons intended in them there are three sorts:—1. Such as are yet open or professed unbelievers. 2. Such as make profession of the faith, profess themselves to believe, but indeed do not so in a due and saving manner; who also admit of many respective considerations. 3. True believers. For the subject-matter of them, they may be referred unto these two general heads:—1. Such as express displeasure to be exercised in temporary things. 2. Such as denounce everlasting wrath and punishment. According to this distribution we may consider what is or ought to be their influence on the minds of men with respect unto the fear which we inquire about.

1. Some gospel comminations respect, firstly, properly, and directly, *professed unbelievers*, as such, and so continuing. As the sum of all promises is enwrapped in those words, "He that believeth shall be saved," Mark xvi. 16, so that of all these threatenings is [enwrapped] in those that follow, "He that believeth not shall be damned." An alike summary of gospel promises and threatenings we have, John iii. 36, "He that believeth on the Son hath everlasting life: and he that believeth not the Son shall not see life; but the wrath of God abideth on him." And threatenings of this nature are frequently scattered up and down in the New Testament. See Rom. ii. 8, 9; 2 Thess. i. 6–10; 1 Pet. iv. 17, 18. And these threatenings may be so far called evangelical, inasmuch as they are proper to the gospel, and distinct from all the threatenings of the law. The law knows no more of gospel threatenings than of gospel promises. The threatenings of the law lie against sinners for sins committed; the threatenings of the gospel are against sinners for refusing the remedy provided and tendered unto them. They are superadded unto those of the law; and in them doth the gospel, when rejected, become "death unto death," 2 Cor. ii. 16, by the addition of that punishment contained in its threatenings unto that which is contained in the threatenings of the law. Now the end of these threatenings,—(1.) On the part of *Christ*, the author of the gospel, is the manifestation of his power and authority over all flesh, with his holiness, majesty, and glory, 2 Thess. i. 6–10. (2.) On the part

of the *gospel* itself,—[1.] A declaration of the necessity of believing; [2.] Of the worth and excellency of the things proposed to be believed; [3.] Of the price and esteem which God puts upon their acceptance or refusal,—and in all, the certain and infallible connection that is between unbelief and eternal destruction; [4.] The vindication of it from contempt, 2 Cor. x. 6.   (3.) On the part of *unbelievers*, to whom they are denounced, the end and design of them is to ingenerate fear in them:—[1.] A fear of dread and terror, with respect unto the authority and majesty of Christ, their author; [2.] A fear of anxiety, with respect unto their present state and condition; [3.] A fear of the punishment itself to be inflicted on them.   And these things do well deserve a more full handling, but that they are not here directly intended.

2. Gospel threatenings may be considered with respect unto all sorts of *unsound and temporary believers.*   For, besides that this sort of persons, continuing such, do and will finally fall under the general threatenings against unbelief and unbelievers, there are peculiarly two sorts of threatenings in the gospel that lie against them:—(1.) Such as respect their present, and, (2.) Such as respect their future condition.   (1.) Of the first sort are those severe intimations of anger and displeasure which our Lord Jesus Christ gave out unto sundry members of the churches in the Revelation, notwithstanding the profession that they made.   He discovers their hypocrisy and falseness under all their pretences, and threatens to cut them off if they repent not, chap. ii. 14–16, 20–23, iii. 1–3, 15–18. And this duty is always incumbent on them to whom the dispensation of the gospel is committed, namely, to declare these threatenings unto all that may be found in their condition.   For not only may they justly suppose that such there are, and always will be, in all churches, but also many do continually declare and evidence themselves to be in no better state.   And the discovery hereof unto them by the word is a great part of our ministerial duty.

(2.) There are such as respect their *future condition,* or threatenings of eternal wrath and indignation with especial regard unto that apostasy whereunto they are liable.   It is manifest that there are such comminations denounced against deserters, apostates, such as forsake the profession which they have made; which we shall have occasion to speak unto in our progress, for they abound in this epistle.   Now these, in the first place, respect these unsound professors of whom we speak.   And this for two ends:—[1.] To deter them from a desertion of that profession wherein they are engaged, and of that light whereunto they have attained; for although that light and profession would not by and of themselves eternally save them, yet,—1*st.* They lie in order thereunto, and engage them into the use of those means which may ingenerate that faith and grace which will produce that effect; 2*dly.* The deserting of them casts them both meritoriously and irrecoverably into destruction. [2.] To stir them up unto a consideration of the true state and condition wherein at present they are. Men may as well fail in their profession, or come short of that grace which they own, Heb. xii. 15, as fall from that profession which they have made. And these threatenings are denounced against the one miscarriage as well as the other.

The general end of these gospel comminations, with respect unto these unsound professors, is *fear.* Because of them they ought to fear. And that,—(1.) With a *fear of jealousy* as to their present condition. The consideration of the terror of the Lord declared in them ought to put them on a trembling disquisition into their state, and what their expectations may be. (2.) A *fear of dread* as to the punishment itself threatened, so far as they fall under conviction of their being obnoxious thereunto.

3. Gospel threatenings may be considered as they respect believers themselves; and in that sense we may consider what respect they have unto God, and what unto believers, with what is the proper effect of them designed of God to be accomplished in their spirits.

There is a difference between the promises and threatenings of the gospel; for the promises of God are declarative of his purposes unto all believers that are "called according to his purpose," Rom. viii. 28–31. The threatenings are not so to all unbelievers, much less to believers; but they are means to work the one sort from their unbelief, and to confirm the other in their faith. Only, they are declarative of God's purposes towards them who have contracted the guilt of the unpardonable sin, and declare the event as to all finally impenitent sinners.

(1.) They have a respect unto the nature of God, and are declarative of his condemning, hating, forbidding of that sin which the threatening is denounced against. It is an effectual way to manifest God's detestation of any sin, to declare the punishment that it doth deserve, and which the law doth appoint unto it, Rom. i. 32.

(2.) They have respect unto the will of God, and declare the connection that is, by God's institution, between the sin prohibited and the punishment threatened; as in that word, "He that believeth not shall be damned." God by it declares the infallible connection that there is, by virtue of his constitution, between infidelity and damnation. Wherever the one is final the other shall be inevitable. And in this sense they belong properly to believers; that is, they are to be declared and preached unto them, or pressed upon their consciences; for,—

[1.] They are annexed to *the dispensation of the covenant of grace,* as an instituted means to render it effectual, and to accomplish the ends of it. The covenant of works was given out or declared in a threatening: "The day that thou eatest, thou shalt die;" but in that threatening a promise was included of life upon obedience. And the covenant of grace is principally revealed in a word of promise; but in that promise a threatening is included, in the sense and to the purposes before mentioned. And, as we have showed before, these threatenings are variously expressed in the gospel. And they are of two sorts:—1st. Such as whose matter in the event hath no absolute inconsistency with the nature and grace of the covenant. Such are all the intimations of God's severity to be exercised towards his own children, in afflictions, chastisements, trials, and desertions. For although these things and the like, in respect of their principle and end, belong unto love and grace, and so may be promised also, yet in respect of their matter, being grievous, and not joyous, afflictive to the inward and outward man, such as we may and ought to pray to be kept or delivered from, they are proposed in the threatenings annexed to the dispensation of the covenant. See Ps. lxxxix. 30–33; Rev. ii., iii. And this sort of threatenings is universally and absolutely annexed to the dispensation of the covenant of grace, both as to the manner of their giving and the matter or event of them. And that because they are every way consistent with the grace, love, and kindness of that covenant, and do in the appointment of God tend to the furtherance of the obedience required therein. 2dly. Such as, in respect of the event, are inconsistent with the covenant, or the faithfulness of God therein; as the comminations of eternal rejection upon unbelief or apostasy, which are many. Now these also belong to the dispensation of the covenant of grace, so far as they are declarative of the displeasure of God against sin, and of his annexing punishment unto it; which declaration is designed of God and sanctified for one means of our avoiding both the one and the other. And whatever is sanctified of God for a means of delivery from sin and punishment, belongs to the dispensation of the covenant of grace.

[2.] This denouncing of threatenings unto believers is suited unto their good and advantage in the state and condition wherein they are in this world; for believers are subject to sloth and security, to wax dead, dull, cold, and formal in their course. These and many other evils are they liable and obnoxious unto whilst they are in the flesh. To awake them, warn them, and excite them unto a renewal of their obedience, doth God set before them the threatenings mentioned. See Rev. ii., iii.

[3.] The proper effect of these threatenings in the souls of believers, whereby the end aimed at in them is attained and produced, is fear,—" Let us therefore fear."

Now, what that fear is, and therein what is the especial duty that we are exhorted unto, may briefly be manifested from what hath been already laid down:—

1. It is not an anxious, doubting, solicitous fear about the punishment threatened, grounded on a supposition that the person fearing shall be overtaken with it; that is, it is not an abiding, perplexing fear of hell-fire that is intended. We are commanded, indeed, to fear him who can cast both body and soul into hell, Luke xii. 4, 5; but the object assigned unto our fear is God himself, his severity, his holiness, his power, and not the punishment of hell itself. It is granted that this fear, with a bondage frame of spirit thereon, doth and will often befall believers. Some deserve, by their negligence, slothfulness, unfruitful walking, and sinful ways, that it should be no better with them. And others also walking in their sincerity, yet by reason of the weakness of their faith, and on many other accounts, are ofttimes detained in such a bondage state and condition, as to fear with dread and terror all the day long. This, therefore, is ofttimes a consequent of some of God's dispensations towards us, or of our own sins; but it is not anywhere prescribed unto us as our duty, nor is the ingenerating of it in us the design of any of the threatenings of God; for,—

(1.) This is contrary unto the end of *all other ordinances of God;* which are appointed to enlighten, strengthen, and comfort the souls of believers,—to bring them to constant, solid, abiding peace and consolation. It cannot be, therefore, that at the same time God should require that as a duty at their hands which stands in a full contrariety and opposition to the end assigned by himself unto all his ordinances whereby he communicates of himself and his mind unto us. See Rom. viii. 15; 2 Tim. i. 7.

(2.) This fear is no effect or fruit of that *Spirit of life* and holiness which is the author of all our duties, and all acceptable obedience unto God. That this is the principle of all new-covenant obedience, of all the duties which, according unto the rule and tenor thereof, we do or ought to perform unto God, is evidently manifest in all the promises thereof. Now this fear of hell,—that is, as that punishment lies in the curse of the law,—neither is nor can be a fruit of that Spirit, given and dispensed in and by the gospel; for "where the Spirit of the Lord is, there is liberty," 2 Cor. iii. 17.

(3.) This kind of fear is not useful unto the confessed end of God's threatenings, namely, to excite and encourage men unto diligence and watchfulness in obedience. For if this were its nature and tendency, the more it is heightened as to its degrees, the more effectual would it be unto its proper end. But we see, on the contrary, that in those in whom it hath been most prevalent it hath produced effects utterly of another nature. So it did in Cain and Judas, and so it doth constantly, where it is absolutely prevalent. It appears, then, that its own *proper effect* is to drive them in whom it is from God;

and when it befalls any believers in any degree, it is the efficacy of
the Spirit of grace in other fruits of it which prevents its dangerous
effects. We may add unto what hath been spoken, that this fear is
directly opposite to the life of faith, being indeed that bondage for
fear of death which the Lord Christ died to deliver believers from,
Heb. ii. 15; this is that fear which perfect love casts out, 1 John iv. 18.

2. There is a watchful, careful fear, with respect unto the use
of means; and this is that which is here intended, and which is
our duty, on the consideration of the threatenings of God and instances of his severity against sinners. And this will appear by the
consideration of what is required unto this fear, which are the things
that follow:—

(1.) There is required hereunto a serious *consideration of the due
debt of sin* and the necessary vindication of God's glory. This is
that which is directly in the first place presented unto us in the
threatenings of the gospel, and ought in the first place to be the object of our faith and consideration. This we have evinced to be the
nature of divine comminations, namely, to declare that it is the
"judgment of God, that they which commit such sin are worthy of
death;" that "the wages of sin is death;" and that this depends on
the holiness of God's nature, as well as on the constitution and sanction of his law, Rom. i. 32, vi. 23. Here may we see and know the
desert of sin, and the concernment of the glory and honour of God in
its punishment,—the end why God originally gave the law with fire,
and thunderings, and terror. An instance hereof we have in Noah,
when he was warned of God concerning the deluge that he was
bringing on the world for sin,—" being moved with fear he prepared
an ark," Heb. xi. 7. A due apprehension of the approaching judgment due unto sin, and threatened by God, made him wary,—
εὐλαβηθείς, he was moved from hence, by this careful fear, to use the
means for his own deliverance and safety. This, therefore, is the
first ingredient in this fear.

(2.) There belongs unto it a due *consideration of the greatness,
terror, and majesty of God,* who is the author of these comminations, and who in them and by them doth express unto us those
glorious properties of his nature. So our apostle adviseth us to "serve
God with reverence and godly fear," because he is " a consuming
fire," Heb. xii. 28, 29. The consideration of his infinitely pure and
holy nature ought to influence our hearts unto fear, especially when
expressed in a way meet to put a peculiar impression thereof upon
us. Threatenings are the beamings of the rays of the holiness of
God in them. And this the same apostle intends, when he gives an
account of that " terror of the Lord" which he had regard unto in
dealing with the souls of men, 2 Cor. v. 11; that is, " how dreadful
a thing it is to fall into the hands of the living God." This also influenceth the fear required of us.

(3.) *A conviction and acknowledgment that in the justice and righteousness of God the punishments threatened might befall us.* So was it with the psalmist: Saith he, " If thou, LORD, shouldest mark iniquities, O Lord, who shall stand?" Ps. cxxx. 3; and again, "Enter not into judgment with thy servant: for in thy sight shall no man living be justified," Ps. cxliii. 2. Without a due consideration hereof, the mind will not be subdued into that contrite and humble frame which in this matter is required.

(4.) *An abhorrency of sin,* as on other reasons, so also *with respect unto its proper end and tendency,* represented in the threatenings of God. There are many other reasons whereon sin is and ought to be everlastingly abhorred; but this is one, and that such a one as ought never to be neglected. God hath, as we have showed, declared in his threatenings what is the desert of sin, and what will be its event in the sinner, if continued in. This ought always to be believed and weighed, so that the mind may be constantly influenced unto an abhorrency of sin on that account, namely, that it ends in death, in hell, in the eternal indignation of God.

(5.) The *nature of this fear,* as discovering itself in its effects, consists principally in a *sedulous watchfulness against all sin,* by a diligent use of the means appointed of God for that purpose. This is the direct design of God in his comminations, namely, to stir up believers unto a diligent use of the means for the avoidance of the sin declared against; and to this purpose are they sanctified and blessed, as a part of the holy, sanctifying word of God. This, therefore, is that which the fear prescribed unto us is directly and properly to be exercised in and about. What is the mind, aim, and intention of God, in any of his comminations, either as recorded in his word, or as declared and preached unto us by his appointment ? It is this and no other, that considering the " terror of the Lord," and the desert of sin, we should apply ourselves unto that constancy in obedience which we are guided unto under the conduct of his good Spirit, whereby we may avoid it. And hence followeth,—

(6.) A constant *watchfulness against all carnal confidence and security.* "Thou standest by faith," saith the apostle; "be not high-minded, but fear," Rom. xi. 20. And whence doth he derive this caution? From the severity of God in dealing with other professors, and the virtual threat contained therein: " For if God spared not the natural branches, take heed lest he also spare not thee," verse 21. This fear is the great preventive of carnal security; it stands upon its watch to obviate all influencing of the mind by the sloth, or negligence, or other lusts of the flesh; or by pride, presumption, elation of heart, or other lusts of the spirit. And therefore this fear is not such a dread as may take a sudden impression on believers by a surprisal, or under some especial guilt contracted by them, but

that which ought to accompany us in our whole course, as the apostle
Peter adviseth us. " See," saith he, " that ye pass the time of your
sojourning here in fear," 1 Pet. i. 17. And it being undoubtedly
of great importance unto us, I have the longer insisted on it; and
shall now proceed with the remaining words.

Μή ποτε καταλειπομένης ἐπαγγελίας. The intention of these words
is variously apprehended by interpreters; neither will   Καταλιπο-
they of themselves, absolutely considered, give us a   μένης ἐπαγγι-
precise and determinate sense. By some it is reported   λίας.
to this purpose: ' Seeing God hath left a promise unto us now
under the gospel.' And this sense is followed by our translators,
who, to make it plain, supply " to us" into the text. This way, the
caution intended in the words, expressed in μή ποτε, " lest," or " lest
at any time," is transferred to the end of the sentence, with respect
unto the evil of the sin that we are cautioned against. And this must
be supposed to be the natural order of the words: " Seeing there is
a promise left unto us of entering into the rest of God, let us fear
lest any of us seem to come short." And this sense is embraced by
sundry expositors. Others take the words to express the evil of the sin
that we are cautioned against, whereof the following clause expresseth
the punishment, or what will befall men on a supposition thereof;
as if the apostle had said, ' We ought to fear, lest, the promise
being left (or forsaken), we should seem to come short of entering
into the rest of God.' For this was the punishment that befell
them of old who rejected the promise; and this way the sense is
carried by most expositors. The difference comes to this, whether
by καταλειπομένης, the act of God in giving the promise, or the neglect of men in refusing of it, be intended.

Καταλείπω is of an ambiguous signification. Sometimes it is used
for " desero," " negligo," to " desert," " neglect," or " forsake" in a
culpable manner. Frequent instances of this sense occur in all authors. And if that sense be here admitted, it confines the meaning
of the words unto the latter interpretation ; "Lest the promise being
forsaken" or " neglected." And the sin intended is the same with
that, chap. ii. 3, Τηλικαύτης ἀμελήσαντες σωτηρίας, "Neglecting so great
salvation." Sometimes it is no more than " relinquo ;" which is a
word ἐκ τῶν μέσων, of a middle or indifferent signification, and is ofttimes used in a good sense. To leave glory, riches, or honour to
others that come after us, is expressed by this word. Καταλείπειν τὴν
δόξαν, is to leave glory unto posterity. So Demosthen. contra Mid.,
Εἰσφέρων ἀπὸ τῆς δόξης ὧν ὁ πατήρ μοι κατέλειπε·—" The glory of the
things which my father left unto me." And Budæus observes, that
καταλείπειν absolutely is sometimes as much as " hæredem instituere,"
"to make" or "leave an heir;" opposed to παραλείπειν,—for παραλείπειν
ἐν ταῖς διαθήκαις is " to pass any one by in a testament" without a

legacy or share in the inheritance. Hence καταλειμμα is "resi-
duum," "quod reliquum est," "reliquiæ," Rom. ix. 27. So is λειμμα,
"a remnant," Rom. xi. 5. Thus the apostle renders הִשְׁאַרְתִּי, 1 Kings
xix. 18, which is "to leave a remnant," "to leave some remaining,"
by κατέλιπον, Rom. xi. 4. See Acts xv. 17. In this sense the word
may here well denote the act of God in leaving or proposing the
promise unto us;—a *promise remaining* for us to mix with faith.

I see not any reason so cogent as should absolutely determine my
judgment to either of these senses with a rejection of the other; for
whether soever of them you embrace, the main design of the apostle
in the whole verse is kept entire, and either way the result of the
whole is the same. Each of them, therefore, gives a sense that is true
and proper to the matter treated of, though it be not evident which of
them expresseth the peculiar meaning of the words. I shall therefore
represent the intention of the apostle according to each of them.

In the first way, this is the sum of the apostle's exhortation: 'The
promise that was made unto the people of old as to their entrance
into the rest of God, did not belong absolutely and universally unto
them alone, as is manifest from the psalm where it is called over,
and as will afterwards be made to appear. This promise, for their
parts, and as to their concern in it, they disbelieved, and thereby
came short of entering into the promised REST. The same promise,
or rather a promise of the same nature, of entering into the rest of
God, remaining, continuing, and being proposed unto us, the same
duties of faith and obedience are required of us as were of them.
Seeing, therefore, that they miscarried through contumacy and unbelief, let us fear lest we fall into the same sins also, and so come
short of entering into the rest now proposed unto us.'

In the second way, what is said in the former exposition to be
expressed in the words is taken to be granted, supposed, and included in them; namely, that a promise of entering into the rest of
God is given unto us no less than it was to them of old, which is
further also confirmed in the next verse. On this supposition, caution is given to the present Hebrews, lest neglecting, rejecting,
despising that promise, through unbelief, they fall short of the rest
of God, under his righteous indignation and judgments; as if the
apostle had only said, 'Take heed, lest, by your unbelief rejecting
the promise, you fall short of the rest of God.'

I shall not absolutely determine upon either sense, but do incline
to embrace the former, upon a threefold account:—1. Because the
apostle seems in these words to lay down the foundation of all his
ensuing arguments and exhortations in this chapter; and this is,
That a promise of entering into the rest of God is left unto us now
under the gospel. On this supposition he proceeds in all his following discourses, which therefore seems here to be asserted. 2. The

last clause of the words, "Lest any of you should seem to come short of it," doth primarily and directly express the sin, and not the punishment of unbelievers, as we shall see afterwards; the promise, and not the rest of God, is therefore the object in them considered. 3. The apostle, after sundry arguments, gathers up all into a conclusion, verse 9, "There remaineth therefore a rest to the people of God;" where the word ἀπολείπεται (of the same root with this) is used in the sense contended for in the first interpretation.

This, therefore, I shall lay down as the import of these words,— 'There is yet on the part of God a *promise* left unto believers of entering into his rest.'

"Of entering into his rest." What is this rest, this rest of God, the promise whereof is said to "be left unto us,"—that is, unto them to whom the gospel is preached,—is nextly to be inquired into.

Εἰσελθεῖν εἰς τὴν κατάπαυσιν αὐτοῦ.

Expositors generally grant that it is the rest of glory which is here intended. This is the *ultimate rest* which is promised unto believers under the gospel. So they who are in glory are said to "rest from their labours," Rev. xiv. 13, and to have "rest," 2 Thess. i. 7,—the rest of believers in heaven, after they have passed through their course of trials, sufferings, faith, and obedience, in this world. This rest they take it for granted that the apostle insists on throughout this chapter, and they make a supposition thereof the ground of their exposition of the several parts of it, regulating the whole thereby. But I must take the liberty to dissent from this supposition, and that upon the reasons following:—

First, The "rest" here proposed is *peculiar to the gospel* and the times thereof, and contradistinct unto that which was proposed unto the people under the economy of Moses; for whereas it is said that the people in the wilderness failed and came short of entering into rest, the rest promised unto them, the apostle proves from the psalmist that there is another rest, contradistinct unto that, proposed under the gospel. And this cannot be the eternal rest of glory, because those under the old testament had the promise thereof no less than we have under the gospel; for with respect thereunto doth our apostle in the next verse affirm that "the gospel was preached unto them, as it is unto us,"—no less truly, though less clearly and evidently. And this rest multitudes of them entered into. For they were both "justified by faith," Rom. iv. 3, 7, 8, and had the "adoption of children," Rom. ix. 4; and when they died they entered into eternal rest with God. They did, I say, enter into the rest of God; that is, at their death they went unto a place of refreshment under the favour of God: for whatever may be thought of any circumstances of their condition,—as that their souls were only in "loco refrigerii," in a place of refreshment, and not of the enjoyment of the immediate presence of God,—yet it cannot be denied but that they entered into peace, and rested, Isa. lvii. 2. This, therefore, cannot be that other rest which is provided under the gospel, in opposition to that proposed under the law, or to the people in the wilderness.

Secondly, The apostle plainly carrieth on in his whole discourse an antithesis consisting of many parts. The principal subject of it is the *two people*,—that in the wilderness, and those Hebrews to whom the gospel was now preached. Concerning them he manageth his opposition as to the *promises* made unto them, the *things promised*, and the *means or persons* whereby they were to be made partakers of them, namely, Moses and Joshua on the one hand, and Jesus Christ on the other. Look, then, what was the rest of God which they of old entered not into, and that which is now proposed must bear its part in the antithesis against it, and hold proportion with it. Now that rest, as we have proved, whereinto they entered not, was the quiet, settled state of God's solemn worship in the land of Canaan, or a peaceable church-state for the worship of God in the land and place chosen out for that purpose.

Now, it is not the rest of heaven that, in this antithesis between the *law* and the *gospel*, is opposed hereunto, but the rest that believers have in Christ, with that church-state and worship which by him, as the great prophet of the church, in answer unto Moses, was erected, and into the possession whereof he powerfully leads them, as did Joshua the people of old into the rest of Canaan.

Thirdly, The apostle plainly affirms this to be his intention, for, verse 3, he saith, " For we which have believed do enter into rest." It is such a rest, it is that rest which true believers do enter into in this world; and this is the rest which we have by Christ in the grace and worship of the gospel, and no other. And thus the rest which was proposed of old for the people to enter into, which some obtained, and others came short of by unbelief, was a rest in this world, wherein the effects of their faith and unbelief were visible; and therefore so also must that be wherewith it is compared. And this consideration we shall strengthen from sundry other passages in the context, as we go through with them in our way.

Fourthly, Christ and the gospel were promised of old to the people as a *means* and *state of rest;* and in answer unto those promises they are here actually proposed unto their enjoyment. See Isa. xi. 1–10, xxviii. 12; Ps. lxxii. 7, 8, etc.; Isa. ix. 6, 7, ii. 2–4; Gen. v. 29; Matt. xi. 28; Isa. lxvi.; Luke i. 70–75. This was the principal notion which the church had from the foundation of the world concerning the kingdom of the Messiah, or the state of the gospel, namely, that it was a state of spiritual rest and deliverance from every thing that was grievous or burdensome unto the souls and consciences of believers. This is that which the people of God in all ages looked for, and which in the preaching of the gospel was proposed unto them.

Fifthly, The true nature of this rest may be discovered from the promise of it; for a promise is said to *remain of entering into this rest.* Now, this promise is no other but the gospel itself as preached unto us. This the apostle expressly declares in the next verse. The want of a due consideration hereof is that which hath led expositors into their mistake in this matter; for they eye only the promise of eternal life given in the gospel, which is but a part of it, and that consequential unto sundry other promises. That promise concerns only them who do *actually believe;* but the apostle principally intends them which are proposed unto men as the prime object of their faith, and encouragement unto believing. And of these the principal are the promise of Christ himself, and of the benefits of his mediation. These sinners must be interested in before they can lay claim to the promise of eternal life and salvation.

Sixthly, The whole design of the apostle is not to *prefer heaven,* immortality, and glory, above the law and that rest in God's worship which the people had in the land of Canaan, for none ever doubted thereof, no, not of the Hebrews themselves; nay, this is far more excellent than the gospel state itself: but it is to set out the excellency of the gospel, with the worship of it and the church-state whereunto therein we are called by Jesus Christ, above all those privileges and advantages which the people of old were made partakers of by the law of Moses. This we have already abundantly demonstrated; and if it be not always duly considered, no part of the epistle can be rightly understood. The rest, therefore, here intended is that rest which believers have an entrance into by Jesus Christ in this world.

This being the rest here proposed, as promised in the gospel, our next inquiry is into the nature of it, or wherein it doth consist. And we shall find the concernments of it reduced into these five heads:—

First, In *peace with God,* in the free and full justification of the persons of believers from all their sins by the blood of Christ: Rom. v. 1, "Being justified by faith, we have peace with God;" Eph. i. 7, "In whom we have redemption through his blood, the forgiveness of sins." This is fully expressed, Acts xiii. 32, 33, 38, 39, "We declare unto you glad tidings, how that the promise which was made unto the fathers, God hath fulfilled the same unto us their children, in that he hath raised up Jesus again. . . . . Be it known unto you therefore, men and brethren, that through this man is preached unto you the forgiveness of sins: and by him all that believe are justified from all things, from which ye could not be justified by

the law of Moses." The whole of what we contend for is expressed
in these words. The promise given unto the fathers, but not accomplished unto them, is no other but the promise of rest insisted on.
This now is enjoyed by believers, and it consists in that justification
from sin which by the law of Moses could not be attained. This,
with its proper evangelical consequents, is the foundation of this
rest. Nor is it of force to except, that this was enjoyed also under
the old testament; for although it was so in the substance of it,
yet it was not so as a complete rest. Neither was it at all attained
by virtue of their present promises, their worship, their sacrifices,
or whatever other advantage they had by the law of Moses; but by
that respect which those things had to the gospel. Justification, and
peace with God thereon, are properly and directly ours; they were
theirs by a participation in our privileges, "God having ordained
some better thing for us, that they without us should not be made
perfect," Heb. xi. ult. Neither had they it clearly or fully, as an
absolutely satisfactory spiritual rest. God revealed it unto them in
and by such means as never made them perfect in this matter, but
left them under a renewed sense of sin, Heb. x. 1–4; but under the
gospel, life and immortality being brought to light, 2 Tim. i. 10,
and the eternal life which was with the Father being manifested
unto us, 1 John i. 2, the veil being removed both from the face of
Moses and the hearts of believers by the Spirit, 2 Cor. iii. 13–18,
they have now a plerophory, a full assured persuasion of it, at least
in its causes and concomitants.

Secondly, In our freedom from a *servile, bondage frame of spirit
in the worship of God.* This they had under the old testament;
they had the spirits of servants, though they were sons. "For the
heir as long as he is νήπιος," "an infant," unable to guide himself,
"differeth nothing from a servant, but is under tutors and governors
until the time appointed of the father." So were these children
in their legal state in bondage, ὑπο τὰ στοιχεῖα τοῦ κόσμου, under the
very first rudiments of instruction which God was pleased to make
use of towards his children in this world, Gal. iv. 1–3. And this
had particular respect unto that "spirit of bondage unto fear," Rom.
viii. 15, which they were under in the worship of God; for it is
opposed unto that liberty, freedom, and filial boldness, which under
the gospel believers are made partakers of, by the "Spirit of adoption" enabling them to cry, "Abba, Father," Gal. iv. 6, Rom. viii.
15, 16. And this kept them from that full and complete rest which
now is to be entered into. For this cannot be, namely, a rest in the
worship of God, but where there is liberty; and this is only where
is the Spirit of Christ and the gospel, as our apostle discourseth at
large, 2 Cor. iii. 14–18. The Son making of us free, we are free
indeed; and do, by the Spirit of that Son, receive spiritual liberty,

boldness, enlargedness of mind, and plainness of speech, in crying, "Abba, Father."

Thirdly, Evangelical rest consists in a *delivery from the yoke and bondage of Mosaical institutions.* For as the people of old had a spirit of bondage within them, so they had without upon them ζύγον, "a yoke;" and that not only in itself δυσβάστακτον, "heavy and grievous to be borne," but such as eventually they could not bear, Acts xv. 10. They could never so bear or carry it as to make comfortable work under it. 'Ο νόμος τῶν ἐντολῶν ἐν δόγμασι, "the law of commands," that principally consisted in commandments, and those greatly multiplied, as we have showed elsewhere, being also positive, absolute, severe, or dogmatical, was burdensome unto them, Eph. ii. 15. This yoke is now taken away, this law is abrogated, and peace, with rest in Christ, in whom we are "complete," Col. ii. 10, and who "is the end of the law for righteousness," are come in the room of them. And this rest in the consciences of men from an obligation unto an anxious, scrupulous observation of a multitude of carnal ordinances, and that under most severe revenging penalties, is no small part of that rest which our Saviour makes that great encouragement unto sinners to come unto him, Matt. xi. 28–30.

Fourthly, This rest consists in that *gospel-worship* whereunto we are called. This is a blessed rest on manifold accounts:—1. Of that *freedom* and liberty of spirit which believers have in the obedience of it. They obey God therein, not in the "oldness of the letter," ἐν παλαιότητι γράμματος,—in that old condition of bondage wherein we were when the law was our husband, that rigorously ruled over us, —but ἐν καινότητι Πνεύματος, in the "newness of the Spirit," or the strength of that renewing Spirit which we have received in Christ Jesus, Rom. vii. 6, as was before declared. 2. Of the *strength and assistance* which the worshippers have for the performance of the worship itself in a due and acceptable manner. The law prescribed many duties, but it gave no strength to perform them spiritually. Constant supplies of the Spirit accompany the administration of the gospel in them that believe. There is an ἐπιχορηγία τοῦ Πνεύματος, Phil. i. 19, "a supply of the Spirit," continually given out to believers from Christ, their head, Eph. iv. 15, 16. Χορηγία, or χορήγημα, is a sufficient provision administered unto a person for his work or business; and ἐπιχορηγία is a continual addition unto that provision, for every particular act or duty of that work or business; "prioris sup-peditationis corollarium,"—a complemental addition unto a former supply or provision. This believers have in their observance of gospel-worship. They do not only receive the Spirit of Christ, fitting and enabling their persons for this work in general, but they have continual additions of spiritual strength, or supplies of the Spirit, for and unto every special duty. Hence have they great peace, ease, and rest, in the whole course of it.   3. The *worship* itself, and the obedience required therein, is not grievous, but easy, gentle, rational, suited unto the principles of the new nature of the worshippers. Hence they never more fully partake of spiritual rest, nor have clearer evidences of their interest and entrance into eternal rest, than in and by the performance of the duties of it.

Fifthly, This is also *God's rest;* and by entering into it believers enter into the rest of God.   For,—1. God *resteth ultimately and absolutely*, as to all the ends of his glory, in Christ, as exhibited in the gospel,—that is, he in whom his "soul delighteth," Isa. xlii. 1, and "in whom he is well pleased," Matt. xvii. 5.   In him his wisdom, righteousness, holiness, and grace, do rest, as being exalted and glorified according to his purpose. 2. Through him he *rests in his love* towards believers also. As of old, in the sacrifices which were types of him, it is said that he "smelled a savour of rest," Gen. viii. 21, so that on his account he would not destroy men, though sinners; so in him he is expressly said to "rest in his love" towards them, Zeph. iii. 17. 3. This is that worship which he ultimately and unchangeably requires in this world. He always gave out rules and commands for his outward worship, from the foundation of the world; but he still did so with a declaration of this reserve, to add what he pleased unto former institutions, and did accordingly, as we have declared on the first verse of this epistle. Moreover, he gave intimation that a time of reformation was to come, when all those institutions should expire and be changed. Wherefore in them the rest of God could not absolutely consist, and which on all occasions he did declare. But now things are quite otherwise with respect unto gospel-worship; for neither will God ever make any additions unto what is already instituted and appointed by Christ, nor is it liable unto any alteration or change unto the consummation of all things. This, therefore, is God's rest and ours.

Obs. IV. It is a matter of great and tremendous consequence, to have the promises of God left and proposed unto us.

From the consideration hereof, with that of the threatening included in the severity of God towards unbelievers before insisted on, doth the apostle educe his monitory exhortation, "Let us fear, therefore." He knew the concernment of the souls of men in such a condition, and the danger of their miscarriages therein. When Moses had of old declared the law unto the people, he assured them that he had set life and death before them, one whereof would be the unquestionable consequent of that proposal. Much more may this be said of the promises of the gospel. They are a "savour of life unto life," or of "death unto death," unto all to whom they are revealed and proposed. In what sense the promise is or may be left unto any hath been declared before in general: That there is a promise of entering into the rest of God yet remaining; that this promise be made known and proposed unto us in the dispensation of the word; that a day, time, or season of patience and grace be left unto us, are required hereunto.   When these things are so, it is a trembling concern unto us to consider the issue; for,—

1. The *matter of the promise* is about the eternal concernments of the glory of God and the good or evil state of the souls of men. The matter of the promise of old was in part typical, and related immediately to things temporal and carnal,—a rest from bondage in the land of Canaan.   But even this being neglected by them to whom it was left and proposed, exposed them to the high displeasure and indignation of God.   And what will be the event of the neglect of such a promise, whose matter is high above the other as heaven is above the earth, excelling it as things spiritual and eternal do things temporal and carnal?   God will have a strict account of the entertainment that is given unto gospel promises amongst the sons of men.   This is no slight matter, nor to be slighted over, as is the manner of the most that are dealt withal about it.   An eternity in blessedness or misery depends singly on this treaty that God hath with us in the promises.   Hence are those frequent intimations of eternal severity which are recorded in the Scripture against those who reject the promise that is left unto them; as Heb. ii. 3, "How shall we escape, if we neglect so great salvation?"   1 Pet. iv. 17, "What shall the end be of them that obey not the gospel of God?" and the like everywhere.

2. The whole *love, goodness, and grace* of God towards mankind, the infinite wisdom of the counsel of his will about their salvation, are contained and exhibited unto us in the promise.   This is the way that God from the beginning fixed on to propose and communicate the effects of these things unto us.   Hence the gospel, which is an explication of the promise in all the causes and effects of it, is termed ἐπιφάνεια τῆς χάριτος τῆς σωτηρίου τοῦ Θεοῦ, Tit. ii. 11,—the "illustrious appearance of the saving grace of God;" and ἐπιφάνεια τῆς χρηστότητος καὶ τῆς φιλανθρωπίας τοῦ Σωτῆρος ἡμῶν Θεοῦ, chap. iii. 4,— the "glorious manifestation of the goodness" (kindness, benignity) "and love of God our Saviour;" and εὐαγγέλιον τῆς δόξης τοῦ μακαρίου Θεοῦ, 1 Tim. i. 11; as also εὐαγγέλιον τῆς δόξης τοῦ Χριστοῦ, 2 Cor. iv. 4;—that is, either, by a Hebraism, εὐαγγέλιον ἔνδοξον, the "glorious gospel," so called from the nature and effects of it; or the gospel which reveals, declares, makes known, the great and signal glory of God, that whereby he will be exalted upon the account of his goodness, grace, love, and kindness.

Now, even amongst men it is a thing of some hazard and consequence for any to have an offer made them of the favour, love, and kindness of potentates or princes.   For they do not take any thing more unkindly, nor usually revenge more severely, than the neglect of their favours. They take themselves therein, in all that they esteem themselves for, to be neglected and despised; and this they do though their favour be of little worth or use, and not at all to be confided in, as Ps. cxlvi. 3, 4. And what shall we think of this tender of all that grace, love, and kindness of God? Surely we ought well to bethink ourselves of the event, when it is made unto us. When our Saviour sent his disciples to tender the promise unto the inhabitants of any city or house, he ordered them that upon its refusal they should " shake off the dust of their feet," Matt. x. 14, " for a testimony against them;" Mark vi. 11. [They were to] shake off the dust of their feet, as a token of God's dereliction and indignation,—a natural symbol to that purpose. So Nehemiah shook his lap against them that would not keep the oath of God, saying, "So God shake out every man from his house, and from his labour, that performeth not this promise," Neh. v. 13. And it was the custom of the Romans, when they denounced war and desolation on any country, to throw a stone into their land. So Paul and Barnabas literally practised this order: Acts xiii. 51, " They shook off the dust of their feet against them." And what they intended thereby they declared in their words unto them that refused the promise, verse 46, "Seeing ye put the word from you, and judge yourselves unworthy of everlasting life, lo, we turn to the Gentiles;" that is, ' we leave you to perish everlastingly in your sins.' And this they did " for a testimony against them,"—a sign and witness, to be called over at the last day, that the promise had been tendered unto them, and was rejected by them. And that this is the meaning of that symbol, and not a mere declaration that they would accept of nothing from them, nor carry away aught of them, not so much as the dust of their feet, as some suppose, is evident from the interpretation of it, in the following words of our Saviour, Matt. x. 15, "Verily I say unto you, It shall be more tolerable for the land of Sodom and Gomorrha in the day of judgment, than for that city;" that is, ' By so doing you shall give them an infallible sign of that certain and sore destruction which shall befall them for their sins.' Severe, therefore, will be the issue of so much love and kindness despised as is exhibited in the promise. See more hereof on chap. ii. 2, 3.

3. This proposal of the promise of the gospel unto men is *decretory* and *peremptory*, as to God's dealings with them about their salvation. " He that believeth not shall be damned," Mark xvi. 16. There is no other way for us to escape " the wrath to come." God hath indispensably bound up mankind to this rule and law: here they must close, or perish for ever. From all which it appears what thoughts men ought to have of themselves and their condition, when the gospel in the providence of God is preached unto them. The

event, one way or other, will be very great. Everlasting blessedness or everlasting woe will be the issue of it, one way or the other. "Let us therefore fear, lest, a promise being left unto us," etc. Again,—

Obs. V. The failing of men through their unbelief doth no way cause the promises of God to fail or cease.

Those to whom the promise mentioned in this place was first proposed came short of it, believed it not, and so had no benefit by it. What then became of the promise itself? did that fail also, and become of none effect? God forbid; it remained still, and was left for others. This our apostle more fully declares, Rom ix. 4, 5; for having showed that the promises of God were given unto the Israelites, the posterity of Abraham, he foresaw an objection that might be taken from thence against the truth and efficacy of the promises themselves. This he anticipates and answers, verse 6, "Not as though the word of God" (that is, the word of promise) "hath taken none effect;" and so proceedeth to show, that whosoever and how many soever reject the promise, yet they do it only to their own ruin; the promise shall have its effects in others, in those whom God hath graciously ordained unto a participation of it. And so also Rom. iii. 3, "For what if some did not believe? shall their unbelief make the faith of God without effect? God forbid." The "faith of God" (that is, his glory in his veracity, as the apostle shows in the next words, "Yea, let God be true, and every man a liar") is engaged for the stability and accomplishment of his promises. Men by their unbelief may disappoint themselves of their expectation, but cannot bereave God of his faithfulness. And the reason on the one hand is, that God doth not give his promises unto all men, to have their gracious effect upon them, whether they will or no, whether they believe them or reject them; and on the other, he can and will raise up them who shall, through his grace, "mix his promises with faith," and enjoy the benefit of it. If the natural seed of Abraham prove obstinate, he can out of stones raise up children unto him, who shall be his heirs and inherit the promises. And therefore, when the gospel is preached unto any nation, or city, or assembly, the glory and success of it do not depend upon the wills of them unto whom it is preached; neither is it frustrated by their unbelief. The salvation that is contained in it shall be disposed of unto others, but they and their house shall be destroyed. This our Saviour often threatened unto the obstinate Jews; and accordingly it came to pass. And God hath blessed ends in granting the *outward dispensation of the promises* even unto them by whom they are rejected, not here to be insisted on. Hence our apostle tells us that those who preach the gospel are a sweet savour of Christ unto God, as well in them that perish as in them that are saved, 2 Cor. ii. 15. Christ is glorified, and God in and by him, in the dispensation of it, whether men receive it or no. Again it follows from these words, that,—

Obs. VI. The gospel state of believers is a state of assured rest and peace.

It is the rest of God. But this will more properly fall under our consideration on verse 3, as to what is needful to be added to the preceding discourse.

The caution enforcing the exhortation insisted on remains to be opened, in the last words of the first verse, " Lest any of you should seem to come short of it."

Τίς ἐξ ὑμῶν.   Τίς ἐξ ὑμῶν,—" Any one of you," " Any one from amongst you." This expression the apostle used before, chap. iii. 12, ἔν τινι ὑμῶν, " in any of you." He respected them all so in general, as that he had a regard to every one of them in particular. Some here read ἡμῶν, " of us." And this seems more proper, for it both answers the preceding caution, " Let us fear," namely, " lest any one of us," and continues the same tenor of speech unto what ensues, " for unto us was the gospel preached." If we read ἡμῶν, the sense of the caution is that ' every one of us should take heed to ourselves;' if we retain ὑμῶν, with the most copies and translations, the intendment is that we all ought to take care of one another, or fear the dangers and temptations of one another, labouring to prevent their efficacy by mutual brotherly care and assistance. And this is most answerable unto the apostle's treating of them in sundry other places of this epistle, as chap. iii. 12, 13, x. 23, 24, xii. 15.

Δοκῇ.   Δοκῇ, " should seem." It refers unto μή ποτε, " lest at any time." There is a threefold probable sense of this word or expression:—1. Some suppose it to be added merely to give an emphasis to the caution. And so there is no more intended but that " none of you come short of it." And this manner of speech is not unusual,—" Lest any seem to come short;" that is, lest any do so indeed. See 1 Cor. xi. 16, xii. 22; 2 Cor. x. 9. 2. Some suppose that by this word the apostle mitigates the severity of the intimation given them of their danger, by a kind and gentle expression,—' Lest any of you should seem to incur so great a penalty, fall under so great a destruction, or fall into so great a sin as that intimated;' without this the admonition seems to have some harshness in it. And it is a good rule, that all such warnings as have threatenings for their motive, or any way included in them, ought to be expressed with gentleness and tenderness, that the persons warned take no occasion of being provoked or irritated. " A soft answer" (and so a soft admonition) " turneth away wrath; but grievous words stir up anger," Prov. xv. 1. See the proceeding of our apostle in this case, chap. vi. 7–10, with what wisdom he alleviates the appearing sharpness of a severe admonition. But, 3. The apostle rather intends to warn them against all appearance of any such failing or falling as he cautioneth them against. He desires them to take heed that none of them do, by foregoing their former zeal and diligence, give any umbrage or appearance of a declension from or desertion of their profession. This is his intention: 'Let there be no semblance or appearance of any such thing found amongst you.'

Ὑστερηκέναι,—"To come short;" "To be left behind;" "To have been left behind;" that is, in the work of first receiving the promise when proposed. If men fail in the beginning, probably they will quite give over in their progress. Ὑστερέω is "posterior sum," "to be behind," in time, in place, in progress. Vulg. Lat., "deesse," "to be wanting;" which renders not the word, nor gives any direct sense. Syr., דְּפָאֵשׁ, "qui cesset," "qui frustretur," "qui deficeret," so is it variously rendered,—any one that should "cease," "fail," "be frustrated," "give over:" whereunto it adds, מֵן דִּלְמֵעַל, "ab ingressu," "from entering in;"—that is, into the rest contained in the promise; making that, and not the promise itself, to be intended; and so the dehortation to be taken from the punishment of unbelief, and not the nature of the sin itself. Ὑστερέω also signifies "frustrari," "non assequi,"—"to be disappointed," and not to attain the thing aimed at. So Thucydid. lib. iii., Ἐπειδὴ τῆς Μιτυλήνης ὑστερήκει,—"After that he missed of Mitylene," or was disappointed in his design of putting in there. And in Isocrates, Ὑστερεῖν τῶν καιρῶν, καὶ πράγματων, is "to be disappointed," or to fail of occasions for the management of affairs. The word also signifies "to want," or "to be wanting." Τῷ ὑστεροῦντι περισσοτέραν δοὺς τιμήν, 1 Cor. xii. 24,—"Giving honour to that which wanteth," "is wanting." Ὑστερήσαντος οἴνου, John ii. 3, "When wine failed," "was wanting," "when they lacked wine." So also to be "inferior," Ὑστερηκέναι τῶν ὑπὲρ λίαν ἀποστόλων, 2 Cor. xi. 5,—"To come behind the chiefest apostles;" that is, be inferior unto them in any thing.

Generally, expositors think there is an allusion unto them who run in a race. Those who are not speedy therein, who stir not up themselves, and put out their utmost ability and diligence, do fail, come behind, and so fall short of the prize. So ὑστερεῖν is "ultimus esse," "deficere in cursu," "à tergo remanere,"—"to be cast," "to faint or fail in the race," "to be cast behind the backs of others." And this is a thing which our apostle more than once alludes unto, and explains, 1 Cor. ix. 24, 25.

But the allusion is taken from the people in the wilderness, and their passing into the land of Canaan. Most of them were heavy through unbelief, lagged in their progress, and were, as it were, left behind in the wilderness, where they perished and came short of entering into the promised land. These words, therefore, "Lest

any of you should come short of it," are as if he had said, 'Lest it
fall out with you in reference unto the promise left unto you, as it
did with the people in the wilderness with respect unto the promise as proposed and preached unto them. For by reason of their
unbelief they fell short, and enjoyed not the promise, nor did enter
into the land promised unto them, or the rest of God. And take
you heed, lest by the same means you fall short of the promise now
preached unto you, and of entering into the rest of God in the gospel.' The word, therefore, directly respects the promise, " fall short
of the promise," consequentially the things promised, or the rest of
God in the gospel. The scope and intention of this latter part of
the verse may be summed up in the ensuing observations.

Obs. VII. Many to whom the promise of the gospel is proposed and
preached do, or may, through their own sins, come short of the enjoyment of the things promised.

The caution here given unto the Hebrews, with the foundation of
it in the example of those who did so miscarry, not only warrants,
but makes necessary this observation from the words. And I wish
it were a matter of difficulty to confirm the truth of what is here
observed. But what is affirmed is but expressive of the state and
condition of most of those in the world to whom the gospel is preached.
They come short of all benefit or advantage by it. It ever was so,
and it may be, for the most part, ever will be so in this world.
That sentence of our Saviour contains the lot and state of men under
the dispensation of the gospel: " Many are called, but few are
chosen." It is true, " faith cometh by hearing," but bare hearing
will denominate no man a believer ; more is required thereunto.
Men, indeed, would probably much esteem the gospel, if it would
save them merely at the cost and pains of others in preaching it.
But God hath otherwise disposed of things; their own faith and
obedience are also indispensably required hereunto. Without these,
the promise considered in itself will not profit them; and as it is
proposed unto them it will condemn them. What are the ways
and means whereby men are kept off from enjoying the promise,
and entering by faith into the rest of God, hath been declared on
chap. iii. 12. Again,—

Obs. VIII. Not only backsliding through unbelief, but all appearances of tergiversation in profession and occasions of them, in times
of difficulty and trials, ought to be carefully avoided by professors:
"Lest any of you should seem." Not only a profession, but the
beauty and glory of it is required of us.

We have often observed that it was now a time of great difficulty
and of many trials unto these Hebrews. Such seasons are of great
concernment to the glory of God, the honour of the gospel, the edification of the church, and the welfare of the souls of men. For in

them all the things of God, and the interests of men in them, have
a public, and as it were *a visible transaction* in the world. Now,
therefore, the apostle would not have the least appearance of tergiversation, or drawing back, in them that make profession of the truth
So he gives us caution elsewhere with the same respect, Eph. v.
15, 16, " Walking circumspectly, redeem the time, because the days
are evil." The reason of both the duties enjoined is taken from the
consideration of the evil of the days, filled with temptations, persecutions, and dangers. Then in all things professors are to walk
ἀκριβῶς, " exactly," " circumspectly," " accurately." And there are
two heads of circumspect walking in profession during such a season.
The first is, to " adorn the doctrine of God our Saviour in all things,"
Tit. ii. 10; κοσμοῦντες τὴν διδασκαλίαν,—rendering beautiful, lovely,
comely, the doctrine of truth which we profess. Κοσμέω is so "to
adorn" any thing, as a bride decketh or adorneth herself with her
jewels, to appear lovely and desirable,—an allusion which the Scripture elsewhere maketh use of, Isa. lxi. 10, and by which Solomon
sets out the spiritual glory and beauty of the church in his mystical
song. This is a season wherein, by all accurate circumspection in
their walking and profession, believers ought to render what they
believe and profess glorious and amiable in the eyes of all. And
this for two ends:—1. That those who are of " the contrary part,"
those that trouble and persecute them, may have μηδὲν φαῦλον to say
of them, Tit. ii. 8,—" nihil improbum aut stultum,"—no wicked, no
foolish matter to lay to their charge. And though the conviction that
falls upon ungodly men may have no effect upon them, but a secret
shame that they should pursue them with wrath and hatred against
whom they have no evil or foolish matter to say, but are forced
openly to fall upon them in things only " concerning the law of
their God," as Dan. vi. 5, yet God makes use of it to check and
restrain that wrath, which if it brake forth would not turn to his
praise, 1 Pet. iii. 16. 2. That others, who by their trials may be
occasioned to a more diligent consideration of them than at other
times, may, by the ornaments put upon the truth, be brought over
to a liking, approbation, and profession of it. In such a season believers are set upon a theatre and made a spectacle to all the world,
1 Cor. iv. 9–13;—all eyes are upon them, to see how they will acquit
themselves. And this is one reason whence times of trouble and
persecution have usually been the seasons of the church's growth
and increase. All men are awakened to serious thoughts of the
contest which they see in the world. And if thereon they find the
ways of the gospel rendered glorious and amiable by the conversation
and walking of them that do profess it, it greatly disposeth their
minds to the acceptance of it. At such a season, therefore, above
all others, there ought to be no appearances of tergiversation or de-

cays. The next head of circumspect walking in such a condition, that no semblance of "coming short" may be given, is, a diligent endeavour to avoid "all appearance of evil," 1 Thess. v. 22,—every thing that may give occasion unto any to judge that we are fainting in our profession. Things that, it may be, are lawful or indifferent at another time, things that we can produce probable and pleadable reasons for, yet if, through the circumstances that we are attended with, they may be looked on by persons of integrity, though either weak or prejudiced, to have an eye or show of evil in them, are carefully to be avoided.

Now, there are two parts of our profession that we are to heed, lest we should seem to fail when times of difficulty do attend us. The first is *personal holiness*, righteousness, and upright universal obedience. The other is the *due observance of all the commands*, ordinances, and institutions of Christ in the gospel. The apostle Peter joins them together, with respect unto our accurate attendance unto them in such seasons, 2 Epist. iii. 11, "Seeing that all these things shall be dissolved, what manner of persons ought ye to be, ἐν ἁγίαις ἀναστροφαῖς, καὶ εὐσεβείαις,"—"in holy conversations;" that is, in every instance of our converse or walking before God in this world. Herein we meet with many changes, many temptations, many occasions, duties, and trials, in all which there ought a thread of holiness to run through in our spirits and actings. Hence it is expressed by "holy conversations,"—which we have rendered by supplying "all" into the text,—καὶ εὐσεβείαις and "godlinesses." The word principally respects the godliness that is in religious worship, which constitutes the second part of our profession. And although the worship of God in Christ be one in general, and no other worship are Christians to touch upon, yet because there are *many duties* to be attended unto in that worship, many *ordinances* to be observed, and our diligent care is required about each particular instance, he expresseth it in the plural number, "godlinesses" or "worships;" or, as we, "all godliness." About both these parts of profession is our utmost endeavour required, that we seem not to fail in them. Men may do so, and yet retain so much integrity in their hearts as may at last give them an entrance, as it were through fire, into the rest of God; but yet manifold evils do ensue upon the appearance of their failings, to the gospel, the church of God, and to their own souls. To assist us, therefore, in our duty in this matter, we may carry along with us the ensuing directions:—

Have an equal respect *always to both the parts of profession mentioned*, lest failing in one of them we be found at length to fail in the whole. And the danger is great in a neglect hereof. For example,—it is so, lest whilst we are sedulous about the due and strict observance of the *duties of instituted worship*, a neglect or decay should grow upon us as to holiness, moral righteousness, and obedience. For,—

(1.) Whilst the mind is deeply engaged and exercised about those duties, either out of a peculiar bent of spirit towards them, or from the *opposition* that is made unto them, the whole man is oftentimes so taken up therewith as that it is regardless of personal holiness and righteousness. Besides the innumerable instances we have hereof in the Scripture, wherein God chargeth men with their wickedness, and rejects them for it, whilst they pretended highly to a strict observance of oblations and sacrifices, we have seen it manifoldly exemplified in the days wherein we live. Whilst men have contended about ordinances and institutions, forms and ways of religion, they have grown careless and regardless as unto personal holy conversation, to their ruin. They have seemed like keepers of a vineyard, but their own vineyard they have not kept. How many have we seen withering away into a dry, sapless frame, under a hot, contending, disputing spirit about ways and differences of worship! Whilst they have been intent on one part of profession, the other of more importance hath been neglected.

(2.) Corrupt nature is apt to *compensate in the conscience* the neglect of one duty with diligence in another. If men engage into a present duty, a duty as they judge exceeding acceptable with God, and attended with difficulty in the world, they are apt enough to think that they may give themselves a dispensation in some other things; that they need not attend unto universal holiness and obedience with that strictness, circumspection, and accuracy, as seems to be required. Yea, this is the ruin of most hypocrites and false professors in the world.

Let it therefore be always our care, especially in difficult seasons, in the first place to secure the first part of profession, by a diligent attendance unto all manner of holiness, in our persons, families, and all our whole conversation in this world. Let faith, love, humility, patience, purity, charity, self-denial, weanedness from the world, readiness to do good to all, forgiving of one another, and our enemies, be made bright in us, and shine in such a season, if we would not seem to come short. And this,—

(1.) Because the difficulties in, and oppositions that lie against, the other part of our profession, with the excellency of the duties of it in such a season, are apt to surprise men into an approbation of themselves in a neglect of those important duties, as was before observed. It is a sad thing to see men suffer for gospel truths with worldly, carnal hearts and corrupt conversations. If we give our bodies to be burned, and have not charity, or are defective in grace, it will not profit us; we shall be but "as sounding brass or a tinkling cymbal," 1 Cor. xiii. 1–3. (2.) God hath no regard to the observance of ordinances, where duties of holiness, righteousness, and love are neglected, Isa. i. 13–17. And in this state, whatever use we may be of in the world or unto others, all will be lost as to ourselves, Matt. vii. 21–23.   (3.) We can have no expectation of strength or assistance from God, in cleaving to the truth and purity of worship against oppositions, if we fail in our diligent attendance unto universal holiness. Here hath been the original of most men's apostasy. They have thought they could abide in the profession of the truths whereof they have been convinced; but growing cold and negligent in personal obedience, they have found their locks cut, and they have become weak and unstable as water. God, for their sins, justly withholding the assistances of his Spirit, they have become a prey to every temptation.   (4.) What is it that we intend and aim at in our profession and our constancy in it? is it not that therein and thereby we may give glory unto God, and honour to the Lord Jesus Christ and his gospel? If this be not our aim, all our religion is in vain. If it be so, we may easily see that without personal universal holiness we do on many accounts dishonour God, Christ, and the gospel by our profession, be it what it will. Here, therefore, let us fix our principal diligence, that there be no appearance of any failure, lest we should seem to come short of the promise.

Secondly, The other part of our profession consists in our *adherence unto a due observation of all gospel institutions and commands,* according to the charge of our Lord Jesus Christ, Matt. xxviii. 20. The necessity hereof depends on the importance of it, the danger of its omission unto our own souls, the dependence of the visible kingdom of Christ in this world upon it; which things may not here be insisted on.

Obs. IX. They who mix not the promises of the gospel with faith shall utterly come short of entering into the rest of God. And this the apostle further demonstrates in the next verse which follows:—

Ver. 2.—"For unto us was the gospel preached, even as unto them [*we were evangelized, even as they*]: but the word of hearing [*the word which they heard*] did not profit them, not being mixed with faith in them that heard."

The signification of the original words, as rendered by translators, hath been already considered.

In this verse the apostle confirms the *reasonableness* of the exhortation drawn from the instance before insisted on. And this he doth on two grounds or principles:—First, The *parity of condition* that was between them of old, represented in the example, as to privilege and duty, and those to whom now he wrote, in the first words of the verse, " For we were evangelized, even as they." Secondly, The *event of that privilege* and call to duty which befell them of old, which he would dehort the present Hebrews from, " The word which they heard profited them not, because," etc.

His first ground must in the first place be opened and improved.

Καὶ γάρ, "etenim." The conjunction of these particles manifests a relation unto what went before, and the introduction of a new reason for its confirmation. And καὶ in this place is not so much a copulative (as usually it is), as an illative particle. So it is used Mark x. 26, Καὶ τίς δύναται σωθῆναι; "And who can be saved?" which we render rightly, "Who then can be saved?" for an inference is intended from the former words, expressed by way of interrogation. And the same particle is sometimes causal; not respecting a conjunction with what went before, nor an inference from it, but is introductory of an ensuing reason. See Luke i. 42, and John vi. 54. Here, as having γάρ, "for" or "because," joined unto it, it signifies the induction of a reason for the confirmation of what was spoken before.

Καὶ γάρ.

'Εσμὲν εὐηγγελισμένοι. Εὐαγγελίζομαι is of a various construction in the New Testament. It is mostly used in an active sense, and when spoken with respect unto persons it hath a dative case, signifying "them," annexed unto it. Luke iv. 18, Εὐαγγελίζεσθαι πτωχοῖς,—"To preach the gospel to the poor;" Rom. i. 15, Τοῖς ἐν 'Ρώμῃ εὐαγγελίσασθαι,—"To preach the gospel to them at Rome;" so frequently. Sometimes it hath the subject of it joined unto it in the accusative case: Acts v. 42, They ceased not teaching from house to house, καὶ εὐαγγελιζόμενοι 'Ιησοῦν τὸν Χριστόν, "and preaching Jesus to be the Christ." So also chap. viii. 4; Eph. ii. 17. And sometimes the object is expressed by the same case. Εὐηγγελίζετο τὸν λαόν, "He evangelized the people," "preached unto them:" so Luke iii. 18. And commonly it is used neutrally or absolutely, "to preach the gospel," without the addition either of subject or object. Sometimes it is used passively; and that either absolutely, as 1 Pet. iv. 6, or with the nominative case of those that are the object of it, Matt. xi. 5, Πτωχοὶ εὐαγγελίζονται,— "The poor are evangelized," or "have the gospel preached unto them." And in this sense and construction is it here used. For the nominative case, ἡμεῖς, is included in the verb substantive, ἐσμέν, "We are evangelized," "we have the gospel preached unto us." And in what way or sense soever the word is used, it doth nowhere denote the receiving of the gospel in the power of it by them who are evangelized; that is, it includes not the faith of the hearers, but only expresseth the act of preaching, and the outward enjoyment of it. The gospel, and therein the promise of entering into the rest of God, is preached unto us.

'Εσμὲν εὐηγγελισμένοι.

Καθάπερ κἀκεῖνοι, "even as they." It is plain from the context who are those whom this relative, κἀκεῖνοι, directs unto, namely, the fathers in the wilderness, who were before treated of; Καθάπερ κἀ- those who had, those who disbelieved and rejected, the κεῖνοι. promise of God, and came short of entering into his rest. And three things are to be inquired into for the opening of these words:—1. Wherein consists the comparison expressed in the word καθάπερ, "even as." 2. How was the gospel preached unto them. 3. How unto us.

1. The comparison is not between the subject of the preaching mentioned, as though they had *one gospel preached* unto them and we another; as if he had said, 'We have a gospel preached unto us, as they had one before us.' For the gospel is one and the same unto all, and ever was so from the giving out of the first promise. Nor, secondly, is the comparison between two several ways, modes, or manners of preaching the gospel: for if so, the preaching of the gospel unto them hath the pre-eminence above the preaching of it unto us, inasmuch as in the comparison it should be made the rule and pattern of ours, "The gospel was preached unto us as unto them;" but the preaching of the gospel by the Lord Jesus Christ and his apostles, which the Hebrews now enjoyed (if that be here understood) was far more excellent, as to the manner of it, than that which their forefathers were made partakers of. The comparison intended, therefore, is merely between the persons, *they* and *we*. 'As they enjoyed the gospel, so do we; as it was preached to them, so to us:' that it is in a far more excellent and eminent manner declared unto us than unto them he further declares afterwards; yet, as I shall show, though this be true, it is probably not the sense of this place.

2. It is supposed and granted that the gospel was preached unto the *people in the wilderness.* The apostle doth not here directly assert it; it is not his intention to prove it; it was not the design or subject-matter that he had in hand; nor would the confirmation of it have been subservient unto his present purpose. It is our privilege and duty, and not theirs, which he is in the immediate consideration of. But the matter being so indeed, a supposition of it, namely, that the gospel was preached unto them, was necessary to his purpose. How this was done we must now inquire; and concerning it we observe,—

(1.) That the promise made unto Abraham did contain the substance of the gospel. It had in it the covenant of God in Christ, and was the confirmation of it, as our apostle disputes expressly, Gal. iii. 16, 17. He says that the promise unto Abraham and his seed did principally intend Christ, the promised seed, and that therein the covenant was confirmed of God in Christ. And thence it was attended with blessedness and justification in the pardon of sin,

Rom. iv.; Gal. iii. 14, 15. So that it had in it the substance of the
gospel, as hath been proved elsewhere. (2.) This covenant, or promise made unto Abraham, was confirmed and established unto his
seed, his posterity, as the Scripture everywhere testifieth. And
hereby had they the substance of the gospel communicated unto
them; therein were they "evangelized." (3.) All the *typical institutions* of the law that were afterwards introduced had in themselves no other end but to instruct the people in the nature,
meaning, and manner of the accomplishment of the promise. To
this purpose they served until the time of reformation. They were,
indeed, by the unbelief of some, abused unto a contrary end; for
men cleaving to them as in themselves the means of righteousness,
life, and salvation, were thereby in their minds diverted from the
promise and the gospel therein contained, Rom. ix. 31, 32, x. 3.
But this was but an accidental abuse of them; properly and directly
they had no other end but that expressed. Nor had the whole law
itself, in its Mosaical administration, any other end but to instruct
the people in the nature, meaning, and manner of the accomplishment of the promise, and to lead them to the enjoyment of it, Rom.
x. 4, and to compel them to betake themselves unto it for life and
rest, Gal. iii. 18–20. (4.) With the spiritual part of the promise
made unto Abraham there was mixed, or annexed unto it, a promise
of the inheritance of the land of Canaan, Gen. xii. 3, 7; and this,—
[1.] That it might instruct him and his seed in the nature of faith,
to live in the expectation of that which is not theirs in possession,
Heb. xi. 8, 9. [2.] That it might be a visible pledge of the love,
power, and faithfulness of God in performing and accomplishing the
spiritual and invisible part of the promise, or the gospel, in sending
the blessing and blessed Seed to save and deliver from sin and death,
and to give rest to the souls of them that do believe, Luke i. 72–75.
[3.] That it might be a place of rest for the church, wherein it
might attend solemnly unto the observance of all those institutions
of worship which were granted unto it or imposed upon it, to direct
them unto the promise. Hence, (5.) The declaration of the promise
of entering into Canaan, and the rest of God therein, became in an
especial manner the preaching of the gospel unto them, namely,—
[1.] Because it was appointed to be the great *visible pledge* of the
performance of the whole promise or covenant made with Abraham.
The land itself and their possession of it was sacramental; for [2.]
It had in itself also a *representation* of that blessed spiritual rest
which, in the accomplishment of the promise, was to be asserted.
[3.] Because by the land of Canaan, and the rest of God therein,
not so much the place, country, or soil, was intended or considered,
as the worship of God in his ordinances and institutions therein
solemnly to be observed. And by these ordinances, or through

faith in the use of them, they were led unto a participation of the benefits of the promise of the gospel.

From what hath been spoken it appears how the gospel was preached unto the fathers in the wilderness, or how they were evangelized. It is not a *typical gospel,* as some speak, that the apostle intends, nor yet a mere institution of types; but the gospel of Jesus Christ, as it was in the substance of it proposed unto them in the promise; the entering into the land of Canaan being the especial instance wherein their faith was to be tried.

3. We may inquire how the gospel is said to be "preached unto us," which is the thing that is directly asserted. And, (1.) By *us,* in the first place, the Hebrews of that time were principally intended. But this, by due analogy, may in the application and use of it be extended unto all others who hear the word. (2.) The apostle had before declared that the gospel, in the full, free, open, and clear dispensation of it, had been preached unto them, and confirmed with signs and wonders amongst them; so that no doubt can be made of the gospel's being preached unto them. And with respect unto this sense and interpretation of the words were the cautions given, at the entrance, about the terms of comparison which seem to be in them. Notwithstanding this, I do at least doubt whether that were the preaching intended by the apostle. The same declaration of it to them of old, and these present Hebrews, their posterity, seems rather to be intended. The words, " For unto us was the gospel preached, even as unto them," seem to be of this importance, that we are no less concerned in the declaration of the gospel made to them, and the promise proposed unto them, than they were. Otherwise the apostle would have rather said, 'The gospel was preached to them, even as to us;' seeing of its preaching unto the present Hebrews there could be no doubt or question: and as we have now often declared, he is pressing upon these Hebrews the example of their progenitors. Therein he minds them that they had a promise given unto them of entering into the rest of God, which because of unbelief they came short of, and perished under his displeasure. Now, whereas they might reply, 'What is that unto us, wherein are we concerned in it, can we reject that promise which doth not belong unto us?' the apostle seems in these words to obviate or remove that objection. To this purpose he lets them know, that even *unto us,*—that is, to themselves,—to all the *posterity of Abraham* in all generations, the gospel was preached in the promise of entering into the rest of God, and may no less be sinned against at any time by unbelief than it was by them unto whom it was at first granted. This sense the words, as was said, seem to require, " To us was the gospel preached, even as unto them ;" that is, wherein and when it was preached unto them, therein and then it was preached unto us also. But it may be

said, that these Hebrews could not be concerned in the promise of entering into the land of Canaan, whereof they had been now possessed for so many generations. I answer, They could not do so, indeed, had no more been intended in that promise but merely the possession of that land; but I have showed before that the covenant-rest of God in Christ was in that promise. Again, it might concern them as much as it did those in the time of David, who were exhorted and pressed, as he manifests out of the psalm, to close with that promise, and to enter into the rest of God, when they were in a most full and quiet enjoyment of the whole land. And if it be said that the promise might belong unto those in the days of David, because that worship of God which had respect unto the land of Canaan was in all its vigour, but now, as unto these Hebrews, that whole worship was vanishing and ready to expire, I answer, That whatever *alterations in outward ordinances and institutions of worship* God was pleased to make at any time, the promise of the gospel was still one and the same; and therein "Jesus Christ, the same yesterday, and to-day, and for ever," Heb. xiii. 8. This, then, I take to be the sense of the words, namely, that as the first preaching of the gospel unto their forefathers belonged in the privilege of it unto these Hebrews, by virtue of the covenant of God with them, so the obligation to faith and obedience thereon was no less on them than on those to whom it was first preached. And the present dispensation of the gospel was but the carrying on of the same revelation of the mind and will of God towards them. And we may now take some observations from the words.

Obs. I. It is a signal privilege to have the gospel preached unto us, to be "evangelized."

As such it is here proposed by the apostle, and it is made a foundation of inferring a necessity of all sorts of duties. This the prophet emphatically expresseth, Isa. ix. 1, 2, "Nevertheless the dimness shall not be such as was in her vexation, when at the first he lightly afflicted the land of Zebulun, and the land of Naphtali, and afterward did more grievously afflict her by the way of the sea, beyond Jordan, in Galilee of the nations. The people that walked in darkness have seen a great light: they that dwell in the land of the shadow of death, upon them hath the light shined." The connection of this prophetical discourse is judged by many obscure and difficult; but the general design of it, as applied by the evangelist, Matt. iv. 15, 16, is not so. For reckoning the various afflictions and distresses that God at several times brought upon the Galilean parts of the land, which lay exposed in the first place to the incursion of their enemies, and whose people were first carried away into captivity, whereby outward darkness and sorrow came upon them, he subjoins that consideration which, though future, and for many ages

to be expected, should recompense and out-balance all the evil that
had in an especial manner befallen them. And this consisted in
that great privilege, that these people were the *first* that had the
gospel preached unto them, as the evangelist manifests in his application of this prophecy.

Hereunto he adds the *nature of this privilege,* and showeth
wherein it doth consist, in a description of their condition before they
were partakers of it, and in the relief which they had thereby. Their
state was, that they "walked in darkness," and "dwelt in the land
of the shadow of death;" than which there can be no higher description of a condition of misery and disconsolation. When the psalmist
would express the utmost distress that could befall him in this world,
he doth it by this supposition, "Though I walk through the valley
of the shadow of death," Ps. xxiii. 4. And these persons are said
to "dwell" in that land which he thought it so dreadful and horrible
to "walk through." And it denotes the utmost of temporal and spiritual misery. And these people are but occasionally singled out as
an instance of the condition of all men without the light of the gospel. They are in hideous darkness, under the shades of death, which
in its whole power is ready every moment to seize upon them. Unto
these the gospel comes as אוֹר גָּדוֹל, "a great light;" as the light of
the sun, called הַמָּאוֹר הַגָּדֹל, "the great light," in its first creation,
Gen. i. 16. In allusion whereunto the Lord Christ in the preaching of the gospel is called שֶׁמֶשׁ צְדָקָה, Mal. iii. 20, "the Sun of righteousness," as he who brings righteousness, "life, and immortality to
light by the gospel." Now, what greater privilege can such as have
been kept all their days in a dungeon of darkness, under the sentence of death, be made partakers of, than to be brought out into
the light of the sun, and to have therewith a tender of life, peace,
and liberty made unto them? And this is so much more in this
matter, as *spiritual darkness,* in an inevitable tendency to *eternal
darkness,* is more miserable than any outward, temporal darkness
whatever; and as spiritual light, "the light of the knowledge of the
glory of God in the face of Jesus Christ," excelleth this outward
light directing the body in the things of this world. Hence Peter
expresseth the effect of the gospel by this, that God by it "calleth
us out of darkness into his marvellous light," 1 Pet. ii. 9; and this is
but one instance of the greatness of this privilege for men to be
evangelized. It is the gospel alone that brings the light of God, or
life and blessedness unto men, who without it are under the power
of darkness here, and reserved for everlasting darkness and misery
hereafter. And more I shall not add; let them consider this by
whom it is not prized, not valued; by whom it is neglected, or not
improved.

Obs. II. Barely to be evangelized, to have the gospel preached unto any, is a privilege of a dubious issue and event. All privileges depend, as to their issue and advantage, on their usage and improvement. If herein we fail, that which should have been for our good will be for our snare. But this hath in part been spoken to before.

Obs. III. The gospel is no new doctrine, no new law; it was preached unto the people of old.

The great prejudice against the gospel at its first preaching was, that it was generally esteemed to be καινὴ διδαχή, a "new doctrine," Acts xvii. 19,—a matter never known before in the world. And so was the preaching of Christ himself charged to be, Mark i. 27. But we may say of the whole gospel what John says of the commandment of love. It is "a new commandment," and it is "an old commandment which was from the beginning," 1 John ii. 7. 8. In the preaching of the gospel by the Lord Jesus himself and his apostles, it was new in respect of the manner of its administration, with sundry circumstances of light, evidence, and power, wherewith it was accompanied. So it is in all ages, in respect of any fresh discovery of truth from the word, formerly hidden or eclipsed.

But as to the substance of it, the gospel is "that which was from the beginning," 1 John i. 1. It is the first great original transaction of God with sinners, from the foundation of the world. Hence the Lord Christ is said to be a "Lamb slain ἀπὸ καταβολῆς κόσμου," Rev. xiii. 8,—"from the foundation of the world." It is not of the counsel and purpose of God concerning him that the words are spoken, for that is said to be πρὸ καταβολῆς κόσμου, Eph. i. 4,—" before the foundation of the world;" that is, from eternity. And, 1 Pet. i. 20, he is said expressly to be " fore-ordained πρὸ καταβολῆς κόσμου,"— " before the foundation of the world;" that is, eternally in the counsel of God. But this ἀπὸ καταβολῆς κόσμου is as much as " presently after" or "from the foundation of the world." Now, how was the Lord Christ a lamb slain presently upon the foundation of the world? Why, this καταβολὴ κόσμου, the " foundation of the world," contains not only the beginning, but also the completing and finishing of the whole structure. So is the whole creation expressed, Ps. cii. 25, 26; Heb. i. 10; Gen. ii. 2, 3. Now, upon the day of the finishing the world, or of completing the fabric of it, upon the entrance of sin, the promise of Christ was given,—namely, " That the seed of the woman should break the serpent's head," Gen. iii. 15. In this promise the Lord Christ was a " lamb slain," though not actually, yet as to the virtue of his incarnation whereby he became a *lamb*, the " *Lamb* of God," and of his death, wherein he was slain to take away the sins of the world. Now, the declaration of the Lord Christ as the Lamb of God slain to take away the sins of the world, is the sum and substance of the gospel.

This, then, having been given out and established ἀπὸ καταβολῆς κόσμου, " from the very beginning of the world," this was the rise of the gospel, which ever since hath been the ground, rule, and measure of all God's transactions with the children of men. Whatever new declarations have been made of it, whatever means have been used to instruct men in it, yet the gospel was still the *same* throughout all times and ages. The Gentiles, therefore, had no true ground to object against the doctrine of it that it was new: for though, by the sin and unbelief of themselves and their forefathers, who had lost, despised, and totally rejected, the first revelation of it, it was new to them; yea, and God, in his just and righteous judgments, had hid it from them, and rendered it at length μυστήριον χρόνοις αἰωνίοις σεσιγημένον, Rom. xvi. 25,—"a mystery," the declaration whereof was "silenced from the past ages of the world," or all the secula that had passed from the beginning; yet in itself it was not new, but the same that was revealed from the foundation of the world by God himself. And this is for the honour of the gospel; for it is a certain rule, "Quod antiquissimum, id verissimum,"—"That which is most ancient is most true." Falsehood endeavours by all means to countenance itself from antiquity, and thereby gives testimony to this rule, that truth is most ancient. And this discovers the lewdness of that imagination, that there have been several ways, in several seasons, whereby men came to the knowledge and enjoyment of God. Some, they say, did so by the *law*, some by the *light of nature*, or the *light within them*, or by philosophy, which is the improvement of it. For God having from the " beginning," from the " foundation of the world," declared the gospel in the manner before proved, as the means whereby sinners might know him, live unto him, and be made partakers of him, shall we think that when this way of his was despised and rejected by men, he himself would do so also, and follow them in their ways, indeed their delusions, which they had chosen, in opposition to his truth and holiness? It is fond and blasphemous once so to imagine.

The Jews, with whom our apostle had to do peculiarly, derived their privileges from the giving of the law, and concluded that because the law was given unto them of God, according to the *law* they were to worship him, and by the *law* they were to be saved. How doth he convince them of their error and mistake in this matter? He doth it by letting them know that the covenant, or the promise of the gospel, was given unto them long before the law, so that whatever the end and use of the law were (which what they were he here declares), it did not, nor could disannul the promise; that is, take its work away, or erect a new way of justification and salvation. Gal. iii. 17, " And this I say, that the covenant, that was confirmed before of God in Christ " (that is, the promise given unto Abraham, verse 16), "the law, which was four hundred and thirty years after, cannot disannul, that it should make the promise of none effect." As if he had said, 'God made a promise to Abraham, or made a covenant with him, whereby he was evangelized, and the way of life and salvation by Christ made known unto him. Now, if the end of the law was to justify sinners, to give them life and salvation, then the way of the promise and covenant instituted by God four hundred and thirty years before must be disannulled. But this the faithfulness and unchangeableness of God will not admit.' And the apostle insists only on the *precedency* mentioned, and not that *priority* which it had of the law of Moses, in that it was preached from the foundation of the world; because dealing with the Jews, it was sufficient for him to evince that even in their relation unto God, and God's especial dealings with them, the gospel had the precedency of the law. What, then, John the Baptist said of the Lord Christ and himself, "He that cometh after me is preferred before me, for he was before me," John i. 15,—though he came after him in his *ministry*, yet he was above him in *dignity*, because he had a *pre-existence* in his divine nature unto him,—the like in another sense may be said of the law and gospel as preached by Christ and his apostles. Though it came after the law, yet it was preferred above it or before it, because it was before it. It was, in the substance and efficacy of it, revealed and declared long before the giving of the law, and therefore in all things was to be preferred before it.

It appears, then, that from first to last *the gospel is, and ever was, the only way of coming unto God;* and to think of any other way or means for that end, is both highly vain and exceedingly derogatory to the glory of God's wisdom, faithfulness, and holiness.

And these things have we observed from the first part of the confirmation of the preceding exhortation, taken from the parity of state and condition between the present Hebrews and those of old, inasmuch as they had both the same gospel preached unto them. The latter part of it is taken from the especial event of giving the promise unto the fathers. And hereof also are two parts:—1. An *absolute assertion* that the word that was preached unto them "did not profit them." 2. That there might be no semblance of reflecting disrespect on the promise of God, as though it could not profit them that heard it, to whom it was preached, the reason of this event and miscarriage is subjoined in these words, "not being mixed with faith in them that heard."

The subject spoken of in the first proposition is, ὁ λόγος τῆς ἀκοῆς, "the word of hearing;" which expression being general, is limited by ἐπαγγελία, the "promise," in the verse foregoing. Some would have the report of the spies, especially of Joshua and Caleb, to be intended in this expres-

'Ο λόγος τῆς ἀκοῆς.

sion. The people believed not the report which they made, and the
account which they gave of the land that they had searched. But,
as was said, it is plainly the same with the ἐπαγγελία, or the " promise," in the other verse, as the coherence of the words doth undeniably evince: " The word of hearing." *Hearing* is the only way
and means whereby the benefits contained in any word may be
conveyed unto us. The intendment, then, of this expression is that
which is declared, Rom. x. 17, "Αρα ἡ πίστις ἐξ ἀκοῆς· ἡ δὲ ἀκοὴ διὰ
ῥήματος Θεοῦ,—" Wherefore faith is from hearing, and hearing is by
the word of God." This is the series of these things. The end of
the word of God is to ingenerate faith in the hearts of men: this it
doth not immediately and absolutely, but by the means of hearing;
men must hear what they are to believe, that they may believe.
Hence, although the term of *hearing* be in itself indifferent, yet in
the Scripture it is used sometimes for the effect of it in faith and
obedience, as was observed on the last chapter; and sometimes for
the proper cause of that effect whereof itself is the means; that is, the
word itself. So ἀκοή expresseth שְׁמוּעָה. So Jer. x. 22, קוֹל שְׁמוּעָה,—
" vox auditus," the " voice of hearing;" that is, of the word to be
heard. And Isa. liii. 1, מִי הֶאֱמִין לִשְׁמֻעָתֵנוּ,—" Who hath believed our
hearing?" that is, ' the word which we propose to them to be heard
and believed.' Neither doth ἀκοή barely signify " auditus," the
" hearing," or the sense of it, which is all that properly is denoted
by that Latin word; but it is used sometimes for the reports of
words themselves which are heard: Matt. xxiv. 6, Μελλήσετε ἀκούειν
πολέμους, καὶ ἀκοὰς πολέμων,—" Ye shall hear of wars, and" (not
hearings but) " reports and rumours of wars." And our translators
have made use of a good word in this matter,—namely, report;
which may denote either what is spoken by men, or what is spoken
of them.

And so these words may be distinguished; ὁ λόγος is the word
materially, that is here *the word of promise*, namely, of entering
into the rest of God; and ἡ ἀκοή expresseth *the manner of its declaration* unto men according to the appointment of God; namely,
by preaching, so as that it may be heard. And hereon depends our
concernment in it. " The word," ὁ λόγος, may be ἐπαγγελία, a " promise" in itself, but if it be not ὁ λόγος τῆς ἀκοῆς, " the word of hearing,"—that is, so managed by the appointment of God as that we
may hear it,—we could have no advantage thereby. In sum, ὁ λόγος
τῆς ἀκοῆς, is ἐπαγγελία εὐαγγελιζομένη, " the promise preached," and
as preached.

Of this word it is said, Οὐκ ὠφέλησεν ἐκείνους,—" It
profited them not," they had no advantage by it. For
we find that notwithstanding the promise given of entering into the rest of God, they entered not in. And there seems to

Οὐκ ὠφίλησεν
ἐκείνους.

be a μείωσις, in the words also. It was so far from benefiting of them, that occasionally it became their ruin. As if he had said, ' Consider what befell them, how they perished in the wilderness under the indignation of God, and you will see how far they were from having any advantage by the word which they heard. And such will be the issue with all that shall neglect the word in like manner.'

The account of this event closeth the words: Μὴ συγκεκραμένος τῇ πίστει τοῖς ἀκούσασι. I observed before that there is some difference, though only in one letter, in some copies, about these words. The Complutensian, with the editions that follow it, reads συγκεκραμένους, the most συγκεκραμένος, which is followed by our translation. And this now translators and expositors do generally embrace, though Chrysostom, Theophylact, and Œcumenius are on the other side.

Μὴ συγκεκρα-
μένος.

The Vulgar Latin renders the last words, "Fidei ex iis quas audiverunt," as though its author had read τοῖς ἀκουσθεῖσιν, " the things that were heard." 'It did not profit them, because they believed not the things which were heard.' This, though it much changes the words, yet it makes no great alteration in the sense. I shall consider what proper sense the words will bear, take them either way, according to the difference of the reading, and then show that which is most proper, according to the mind of the Holy Ghost.

If we read συγκεκραμένους, it refers to ἐκείνους, and is regulated thereby: "Those who were not mixed with the faith of them that heard." And this seems to exclude the interpretation of Chrysostom, which Theophylact, who not only follows him almost constantly, but also transcribes from him, professeth that he could not understand. For he would have "those who were not mixed" (for he refers it to the persons of men, and not the word preached) to be Caleb and Joshua; who, saith he, mixed not themselves with the company of the rebellious and disobedient upon the return of the spies. And this, he saith, "they did by faith;" they kept themselves from the company of them who heard the word and were disobedient. But this interpretation overthrows itself; because if συγκεκραμένους be regulated by ἐκείνους, it is evident that those who did not so mix themselves had no profit by the word. For the word preached did not profit them who were not mixed; which could not be spoken of Joshua and Caleb. But it may not be amiss to consider the words themselves of these authors, which yet I do not usually. Thus, therefore, treats Chrysostom on the place: Ἤκουσαν κἀκεῖνοι, φησίν, ὥσπερ ἡμεῖς ἀκούομεν, ἀλλ' οὐδὲν ὄφελος αὐτοῖς γέγονε· μὴ τοίνυν νομίσατε ὅτι ἀπὸ τοῦ ἀκούειν τοῦ κηρύγματος ὠφελήσεσθε· ἐπεὶ κἀκεῖνοι ἤκουσαν ἀλλ' οὐδὲν ἀπώναντο, ἐπειδὴ μὴ ἐπίστευσαν· οἱ οὖν περὶ Χάλεβ καὶ Ἰησοῦν ἐπειδὴ μὴ συνεκράθησαν τοῖς ἀπιστήσασι, τουτέστιν, οὐ συνεφώνησαν, διέφυγον τὴν κατ' ἐκείνων ἐνεγχθεῖσαν τιμωρίαν· καὶ ὅρα τι

Συγκεκρα-
μένους.

Θαυμαστόν· οὐκ εἶπεν οὐ συνεφώνησαν ἀλλ᾽, οὐ συνεκράθησαν· τουτέστιν ἀστα-
σιάστως διέστησαν ἐκείνων πάντων μίαν καὶ τὴν αὐτὴν γνώμην ἐσχηκότων·—
"They also heard, even as we hear; but it profited them not. Do
not therefore suppose that you shall have any benefit from a mere
hearing of preaching; for they also heard, but it profited them not,
because they believed not. But Caleb and Joshua, because they con-
sented not unto them who believed not, escaped the punishment
which was inflicted on them. And this is admirable: he says not
they did not consent, but they were not mixed; that is, without sedition they separated themselves from them who were of one and the
same mind." It is evident that he refers "mixed" to persons, not
things, and so seems to have read συγκεκραμένους. But those who
were not so mixed he makes to be Caleb and Joshua, when it is
plain that the word profited not them who were not so mixed, if
that term be to be applied to persons. Hence was the modest
censure of Theophylact upon this passage; for having repeated it, he
adds, Τοῦτο δὲ, κατὰ τὴν μεγάλην αὐτοῦ καὶ βαθεῖαν σοφίαν, ὁ ἅγιος οὗτος
εἶπεν· ἐμοὶ γοῦν ἀναξίῳ οὐκ ἔδωκε νοῆσαι πῶς αὐτὸ εἶπεν·—"Thus speaks
that holy man, according to his great and deep wisdom; but to me
unworthy, it is not given to understand in what sense he spake it."
His own sense he otherwise expresseth; saith he, Μὴ συγκεκραμένους
τῇ πίστει τοῖς ἀκούσασι, τοῦτ᾽ ἔστι μὴ ἐνωθέντας, μὴ συμφρονήσαντας περὶ τῆς
πίστεως τοῖς ἀκούσασιν, ἀλλ᾽ ἀποῤῥαγέντας αὐτων·—that is, "They were
not united, they agreed not in faith with them which heard, but were
divided from them." Sundry others follow this interpretation. And
according to it τοῖς ἀκούσασι denotes the "obedient hearers,"—those
who so heard the word of promise as to believe it, and to yield obedience unto God on that account. According to which construction
this must be the importance of the words: 'The word preached profited them not, because they did not associate, or join themselves to,
or mix themselves with, those who, hearing the word, believed and
obeyed the voice of God.'

If this be the sense of the words, the whole congregation is blamed
for a wicked separation from two single persons, who abode constant
in the faith of the promise of God. They sinned in that they would
not join themselves unto them, nor unite with them in that profession of faith and obedience which they made. Neither their number nor their agreement among themselves could free them from
schism, sin, and punishment. They would not unite themselves
unto those two persons who abode in the truth, and so perished
under the indignation of God thereon.

And these things are true; but I judge them not to be directly
intended in this place. For the reading before mentioned, of συγκεκραμένος, which must refer to ὁ λόγος τῆς ἀκοῆς, "the word preached,"
and not to any person or persons, is confirmed by most ancient

copies, and followed by most ancient translations. Besides, the sense of the words, which in the other way is dark and involved, in this is full, clear, and proper; for,—

1. The other sense binds up the intention of the words unto that *particular time*, season, and action, when the people murmured upon the return of the spies that went to search the land. This, indeed, was a signal instance of their unbelief, yet the whole of it in refusing the promise is not to be restrained unto that instance. For our apostle is declaring that in their whole course they did totally and finally reject the promise.

2. If the persons spoken of be to be understood, the text doth not say they were not mixed with them that believed, were not united unto them, or conjoined with them, but not mixed τῇ πίστει, "to the faith." Now, there are two difficulties not easily removable that do attend this sense and construction of the words:—(1.) How men can be said to be mixed with the faith of others. Cameron answers, that it may be understood to be "joined with them in the communion of the same faith." I acknowledge this is a good and fair sense, but such as plainly makes the persons, and not their faith, to be the immediate object of this conjunction, which the words will not allow. (2.) How harsh is this construction, Συγκεκραμένους τῇ πίστει, τοῖς ἀκούσασι,—two dative cases joined in apposition without the intervention of any preposition, the one denoting the act, the other the persons: "Joined to the faith to them that heard it!" But as we shall see in the other more usual and approved reading, referring the word "mixed" to the principal subject of the whole proposition, or "the word preached," the sense will appear full and satisfactory.

Μὴ συγκεκραμένος, "the word not being mixed." Συγκεράννυμι is sometimes taken in a natural sense for to "mix" or "mingle" one thing with another, as water and wine; or to mix compositions in cordials or in poisons: Herodian, lib. i. cap. liv., Ἐμβαλοῦσα εἰς κύλικα τοῦ φαρμάκου, οἴνῳ τε κεράσασα εὐώδει δίδωσι,—"Gave him poison mixed with most savoury wine." So Plutarch, Sympos. lib. iv. quæst. 1: Ὁμοῦ μεταλλικὰ καὶ βοτανικὰ, ... εἰς τὸ αὐτὸ συγκεραννύντας. This mixture, which was properly of a cup to drink, was sometimes so made to give it strength and efficacy, to inebriate or give it any pernicious event. Hence "a cup of mixture" is expressed as an aggravation: Ps. lxxv. 8, "For in the hand of the LORD there is a cup, and the wine is red, מָלֵא מֶסֶךְ,"—"full of mixture." A "cup" sometimes signifies divine vengeance, as Jer. li. 7; and "wine" often. The vengeance here threatened being to arise unto the utmost severity, it is called a "cup," and that of "wine," of "red wine," and that "full of mixtures," with all ingredients of wrath and indignation. Sometimes the mixture was made to temperate and alleviate, as water mixed with strong inebriating wine. Hence a " cup without mixture" is an expression of great indignation, Rev. xiv. 10 ; nothing being added to the " wine of fury and astonishment" to take off its fierceness. Amongst physicians σύγκραμα is a " mixed potion." The word therefore signifies to mix two or more things together, so as they may inseparably incorporate, for some certain ends, acts, or operations; as wine and water to drink; several ingredients to make a useful cordial.

This being the importance of the word, expositors illustrate the whole sense by various allusions, whence they suppose the expression to arise. Some to the mixture of things to be eaten and drunk, that they may be made suitable and useful to the nourishment of the body; for so are the promises made by faith to the nourishment of the soul. Some to the mixture of the natural ferment of the stomach with meat and drink, causing digestion and nourishment thereby. And this latter allusion seems well to represent the nature of faith in this matter. The word of God, especially the word of promise, is the food of the souls of men: so is it often called, and thereunto frequently compared. Our apostle distributes the whole word, with respect unto them that hear it, or receive it, into " strong meat" and " milk," Heb. v. 13, 14. The whole is food, and in the whole is suited to the various conditions of believers in this world, whether strong and increased in spiritual light and experience, or whether young and weak. And so the same word is by Peter called " sincere milk;" which those who are born again ought to desire and make use of as their principal food, 1 Pet. ii. 1, 2. And with respect hereunto is faith sometimes expressed by *tasting*, which is the sense exercised about our food; which manifests, it may be, that more of experience is included in it than some will allow: 1 Pet. ii. 3, " If so be ye have tasted that the Lord is gracious." And wherein do we taste of the grace of God? In his word, as the psalmist declares, Ps. cxix. 103, "How sweet are thy words unto my taste !" And in pursuit of the same metaphor, the word is said to be sweet, "sweeter than honey and the honey-comb," Ps. xix. 10, cxix. 103. And frequently it is expressed by *eating*, wherein consists the life of the sacramental notion of eating the flesh and drinking the blood of Christ, whereby the especial actings of faith on that peculiar subject of the promise, Christ crucified for us, is expressed. The sum is, *spiritual truths*, being savingly believed, are united with that faith which receives them,—so incorporated with it as that they come to be realized in the soul, and to be turned into the *principle* of that new nature whereby we live to God. Want hereof is charged on the people to whom the gospel was declared in the wilderness. The word which they heard was not so really and savingly received by faith as to be incorporated therewith, and to become in them a living principle enabling and strengthening them unto obedience. It is not the intention of the words to declare barely and nakedly that they did not believe in any sort or sense, but that these hearers did not receive and improve the word of promise in such a way and manner as to obtain the full benefit and advantage of it. They had, as we find, an apprehension of the truth of the promise, which did so far prevail upon them that sometimes they professed that they would place their confidence in it, and regulate their obedience accordingly. But they were not steadfast herein, because, notwithstanding all their profession, their faith and the word of God were never solidly united, mixed, and incorporated in their souls. They *tasted* sometimes a little sweetness in it, but took it not down to *digest* it, that it might have a subsistence, power, and efficacy in them. This caused the word to fail of its end towards them,—it did not profit them; and them to fail of their end by it,—they entered not into the rest of God. And with the consideration hereof doth the apostle press the Hebrews, and us with them. And it is of great weight. The same promise being left unto us as to them, and this being the way whereby they came short of it, we have reason to be watchful against the like miscarriages in ourselves. And the truths doctrinally declared in this latter part of the verse may be comprised in the ensuing observations:—

Obs. IV. God hath graciously ordered that the word of the gospel shall be preached unto men; whereon depends their welfare or their ruin.

To them and to us was the word preached; and this as a great effect of the love, care, grace, and goodness of God towards them and us. The word is like the sun in the firmament. Thereunto is it compared at large, Ps. xix. It hath virtually in it all spiritual light and heat. But the preaching of the word is as the motion and beams of the sun, which actually and effectually communicate that light and heat unto all creatures which are virtually in the sun itself.

The explanation of this similitude is expressly insisted on by our apostle, Rom. x. 18. And because of this application doth the apostle make that alteration in the expression. For whereas in the psalm it is said קַוָּם, "their line is gone forth into all the earth," with respect in the first place and literally to the line or orderly course of the sun and other celestial bodies, he renders that word by φθόγγος, "their sound," "voice," or "speaking," respecting the mystical sense of the place, and application of the words to the preaching of the gospel, which was principally intended in them. And this is the true reason of that variety which many critics have troubled themselves and others about to little purpose. What, then, the motion and beams of the sun are to the natural world, that is the preaching of the gospel to the spiritual world,—to all who intend to live unto God here, or to enjoy him hereafter. Of old the preaching of the gospel was by many wise men, or those that thought or boasted themselves so to be, esteemed folly, 1 Cor. i.,—that is, a thing needless and useless; and the wiser any one would have himself esteemed to be, the more vehemently would he condemn preaching as folly. But notwithstanding all their pride, scorn, and opposition, it proved the "foolishness of God," which was wiser than all their wisdom; that is, what God chose to compass his end by, which seemed unto them "foolishness," but was indeed the "wisdom and power of God." And it is that which the eternal welfare or ruin of men depends upon: as the apostle in this place declares, and as the Scriptures testify everywhere. And this may direct us to make a right judgment both of that contempt and neglect of it which are found amongst many who ought to have other thoughts about it. The whole work is by some despised and decried; and few there are who labour in it with diligence as they ought. But they shall all bear their own judgment.

Obs. V. The sole cause of the promise being ineffectual unto salvation in and towards them to whom it is preached, is in themselves and their own unbelief.

This the apostle expressly asserts. It is granted that "the word did not profit them." But what was the reason of it? Was it weak or insufficient in itself? Was it like the law, that made nothing perfect? that could not take away sin, nor justify the souls of men? No; but the sole cause hereof was that it was "not mixed with faith." God hath not appointed to save men whether they will or no; nor is the word of promise a means suited unto any such end or purpose. It is enough that it is every way sufficient unto the end whereunto of God it is designed. If men believe it not, if they refuse the application of it to themselves, no wonder if they perish in their sins.

Obs. VI. There is a failing, temporary faith with respect to the promises of God, which will not advantage them in whom it is.

It is known how often the people of old professed that they did believe, and that they would obey accordingly; but, saith the apostle, notwithstanding all their pretensions and professions, notwithstanding all the convictions they had of the truth of the word, and the resolutions they had of yielding obedience, wherein their temporary faith did consist, yet they perished in their sins, because "the word was not mixed with faith in them;" that is, truly and really believed.

Obs. VII. The great mystery of useful and profitable believing consists in the mixing or incorporating of truth and faith in the souls or minds of believers.

This being a truth of much importance, I shall a little insist on the explanation and improvement of it, and that in the ensuing observations:—

1. There is a great respect, relation, and union, between the faculties of the soul and their proper objects, as they act themselves. Thus truth, as truth, is the proper object of the understanding. Hence, as it can assent unto nothing but under the notion and apprehension of truth, so what is so indeed, being duly proposed unto it, it embraceth and cleaveth unto necessarily and unavoidably. For truth and the understanding are, as it were, of the same nature, and being orderly brought together do absolutely incorporate. Truth being received into the understanding doth no way affect it nor alter it, but only strengthen, improve, enlarge, direct, and confirm it, in its proper actings. Only it implants a type and figure of itself upon the mind; and hence those things or adjuncts that belong unto one of these are often ascribed unto the other. So we say such a doctrine or proposition is *certain*, from that certainty which is an affection of the mind; and our apprehension of any thing to be *true*, from the truth of that which we do apprehend. This is that which we call knowledge; which is the relation, or rather the union, that is between the mind and truth, or the things that the mind apprehends as true. And where this is not, when men have only fluctuating conceptions about things, their minds are filled with opinions, they have no true knowledge of any thing.

2. The truth of the gospel, of the promise now under especial consideration, is peculiar, divine, supernatural; and therefore for the receiving of it God requireth in us, and bestoweth upon us, a peculiar, divine, supernatural habit, by which our minds may be enabled to receive it. This is *faith*, which is "not of ourselves, it is the gift of God." As the mind acts naturally by its reason to receive truths that are natural and suited to its capacity, so it acts spiritually and supernaturally by faith to receive truths spiritual and supernatural. Herewith are these truths to be mixed and incorporated. Believing doth not consist in a mere assent to the truth of the things proposed to be believed, but in such a reception of them as gives them a real *subsistence* and *inbeing* in the soul by faith. We shall make things more fully to appear, and the better explain them, if we show,—(1.) *How* this is expressed in the Scripture, with respect to the nature, acts, and effects of faith ; (2.) By *what means* it comes to pass that faith and the promise do so incorporate.

(1.) [1.] For *faith* itself; it is by our apostle said to be ἐλπιζομένων ὑπόστασις, Heb. xi. 1,—"the substance of things hoped for." Now the ἐλπιζόμενα here, "the things hoped for," are so termed with respect unto their *goodness* and their *futurition*, in which respects they are the objects of hope. But they are proposed unto faith, and respected by it, as true and real. And as such it is the

ὑπόστασις, or "substance" of them; not absolutely and physically, but
morally and in respect of use. It brings them into, makes them
present with, and gives them a subsistence, as to their use, efficacy,
and comfort, in the soul. This effect of faith is so far of the
nature of it, that the apostle makes use of it principally in that
description which he gives us of it. Now, this giving a *subsistence
in the mind* unto the things believed, that they shall really operate
and produce their immediate effects therein, of love, joy, and obedience, is that spiritual mixture and incorporation whereof we speak.
And here lies the main difference between saving faith and the
temporary persuasion of convinced persons. This latter gives no
such subsistence unto the things believed in the minds of men, as
that they should produce their proper effects therein. Those in
whom it is believe the promise, yet not so as that thereby the things
promised should have such an existence in their minds as to produce
in them and upon them their proper effects. It may be said of
them, as it is of the law in another sense, "They have the shadow
of good things to come, but not the very image of the things."
There is not a real reflection of the things they profess to believe
made upon their minds. For instance, the death of Christ, or
"Christ crucified," is proposed unto our faith in the gospel. The
genuine proper effect hereof is to destroy, to crucify, or mortify sin
in us. But where this is apprehended by a temporary faith only, this
effect will not at all be produced in the soul. Sin will not be mortified, but rather secretly encouraged; for it is natural unto men of
corrupt minds to conclude that they may continue in sin, because
grace doth abound. On the other side, where faith gives the subsistence mentioned unto the death of Christ in the soul, it will
undoubtedly be the death of sin, Rom. vi. 3–14.

[2.] Faith in its *acting* towards and on the promise is also
said to receive it. By it we receive the word; that is, it takes it
into the soul and incorporates it with itself. There is more herein
than a mere assent to the truth of what is proposed and apprehended.
And sometimes we are said by it to receive the word itself, and
sometimes to receive the things themselves which are the subject-
matter of it. So are we in the first way said to "receive with meekness the ingrafted word," James i. 21; to "receive the promises,"
Heb. xi. 13; "having received the word," 1 Thess. i. 6, ii. 13. In
the latter way to "receive Christ" himself, John i. 12, and "the atonement" made by him, Rom. v. 11; which are the principal subjects of
the gospel. And herein lies the life of faith; so that it is the proper description of an unbeliever, that "he doth not receive the things
of the Spirit of God," 1 Cor. ii. 14. And unbelief is the not receiving of Christ, John i. 11. There may be a tender made of a
thing which is not received. A man may think well of that which

is tendered unto him, and yet not receive it. But what a man doth receive duly and for himself, it becomes properly his own. This work of faith, then, in receiving the word of promise, with Christ and the atonement made by him therein, consists in its giving unto them a *real admittance* into the soul, to abide there as in their proper place; which is the mixture here intended by the apostle.

[3.] Hence and hereon the word becomes an *ingrafted word*, James i. 21, " Wherefore, lay apart all filthiness, and superfluity of naughtiness, and receive with meekness the ingrafted word, which is able to save your souls." The exhortation is unto reality and growth in believing. To this end the word is proposed, as that which is to be brought into the soul. And to that purpose room is to be made for it, by the casting out of such things as are apt to possess the mind and leave no admittance for the word. Now the ρυπαρία and περισσεία κακίας, " filth" and "superfluity of evil," here intended, are those corrupt, carnal lusts which by nature possess the minds of men, and render them " enmity against God," Rom. viii. 7. These are so fixed in the mind, so incorporated with it, that from them it is denominated "fleshly" and " carnal." And they are to be put away, cast out, separated from the mind, uprooted and rejected, that the word may be brought in and received. And how is that to be received? As a word that is to be ἔμφυτος, " implanted" or " ingrafted" into the mind. Now, we all know that by ingrafting there comes an incorporation, a mixture of the natures of the stock and graft into one common principle of fruit-bearing. So is the word received by faith, that being mixed with itself, both of them become one common principle of our obedience. And on this account doth our Saviour compare the word of the gospel unto *seed*, Matt. xiii. Now *seed* brings forth no fruit or increase unless falling into the earth, it *incorporate* with the fructifying virtue thereof. And with respect hereunto it is said that God writes his law in our hearts, Jer. xxxi. 33. As our apostle expounds it, 2 Cor. iii. 3: " The word of the gospel is by the Spirit of the living God written, not in tables of stone, but in the fleshy tables of the heart." So is it ingrafted, when it is as really, by the help of faith, communicated unto and implanted on the heart, as written words are in their engravement on tables of stone.

[4.] The effect of this ingrafting of the word, which belongs also to this spiritual incorporation, is the casting of the soul into the *mould, type, image*, or *figure* of the doctrine of it, as our apostle expresseth it, Rom. vi. 17: " Ye have obeyed from the heart εἰς ὃν παρεδόθητε τύπον διδαχῆς,"—"that form of doctrine that ye have been delivered up unto," that ye have been cast into. This is that transformation of mind which we are exhorted to look after in the renovation that it receives by believing, Rom. xii. 2. As the scion, being grafted or inoculated into the stock, turns and changes the natural juice of the stock into another kind of fructifying nutriment than it had before, so the word being by its mixture with faith ingrafted into the soul, it changeth the natural operation of it to the production of spiritual effects, which before it had no virtue for. And it *transforms* also the whole mind, according to the allusion, Rom. vi. 17, into a new shape, as wax is changed by the impression of a seal into the likeness of it.

[5.] The expression of faith by *eating* and *drinking*, which is frequent in Scripture, as before intimated, gives further light into the spiritual incorporation that we inquire after. Thus the word is said to be "food," "strong meat," and "milk," suited to the respective ages and constitutions of believers. And the Lord Christ, the principal subject of the word of the gospel, says of himself, that he is "the bread that came down from heaven," that "his flesh is meat indeed, and his blood drink indeed." Faith is the eating of this food, this milk, this meat, this flesh. Now in eating, when food is prepared, it is received, and by a due digestion turned into the very substance of the body of him that eats. Supplies proceed from thence unto the flesh, blood, and spirits of the eater, according as the principles of nature require and direct. So also must it be in this matter spiritually. This the Capernaites not understanding of old, but taking the words of our Saviour in a carnal manner, thinking he would have them eat his flesh with their teeth, and pour his blood down their throats, were offended at him, and perished in their unbelief, John vi. 52, 59. But he lets his disciples know that the whole mistake lay in the *carnal imagination* of those wretches. He understood no more but the *spiritual union* of himself unto the souls of believers by faith,—which is no less real and sure than the union that is between the body and the meat it receives when duly digested, verse 56; that "the flesh," in the carnal sense, was of no use or profit, but that his words were "spirit and life," verse 63. From an ignorance also of this spiritual incorporation of Christ in the promise and faith is it that the church of Rome hath feigned their monstrous carnal eating with their teeth of the flesh or body of Christ, though he had foretold them that it should profit them nothing. Wherefore, the word being prepared as spiritual food for the soul, faith receives it, and by a spiritual eating and digestion of it, turns it into an increase and strengthening of the vital principles of spiritual obedience. And then doth the word profit them that hear it.

Hence is the word of Christ said to *dwell* or *inhabit* in us: Col. iii. 16, "Let the word of Christ dwell in you richly in all wisdom." This *inhabitation* of the word, whereby it makes its residence and abode in the souls of men, is from this spiritual incorporation or mixing with faith. Without this it may have various effects upon the mind and conscience, but it comes to no abiding habitation. With some it casts its beams and rays for a season into their minds, φαίνει, but is not "received" nor "comprehended," John i. 5; and therefore οὐκ αὐγάζει, it "doth not enlighten them," though it shines unto them, 2 Cor. iv. 4. It comes and departs almost like lightning, which rather amazeth than guideth. With some it makes a transient impression upon the affections; so that they hear it and admit of its dispensation with joy and some present satisfaction, Matt. xiii. 20. But it is but like the stroke of a skilful hand upon the strings of a musical instrument, that makes a pleasant sound for the present, which insensibly sinks and decays until a new stroke be given; it hath no abode or residence in itself or the strings. No more hath the word that strikes on the affections only, and, causing a various motion and sound in joy, or sorrow, or delight, vanisheth and departeth. With some it lays hold on their consciences, and presseth them unto a reformation of their conversation, or course in this world, until they do many things gladly, Mark vi. 20; but this is by an efficacious impression from without. The word doth not abide, inhabit, or dwell in any, but where it hath a subsistence given unto it in the soul by its incorporation with faith, in the manner described.

This, then, is savingly and profitably to believe. And thus is it with very few of the many that make profession so to do. It is but in one sort of ground where the seed incorporates so with the earth as to take root and to bring forth fruit. Many pretend to believe, few believe indeed, few mix the word preached with faith; which should give us all a godly jealousy over our hearts in this matter, that we be not deceived.

(2.) It is therefore worth our inquiry how, or by what means, faith is assisted and strengthened in this work of mixing the word with itself, that it may be useful and profitable unto them that hear it. For although it is in and of the nature of faith thus to do, yet of itself it doth but begin this work, or lay the foundation of it, there are certain ways and means whereby it is carried on and increased. And among these,—

[1.] Constant *meditation*, wherein itself is exercised, and its acts multiplied. Constant fixing the mind by spiritual meditation on its proper object, is a principal means whereby faith mixeth it with itself. This is κατοπτρίζεσθαι, to behold steadfastly the glory of God in Jesus Christ, expressed in the gospel as in a glass, 2 Cor. iii. 18; for the meditation of faith is an *intuition* into the things that are believed, which works the *assimilation* mentioned, or our being "changed into the same image," which is but another expression of the incorporation insisted on. As when a man hath an idea or projection of any thing in his mind that he will produce or effect, he casteth the image framed in his mind upon his work, that it shall exactly answer it in all things; so, on the other side, when a man doth diligently contemplate on that which is without him, it begets an idea of it in his mind, or casts it into the same image. And this meditation which faith worketh by, for to complete the mixture or composition intended, is to be fixed, intuitive, constant, looking into the nature of the things believed. James tells us, that "he who is a mere hearer of the word is like a man considering his natural face in a glass, who goeth away, and immediately forgetteth what manner of man he was," chap. i. 23, 24. It is so with a man that takes but a slight view of himself; so is it with men that use a slight and perfunctory consideration of the word. But saith he, 'O παρακύψας εἰς νόμον τέλειον,—" He that diligently bows down, and inquires into the law of liberty," or the word (that is, by the meditation and inquiry mentioned), " that man is blessed in all his ways." So doth that word signify, 1 Pet. i. 12, where alone again it is used in this moral sense, of diligent inquiry, it signifying properly "to bow down." This is that which we aim at. The soul by faith meditating on the word of promise, and the subject-matter of Christ and his righteousness, Christ is thereby formed in it, Gal. iv. 19, and the word itself is inseparably mixed with faith, so as to subsist with it in the soul, and to produce therein its proper effects. This is to be " spiritually minded;" and φρονεῖν τά ἄνω, Col. iii. 2, to "mind the things that are above," as those which yield the best relish and savour to the soul; which being constant will assert a mixture, incorporation, and mutual conformity between the mind and the object of it.

[2.] Faith sets *love* at work upon the objects proposed to be believed. There is in the gospel, and the promises of it, not only the *truth* to be considered which we are to believe and assent unto, but also the *goodness*, excellency, desirableness, and suitableness unto our condition, of the things themselves which are comprised in them. Under this consideration of them, they are proper objects for love to fix on, and to be exercised about. And " faith worketh by love," not only in acts and duties of mercy, righteousness, and charity towards men, but also in adhesion unto and delight in the things of God which are revealed to be lovely. Faith makes the soul in love with spiritual things. Love engages all other affections into their proper exercise about them, and fills the mind continually with thoughtfulness about them and desires after them; and this mightily helps on the spiritual mixture of faith and the word. It is known that love is greatly effectual to work an assimilation between the mind and its proper object. It will introduce its idea into the mind, which will never depart from it. So will carnal love, or the impetuous working of men's lusts by that affection. Hence Peter tells us that some men have ὀφθαλμοὺς μεστοὺς μοιχαλίδος καὶ ἀκαταπαύστους ἁμαρτίας, 2 Epist. chap. ii. 14,—"eyes full of an adulteress." Their lust hath so wrought by their imagination as to introduce a constant idea of the object into their minds, as if there were an image of a thing in their eye, which continually represented itself unto them as seen, whatever they looked on: therefore are they constantly unquiet, and "cannot cease to sin." There is such a mixture of lust and its object in their minds, that they continually commit lewdness in themselves. Spiritual love, set on work by faith, will produce the like effect. It will bring in that idea of the beloved object into the mind, until the eye be full of it, and the soul is continually conversant with it. Our apostle, expressing his great love unto Christ, above himself and all the world, as a fruit of his faith in him, Phil. iii. 8, 9, professeth that this was that which he aimed at, namely, that he "might know him, and the power of his resurrection, and the fellowship of his sufferings, being made conformable unto his death," verse 10. The resurrection, with the sufferings and death of Christ which preceded it, he knew before and believed: but he aims at more, he would have a further inward experience of "the power of his resurrection;" that is, he would so mix it with faith working by love to Christ, as that it might produce in him its proper effects, in an increase of his spiritual life, and the quickening of him unto all holiness and obedience. He would also be yet further acquainted with "the fellowship of his sufferings," or obtain communion with him in them; that the sufferings of Christ subsisting in his spirit by faith, might cause sin to suffer in him, and crucify the world unto him, and him unto the world. By all which he aimed to be made completely "conformable unto his death;" that is, that whole Christ, with his life, sufferings, and death, might so abide in him that his whole soul might be cast into his image and likeness. I shall add no more concerning this truth, but only that it is best manifested, declared, and confirmed, in the minds and consciences of them who know what it is really to believe and to walk with God thereon.

VERSE 3.

Many have variously reasoned and conjectured about the coherence of this part of the apostle's discourse with that which immediately goeth before. It is not my way to propose the interpretations or analyses of others, much less to contend about them, unless necessity for the vindication of some important truth do require it of me. That, therefore, which in the words and design of the apostle seems to be most natural and genuine, as to the coherence of his discourse, I shall alone explain and confirm.

The work here engaged in is evidently to explain and improve the testimony cited out of David in the foregoing chapter. His purpose, also, is to draw out of it whatever was enwrapped in it by the wisdom of the Holy Ghost for the instruction of these Hebrews; which could not be clearly understood by them under the old testament, as designed for their peculiar use and direction now under the dispensation of the gospel. Having, therefore, declared unto them the danger of unbelief, by laying down graphically before them the sin and punishment of others, in and from the words of the psalm, he proceeds from the same words and example to give them encouragements unto faith and obedience; but withal foreseeing that an objection might be raised against the very foundation of his arguments and exhortations, he diverts to the removal of it, and therein wonderfully strengthens, carrieth on, and confirmeth his whole purpose and design.

The foundation of the whole ensuing discourse lies in this, that there is a promise left unto us of entering into the rest of God, verse 1. This, therefore, we ought to take heed that we come not short of by unbelief. Hereunto the Hebrews might object (as was before observed) that they were not now any way concerned in that promise; for consider whatever is said of the rest of God in the Scripture, and it will appear that it doth not belong unto us, especially not what is said of it in the psalm insisted on. The rest of the land of Canaan, and the rest of the Sabbath, are so called; but these are already past, or we are in the present enjoyment of them, so that it is to no purpose to press us to enter into rest.' The removal of this objection the apostle here designs from the words of David, and therein the establishment of his present exhortation. He manifests, therefore, that besides those mentioned there was yet another rest remaining for the people of God, and that directed unto in the words of the psalmist. This he proves and evinceth at large, namely, that there was a spiritual rest yet abiding for believers, which we are called and obliged to seek an entrance into. This, in general, is the design and method of the apostle's discourse in this place.

In this third verse three things are laid down:—First, An *assertion* comprising the whole intendment of the apostle, in these words, " For we which have believed do enter into rest." Secondly, A *proof* of that assertion from the words of the psalmist, " As he said, As I have sworn in my wrath, if they shall enter into my rest." Thirdly, An *elliptical* entrance into a full confirmation of his assertion, and the due application of his proof produced unto what he had designed it: " Although the works were finished from the foundation of the world."

Ver. 3.—Εἰσερχόμεθα γὰρ εἰς τὴν κατάπαυσιν οἱ πιστεύσαντες, καθὼς εἴρηκεν· Ὡς ὤμοσα ἐν τῇ ὀργῇ μου· Εἰ εἰσελεύσονται εἰς τὴν κατάπαυσίν μου· καίτοι τῶν ἔργων ἀπὸ καταβολῆς κόσμου γενηθέντων.

The words need little explication. Εἰσερχόμεθα γάρ. One old manuscript reads εἰσερχώμεθα οὖν, of which afterwards. Vulg. Lat., Ar., "ingrediemur;" Rhemists, "shall enter;" Eras., Beza, Syr., "ingredimur," "introimus,"—"do enter." The word is in the present tense; and though in that form it may sometimes be rendered by the future, yet here is no necessity why it should so be. "Do enter."

Οἱ πιστεύσαντες. Vulg. Lat., "qui credidimus;" Arias, "credentes;" Syr., "qui credimus;"—"who do believe," "who have believed."

Of the following words, see chap. iii. 11, 18.

Καίτοι, "et quidem," "and truly;" Beza, "quamvis," "although;" Eras., "quanquam;" so the Syriac.

Ἀπὸ καταβολῆς κόσμου. Ar., "a fundatione mundi," "from the foundation of the world;" Syr., "from the beginning of the world;" Beza, "a jacto mundi fundamento," properly; which we can no way render but by "from the foundation of the world."

Γενηθέντων, "genitis,"' 'factis," "perfectis,"—"made," "finished," "perfected." [1]

Ver. 3.—For we do enter into rest who have believed; as he said, As I have sworn in my wrath, if they shall enter into my rest: although the works were finished from the foundation of the world.

The assertion laid down in the entrance of the verse is FIRST to be considered; and therein,—

First, The *causal connection*, γάρ, "for." Now this, as we have showed, doth not refer precisely to any particular passage foregoing. Only it makes way to the further improvement of the whole design of the apostle; which use of that particle we have before observed: 'The promise, threatening, example, duty, treated of, belong unto us; and this appears from hence, that we are entered into rest who have believed.'

Secondly, The *subject of the proposition*, or persons spoken of, are οἱ πιστεύσαντες, "who have believed." The persons included in the verb εἰσερχόμεθα, regulating also this participle, are transferred over unto it in the translation, "we who have believed." Believing in general is only mentioned; the object of it, or what we believe, is implied, and it is to be taken from the subject-matter treated of. Now this is the gospel, or Christ in the gospel. This is that which he proposeth unto them, and which he encourageth them in from his own example. With respect hereunto men in the New Testament are everywhere termed πιστεύοντες, πιστοί, or ἄπιστοι, "believers," or "unbelievers:" 'We who have believed in Jesus Christ through the preaching of the gospel.'

Εἰσερχόμεθα. We observed before that one old manuscript reads Εἰσερχώμεθα οὖν, "Let us therefore enter;"

---

[1] EXPOSITION.—Ebrard takes a peculiar view of the last clause of this verse: "It is self-evident that the *works* here are antithetically opposed to *faith*. It is surprising how all critics should have supposed that *the works of God* are here meant, and especially his works of *creation*."—ED.

making it answer unto Φοϐηθῶμεν οὖν, verse 1, " Let us fear, therefore;" and Σπουδάσωμεν οὖν, verse 11, "Let us therefore labour." But
the sense in this place will not admit of this reading, because of the
addition of οἱ πιστεύσαντες, " who have believed." The Vulgar Latin
renders it "ingrediemur," in the future tense; which sense is allowed
by most expositors. But that which induced them to embrace it was
a mistake of the rest here intended. The word expresseth a present
act, as a fruit, effect, or consequent of believing. That it is which
in a spiritual way answers unto the Israelites entering into the land
of Canaan under the conduct of Joshua. Wherefore this entering,
this going in, is an allusion taken both in general from the entrance
that a man makes into his land or house to take possession of it, and
in particular, unto the entrance of the Israelites which were not rebellious or disobedient into the land of Canaan.

Εἰς τὴν κατάπαυσιν, "into that rest," the promised rest.

Εἰς τὴν κατά-
παυσιν.
What the rest here intended is hath been declared on
the first verse of this chapter; but because the right
stating hereof is the *basis* on which the whole ensuing exposition of
the apostle's discourse is founded, and the *hinge* on which it turns,
I shall further confirm the interpretation of it before laid down,
principally with such reasons as the present text doth suggest. This
rest, then, we say, firstly and principally, is that *spiritual rest of
God, which believers obtain an entrance into by Jesus Christ, in
the faith and worship of the gospel,* and is not to be restrained unto
their eternal rest in heaven. Supposing, then, what hath been argued
on the first verse, I add,—

First, That the express words here used do assign a *present entrance* into rest unto them that do believe, or have believed: Εἰσερχόμεθα,—" We do enter in." It may be said, and it is confessed that
the present tense doth sometimes express that which is instantly
future; as some think it may be proved from Luke xxii. 20, " This
cup is the new testament in my blood, τὸ ὑπὲρ ὑμῶν ἐκχυνόμενον,"—
" which is shed for you." So also is the same word used, Matt. xxvi.
28. The Vulgar Latin renders the word in each place " effundetur,"
" shall be shed" (or " poured out") " for you," with respect unto the
death of Christ, which was shortly to ensue. I will not deny, as was
said, but that the present tense is sometimes put for the future, when
the thing intended is immediately to ensue; but yet it is not proved
from this place. For our Saviour speaks of the virtue of his blood,
and not of the time of shedding it. It was unto them, in the participation of that ordinance, as if it had been then shed, as to the
virtue and efficacy of it. But ἔρχεται seems to be put for ἐλεύσεται,
John iv. 21, " is come," for " shall come" speedily; and ὁ ἐρχόμενος
is sometimes " he that is to come." But whenever there is such an
enallage of tenses, the instant accomplishment of the thing supposed

future is intended; which cannot be said with respect unto eternal rest in heaven. So this change is not to be supposed or allowed, but where the nature of the thing spoken of doth necessarily require it. This tense is not to be imposed on the places where the proper signification of a word so timed is natural and genuine, as it is in this place. It is here, then, plainly affirmed that believers do here, in this world, enter into rest in their gospel-state.

Secondly, The apostle is not primarily in this place exhorting sincere believers unto perseverance, that so at last they may be saved, or enter into eternal rest; but professors, and all to whom the word did come, that they would be sincere and sound in believing. He considers them in the same state with the people in the wilderness when the promise was proposed unto them. Their faith then in it, when they were tried, would have given them an immediate entrance into the land of Canaan. Together with the promise, there was a rest to be instantly enjoyed on their believing. Accordingly, considering the Hebrews in the like condition, he exhorts them to close with the promise, whereby they may enter into the rest that it proposed unto them. And unto perseverance he exhorts them, as an evidence of that faith which will give them an assured entrance into this rest of God; as chap. iii. 14, "We are made partakers of Christ, if we hold the beginning of our confidence steadfast unto the end."

Thirdly, The rest here intended is that whereof the land of Canaan was a type. But there were no types of heaven absolutely as a future state of glory. But both the land and all the institutions to be observed in it were types of Christ, with the rest and worship of believers in and by him. They were "shadows of things to come, the body whereof was Christ," Col. ii. 17. The whole substance of what was intended in them and represented by them was in Christ mystical, and that in this world, before his giving up the kingdom unto the Father at the end, that God may be all in all. Our apostle, indeed, declares that the most holy place in the tabernacle and temple did represent and figure out heaven itself, or the "holy place not made with hands;" as we shall see at large afterwards, Heb. ix. 6–12. But there heaven is not considered as the place of eternal rest and glory to them that die in the Lord, but as the place wherein the gospel-worship of believers is celebrated and accepted, under the conduct and ministration of our high priest, the Lord Jesus Christ; which office ceaseth when his saints are brought into glory. The rest, therefore, here intended being that which was typed out and represented by the land of Canaan, is not the rest of heaven, but of that gospel-state whereinto we are admitted by Jesus Christ. Hereof, and not of heaven itself, was the whole Mosaical economy typical, as shall elsewhere be at large demonstrated.

This, therefore, is the sense and importance of the apostle's assertion in this verse, 'We who have believed in Jesus Christ, through
the gospel, have thereby an admittance and entrance given unto us
into that blessed state of rest in the worship of God which of old
was promised,' Luke i. 69–73. It remains only that we inquire
into the nature of this rest, what it is and wherein it doth consist.
Now this we have done also already on the first verse; but the whole
matter may be further explained, especially with respect unto the
principal consideration of it. And this is, on what account this gospel-state is called God's rest, for so it is in this verse, "If they shall
enter into my rest."

First, It is the rest of God upon the account of the *author* of it, in
whom his soul doth rest. This is Jesus Christ, his Son. Isa. xlii. 1, "Behold," saith God the Father of him, "my servant, whom I uphold; בְּחִירִי
רָצְתָה נַפְשִׁי," "mine elect; my soul delighteth (resteth) in him." Matt.
iii. 17, "This is my beloved Son, ἐν ᾧ εὐδόκησα," אֲשֶׁר־חָפֵצִי בּוֹ. Both
the words contain more than we can well express in our language.
The full satisfaction of the mind of God, with that delight and rest
which answer the propensity of the affections towards a most suitable
object, is intended in them. The same with that of Prov. viii. 30,
" I was by him, as one brought up with him, and I was daily his
delight, rejoicing always before him." In which words the infinite,
intimate affection and mutual satisfaction between the Father and
the Son are expressed. Now God is said to rest in Christ on a twofold account.

1. Because in him, in the glorious mystery of his person as *God*
and *man*, he hath satisfied and glorified all the holy properties
of his nature, in the exercise and manifestation of them. For all
the effects of his wisdom, righteousness, holiness, grace, and goodness, do centre in him, and are in him fully expressed. This is
termed by our apostle, 'Η δόξη τοῦ Θεοῦ ἐν προσώπῳ Ἰησοῦ Χριστοῦ,
2 Cor. iv. 6;—"The glory of God, in the face" (or " person") " of
Jesus Christ;" that is, a glorious representation of the holy properties of the nature of God is made in him unto angels and men.
For so " it pleased the Father that in him all fulness should dwell,"
Col. i. 19; that he might have "the pre-eminence in all things,"
verse 18, especially in the perfect representation of God unto the
creation. Yea, the "fulness of the Godhead dwelt in him bodily,"
Col. ii. 9, in the union of his person,—the highest and most mysterious effect of divine wisdom and grace, 1 Tim. iii. 16; 1 Pet. i. 11,
12. In this sense is he said to be " the image of the invisible God,"
Col. i. 15; which though it principally respects his divine nature,
yet doth not so absolutely, but as he was incarnate. For an image
must be in a sort aspectable, and represent that which in itself is
not seen, which the divine nature of the Son, essentially the same

with the Father's, doth not do. God doth, maketh, worketh all things for himself, Prov. xvi. 4; that is, for the satisfaction of the holy perfections of his nature in acts suitable unto them, and the manifestation of his glory thereon. Hence in them all God in some sense doth rest. So when he had finished his works in the creation of the world, he saw that they were "good,"—that is, that they answered his greatness, wisdom, and power; and he rested from them, Gen. ii. 2. Which rest, as it doth not include an antecedent lassitude or weariness, as it doth in poor finite creatures, so it doth more than a mere cessation from operation, namely, complacency and satisfaction in the works themselves. So it is said, Exod. xxxi. 17, that "on the seventh day God rested, and was refreshed;" which expresseth the complacency he had in his works. But this rest was but partial, not absolute and complete; for God in the works of nature had but partially acted and manifested his divine properties, and some of them, as his grace, patience, and love, not at all. But now, in the person of Christ, the author of the gospel, who is "the brightness of his glory, and the express image of his person," God doth absolutely and ultimately rest, and that in the manifestation of all his glorious properties, as hath been declared. Hence, in the sacrifices that were typical of him it is said וַיָּרַח יְהֹוָה אֶת־רֵיחַ הַנִּיחֹחַ, Gen. viii. 21,— "God smelled a savour of rest," as prefiguring that and foregoing it, wherein he would always rest; for,—

2. As in the *person*, so also in the *work* of Christ, doth God perfectly rest,—namely, in the work of his mediation. He so rests in it, that as it needeth not, so he will never admit of any addition to be made unto it, any help or assistance to be joined with it, for any ends of his glory. This is the design of our apostle to prove, Heb. x. 5–7. God designed the sacrifices of the law for the great ends of his glory in the typical expiation of sin; but he manifested by various means that he did never absolutely rest in them. Ofttimes he preferred his moral worship before them; ofttimes he rebuked the people for their carnal trust in them, and declared that he had appointed a time when he would utterly take them away, Heb. ix. 10. But as to the mediation and sacrifice of Christ things are absolutely otherwise. Nothing is once named in competition with it; nay, the adding of any thing unto it, the using of any thing with it to the same end and purpose, is, or would be, ruinous to the souls of men. And as for those who will not take up their rest herein, that accept not of the work that he hath wrought, and the atonement that he hath made, by faith, there remains no more sacrifice for their sin, but perish they must, and that for ever. Two ways there are whereby God manifesteth his absolute rest in the person and mediation of Christ:—

(1.) By giving unto him "all power in heaven and in earth" upon his exaltation. This power, and the collation of it, we have discoursed of on the first chapter. It was as if God had said unto him, ' My work is done, my will perfectly accomplished, my name fully manifested,—I have no more to do in the world: take now, then, possession of all my glory,—sit at my right hand; for in thee is my soul well pleased.'

(2.) In the command that he hath given unto angels and men, to worship, honour, and adore him, even as they honour the Father; whereof we have elsewhere treated. By these ways, I say, doth God declare his plenary rest and soul-satisfaction in Jesus Christ, the author of this gospel rest, and as he is so.

Secondly, It is God's rest, because he will never *institute any new kind or sort of worship* amongst men, but only what is already ordained and appointed by him in the gospel. God dwells among men in and by his solemn worship: Exod. xxv. 8, " Let them make me a sanctuary, that I may dwell among them." God dwells in the place of his worship, by it. Hence, when he fixed his worship amongst the people for a season in the land of Canaan, he called it his rest. Thence was that prayer on the motions of the ark, " Arise, O LORD, into thy rest, thou, and the ark of thy strength," Ps. cxxxii. 8; 2 Chron. vi. 41: which was the principal thing aimed at in all God's dealings with that people, the end of all his mighty works, Exod. xv. 17. And in this worship of the gospel, the tabernacle which he hath made for himself to dwell in, the sanctuary which his hands have established, is again with men, Rev. xxi. 3. He hath in it set up again the tabernacle of David, so that it shall fall no more, Acts xv. 16. This worship he will neither add to, nor alter, nor take from; but this is his rest and his habitation amongst men for ever. He is pleased and satisfied with it by Christ.

Thirdly, God also is at peace with the *worshippers*, and rests in them. He sets up his tabernacle amongst men, that he may " dwell amongst them, and be their God, and that they may be his people," Rev. xxi. 3; and herein " he rejoiceth over them with joy, and resteth in his love," Zeph. iii. 17. Thus the whole work of God's grace in Christ being accomplished, he ceaseth from his labour, and entereth into his rest.

I have added these things to show that it is God's rest which believers do enter into, as it is here declared. For the nature of the rest itself, as it is by them enjoyed, it hath fully been opened on the first verse, and need not here be again insisted on. And this is that rest which is principally intended both here and in the whole chapter. It is not, indeed, absolutely intended, or exclusively unto all other spiritual rests, or to an increase and progress in the same kind; but it is principally so: for this rest itself is not absolute, ultimate, and complete, but it is initial, and suited to the state of believers in this world. And because it hath its fulness and perfection in eternal rest, in the immediate enjoyment of God, that also may seem to be included therein, but consequentially only.

There remains, for the full explication of this assertion of the apostle, only that we show what it is to enter into this rest. And these two things may be observed to that purpose:—1. That it is *an entrance* which is asserted. 2. That it is *but an entrance.*

1. It is an entrance, which denotes a right executed. There was a right proposed in the promise, and served therein for believers indefinitely. But it is not executed, nor is possession given but by believing. "A rest remaineth for the people of God,"—that is, in the promise; and "we who have believed do enter into it." It is faith which gives us "jus in re," a right in possession, an actual, personal interest, both in the promises and in the rest contained in them, with all the privileges wherewith it is attended.

2. It is but an entrance into rest,—(1.) Because the rest itself is not absolute and complete, as we have declared. Look to what is past, what we are delivered and secured from, and it is a glorious rest. Look unto what is to come, and it is itself but a passage into a more glorious rest. It is an "abundant ministration of an entrance into the everlasting kingdom of our Lord and Saviour Jesus Christ," 2 Pet. i. 11. (2.) Because we meet with contests and oppositions in this state: as the Israelites after they had passed over Jordan, and, according to the promise, were entered into the rest of God, yet had great work to do in securing and preserving the possession which they had taken by faith; yea, they had great enemies to contend withal and to subdue. Much diligence and wisdom were yet to be used for their settlement. And it is not otherwise with us as to our entrance into the rest of God in this world. We have yet spiritual adversaries to conflict withal; and the utmost of our spiritual endeavours are required to secure our possession, and to carry us on to perfection.

Obs. I. The state of believers under the gospel is a state of blessed rest; it is God's rest and theirs.

So much was necessary to be spoken concerning the nature of this rest in the opening of the words, that I shall treat but briefly on this observation, though the matter of it be of great importance. God created man in a state of present rest. This belonged unto that goodness and perfection of all the works of his hands which God saw in them, and blessed them thereon. And as a token of this rest did God institute the rest of the seventh day; that man, by his example and command, might use and improve the state of rest wherein he was made, as we shall see afterwards. Now, this rest consisted in three things:—1. Peace with God; 2. Satisfaction and acquiescency in God; 3. Means of communion with God. All these were lost by the entrance of sin, and all mankind were brought thereby into an estate of trouble and disquietment. In the restoration of these, and that in a better and more secure way and manner, doth this gospel-state of believers consist.

First, Without it our *moral state*, in respect of God, is an estate of *enmity and trouble*. There is no peace between God and sinners. They exercise an "enmity against God" by sin, Rom. viii. 7; and God executeth an enmity against them by the curse of the law, John iii. 36. Hence nothing ensues but trouble, fear, disquietment, and anguish of mind. The relief that any find, or seem to find, or pretend to find, in darkness, ignorance, superstition, security, self-righteousness, false hopes, will prove a refuge of lies, a covering too short and narrow to hide them from the wrath of God, which is the principal cause of all trouble to the souls of men. All this is removed by the gospel; for, "being justified by faith, we have peace with God," Rom. v. 1. Jesus Christ therein is "our peace, who hath reconciled us unto God by the cross, having slain the enmity thereby," Eph. ii. 14, 16. And as for the law, which is the means and instrument whereby God gives in trouble to the souls of men, the power and curse whereof constitute them in a state of unrest and trouble, he hath undergone the curse of it, Gal. iii. 13, and fulfilled the righteousness of it, Rom. viii. 3; whence the covenant of it is abolished, Heb. viii. 13, and the condemning power of it is taken away, 1 Cor. xv. 56, 57. The benefit of all which grace being communicated to believers in and by the gospel, they are instated in peace with God; which is the foundation and first part of our rest, or our interest in this rest of God.

Secondly, There is in all men, before the coming of the gospel, a want of an *acquiescency and satisfaction in God*. This is produced by the corrupt principle and power of sin, which having turned off the soul from God, causeth it to wander in endless vanities, and to pursue various lusts and pleasures, seeking after rest which always flies from it. This is the great, real, active principle of unrest or disquietment unto the souls of men. This makes them "like a troubled sea, which cannot rest." The "ignorance that is in them alienates them from the life of God," Eph. iv. 18. And their fleshliness or sensuality fills them with a dislike and hatred of God; for "the carnal mind is enmity against God," Rom. viii. 7, 8. And the "vanity of their minds" leads them up and down the world after "divers lusts and pleasures," Eph. iv. 17. And is there, can there be, any peace, any rest in such a condition? But this also is removed by the gospel; for its work is to destroy and ruin that power of sin which hath thus turned off the soul from God, and so again to renew the image of God in it, that it may make him its rest. This is the effect of the gospel, to take men off from their principle of alienation from God, and to turn their minds and affections unto him as their rest, satisfaction, and reward; and other way for these ends under heaven there is none.

Thirdly, Unto peace with God, and acquiescency in him, a way of *intercourse* and communion with him is required, to complete a state of spiritual rest. And this also, as it was lost by sin, so it is restored unto us in and by the gospel. This our apostle discourseth of at large in the ninth and tenth chapters of this epistle, whither we refer the consideration of it.

But yet I must acknowledge that the truth insisted on is liable to some important objections, which seem to have strength communicated unto them both from the Scriptures and from the experience of them that do believe. Some of the principal, therefore, of them, as instances of the rest, must be removed out of the way. And it will be said,—

1. ' That the description given us of the *state of believers* in this world lies in direct contradiction to our assertion; for doth not our Saviour himself foretell all his disciples that " in this world they shall have trouble;" that they should be "hated," and "persecuted," and "slain?" See John xv. 19–21, xvi. 2, 33. And did not the apostles assure their hearers that "through much tribulation they must enter into the kingdom of God ?" Acts xiv. 22. Hence it is the notation of believers, " them that are troubled," to whom future rest is promised, 2 Thess. i. 7. And when they come to heaven, they are said to "come out of great tribulation," Rev. vii. 14; yea, they are warned not to think strange of " fiery trials," the greatest, the highest imaginable, as that which is the common lot and portion of all that believe in Jesus, 1 Pet iv. 12. And do not, have not believers in all ages found this in their own experience to be their state and condition ? And is it not the very first lesson of the gospel, for men to "take up the cross," and to "deny themselves" in all their desires and enjoyments ? And how can this be esteemed to be an estate of rest, which, being denominated from the greater part of its concernments and occurrences, may be called a state of trouble or tribulation, which is directly contrary to a state of rest ?'

(1.) It is not difficult to remove this objection. Our Lord Jesus Christ hath done it for us, in these words of his to his disciples, "In the world ye shall have trouble; but in me ye shall have peace," John xvi. 33. The rest we treat of is spiritual; God's rest, and our rest in God. Now spiritual, inward rest, in and with God, is not inconsistent with outward, temporal trouble in the world. We might go over all those things wherein we have manifested this gospel-rest to consist, and easily evince that no one of them can be impeached by all the troubles that may befall us in this world; but our apostle hath summarily gone through with this work for us: Rom. viii.

35–39, "Who shall separate us from the love of Christ? shall tribulation, or distress, or persecution, or famine, or nakedness, or peril, or
sword ?..... Nay, in all these things we are more than conquerors,
through him that loved us. For I am persuaded that neither death,
nor life, nor angels, nor principalities, nor powers, nor things present,
nor things to come, nor height, nor depth, nor any other creature,
shall be able to separate us from the love of God, which is in Christ
Jesus our Lord." The sum of all is this, that no outward thing,
no possible opposition, shall prevail to cast us out of that rest which
we have obtained an entrance into, or impede our future entrance
into eternal rest with God.

(2.) Moreover, one part of this rest whereinto we are entered
consists in that *persuasion* and assurance which it gives us of eternal
rest, wherewith believers may support their souls under their
troubles, and balance all the persecutions and afflictions that they
meet withal in this world. And this also our apostle directs us
unto, 2 Cor. iv. 16–18: "For which cause," saith he, " we faint not;
but though our outward man perish, yet the inward man is renewed
day by day. For our light affliction, which is but for a moment,
worketh for us a far more exceeding and eternal weight of glory;
while we look not at the things which are seen, but at the things
which are not seen; for the things which are seen are temporal, but
the things which are not seen are eternal." That persuasion which
we have in this gospel-state of an assured enjoyment of eternal, invisible things, an " eternal weight of glory," casts out of consideration
all the momentary sufferings which in this world we may be exposed
unto. As our peace with God by Christ, our interest in him, our
communion with him, and acceptance in our worship through the
blood of Jesus, the spiritual freedom and liberty of spirit which we
have through the Holy Ghost in all that we have to do with him,
and the like spiritual mercies, wherein this rest doth consist, can
neither be weakened nor impaired by outward troubles; so it supplies us with such present joy, and infallible future expectation, as
enable us both to glory in them and triumph over them, Rom. v.
3–5. Yea,—

(3.) Further, God is pleased so to order and dispose of things,
that this rest is never more assured, more glorious and conspicuous,
than when those who are entered into it are under reproach, trouble,
and sufferings, upon the account of their profession of it. So saith
the apostle, 1 Pet. iv. 14, " If ye be reproached for the name of
Christ, happy are ye; for the Spirit of glory and of God resteth upon
you." Whatever may befall us of evil and trouble upon the account
of the gospel, it adds unto that blessed state of rest whereinto we
are entered; for therein "the Spirit of glory and of God resteth
on us." There is more in the words than that one expression should

serve merely to explain the other, as if he had said, 'The Spirit of glory, that is, of God;' nor is it a mere Hebraism for the glorious Spirit of God; but the especial work of the Spirit of God in and upon believers in such a season is intended. 'He shall work gloriously in them, and by them; supporting, comforting, and powerfully enabling them to maintain and preserve their souls in that rest whereinto they are called.' This state of rest, therefore, cannot be impeached by any outward troubles.

2. 'But it seems not inwardly and spiritually to answer the description that hath been given of it; for, (1.) There are many true believers who all their days never come to any abiding sense of *peace with God*, but are filled with trouble, and exercised with fears and perplexities, so that they go mourning and heavily all their days. These find it not a place of rest. (2.) There are no believers but are exercised with continual troubles from the *remainders of sin* yet abiding in them. These keep them in a continual conflict, and make their lives a warfare, causing them to cry out and complain because of their trouble, Rom. vii. 24. And it may be said, How can these things consist with a state of rest?

Some few distinctions will clear our way also from the cumbrance of this objection. As,—

(1.) It is one thing *to be in a state of rest*, another *to know* that a man is so. Believers are by faith instated in rest, and have every one of them "peace with God," being "reconciled unto him by the blood of the cross;" but as to what shall be the measure of their own understanding of their interest therein, this is left to the sovereign grace and pleasure of God.

(2.) There is a difference between a *state of rest* in general and actual rest in all particulars. A state of rest, denominated from all the principal concernments of it, may admit of much actual disquietment, whereby the state itself is not overthrown or changed, nor the interests of any in it disannulled. And the contests of indwelling sin against our spiritual rest are no other.

(3.) There is a difference between a *state itself* and men's *participation* of that state. This gospel-state in and of itself is an estate of complete peace and rest; but our participation of it is various and gradual. Rest in it is provided, prepared, and exhibited; this we receive according to our several measures and attainments.

(4.) Let it be remembered that our whole interest in this rest is called our *entrance;* we do enter, and we do *but enter:* we are so possessed as that we are continually entering into it; and this will admit of the difficulties before insisted on without the least impeachment of this state of rest.

Obs. II. It is faith alone which is the only way and means of entering into this blessed state of rest. "We who have believed do enter."

This is that which all along the apostle both asserteth and proveth. His whole design, indeed, is to manifest, by testimonies and examples, that unbelief cuts off from, and faith gives an entrance into, the rest of God. Only, whereas it is evident that the unbelief which cut them off of old, did produce and was attended with disobedience,—whence, as we observed, the apostle expresseth their sin by a word that may signify either the one or the other, the cause or the effect, unbelief or disobedience,—so the faith which gives us this admission into the rest of God, is such as produceth and is accompanied with the obedience that the gospel requireth. But yet neither doth this obedience belong to the *formal nature* of faith, nor is it the condition of our entrance, but only *the due manner of our behaviour* in our entering. The entrance itself depends on faith alone; and that both negatively, so that without it no entrance is to be obtained, whatever else men may plead to obtain it by; and positively, in that it alone effects it, without a contribution of aid or strength in its so doing from any other grace or duty whatever. This is not a purchase for silver or gold to prevail for, as men may buy a rest from purgatory: works of the law, or of supererogation, if they might be found, will not open this way unto us; it is faith alone that gives this entrance: "We which have believed do enter into rest;" which is the apostle's assertion in this place.

The SECOND thing in these words is the proof produced by the apostle in the confirmation of the foregoing assertion. And this lies in the next part of the verse: "As he said, As I have sworn in my wrath, if they shall enter into my rest." The exposition of these words, absolutely considered, we have passed through on the former chapter. Our present inquiry is only into their use in this place. And it is evident that they are intended by the apostle for a confirmation of what he had before affirmed. But yet it is certain, that this at the first view they do not seem to do. For how is it proved that "we who believe do enter into rest," because God sware concerning others, that "they should not so do?" This difficulty we must remove by a due application of these words unto the apostle's purpose.

The words may be considered two ways. 1. Logically, merely as to the rational and artificial form of the argument in them. 2. Theologically, as to their force and intention according to the analogy of faith. And both ways we shall find the apostle's intention and assertion evinced by them.

For the first, the apostle's argument depends upon a known rule, namely, that *unto immediate contraries*, or things immediately contrary one to another, *contrary attributes may be certainly ascribed:* so that he who affirms the one at the same time denies the other; and on the contrary, he that denies the one affirms the other. He that says, ' It is day,' doth as really say it is not night as if he had used these formal words. Now, the proposition laid down by the apostle in proof of his assertion is this, 'They who believed not did not enter into God's rest; for God sware that they should not, and that because they believed not. Hence it follows inevitably, in a just ratiocination, that they who do believe do enter into that rest.' Supposing what he hath already proved, and intends further to confirm, namely, that the promise belongs unto us as well as unto them, —the promise is the same, only the rest is changed; and supposing also what he hath already fully proved, namely, that the enjoying of the promise, or entering into rest, depends on the mixing of it with faith, or believing; and his proof that those who do believe do enter into rest, because God hath sworn that those who believe not shall not enter, is plain and manifest. For, the promise being the same, if unbelief exclude, faith gives entrance; for what is denied of the one is therein affirmed of the other. Some expositors of the Roman church do greatly perplex themselves and their readers in answering an objection which they raise to themselves on this place. For say they, ' By the rule and reason of contraries, if *unbelief* alone exclude from the rest of God,—that is, the glory of God in heaven,—then *faith* alone gives admission into glory.' This they cannot bear, for fear they should lose the advantage of their own merits. And they are incompetent to salve their own objection. For the rule they respect will inevitably carry it, that in what sense soever unbelief excludes, faith gives admission. But the truth is, that both their objections and their answers are in this place importune and unseasonable; for it is not the rest of glory that is here intended, and that faith alone gives us admission into a gospel-state of rest, they will not deny.

And here by the way we may take notice of the use of reason, or logical deductions, in the proposing, handling, and confirming of sacred, supernatural truths, or articles of faith. For the validity of the apostle's proof in this place depends on the certainty of the logical maxim before mentioned, whose consideration removes its whole difficulty. And to deny this liberty of deducing consequences, or one thing from another, according to the just rules of due ratiocination, is quite to take away the use of the Scripture, and to banish reason from those things wherein it ought to be principally employed.

Secondly, The words may be considered *theologically;* that is, by other rules of Scripture, according to the analogy of faith. And thus the force of the apostle's proof springs out of another root, or there lies a reason in the testimony used by him taken from another consideration. And this is from the nature of God's covenant with us, and the end thereof. For whereas the covenant of God is administered unto us in promises and threatenings, they have all of them the same end allotted to them, and the same grace to make them effectual. Hence every threatening includes a promise in it, and every promise hath also the nature of a threatening in its proposal. There is a mutual inbeing of promises and threatenings in reference unto the ends of the covenant. God expressing his mind in various ways, hath still the same end in them all. The first covenant was given out in a mere word of threatening: "The day thou eatest thou shalt die." But yet none doubteth but that there was a promise of life upon obedience included in that threatening, yea, and principally intended. So there is a threatening in every promise of the gospel. Whereas, therefore, there is a great threatening, confirmed with the oath of God, in these words, that those who believe not should not enter into his rest; there is a promise included in the same words, no less solemnly confirmed, that those who do believe should enter into rest: and thence doth the apostle confirm the truth of his assertion. From what hath been discoursed we may observe, that,—

Obs. III. There is a mutual inbeing of the promises and threatenings of the covenant, so that in our faith and consideration of them they ought not utterly to be separated.

Wherever there is a promise, there a threatening in reference unto the same matter is tacitly understood. And wherever there is a threatening, that is no more than so, be it never so severe, there is a gracious promise included in it; yea, sometimes God gives out an express threatening for no other end but that men may lay hold on the promise tacitly included. The threatening that Nineveh should perish was given out that it might not perish. And John Baptist's preaching that the axe was laid to the root of the trees was a call to repentance, that none might be cut down and cast into the fire. And the reasons hereof are,—

1. Because they have both of them the *same rise* and spring. Both promises and threatenings do flow from, and are expressive of the holy, gracious nature of God, with respect unto his actings towards men in covenant with himself. Now, though there are distinct properties in the nature of God, which operate, act, and express themselves distinctly, yet they are all of them essential properties of one and the same nature; and what proceeds from them hath the same fountain. So declaring his nature by his name, he ascribes that unto his one being which will produce contrary effects, Exod. xxxiv. 6, 7 : That he is "gracious, long-suffering, abundant in goodness and truth, keeping mercy for thousands, forgiving iniquity, transgression, and sin," he expresseth in and by his promises; that he "will by no means clear the guilty," but "visit iniquity," he expresseth by his threatenings. They do both of them but declare the actings of the one holy God, according to the distinct properties of his nature, upon distinct objects. This is the foundation of that

mutual inbeing of promises and threatenings whereof we discourse.

2. Both of them, as annexed to the covenant, or as the covenant is administered by them, have the *same end.* God doth not design one end by a promise, and another by a threatening, but only different ways of compassing or effecting the same end. The end of both is, to increase in us faith and obedience. Now, this is variously effected, according to the variety of those faculties and affections of our souls which are affected by them, and according to the great variety of occasions that we are to pass through in the world. Faith and obedience are principally in our minds and wills; but they are excited to act by our affections. Now, these are differently wrought upon by promises and threatenings, yet all directing to the same end. The use of divine threatenings is, to make such a representation of divine holiness and righteousness to men, as that, being moved by fear, an affection suited to be wrought upon by the effects of them, they may be stirred up unto faith and obedience. So Noah, upon God's warning, that is, his threatening the world with destruction, being "moved with fear, prepared an ark," Heb. xi. 7; which our apostle instanceth in as an effect of his faith and evidence of his obedience. The threatenings of God, then, are not assigned unto any other end but what the promises are assigned unto, only they work and operate another way. Hereon faith coming unto the consideration of them, finds the same love and grace in them as in the promises, because they lead to the same end.

3. Again, threatenings are *conditional;* and the nature of such conditions is, not only somewhat is affirmed upon their supposal, and denied upon their denial, but the contrary unto it is affirmed upon their denial; and that because the denial of them doth assert a contrary condition. For instance, the threatening is, that he who believeth not shall not enter into the rest of God. Upon a supposition of unbelief, it is affirmed herein that there shall be no entrance into rest. Upon the denial of that supposal, not only it is not averred that there shall be no such entrance, but it is also affirmed that men shall enter into it. And this because the denial of unbelief doth include and assert faith itself, which plainly gives the threatening the nature of a promise, and as such may it be used and improved.

4. The same grace is administered in the covenant to make the one and the other *effectual.* Men are apt to think that the promises of the gospel are accompanied towards the elect with a supply of effectual grace to render them useful, to enable them to believe and obey. This makes them hear them willingly, and attend unto them gladly. They think they can never enough consider or meditate upon them. But as for the threatenings of the gospel, they suppose that they have no other end but to make them afraid; and so they

may be freed from the evil which they portend, they care not how little they converse with them. As for any assistance in their obedience to be communicated by them, they do not expect it. But this is a great mistake. Threatenings are no less sanctified of God for the end mentioned than promises are; nor are they, when duly used and improved, less effectual to that purpose. God leaves no part of his word, in its proper place, unaccompanied with his Spirit and grace; especially not that which is of so near a concernment unto his glory. Hence many have had grace administered unto them by threatenings, on whom the promises have made no impression: and this not only persons before conversion, for their conviction and humiliation, but even believers themselves, for their awakening, recovery from backsliding, awe and reverence of God in secret duties, encouragement in sufferings, and the like. Now, from what hath been spoken, it follows that faith, being duly exercised about and towards gospel threatenings, yea, the most severe of them, may find the same love and the same grace in them as in the most sweet and gracious promises. And there can be no reason why men should dislike the preaching and consideration of them, but because they too well like the sins and evils that are the condition of their execution.

We shall now proceed to the opening of the last clause of this verse, wherein the apostle illustrates and confirms the truth of the proof he had produced, by evincing that he had made a right application of the testimony used to that purpose. For proving that those who believe under the gospel do enter into rest, from these words of the psalmist, "If they shall enter into my rest," it was incumbent on him to manifest that the rest intended in these words had respect unto the rest of the gospel, which was now preached unto all the Hebrews, and entered into by all that believed. Whereas, therefore, a rest of God is mentioned in that testimony, he proceeds to consider the various rests that, on several accounts, are so called in the Scripture, "the rests of God." From the consideration of them he concludes, that after all other rests formerly enjoyed by the people of God were past, there *yet remained a rest* for them under the Messiah, which was principally intended in the prophetical words of David. This is the design of his ensuing discourse, which here he makes an entrance into with some seeming abruptness, or at least with an elliptical phrase of speech, in these words, "Although the works were finished from the foundation of the world."

Καίτοι.   Καίτοι. Some render it "et quidem," "and truly;" some "quamvis," and "quanquam," "although;" some "sed," "but;" the Syriac, אֶלָּא, "quia ecce," or "et ecce," "and behold." The addition of the particle τοι to the conjunction causeth this variety. And καίτοι is variously used and variously rendered

out of other authors; which I should not mention, as seeming too
light a matter here to be insisted on, but that various interpretations
do often depend on the different acceptation of these particles. The
common use of it is " quamvis:" so is it here rendered by Erasmus
and Beza, who are followed by ours, " although." So Demosthenes,
Καίτοι τόγε αἰσχρὸν ὁμοίως, "Quamvis et id similiter turpe,"—"Although
that be dishonest in like manner." What this exception intends
shall be afterwards declared.

Τῶν ἔργων, "the works;" that is, of God's creation: the works of the
creation. So the Syriac, עֲבְדוֹהִי דַּאלָהָא,—"the works
of God himself;" that is כָּל מְלַאכְתּוֹ אֲשֶׁר בָּרָא אֱלֹהִים לַעֲשׂוֹת,   Τῶν ἔργων.
—" all his work that God created and made," or that he designed
to make in that first creation.

Γενηθέντων, "perfectis,"—" were perfected," or "finished." Syr, הֲווֹ,
"fuerunt," or "facta sunt,"—" were," or " were made."
"Genitis," "being born," from אֵלֶּה תוֹלְדוֹת, Gen. ii. 4; or   Γενηθέντων.
" created," " finished," " perfected," from וַיְכֻלּוּ, Gen. ii. 1,—" were
finished." The end of עָשָׂה, "he made." There was, in the creation,
God's design, לַעֲשׂוֹת, to " make all things;" according thereunto, בָּרָא
or עָשָׂה, he " created" or " made;" the end whereof was יְכֻלּוּ, they
" were finished." For the apostle in these words applies the first
three verses of the second chapter of Genesis to his own purpose.

The season of the whole is added, ἀπὸ καταβολῆς κόσμου, " a
jacto mundi fundamento," " a jactis mundi fundamen-
tis," " ab institutione mundi," " a constitutione mundi,"   Ἀπὸ καταβο-
—" from the foundation of the world." Syr., מֶן שׁוּרָיֵהּ   λῆς κόσμου.
דְעָלְמָא,—" from the beginning of the world." Καταβολή is properly
" jactus ex loco superiore," a casting of any thing from above,
thither where it may abide. Hence Chrysostom on Eph. i. 3, on
the same word: Ὡς ἀπό τινος ὕψους καταβεβλημένον μεγάλου αὐτὸν
δεικνύς·—the founding of the word comes from above, from the
power of God over all. The word is but once in the New Testament applied unto any other purpose, Heb. xi. 11; but frequently
in that construction here used, καταβολὴ κόσμου. See Matt. xiii. 35,
xxv. 34; Luke xi. 50; John xvii. 24; Eph. i. 4; Heb. ix. 26; 1 Pet.
i. 20; Rev. xiii. 8, xvii. 8. Twice with πρό, that is, " before," Eph.
i. 4; 1 Pet. i. 20, "Before the foundation of the world;" else with ἀπό,
"from" it, denoting the beginning of time, as the other doth eternity.

" Although the works were finished from the foundation of the
world."

I do acknowledge that these words, as they relate to the preceding and ensuing discourses of the apostle, are attended with great
difficulties; for the manner of the ratiocination or arguing here used
seems to be exceedingly perplexed. But we have a relief against
the consideration of the obscurity of this and the like passages of

holy writ; for the things delivered obscurely in them, as far as they are needful for us to know or practise, are more fully and clearly explained in other places. Nor is there the least semblance that any thing contained in this place should have an inconsistency with what is elsewhere declared. The principal difficulties lie in the discovery of the especial design of the apostle, with the force of the arguments, reasons, and testimonies, whereby he confirmeth his purpose;—that is, that we may clearly discern both what it is which he intends to prove and how he proves it; for the sense of the words is obvious. These are the things that we are to inquire into, with what spiritual skill and diligence God is pleased to impart. And here, because the words under consideration do give an entrance into the whole ensuing discourse, I shall on them lay down the general principles of it, which I would desire the reader a little to attend unto, and afterwards to consider how they are severally educed from the particular passages of it:—

First, It is evident that the apostle here engageth into the confirmation of what he had laid down and positively asserted in the foregoing verses. Now this is, ' That there is yet, under the gospel, a promise of entering into the rest of God left or remaining unto believers; and that they do enter into that rest by mixing the promise of it with faith.' This he declares, and the declaration of it was useful unto and necessary for these Hebrews. For he lets them know, as hath been showed, that, notwithstanding their enjoyment of the rest of Canaan, with the worship and rest of God therein, which their forefathers fell short of by their unbelief, they were now under a new trial, a new rest being proposed unto them in the promise. This he proves by a testimony out of the 95th psalm. But the application of that testimony unto his purpose is obnoxious unto a great objection. For the rest mentioned in that psalm seems to be a rest long since past and enjoyed, either by themselves or others; so that they could have no concernment in it, nor be in any danger of coming short of it. And if this were so, all the arguments and exhortations of the apostle in this place might be rejected as groundless and incogent, as drawn from a mistaken and misapplied testimony.

To remove this objection, and thereby confirm his former assertion and exhortation, is the present design of the apostle.

Secondly, To the end mentioned, he proceeds unto the exposition and vindication of the testimony which he had cited out of the psalm. And herein he shows, from the *proper signification* of the words, from the *time* when they were spoken, and *persons* to whom, that no other rest is intended in them but what was now proposed unto them, or the rest of God and of his people in the gospel. This he proves by various arguments, laying singular weight upon this matter; for if there was a new rest promised, and now proposed unto them, if they mixed not the promise of it with faith during the time of their day, or continuance of God's patience towards them, they must perish, and that eternally.

Thirdly, The general argument to his purpose which he insists on, consists in an enumeration of all the several rests of God and his people which are mentioned in the Scripture; for from the consideration of them all he proves that no other rest could be principally intended in the words of David but only the rest of the gospel, whereinto they enter who do believe.

Fourthly, From that respect which the words of the psalmist have unto the other foregoing rests, he manifests that those also were representations of that spiritual rest which was now brought in and established. These things comprise the design of the apostle in general.

In pursuit hereof he declares in particular,—1. That the rest mentioned in the psalm is not that which ensued *immediately on the creation.* This he evinceth because it is spoken of afterwards, a long time after, and that to another purpose, verses 4, 5. 2. That it is not the rest of the *land of Canaan,* because that was not entered into by them unto whom it was promised, for they came short of it by their unbelief, and perished in the wilderness; but now this rest is offered afresh, verses 6, 7. 3. Whereas it may be objected, that although the wilderness-generation entered not in, yet their posterity did, under the conduct of Joshua, verse 8; he answers, that this rest in the psalm being promised and proposed by David so long a time (above four hundred years) after the people had quietly possessed the land whereinto they were conducted by Joshua, it must needs be that another rest, yet to come, was intended in those words of the psalmist, verse 9. And, 4. To conclude his argument, he declareth that this new rest hath a *new, peculiar* foundation, that the other had no interest or concernment in, namely, his ceasing from his own work and entering into his rest who is the author of it, verse 10. This is the way and manner of the apostle's arguing, for the proof of what he had said before in the beginning of the chapter, and which he issueth in the conclusion expressed, verse 9.

But we are yet further to inquire into the nature of the several rests here discoursed of by the apostle, with their relation one to another, and the especial concernments of that rest which he exhorts them to enter into, wherein the principal difficulties of the place do lie. And some light into the whole may be given in the ensuing propositions:—

1. *The rest of God* is the foundation and principal cause of our rest. So it is still called God's rest: "If they shall enter into my rest." It is, on some account or other, God's rest before it is ours.

2. God's rest is not spoken of absolutely with respect unto himself only, but with reference to the rest that ensued thereon for the church to rest with him in. Hence it follows that the rests here mentioned are as it were double,—namely, the rest of God, and the rest that ensued thereon for us to enter into. For instance, at the finishing of the works of creation, which is first proposed, " God ceased from his work, and rested;" this was his own rest. He "rested on the seventh day." But that was not all; he "blessed it" for the rest of man, a rest for us ensuing on his rest: that is, an expressive representation of it, and a figure or means of our entering into, or being taken into a participation of the rest of God ; for the sum of all that is proposed unto us, is an entrance into the rest of God.

3. The apostle proposeth the *threefold state of the church* of God unto consideration:—(1.) The state of it under *the law of nature* or creation; (2.) The state of it under *the law of institutions* and carnal ordinances; (3.) That now introducing *under the gospel.* To each of these he assigns a distinct rest of God, a rest of the church entering into God's rest, and a day of rest as a means and pledge thereof. And withal he manifests that the former two were ordered to be previous representations of the latter, though not equally nor on the same account.

(1.) He considers the church and the state of it under the *law of nature*, before the entrance of sin. And herein he shows, first, that there was a *rest of God;* for " the works," saith he, " were finished from the foundation of the world, and God did rest from all his works," verses 3, 4. This was God's own rest, and was the foundation of the *church's rest.* For, [1.] It was the duty of man hereon to enter into the rest of God,—that is, to make God his rest, here in faith and obedience, and hereafter in immediate fruition; for which end also he was made. [2.] *A day of rest,* namely, the seventh day, was blessed and sanctified, for the present means of entering into that rest of God, in the performance of his worship, and a pledge of the eternal fulness and continuance thereof, verses 3, 4. So that in this state of the church there were three things considerable:—[1.] God's rest; [2.] Men's entering into God's rest by faith and obedience; [3.] A day of rest, or a remembrance of the one and a pledge of the other. And in all this there was a type of our rest under the gospel (for which end it is mentioned), wherein he who is God did cease from his work, and therein lay the foundation of the rest that ensued, as we shall see.

(2.) He considers the church under the *law of institutions.* And herein he representeth the rest of Canaan, wherein also the three distinct rests before mentioned do occur. [1.] There was in it a rest of God. This gives denomination to the whole, for he still calls it

" my rest;" for God wrought about it works great and mighty, and ceased from them only when they were finished. And this work of his answered in its greatness unto the work of creation, whereunto it is compared by himself, Isa. li. 15, 16, " I am the LORD thy God, that divided the sea, whose waves roared; The LORD of hosts is his name. And I have put my words in thy mouth, and I have covered thee in the shadow of mine hand, that I may plant the heavens, and lay the foundations of the earth, and say unto Zion, Thou art my people." The " dividing of the sea, whose waves roared," is put by a synecdoche for the whole work of God preparing a way for the church-state of the people in the land of Canaan, the whole being expressed in one signal instance: and this he compares unto the works of creation, in " planting the heavens, and laying the foundations of the earth;" for although those words are but a metaphorical expression of the church and political state of the people, yet there is an evident allusion in them unto the original creation of all things. This was the work of God, upon the finishing whereof he entered into his rest; for after the erection of his worship in the land of Canaan, he said of it, "This is my rest, and here will I dwell."

[2.] God being thus entered into his rest, in like manner as formerly, two things ensued thereon:—1st. That the people are invited and encouraged to enter into his rest. And this their entrance into rest was their coming by faith and obedience into a participation of his worship, wherein he rested; which though some came short of by unbelief, yet others entered into under the conduct of Joshua. 2dly. Both these God expressed by appointing a day of rest; for he did so, both that it might be a token, sign, and pledge of his own rest in his instituted worship, and be a means, in the solemn observation of that worship, to further their entrance into the rest of God. These were the ends of God's instituting a day of rest among his people, whereby it became a peculiar sign or token that he was their God, and that they were his people. It is true, this day was the same in order of the days with that before observed from the foundation of the world, namely, the seventh day from the foundation of the creation; but yet it was now re-established, upon new considerations and unto new ends and purposes. The time of the change and alteration of the day itself was not yet come; for this work was but preparatory for a greater. And so, whereas both these rests, that of old, from the foundation of the world, and this newly instituted in the land of Canaan, were designed to represent the rest of the gospel, it was meet they should agree in the common pledge and token of them. Besides, the covenant whereunto the seventh day was originally annexed was not yet abolished, nor yet to be abolished; and so that day was not yet to be changed. Hence the seventh day came to fall under a double consideration:—(1st.) As it was such a proportion of time as was requisite for the worship of God, and appointed as a pledge of his rest under the law of creation, wherein it had respect unto God's rest from the works of creation alone; (2*dly*.) As it received a new institution, with superadded ends and significations, as a token and pledge of God's rest under the law of institutions; but materially the day was to be the same until that work was done, and that rest was brought in, which both of them did signify. Thus both these states of the church had these three things distinctly in them:—a rest of God for their foundation; a rest in obedience and worship for the people to enter into; and a day of rest, as a pledge and token of both the others.

(3.) The apostle proves, from the words of the psalmist, that yet there was to be a *third state* of the church,—an especial state under the Messiah, or of the gospel, whereof the others were appointed to be types and shadows. And thence he likewise manifests that there is yet remaining also another state of rest, belonging unto it, which is yet to be entered into. Now, to the constitution of this rest, as before, three things are required:—[1.] That there be some *signal work of God* which he must have completed and finished, and thereon entered into his rest. This must be the foundation of the whole new church-state to be introduced, and of the rest to be obtained therein. [2.] That there be a *spiritual rest* ensuing thereon, and arising thence, for them that believe to enter into. [3.] That there be a new or a *renewed day of rest*, to express the rest of God unto us, and to be a means and pledge of our entering into it.

And that all these do concur in this new state of the church it is the apostle's design to demonstrate, which also he doth; for he showeth,—[1.] That there is a *great work of God*, and that finished, for the foundation of the whole. This he had made way for, chap. iii. 3, 4, where he both expressly asserts Christ to be God who made all things, and shows the analogy and correspondency that is between the creation of all things and the building of the church. As God, then, wrought in the creation of all, so Christ, who is God, wrought in the setting up of this new church-state; and upon his finishing of it he entered into his rest, ceasing from his works, as God also did upon the creation from his, chap. iv. 10: for that the words of that verse contain the foundation of the gospel church-state, in the work of Christ and rest that ensued thereon, shall be declared in its proper place. [2.] That there is hence arising " a *rest for the people of God*," or believers, to enter into. This is the main of his design to prove, and he doth it invincibly from the testimony of the psalmist. [3.] It remains that there must be a *new day of rest*, suited and accommodated to this new church-state. And this new day must arise from the rest that the Lord Christ entered into, when he had finished the work whereby that new church-state was founded.

This is the "sabbath-keeping" which the apostle concludes that he had evinced from his former discourse, verse 9.

And concerning this day we may observe,—1*st.* That it hath this in common with the former days, that it is a sabbatism, or *one day in seven;* for this portion of time to be dedicated unto rest, having its foundation in the light and law of nature, was equally to pass through all estates of the church. 2*dly.* That although both the former states of the church had one and the same day, though varied as to some ends of it in the latter institution, now *the day itself* is changed; because it now respects a work quite of another nature as its foundation than that day did which went before. And therefore is the day now changed, which before could not be so. 3*dly.* That the observation of it is suited unto the spiritual state of the church under the gospel, delivered from *the bondage frame of spirit* wherewith it was observed under the law.

These are the rests the apostle here discourseth of, or a three-fold rest, under a threefold state of the church; and if any of these be left out of our consideration, the whole structure of the discourse is loosened and dissolved.

The involvedness of this context, with the importance of the matter treated of in it, with the consideration of the very little light which hath been given unto it by any expositors whom I could as yet attain to the sight of, hath caused me to insist thus long in the investigation of the true analysis of it. And if the reader obtain any guidance by it into an understanding of the mind of the Holy Ghost, he will not think it tedious; nor yet the repetition of sundry things which must necessarily be called over again in the exposition of the several passages of the context, whereby the whole will be further opened and confirmed.

Having taken a prospect into the whole design of this place, I shall now return to the consideration of those particular passages and testimonies by which the whole of what we have observed from the context is cleared and established. And first we must view again the preface, or entrance into the discourse, as it is expressed in the close of the third verse:—

"Although the works were finished from the foundation of the world."

In these words the apostle begins his answer unto such objections as his former assertion, concerning the entrance of believers into God's rest now under the gospel, seems to be liable unto. And therein he clears it by a further exposition of the testimony produced out of the psalmist unto that purpose, compared with other places of Scripture wherein mention is made of the rest of God in like manner. Now, all rest supposeth work and labour. The first notion of it is a cessation from labour, with the trouble or weariness thereof. Wherefore every rest of God must have some work of God preceding it. That labour and rest are not properly ascribed unto God is evident. They include that lassitude or weariness upon pains in labour, that ease and quiet upon a cessation from labour, whereof the divine nature is not capable. But the effect of God's power in the operation of outward works, and an end of temporary operations, with the satisfaction of his wisdom in them, are the things that are intended in God's working and resting. Here the first is mentioned, τὰ ἔργα, "the works;" מַעֲשֵׂה, "the work,"—that is, of God. So he calls the effect of his creating power, his "work," yea, "the work of his hands" and "fingers," Ps. viii. 3, 6; in allusion to the way and manner whereby we effect our works. And the works here intended are expressed summarily, Gen. ii. 1, " The heavens and the earth, and all the host of them;" that is, the whole creation, distributed into its various kinds, with reference unto the season or distinct days of their production, as Gen. i.

Of these works it is said they were "finished." "The works were finished;" that is, so effected and perfected as that God would work no more in the same kind. The continuation of things made belongs unto God's effective providence; from the making more things, kinds of things, new things, "in rerum naturâ," God now ceased. So are the words usually interpreted, namely, that God now so finished and perfected all kinds of things, as that he would never more create any new kind, race, or species of them, but only continue and increase those now made, by an ordinary work upon them and concurrence with them in his providence. It may be this is so; it may be no instance can be given of any absolutely *new kind of creature* made by God since the finishing of his work at the foundation of the world: but it cannot be proved from these words; for no more is expressed or intended in them, but that, at the end of the sixth day, God finished and put an end unto that whole work of creating heaven and earth, and all the host of them, which he then designed, made, and blessed. These works, therefore, the works of the first creation, were finished, completed, perfected; and this,—

"From the foundation of the world." The words are a periphrasis of those six original days wherein time and all things measured by it and extant with it had their beginning. It is sometimes absolutely called "the beginning," Gen. i. 1, John i. 1; that is, when a beginning was given unto all creatures by Him who is without beginning. And both these expressions are put together, Heb. i. 10, κατ᾿ ἀρχάς. So the apostle renders לְפָנִים, Ps. cii. 25, "In the beginning thou hast laid the foundation." By "the foundation," then, is not intended absolutely the *first beginning* or foundation of the work, as we call that the foundation of a house or building which is first laid, and on which the fabric is raised. But the word is to be taken ἐν πλάτει, for the whole building itself; or formally for the building, which extends itself to the whole equally, and not materially to any part of it, first or last. For it is said that from this laying of the foundation " the works were finished." Καταβολὴ κόσμου is the erecting of the whole building of the creation on the stable foundation of the power of God put forth therein.

This is the first thing that the apostle fixeth as a foundation unto his ensuing discourse, namely, that in the first erection of the church in the state of nature, or under the law of creation, the beginning of it was in the work of God, which he first finished, and then entered into his rest; as he proves in the next verse. But we may here rest, and interpose some doctrinal observations; as first,—

Obs. IV. God hath showed us in his own example that work and labour is to precede our rest.

The first appearance of God to any of his rational creatures was working, or upon his works. Had any of them been awakened out of their nothing, and no representation of God been made unto them but of his essence and being in his own eternal rest and self-satisfaction, they could have had no such apprehensions of him as might prepare them for that subjection and obedience which he required of them. But now, in the very first instant of their existence, they found God gloriously displaying the properties of his nature, his wisdom, goodness, and power, in the works of his hands. This instructed them into faith, fear, and subjection of soul. When the angels were first created, those creatures of light, they found God as it were laying the foundations of the heavens and earth; whereon all those "sons of God shouted for joy," Job xxxviii. 7. They rejoiced in the manifestation that was made of the power and wisdom of God in the works which they beheld. Hence it is justly supposed that they were made on the first day, when only the foundations of this glorious fabric were laid, Gen. i. 2; wherein they were able to discern the impressions of his wisdom and power. Man was not created until more express representations were made of them in all other creatures, suited unto his institution. After God had done that which might satisfy them and men, in the contemplation of his works, he enters into his rest, returns as it were into his own eternal rest, and directs them to seek rest in himself.

And herein the design of God was to set us an example of that course which, "according to the counsel of his will," he intended by his command to guide us unto; namely, that a course of work and labour might precede our full enjoyment of rest. This he plainly declares in the fourth commandment, where the reason he gives why we ought, in a returning course, to attend unto six days of labour before we sanctify a day of rest, is, because he wrought himself six days, and then entered into his rest, Exod. xx. 8–11. The command instructs us in, and gives us the force and use of the example he sets us. Thus he dealt with Adam; he set him to work so soon as he was made: " He took the man, and put him into the garden of Eden, to dress it and to keep it," Gen. ii. 15. And this he was to do antecedently unto the day of rest which was given him; for it was upon the sixth day, yea, before the creation of the woman, that he was designed unto and put into his employment, and the rest was not sanctified for him until the day following. And this day of rest was given unto him as a pledge of eternal rest with God. So both the whole course of his obedience and his final rest after it were represented by his days of work and rest.

But here now there is an alteration under the gospel. The day of rest under the law, as a pledge of final rest with God, was the *last day* of the seven, the *seventh day;* but under the gospel it is the *first day* of the seven. Then the week of labour went before, now it follows after. And the reason hereof seems to be taken from the different state of the church. For of old, under the covenant of works, men were absolutely to labour and work, without any alteration or improvement of their condition, before they entered into rest. They should have had only a continuance of their state wherein they first set out, but no rest until they had wrought for it. The six days of labour went before, and the day of rest, the seventh day, followed them. But now it is otherwise. The first thing that belongs unto our present state is an entering into rest initially; for we enter in by faith. And then our working doth ensue; that is, " the obedience of faith." Rest is given us to set us on work; and our works are such as, for the manner of their performance, are consistent with a *state of rest.* Hence our day of rest goes before our days of labour: it is now the first of the week, of the seven, which before was the last. And those who contend now for the observation of the seventh day do endeavour to bring us again under the covenant of works, that we should do all our work before we enter into any rest at all. But it will be objected, that this is contrary to our observation before laid down, namely, that, after the example of God, we must work before we enter into rest; for now it is said that we enter into rest antecedently unto our works of obedience.

Ans. 1. The rest intended in the proposition is absolute, complete, and perfect,—the rest which is to be enjoyed with God for ever. Now, antecedent unto the enjoyment hereof all our works performed in a state of initial rest must be wrought. 2. There are works also which must precede our entering into this initial or gospel rest, though they belong not to our state, and so go before that sabbatical rest which precedes our course of working. Neither are these works such as are absolutely sinful in themselves and their own nature; which sort of works must be necessarily excluded from this whole discourse. Thus, our Saviour calling sinners unto him, with this encouragement, that in him they should find rest and enter into it, as hath been declared, he calls them that "labour and are heavy laden," Matt. xi. 28, 29. It is required that men labour under a sense of their sins, that they be burdened by them and made weary, before they enter into this initial rest. So that in every condition, both from the example of God and the nature of the thing itself, work and labour is to precede rest. And although we are now here in a state of rest, in comparison of what went before, yet this also is a state of working and labour with respect unto that fulness of everlasting rest which shall ensue thereon. This is the condition, that, from the example and command of God himself, all are to accept of. Our works and labours are to precede our rest. And whereas the divine nature is no way capable of lassitude, weariness, sense of pain or trouble in operation, it is otherwise with us,—all these things are in us attended with trouble, weariness, and manifold perplexities. We are not only to do, but to suffer also. This way is marked out for us, let us pursue it patiently, that we may answer the example, and be like unto our heavenly Father. Again,—

Obs. V. All the works of God are perfect.

He "finished" them, and said that they were "good." "He is the Rock, and his work is perfect," Deut. xxxii. 4. His infinite wisdom and power require that it should be so, and make it impossible that it should be otherwise. The conception of them is perfect, in *the infinite counsel of his will;* and the operation of them is perfect, through his *infinite power.* Nothing can proceed from him but what is so in its own kind and measure, and the whole of his works is so absolutely. See Isa. xl. 28. As when he undertook the work of creation, he finished it, or perfected it, so that it was in his own eyes "exceeding good;" so the works of grace and providence, which are yet upon the wheels, shall in like manner be accomplished. And this may teach us at all times to trust him with his own works, and all our concerns in them, whether they be the works of his grace in our hearts, or the works of his providence in the world. He will "perfect that which concerneth us," because "his mercy endureth for ever," and will "not forsake the work of his own hands," Ps. cxxxviii. 8.

Obs. VI. All the works of God in the creation were wrought and ordered in a subserviency unto his worship and glory thereby. This we have cleared in our passage.

VERSE 4.

The next verse gives the reason of the preceding mention of the works of God and the finishing of them. Now this was not for their own sakes, but because of a rest that ensued thereon,—the rest of

God, and a day of rest as a token of it, and a pledge of our interest therein, or entrance into it. That such a rest did ensue he proves by a testimony taken from Gen. ii. 2, 3, "And on the seventh day God ended his work which he had made; and he rested on the seventh day from all his work which he had made. And God blessed the seventh day, and sanctified it; because that in it he had rested from all his work which God created and made." The rest of God himself is intended solely neither in this place of Genesis nor by our apostle, although he repeats only these words, "And God did rest the seventh day from all his works." But the blessing and sanctifying of the seventh day, that is, the institution of it to be a day of rest unto man, and a pledge or means of his entering into the rest of God, is that which is also aimed at in both places. For this is that wherein the apostle is at present concerned.

Ver. 4.—Εἴρηκε γάρ που περὶ τῆς ἑβδόμης οὕτω· Καὶ κατέπαυσεν ὁ Θεὸς ἐν τῇ ἡμέρᾳ τῇ ἑβδόμῃ ἀπὸ πάντων τῶν ἔργων αὐτοῦ.

Εἴρηκε, "dixit," "said;" the nominative case is not expressed: 'The Scripture hath said.' This is a usual form of speech in the New Testament: John vii. 38, Καθὼς εἶπεν ἡ γραφή, verse 42. But most frequently the speaking of the Scripture is expressed by λέγει, John xix. 37, Rom. iv. 3, ix. 17, x. 11, xi. 2, Gal. iv. 3, James iv. 5: sometimes by λαλεῖ, Rom. iii. 19; here by εἴρηκε: all the words used in the New Testament to express *speaking* by. For it is not dead and mute, but living and vocal, even the voice of God to them who have ears to hear. And *speaking* is applied unto it both in the preterperfect tense, "hath said," "hath spoken," as John vii. 38, 42, to denote its original record; and in the present tense, to signify its continuing authority. Or, it may be that τίς should be here supplied, "A certain man said;" for our apostle hath already used that form of speech in his quotation, chap. ii. 6, Διεμαρτύρατο δέ που τίς, —"One testifieth in a certain place." Or, "He hath said;" that is, God himself, the Holy Ghost, whose authority in the Scripture in all this discourse and debate we rely upon. Or it is taken impersonally, for "dicitur," "It is said." Που, "alicubi," "in quondam loco,"—" somewhere," "in a certain place." The Syriac omits this που. Arab., "in a certain section." Περὶ τῆς ἑβδόμης. Translators generally, "de die septimo,"—" of the seventh day." The Syriac, כֹּל שַׁבְּתָא, —"concerning the Sabbath." Οὕτω or οὕτως,—" so," "after this manner." But there is little of difficulty in or difference about the translation of these words.

Ver. 4.—For he spake in a certain place [*somewhere*] of the seventh day on this manner, And God did rest the seventh day from all his works.

The verse hath two parts: the one expressing the *manner* of the introduction of an intended testimony; the other containing the *testimony* itself. The first is in these words: "For he spake in a certain place concerning the seventh day."

Γάρ.   Γάρ, "for," a note of illation, showing that in the ensuing words the apostle designed the proof of what he had elliptically expressed in the verse foregoing; the importance whereof we have before declared. The sum is, that there was a rest of God and his people, and a day of rest, from the foundation of the world; which was not the rest here mentioned by the psalmist. "For he saith."

Εἴρηκε, "he spake," or "said." Who or what this refers unto hath been showed already.   *Εἴρηκι.*

Πoυ, "somewhere," "in a certain place." As he allegeth not his author expressly, no more doth he the particular place where the words are recorded. He only refers the   *Πoυ.* Hebrews to the Scripture, which was the common acknowledged principle of truth between them, which he and they would acquiesce in, and wherein they were expert. Especially were they so in the books of Moses; and particularly in the history of the creation of the world, whence these words are taken. For this was their glory, that from thence they were in the clear light of the original of the universe, which was hidden in darkness from all the world besides.

Περὶ τῆς ἑβδόμης. This is the subject concerning which the ensuing testimony is produced. Generally the words are rendered, "de die septima," or "de septima;"—"of the   *Περὶ τῆς ἑβδό-* seventh day." Only the Syriac, as was observed, renders   *μης.* it "of the Sabbath day;" and this not unduly, as expressing the intention of the place. For ἑβδόμη, "the seventh," may be used either naturally and absolutely for the seventh day, ἡ ἡμέρα ἡ ἑβδόμη, as it is expressed in the words following, "the seventh day," that is from the beginning of the creation, wherein the first complete returning course of time was finished, after which a return is made to the first day again; or, it may be used τεχνικῶς, "artificially," as a notation of a certain day peculiarly so called; or as the name of one day, as most nations have given names to the weekly course of days. For at that time ἡ ἑβδόμη, "the seventh," was the name whereby the Hellenists called the Sabbath day. So it is always termed by Philo, as others have observed; which also gives evidence unto the writing of this epistle originally in the Greek tongue. So in the gospel, μία σαββάτων, "one," or "the first of the week," is the notation of the Lord's day; and it is the Sabbath which the apostle is speaking of. And this respects both the rest of God, and the rest appointed for us thereon. For the proof hereof is that which he now and in these words designs. He proves that, under the law of creation, God did rest when he had finished his work, made way for his creatures to enter into his rest, and gave them a day as a pledge thereof.

Οὕτω, "on this wise," or "to this purpose;" so it may be rendered, either as precisely denoting the words   *Οὕτω.* reported, or as respecting the substance and design of them, "thus," or "to this purpose."

Secondly, The *testimony* itself ensues: "And God rested the

seventh day from all his works." The words, as was observed, are
taken from Gen. ii. 2. But the apostle intends not only to use the
words by him cited, but in them he directs us to the whole passage
whereof they are a part. For it would not answer his purpose to
show merely that God rested from his works, which these words
affirm; but his aim is to manifest, as hath been now often observed,
that thereon there was a rest provided for us to enter into, and a day
of rest appointed as a pledge thereof. And this is fully expressed
in the place directed unto; for God upon his own rest "blessed the
seventh day, and sanctified it." We shall open the words as far as
is needful, and then consider what is confirmed by them.

Κατέπαυσιν.   Κατέπαυσεν ὁ Θεός, "God rested." The apostle adds
ὁ Θεός, "God," from the beginning of the verse, וַיְכַל
אֱלֹהִים, "and God finished;" for afterwards it is only, "he rested,"—
וַיִּשְׁבֹּת, "et requievit." A *cessation* from work, and not a *refreshment* upon weariness, is intended. God is not weary: he was no
more so in the works of creation than he is in the works of providence. Isa. xl. 20, "The Creator of the ends of the earth fainteth
not, neither is weary." He laboureth not in working; and therefore
nothing is intended in this word but a cessation from operation. And
this fully satisfies the sense of the word. But yet, Exod. xx. 11, it
is said, וַיָּנַח; which signifies such a rest or resting as brings refreshment with it unto one that is weary. There may, therefore, an anthropopathy be allowed in the word, and rest here be spoken of
God with allusion unto what we find in ourselves as to our refreshment after labour. This is thus expressed for our instruction and
example; though in God nothing be intended but the cessation from
exerting his creating power to the production of more creatures, with
his satisfaction in what he had already done. And in this word,
וַיִּשְׁבֹּת, lies the foundation of the "Sabbath," both name and thing.
For as the name שַׁבָּת, is from this יִשְׁבֹּת, here first used, so herein
also lie both the occasion and foundation of the thing itself. So in the
command, "Remember the Sabbath day, to sanctify it: six days shalt
thou labour and do all thy work;" the reason of the command en-
sues, וְיוֹם הַשְּׁבִיעִי שַׁבָּת לַיהוָה אֱלֹהֶיךָ,—"for the seventh day is the sabbath
to the LORD thy God:" that is, "his rest" was on that day, on the
account whereof he commands us to keep a day of rest. Hence our
apostle in this place expresseth our rest, or day of rest under the
gospel, by σαββατισμός, "a sabbatism;" of which afterwards.

'Εν τῇ ἡμέρᾳ ἑβδόμῃ.   God rested ἐν τῇ ἡμέρᾳ ἑβδόμῃ, "on that seventh day,"
—בַּיּוֹם הַשְּׁבִיעִי. The translation of the LXX. hath a
notable corruption in it about the beginning of this
verse in Genesis; for whereas it is said that God finished his work
"on the seventh day," it saith that God did so ἐν τῇ ἡμέρᾳ τῇ ἕκτῃ,
"on the sixth day:" and the mistake is ancient, and general in all

copies, as also followed by some ancient translations, as the Samaritan and the Syriac. The occasion of this corruption was to avoid a pretended difficulty in the text, seeming to assert that God rested on the seventh day, and yet that he finished his work on that day. Besides, the story of the creation doth confine it to six days, and no more. But this expression, " He finished his work on the seventh day," seems to denote the continuance of his operation on that day; and indeed the Jews have many odd evasions, from an apprehension of a difficulty in this place. And Jerome thinks, though very unduly, that from this expression in the original they may be pressed with an argument against their sabbatical rest. But there is a double resolution of this difficulty, either of them sufficient for its removal, and both consistent with each other. The first is, that the Hebrew word, by the conversive prefix having a sense of what is past given unto it, may well be rendered by the preterpluperfect tense. And so it is by Junius: " Cum autem perfecisset Deus die septimo opus suum quod fecerat, quievit;"—" And when God had perfected his work, on the seventh day he rested." Thus the seventh day is not expressed as a time wherein any work was done, but as the time immediately present after it was finished. And " finis operis non est ipsum opus;"—" the term, end, or complement of a work, is not the work itself." Again, the word here used, כָּלָה, doth not properly signify " to work" or " effect," but " to complete," " perfect" or "accomplish." וַיְכַל מְלַאבְתּוֹ אֲשֶׁר עָשָׂה;—" Had perfected his work that he had made." So that on the seventh day there was no more work to do.

By this discourse the apostle seems only to have proved that the works were finished, and that God rested, or ceased from his work, on the seventh day. But this seemeth not to answer his intention, for he treats not absolutely about the rest of God (for that would not have been to his present purpose), but such a rest as his obedient creatures might enter into, whereof that rest of God was the foundation,—such as the rests were which he afterwards mentions in the land of Canaan, and under the gospel. Wherefore in this quotation he includes the sense of the whole words before laid down, namely, that upon and because of the rest of God on the seventh day, he sanctified and blessed that day to be a day of rest unto them that worship him, and a pledge of their entering into rest with him. Here, therefore, the command and appointment of the seventh day to be a Sabbath, or a day of rest unto men, from the foundation of the world, is asserted, as hath been proved elsewhere.

This, then, is the sum of what is here laid down, namely, that from the beginning, " from the foundation of the world," there was a work of God, and a rest ensuing thereon, and an entrance proposed unto men into that rest, and a day of rest as a pledge thereof, given unto them; which yet was not the rest intended by the psalmist, which is mentioned afterwards, as in the next verse.

Before we proceed, according to our designed method, we may take notice of the ensuing observations:—

Obs. I. Whatever the Scripture saith in any place, being rightly understood and applied, is a firm foundation for faith to rest upon, and for arguments or proofs in the matter of God's worship to be deduced from.

Thus the apostle here confirms his own purpose and intention. His aim is to settle the judgment of these Hebrews in things pertaining to the worship of God; and to supply them with a sufficient authority which their faith might be resolved into. This he doth by referring them to a certain place of Scripture, where the truth he urgeth is confirmed. For, as I have showed before, he designed to deal with these Hebrews, not merely upon his *apostolical authority*, and the revelations that he had received from Jesus Christ, as he dealt with the churches of the Gentiles, but on the *common principles of the Scriptures of the Old Testament*, which were mutually acknowledged by him and them. And a great work it was that he had undertaken, namely, to prove the abolishing of the worship of the Old Testament, and the introduction of a new kind of worship in the room of it, from testimonies of the Old Testament itself;—a matter, as of great appearing difficulties in itself, so exceedingly suited to the conviction of the Jews, as utterly depriving them of all pretences for the continuance in their Judaism. And this, through the especial wisdom given unto him and skill in holy writ, he hath so performed as to leave a blessed warranty unto the church of Christ for the relinquishment of the whole system of Mosaical worship, and a rock for the obstinate Jews to break themselves upon in all ages. And this should encourage us,—1. To be diligent in searching of the Scriptures, whereby we may have in readiness wherewith at all times to confirm the truth and to stop the mouths of gainsayers; and without which we shall be easily tossed to and fro with every wind of doctrine. 2. Not to fear any kind of opposition unto what we profess in the ways and worship of God, if we have a word of truth to secure us, namely, such a word of prophecy as is more firm than a voice from heaven. It is utterly impossible that, in things concerning religion and the worship of God, we can ever be engaged in a cause attended with more difficulties, and liable to more specious opposition, than that was which our apostle was now in the management of. He had the practice and profession of the church, continued from the first foundation of it, resolved into the authority of God himself as to its institution, and attended with his acceptation of the worshippers in all ages, with other seeming disadvantages, and prejudices innumerable, to contend withal; yet this he undertakes on the sole *authority of the Scriptures*, and testimonies to his purpose thence taken, and gloriously accomplisheth his design. Certainly whilst we have the same warranty of the word for what we avow and profess, we need not despond for those mean artifices and pretences wherewith we are opposed, which bear no proportion to those difficulties which by the same word of truth have been conquered and removed. For instance, what force is there in the pretence of the Roman church, in their profession of things found out, appointed, and commanded by themselves, in comparison of that of the Hebrews for theirs, begun and continued by the authority of God himself? And if this hath been removed and taken away by the light and authority of the Scriptures, how can the other, "hay and stubble," stand before it?

Obs. II. It is to no purpose to press any thing in the worship of God, without producing the authority of God for it in his word.

Our apostle takes no such course, but still minds the Hebrews what is spoken in this and that place to his purpose. And to what end serves any thing else in this matter? is there any thing else that we can resolve our faith into, or that can influence our consciences into a religious obedience? and are not these things the life and soul of all worship, without which it is but a dead carcass and an abomination to God and them that are his?

Obs. III. What the Scripture puts an especial remark upon is especially by us to be regarded and inquired into.

Here the apostle refers to what was in a peculiar manner spoken concerning the seventh day; and what blessed mysteries he thence educeth we shall endeavour to manifest in our exposition of that part of his discourse wherein it is handled.

These things being thus fixed, we may with much brevity pass through the remaining verses wherein the apostle treats of the same subject. Unto what, therefore, he had affirmed of God's entering into his rest upon the finishing of the works from the foundation of the world, he adds,—

VERSE 5.

Καὶ ἐν τούτῳ πάλιν· Εἰ εἰσελεύσονται εἰς τὴν κατάπαυσίν μου.

Καὶ ἐν τούτῳ, " and in this," or " here," ἐν τούτῳ τῷ ψαλμῷ, " in this psalm :" or τόπῳ, " in this place ;" that is, in the place of Scripture under consideration and exposition, namely the 95th Psalm, or the words of the Holy Ghost by David therein. The expression is elliptical, and the sense is to be supplied from the beginning of the fourth verse : " For he spake in a certain place ; and again he speaks in this place."

Πάλιν, "again ;" that is, after he had said before that upon the finishing of his works God rested the seventh day, and blessed it for a day of rest unto his creatures, he (that is, the same Holy Ghost) says yet again, upon another occasion, " If they shall enter into my rest."

Ver. 5.—And in this again, If they shall enter into my rest.

" If they shall enter into my rest." We have showed before that from these words, not absolutely considered, but as used and applied in the discourse of the psalmist, he proveth that there is yet a promise of entering into rest remaining to the people of God. This is included in them, as they are taken from the historical record in Moses and prophetically applied in David. And this he takes here for granted, namely, that an entrance into the rest of God for some is intended in those very words whereby others were excluded. His present argument is from the *time* and *place* when and where these words were spoken, which include a rest of God to be entered into. Now this was in the time of Moses, and in the wilderness; so that they cannot intend the sabbatical rest from the foundation of the world. ' For the works,' saith he, ' were finished in six days, and the seventh day was blessed and sanctified for a day of rest,' as Moses testifieth, Gen. ii. 1–3. This rest was tendered unto and entered into by some from the foundation of the world. It must, therefore, of necessity, be " another rest" that is spoken of by the psalmist, and which the people were afresh invited to enter into, as afterwards he more clearly asserts and proves. And they who deny a sabbatical rest from the beginning, do leave no foundation for nor occasion unto the apostle's arguments and discourse; for if there were no such rest from the foundation of the world, what need he prove that this in David was not that which, on this supposition, was not at all? This, therefore, is his purpose in the repetition of this testimony, namely, to show that the rest mentioned therein was not that which was appointed from the beginning of the world, but another, whose proposal yet remained. So then there was another rest of God besides that upon the creation of all, as is evident from this place, which he further confirms in the next verse. And we may hence learn, that,—

Obs. Many important truths are not clearly delivered in any one singular testimony or proposition in the Scripture, but the mind of God concerning them is to be gathered and learned by comparing of several scriptures, their order and respect unto one another.

Considering, as the apostle here doth, what is said τοὺ, and what again ἐν τούτῳ, what in one place, and what in another, then comparing them together with their mutual respect, with the due use of other means, we shall, under the conduct of God's Spirit and grace, come to an acquaintance with his mind and will. The heathens saw and acknowledged that all truth lies deep. And the wise man adviseth us to dig and search after it as after gold and silver and precious stones. Now, the deep mine of all spiritual truth is in the word of

God: here must we search for it if we intend to find it. And one principal way and means of our search is, the comparing together of divers places treating concerning the same matter or truth. This by some is despised, by the most neglected; which causeth them to know little and mistake much in the holy things of God.

VERSE 6.

Having thus removed an objection that might arise against the new proposal of a rest of God distinct from the sabbatical rest, which was appointed from the foundation of the world, and manifested that although there was in the state of nature, or under the law of our creation, a working and rest of God, and a rest for men to enter into, and a day set apart as a pledge of that rest, yet this was not the *rest* which he now inquired after,—the apostle in this and the following verses proceedeth to improve his testimonies already produced to a further end, namely, to prove that although after the original rest now mentioned there was a second rest promised and proposed unto the people of God, yet neither was that it which is proposed in this place of the psalm, but a third, that yet remained for them, and was now proposed unto them, and that under the same promises and threatenings with the former; whence the carriage and issue of things with that people with respect thereunto is greatly by us to be considered.

Ver. 6.—'Επεὶ οὖν ἀπολείπεταί τινας εἰσελθεῖν εἰς αὐτὴν, καὶ οἱ πρότερον εὐαγγελισθέντες οὐκ εἰσῆλθον δι' ἀπείθειαν·

'Επεὶ οὖν, " quoniam igitur,"—" seeing therefore," " whereas therefore;" or as Beza, " quia, igitur,"—" therefore," " because." The words are the notes or signs of an inference to be made from what was spoken before, or a conclusion to be evinced from what follows after.

'Απολείπεται, " superest," " reliquum est;" impersonally, " it remaineth." The word may have respect unto the form of the argument, or to the matter of it. In the first way, it denoteth what he hath evinced by his former reasonings and testimonies, namely this, " that some must enter into rest;" which way the words look as expressed in our translation : in the latter, it intendeth no more but that there are some yet to enter into rest, or this work of entering into the rest of God yet remaineth. Neither is this difference so great as that we need precisely to determine the sense either way.

Τινὰς εἰσελθεῖν εἰς αὐτήν, " quosdam introire in eam," " ut aliqui introeant in eam;" " that some enter into it." The Syriac changeth both the words and sense in this place: מְטוּל הָכִיל דְּאִית הֲוָא אַתְרָא הוֹא דְּאֱנָשׁ אֲנָשׁ נֵעוּל לְה; " seeing therefore there was a place into which any man might enter," or " every man,"—" a man," " man." It seemeth precisely to respect the land of Canaan, as that rest whereinto some may, do, or must enter ; whereas the apostle is proving that it was not that, but another. Arab., " seeing some remain that must enter into it."

Καὶ οἱ πρότερον εὐαγγελισθέντες. Vulg. Lat., " quibus prioribus annunciatum est;" that is, πρώτοις : it refers the word to the persons, and not to the thing or the preaching itself. Rhem., " and they to whom first it was preached," instead of "they to whom it was first preached." Πρότερον, " prius," " first;" not absolutely, but with respect unto what follows.

The remainder of the words have been opened before.

Ver. 6.—Whereas, therefore, it remaineth that some enter into it, and those to whom it was first preached [*who were first evangelized*] entered not in, because of unbelief, [or *disobedience.*]

The words contain an *assertion*, and a particular *assumption* from it. The assertion is, that " some must" (or " shall") " enter into the rest of God." This he concludes as evinced and proved by his former arguments and testimonies. And this is not the rest of God and the Sabbath from the foundation of the world ; for express mention is made afterwards, and on another occasion, of another rest of God, whereinto an entrance was to be obtained. This he proves from those words of the psalmist, as cited out of Moses, " If they shall enter into my rest." For although he cites the words immediately out of the psalm, yet he argues from them as first recorded in Moses; for he proves in the next verse that David intends another rest than that which was before spoken of, although typically included in the former. So the words prove that there is yet a remaining entrance into a rest of God. Not as if these particles, אם and εἰ, used here, had in the same place a contrary signification, and might be interpreted negatively or affirmatively, " If they shall," that is, ' they shall not,'—for that was the intention of the words towards them concerning whom they were first spoken,—and, " They shall enter," ' some shall,' as the apostle applies them; but that a promise is included in every conditional threatening, as we have before declared. The sense of these words, then, is, ' That from what hath been spoken, it is evident that some must yet enter into another rest of God besides that which was in the Sabbath appointed from the foundation of the world.'

Secondly, He assumes that those to whom that rest was first preached " entered not in, because of their disobedience." It is manifest whom the apostle intends in these words, namely, those who came out of Egypt under the conduct of Moses, whose sin and punishment he had so fully expressed in the foregoing chapter. Now to these was the rest of God first declared, they were first evangelized with it. And hereby the apostle shows what rest it is that he intends, namely, not absolutely the *spiritual rest of the promise,* for this was preached and declared unto believers from the foundation of the world; but it was the *church rest* of the land of Canaan, that was first preached unto them;—that is, the accomplishment of the promise, upon their faith and obedience, was first proposed unto them; for otherwise the promise itself was first given to Abraham, but the actual accomplishment of it was never proposed unto him, on any condition. Into this rest they entered not, by reason of their unbelief and disobedience, as hath been at large declared on the third chapter, which the apostle here refers unto.

This, therefore, is the substance of this verse: Besides the rest of God from the foundation of the world, and the institution of the *seventh-day Sabbath* as a pledge thereof, there was another rest for men to enter into, namely, the rest of God and his worship in the land of Canaan. This being proposed unto the people of old, they entered not into it, by reason of their unbelief.

And in proportion unto what was declared before, concerning the rest of God after the finishing of his works from the foundation of the world, we may briefly consider what this rest was, which those to whom it was first proposed entered not into. For it is not observed that they entered not into it to manifest that the same rest which they entered not into did still remain for those that now would enter into it by faith; for the apostle plainly proves afterwards that it is another rest that he treats of, and that although some did enter into that rest under the conduct of Joshua, yet there was still another rest besides that prophesied of in the psalm: but this is called over in the pursuit of his former exhortation, that we should take heed lest we come short of the rest proposed unto us, as they came short of that which was then proposed unto them. We may therefore here consider what was that rest which God calls "his rest;" and which he invited them to enter into, and what did concur in the constitution of it. And these things, although they have been mentioned before, must here be laid down in their proper place.

First, This being a *rest of God,* there must be some *work of God* preceding it, with respect whereunto it is so called. Now this was the mighty work of God in erecting the church-state of the Israelites, compared unto his work in the creation of heaven and earth, whereby he made way for the first state of rest before mentioned, Isa. li. 15, 16; and this it every way answered unto. And this work of God had two parts; or two sorts of works concurred thereunto:— 1. Such as were *preparatory* unto it, namely, the works that he wrought for the delivery of the people out of Egypt. These were effected "by temptations, by signs, and by wonders, and by war, and by a mighty hand, and by a stretched-out arm, and by great terrors," Deut. iv. 34. These things of dread and terror answer the creation of the first matter, which was "void, and without form." 2. *Perfective* of it, in the giving of the law with all its statutes and ordinances, and the whole worship of God to be observed among that people. This was the especial and particular forming of the church into such a state as wherein God might rest, Ezek. xvi. 8-13, answering the six days' work, wherein God made and formed all kind of creatures out of the first created, informed [that is, formless] mass. For as on their finishing God looked on them, and saw that they were "good," and declared them so to be, Gen. i.; so upon the erection of this church-state and disposition of the people, he saw that it was good, and declared it so to be: Ezek. xvi. 14, "Thy renown went forth among the heathen for thy beauty; for it was perfect, through my honour that I put upon thee." So was the work of the creation of that church-state, the generation of these heavens and earth, and all the host of them, finished.

Secondly, This thing done, God rests or enters into his own rest: "He and the ark of his strength arose, and entered into his rest," in answer to his rest after his finishing of the works of the first creation, Ps. cxxxii. 8. The settlement of his worship, and the typical representation of his presence among the people therein, shadowing out his glorious presence in Him in whom the fulness of the Godhead was to dwell bodily, he calls it "his rest," and "his own rest." And hereon ensued a double rest proposed to the people:—1. A *spiritual rest in God*, as having entered into a special covenant with them. Upon God's rest on the creation, men were invited to enter into God's rest as *the God of nature*, upon the terms and according unto the law of creation; but by sin this rest was rendered useless and unprofitable unto all mankind, and the covenant itself lost all its power of bringing men unto God. But now, in this erection of a new church-state among the posterity of Abraham, the foundation of it was the promise made unto Abraham, which contained in it the substance of another covenant, whereinto God through Jesus Christ would enter and rest therein; whereon he invites them by faith and obedience to enter into it also, into the rest of God. 2. There was a pledge of this spiritual rest proposed unto the people; and this was the *land of Canaan*, and the quiet possession thereof, and exercise of the worship of God therein. By this and their respect unto it God tried their faith and obedience as to that spiritual rest which, as it were, lay hid under it. And herein it was that they failed, whose example is proposed and considered in this chapter.

Thirdly, God's rest after the creation of the world at first was on the first *seventh day;* which he therefore "blessed and sanctified," that it might be a pledge and token both of his own acquiescency in his works and in the law of obedience that he had assigned unto them all; as also unto men of that eternal rest which was in himself prepared for them, upon the observance of that law whose institution he himself rested in, and also that they might have an especial time and season solemnly to express their faith and obedience. And this day he again, for the same ends, renewed unto the people of Israel, and that without any change of it, both because the time was not yet come wherein the *great reformation of all things* was to be wrought, and because the first covenant, whereunto that day's rest was annexed, was materially revived and represented anew unto that people. And this day of rest, or the institution of the seventh-day Sabbath in the church of the Jews, is necessarily included in this verse: for without the consideration of it this rest doth not answer the rest of God before insisted on, and which is the rule and measure of all that follow; for therein there was a day of rest, which is mentioned synecdochically for the whole rest of God, in these words, " For one speaking of the seventh day;" and therefore our apostle, in his next review of this testimony, doth not say there was another rest, but only that "another day" was determined, which extends both to the general season wherein the rest of God is proposed to any, as also to the especial day, which was the visible pledge of the rest of God, and whereby the people might enter into it, as in the ensuing words will be made manifest.

This, then, is that which the apostle hath proved, or entered upon the proof of, towards his main design in these verses,—namely, that there being a rest of God for men to enter into, and this not the rest of the land of Canaan, seeing they who had it proposed and offered first unto them did not enter into it, there must be yet that other rest remaining which he provokes the Hebrews to labour for an entrance into. And the ground of his argument lies herein, in that the rest of Canaan, although it was a distinct rest of itself, yet it was typical of that other rest which he is inquiring after, and the good things of this new rest were obscurely represented unto the people therein; so that by rejecting that rest they rejected the virtue and benefits of this also. And we may hence observe, that,—

Obs. I. The faithfulness of God in his promises is not to be measured by the faith or obedience of men at any one season, in any one generation, or their sins whereby they come short of them, nor by any providential dispensations towards them.

The people in the wilderness having a promise proposed unto them of entering into the rest of God, when they all failed and came short of it, there was an appearance of the failure of the promise itself. So they seem themselves to have tacitly charged God, when he denounced the irrevocable sentence against their entering into the land of promise: for after the declaration of it he adds, " And ye shall know my breach of promise," Num. xiv. 34; which is a severe and ironical reproof of them. They seem to have argued, that if they entered not, God failed in his promise, and so reflected on his truth and veracity. 'That,' saith God, 'shall be known when you are utterly destroyed;' (for then it was that it should be accomplished.)

'Ye shall know that it is your sin, unbelief, and rebellion, and not any failure on my part.'

Our apostle manageth a great argument on this subject in another place. Upon the preaching of the gospel, it was seen that, the Gentiles being called, the generality of the Jews were rejected, and not taken into a participation of the benefits thereof. Hence there was an appearance that the promise of God unto the seed of Abraham, and the faithfulness of God therein, were failed. This objection he proposeth to himself by way of anticipation, Rom. ix. 6, "Not as though the word of God hath taken none effect." The "word of God" intended is the word of promise, as is declared, verse 8. This seemed to fail, in that the seed of Abraham were not universally, or at least generally, made partakers of it. 'It is not so,' saith he; 'the promise is firm and stable, and hath its effect, notwithstanding this appearing failure.' Thereon he proceeds at large in the removal of that objection, by manifesting that in the fleshly seed of Abraham the promise was effectual, according to the eternal counsel of God and his purpose of election.

And thus it frequently falls out among the people of God. Having, it may be, made some undue applications of promises unto themselves; it may be, misinterpreted or misunderstood them; or, it may be, supposed that they were in a greater forwardness towards their accomplishment than indeed they were; upon their own personal trouble, or calamities of the whole church, they have been ready at least to expostulate with God about the truth and stability of his promises. See Ps. cxvi. 11; 1 Sam. xxvii. 1; Jer. xii. 1; Hab. i. 2-4, 13. The greatness of their troubles, and the urgency of their temptations, cast them on such expressions. The psalmist gives one corrective to all such failings, Ps. lxxvii. 10, "I said, This is my infirmity; but I will remember the years of the right hand of the Most High;"—'All my troublesome apprehensions of God's dispensations, and the accomplishment of his promises, are fruits and effects of my own weakness. To relieve me against them for the future, I will consider the eternity, and power, and sovereignty of God; which will secure me from such weak apprehensions.' And to help us in the discharge of our duty herein, we may take the help of the ensuing observations and rules:—

Obs. II. 1 The promises of God are such as belong only to the grace of the covenant, or such as respect also the outward administration of it in this world. Those of the first sort are always, at all times, actually fulfilled and made good unto all believers, by virtue of their union unto Christ, whether themselves have the sense and comfort of that accomplishment in their own souls at all times or no; but of this sort of promises we do not now treat peculiarly. Besides these, there are promises which respect the outward administration of the covenant, under the providence of God in this world. Such are all those which concern the peace and prosperity of the church, in its deliverance out of trouble, the increase of light and truth in the world, the joy and comfort of believers therein, with others innumerable of the like importance; and it is those of this kind concerning which we speak.

Obs. III. 2. Some, yea, many promises of God, may have a full accomplishment when very few know or take notice that so they are,—it may be none at all. And this falls out on sundry reasons; for,—(1.) Such things may, in the providence of God, fall out in and with the accomplishment of them, *as may keep men from discerning and acknowledging of it.* Great wisdom and understanding were ever required to apprehend aright the accomplishment of such promises as are mixed with God's dispensations in the affairs of this world, Rev. xiii. 18; nor was this wisdom ever attained in any age by the generality of professors. Thus, when God came to fulfil his promise in the deliverance of his people from Egypt, he suffered at the same time their bondage and misery to be so increased that they could not believe it, Exod. v. 21–23. See chap. iv. 31, compared with chap. vi. 9. Believers, according to their duty, pray for the accomplishment of the promise of God, it may be in their great distress. God answers their desires. But how? "By terrible things in righteousness," Ps. lxv. 5. It is "in righteousness" that he answers them; that is, the righteousness of fidelity and veracity in the accomplishment of his promises. But withal he sees it necessary, in his holiness and wisdom, to mix it with such "terrible things" in the works of his providence as make their hearts to tremble; so that at the present they take little notice of the love, grace, and mercy of the promise. There are many wonderful promises and predictions in the Revelation that are unquestionably fulfilled. Such are those which concern the destruction of the Pagan-Roman empire, under the opening of the six seals, chap. vi. Yet the accomplishment thereof was accompanied with such terrible things, in the ruin of nations and families, that very few, if any one individual person, took notice of them, at the time when they were under their completion. (2.) It so falls out from the *prejudicate opinions* that men may and oftentimes do conceive concerning the sense and meaning of the promises, or the nature of the things promised. They apprehend them to be one thing, and in the event they prove another; which makes them either utterly reject them, or not to see their accomplishment. So was it in the exhibition or coming of the Lord Christ in the flesh, according to the promise. The Jews looked for it, and longed after it continually, Mal. iii. 1, 2. But they had framed a notion of the promise and the thing promised unto themselves which was no way answered thereby. They ex-

pected he should come in worldly honour, power, and glory, to satisfy them with peace, dominion, wealth, and prosperity; but he
comes quite in another manner, and for other ends: hence they received him not, nor would at all believe the promise to be fulfilled when it had its exact and complete accomplishment. It may
be so with others. They may misunderstand the promises, and look
for such things by them as are not indeed intended in them. So
many men miscarry, when they overlook the true spiritual importance and intention of prophetical promises, to take up with the
carnal things which in the letter they are shadowed out by. (3.)
Unbelief itself hides the accomplishment of promises from the eyes
of men. So our Lord Christ, speaking of his coming to avenge his
elect, adds unto it, " Nevertheless, when the Son of man cometh,
shall he find faith on the earth?" Luke xviii. 8. Men will not apprehend nor understand his work through unbelief.

And this one consideration should teach us great moderation in
our judgments concerning the application of promises, prophecies,
and predictions, unto their seasons. I am persuaded that many have
contended (thereby troubling themselves and others) about the
seasons and time wherein some prophecies are to be fulfilled, which
have long since received their principal accomplishment, in such a
way as those who now contend about them think not of. Such are
many of those which are by some applied unto a future estate of the
kingdom of Christ in this world, which were fulfilled in his coming
and erection of his church. And whereas many of that nature do
yet doubtless remain upon record, which shall be accomplished in
their proper season, yet when that is come, it may possibly very
little answer the notions which some have conceived of their sense
and importance. Experience also hath sufficiently taught us that
those computations and conjectures at the times of fulfilling some
promises which seem to have been most sedate and sober, have
hitherto constantly disappointed men in their expectations. That
God is faithful in all his promises and predictions; that they shall
every one of them be accomplished in their proper season; that the
things contained in them and intended by them are all of them
fruits of his love and care towards his church; that they all tend
unto the advancement of that glory which he hath designed unto
himself by Jesus Christ; are things that ought to be certain and
fixed with us. Beyond these we ought to be careful, (1.) That we
affix *no sense* unto any promise which we conceive as yet unaccom-
plished, that is, [1.] In any thing unsuited to the *analogy of faith*,—
like those who dreamed of old of such a promised kingdom of Christ
as wherein all the Mosaical worship and rites should be restored;
[2.] That debaseth spiritual promises unto *carnal lusts* and interests,—like them who, in the foregoing age, under a pretence of

filling up Christ's promised kingdom, gave countenance thereby unto their own violence, rapine, and filthiness: (2.) That we be not *peremptory*, troubling our own faith and that of others about the future accomplishment of such promises as probably are fulfilled already, and that in a sense suited to the analogy of faith and tenor of the new covenant: (3.) That in such as wherein we have a well-grounded assurance that they are yet to be fulfilled, we wait quietly and patiently for the salvation of God; not making our understanding of them the *rule of any actions* for which we have not a plain warranty in the prescription of our duty in other places of Scripture.

Obs. IV. 3. Some promises of God, as to their full accomplishment, may be confined unto some certain time and season, although they may have, and have, their use and benefit in all seasons; and until this is come there can be no failure charged, though they be not fulfilled. Thus was it with the great promise of the coming of Christ before mentioned. It was given out from the foundation of the world, Gen. iii. 15, and in the counsel of God confined to a certain period of time, determined afterwards in the prophecies of Jacob, Daniel, Haggai, and otherwise. This all the saints of God were in expectation of from the first giving of the promise itself. Some think that Eve, upon the birth of Cain,—concerning whom she used these words, " I have obtained a man from the LORD," which they contend should be rendered, " the man the LORD,"—did suppose and hope that the promise of the exhibiting of the blessing Seed was accomplished. And if they looked for him on the nativity of the first man that was born in the world, it is very probable that their hearts were frequently made sick, when their hopes were deferred for four thousand years. See Gen. v. 29, xlix. 18, compared with Luke ii. 30, Exod. iv. 13. And many a time, no doubt, they were ready to call the truth of the promise, and therein the faithfulness of God, into question. Great desires they had, and great expectations, which were frustrated. Hence our Saviour tells his disciples, that " many prophets and righteous men desired to see the things which they saw, and saw them not," Matt. xiii. 17. They desired, hoped, prayed, that the promise might be fulfilled in their days; which yet it was not. Hence our apostle tells us that " these all died in faith, not having received the promise," Heb. xi. 13; that is, not the accomplishment of it. Yet this their disappointment did not in the least shake the stability of the promise; for although it was not yet actually fulfilled, yet they had benefit from it, yea, life and salvation by it. And this God hath provided, in reference unto those promises whose actual accomplishment is confined unto a certain season, which a present generation shall not be made partakers of:— there is that grace and consolation in them, for and unto them that do believe, that they have the full benefit of the merciful and spiritual part of them, when they are utterly useless to them who have only a carnal expectation of their outward accomplishment. Thus, that other promise made unto Abraham, for the delivery of his posterity out of thraldom, was limited to the space of four hundred years, Gen. xv. 13, 14. Very probable it is that the Israelites, during their bondage in Egypt, were utterly unacquainted with the computation of this time, although they knew that there was a promise of deliverance; for, as it is most likely they had lost the tradition of the revelation itself, or at least knew not how to state and compute the time, so did God order things that they should depend on his absolute sovereignty, and neither make haste nor despond. And yet, doubtless, through the delay they apprehended in the accomplishment of the promise, some of them fell into one of these extremes, and some of them into the other;—the first way the children of Ephraim seem to have offended, "whom the men of Gath who were born in the land slew," when "they came down to take away their cattle," 1 Chron. vii. 21. Probably these sons of Ephraim would have been entering upon Canaan, and spoiling of the Amorites before the appointed and full time came; and they perished in their undertaking. Others again, no doubt, in their great distresses and anguish of soul, were exercised with many fears lest the promise had utterly failed. But there was no alteration in God or his word all this while. This made the holy men afterwards have a great respect unto the set time of the fulfilling of promises, when by any means it was infallibly discovered, and then to fix themselves to such duties as might be meet for their season. So the psalmist prays that "God would arise and have mercy upon Zion, because the time to favour her, yea, the set time," the time fore-designed and appointed, "was come," Ps. cii. 13. And when Daniel understood, by the books of Jeremiah the prophet, that the time of the fulfilling of the promise for returning the captivity of Judah was at hand, he set himself to prayer, that it might be done accordingly, Dan. ix. 2, 3, 17. But what shall men do in reference unto such promises, when they know not by any means the set time of their accomplishment?

Ans. Believe, and pray; and then take the encouragement given, Isa. lx. 22, "I the LORD will hasten it in its time." It hath its appointed time, which cannot be changed; but if you will consider the oppositions that lie against it, the unlikelihood and improbability of its accomplishment, the want of all outward means for it, upon faith and prayer it shall be hastened. Thus in the days of the gospel there are signal promises remaining concerning the calling of the Jews, the destruction of Antichrist, the peace and glory of the churches of Christ. We know how men have miscarried in these things: some have precipitately antedated them, some unwarrant-

ably stated the times of them; whose disappointment and their own
unbelief and carnal wisdom have brought the generality of men to
look no more after them, and either to think that the promises of
them are failed, or that indeed such promises were never made,—
wherein unbelief hath found very learned advocates. But it is certain that there are periods of time affixed unto these things. "The
vision of them is yet for an appointed time, but at the end it shall
speak, and not lie; though it tarry," and be delayed beyond the computation of some, and the expectation of all, yet "wait for it, because
it will surely come." It will not tarry one moment beyond the time
of old prefixed unto it, as Hab. ii. 3. In the meantime God hath
given us certain directions, in general computations of the times to
come; from whence yet the most diligent inquirers have been able
to learn nothing stable and certain, but that the time must needs be
long from the first prediction, and that it is certainly stated for its
accomplishment in the counsel of God. The rule, therefore, confirmed by these instances, duly considered, may evidence the stability
of God's promises, notwithstanding the intervening of cross providential dispensations.

Obs. V. 4. There are many promises whose signal accomplishment
God hath not limited unto any especial season, but keeps it in his own
will to act according to them towards his church as is best suited to
his wisdom and love. Only there is no such promise made but God
will at one time or other verify his word in it, by acting according
to it, or fulfilling of it. And God hath thus disposed of things,—
(1.) That he may always have in a readiness wherewith to manifest his displeasure against the sins of his own people; (2.) That he
may have wherewith to exercise their faith; and, (3.) To encourage
them to prayer, expectation, and crying unto him in their distresses.
Thus setting aside the promises that are limited unto a certain period of time, there are enough of these promises at all times to satisfy
the desires and prayers of the church. When God hath limited his
promises to a certain season and time, let the men of that age, time,
and season, be what they will, "the decree will bring forth," and the
faithfulness of God requires the exact accomplishment of such determinate promises. Thus the promise of the coming of Christ
being limited and determined, he was to come, and he did come
accordingly, whatever was the state with the church, which was as
bad as almost it could be in this world; so that one of themselves
confessed not long after, that if the Romans had not destroyed them,
he thought "God would have sent fire upon them from heaven, as
he did on Sodom and Gomorrah." But then was Christ to come,
according to the time fore-appointed, and then he did come amongst
those murderers. So God had limited the time of the bondage of
Abraham's posterity unto four hundred and thirty years. When

that time was expired, the people were wicked, unbelieving, murmuring, and no way prepared for such a mercy; yet in the "very same night" whereunto the promise was limited they were delivered. But now as to their entrance into Canaan, God left the promise at a greater latitude. Hence they are brought to the very door and turned back again, by reason of their sins and unbelief; and yet the promise of God failed not, as it would have done had they not been delivered from the Egyptians at the end of four hundred and thirty years, whatever their sins or unbelief were. And of this sort, as was said, there are promises recorded in the Scripture innumerable; and there is not one of them but shall at one time or other be accomplished. For although, as to their accomplishment at this or that season, they depend much upon the faith, repentance, and obedience of the church, yet they have not absolutely a respect unto that condition that shall or may never be performed, that so they should come to be utterly frustrated. God, therefore, doth by them try and exercise the faith of his people in this or that age, as he did those in the wilderness by the promise of entering into rest; but yet he will take care, in the administrations of his grace, that his church at one season or another shall be made partaker of them, that his word do not fall to the ground.

Obs. VI. 5. Some concerns of the glory of God in the world may suspend the full and outward accomplishment of some promises for a season. Thus there are many promises made to the church of deliverance out of afflictions and persecutions, and of the destruction of its adversaries. When such occasions do befall the church, it may and ought to plead these promises of God, for they are given and left unto it for that purpose. But yet it often falls out that the fulfilling of them is for a long time suspended. God hath other ends to accomplish by their sufferings than are yet brought about or effected. It is needful, it may be, that his grace should be glorified in their *patience*, and the truth of the gospel be confirmed by their *sufferings*, and a testimony be given to and against the world. It may be, also, that God hath so ordered things, that the straits and persecutions of the church shall tend more to the furtherance of the gospel and the interest of Christ than its peace and tranquillity would do. And in such a season God hath furnished his people with other promises, which they ought to "mix with faith," and which shall be accomplished. Such are those of his presence with them, abiding by them, owning and supporting of them, comforting them in their distresses, and of ordering all things to their good and satisfaction. Besides, they have relief and consolation in the goodness, faithfulness, and tenderness of God, in those other promises whose fulfilling and performance he hath reserved unto his own sovereignty. Herein in all their tribulation do they rejoice, as Abraham did in his foresight of the day of Christ, then so many generations distant. And the consideration of these rules will evidence that neither the sons of men, nor any other troubling intervenings of providence, can any way shake the truth and stability of the promises of God. And we may hence learn,—

(1.) In any condition wherein we judge ourselves to be called to *plead any promises of God,* and to have an expectation of their accomplishment, not to make haste. This is the great rule given the church in reference unto the greatest promise that ever was given unto it, " He that believeth shall not make haste," Isa. xxviii. 16. A promise of the sending of Christ is given in the words foregoing: "Behold, I lay in Zion for a foundation a stone, a tried stone, a precious corner-stone, a sure foundation." This might well raise up a great expectation in the hearts of the people in their distressed and troublous condition. But, alas! this was not actually fulfilled until many generations after. Here patience is required. " He that believeth shall not make haste;" that is, impatiently press after the future accomplishment of the promise, unto the neglect of present duties. So are we all apt to do. When our condition is grievous and burdensome, and there are promises on record of better things for them that fear God, we are apt to give place to impatient desires after them, unto the neglect of present duties. The same advice is given us in reference unto any providences of God wherein his church is concerned that fall under any promises. Such are those before mentioned about Antichrist and his destruction; with respect unto them also we are to wait, and not make haste, Hab. ii. 3. We see how many occasions there may be of retarding the actual accomplishment of promises. Our wisdom and duty therefore is, to leave that unto his sovereign pleasure, and to live upon his truth, goodness, and faithfulness in them. They shall all be " hastened in their appointed time." I could easily instance in evils great and fatal that would ensue on our miscarriage in this thing. I shall name that which is the greatest amongst them: This is that which puts men upon irregular ways to partake of the promise; which when they fail in, as God will blast such ways, they begin to question, yea, to disbelieve the promise itself.

(2.) Again; when the accomplishment of promises seemeth to be deferred, we are not to faint in our duty. The benefit and advantage which we have in and by the accomplishment of promises is not the sole end why they are given unto us of God; but he intends in and by their proposal unto us to try and exercise all our graces,—our faith, patience, obedience, and submission unto him. So he dealt with those Israelites in the wilderness, proposing unto them the promise of entering into rest, he tried them how they would trust him, and cleave unto him, and fully follow after him. Failing herein, they came short of the promise. So God deals with us; he will exercise and prove us, whilst we are waiting for the actual performance of the promise. Now, if we find this deferred beyond our hopes, and it may be our fears, and we do begin to faint, as though the promise itself did fail, it is the readiest way to cause us to come short of it. Something of this nature befell the father of the faithful himself. He had received the great promise, that ".in his seed all the nations of the earth should be blessed." Many years after this he was childless, until his own body was in a manner dead, and so was Sarah's womb also. The hope that he had remaining was above hope, or all rational appearing grounds of it. This once put him so to it as that he cried, " Lord GOD, what wilt thou give me, seeing I go childless?" All this while God was bringing him to his foot, training him up to obedience, submission, and dependence upon himself. When, therefore, we consider of any promises of God, and do not find that we are actually possessed of the things promised, nor do know when we shall be so, our duty is to apply ourselves unto what in our present station is required of us. We may see and learn the love and goodness that is in every promise, what grace and kindness it proceeds from, what faithfulness it is accompanied withal; which is the sum of what the saints under the old testament had respect unto in the promise of the Messiah. Moreover, what God requires at our hands, what patience, waiting, submission, we must be searching into. These, I say, and the like, are our duties in this case; and not to faint, or charge the Lord unjustly, all whose ways are mercy and truth, and all whose promises are firm and steadfast.

VERSE 7.

Πάλιν τινὰ ὁρίζει ἡμέραν, Σήμερον, ἐν Δαβὶδ λέγων, μετὰ τοσοῦτον χρόνον, καθὼς εἴρηται, Σήμερον, ἐὰν τῆς φωνῆς αὐτοῦ ἀκούσητε, μὴ σκληρύνητε τὰς καρδίας ὑμῶν.

Some MSS. for εἴρηται, " said," or "spoken," read προείρηται, "forespoken," or "foretold." Μετὰ τοσοῦτον χρόνον, " post tantum tempus," or " temporis," as the Vulg. Lat.; that is, " tantum temporis spatium elapsum," " after so great a space of time past." Syr., "from after so much time;" and adds, " as it is said above that David said."

Πάλιν, "again." It may denote either the repetition of an old act, or the introduction of a new testimony. Our apostle often useth this word on this latter occasion. So he doth several times, chap. i. And here it may seem to be so applied: ' "Again," to confirm further what hath been spoken.' But it doth rather express in this place the repetition of the thing spoken of, and is to be joined in construction with " he limiteth:" 'After the determination, limiting, or appointing the day before mentioned, the day of rest,—that is, the rest itself, and a " certain day" for the representation of it and entering into it, with all that concerned it and fell out about it, both at the beginning of the world, and also at the entrance of the people into Canaan,—" again he limiteth," or " he limiteth again."'

Ὁρίζει, " he limiteth;"—that is, absolutely God doth so, whose authority alone in these things is the rule of our faith and obedience; particularly the Holy Ghost, this limitation being made in the Scriptures, which were given by his immediate and peculiar inspiration, 2 Pet. i. 21. "Limiteth;" that is, either describes or defineth it in a prophetical prediction, or determineth and appoints it by an authoritative institution. He describes it in itself, and appoints it unto us. The word may comprise both, and we have no ground to exclude either.

Τινὰ ἡμέραν, " a certain day;" that is, another determinate day, in answer to the days forementioned, and whose season was now elapsed and past. It is certain that the apostle doth principally intend to evince the new rest of God under the gospel, and to persuade the Hebrews to secure their entrance into it, and possession of it. But he here changeth his terms, and calls it not a " rest," but proposeth it from the psalmist under the notion of a " day." And this he doth because he had before proved and illustrated the rest of God, from the day that was set apart as a pledge and means of it, as also because he designs to manifest that there is another day determined, as a pledge and representation of this new rest, or as an especial season for the enjoyment of the privileges thereof.

Σήμερον. The day he intends is that which in the psalmist is called הַיּוֹם, or σήμερον, " to-day." The former day he called ἑβδόμην, " the seventh day." This was the day of rest from the foundation of the world unto the giving of the law, as also under the law itself; but now there is to be " another day," expressive of the other rest promised. The seventh day from the beginning of the creation was separated to this purpose, with respect unto the rest proposed to man in the state of innocency, and the typical rest promised to the people under the law; but this new, spiritual rest in Christ by the gospel, is to have " another day" to express and declare it. Thus is σήμερον, " to-day," in the psalmist, left at liberty to be any day in the prophecy, but limited to the first by the resurrection of Christ. " Again, he limiteth a certain day," called σήμερον, " to-day."

Λέγων ἐν Δαβίδ, " speaking in David," who was the person by whom this matter was revealed to the church, in a psalm that he composed by divine inspiration for that purpose. And "David" may be here taken properly for the *person of David* himself; and so this expression declares the way and manner whereby he came to reveal this thing. It was from the speaking of the Holy Ghost *in* him, whereby he was ὑπὸ Πνεύματος ἁγίου Φερόμενος, 2 Pet. i. 21,—acted by him to receive and deliver his inspirations. So the apostle by ἐν renders the intention of the Hebrew בְ. He spake in them; as David of himself, רוּחַ יְהוָה דִּבֶּר־בִּי, 2 Sam. xxiii. 2,— " The Spirit of the LORD spake in me." And so our apostle, in the beginning of this epistle, " God spake ἐν τοῖς προφήταις, and ἐν Υἱῷ,"—" in the prophets, and in the Son." So, as was said, the words not only express the revelation itself, but the manner of it also. The Holy Ghost spake in them whom he employed as his instruments; using their minds, tongues, and pens, for the receiving and declaring his sense and words, without leaving any thing unto their own inventions and memories. So David adds in the foregoing place, וּמִלָּתוֹ עַל־לְשׁוֹנִי,—" He spake in me, and his word was upon my tongue." Or, secondly, the name "David" may be taken by a metonymy for the psalm itself, whereof he was the penman: " Speaks in the psalm which David wrote." Thus not his inspiration of David is intended, or his speaking in his person, but the continued speaking of the Holy Ghost unto the church in that psalm, as in and by all other Scriptures: for the Scripture is the voice of God, and he always speaks unto us thereby; and itself is said to speak, because of God's speaking in it.

Μετὰ τοσοῦτον χρόνον, " after so long a time," namely, spent and bygone. The date of this time is to be taken from the coming of the Israelites out of Egypt, or from the second year after, when the spies were sent to search the land, and all that ensued thereon, which our apostle hath so considered and improved. From thence to the time of David was about five hundred years: so that our apostle might well call it τοσοῦτον χρόνον, " so long a time," or so great a space of time. The remaining words of this verse have been opened before.[1]

Ver. 7.—He limiteth a certain day again, saying in David, To-day, after so long a time; as it is said, To-day, if ye will hear his voice, harden not your hearts.

The design of the apostle in these words, is to confirm what he had before asserted about a new rest, and new day of rest, now remaining for the people of God to enter into and to possess. And there are three things considerable in them:—1. The *proposition* of his argument, wherein its strength lies; 2. An *enforcement* of it from a considerable circumstance; 3. The *confirmation* of it, by an introduction of the divine testimony from whence it is taken :—

1. His argument lies in this, that after the constitution of the sabbatical rest from the beginning of the world, and the proposition of the rest of Canaan to the people in the wilderness, God, besides them, hath "limited," determined, designed another " certain day," which was neither of the former. This must needs, therefore, be " another day ;" and that can be no other but the day of the gospel. And, as we observed before, he calls it not merely a " rest," but a " day;" that it may fully and in all particulars answer the rests before insisted on, that were types and shadows of it.

2. His enforcement of this argument is taken from the circumstance of time, when this day was limited and determined. Had the words here recorded been spoken at or near the time when the people's entering into the other typical rest of Canaan was under consideration, they might have been thought to have pertained thereunto, and to have contained an exhortation unto them to make use of their season. But now, whereas God speaks these words, wherein a day of rest is limited, so long a space of time after, namely, five hundred years or thereabouts, it cannot be but that another day of rest must be intended in them; and therefore there is still a promise remaining of entering into the rest of God, which we must take heed that we come not short of by unbelief and disobedience.

3. He confirms his proposition by repeating the divine testimony which it is built upon, " As it is said, To-day, if ye will hear his voice." Much use hath the apostle made of these words in these chapters. It is only one word of them that he now builds on,

---

[1] VARIOUS READING.—Lachmann and Tischendorf insert προείρηται in the text, as undoubtedly the true reading; Griesbach marks it as a reading of great value. EXPOSITION.—The words καθὼς προείρηται connect grammatically with λέγων, and indicate that the words had already been cited, chap. iii. 7, 15. Others take the first σήμερον as the object of λέγων, "inasmuch as in David he calls it (the day), a to-day." Others, as Calvin, Beza, Grotius, Bleek, take σήμερον as apposition to ἡμέραν τινά, " he defines again a day, a to-day." This entire treatment of σήμερον is *modern.—Ebrard.—*ED.

namely, "to-day," whence he educeth the great mysteries of a gospel rest, and the answering of it both to the rest under the old testament and the day whereby it was expressed. Sundry doctrinal observations may be hence taken, namely, from the manner of the expressions here used; the matter hath been spoken unto already.

Obs. I. In reading and hearing the Scripture, we ought to consider God speaking in it and by it unto us.

"He saith;" that is, God saith, or more especially the Holy Ghost. He both spake "in David," in the inspiration of that psalm; and "by David," or in the psalm, he speaks unto us. This alone will give us that reverence and subjection of soul and conscience unto the word of God which are required of us, and which are necessary that we may have benefit and advantage thereby. In that kind of careless and "way-side" deportment whereby men enjoy or hear the word and immediately lose it, this is not the least evil, that they do not sufficiently consider whose word it is, and who speaks immediately unto them. Our apostle commends the Thessalonians, that they "received the word, not as the word of men, but as it is in truth, the word of God," 1 Thess. ii. 13. They considered whose word it was, and whilst the apostle spake to their outward ears, they attended unto God speaking to their hearts; which made them receive it in a due manner, with faith and obedience. So God promiseth to look graciously unto him that "trembleth at his word," Isa. lxvi. 2; which frame of heart proceedeth alone from a due consideration of its being his. Customariness, negligence, and sloth, are apt to spoil us of this frame, of this grace, and so to deprive us of the benefit of the word. And to prevent this, God doth not only preface what he speaks with "Thus saith the LORD," but ofttimes adjoins such of his attributes and excellencies as are suited to beget an awe and reverence in our hearts, both of him that speaketh and of that which is spoken. See Isa. xxx. 15, lvii. 15. Let a man but consider that it is God, the great and holy one, that speaketh unto him in his word, and it cannot but excite in him faith, attention, and readiness unto obedience; as also work in him that awe, reverence, and trembling, which God delighteth in, and which brings the mind into a profiting frame.

And this concerns the word preached as well as read. Provided, —1. That those that preach it are sent of God; 2. That what is preached be according to the analogy of faith; 3. That it be drawn from the written word; 4. That it be delivered in the name and authority of God.

Obs. II. Divine inspiration, or the authority of God speaking in and by the penmen of the Scripture, is the ground and foundation of our faith, that which gives them authority over our consciences and efficacy in them. This hath been argued elsewhere.

Obs. III. The holy Scripture is an inexhaustible treasury or repository of spiritual mysteries and sacred truths. And,—

Obs. IV. Many important truths lie deep and secret in the Scripture, and stand in need of a very diligent search and hard digging in their investigation and for their finding out.

These two propositions are nearly related, and do both arise from the same consideration of the text. How many deep and mysterious truths, and those of great importance and of signal use, hath our apostle found out in the words of the psalm produced by him! and how doth he here, by stating aright the true intention of one single word or expression,—and that gathered from the consideration of all its circumstances, as by *whom* it was spoken, *when* it was spoken, and *to what purpose*,—make the eminent conclusion we have insisted on! And these things are for our instruction.

First, it is hence collected, That the holy Scripture is an inexhaustible treasury or repository of spiritual mysteries and sacred truths. We had never known what had been in the Old Testament had it not been for the New, and the Spirit of it, Luke xxiv. 45; and we should never know fully what is in the New Testament, were it not for heaven and glory, where "we shall know even as we are known," 1 Cor. xiii. 12. It may be some will say, they can see none of these stores, can find little or nothing of the riches pretended here to be laid up. It may be so; for this treasure is such as men can see little of it, if they have not a guide and a light. Let a treasury that is made deep, or closely immured, be filled never so full with gold and precious things, yet if you turn a man into it in the dark, he can see nothing that is desirable, but rather feel a horror and a fear come upon him. The Jews have at this day the Old Testament, wherein a great part of this treasure is contained, and they have a general faith that it is full of mysteries and truths; but being utterly destitute of the Spirit and all heavenly light, they see nothing of it, but search for I know not what ridiculous fancies, rather than sacred mysteries, in the words and letters of the book. This account our apostle gives, 2 Cor. iii. 14, 15, "Their minds are blinded, for until this day remaineth the veil untaken away in the reading of the Old Testament; which veil is done away in Christ. But even unto this day, when Moses is read, the veil is upon their heart." Poor creatures! they put a veil when they read the Scripture upon their hats or their heads, but there is one indeed upon their hearts; whence their minds are blinded, that they can discern no part of the mysterious treasures that are laid up therein. It is by the Spirit of Christ and light of the gospel that this veil of darkness and blindness is taken away. Wherefore, to make the truth of what we have asserted the more evident, we may consider that the whole counsel of God, concerning all his ways and works that are outwardly of him, is contained in this book, Acts xx. 27. If a wise man, and of great experience in the world, should commit,—if Solomon had committed all his counsels, all the effects of his wisdom unto writing, it would be, it would have been justly valued, and much inquired into. But here we have all the counsel of the infinitely wise God himself concerning his ways and works. To give some instances hereof:—

1. Here is expressed and contained the *mystery of his love, grace, wisdom, righteousness, and holiness,* in Christ Jesus. Now what heart can search into the bottom of these things, what mind can fully receive or comprehend them, what tongue can express them,—the things which God himself delighteth in, and which the angels desire to bow down and look into? This he calls the "riches of his grace, wherein he hath abounded toward us in all wisdom and prudence," Eph. i. 7, 8; the "mystery of his will," verse 9; the "riches of glory," verse 18; the "exceeding riches of his grace," chap. ii. 7; the "mystery which from the beginning of the world was hid in him," but by the gospel is manifested unto "principalities and powers in heavenly places," even "the manifold wisdom of God," chap. iii. 9, 10. These riches, these treasures, these mysterious truths, are rather by us to be admired and adored than fully comprehended in this life; yet here are they deposited, revealed, declared, and laid up safe, for the use, instruction, and edification of the church in all ages. Some men pass by the door of this treasury, and scarce deign to look aside towards it. There is nothing that they do more despise. Some look into it superficially and cursorily, and see nothing in it that they can much delight in or desire to know more of. But humble, believing souls, whom God by his Spirit leads into the secret stores of divine truth, they behold the riches of God, admire his bounty, and take out for their own use continually. Whilst the mystery of this love and grace is contained in the Scripture, it may well be esteemed a treasure rich and absolutely inexhaustible; and our beholding of it, our acquaintance with it, make us partakers of it, 2 Cor. iii. 18.

2. There is in it the *whole counsel of God* concerning his own worship, and the whole of that obedience which he requires of us that we may come to be accepted with him here, and to the eternal enjoyment of him in glory. For "all Scripture is given by inspiration of God, and is profitable for doctrine, for reproof, for correction, for instruction in righteousness; that the man of God may be perfect, throughly furnished unto all good works," 2 Tim. iii. 16, 17. 'Here is all,' say some; 'Here is enough,' say most: and I am sure that whoever walketh according to this rule, mercy and peace shall be on him, as on the whole Israel of God. This increaseth the riches of this treasury. Here we may find all that God would have us do that we may please him,—all that he requires of us in this world,

our whole duty with reference unto eternity. Here is our guide, our rule, ready to direct us in all stated duties, on all occasions and emergencies; so that nothing can befall us, nothing can be required of us in the worship of God, in the course, ways, and actions of our lives, but what we may have here light, guidance, and direction for. It is the word of his wisdom, will, and grace, who made us these souls, and who foreknew every thought that would be in them to eternity, and hath secretly laid up in his word that which shall suit and answer unto every occasion of all that believe in him. Whence one cried out of old, "Adoro plenitudinem Scripturarum,"—"I adore the fulness of the Scripture;" in which posture of holy admiration I desire my mind may be found whilst I am in this world.

3. There is in it a glorious discovery of the *eternal being* or nature of God, with its glorious essential excellencies, so far as we are capable of an encouraging contemplation of them in this world. It is true, that the being, nature, and properties of God, may be known by the light of nature, and from the consideration of those works which are the certain product of his power and goodness. But how dark, weak, obscure, and imperfect, is that discovery, in comparison of that which is made unto us in the word! Of many things indispensably necessary to be known of God, it knows nothing at all, as of the eternal existence of the one individual nature of God in three persons; and what it doth teach, it doth so marvellous unevenly, unsteadily, and darkly. Consult the writings of them who have most improved the light of nature in their disquisitions after the being and nature of God, who have most industriously and curiously traced the footsteps of nature towards its eternal spring and fountain. Men they were, wise, learned, sagacious, contemplative almost to a miracle, and wonderfully skilful to express the conceptions of their minds in words suited to intimate their senses, and to affect the readers. But when and where they are in the highest improvement of their reason, their fancies most raised, their expressions most reaching, generous, and noble, bring it all to one leaf of divine revelation, expressed by a poor illiterate shepherd or a fisherman, and you shall quickly find their candle before this sun first to lose its rays and lustre, then its light, and lastly utterly to expire as useless. Hence our apostle fears not to declare, that even in their disquisitions after God, "they waxed vain in their imaginations," and that "their foolish hearts were darkened," Rom i. But in his word it is that God hath made that revelation of himself wherein the souls of men may fully acquiesce; upon it hath he left an impression of all his excellencies, that we might learn to "glorify him as God." And what stores of truth are needful to this purpose, who can express?

4. The souls of them that believe are carried by it out of this world, and have *future eternal glories* presented unto them. Here are they instructed in the hidden things of immortality; which is darkness itself unto them who are destitute of this guide. It is true, we have but a very low and obscure comprehension of the things of the other world; but this is from our weakness and imperfection, and not out of any defect in their scriptural revelation. There we are told that " we shall be ever with the Lord," " like him, seeing him as he is," " beholding his glory," in " mansions" of rest and blessedness, receiving a reward in " a crown of glory that fadeth not." If we know but little of what is in these things, as we do but very little; if we cannot comprehend them, nor fill our minds steadfastly with them, it is, as was said, from our own weakness and imperfection; the truth and excellency of them are stored in this sacred treasury. Now, how large, how extensive and unsearchable, must that repository of mysterious truths be, wherein all these things, with all the particulars whereinto they branch themselves, all the whole intercourse between God and man in all ages, and always, are laid up and stored! O heavenly, O blessed depositum of divine grace and goodness!

I confess, some think it strange that this one book, and that whereof so great a part is taken up in genealogies, histories, and laws, antiquated as to their original use, should contain all sacred spiritual truth; and therefore they have endeavoured to help it with a supply of their own traditions and inventions. But they do not consider the hand whereby these things are stored. They are laid up in God's method, wrapped up in his words, which, in infinite wisdom, he hath given a capacity unto to receive and contain them all. Those " secrets of wisdom are double unto what can be comprehended," Job xi. 6. Hence, although every humble soul may learn and receive from it what is absolutely sufficient for itself on all occasions, with respect to its own duty and eternal welfare, yet the whole church of God, neither jointly nor severally, from the beginning to the end of the world, have been, are, or shall be, able to examine these stores to the bottom, and to find out perfectly all the truths, in all their dimensions, concerns, and extent, that are contained herein.

From hence the truth of our second proposition is evident, namely, That many important truths lie deep and secret in the Scripture, standing in need of very diligent search in their investigation and for their finding out. And the reason why in this place I insist on these things, is not so much to explain the sense of it as to vindicate the way of our apostle's arguing and citing of testimonies out of the Scripture, with his exposition and explication of them; which some in our days are not afraid nor ashamed to charge with obscurity and perplexity, not understanding what the nature of these things doth require.

And thus shall we find it in this place. And many instances of the like nature may we meet withal in this epistle; wherein the obscurity of the apostle is not to be blamed, but his wisdom admired. Hence is the direction and command of our Saviour, John v. 39, 'Ερευνᾶτε τὰς γραφάς,—" Search the Scriptures;" dig into them, accomplish a diligent search, as 1 Pet. i. 11, Acts xvii. 11,—as men seek after rubies, silver, and gold, as the wise man expresseth it, Prov. ii. 3–5, iii. 14, 15. The sum of these words is,—Without humility, industry, prayer, and diligence, proceeding from desires, it is in vain to think of obtaining divine wisdom. They that search for silver and hid treasures go about it with inflamed desires, pursue it with unconquerable and unwearied industry, and rejoice in them when they are found, Matt. xiii. 44. And David describeth his blessed man to be one that " delighteth in the law of the LORD, and meditateth in it day and night," Ps. i. 2. So God expressly commanded Joshua: " This book of the law shall not depart out of thy mouth, but thou shalt meditate therein day and night," chap. i. 8,— that is, constantly and diligently; making it manifest that great and sedulous inquiry is to be made after the mind and will of God therein. And this carried David to pray that God would " open his eyes, that he might behold wondrous things out of his law," Ps. cxix. 18. It must be when men take a transient view of the Scripture, in their own light and strength, that they can see no great nor excellent thing in it, Hos. viii. 12; but he who in the light of God, his eyes being opened thereby, searcheth deeply and attentively into it, shall find "wondrous" or marvellous "things in it," excellent and glorious things, that others are not acquainted withal, and be made wiser than others thereby.

That which we are therefore to inquire into, for our own advantage, is the ways and means whereby a due search may be made into the Scriptures, and what is necessarily required thereunto, so that we may not fail of light and instruction. And they are, amongst others, these that follow:—

1. A *peculiarly humble frame of spirit*, which is teachable. As there is no grace that is either more useful unto our own souls or more acceptable with God than humility, 1 Pet. iii. 4, so it is in an especial manner required as a qualification in them who would be instructed in the mind of God out of his word. So the promise is, Ps. xxv. 9, "The meek will he guide in judgment; and the meek will he teach his way;"—עֲנָוִים, that is, the humble and contrite ones. And it is the same that is twice expressed in that psalm by " fear:" verse 12, " What man is he that feareth the LORD ? him shall he teach in the way that he shall choose;" and verse 14, " The secret of the LORD is with them that fear him; and he will shew them his

covenant." Now, these promises of instruction in "judgment," or
the ordinances of God, in his " way," his " covenant," and of the
communication of his "secret counsel" (that is, סוֹד יְהוָֹה, " the secret
counsel of the LORD"), are not given merely unto such as are personally " meek" and " humble," but unto such as bring meekness
and humility, self-diffidence and submission of soul, unto the word
in their studying of it, Isa. xxviii. 9, with Ps. cxxxi. 2.   In Job xxviii.
there is a great inquiry made after wisdom; it is sought for amongst
men "in the land of the living," by mutual converse and instruction,
verse 13; and in the " depths of the sea," verse 14, among the secret
works of nature; but " it is hid close from all living."   What then
shall a man do ? lie down and utterly despair ?   No; saith he, verse
28, " Unto man he said, Behold the fear of the Lord, that is wisdom."   This is the only way to attain it, for such only God will teach.
Hence are we enjoined to " receive with meekness the ingrafted
word," James i. 21.   When men come to the reading and studying of the Scriptures in the confidence of their own skill, wisdom,
parts, learning, and understanding, God scorneth to teach them, he
" beholds them afar off."   The fruits and effects of this state of
things, in the pride of men, and the severity of God in giving them
up to darkness and blindness, we may behold every day.   Hence
that came to pass of old which is yet observable, mentioned by our
apostle, 1 Cor. i. 26, 27.   And sometimes none presume more in
this kind than those who have as little reason as any to trust to
themselves.   Many an illiterate person hath an arrogance proportionable unto his ignorance, 2 Pet. iii. 16.   And hence sundry from
whom it was expected, on the account of their condition, that they
should be very humble and lowly in mind in their reading of the
word, have been discovered in the issue, by their being given up to
foolish and corrupt errors, to have had their minds filled with pride
and self-conceit; without which they would not have been so.

This is the great preparation for the soul's admittance into the
treasury of sacred truths: Go to the reading, hearing, studying of
the Scripture, with hearts sensible of your own unworthiness to be
taught, of your disability to learn, ready to receive, embrace, and submit unto what shall be made known unto you,—this is the way to be
taught of God.   And in this way if you learn not so much as others,
yet that which you do learn shall be of as much use, benefit, and
advantage unto you, as theirs shall be who attain unto the greatest
degrees of spiritual light and knowledge.   The word, thus inquired
into, will be as manna to them that gathered it, Exod. xvi. 18.

2. *Earnest prayer for the guidance, direction, assistance, and illumination of the Holy Ghost,* to enable us to find out, discern, and
understand, " the deep things of God."   Where this is neglected,
whatever we know, we know it not as we ought.   David's prayer
was, as we observed before, "Open thou mine eyes, that I may behold

wondrous things out of thy law," Ps. cxix. 18.   This opening of our
eyes is the immediate work of the Holy Ghost.   Without this we
shall never be able to discern the wondrous, mysterious things that
are in the word of God, 2 Cor. iii. 18, iv. 6.   The Lord Christ promiseth that "the Comforter shall teach us all things," John xiv. 26;
and, as " the Spirit of truth, guide us into all truth," chap. xvi. 13.
And although there may be somewhat peculiar in these promises
unto the apostles, namely, to guide them by extraordinary inspiration and revelation, yet also there is grace promised in them to all
his disciples, that they also shall be guided into the truth by the
word through his instruction; for, as he tells all believers that " his
Father will give the Holy Spirit unto them that ask him of him,"
so John tells them that "they have an unction from the Holy One,"
1 John ii. 20, " which abideth in them, and teacheth them all
things," verse 27,—that is, which God would have them know in
their stations, and which are needful for them.   That this is the
only way whereby we may come to know the things of God, the
great and wondrous things of God laid up in the word, our apostle
discourseth at large, 1 Cor. ii.: The "natural man," he tells us,—that
is, such an one as hath not the help and assistance of the Spirit of
God,—cannot receive the things that are of God, verse 14.   He can
neither find them out himself, nor own them when they are discovered by others.   But " the Spirit searcheth the deep things of
God," verse 10.   Many of the things of God in the Scripture are
" very deep," so that they cannot be discovered but by the help of
the Spirit of God; as he shows they are to believers, verses 11, 12,
15, 16.   And to this purpose are we directed to pray by the example
of our apostle, Eph. i. 16–20, iii. 16–19; Col. ii. 2.   Now what is
the work of the Holy Spirit in this matter, by what way and means
he leads us to the knowledge and acknowledgment of sacred truths,
how he guides and directs us into the discovery of the sense and
meaning of God in his word, shall, if God will and I live, be
handled apart in another discourse,[1] and shall not therefore be now
insisted on.   But this is the great and principal rule, which is to be
given unto those who would find out the mind of God in the Scripture, who would search out the mysterious truths that are contained
in it, and would be kept from errors in their so doing, and that both
to understand things aright for their own advantage, and interpret
the word aright for the advantage and edification of others: Let
them be earnest, diligent, constant, fervent in their supplications
and prayers, that God, according to his promise, would graciously
send his Holy Spirit, to guide, lead, instruct, and teach them, to
open their understandings, that they may understand the Scriptures,

---

[1] See " Causes, Ways, and Means of Understanding the Word of God," in
vol. iv. of the author's works.—ED.

as our Lord Jesus did for the disciples by the way, and to preserve them from mistakes and errors. Unless we have this guidance we shall labour to little purpose in this matter; yea, woe be to him who leans to his own understanding herein !¹ And these prayers ought to be,—(1.) A constant part of our *daily supplications;* (2.) *Brief elevations* of soul unto God, whenever occasionally or statedly we read the word, or hear it; (3.) *Solemn or appointed seasons.*

3. *Endeavour, in all inquirings into the word, to mind and aim at the same ends which God hath in the giving and granting of it unto us.* Then do we comply with the will of God in what we do, and may comfortably expect his gracious assistance. Now, in general God had a fivefold end in granting this inestimable privilege of the Scripture unto the church:—

(1.) That it might be such a *revelation of himself,* his mind and will unto us, as that we might so know him as to believe in him, fear him, love him, trust in him, and obey him in all things. This is the great and principal end of the Scripture, Deut. xxix. 29. Without this, all things concerning God and our duty, since the entrance of sin, are wrapped up in darkness and confusion, as is manifest at this day in all nations and places left destitute of it. And this, therefore, is to be our principal aim in our study of the Scripture. That we may know God as he hath revealed and declared himself; that we may come to an acquaintance with him by a rule and light infallible, given us by himself for that purpose, that so in all things we may glorify him as God, and live unto him, is the first thing which in this matter we ought to aim at. And a due consideration hereof will be exceeding useful and effectual to curb the vanity and curiosity of our minds, which are apt to turn us aside towards corrupt, unprofitable, and sinister ends.

(2.) Another end of God was, that we might have a *safe rule* and *infallible guide* for the due performance of all the duties, towards himself and one another, which he requires of us in the whole course of our obedience, 2 Tim. iii. 15–17. God hath, in infinite wisdom, treasured up in this book every thing that, either for the matter or manner of its performance, is any way necessary for us to know or do, that we may be wise unto salvation, and thoroughly furnished for every duty that he requireth at our hands. And here lies our next end. We come to the Scripture to learn these things; and nowhere else can we so learn them as to attain either assurance and peace in our souls, or so perform them as that they should be

---

¹ In his edition of this work, Dr Wright very properly transfers the three lines which follow, from their place, in the original edition, at the close of the fifth particular under the next division. We adopt his emendation, as obviously required by the subject of these lines, which have evidently a connection with the paragraph above.—ED.

acceptable unto God. This mind, therefore, ought to be in us, in all wherein we have to do with the Scriptures. We go to them, or ought so to do, to learn our own duty, to be instructed in the whole course of our obedience, in what God requires of us in particular. With this design we may go on and prosper.

(3.) God hath given us his word to guide and direct us in our *ways* under all dispensations of his providence, that we sin not against him, nor hurt or damage ourselves, Ps. cxix. 24. The providences of God towards us, as to our course in this world, do oftentimes bring us into great straits and difficulties, so that we know not well how to steer our course, so as neither to sin against God, nor to prejudice or ruin ourselves without just and cogent reasons. God hath given us his word to counsel us in this matter; and by a diligent attendance unto it we shall not fail of blessed guidance and directions. Here we ought to seek it; and here we may find it, if we seek in a due manner.

(4.) The Scriptures are given us of God to administer unto us *consolations and hope* in all our distresses and tribulations, Rom xv. 4; Ps. cxix. 92. In them hath God graciously treasured up whatever is useful or needful to this purpose. Whatever be our distresses, fears, disconsolations, as to what hath, doth, or may befall us in this world, God hath designed a relief under it and against it in his word. That we may be always furnished with this blessed and precious provision, ought to be one end also that we aim at in our considerations of it.

(5.) God hath done this, that he might give us *infallible assurance of eternal life* when we shall be here no more, with some prospect into the glories of it and foretastes of its sweetness, 2 Tim. i. 10. This as we stand in need of, so the constant fixing of our eye upon it as our utmost end, will be a safe and blessed guidance unto us in our whole course. These are the ends of God in giving us his word, and these ought to be ours continually in our search into it; and the want hereof, whilst some have indulged their fancies in the pursuit of unuseful notions and speculations, hath caused them to err from the truth.

4. They that would search the Scriptures to find out the sacred truths that lie hid in them, ought to take *care that they entertain no corrupt lusts in their hearts or minds;* which will certainly refuse to give admittance unto spiritual truth when it is tendered unto them. Hence is that advice of the apostle James, chap. i. 21. They that will " receive the word " so as to have it an " ingrafted word," to effect in them the work and end whereunto it is designed, must " cast out all filthiness and superfluity of naughtiness." Fleshly and corrupt lusts indulged unto in the hearts and minds of men will make their most industrious search into the Scripture of no ad-

vantage to themselves. Love of sin will make all study of the Scripture to be mere lost labour. Hearts pure and undefiled, minds serene and heavenly, so far as by the grace of God we can attain to them, are required to this work. And it ought to be one great motive unto an endeavour after them, that we may be the more able to discern the mind of God in his word.

5. *Sedulity and constancy in this duty* are great helps to a profitable discharge of it. When men read the word but seldom, so that the things of it are strange to them, or not familiar with them, they will be continually at a loss in what they are about. This is that which the wise man directs us unto, Prov. vii. 1–4. Constant reading and meditation on the word will create a familiarity between our minds and it, when occasional diversions only unto it will make an estrangedness between them. Hence our apostle commends it in his Timothy, that "from a child he had known the holy Scriptures," 2 Tim. iii. 15; whereby being made familiar unto him, he was much assisted in the right understanding and use of them. And there is not any thing in our walking before God that is more acceptable unto him. For this expresseth somewhat of that reverence which we ought to have of the greatness and holiness of Him with whom we have to do. The Jews' frontispiece to their great Bible is that saying of Jacob upon the vision of God that he had at Bethel, " How dreadful is this place! This is none other but the house of God, and this is the gate of heaven." So ought we to look upon the word, with a holy awe and reverence of the presence of God in it. Our faith and dependence on him, with our valuation of the knowledge of his mind and will, are hereby expressed; and hereby also do we give glory to him.

6. In our search after truth our minds are greatly to be influenced and guided by the analogy of faith. He that " prophesieth," —that is, interpreteth Scripture,—must do it κατὰ τὴν ἀναλογίαν τῆς πίστεως, Rom. xii. 6; "according," say we, "to the proportion of faith." There is a harmony, an answerableness, and a proportion, in the whole system of faith, or things to be believed. Particular places are so to be interpreted as that they do not break or disturb this order, or fall in upon their due relation to one another. This our apostle calls ὑποτύπωσιν ὑγιαινόντων λόγων, 2 Tim. i. 13,—a fixed, and as it were an " engraved form of sound, wholesome, or healing words or doctrines," or a summary of fundamental truths; ὑγιαινοῦσα διδασκαλία,—" the sound doctrine of the gospel," chap. iv. 3. And this, probably, is that which he intends by his μόρφωσις εὐσεβείας, ·chap. iii. 5, a " form " or " delineation of godliness," in the doctrines of it; which many may have, who, as we say, are orthodox and sound in the faith, who yet in their hearts and lives deny the power of it. This "proportion of faith," this " form of sound words," is continually

to be remembered in our inquiry after the mind of God in any particular place of the Scripture; for all the Scripture is from the same
spring of divine inspiration, and is in all things perfectly consistent
with itself. And the things that are of greatest importance are delivered in it plainly, clearly, and frequently. Unto these the sense
of every particular place is to be reduced; none is to be assigned unto
it, none to be pretended from it, that falls in upon any of the truths
elsewhere clearly and fully confirmed. For men to come to a place
of Scripture, it may be dark and obscure in itself, and, through I
know not what pretences, draw a sense from it which is inconsistent
with other doctrines of faith elsewhere plainly revealed, is openly to
corrupt the word of God. And as indeed there is no place which
doth not afford a sense fairly reconcilable unto the analogy of faith,
so, if it do not appear unto us, we must sit down in the acknowledgment of our own darkness and ignorance, and not admit of any such
sense as riseth up in contradiction thereunto. Want of a due attendance unto this rule is that which hath produced the most pestilent
heresies in the church. Thus the Papists, taking up these words,
" This is my body," without a due consideration of the analogy of
faith about the human nature of Christ, the spirituality of the union
and communion of believers with him, the nature of sacramental
expressions and actions, which are elsewhere evidently declared, by
which the interpretation, according to the apostle's rule, is to be regulated and squared, have from them fancied the monstrous figment
of their transubstantiation, absolutely destructive of them all. It is
the known way of the Quakers amongst ourselves, if they can get
any one single text of Scripture which, in the sound of the words, or
on any other account, seems to favour some fancy they have a mind
unto, instantly they take it up, not once considering whether it do
not dissolve the whole proportion of faith, and overthrow the most
fundamental articles of Christianity: so from the outward sound of
that one text, John i. 9, "That was the true Light, which lighteth
every man that cometh into the world," they fear not to take up a
pretended sense of them, destructive to what is taught about the
nature of Christ, the work of the Holy Spirit, of faith, grace, conversion to God, plainly and evidently in a thousand other places.
Our apostle doth not so; for although he deduces great and mysterious truths out of the Scriptures of the Old Testament, yet they are
such as answer the whole system of divine revelation, and have a
due place and order in the "form of sound words."

7. *A due consideration of the nature of the discourse wherein
any [dark ?] words are used*, tends much to give light into their
sense and importance. And the discourses in the Scripture may be
referred materially to four general heads; for they are either historical, or prophetical, or dogmatical, or hortatory. And for the way

or form of writing used in them, it is in general either proper and literal, or figurative and allegorical, as is the whole book of Canticles, and many other parts or passages in the Scripture. Now these things are duly to be weighed by them who intend to dig deep into this mine of sacred truth. But particular directions in reference unto them are too many here to be insisted on.

8. The proper *grammatical sense* of the words themselves is duly to be inquired into and pondered. This principally respects them who are able to pursue this search after truth in the original languages. Others also may have much help by comparing parallel places, even in translations; whence the proper sense or usual acceptation of any words may be learned. And of this nature many other particular rules might be added, which are by others commonly insisted on, and therefore may be here omitted.

This that hath been spoken may serve, as for the reproof of some, so for the direction of others. Whence is it that some receive so little benefit by their studying of the Scripture, at least in their pretending so to do? Alas! their manifold miscarriages are manifest unto all. Without diligence, without humility, without watching unto prayer, they go in the confidence of their own strength and abilities to search and expound it; which is to attempt the opening of brazen doors without a key, and the digging of mines for hid treasures with men's nails and fingers. It is true there are sundry things that are common to the Scripture, as it is a writing consisting of propositions and reasonings, with all other writings; an apprehension and understanding of many of these lieth obvious to every superficiary reader: but to come to a clear understanding of the secrets of the mind of God, and mysteries of his will, this is not to be attained without the sedulous, diligent use of the means before mentioned. And what guidance lies in them, and other particular rules to the same purpose, is, though in great weakness, looked after in this Exposition.

VERSE 8.

In this verse the apostle gives a further confirmation unto his argument by a particular application of it unto the especial matter in hand. Herewithal he removeth or preventeth an objection that might probably be raised against one part of his discourse. And the preventing of such objections as whereunto what we affirm and teach is at first view liable, is as needful as the raising of objections which possibly would never come to the minds of our hearers or readers is needless and foolish.

Ver. 8.—Εἰ γὰρ αὐτοὺς Ἰησοῦς κατέπαυσεν, οὐκ ἂν περὶ ἄλλης ἐλάλει μετὰ ταῦτα ἡμέρας.

Εἰ γάρ, "for if;" αὐτούς, that is, the people of old, those of whom he hath treated, particularly the new generation that entered Canaan.

Κατέπαυσεν. The apostle in this chapter useth this word both in a neutral and active signification. Verse 4, Κατέπαυσεν ὁ Θεός, " God rested;" here, "caused them to rest," "given them rest." Beza, "in requiem collocasset;" Arias, " requiem præstitisset." The word properly, and usually in other authors, signifies " finem imponere," " cessare facere;" " to put an end," or "to make to cease," as rest puts an end to labour. So the word is used, verse 10, Κατέπαυσεν ἀπὸ τῶν ἔργων, " Hath ceased from his works." Ἰησοῦς, " Jesus,"—that is, Joshua; and by so calling him, the apostle also declares what was the true Hebrew name of Jesus Christ, which the Greeks express by " Jesus." His name was originally הוֹשֵׁעַ, " Hoshea;" the same with that of Hosea the prophet, chap. i. 1. Then when he went to espy out the land his name was changed by Moses into יְהוֹשֻׁעַ, " Jehoshuah," Num. xiii. 16. It is true, in the writing over the story of those times he is called Jehoshua before, as Exod. xvii. 9; but it is most probable that Moses now, by divine direction, changed his name, when he went to view that land whither he was to conduct the people, and writing the story of these things afterwards, he used the name whereby he was then called. Some of those who had most imbibed the Chaldee dialect or tongue during the captivity changed this name into יֵשׁוּעַ, " Jeshua," Ezra ii. 2, Neh. iii. 19; though the prophets Haggai and Zechariah retain the name of Jehoshua, Hag. i. 1, ii. 2, 4, Zech. iii. 1. Now all these names are from the same root, and of the same signification. From הוֹשִׁיעַ in Hiphil (for in Kal the verb is not found), is יֵשַׁע, " Jesha," " salus,"— " health," " help," " salvation." Thence are הוֹשֵׁעַ, " Hoshea;" יְהוֹשֻׁעַ, "Jehoshua;" and יֵשׁוּעַ, " Jeshua;"—"that is, σωτήρ, " salvator," " sospitator," " liberator;" though Cicero affirms that the Greek word cannot be expressed by any one proper Latin word. " Salvator " is coined for that purpose,—" a saviour." Now, as persons on great occasions had their names as to their signification wholly changed, as when in the Old Testament Jacob was called Israel, and Solomon, Jedidiah; and in the New Testament Simon was called Peter, and Saul was called Paul; and divers had double names occasionally given them, as Esther and Hadassah, Daniel and Belteshazzar: so God was pleased sometimes to change one letter in a name (not without a mystical signification): so the name of Abram was changed into Abraham, by the interposition of one letter of the name of God; and that of Sarai into Sarah, by an addition of the same, Gen. xvii. 5, 15: so here the name of Hoshea is changed into Jehoshua, by the addition of one of the letters of the name of God, increasing the signification; and this name was given him as he was a type of Christ, and the typical saviour or deliverer of the people.

The name of יֵשׁוּעַ, " Jeshua," from the Chaldee dialect, prevailed at length in common use, being of the same signification with the other, namely, " a saviour," "one that saveth." Hence, when they came to converse with the Greeks, came the name of Ἰησοῦς, or " Jesus." For the Greeks called Hoshea, Ausis, and Nun his father, Naue, greatly corrupting the original names. But Hoshea and Jehoshua and Jeshua they called Jesus. In יֵשׁוּעַ, " Jeshua," they rejected the guttural ע, as not knowing its right pronunciation, whereon יֵשׁוּ, " Jesu," remained; and then in their accustomed way they added the terminative sigma, and so framed Ἰησοῦς,— as of מָשִׁיחַ, " Messiach," by the rejection of ח and the supplement of ς, they made Μεσσίας, " Messias." Hence the name Jeshua being in common use for and of the same signification with Jehoshua, and that in the Greek pronunciation being turned into Jesus, that was the name whereby the Lord Christ was called: Matt. i. 21, Καλέσεις τὸ ὄνομα αὐτοῦ Ἰησοῦν· αὐτὸς γὰρ σώσει τὸν λαὸν αὐτοῦ ἀπὸ τῶν ἁμαρτιῶν αὐτῶν·—" Thou shalt call his name Jesus; for he shall save his people from their sins." It is plain that the reason of the name is taken from its signification of saving,—" he shall save," be their saviour; so that all the attempts that some have made to derive it from other words are vain and frivolous. And so also are theirs who would deduce the Greek name Ἰησοῦς from ἰάω, ἰάσω, " to heal:" for

Ἰησοῦς is of no signification at all in the Greek tongue, it being only their man-ner of pronunciation of יֵשׁוּעַ, " Jeshua," which is " a saviour ;" which name was given to the Lord Christ because of the work he had to do. So also was it to this Jesus the son of Nun. The wickedness of the perfidious Jews in writing his name יֵשׁוּ, and the horrible abuse they make thereof, are known to the learned, and there is no need to acquaint others with them.

Οὐκ ἂν περὶ ἄλλης ἡμέρας, " concerning another day." The apostle having de-scribed the rest he discourseth of by the especial day of rest that was in the several estates of the church peculiarly to be observed, now by a synecdoche expresseth the whole rest itself and all the concernments of it by the name of a " day."

Ἐλάλει, " he would not have spoken ;" that is, either God absolutely, or the Holy Ghost, whose immediate work the inspiration of the psalmist was, whose words these are.

Μετὰ ταῦτα, " after these things ;" the things which befell the people in the wilderness, and what they afterwards attained under the conduct of Joshua.

Ver. 8.—For if Jesus had given them rest, then would he not after these things have spoken concerning another day.

The confirmation of his principal assertion from the words of David, concerning the rest prepared and proposed in the gospel unto believers, is that which our apostle still insists on, as was declared. Hereon was his whole exhortation of the Hebrews founded, and hereinto was it resolved. And on the same truth depended all the reasonings and motives whereby he enforced his exhortation. This, therefore, was fully to be established and clearly vindicated. And that which, last of all, remained to his purpose was the removal of an objection which, among the Jews, it was evidently liable and ob-noxious unto. And this he doth by the due stating of the time when those words were spoken which he had pleaded in evidence of his assertion. The objection laid down by way of anticipation is plain in the words; and it is this: ' Although the people which came out of Egypt entered not into the rest of God that was pro-mised, by reason of their unbelief and disobedience, as you have proved, yet the next generation, under the conduct of Joshua, went into and enjoyed the rest which they were excluded from. This, therefore, was the rest intended; which we being in the enjoyment of, what ground have you to propose another rest unto us?' This is the force of the objection. And two things are comprised in the apostle's answer unto it:—First, A denial of the supposition on which the objection is founded. This is done virtually in the manner of the proposal of the objection itself: " For if Jesus had given them rest ;"—that is, whatever be pretended and pleaded, he did not do so; that is, not that full and ultimate rest which in all these things God aimed at. Secondly, He gives the reason of this his denial; which is this, that five hundred years after, God in David, and by him, proposeth another rest, or another day of rest, and invites the people

unto an entrance, after they were so long fully possessed of all that
Joshua conducted them into; and whereas there was no new rest
for the people to enter into in the days of David, and the psalm
wherein these words are recorded is acknowledged to be prophetical
of the days of the Messiah, it unavoidably follows that there is yet
a rest and a day of rest remaining for the people of God, which he
lays down as his conclusion in the verse ensuing.

This interpretation of the words perfectly satisfieth the argument
in hand; but yet I judge there is more in them than a mere answer
unto the objection mentioned, though expositors look no farther.
And this is, that the apostle also designs to teach the Hebrews that
all those things which were spoken about the rest of God in the
land of Canaan, and in Mosaical institutions, had not the reality or
substance of the things themselves in them, Heb. x. 1; so that absolutely neither did God rest nor were the people to look for rest in
them. They had no other end nor use, but only to teach them to
look out after and to prepare for that rest which was promised from
of old; so that Joshua did not give them real rest, but only that
which was a typical instruction for that season in what was to come.
And therefore in David the same matter is carried still on, and direction is still given to look out after the rest to come. And we
may learn hence, principally, that,—

Obs. I. There is no true rest for the souls of men but only in Jesus
Christ by the gospel.

Notwithstanding all that was done to and for the Israelites by
Joshua, yet he gave them not rest, he brought them not into the
full and complete rest of God; "God having provided some better
things for us, that they without us should not be made perfect."
And the reasons hereof are:—First, because God himself resteth
not in any thing else, and in his rest alone it is that we can
find rest. It is in vain for us to seek for rest in that wherein
God resteth not. We have seen that at the beginning, when he
had created man, he entered into his rest, in that satisfaction which
he took in the effects of his own power, wisdom, and goodness,
Exod. xxxi. 17. He provided likewise rest in himself for man, and
gave him a day as a pledge of his entrance into it, Gen. ii. 2. In
this condition trouble and disquietment entered into the whole
creation, by the sin and apostasy of Adam. God no more rested
in the works of his hands, but cursed the earth, Gen. iii. 17, 18,
made the whole creation subject to vanity, Rom. viii. 20, and revealed his wrath from heaven against the ungodliness of men, Rom.
i. 18. And hereof he hath in all ages since given signal instances;
as in the flood of waters wherewith he drowned the old world, and
the fire from heaven wherewith he consumed Sodom and Gomorrah. And of the same kind are those severe judgments by

pestilences, famines, earthquakes, inundations, eruptions of sub-
terraneous vapours, conflagrations, and the like; all testifying the
indignation of God against the works of his own hands, because of
the sin of man, to whom he had given them for a possession, and
put them in subjection. For God had decreed from eternity to permit
a disturbance by sin in the first order of things, that he might gather
all things unto a head, with durable rest and peace, in Jesus Christ,
Isa. xlii. 1; Eph. i. 10. Man hath also utterly lost his rest in
that first rest of God; and though he several ways seeks after it,
yet, like the unclean spirit cast out of his habitation, he can find
none. Some seek it in the world, the pleasures and profits of it;
some in the satisfaction of their sensual lusts; some in themselves,
their own goodness and righteousness; some in superstition and vain
ways of religious worship, invented by themselves,—some of them
horrid and dreadful, Mic. vi. 6, 7: all in vain. Man hath lost his
rest by falling off from God; and nothing will afford him the least
quietness but what brings him to him again, which none of these
ways will do. It is in and by Christ alone that our lost rest may
be recovered. For,—

Secondly, Other things will not give rest to the souls of men.
A higher instance hereof we cannot have than in these Israelites.
They had been for sundry ages in bondage unto cruel oppressors,
who ruled over them with unparalleled severity and rage. Such,
besides their hard and continual labour in the furnace, was that of
their having their tender infants, the comfort of their lives and
hope of the continuance of their name and race on the earth, taken
from the womb and cruelly murdered. This they were now delivered from, and all their enemies subdued under them, until they
set their feet upon the necks of kings. Who would not now think
that this would give them rest? And so it did, outward rest and
peace, until it was said that God gave them "rest on every hand." And
many yet in the like condition of bondage with themselves, shut up
in the hands of hard and cruel rulers, are apt to think that a deliverance from that condition would give them perfect rest and
satisfaction. But yet the Holy Ghost tells us that this did not give
them rest; not that rest wherein they might ultimately acquiesce.
Besides, whereas neither they nor their forefathers, for four hundred and thirty years, had ever had either house, or land, or possession, but wandered up and down in those places wherein they were
strangers, and had not one foot's breadth that they might call their
own, but only a cave or two to bury them in when they were dead,
they had now a whole plentiful country given unto them to inhabit
and possess, a fruitful country, "a land flowing with milk and
honey;" and therein cities which they had not walled, houses which
they had not built, vineyards which they did not plant, with all

sorts of riches and substance unspeakable. This might add unto their former satisfaction, especially being suddenly given, and flowing in upon them. And where there is wealth in abundance, and absolute liberty, what can be desired more, to give men rest? But yet it did not so. Yet further; whereas before they lived in a loose, scattered condition, without law or rule of their own, or amongst them, God had now gathered them into a firm, well-compacted political body, and given them a great and righteous law for the rule and instrument of their government, which all nations did admire, Deut. iv. 5, 6. This, as it gave them glory and honour in the world, so it was a means of securing that wealth and liberty which they enjoyed. And where these three things are, there a people may be supposed to be at perfect rest; for liberty, wealth, and rule make up a state of rest in this world. But it was not so with them. Joshua gave them not rest. More than all this; God had established his glorious worship amongst them, intrusted them with his oracles and ordinances, and that whole system of religious honour which he would then accept in the world, Rom. ix. 4, All these things, with other mercies innumerable, they were made partakers of by and under the conduct of Joshua. And yet it is here plainly affirmed and proved that he did not give them rest; that is, the ultimate and chiefest rest which God had provided for his church and people in this world. Why, what was wanting hereunto? what was yet behind? That the apostle declares in this place. The promise was not yet fulfilled, the Messiah was not yet come, nor had finished his work, nor were the glorious liberty and rest of the gospel as yet exhibited and given unto them. It were easy to demonstrate how all these things singly and jointly do come short of true rest; for notwithstanding all these, and in particular the highest of them, namely, the law and ordinances of worship, they had not spiritual liberty, rest, and peace, but were kept in a bondage frame of spirit, and laid up all their hopes and expectations in that which was not yet granted to them. So our apostle tells us that "the law made nothing perfect," and that their sacrifices could never completely pacify their consciences, and therefore were continually renewed, with a remembrance of sin. It is Christ, then, alone, as declared in the gospel, in whom God doth rest, and in whom our souls may find rest. The reasons hereof may be taken from that description which we have given before of this gospel rest which the apostle insisteth on.

It is surely, therefore, our wisdom, in our inquest after rest,—which, whether we take notice of it or no, is the main design of our lives, in all that we project or execute,—not to take up in any thing beneath him or without him. All those things, the enjoyments of the world, the righteousness of the law, the outward ordinances of di-

vine worship, say openly and plainly unto us, that rest is not in
them. If all these in conjunction had been satisfactory to that end,
then had Joshua given the people rest, and there had been no mention of another day. Yea, whatever, lawfully used, they may have
of rest in them, it is no rest in comparison of that which is to be
obtained in Christ Jesus. Hence he invites us unto him under
this very notion, of giving " rest unto our souls," Matt. xi. 28. And
here, in him, there is no want, no defect, no disappointment, no
fadingness, nothing that hinders those other things from giving
complete rest unto men. He that rests in the world, or rests in
himself, or rests in his own righteousness, or rests even in God's
ordinances, will never come to rest until he be deprived of all expectation from them and confidence in them.

Obs. II. The gospel church-state is a state of spiritual rest in
Christ.

This, for the substance of it, hath been handled at large before.
I mention it now only for two ends: first, to show what we ought
to look after in this gospel church-state, and under the enjoyment
of gospel privileges ; and then, secondly, to discover a little how
men deceive themselves in this matter. First, This is that which
distinguisheth our present church-state from that of theirs under the
old testament : Joshua gave them all other things, only he gave
them not rest, the rest of God ; this is now the portion of them that
believe; this all the children of the church are to look after. What
is it, then, that men do seek after, or join themselves to the church
of Christ upon the account of? What do they look for in, the worship, in the ordinances, in the ways of the church? If it be any
thing but only to enter into the rest of God through Christ, they
do but deceive themselves; whatever they take up in short hereof,
they frustrate the whole counsel of God towards themselves in the
gospel. Secondly, How many pretend to an interest in this gospel
church-state, who plainly, openly, and visibly seek after their rest
in other things,—many in their own duties, most in their lusts and
the pleasures of the world! Where is the privilege of such persons
as these above that of the Israelites under the conduct of Joshua?
Can they say, that although in and under all the enjoyments before
mentioned they obtained not rest, yet the Lord Christ hath given
rest unto their souls in the gospel? Alas! they have no rest at all;
and that which they do pursue is such as the gospel hath no concernment in. Did Christ come, think you, to give you rest *in* your
lusts, in your sins, in your pleasures? God forbid; he came to give
you rest *from* these things in himself; which alone is the rest
preached unto you.

Obs. III. It is a great mercy and privilege to have a day of rest
and worship given unto us.

The apostle doth not say here, that 'after these things he speaks of *another rest*,' but of "*another day;*" for from the foundation of the world we were taught our rest in God by a day of rest given unto us. When by sin we forfeited our interest in that rest of God, he might justly have deprived all the world of the knowledge of the day of rest first appointed. And indeed, whilst he left his law standing, as a testimony of his holiness and a rule of his future judgment, but did not by any outward means press it on the consciences and practices of men, all knowledge of a day of rest was lost from amongst mankind, some few excepted, whom God took into his especial care. For to what purpose should they look after a day of rest, who had utterly lost all desires after and all interest in the rest of God itself? But when God would revive in men a hope and expectation of returning unto rest in and with himself, he recalls to their remembrance the day of rest which was at first appointed; but as he then led men into rest only typically, and in order to the representation of a future rest to be brought in, so he renewed unto them the remembrance of the day of rest typically also, that it might be a sign between him and them. But now, the rest of God being again established, he hath appointed unto us "another day," as it is in the text,—a day of rest for the ends which have been often mentioned. And this is a great mercy and privilege; for,—

1. It is a *pledge of our rest in God*, which is the life, happiness, and blessedness of our souls. It is given us to this end and purpose that so it might be; which was the end of a day of rest from the foundation of the world, as hath been declared.

2. It is a pledge of the *recovery of this rest* for us, and that it is not absolutely the same rest in God whereunto we were made, but another rest, a better and more sure. And therefore it is "another day" that is given unto us, and not the same day as of old. God kept the people under the law in an intermediate estate, between the duties of the old covenant and the promises of the new. This kept them to the precise day of the old covenant; for although virtually they were made partakers of that rest of God which is in Jesus Christ, yet the foundation and cause of it being not as yet laid and wrought, they were to content themselves with pledges of it as a thing to come, such as were their sacrifices and ordinances of worship, with the old day typically renewed. But to have another day, which could not be established but with respect to the works of Christ already wrought, and so to be a pledge of what was done before, this they could not have. This God hath reserved for us; and the day we now have being another day, is a pledge of rest already wrought out, and actually prepared.

3. It is given us as a *means* of entering into the rest of God. For hereon hath God ordained that the solemn declaration of his mind

and will concerning his rest, and our entrance into it, should be made unto us. Hereon do we celebrate all that solemn worship of God whereby we express our faith concerning our rest in him, and by which, as means appointed for that end, we are admitted into that rest, and carried on gradually towards its full and eternal enjoyment. And these things the apostle further confirms.

VERSE 9.

Having passed through his testimonies and arguments, the apostle in this and the following verse lays down both what he hath evinced in his whole disputation, as also the general foundation of it, in answer to the principles of his preceding discourse.

Ver. 9.—Ἄρα ἀπολείπεται σαββατισμὸς τῷ λαῷ τοῦ Θεοῦ.

Ἄρα, "itaque," "igitur;" the common note of inferring a conclusion from any argument, whether inartificial or artificial, of both which sorts the apostle makes use in this place. Hereby, therefore, he would mind the Hebrews to attend both to what he was about to assert, and to the dependence of it on the former testimonies and arguments that he had pleaded and vindicated.

Ἀπολείπεται, "relinquitur," "superest,—" "it is left," "it remains," "it is evinced." For this word may refer unto ἄρα, "therefore," and be a part of the induction of the conclusion following. So the verb is to be taken impersonally, "it remaineth therefore," or 'this is that which we have proved.' In this sense ἀπολείπεται is the modification of the conclusion, and is not of the substance of it, or one of the terms of the proposition. And this exposition the Syriac version follows, reading the whole words, מֶדֵין קַיָּם הוּ לְמַשְׁבָּתוּ לְעַמֵּהּ דַּאלָהָא;—" Wherefore it is certain that the people of God ought to sabbatize," or "keep a sabbath,"—'This is certain, a truth that is proved and vindicated; so that the people of God may know their privilege and their duty.' The Ethiopic version renders the words somewhat strangely: "Is the priesthood of the people of God abrogated?" that is, it is not; so that standing still in the same peculiar relation to God as they did of old, when they were a royal priesthood, they ought still to attend unto his worship, and celebrate his ordinances, the great work of the day of their rest. Or ἀπολείπεται may refer unto σαββατισμός following, and be of a neutral signification: "A sabbatism" or "rest remaineth,"—' There is yet another rest remaining and abiding for the people of God to enter into, besides those before mentioned and discoursed of.' "It remaineth;" that is, God hath prepared it, promised it, and invites us to enter into it.

Σαββατισμός. This word is framed by our apostle from a Hebrew original, by the addition of a Greek termination; and so becomes comprehensive of the whole sense to be expressed, which no other single word in either would do. The original of it is the Hebrew שָׁבַת, which signifies " to rest;" and it is first used to express the rest of God after his works of the creation: Gen. ii. 2, וַיִּשְׁבֹּת בַּיּוֹם הַשְּׁבִיעִי;—" And he rested " (or " sabbatized ") "on the seventh day." And this being so of old, the word is used by our apostle to show that the rest which he now asserts for the people of God is founded in the rest of God himself. If this it had not been, it might have been ἀνάπαυσις, " a rest" in general; it could not have been σαββατισμός, " a sabbatism," a " sabbatizing rest," for there is no foundation for any such name or thing but in the rest of God. From the rest of God, this word came to give name unto the day of rest appointed for men, Exod. xx. 10–12. Because God שָׁבַת, " shabbath," rested from his works, he blessed יוֹם הַשַּׁבָּת, "iom hashshabbath," " the day of rest," the sabbath; which he would have us remember to keep. Now, our apostle having proved that the consideration of that original rest of God, as to its first ends and purposes, is removed, and consequently the day itself founded thereon, and another rest introduced, to be expressed in and by another day, he calls it a "sabbatism," to express both the rest itself and the observation of another day likewise, as a pledge and token of that other rest of God, and of our spiritual interest therein. The word, then, doth not precisely intend either a day of rest or a spiritual rest, but the whole of our rest in God with respect unto his, and that day that is the token thereof comprised therein.[1]

Ver. 9.—There remaineth therefore a rest to the people of God.

And hereby the apostle completes the due analogy that is between the several rests of God and his people, which he hath discoursed of in this chapter. For as at the beginning of the world there was first the *work of God* and his *rest* thereon; which made way for a rest for his people in himself, and in his worship, by the contemplation of his works which he had made, and on whose finishing he rested; and a day designed, determined, blessed, and sanctified, to express that rest of God,—whence mention is made of those works in the command for the observation of that day, seeing the worship of God in and on that day consisted principally in the glorifying of God by and for those works of his,—as also to be a means to further men in their entrance into his eternal rest, whereunto all these things do tend; and this was the σαϛϛατισμός of the people of God from the foundation of the world: and as at the giving of the law there was a great work of God, and his rest thereon, in the finishing of his work and the establishing of his worship in the land of Canaan; which made way for the people's entering into his rest in that worship and country, and had a day assigned them to express the one and the other, and to help them to enter finally into the rest of God,—all which were types and shadows of the rest mentioned by David; and this was their σαϛϛατισμός, or sabbatizing rest: so now, under the gospel, there is a sabbatism comprehensive of all these; for there was, as we shall see, a great work of God, and a rest of his own that ensued thereon ; on this is founded the promise of rest, spiritual and eternal, unto them that do believe; and the determination of a new day, expressive of the one and the other,—that is, the rest of God, and our rest in him; which is the sabbatism that our apostle here affirms to remain for the people of God. And what day this is hath been declared, namely, the first day of the week.

---

[1] TRANSLATIONS.—Σαϛ. The celebration of a Sabbath.—*Ebrard.* A Sabbath-rest.—*Boothroyd, De Wette, Tholuck, Craik.* A Sabbath-rest, or, *in extenso,* a keeping of sabbatical rest.—*Conybeare and Howson.* A Sabbath-keeping.—*Scholefield.*—ED.

Now, besides the evidence that ariseth from the consideration of the whole context, there are two things which make it undeniably manifest that the apostle here proves and asserts the granting of an *evangelical Sabbath,* or day of rest, for the worship of God to be constantly observed. This, I say, he doth, though he doth not this *only,* nor separately: which whilst some have aimed to prove, they have failed of their aim, not being able to maintain a Sabbath rest exclusively, in opposition either to a spiritual or eternal rest; for so it is not here considered, but only in the manner and order before laid down.

Now these are, first, the introduction of the seventh day's rest into this discourse, and the mentioning of our gospel rest by the name of a "day." Unless the apostle had designed the declaration of a day of rest now under the gospel, as well as a real spiritual rest by believing, there is no tolerable reason to be given of his mentioning the works of God and his rest, and his appointment of the old Sabbath; which, without respect unto another day, doth greatly obscure and involve his whole discourse. Again; his use of this word, framed and as it were coined to this purpose, that it might both comprise the spiritual rest aimed at, and also express a Sabbath-keeping or observation. When he speaks of our rest in general, he still doth it by κατάπαυσις; adding there was an especial day for its enjoyment. Here he introduceth σαββατισμός, which his way of arguing would not have allowed, had he not designed to express the Christian Sabbath.

Secondly, He shows who they are to whom this sabbatism doth belong, who are to enter into this rest, to enjoy it, with all the privileges that do attend it; and these are ὁ λαὸς τοῦ Θεοῦ,—" the people of God." Those of old to whom the rest of Canaan was proposed were the people of God, and God hath a people still; and wherever he hath so, rest is promised to them and prepared for them. These he had before described by their own grace and obedience, verse 3, "We who have believed do enter into rest." Here he doth it by their relation unto God, and the privilege that depended thereon; they are the "people of God" that are interested in this sabbatism. And the apostle makes use of this description of them upon a double account:—

1. Because their being of "the people of God," that is, in covenant (for where a people is God's people, he is their God, Hos. ii. 23), was the greatest and most *comprehensive privilege* that the Hebrews had to boast of or to trust in. This was their glory, and that which exalted them above all nations in the world. So their church pleads with respect unto all others, Isa. lxiii. 19, "We are thine: thou never barest rule over them; thy name was not called on them;"—that is, they were never called the people of Jehovah, because never taken

into covenant with him.   This privilege whereunto they trusted, the apostle lets them know belongs as well to them that believe under the new testament as it did to them under the old.   Abram was now become Abraham, " a father of many nations."   And as those who were his carnal seed of old were the people of God, so God had now a people in and of all those who were his children according to the faith.   They may see, therefore, that they shall lose nothing, no privilege, by coming over to the gospel state by faith in Christ Jesus.   Upon a new account they become " the people of God;" which interests them and their children in the covenant, with the seals and all the ordinances of it, even as formerly.   For this name, "people," doth not firstly respect *individuals*, but a *collective body* of men, with and in all their relations.   Believers, not singly considered, but they and their seed, or their children, are this people; and where they are excluded from the initial ordinance of the covenant, I know not how believers can be called "the people of God."

2. He proceeds further, and shows them that indeed this privilege is now transferred over from the old estate and *Canaan rest* unto them that shall and do enter into this rest of God under the gospel.   Hence, instead of losing the privilege of being " the people of God" by faith in Christ, he lets them know that they could no longer retain it without it.   If they failed herein, they would be no longer " the people of God;" and as a signification thereof, they would become " no people" at all.   And so hath it fallen out with them.   For ever since they ceased to be God's people they have been " no people," or enjoy no political rule and society in the world. Thus, then, " there remaineth a rest" (or " Sabbath-keeping") " for the people of God."   But yet there is a considerable difficulty that ariseth against the whole design of the apostle: and this is, that this sabbatism of the people of God wanteth a due foundation in an especial work and rest of God.   For as, if God had not done a *new work*, and *rested* in it, at the giving of the law and establishment of his worship, whereby a new world as it were was erected, there could have been no *new rest* for his people to enter into, but all must have regarded the rest that was from the foundation of the world; so, if there be not a *new work* and *rest of God* now wrought and entered into by him, there cannot be a *new rest* and a *new day of rest* for the people of God.   This objection, therefore, the apostle removes, and manifests that there is a new blessed foundation of that rest which he now proposeth to the Hebrews, verse 10, as we shall see.   For the present we may observe, that,—

Obs. I. Believers under the new testament have lost nothing, no privilege that was enjoyed by them under the old.

Many things they have gained, and those of unspeakable excellency, but they have lost nothing at all. Whatever they had of privilege in any ordinance, that is continued; and whatever was of burden or bondage, that is taken away. All that they had of old was on this account, that they were the people of God. To them as such did all their advantages and privileges belong. But they were yet so the people of God as to be kept like servants, under the severe discipline of the law, Gal. iv. 1. Into this great fountain-privilege believers under the gospel are now succeeded. And what was of servitude in reference unto the law is removed and taken away; but whatever was of advantage is continued unto them, as the people of God. This, I suppose, is unquestionable, that God making them to be "his people who were not a people," would not cut them short of any privilege which belonged before to his people as such, Rom. ix. 25, 26. Besides, the state of the gospel is an estate of more grace and favour from God than that under the law, John i. 17. The whole gospel is an ampliation of divine spiritual grace and favour to God's people. So is it a better estate than that which went before, accompanied with "better promises," more liberty, grace, and privileges, than it. Nothing, then, of this nature can be lost therein or thereby to believers, but all privileges at any time granted unto the people of God are made over to them that under the gospel are so. Let men but give one instance to this purpose, and not beg the matter in question, and it shall suffice. Moreover, God hath so ordered all things in the dispensation of his grace and institution of his worship, that Jesus Christ should have the pre-eminence in all. All things are gathered up unto a head in him. And is it possible that any man should be a loser by the coming of Christ, or by his own coming unto Christ? It is against the whole gospel once to imagine it in the least instance. Let it now be inquired whether it were not a great privilege of the people of God of old, that their infant seed were taken into covenant with them, and were made partakers of the *initial seal* thereof? Doubtless it was the greatest they enjoyed, next to the grace they received for the saving of their own souls. That it was so granted them, so esteemed by them, may be easily proved. And without this, whatever they were, they were not a people. Believers under the gospel are, as we have spoken, the people of God; and that with all sorts of advantages annexed unto that condition, above what were enjoyed by them who of old were so. How is it, then, that this people of God, made so by Jesus Christ in the gospel, should have their charter, upon its renewal, razed with a deprivation of one of their choicest rights and privileges? Assuredly it is not so. And therefore if believers are now, as the apostle says they are, "the people of God," their children have a right to the initial seal of the covenant. Again,—

Obs. II. It is the people of God alone who have a right unto all the privileges of the gospel, and who in a due manner can perform all the duties of it.

The rest of the gospel and all that is comprised in it, is for them, and for them only. All others who lay hand on them, or use them, are "agri alieni invasores,"—wrongful invaders of the rights and enclosures of others; and " malæ fidei possessores," or do but unjustly possess what they have injuriously seized on. And the reason hereof is, because all gospel privileges are but adjuncts of and annexed unto the covenant of grace, and the administration of it. Without an interest in that covenant, none can attain the least right unto them; and this they alone have who are the people of God, for by that interest they become so. There is, therefore, great rapine and spoil committed upon the gospel and its ordinances in the world. Every one thinks he is born with a right to the chiefest of them, and cannot be excluded from them without the highest injustice. But ask some whether they are the people of God or no, and they will be ready to deride both name and thing. Custom, and an opinion received by tradition, hath put an esteem and valuation upon the enjoyment of the ordinances of the gospel. These, therefore, or their pretended right unto them, men will by no means forego, nor suffer themselves to be divested of them; but for the true, real, spiritual foundation and use of them, they are generally despised. But all may know that this is the method of the gospel,—first become the people of God, by entering into covenant with him in Jesus Christ, and all other spiritual mercies will be added unto you.

Obs. III. The people of God, as such, have work to do, and labour incumbent on them. Rest and labour are correlates; the one supposeth the other.

Affirming, therefore, that there is a *rest* for them, it includes in like manner that they have *work* to do. What this is cannot here be declared in particular: none that knows in any measure what is their condition in themselves, what their station in the world, what enemies they have to conflict withal, what duties are continually incumbent on them, but knows there is work and labour required of them. Thus our Saviour expresseth his approbation of his churches by, " I know thy works, and thy labour," Rev. ii. 2. The people of God dwell not as Laish, in security; nor are Sybarites, spending their time in sloth, luxury, and riot: but they are an industrious, working people; and I wish that those who profess themselves to be so were less industrious in earthly things, and more in heavenly; although I must say that those who are industrious heavenwards will not be altogether negligent or slothful in their stations in this world. But Christ calls men to work, and that our portion in this world is intermixed withal.

Obs. IV. God hath graciously given his people an entrance into rest during their state of work and labour, to sweeten it unto them, and to enable them for it.

The state of sin under the law is a state of all labour, and no rest; for "there is no peace," or rest, "to the wicked," saith God, Isa. lvii. 21. The future state of glory is all of rest,—*all rest.* The present state of believing and obedience is a mixed state,—partly of labour, partly of rest: of labour in ourselves, in the world, against sin, under affliction and persecution; of rest in Christ, in his love, in his worship, and grace. And these things have a great mutual respect unto one another. Our labour makes our rest sweet, and our rest makes our labour easy. So is God pleased to fill us, and exercise us; all to prepare us duly for eternal rest with himself.

Obs. V. Believers may and do find assured rest in a due attendance unto and performance of the duties of the gospel. This is that which the apostle asserts and proves.

Obs. VI. There is a weekly sacred day of rest appointed for believers under the gospel, as will appear from the next verse.

VERSE 10.

'Ο γὰρ εἰσελθὼν εἰς τὴν κατάπαυσιν αὐτοῦ, καὶ αὐτὸς κατέπαυσεν ἀπὸ τῶν ἔργων αὐτοῦ, ὥσπερ ἀπὸ τῶν ἰδίων ὁ Θεός.

There is no difficulty in these words, nor difference in the translation of them.

Ver. 10.—**For he that is entered into his rest, he also hath ceased from his works, as God from his own.**

So are the words to be read. Speaking of the works of God, he calls them his ἴδια, " his own,"—ἀπὸ τῶν ἰδίων, "from his own;" and of the other compared with him, he says only τὰ ἔργα αὐτοῦ, " his works:" somewhat otherwise than they are rendered in our version.

Expositors generally apply these words unto *believers,* and their entering into the rest of God; whether satisfactorily to themselves or others, either as to their design, coherence, scope, or signification of particular expressions, I know not. Nor is it my way to oppose or confute the expositions of others, unless they are of such as wrest the Scripture to the confirmation of errors and heresies, or pervert the testimonies which in any texts or places are given unto important and fundamental truths of the gospel; such as we have met with many in our passage. But where things spoken or delivered are true with respect unto the analogy of faith, though they may not be rightly or regularly deduced from this or that text in particular, yet they may have their use unto edification, through their conformity unto what is taught in other places;—in such cases

I shall not contend with any, but with all humility propose my own thoughts and reasons to the consideration of them who are wise, learned, and godly. I am not, then, satisfied with the exposition mentioned of this place, but look upon it as that which neither suits the design of the apostle, nor can bear a tolerable sense in its particular application. For, first, supposing believers to be here intended, what are the works they are said to rest from? Their sins, say some; their labours, sorrows, and sufferings, say others; from these they rest in heaven. But how can they be said to rest from these works as God rested from his own? for God so rested from his as to take the greatest delight and satisfaction in them, to be refreshed by them: "In six days the LORD made heaven and earth, and on the seventh day he rested, and was refreshed," Exod. xxxi. 17. He so rested *from them* as that he rested *in them*, and blessed them, and blessed and sanctified the time wherein they were finished. Indeed God's rest from and upon his works, besides a mere cessation of working, consisted principally in the satisfaction and complacency that he had in them. But now, if those mentioned be the works here intended, men cannot so rest from them as God did from his; but they cease from them with a detestation of them as far as they are sinful, and joy for their deliverance from them as far as they are sorrowful. Now, this is not to rest as God rested. Again, when are men supposed to rest from these works? It cannot be in this world, for here we rest not at all from temptations, sufferings, and sorrows; and for that mortification of sin which we attain unto, we are to fight continually, "resisting even unto blood." It must therefore be in heaven that they so rest; and this is affirmed accordingly. But this utterly excludes the rest in and of the gospel from the apostle's discourse, and enervates it, so as that his whole present argument is nothing to his purpose, as we have showed before.

It appears, therefore, that it is the *rest of another* that is here intended, even the *rest of Christ from his works*, which is compared with the rest of God from his at the foundation of the world; for,—

First, The conjunction γάρ, "for," which introduceth this assertion, manifests that the apostle in these words gives an account whence it is that there is a new sabbatism remaining for the people of God. He had proved before that there could be no such rest but what was founded in the works of God, and his rest that ensued thereon. Such a foundation therefore, he saith, this new rest must have; and it hath it. Now this is, and must be, in the works and rest of him by whom the church was built, that is Christ, who is God, as it is expressly argued, chap. iii. 3, 4. For as that rest which all the world was to observe was founded in his works and rest who built or made the world and all things in it; so *the rest of the church of the gospel* is to be founded

in his works and rest by whom the church itself was built, that is
Jesus Christ; for he, on the account of his works and rest, is also
Lord of the Sabbath, to abrogate one day of rest and to institute
another.

Secondly, The apostle here changeth the manner of his expression; from the plural absolutely, " We who believe," or virtually in
the name of a multitude, "the people of God," into that which is absolutely singular: ʽΟ εἰσελθών "He that is entered." A single person is here expressed; one on whose account the things mentioned
are asserted. And of this change of phrase there can no reason be
given, but only to signify the introduction of a singular person.

Thirdly, The rest which he is said to enter into is called "his
rest," absolutely. As God, speaking of the former rest, calls it " my
rest," so this is the " my rest" of another,—" his rest," namely, the
rest of Christ. When the entering of believers into rest is mentioned, it is called either " God's rest,"—" They shall enter into my
rest;" or " rest" absolutely,—" We that believe do enter into rest:"
but not 'their rest,' or 'our rest;' for it is not our own, but God's rest
whereinto we enter, and wherein we rest. The rest here is the rest
of him whose it is, who is the author of it; that is, of Christ.

Fourthly, There is a direct parallel in the whole verse between
the works of the old creation and those of the new, which the apostle
is openly comparing together. 1. For the authors of them: Of the
one it is said to be God,—"As God did from his;" that is, the Creator: of the other, "He," αὐτός; ʽ who is that He of whom we speak,'
saith our apostle, ʽ verse 13,'—for in these words he makes also a
transition to the person of Christ, allowing only the interposition of
an applicatory exhortation, verse 11. 2. The works of the one and
the other are expressed. The works of the Creator are ἴδια ἔργα, " his
proper works," "his own works," the works of the old creation. And
there are the works of him of whom he speaks, τὰ ἔργα αὐτοῦ, " his
works;" those which he wrought in like manner as God did his own
at the beginning,—that is, the work of building the church. For
these works must answer each other, and have the same respect unto
their authors or workers. They must be good and complete in their
kind, and such as rest and refreshment may be taken in as well as
upon. To compare the sins or the sufferings of men with the works
of God, our apostle did not intend. 3. There is the rest of the one
and the other. And these must also have their proportion to one
another. Now God rested from his own works of creation,—(1.) By
ceasing from creating, only continuing all things by his power in
their order, and propagating them to his glory. (2.) By his respect
unto them or *refreshment* in them, as those which set forth his praise
and satisfied his glorious design. And so also must he rest who is here
spoken of. (1.) He must cease from working in the like kind. He

must suffer no more, die no more, but only continue the work of his grace, in the preservation of the new creature, and orderly increase and propagation of it by the Spirit. (2.) In his delight and satisfaction which he taketh in his works, which Jesus Christ hath to the utmost. " He sees of the travail of his soul, and is satisfied," and is in possession of that " glory which was set before him" whilst he was at his work.

From what hath been spoken, I suppose it will appear plainly, to unprejudiced and impartial minds, that it is the person of Jesus Christ that is the subject here spoken of; and we shall confidently allow a supposition thereof to regulate our exposition of this verse. And there is considerable in it,—

First, *The person spoken of,* ὁ εἰσελθών, " He that is entered into his rest;" that is, the Lord Jesus Christ, the builder of 'Ο εἰσελθών. the church, the author of the new creation. And this gives an account of the causal connection, "for:" "There remaineth a sabbatism now for the people of God, for Christ is entered into his rest."

Secondly, There are the *works* that this rest of his respects, which it is said he hath "ceased" or "rested from." These Ἀπὸ τῶν ἔρ- words have been fully opened and declared on the third γων αὐτοῦ. and fourth verses of the third chapter, whither we refer the reader. All that he did and suffered, from his incarnation to his resurrection, as the mediator of the new covenant, with all the fruits, effects, and consequents of what he so did and suffered, belong to these works.

Thirdly, There is the *rest* that he entered into to be considered. Hereof we have seen before in general that there are Εἰς τὴν κατά- two parts:—1. A *cessation* from his works; he hungered παυσιν αὐτοῦ. no more, was tempted no more, in a word, died no more. 2. A *satisfaction* in his works and the product of them. This Christ had in his; whence he says, upon a view of their effects, "The lines are fallen unto me in pleasant places; yea, I have a goodly heritage," Ps. xvi. 6.

Fourthly, His *entrance* into his rest is in like manner proposed unto us. Now this was not his lying down in the grave. His body, indeed, there rested for a while; but that was no part of his mediatory rest, as the founder and builder of the church. For,—1. It was a part of his humiliation; not only his death, but his abode or continuance in the state of death was so, and that a principal part of it. For after the whole human nature was personally united unto the Son of God, to have it brought into a state of dissolution, to have the body and soul separated from each other, was a great humiliation. And every thing of this sort belonged to his works, not his rest. 2. This separation of body and soul under the power of death was penal, part of the sentence of the law which he underwent. And therefore Peter declares that the pains of death were not loosed but in his resurrection, Acts ii. 24: " Whom God," saith he, " hath raised up, loosing the pains of death; because it was not possible that he should be holden of it." Whilst he was held of it, he was under it penally. This therefore could not be his rest, nor any part of it; nor did he in it enter into his rest, but continued his work. Nor, secondly, did he first enter into his rest at his ascension. Then, indeed, he took actual possession of his glory, as to the full public manifestation of it. But to enter into rest is one thing, and to take possession of glory another. And it is placed by our apostle as a remote consequent of the Lord Christ's being "justified in the Spirit," when he entered into his rest, 1 Tim. iii. 16. But this his entrance into rest was in, by, and at his resurrection from the dead. For,— 1. Therein and then was he freed from the sentence, power, and stroke of the law, and discharged of all the debt of our sin, which he had undertaken to make satisfaction for, Acts ii. 24. Then and therein were all types, all prophecies and predictions fulfilled, that concerned the work of our redemption. 3. Then indeed his work was done; I mean that which answered God's creating work, though he still continueth that which answers his work of preservation. Then was the law fully satisfied, Satan absolutely subdued, peace with God made, the price of our redemption paid, and the whole foundation of the church gloriously laid in and upon his own person. Then "the morning stars sang together, and all the sons of God shouted for joy." 4. Then and therein was he "declared to be the Son of God with power," Rom. i. 4; God manifesting to all that this was he concerning and to whom he said, "Thou art my Son, this day have I begotten thee," Acts xiii. 33. This might be further confirmed, but that, as I know, it is not much questioned. Therefore did the Lord Christ enter into his rest, after he had finished and ceased from his works, " on the morning of the first day of the week," when he arose from the dead, the foundation of the new creation being laid and perfected.

Here lieth the foundation of our sabbatizing, of the sabbatism that remains for the people of God. This reason doth the apostle give of it. He had before asserted it; and there remained no more for him to do but to manifest that as those other rests which were past, the one at the beginning of the world, the other at the giving of the law, had their foundation in the works and rests of God, whence a day of rest was given out to the church; so had this new rest a foundation in the works and rest of Christ, who built all these things and is God, determining a day for our use, in and by that whereon himself entered into his rest,—that is, the first day of the week. See hence, that,—

Obs. I. The whole church, all the duties, worship, and privileges of it, are founded in the person, authority, and actions of Jesus Christ.

Obs. II. The first day of the week, the day of the resurrection of Christ, when he rested from his works, is appointed and determined for a day of rest or Sabbath unto the church, to be constantly observed in the room of the seventh day, appointed and observed from the foundation of the world and under the old testament.

This proposition, containing a truth of great importance, and greatly opposed by many on various accounts, that the full discussion of it may not too much interrupt the course of our exposition, is handled apart and at large, in exercitations to that purpose, whereunto the reader in this place is remitted.[1]

VERSE 11.

In this verse we have a return made unto, and an improvement of the principal exhortation which the apostle had before proposed. In the first verse he laid it down in these words, " Let us fear, lest, a promise being left of entering into his rest, any of you should seem to come short of it." Here he declares how that fear there recommended is to act itself, or how it is to be improved and exercised. It appears, therefore, hence, what we observed before, namely, that it was not a fear of dread, terror, or doubting, that might weaken, discourage, or dishearten them, which he enjoined them; but such a reverential respect unto the promises and threatenings of God as might quicken and stir them up unto all diligence in seeking to inherit the one and avoid the other. Here, therefore, the same exhortation is resumed and carried on, and that on sundry suppositions, which he had laid down, explained, and confirmed in his preceding discourse, being all of them effectual enforcements of it. Now these are,—1. That *there is a rest* promised unto us, and yet remaining for us, which is foretold and described in the 95th Psalm; for he hath showed that the rest mentioned therein was not a rest that was past, or enjoyed by any that went before us in any state of the church from the foundation of the world, but it is that which is now declared and proposed in the gospel. 2. That others had a *rest typical* hereof proposed unto them, seeing God never ordained his church in any state without a rest, and a day of rest as a token thereof. 3. That some by sin, or unbelief and disobedience, fell short of the rest proposed to them, and did not enter into it, but were destroyed in the just indignation of God against them. 4. That in their sin and God's displeasure, with the event of the one and effects of the other, there was an *example* set forth

---

[1] See vol. xix. p. 261.

of what would be the event with them, and God's dealings towards them, who through unbelief should neglect the rest now declared and proposed unto them. Unto all these propositions he subjoins a description of this new rest, in the cause, original, and nature of it, with that day of rest wherein it is expressed. Having, therefore, proved and confirmed these things in his expositions and discourses upon the 95th Psalm, he lays them down as the foundation of his exhorting the Hebrews to faith and perseverance, keeping himself unto the notion of a rest, and of entering into it, which the testimony he had chosen to insist upon led him unto.

Ver. 11.—Σπουδάσωμεν οὖν εἰσελθεῖν εἰς ἐκείνην τὴν κατάπαυσιν· ἵνα μὴ ἐν τῷ αὐτῷ τις ὑποδείγματι πέσῃ τῆς ἀπειθείας.

Σπουδάσωμεν. Vulg. Lat., "festinemus;" and the Rhemists, "let us hasten," —that is, σπεύδωμεν. The words are both from the same original; but σπουδάζω is never used for "to hasten;" nor is σπεύδω, for a rash, precipitate haste, such as is condemned by the prophet in the things of God: Isa. xxviii. 16, "He that believeth shall not make haste;" that is, with such a kind of haste as causeth men to miscarry in what they undertake, and gives them disappointment and shame. Hence the apostle renders these words, הַמַּאֲמִין לֹא יָחִישׁ, "He that believeth shall not make haste," by Ὁ πιστεύων ἐπ᾽ αὐτῷ οὐ καταισχυνθήσεται, Rom. ix. 33, "Whosoever believeth on him shall not be ashamed,"—expressing the cause by the effect. Syr., נֶתְחַפַּט, "enitamur, operam demus,"—"let us endeavour it," "do our endeavour." Ours, "let us labour;" Bez., "studeamus," properly,—"let us study," or "studiously endeavour," "sedulously apply our minds."

Εἰσελθεῖν εἰς ἐκείνην τὴν κατάπαυσιν. These words have been all opened before; nor do translators vary in the rendering of them.

Ἵνα μὴ ἐν τῷ αὐτῷ τίς ὑποδείγματι πέσῃ τῆς ἀπειθείας. Vulg. Lat., "ut ne in id ipsum quis incidat incredulitatis exemplum." Rhem., "that no man fall into the same example of incredulity;" somewhat ambiguously. Beza, "ne quis in idem incidat contumaciæ exemplum;" "that no man fall into the same example of stubborn disobedience,"—that is, into the like sin. Erasm., "ne quis concidat eodem incredulitatis exemplo;" to the same purpose: as ours also, "lest any man fall after the same example of unbelief." Syr., "that we fall not after the manner of them who believed not,"—בַּדְמוּתָא, "ad similitudinem," "like unto them." And in all these translations it is left somewhat ambiguous whether it be the sin of the people or their punishment that is proposed to consideration.

Μή τις πέσῃ, or μή τις, "lest any;" and of what is therein included we have spoken before. Πέσῃ, "cadat," that is, into sin; "incidat," into punishment; "concidat," "do fall."

Τῷ αὐτῷ ὑποδείγματι. Ὑπόδειγμα is sometimes as much as παράδειγμα, an "exemplary punishment;" or an example instructive by the evil which befalls others. Of the sense of the words afterwards.

Ver. 11.—Let us labour therefore [or, *diligently endeavour*] to enter into that rest; lest any should fall in the same example of unbelief.

In the words three things may be observed:—First, The *illative particle* οὖν, "therefore;" denoting an inference from and dependence upon what was before discoursed. The things he now introduceth arise from the consideration of what was before alleged and proved, with an especial respect unto that part of the example insisted on which consisted in the sin and punishment of the people of old; " therefore." Secondly, An *exhortation unto duty* ensues. Thirdly, A *motive* thereunto is proposed. In the exhortation there is the duty itself exhorted unto,—which is, to " enter into that rest;" and the manner of its performance,—it is to be done with labour and diligence, " Let us labour to enter into that rest."

First, The duty exhorted unto is expressed in terms whose use is taken from the example before insisted on, " entering into rest." The things intended may be considered two ways, as to the act of the duty, or the duty itself and the effect of it, both included in the words. The duty itself intended is faith and obedience unto the gospel; these were represented of old by the people's Εἰς ἐκείνην τὴν κατάπαυσιν. applying themselves to enter into the promised land of Canaan. Here, therefore, he exhorts them unto their present duty under these terms.. And the effect of this duty, which is a participation of the rest of God, is also included.

And indeed glorious advantages are comprised in all gospel duties. To know God in Christ is " life eternal," John xvii. 3; to believe, is to enter into the rest of God. Again, for the further explication of these words, we may observe that the apostle changeth his expression from what it was in the preceding verse. He tells us, verse 9, that "there remaineth σαββατισμός" (a " sabbatism") " for the people of God;" but here he doth not exhort them to enter εἰς ἐκείνον τὸν σαββατισμόν, (" into that sabbatism,") but changeth it into κατάπαυσιν,—that is, מְנוּחָה, as the other is שַׁבָּתוֹן. And the reason is, because by that word, " sabbatism," he intended to express the rest of the gospel not absolutely, but with respect unto the pledge of it in the day of rest, which is given and determined unto them that believe, for the worship of God and other ends before recounted: but the apostle here returns to exhort the Hebrews to endeavour after an interest in and participation of the whole rest of God in the gospel, with all the privileges and advantages contained in it; and therefore resumes the word whereby he had before expressed the rest of God in general.

Secondly, For the manner of the performance of this duty, the word σπουδάσωμεν doth declare it. Let us "diligently study," " endeavour," or " labour" to this purpose. If we suppose "labour" in our language to be the most proper word (though I had rather use " endeavour"), such a labouring is to be understood as wherein the mind and whole soul is very intently exercised, and that upon the account of the difficulties which in the performance of this duty we shall meet withal. For the apostle, expressing our faith and gospel obedience, with the end of them, by " entering into the rest of God,"

—a phrase of speech taken from the people's entering into the land of Canaan of old,—he minds us of the great opposition which in and unto them we shall be sure to meet withal. It is known what difficulties, storms, and contrary winds, the people met with in their wilderness peregrinations. So great were they, that the discouragements which arose from them were the principal occasions of their acting that unbelief which proved their ruin. Sometimes their want of water and food, sometimes the weariness and tediousness of the way, sometimes the reports they had of giants and walled towns, stirred up their unbelief to murmurings, and hastened their destruction. That we shall meet with the like opposition in our faith and profession the apostle instructs us, by his using this phrase of speech with respect unto the occasion of it, " entering into the rest of God." And we may observe hence,—

Obs. I. That great oppositions will and do arise against men in the work of entering into God's rest; that is, as unto gospel faith and obedience.

First, The very first lessons of the gospel discourage many from looking any farther. So when our Saviour entertained the young man that came to him for instruction with the *lesson of self-denial,* he had no mind to hear any more, but " went away sorrowful," Matt. xix. 22. And the reasons hereof may be taken partly from the nature of the gospel itself, and partly from our own natures to whom the gospel is proposed. I shall but instance in that general consideration, which alone would bear the weight of this assertion;—and this is, that in the gospel there is proposed unto us a " new way" of entering into the rest of God, of acceptation with him, of righteousness and salvation, which is contrary to our natural principle of self-righteousness, and seeking after it "as it were by the works of the law;" for this fills our hearts naturally with an enmity unto it and contempt of it, making us esteem it " foolish" and " weak," no way able to effect what it proposeth and promiseth. But this would be too large a field to enter into at present, and I shall therefore insist only on some particular instances, giving evidence to the proposition as laid down. These I shall take from among the precepts of the gospel, some whereof are very difficult unto our nature as it is weak, and all of them contrary unto it as it is corrupt.

1. Some gospel precepts are exceeding *difficult unto our nature as it is weak.* This our Saviour takes notice of when exhorting his disciples to watchfulness and prayer in an hour of temptation; he tells them that " the spirit is willing, but the flesh is weak," Matt. xxvi. 41; where by " the flesh" he intendeth not that corrupt principle which is in us, that is often called by that name, but our nature in its whole composition with respect unto that weakness whence it is apt to succumb and sink under difficult duties. To fix on one in-

stance among many, of this nature is self-denial, so indispensably required of all in the gospel. The denial of our lusts and corrupt inclinations falls under another consideration, and must on other accounts have violence offered unto them, as afterwards; but in the first place we may weigh this precept as it extends itself unto things in themselves lawful, and which have an exceeding suitableness unto our natures as weak and infirm. We are but dust, and God knows that we are but dust, Ps. ciii. 14. And he hath in his providence provided many things, and allowed us the use of them, which are fitted and suited to our refreshment and relief in our pilgrimage. Such are houses, lands, possessions, the comfort of relations and friends, which he hath given us a right unto and an interest in. And as we are persuaded that, through the weakness and frailty of our natures, we do greatly stand in need of these things, so it is known how our hearts are apt to cleave unto them. But here this gospel precept of self-denial interposeth itself, and requireth two things of us:—

(1.) It requires an undervaluation of them, or at least introduceth a new affection over them and above them, which shall put the heart into a continual readiness and preparedness to part with them at the call and upon the occasions of the gospel, Matt. x. 37. Our acceptance of Christ on gospel terms is like a man's entrance into a marriage relation. It introduceth a new affection, that goes above and regulates all former affections; for " a man must forsake both father and mother, and cleave unto his wife." All others are to be steered and regulated hereby. And he that by his acceptance of Christ would enter into rest, must subordinate all former affections to lawful things unto this new one, which will not abide in any heart but where it is supreme.

(2.) On sundry occasions which the profession of the gospel will present us withal, actually to relinquish and forego them, and to trust our persons, with all their weaknesses and frailties, to the provision that Christ will make for them, Mark viii. 34–37. This is difficult unto our nature, because of its weakness. It is apt to say, ' Let me be spared in this or that,'—to make an intercession for a Zoar. ' What shall become of me when all is lost and gone? What shall I do for rest, for ease, for liberty, for society, yea for food and raiment?' Yet are all these to be conquered by faith, if we intend to enter into the rest of God. We condemn them of old who were afraid of giants and walled towns, which made them murmur and withdraw from their duty. These are our giants and fenced cities; —and, alas! how many are hindered by them from inheriting the promise! The like may be said of that particular branch of the great duty of self-denial, in " taking up the cross," or willingness to undergo all sorts of persecutions for the sake of Jesus Christ. Many of these are exceeding dreadful and terrible to our nature as mortal, weak, and infirm. Peter knew how it is with us in all our natural principles, when he advised his Lord and Master to spare himself, as he was foretelling of his own sufferings. Here the weakness of our nature would betake itself to a thousand pretences to be spared; but the gospel requires severely that they be all discarded, and the cross cheerfully taken up, whenever by the rule of it we are called thereunto. And they do but deceive themselves who engage into a profession of it without a readiness and preparation for these things. It is true, God may spare whom he pleaseth and when he pleaseth, as to the bitterness of them; and some, in his tenderness and compassion, are little, it may be, exercised with them all their days; but this is by especial dispensation and extraordinary indulgence. The rule is plain,—we must be all ready in the school of Christ to say this lesson, and he may call forth whom he pleaseth unto its repetition. We are, it may be, loath to come forth, loath to be brought to the trial; but we must stand to it, or expect to be turned out of doors, and to be denied by the great Master at the last day. We are, for the most part, grown tender and delicate, and unwilling to come (so much as in our minds) to a resolved conversation with these things. Various hopes and contrivances shall relieve our thoughts from them. But the precept is universal, absolute, indispensable, and such as our entrance into the rest of God doth depend on its due observance. By the dread hereof are multitudes kept in the wilderness of the world, wandering up and down between Egypt and Canaan, and at length fall finally under the power of unbelief. These and the like things are very difficult unto our nature as it is weak.

2. All the commands of the gospel are *opposite and contrary to our nature as it is corrupt.* And this hath so large an interest in all men, as to make those things very difficult unto them which are wholly opposite thereunto. A sense hereof hath made some endeavour a composition between the gospel and their lusts, so "turning the grace of God into lasciviousness," by seeking countenance from thence unto their sins, which have no design but to destroy them. From the corruption of our nature it is that the things which the gospel in its precepts requires us severely to cast off and destroy have a treble interest in us, that it is not easy to overcome,—an interest of love, an interest of usefulness, and an interest of power.

(1.) An interest of *love.* Hence we are commanded to pull out right eyes, if they offend us, Matt. v. 29,—things that are as dear unto us as our eye, as our right eye. And it is a proverbial expression to set out the high valuation and dear esteem we have of any thing, to say that it is unto us as our eye;—as God himself, to express his tender care over his people, says, " he that toucheth them toucheth

the apple of his eye," Deut. xxxii. 10, Zech. ii. 8.   And such are the
lusts of the flesh naturally to men; whence the precept of the gospel,
" If thy right eye offend thee, pluck it out, and cast it from thee,"
immediately subjoined to that doctrine of purity and chastity, "Whosoever looketh on a woman to lust after her, hath committed adultery
with her already in his heart," Matt. v. 28.   Now there cannot but
be great difficulty in cutting off and casting away from us such things
as have so great an interest of love in us, as these lusts have in corrupted nature.   Every one is unwilling to part with what he loves;
and the more he loves it the less willing is he to part with it, the
longer and the more earnestly will he hold it.   And there is nothing
that men naturally love more than their carnal lusts.   They will
part with their names, their estates, and venture their lives, all to
satisfy them.

(2.) An interest of *usefulness*.   Nature, as corrupt, would persuade
a man that he cannot live nor subsist in this world without the
help and advantage of some of those things which the gospel forbids
to all them that will enter into the rest of God.   Hence is the command to cut off the right hand, if it offend, Matt. v. 30; that is,
things apprehended as useful unto us as a right hand is to the
common services of life.   Of this kind is that inordinate love of the
world, and all the ways whereby it is pursued, which the gospel doth
so condemn.   These things are to many what Micah's gods were
unto him, who cried out upon the loss of them, when they were
stolen by the Danites, " Ye have taken away my gods, and what
have I more?"   Take away from men their love of this world, and
the inordinate pursuit of it, and they think they have no more; they
will scarce think it worth while to live in the world any longer.
And this interest also is to be overcome, which it cannot be without
great difficulty; and a cleaving unto it is that which hinders multitudes from entering into the rest of God.

(3.) An interest of *power*.   Hence sin is said to have " strongholds"
in us, which are not easily cast down.   But hereof I have treated in
a peculiar discourse.

Secondly, Another reason of the difficulty of this work ariseth
from *the combined opposition* that is made unto it; for as the Egyptians, the Canaanites, and the Amorites, did all of them their utmost to hinder the Israelites from entering into Canaan,—and what
they could not effect really by their opposition, they did morally, by
occasioning the people's unbelief through their fighting against them,
which proved their ruin,—so do our spiritual adversaries deal in
this matter.   If the work of the gospel go on, if men endeavour by
it to enter into God's rest, Satan must lose his subjects, and the
world its friends, and sin its life.   And there is not one instance
wherein they will not try their utmost to retain their interest.   All

these endeavour to hinder us from entering into the rest of God; which renders it a great and difficult work.

It will be said, ' That if there be all these difficulties lying before us, they must needs be so many discouragements, and turn men aside from attempting of it.' I answer,—

1. Of old, indeed, they did so. The difficulties and discouragements that lay in the way of the people quite took off their hearts and minds from endeavouring an entrance into the promised land. But what was the event? The apostle declares at large that on this account the indignation of God came upon them, and "their carcasses fell in the wilderness." And no otherwise will it be with them who are afraid to engage in those spiritual difficulties we have now to conflict withal. They will die and perish under the wrath of God, and that unto eternity. He that shall tell men that their entering into the rest of Christ is plain, easy, suited to nature as it is weak or corrupt, will but delude and deceive them. To mortify sin, subdue our bodies, and keep them in subjection,—to deny ourselves, not only in the crucifying of lusts that have the secretest tendency unto things unlawful, but also in the use of things lawful, and our affections to them, pulling out right eyes, cutting off right hands, taking up the cross in all sorts of afflictions and persecutions,— are required of us in this matter: and they are not at present joyous, but grievous; not easy and pleasant, but difficult, and attended with many hardships. To lull men asleep with hopes of a rest in Christ, and in their lusts, in the world, in their earthly accommodations, is to deceive them and ruin them. We must not represent the duties of gospel faith and obedience as the Jesuits preached Christ to the Indians,—never letting them know that he was crucified, lest they should be offended at it. But we must tell men the plain truth as it is, and let them know what they are to expect from within and from without, if they intend to enter into rest.

2. Notwithstanding all these difficulties, the promise of God, being mixed with faith, will carry us safely through them all. After the unbelieving generation was destroyed in the wilderness the hardships and difficulties still remained; yet their children, believing the promise, passed through them and entered into rest. The power of God, and his faithfulness amongst them and unto them, conquered them all. And it will be so with them infallibly that shall mix the promise with faith in reference unto this spiritual rest. God will both supply them with strength and subdue their enemies, so as that they shall not fail of rest. Whatever, therefore, may be pretended, it is nothing but unbelief that can cause us to come short of rest; and this will do it effectually. Faith in the promise will engage the power of Christ unto our assistance; and where he will work none shall let him. To this end we might consider the various

ways whereby he will make mountains become plains, dry up rivers, yea, seas of opposition, and make all those things light and easy unto us which seem so grievous and insupportable unto our nature, either as weak and frail, or as corrupt and sinful. But we must not too far digress into these things. And I say, *thirdly,* which is a second observation from the words,—

Obs. II. That as the utmost of our labours and endeavours are required to our obtaining an entrance into the rest of Christ, so it doth very well deserve that they should be laid out therein.

'Let us,' saith the apostle, 'endeavour this matter with all diligence,' as the word imports. Men are content to lay out themselves unto the utmost for other things, and to spend their strength for "the bread that perisheth," yea, "for that which is not bread." Every one may see how busy and industrious the world is in the pursuit of perishing things; and men are so foolish as to think that they deserve their whole time and strength; and more they would expend in the same way, if they were intrusted with it. "This their way is their folly." But how easy a thing were it to demonstrate, from the nature of it, its procurement and end, with our eternal concernment in it, that this rest deserves the utmost of our diligence and endeavours. To convince men hereof is one of the chief ends of the preaching of the gospel in general, and so needs not here to be insisted on.

Obs. III. Again, there is a present excellency in and a present reward attending gospel faith and obedience.

They are an entrance into the rest of Christ, or they give us a present interest therein. They are not only a present means of entering into future eternal rest with God, but they give us a present participation of the rest of Christ; which wherein it doth consist hath been before declared.

Thirdly, The latter part of this verse yet remaineth to be explained and applied. Therein unto the precedent exhortation a motive is subjoined: "Lest any fall after the same example of unbelief." These words, as was in part before intimated, do express either the sin to be avoided, or the punishment whereby we should be deterred from it.

The word, "to fall," is ambiguous, and may be applied to either sense; for men may *fall into sin,* and they may *fall into the punishment due to their sin,* when that word is used in a moral sense. Matt. xv. 14, '" The blind lead the blind, ἀμφότεροι εἰς βόθυνον πεσοῦνται,"—"both shall fall into the ditch," of sin or trouble. See Rom. xi. 22, James v. 12. For the prime use of the word is in things natural, and is only metaphorically translated to express things moral. And ὑπόδειγμα is most commonly "a teaching example." So ὑποδείκνυμι is "to teach," or "to instruct" by showing: Matt. iii. 7,

" O generation of vipers, τίς ὑπέδειξεν ὑμῖν,"—"who hath warned" (taught, instructed) "you." Thence ὑπόδειγμα is "documentum." Ταῦτα ὑποδείγματα ἔσται τῷ Πολυδάμνη ὧν δεῖ ἐπιμεληθῆναι·—"These are instructions for Polydamnes, about the things that are to be provided for." But it is also often used as παράδειγμα, "an exemplary punishment;" as ʹΥπόδειγμα τῷ πλήθει ποιῶν αὐτόν·—"Making him an example to the multitude;" that is, in his punishment. And so among the Latins, "exemplum" is often put absolutely for "punishment," and that of the highest nature. Now, if ὑπόδειγμα in this place be taken merely for a "document" or "instruction," which is undoubtedly the most proper and usual signification of the word, then the sense may be, 'Lest any of you should fall into that unbelief whereof, and of its pernicious consequents, you have an instructive example in them that went before, proposed on purpose unto you, that you might be stirred up to avoid it.' If it be taken for παράδειγμα, as sometimes it is, and so include in its signification "an exemplary punishment," then the meaning of the word is, 'Lest any of you, through your unbelief, fall into that punishment, which hath been made exemplary in the ruin of those other unbelievers who went before you.' And this I take to be the meaning of the words: 'You have the gospel, and the rest of Christ therein, preached and proposed unto you. Some of you have already taken upon you the profession of it, as the people did of old at mount Sinai, when they said, "All that the LORD our God shall command, that we will do." Your condition is now like unto theirs, and was represented therein. Consider, therefore, how things fell out with them, and what was the event of their sin and God's dealing with them. They believed not, they made not good their engagement, they persisted not in their profession, but were disobedient and stubborn; and God destroyed them. They "fell in the wilderness," and perished, not entering into God's rest, as hath been declared. If now you, or any amongst you, shall be found guilty of their sin, or the like answering unto it, do not think or hope that you shall avoid the like punishment. An example of God's severity is set before you in their destruction. If you would not fall into it, or fall under it, labour by faith and obedience to enter into the rest of Christ.' And this I take to be the true sense and importance of the words, answering in their coherence and relation unto them that go before; for these words, "Let us labour to enter into that rest," are no more but, 'Let us sincerely believe and obey; wherein we shall find, through Jesus Christ, rest to our souls.' Hereunto this clause of the verse is a *motive:* "Lest any of you fall in the same example of unbelief." Now, if their sense should be, 'Lest any of you, after their example, should fall into unbelief;' then that of the whole must be, 'Let us labour to believe, that we fall not into unbelief,'—which is a mere battology, and remote from our divine author. Hence observe,—

Obs. IV. Precedent judgments on others are monitory ordinances unto us.

They are so in general in all things that fall out in the providence of God in that kind, whereof we may judge by a certain rule. This is the use that we are to make of God's judgments, without a censorious reflection on them in particular who fall under them; as our Saviour teacheth us in the instances of the Galileans, whose blood Pilate mingled with their sacrifices, and those men on whom the tower in Siloam fell. But there are many things peculiar in the examples of this kind given us in the Scripture; for,—1. We have an infallible rule therein to judge both of the sins of men and the respect that the judgments of God had unto them; besides, 2. They are designed instances of the love and care of God towards us, as our apostle declares, 1 Cor. x. 11. God suffered their sins to fall out, and recorded his own judgments against them in his word, on purpose for our instruction; so that as he declared his severity in them towards others, he makes known by them his love and care towards us. This gives them the nature of ordinances, which all proceed from love. To this end, and with a sense hereof, are we to undertake the consideration of them. So are they exceedingly instructive; to which purpose we have treated somewhat on the third chapter, whither we refer the reader. Again,—

Obs. V. It is better to have an example than to be made an example of divine displeasure; yet this will befall us if we neglect the former: for,—

Obs. VI. We ought to have no expectation of escaping vengeance under the guilt of those sins which others, in a like manner guilty of, have not escaped.

We are apt to flatter ourselves, that however it fared with others, it will go well with us; like him who blesseth himself, and says he shall have peace, when he hears the words of the curse. This self-pleasing and security variously insinuates itself into our minds, and tenaciously cleaves unto us; but as we have any care of our eternal welfare, we are to look upon it as our greatest enemy. There is no more certain rule for us to judge of our own condition, than the examples of God's dealings with others in the same. They are all effects of eternal and invariable righteousness; and " with God there is no respect of persons." I might here insist on the ways and means whereby this self-flattery imposeth false hopes and expectations on men; as also on the duties required of us for to obviate and prevent its actings, but must not too often digress from our main purpose and design.

VERSES 12, 13.

These next verses contain a new enforcement of the precedent exhortation, taken from the consideration of the means of the event threatened in case of unbelief. Two things are apt to arise in the minds of men for their relief against the fear of such comminations as are proposed unto them: 1. That their failing in point of duty may not be discerned or taken notice of. For they will resolve against such transgressions as are open, gross, and visible to all; as for what is partial and secret, in a defect of exactness and accuracy, that may be overlooked or not be observed. 2. That threatenings are proposed "in terrorem" only,—to terrify and awe men, but not with a mind or will of putting them into execution. Both these vain pretences and deceiving reliefs our apostle in these verses obviates the way of, or deprives men of them where they have been admitted. For he lets them know that they are to be tried by that, or have to do with Him, who both actually discovers all the secret frames of our hearts, and will deal with all men accordingly. Moreover, herein he informs them how and in what manner it is necessary for them to attend unto his exhortation in the performance of their duty; namely, not in or by a mere outward observance of what is required of them with respect unto profession only, but with a holy jealousy and watchfulness over their hearts, and all the intimate recesses of their souls, the most secret actings of their spirits and thoughts of their minds; seeing all these things are open unto cognizance, and subject unto trial.

Ver. 12, 13.—Ζῶν γὰρ ὁ λόγος τοῦ Θεοῦ, καὶ ἐνεργὴς, καὶ τομώτερος ὑπὲρ πᾶσαν μάχαιραν δίστομον, καὶ διϊκνούμενος ἄχρι μερισμοῦ ψυχῆς τε καὶ πνεύματος, ἁρμῶν τε καὶ μυελῶν, καὶ κριτικὸς ἐνθυμήσεων καὶ ἐννοιῶν καρδίας· καὶ οὐκ ἔστι κτίσις ἀφανὴς ἐνώπιον αὐτοῦ· πάντα δὲ γυμνὰ καὶ τετραχηλισμένα τοῖς ὀφθαλμοῖς αὐτοῦ, πρὸς ὃν ἡμῖν ὁ λόγος.

Ζῶν γάρ, "vivus enim." Syr. הַוְיָא הִי, "vivus est;" it supplies הִי, "est," as do all other translations, though there be an emphasis ofttimes in sundry languages in the omission of the verb substantive. Ours, "quick," improperly; for that word doth more ordinarily signify "speedy," than "living:" and I doubt not but many are deceived in this place through the ambiguity of that word.

Ὁ λόγος, "sermo," "verbum;" so is that word promiscuously rendered by translators, though the first using of "sermo" in John i. 1 caused some stir amongst them who had been long used to "verbum." But these words are promiscuously used, both by the ancients and learned men of latter days. Ours, "The word." Syr., מֶלְּתֵהּ; the same word that it useth John i. 1, where the person of the Son of God is spoken of.

Καὶ ἐνεργής, "et efficax;" so all the Latin translators;—"efficacious," "effectual in operation," "powerful:" but that denotes the habit, this word intends the act, —"effectually operative." Syr. וְכָל סָעַר, "et omnino," or "ad omnia efficax,"—

" altogether efficacious;" for ἐνεργής denotes a very intimate, active, powerful operation or efficacy. Rhem. " forcible."

Καὶ τομώτερος. Vulg. Lat., Ari. Mon., " penetrabilior." Scarce properly, for participles in " bilis," are mostly passive; and in our language, " penetrable" is the description of a thing that may be pierced, or is easy so to be. Hence the Rhem. render it " more piercing," properly. Beza, " penetrantior," as Erasmus. Valla, and from him Erasmus, say they would render it " incidentior," were that a proper Latin word. Ours, " sharper;" not so properly,— " more cutting," or " more piercing." Syr., וְחַרִיפָא טָב, " et longe penetrantior;" " and much more cutting," " sharp," or " piercing." It adds " cal" and " tab," to express the form of the comparative degree used in the original.

Ὑπὲρ πᾶσαν μάχαιραν δίστομον, " super omnem gladium ancipitem," " above any two-edged sword." Ὑπέρ being added to the preceding comparative τομώτερος, eminently exalts one of the comparates above the other. Syr. דִּתְרֵין פּוּמֵיהּ, " before a sword with two mouths." Both the Hebrews and the Greeks call the edge of the sword its mouth,—στόμα τῆς μαχαίρας, " the mouth of the sword,"—it being that wherewith it devours. Beza, " quovis gladio ancipiti." Eras., " utrinque incidente." Arab., " and in cutting sharper than a sword of two edges." Ethiopic, " than a razor." Ours, " than any two-edged sword."

Καὶ διϊκνούμενος, " et pertingens," " et pertinget." Syr., וְעָאֵל, " et ingreditur,"—" and entereth," " reacheth unto," " cometh into," " pierceth into."

Ἄχρι μερισμοῦ ψυχῆς τε καὶ πνεύματος, " usque ad divisionem animæ et spiritus." Beza, " animæ simul ac spiritus," " both of soul and spirit;" expressing the particle τε, which yet in some copies is wanting.

Ἁρμῶν τε καὶ μυελῶν, " compagumque et medullarum," " of the joints and marrow." The Syriac adds וְגַרְמֵא, " and of the bones." Ethiopic, " et discernit animam ab anima, et quod noctescit a nocte; " discerneth one soul from another, and that which is dark from night,"—that is, the most secret things.

Καὶ κριτικός, " et discretor." Vulg. Lat., " et judicat," " et dijudicat;" " judgeth," " discerneth." " Judex," " criticus," " and is a discerner;" that is, one that discerneth by making a right judgment of things.

Ἐνθυμήσεων, " cogitationum." Ethiopic, " cogitationum desiderabilium," " desirable thoughts;" not without reason, as we shall see.

Καὶ ἐννοιῶν καρδίας. Vulg. Lat., Ari., Eras., " intentionum cordis," " of the intentions of the heart." Beza, " conceptuum," " conceptions." Ours, " intents," —a word of a deeper sense. There may be " conceptus" where there is not " intentio" or " propositum." Syr., " the will of the heart." See Eph. ii. 3.

Καὶ οὐκ ἔστι κτίσις, " et non est creatura," " and there is not a creature." Beza, " et nulla est res creata," " and there is no created thing;" more proper in Latin, but a " creature" is common with us.

Ἀφανής. Beza, " non manifesta." Ours, " that is not manifest." Vulg. Lat., " invisibilis." And the Rhem., " invisible," not properly : " not manifestly apparent." Syr., " that is hid."

Πάντα δὲ γυμνά. Beza, " imo omnia nuda," " yea, all things are naked." Ours, " but all things are naked."

Καὶ τετραχηλισμένα. Vulg. Lat., " aperta," " open." Beza, " intime patentia," " inwardly open." Erasm., " resupinata," " laid on their backs," " open." Syr., וּגְלֵא, " and manifest," or " revealed."

Πρὸς ὃν ἡμῖν ὁ λόγος. Beza, " quo cum nobis est negotium;" which ours render, " with whom we have to do." Vulg. Lat., " ad quem nobis sermo." Rhem., " to whom our speech is." Syr., " to whom they give account." And the Arabic to the same purpose, " before whom our trial or excuse must be." What help we may have in the understanding of the words from these various translations of them, we shall see in our consideration of the particulars of the text. The difficulty of the place hath caused me to inquire the more diligently into the sense of translators upon the words themselves.[1]

Ver. 12, 13.—For the word of God is living and power-ful [or *effectual*], and sharper [*more cutting, or cutting more*] than any two-edged sword, piercing even to the dividing asunder of the joints and marrow, and is a discerner [*a discerning judge*] of the thoughts and in-tents [*conceptions*] of the heart. Neither is there any creature that is not [*apparently*] manifest in his sight: but all things are naked and opened unto the eyes of him with whom we have to do, [or *to whom we must give an account.*]

The whole exposition of these words depends on the subject spoken of, verse 12; that, therefore, we must diligently inquire into. This being rightly stated, the things spoken must be duly accommodated unto it; and in these two things doth the due exposition of these words consist. Now this subject is ὁ λόγος τοῦ Θεοῦ, "the word of God." It is known that this name some- ʼΟ λόγος τοῦ Θεοῦ. times in the Scripture denotes the *essential Word of God,* sometimes the *word spoken by him:* or, λόγος Θεοῦ is either οὐσιώδης, that is, the eternal Son of God; or προφορικός, his enuncia-tive word, the word of his will, his declared, written word. And the confounding of these is that which so entangleth the Quakers amongst us; or rather, is that whereby they endeavour to entangle others, and seduce "unlearned and unstable souls." But all sorts of expositors are divided in judgment about which of these it is that is here intended. Amongst the ancients, Ambrose, with many others, contends that it is the *essential and eternal Word of God* which is spoken of. Chrysostom seems rather to incline to the *written word.* The expositors of the Roman church are here also divided. Lyra, Cajetan, Carthusianus, à Lapide, Ribera, with sundry others, pleaded for the *essential Word.* Gatenus, Adamus, Hessetius, Estius, for the *word written.* So do the Rhemists in their annotations, and parti-

<hr>

[1] EXPOSITION.—Three questions are raised by the use of the term λόγος in this passage:—1. Does it refer to the personal or written Word? That the former is the correct exegesis is the opinion of Clericus, Seb. Schmid, Spener, Heinsius, Cramer, Alting, Olshausen, and Tholuck; while the latter view is held by Bengel, M'Knight, M'Lean, Bloomfield, Stuart, Scholefield, Turner, and Ebrard. 2. Do both the 12th and 13th verses apply to the written word? Most of those who hold by the latter of the two views just mentioned, with some exceptions, such as Ebrard, conceive that there is a transition in the 13th verse to God himself,—the pronoun αὐτοῦ referring to the same person to whom our account is to be ren-dered. 3. Opposed to the view that the personal Word is meant, three opinions are held:—(1.) Some writers conceiving "the word" to mean Old Testament threatenings, such as Stuart; (2.) Others, such as Ebrard, New Testament revela-tion; while (3.) Conybeare and Howson understand by it the revelation of God's judgment to the conscience.—ED.

cularly for the word of threatening. Amongst the Protestants, few
judge the *essential Word*, or Son of God, Jesus Christ, to be intended. Jacobus Cappellus and Gomarus I have only met withal
that are positively of that mind. Among the rest, some take it
for the *word of God* preached in general, as Calvin; some for the
threatenings of God, with the Rhemists; and some peculiarly for the
gospel. Crellius waives all these, and contends that it is the decree
of God which is designed; which when he comes to the explanation
of, he makes it the same with his threatenings. I shall inquire with
what diligence I can into the true and direct meaning of the Holy
Ghost herein.

First, I grant that the *name* here used, ὁ λόγος τοῦ Θεοῦ, "the
word of God," is ascribed sometimes to the essential Word of God,
and sometimes to the enunciative word, or the Scripture, as inspired
and written. That the Son of God is so called we shall show afterwards; and that the declaration of the will of God by the penmen
of the Scripture is so termed, is obvious and acknowledged by all
but only our Quakers. But testimonies are full, many, and pregnant to this purpose: Luke v. 1, "The multitude pressed on him to
hear τὸν λόγον τοῦ Θεοῦ,"—"the word of God;" where the word of
God is directly distinguished from him that spake it, which was
Jesus Christ. Chap. viii. 11, "The seed is ὁ λόγος τοῦ Θεοῦ,"—"the
word of God;" that is, the word preached by Jesus Christ, the good
sower of that seed, as the whole chapter declares. Chap. xi. 28,
"Blessed are those that hear τὸν λόγον τοῦ Θεοῦ, καὶ φυλάσσοντες
αὐτόν,"—"the word of God, and keep it;" that is, preserve it in their
hearts, and obey it being heard. Mark vii. 13, "Making void τὸν
λόγον τοῦ Θεοῦ,"—"the word of God by your traditions." The word
of God, that is, in his institutions and commands, is directly opposed
to the traditions and commands of men, and so is of the same general nature. Acts iv. 31, "They were all filled with the Holy Ghost,
and spake out τὸν λόγον τοῦ Θεοῦ,"—"the word of God," the word
which they preached, declaring Jesus Christ to be the Son of God.
When Philip had preached the gospel at Samaria and many believed, it is said, Acts viii. 14, that "the apostles heard that Samaria
had received τὸν λόγον τοῦ Θεοῦ,"—"the word of God," or believed
the doctrine of the gospel preached unto them. Chap. xii. 24, Ὁ δὲ
λόγος τοῦ Θεοῦ ηὔξανε καὶ ἐπληθύνετο,"—"But the word of God grew
and multiplied;" that is, upon the death of Herod it was more and
more preached and received. 1 Cor. xiv. 36, "Did the word of God
go out from you, or came it to you alone?" In like manner is it
used in many other places. I have instanced in these to obviate
the vain clamours of those men who will not allow the Scripture, or
gospel as preached, to be called the word of God. So ὁ λόγος absolutely, "the word," and "the word of the gospel," "the word

preached," "the word of Christ," are common notations of this declared word of God.

Secondly, It is granted that the *attributes and effects* that are
there ascribed unto the word of God may, in several senses, be applied to the one and the other of the things mentioned. That they
are properly ascribed unto the eternal Son of God shall be afterwards declared. That in some sense also they may be applied unto
the written word, other places of the Scripture, where things of the
same nature are ascribed unto it, do manifest. Isa. xlix. 2; Ps. xlv. 5,
cv. 19, cvii. 20, cxlvii. 15, 18; Isa. xl. 8, lv. 11, are cited by Grotius to
this purpose, whereof yet more do clearly confirm the assertion. For
though the word of God be mentioned in them, yet in some of the
places the essential Word of God, in most of them his providential
word, the word of his power, is unquestionably intended. But see
Hos. vi. 5; 1 Cor. xiv. 24, 25.

Thirdly, It must be acknowledged, that if the things here mentioned be ascribed unto the written word, yet they do not *primarily*
and absolutely belong unto it upon its own account, but by virtue
of its relation unto Jesus Christ, whose word it is, and by reason of
the power and efficacy that is by him communicated unto it. And
on the other hand, if it be the Son, or the eternal Word of God, that
is here intended, it will be granted that the things here ascribed
unto him are such as for the most part he effects by his word in and
upon the hearts and consciences of men. Hence the difference that is
between the various interpretations mentioned in the issue concurs in
the same things, though the subject primarily spoken of be variously
apprehended. Now that this is the *word of God's will*, his enunciative word, his word written, spoken, preached, is by very many
contended and pleaded on the ensuing reasons:—

1. From the *subject;* 'Because the Son of God, or Christ, is nowhere
in the Scripture called ὁ Λόγος τοῦ Θεοῦ, " the Word," or " Word of
God," but only in the writings of John the apostle, as in his Gospel
and the Revelation. By Paul he is everywhere, and in an especial
manner in this epistle, called the Son, the Son of God, Jesus Christ;
and nowhere is he termed by him the Word, or the Word of God.'
This argument is made use of by all that are of this mind; but that
it is not available to evince the conclusion intended shall immediately be made manifest.

2. From its *attributes.* They say, ' The things here spoken of, and
attributed unto the word of God, as that it is " powerful, sharper
than a two-edged sword, piercing to the dividing asunder of the
soul and spirit," are not personal properties, or such things as may
properly be ascribed unto a person, as the eternal Word of God is,
but rather belong unto things, or a thing, such as is the word
preached.' Now this must be particularly examined in our expo-

sition of the words; wherein it will be made to appear, that the things here ascribed unto the word of God, taken together in their order and series, with respect unto the end designed, are such as cannot firstly and properly belong to any thing but a person, or an intelligent subsistence, though not merely as a person, but as a person acting for a certain end and purpose, such as the Son of God is; and this will also be evinced in our exposition of the words.

3. From the *context*. It is objected by Estius, ' That the mentioning or bringing in of Christ, the Son of God, in this place is abrupt, and such as hath no occasion given unto it; for the apostle in the precedent verses is professedly treating about the gospel, and the danger they were in that should neglect it, or fall away from the profession of it. Hence it naturally follows, that he should confirm his exhortation by acquainting them with the power and efficacy of that word which they did despise.' But neither is there any force in this consideration: for,—(1.) We shall see that there is a very just occasion to introduce here the mention of the Lord Christ, and that the series of the apostle's discourse and arguing did require it. (2.) It is the way and manner of the apostle, in this epistle, to issue his arguings and exhortations in considerations of the person of Christ, and the respect of what he had insisted on thereunto. This we have already manifested in several instances. (3.) Thus, in particular, when he had treated of the word of the law and of the gospel, he closeth his discourse by minding them of the punishment that should and would befall them by whom they were neglected. Now punishing is the act of a person, and not of the word, chap. ii. 1–3. And there is the same reason for the introduction of the person of Christ in this place. (4.) Estius himself doth, and all must confess, that it is either God or Christ that is intended, verse 13, " with whom we have to do," and " before whose eyes all things are opened and naked." And if the order of the discourse admit of the introduction of the person of Christ in verse 13, no reason can be assigned why it may not do so in verse 12. Yea, it will be found very difficult, if possible, to preserve any tolerable connection of speech, and so to separate those verses that what is spoken of in the one should not be the subject of the other also.

4. Cameron argues, from the connection of the words, to prove the preaching of the word, and not the person of Christ, to be intended. For saith he, ' The conjunction, καί, noteth the reason of the thing spoken of before; but that which precedes is a dehortation from the contempt of the gospel. And the reason hereof the apostle gives in these verses, in that those who forsake the gospel which they have once embraced are wont to be vexed in their consciences, as those who have denied the known truth. And although they seem to be quiet for a season, yet it is stupidness, and not peace,

that they are possessed with. Now this judgment is often ascribed unto the word of God.'

Ans. These things are somewhat obscurely proposed. The meaning seems to be, that the apostle threatens the Hebrews with the judging and disquieting power of the word when it is by any rejected. But this is inconsistent with the true design of the words, which we before laid down. Having exhorted them to perseverance, and to take heed that they neglected not the promise of entering into the rest of God through unbelief, he presseth them further to care, diligence, sincerity, and constancy, in the performance of the duty that he had exhorted them unto. And this he doth from the consideration of the person of Christ, the author of the gospel; as his manner is in all his arguings, to bring all to that point and centre. And as to his present purpose, suitably unto his exhortation and the duty which he enjoined them, he insists upon his ability to discern and discover all the secret frames and actings of their spirits, with all the ways and means whereby a declension in them might be begun or carried on.

I do judge, therefore, that it is the *eternal Word of God*, or the *person of Christ*, which is the subject here spoken of, and that upon the ensuing reasons:—

First, ὁ Λόγος, and ὁ Λόγος τοῦ Θεοῦ, "the Word," and "the Word of God," is the proper name of Christ in respect of his divine nature, as the eternal Son of God. So is he called expressly, John i. 1, 2; Rev. xix. 13, Καλεῖται τὸ ὄνομα αὐτοῦ, ὁ Λόγος τοῦ Θεοῦ, "His name is called" (or, "this is his name,") "the Word of God." This, therefore, being the name of Christ, where all things that are spoken of it do agree unto him, and there be no cogent reasons in the context to the contrary, he is presumed to be spoken of, nor will any rule of interpretation give countenance to the embracing of another sense.

It is, as we heard before, excepted against this first reason, that Christ is called ὁ Λόγος, "the Word," only in the writings of John the evangelist, and nowhere else in the New Testament, particularly not by our apostle in any of his epistles.

Ans. 1. This observation can scarcely be made good; I am sure not convincingly. Luke the evangelist tells us that some were ἀπ' ἀρχῆς αὐτόπται καὶ ὑπηρέται τοῦ Λόγου, chap. i. 2,—"from the beginning eye-witnesses and ministers of the Word:" that is, of the person of Christ; for these words are expounded, 1 John i. 1, "That which was from the beginning, which we have heard, which we have seen with our eyes, which we have looked upon, and our hands have handled of the Word of life." They were αὐτόπται τοῦ Λόγου,—"eye-witnesses of the Word." How they could be said to be eye-witnesses of the word preached is not evident. Jerome renders the words, "Sicut tradiderunt nobis, qui ab initio viderunt

Sermonem et ministraverunt ei," Præfat. in Evangel.;—"As they delivered unto us, who from the beginning themselves saw the Word, and ministered unto him." And ὑπηρέται must respect a person to whom those so called do minister, and not the word that is administered. In the same sense the word is used again most probably, Acts xx. 32: Παρατίθεμαι ὑμᾶς, ἀδελφοί, τῷ Θεῷ, καὶ τῷ Λόγῳ τῆς χάριτος αὐτοῦ, τῷ δυναμένῳ ἐποικοδομῆσαι καὶ δοῦναι ὑμῖν κληρονομίαν·— "I commend you, brethren, to God, and to the Word of his grace, which is able to build you up, and give you an inheritance." To be able to build us up, and give us an inheritance, is the property of a person; nor can they be ascribed to the word preached, without a forced prosopopœia, and such as is unusual in Scripture. Therefore this Λόγος τῆς χάριτος τοῦ Θεοῦ is the Son of God. And he is called "the Word of his grace," either because he was given unto us of his mere grace, as he is elsewhere called "the Son of his love;" or τῆς χάριτος may be "genitivus effecti," the Word that is the author and cause of grace; as God himself is called "the God of peace and love," 2 Cor. xiii. 11. To him, therefore, are believers committed and commended by the apostle, as a recommendation is made of one man unto another in or by an epistle. See its sense in Acts xiv. 23; 1 Tim. i. 18; 1 Pet. iv. 19. Now, the word of the gospel is said to be committed or commended unto us, 2 Tim. ii. 2; so as we cannot, unless it be exceeding abusively,[1] be said to be committed and commended thereunto. And if any will not admit the person of Christ to be here intended by "the Word of God's grace," I would supply an ellipsis, and read the text, "I commend you to God, and the Word of his grace, even to him that is able;" which I acknowledge the manner of the expression by the article τῷ δυναμένῳ will bear.

2. But whatever may be spoken concerning this phraseology in other places and in other epistles of this apostle, there is peculiar reason for the use of it here. I have observed often before, that in writing this epistle to the Hebrews, our apostle accommodates himself to the apprehensions and expressions that were then in use among the Hebrews, so far as they were agreeable unto the truth, rectifying them when under mistakes, and arguing with them from their own concessions and persuasions. Now at this time there was nothing more common or usual, among the Hebrews, than to denote the *second subsistence in the Deity* by the name of "The Word of God." They were now divided into two great parts; first, the inhabitants of Canaan, with the regions adjoining, and many old remnants in the east, who used the Syro-chaldean language, being but one dialect of the Hebrew; and, secondly, the dispersions under the

---

[1] That is, in a sense remote from the proper use of the word.—ED.

Greek empire, who are commonly called Hellenists, who used the Greek tongue. And both these sorts at that time did usually, in their several languages, describe the second person in the Trinity by the name of " The Word of God." For the former sort, or those who used the Syro-chaldean dialect, we have an eminent proof of it in the translation of the Scripture which, at least some part of it, was made about this time amongst them, commonly called the Chaldee Paraphrase; in the whole whereof the second person is mentioned under the name of מימרא דיי, " Memra da-Iova," or the " Word of God." Hereunto are all *personal properties* and all *divine works* assigned in that translation; which is an illustrious testimony to the faith of the old church concerning the distinct subsistence of a plurality of persons in the divine nature. And for the Hellenists, who wrote and expressed themselves in the Greek tongue, they used the name of ὁ Λόγος τοῦ Θεοῦ, the " Word of God," to the same purpose; as I have elsewhere manifested out of the writings of Philo, who lived about this time, between the death of our Saviour and the destruction of Jerusalem. And this one consideration is to me absolutely satisfactory as to the intention of the apostle in the using of this expression, especially seeing that all the things mentioned may far more properly and regularly be ascribed unto the person of the Son than unto the word as written or preached. And whosoever will take the pains to consider what occurs in the Targums concerning their מימרא דיי, the " Word of God," and compare it with what the apostle here speaks, and the manner of its introduction, will, if I greatly mistake not, be of the same mind with myself. But I shall add yet some further considerations.

3. The introduction of ὁ Λόγος, or " the Word," here, is with respect unto a commination or an *admonition;* for the design of it is to beget a reverence or fear in the minds of men about their deportment in the profession of the gospel, because of the consequents of disobedience in punishment and revenge. Now the Lord Christ is particularly termed the " Word of God" with respect unto the judgments that he exerciseth with regard unto his church and his gospel, Rev. xix. 13. That administration, therefore, being here respected, gives occasion unto a peculiar ascription of that name unto him, the " Word of God," who will destroy all the opposers and forsakers of the gospel.

4. It cannot be denied, nor is it by any, but that it is the *person of the Son,* or of the Father, that is intended, verse 13. Indeed it is directly of the Son, as we shall manifest from the close of the words; but all confess God to be intended. Nor can these expressions, of " all things manifest in his sight," and being " opened and naked unto his eyes," be applied unto any other, or intend any other but God; and that it is the Son who is especially intended the close

of the verse doth evince, πρὸς ὃν ἡμῖν ὁ Λόγος. He speaks of "him with whom we have to do." Some take πρὸς ὃν here for περὶ οὗ, "concerning whom;" ἡμῖν ὁ λόγος, "nostra oratio est," "our discourse is:" which must needs denote the Son, concerning whom in this whole epistle he treats with the Hebrews. Ours, "with whom we have to do;" that is, in this matter,—who hath a concernment in us and our steadfastness or declension in profession. And this also properly and immediately designs the person of the Son. The precise sense of the words is, "cui a nobis reddenda ratio est,"—"to whom we must give an account," both here and hereafter. So Chrysostom and the Syriac translation expressly. Principally this respects the last day's account, called our λόγος, or "ratiocinium:" Heb. xiii. 17, "They watch for your souls, ὡς λόγον ἀποδώσοντες,"—"as those that must give an account." Luke xvi. 2, 'Απόδος τὸν λόγον,— "Give an account of thy stewardship." Rom. xiv. 12, "Every one of us λόγον δώσει,"—"shall give an account of himself unto God." 1 Pet. iv. 5, Οἱ ἀποδώσουσι λόγον,—"Who shall give an account unto him who is ready to judge the quick and the dead." And this account is certainly to be given up immediately to Jesus Christ, Acts xvii. 31, Rom. xiv. 9, 10. Nor is it any way obstructive to the embracing of this sense, that ὁ λόγος should be taken so diversely in the beginning of the 12th and end of the 13th verse, during the continuation of the same discourse. For such an antanaclasis is not only very frequent but very elegant: 'Ο Λόγος τοῦ Θεοῦ, πρὸς ὃν ἡμῖν ὁ λόγος. See Matt. viii. 22, 2 Cor. v. 21, John i. 11. It is therefore the person of Christ which is undeniably intended in the 13th verse, even he to whom we must give an account of our profession, of our faith and obedience. And the relative, αὐτοῦ, in the first clause of that verse, in "his sight," can refer to nothing properly but ὁ Λόγος or "Word of God," verse 12. And its dependence is clear thereon: "Is a discerner of the thoughts and intents of the heart; neither is there any creature that is not manifest in his sight." So a reason is assigned in the beginning of the 13th verse of what was affirmed in the close of the 12th: he is "a discerner of the thoughts of the heart," because "all things are manifest unto him."

5. The *attributes* here ascribed to the word, verse 12, do all of them properly belong unto the person of Christ, and cannot firstly and directly be ascribed to the gospel. This shall be manifested in the ensuing explication of the words:—

(1.) It is said to be ζῶν, "vivus," "vivens,"—"living;" which, as was observed, we have translated ambiguously, "quick." Zῶν is applied to God himself, as expressing a property of his nature, Matt. xvi. 16, 1 Tim. iv. 10, Heb. iii. 12. And it is also peculiarly ascribed unto Christ the mediator, Rev. i. 18. And he is ὁ ζῶν, "the living one." And two things are intended in it:—[1.] That he who is so "hath life in himself." [2.] That he is the "Lord of life" unto others. Both which are emphatically spoken of the Son. [1.] He "hath life in himself," John v. 26; and, [2.] He is the "Prince of life," Acts iii. 15, or the author of it. He hath the disposal of the life of all, whereunto all our concernments temporal and eternal do belong. See John i. 4. And it is evident how suitable unto the purpose of the apostle the mention hereof at this time is. He minds the Hebrews that he with whom they have to do in this matter is "the living one." As in like manner he had before exhorted them to "take heed of departing from the living God," and afterwards warns them how "fearful a thing it is to fall into the hands of the living God," chap. x. 31; so here, to dissuade them from the one and to awe them with the other, he minds them that "the Word of God," with whom in an especial manner they have to do, is "living." What is contained in this consideration hath been declared on chap. iii. 13. Now this cannot properly be ascribed unto the word of the gospel. It is, indeed, the instrumental means of quickening the souls of men with spiritual life, or it is the instrument that the Lord Christ maketh use of to that purpose; but in itself it is not absolutely "living,"—it hath not life in itself, nor in its power. But Christ hath so; for "in him is life, and the life is the light of men," John i. 4. And this one property of him with whom we have to do contains the two great motives unto obedience; namely, that on the one side he is able to support us in it, and reward us eternally for it; on the other, that he is able to avenge all disobedience. The one will not be unrewarded, nor the other unrevenged; for he is "the living one" with whom in these things we have to do.

(2.) It is ἐνεργής, "powerful." Power for operation is an act of life; and such as is the life of any thing, such is its power for operation. These things, life, power, and operation, answer one another. And this power signifies *actual power*, power acted or exerted,—actuated power, or power effectual in actual operation. Having therefore first assigned life to the Word of God, that is the principle of all power, life in himself, as being "the living one," our apostle adds that he exerts that power of life in actual operation, when, where, and how he pleaseth. He is ἐνεργής. 'Ενεργέω, I confess, is a common word, signifying the efficacy of any thing in operation according to its principle of power; but it is that also whereby our apostle most frequently expresseth the almighty, effectual, operating power of God in and about spiritual things, 1 Cor. xii. 6, 11, Gal. ii. 8, iii. 5, Eph. i. 11, Phil. ii. 13, 1 Thess. ii. 13, Eph. i. 19, Col. ii. 12, and elsewhere. And this was necessary to be added to the property of life, to manifest that the Lord Christ, the Word of God, would effectually put forth his power in dealing with professors according to their deportment; which afterwards is expressed in sundry instances. And herein the apostle lets both the Hebrews and us know that the power that is in Christ lies not idle, is not useless, but is continually exercising itself towards us as the matter doth require. There is also, I acknowledge, an energy, an operative power in the word of God as written or preached; but it is not in it primarily, by virtue of a life or principle of power in itself, but only as a consequent of its being his word who is " the living one," or "as it is indeed the word of the living God."

The original of the power of Christ in *life,* and the efficacy of it in *operation,* being laid down, he further declares it,—(1.) By its *properties;* (2.) By its *effects.*

(1.) The *property* of the Word, with respect unto the exercise of his power, is, that it is τομώτερος ὑπὲρ πᾶσαν μάχαιραν δίστομον. From τέμνω, to "cut" or "divide," is τομός, "scindens," " incidens,"—" cleaving," " cutting," or that which is " vi incisoriâ præditus," endued with a cutting power; τομώτερος, in the comparative degree. Valla says he would render it " incidentior," were that word used. So in Phocylides,—

Τομώτερος.

"Οπλον τοι λόγος ἀνδρὶ τομώτερόν ἐστι σιδήρῳ.

" Telum ferro penetrantius;" " acutior," " penetrantior" (see the different translations of the word before); " sharper," " more piercing." Ὑπὲρ πᾶσαν μάχαιραν δίστομον. The preposition ὑπὲρ πᾶσαν added to the comparative degree increaseth the signification; for it might have been said, τομὸς ὑπὲρ πᾶσαν, or τομώτερος πάσης μαχαίρας: but the construction used expresseth the greatest distance between the comparates,—" than any two-edged sword." Δίστομος, that is, ἀμφίστομος,— " gladius biceps, anceps, utrinque incidens;" "double-edged or mouthed, cutting every way." פִּי־חָרֶב, " the mouth of the sword," is a Hebraism, with such an elegance in the allusion as most languages have admitted it. The metaphor is doubtless taken from wild beasts, whom mankind first feared, that devour with their mouths; which when the sword began to be used for destruction, gave them occasion to call its edge by the name of its "mouth:" δίστομος, "double-mouthed," cutting each way, that leaves nothing unpierced whereunto it is applied. Christ in the exercise of his power is said to be " more piercing than any two-edged sword;" for so doth God oftentimes set forth himself and his power, with an allusion to things sensible, thereby to convey a notion and apprehension of them to our understandings. So he is said to be "a consuming fire," and that he will be "as a lion;" things of great terror to men. This of a " sword" is often mentioned with respect unto the Lord Christ, Isa. xlix. 2; Rev. i. 16, " Out of his mouth went a sharp two-edged sword." And it is principally assigned unto him with respect unto the exercise of his power in and

Ὑπὲρ πᾶσαν μάχαιραν δίστομον.

by his word, which is called "the sword of the Spirit," Eph. vi. 17;
the "sword that is on his thigh," Ps. xlv. 3, which he hath in
readiness when he goeth forth to subdue the souls of men to himself; as it is also "the rod of his power," Ps. cx. 2. But it is Christ
himself who makes the word powerful and sharp: the principal efficiency is in himself, acting in and with it. That then which is
here intended, is the spiritual, almighty, penetrating efficacy of the
Lord Christ, in his dealing with the souls and consciences of men
by his word and Spirit. And whereas there is a twofold use of
a sword; the one natural, to cut or pierce through all opposition,
all armour of defence; the other moral, to execute judgments and
punishments, whence the sword is taken for the right and authority
of punishing, and ofttimes for punishment itself, Rom. xiii. 4; here
is an allusion unto it in both senses. The Lord Christ, by his word
and Spirit, pierceth into the souls of men (as we shall see in the
next clause), and that notwithstanding all the defence of pride,
security, obstinacy, and unbelief, which they wrap up themselves in,
according to the natural use of the sword. Again, he by them executes judgments on wicked men, hypocrites, false professors, and
apostates. He "smites the earth with the rod of his mouth, and
slays the wicked with the breath of his lips," Isa. xi. 4. He cuts
off the life of their carnal hopes, false peace, worldly security, whatever they live upon, by the "two-edged sword" that proceeds out
of his mouth. And the minding of the Hebrews hereof was exceedingly suited to his present purpose, as hath been declared. And
in the pursuit of this double allusion are the ensuing expressions
accommodated to the matter intended.

(2.) This power of the Word is described by its *effects:* Διϊκνούμενος
ἄχρι μερισμοῦ ψυχῆς τε καί πνεύματος, ἁρμῶν τε καί μυελῶν· καί κριτικός
ἐνθυμήσεων καί ἐννοιῶν καρδίας. The *act* itself intended is in the first
word, διϊκνούμενος. The *object* of that act is doubly expressed,—[1.]
By "soul and spirit;" [2.] "Joints and marrow;" and [3.] There is
the extent of this act with reference unto that object, expressing the
effect itself, ἄχρι μερισμοῦ,—"to the dividing of them."

Διϊκνούμενος, "perveniens," "penetrans;" "piercing," say we, in
answer to the sharpness before expressed. The word in
other authors is variously rendered by "pervado," "per-
meo," "pervenio," "attingo,"—"to pass through," "to reach unto,"
"to attain an end;" from ἵκω, "to come." It is here, in the pursuit
of the former allusion, used elegantly to express the power of Christ,
as a sword piercing into the soul. And the meaning of the following expressions is, that it doth so into the innermost recesses, and
as it were the secret chambers of the mind and heart. And this
word is nowhere else used in the Scripture.

The *object* of this piercing is the "soul and spirit." Some think

that by ψυχή, the natural and unregenerate part of the soul is intended; and by πνεῦμα, that which is in it renewed
and regenerate. And there is some ground for that explication of this distinction; for hence is a man wholly
unregenerate called ψυχικός, 1 Cor. ii. 14; say we, "the natural
man." And though ψυχή, absolutely used, doth denote either the
being of the rational "soul," or "life," which is an effect thereof;
yet as it is opposed to the "spirit," or distinguished from it, it may
denote the unregenerate part, as σάρξ, the "flesh," doth, though absolutely it signifies one part of the material substance of the body.
From hence is an unregenerate person denominated ἄνθρωπος ψυχικός. So the spiritual part is frequently called πνεῦμα, the "spirit,"
as John iii. 6; and a regenerate person πνευματικός, the "spiritual
man," 1 Cor. ii. 15. According to this interpretation, the sense of
the words is, that the Word of God, the Lord Christ, by his word
and Spirit pierceth into the state of the soul, to discover who or
what is regenerate amongst us or in us, and who or what is not
so. The principles of these things are variously involved in the
souls of men, so that they are not ofttimes discernible unto them in
whom they are, as to whether of them is predominant. But the
Lord Christ makes a μερισμός, a "division" with a distribution, referring all things in the soul to their proper source and original.
Others judge, that whereas our apostle makes a distinction between
soul and spirit, as he doth in other places, he intends by ψυχή, "the
soul," the affections, the appetites, and desires; and by πνεῦμα, "the
spirit," the mind or understanding, the τὸ ἡγεμονικόν, the "conducting
part" of the soul. And it is most probable that he here intends the
same: for setting out the penetrating power of the Word of God with
reference unto the souls of men, he distributes the soul into as it
were its principal constituent parts, or faculties of it; that is, the
mind, that leads, conducts, and guides it; and the passions, that
steer and balance it, wherein all the most secret recesses and springs
of all its actings do lie. And this sense is confirmed from the following words, wherein the same thing is asserted under a different
notion,—namely, of the "joints and marrow." That which in the
soul answers the joints and marrow in the body, by way
'Ἁρμῶν τε
καὶ μυελῶν.
of allusion, is that which is intended. Joints and marrow in themselves are things sensual and fleshly, that
have no concern in this matter; but in the body they are doubly
considerable,—

[1.] Upon the account of their *use;* and so they are the ligaments
of the whole, the principal and only means of communication to the
members from the head, and among themselves. So this use of
them is translated to spiritual things, Eph. iv. 16. And by a luxation
or discontinuation of them the whole body will be dissolved.

[2.] On the account of their *hiddenness* and secrecy. They are undiscernible unto the eye of man, and it must be a sharp instrument or sword that pierceth unto them so as to divide them one from the other, whereby natural life will be destroyed. As these things are in the body for use and hiddenness, with respect unto their being pierced with a sword, so would the apostle have us to understand what he speaks of in reference unto the soul, the most useful and secret parts whereof are pierced and divided by the power of Christ; whence, if it be in a way of punishment, spiritual death doth ensue. And this is yet further confirmed in the last description which the apostle gives us of the Word of God from his actings and effects,—he is "a discerner of the thoughts and intents of the heart;" which yet he more clearly explains in the next verse, as we shall see in the opening of it. That, then, which in all these expressions is intended, is the absolute power and ability of the Son of God to judge of the rectitude and crookedness of the ways and walkings of the sons of men under their profession, from the inward frames of their minds and hearts unto all their outward duties and performances, either in perseverance or backsliding.

The last expression, *κριτικὸς ἐνθυμήσεων καὶ ἐννοιῶν καρδίας*,—"is a discerner of the thoughts and intents of the heart,"—is plainly declarative of what is elsewhere ascribed unto $Κριτικός.$ him, namely, that he is *καρδιογνώστης*,—he that "knoweth and searcheth the hearts of men." This is a peculiar property of God, and is often affirmed so to be, Jer. xvii. 10; 1 Sam. xvi. 7; Ps. vii. 9; and this in an especial manner is ascribed to the Lord Christ, John ii. 24, 25, xxi. 17; Rev. ii. 23. This is eminently expressed in that confession of Peter, "Lord, thou knowest all things, thou knowest that I love thee;"—'By virtue of thine omniscience, whereby thou knowest all things, thou knowest my heart, and the love which I have therein unto thee.' *Κριτικός*, "judex," "discretor;" one that, upon accurate inspection and consideration, judgeth and giveth sentence concerning persons and things. It differs from *κριτής*, a "judge," as adding the act of judging unto the right and power of judgment. And this word alone, as it is here used, is sufficient to evince that the person of Christ is here principally intended, seeing it cannot be accommodated to the word as written or preached, in any tolerable manner.

Καρδίας. By the "heart," as I have showed before, $Καρδίας.$ the whole soul and all the faculties of it, as constituting one rational principle of moral actions, is intended, and so includes the "soul and spirit" before mentioned. Here two things are ascribed unto it:—

[1.] *'Ενθυμήσεις*, "thoughts," "cogitations," whatever is inwardly conceived, *ἐν τῷ θυμῷ*, "in the mind;" with a peculiar $'Ενθυμήσιων.$ respect unto the irascible appetite called יֵצֶר מַחֲשֶׁבֹת לֵב,

Gen. vi. 5, "the figment of the cogitations of the heart,"—the thoughts which are suggested by the inclinations of the affections, with their commotions and stirrings in the heart or mind.

[2.] Ἔννοιαι, "designs" or "purposes," inwardly framed ἐν τῷ νόῳ, "in the understanding." Sometimes this word signifies the moral principles of the mind, by which it is guided in its actings. Hence are the κοιναὶ ἔννοιαι, or "common principles" that men are directed by in what they do. And here it denotes the principles that men are guided by in their actings, according to which they frame their actual purposes and intentions. Upon the whole matter, the design of the apostle in these words is to declare the intimate and absolute acquaintance that the Word of God hath with the inmost frames, purposes, desires, resolutions, and actings of the minds of professors; and the sure, unerring judgment which he makes of them thereby.

Ἐννοιῶν.

Ver. 13.—The 13th verse contains a confirmation of what is asserted in that foregoing. There the apostle declared how the Word of God pierceth into the hearts, minds, and souls of men, to discern and judge them. That they to whom he wrote might not doubt hereof, he confirms it by showing the ground of his assertion, which is the natural omniscience of the Word of God: 'It cannot be otherwise than as I have declared, seeing he of whom we speak, "with whom we have to do," to whom we must give an account, this "Word of God," seeth and knoweth all things, nor can any thing possibly be hid from him.' This is the natural coherence of the words, and upon a supposition of a different subject to be spoken of in this from the foregoing verse, no man can frame a tolerable transition in this contexture of words from the one unto the other. I shall therefore proceed in the explication of them, as words of the same design, and used to the same purpose.

Καὶ οὐκ ἔστι κτίσις ἀφανὴς ἐνώπιον αὐτοῦ. The manner of the expression is by a double negation: the one expressed, οὐκ ἔστι, "there is not;" the other included in the privative α in ἀφανής. And these expressions do emphatically assert the contrary to what is denied: "There is not a creature that is not manifest;" that is, every creature is eminently, illustriously manifest.

Οὐκ ἔστι.

Οὐκ ἔστι κτίσις, "there is not a creature," any thing created: that is, every creature whatever, whether they be persons or things,—angels, men, devils, professors, persecutors, all men of all sorts; and all things concerning them,—their inward frames of mind and heart, their affections and temptations, their state and condition, their secret actings, their thoughts and

Ἔστι κτίσις.

inclinations. This confirms and carries on the foregoing attributions to the Word of God.

'Αφανής. Φαίνω is "to appear," "to shine forth;" and ἀφανής is opposed to ἐπιφανής, "illustrious," "perspicuous," "eminently manifest;"—so it is "hid," "obscure," not *'Aφανής.* openly or evidently appearing. It is more than ἄφαντος, which is merely "one out of sight," Luke xxiv. 31. This negation includes a plain, clear, illustrious appearance, nothing shrouding, hiding, interposing itself to obscure it.

'Ενώπιον αὐτοῦ, "before him," "in conspectu ejus," "in his sight." Every creature is continually under his view. Αὐτοῦ *'Ενώπιον αὐτοῦ.* must refer to ὁ Λόγος τοῦ Θεοῦ, "the Word of God," in the beginning of verse 12; and cannot respect πρὸς ὃν, in the end of this verse. For the interposition of the adversative particle δέ, "but," and the introduction of the relative αὐτοῦ again, do necessarily refer this αὐτοῦ to ὁ Λόγος, and proves the same person to be all along intended.

Πάντα δὲ γυμνὰ καὶ τετραχηλισμένα. The unusual application of the word τραχηλίζομαι in this place hath made work more than enough for critics. But the design of the *Γυμνὰ καὶ τε-* apostle is open and plain, however the use of the word *τραχηλισμένα.* be rare, with some especial allusion. All agree that τετραχηλισμένα is as much as πεφανερωμένα, "absolutely open" or "manifest." Only Œcumenius hath a peculiar conceit about it. It is, saith he, κάτω κύπτοντα, καὶ τὸν τράχηλον ἐπικλίνοντα, διὰ τὸ μὴ ἰσχύειν ἀτενίσαι τῇ δόξῃ ἐκείνῃ τοῦ κριτοῦ καὶ Θεοῦ ἡμῶν Ἰησοῦ·—"bowing down, and declining or turning aside the neck, as not being able to behold the glory of Jesus, our Judge and God." But he gives us another signification of the word himself. Τράχηλος, "the neck," is a word commonly used in Scripture, and in all authors. Thence τραχηλίζομαι, in the sense here used, "to be manifest," must receive its signification from some posture of the neck; and as joined here with γυμνός, "naked," it may have respect unto a double allusion. First, unto wrestlers and contenders in games. First they were made naked, or stripped of their clothes; whence, as it is known, comes γυμνάζω and γυμνάσιον, "vigorously to exercise," and a place of such exercise. Then, in their contending, when one was thrown on his back, when he was "resupinatus," he was τραχηλιζόμενος, "laid open, with his throat and neck upwards." Hence the word comes to signify things that are "open, naked, evident, manifest." The face and neck of a naked person being turned upwards, it is manifest who he is. This is to have "os resupinatum;" and, as he speaks, "aulam resupinat amici" [Juv., Sat. iii. 112], of him who sees what is in it to the bottom. There is yet another allusion that may be intended, and this is taken from beasts that are slain, and, being stripped of their

skins, are hanged by the neck, that all may see and discern them. This
is also mentioned by Œcumenius. And Varinus gives us a further
sense, and says that τραχηλίζειν is as much as διχοτομεῖν, "to divide
into parts;" or διὰ τῆς ῥάχεως σχίζειν, "to cut," "cleave," or "divide
through the back-bone," that all may be discovered. And from these
two significations I suppose the design of the apostle in this allusion may most probably be collected. It is evident that he hath
great regard unto, and doth much instruct the Hebrews by and
from the customs in use amongst themselves. Unto one of them
doth he here seem to have respect, namely, the beasts that were
sacrificed. The first thing that was done with the body of it, after
it was slain, was its being flayed. This work was done by the priests.
Hereby the carcass of the beast was made γυμνόν, "naked," laid open
to the view of all. Then were all its entrails opened, from the neck
down to the belly; after which the body was cut into its pieces
through the chine-bone: whereby in both the senses mentioned, both
of opening and division, it became τετραχηλισμένον, "opened and
divided," so that every part of it was exposed to view. Hence the
apostle, having compared the Word of God before in his operations
to a "two-edged sword, that pierceth to the dividing asunder of
the joints and marrow," as did the sharp knife or instrument of the
sacrificer; here affirms that "all things" whatever, and so consequently the hearts and ways of professors, were "evident, open, and
naked before him," as the body of the sacrificed beast was to the
priests when flayed, opened, and cut to pieces. This is the most
probable account of these expressions in particular, whose general
design is plain and evident. And this appears yet further from the
next words.

Τοῖς ὀφθαλμοῖς αὐτοῦ, "to the eyes of him." He followeth on his
former allusion; and having ascribed the evidence of all

*Τοῖς ὀφθαλ-
μοῖς αὐτοῦ.* things unto the omniscience of the Word, by the similitude before opened, in answer thereunto he mentions
his eyes wherewith he beholds the things so naked and open before
him. Both expressions are metaphorical, containing a declaration
of the omniscience of Christ, whom he further describes in the last
words, by our respect unto him in all these things.

Πρὸς ὃν ἡμῖν ὁ λόγος. How variously these words are rendered,
and thereby what various senses are put upon them, hath been declared. But both the proper signification of them and the design
of the place direct us to one certain sense, namely, "to whom we
must give an account." Λόγος is "an account;" there is no other word
used in the New Testament to express it. Πρὸς ὃν is properly "unto
whom," and not "of whom," or "concerning whom;" that is, it
expresseth the *object* of the action here mentioned, and not the *subject* of the proposition. And the whole is rightly rendered, "to

whom we must give an account;" or, "before whom our account is to be made." And this answers the design of the apostle in the place. For evidencing unto them the efficacy and omniscience of the Word of God, trying all things, and discerning all things, he minds them of their near concernment in these matters, in that he and they must all give up their final accounts unto and before him who is so intimately acquainted with what they are, and with whatsoever they shall do in this world.

There are many things remaining to be observed from these words, which are both of great importance in themselves, and do also serve to the further explanation of the mind of the Holy Ghost in these words, as to what of our instruction is particularly intended in them. And from the properties that are assigned to the Word of God, verse 12, we may observe, that,—

Obs. I. It is the way of the Spirit of God, to excite us unto especial duties by proposing unto us and minding us of such properties of God as the consideration whereof may in an especial manner incline us unto them.

Here the Hebrews are minded that the Word of God is *living*, to give unto their hearts that awe and reverence of him which might deter them from backsliding or falling away from him. Our whole duty in general respects the nature of God. It is our giving glory to him because he is God, and as he is God, "glorifying him as God," Exod. xx. 2; Isa. xlii. 8; Deut. xxviii. 58; Rom. i. 21. It is our giving him the honour which is due to his being. That is the formal reason of all divine worship and obedience. And as this duty in general brancheth itself into many particular duties in the kinds of them, all which in various instances are continually to be attended unto; so God hath not only revealed his being unto us in general, but he hath done it by many distinct properties, all of them suited to promote in our minds our whole duty towards God, and this or that duty in particular. And he often distinctly presseth upon us the consideration of those properties, for to stir us up unto those distinct duties which they direct unto. God in his nature exists in one simple essence or being; nor are there any things really different or distinct therein. His nature is all his properties, and every one of his properties is his whole nature; but in the revelation of himself unto us he proposeth his nature under the notion of these distinct properties, that we may the better know the nature of the duty which we owe unto him: Hosea iii. 5, "Fear the LORD and his goodness." So in places innumerable doth he mind us of his power and greatness; that upon our thoughts and apprehensions of them we might be stirred up to fear him, to trust in him, to get our hearts filled with a due awe and reverence of him, with many other duties of the like nature with them, or evidently proceeding

from them:—to trust, Isa. xxvi. 4; fear, Jer. x. 6, 7. His goodness, grace, bounty, patience, are all of them distinctly proposed
unto us; and they all lead us unto especial duties, as the apostle
speaks, Rom. ii. 4, "The goodness of God leadeth to repentance."
From these, or the efficacy of the consideration of them upon our
souls, ought to proceed our love, our gratitude, our delight in God,
our praise and thankfulness; and by them ought they to be influenced. So his holiness ingenerates terror in the wicked, Isa. xxxiii.
14; and holy reverence in others, Heb. xii. 28, 29. The like may
be spoken of the rest of the properties of God, with respect unto the
remainder of our duties. In like manner, and to the same purpose,
did God of old reveal himself by his name. He still ascribed such
a name to himself as might be prevalent on the minds of men unto
their present duties. So when he called Abraham to "walk before
him," in the midst of many difficulties, temptations, hardships, and
dangers, he revealed himself unto him by the name of *God Almighty*,
thereby to encourage him to sincerity and perseverance, Gen. xvii. 1.
Hence, in his greatest distress he peculiarly acted his faith on the
power of God, Heb. xi. 19. And when he called his posterity to
comply in their faith and obedience with his faithfulness in the
accomplishment of his promises, he revealed himself unto them by
his name *Jehovah;* which was suited to their especial encouragement
and direction, Exod. vi. 3. To the same end are the properties of
the Word of God here distinctly proposed unto us. We are called
to the faith and profession of the gospel. Herein we meet with
many difficulties without, and are ofttimes ready to faint in ourselves, or otherwise to fail and miscarry. In this matter we have to
do with the Lord Christ; to him we must one day give an account.
Wherefore, to stir us up to carefulness, diligence, and spiritual watchfulness, that we give not place to any decays or declensions in our
profession, we are especially minded that he is the *living one,* and
one that continually exerciseth acts of life toward us. And in all
duties of obedience, it will be our wisdom always to mind that respect which the properties of God or of Christ have unto them.
Again, the Word of God is so *living* as that also it is *powerful,* or
actually always exercising itself in power, actually efficacious toward
the ends mentioned,—ἐνεργής. So that,—

Obs. II. The life and power of Christ are continually exercised
about the concernments of the souls of professors; are always actually
efficacious in them and upon them.

And this power he putteth forth by his word and Spirit; for we
declared, in the opening of the words, that the effects here ascribed
unto the *essential Word* are such as he produceth by the *word
preached,* which is accompanied with and made effectual by the
dispensation of the Spirit, Isa. lix. 21. And the power here intended

is wholly clothed with the word; thereby it is conveyed to the souls of men; therein is "the hiding of his power," Hab. iii. 4. Though it seems weak, and is despised, yet it is accompanied with the hidden power of Christ, which will not fail of its end, 1 Cor. i. 18. And the word preached is not otherwise to be considered, but as that which is the conveyance of divine power to the souls of men. And every impression that it makes on the heart is an effect of the power of Christ. And this will teach us how to value it and esteem it, seeing it is the only way and means whereby the Lord Christ exerciseth his mediatory power towards us on the behalf of God; and effectual it will be unto the ends whereunto he designs it. For he is in it "sharper than any two-edged sword." So that,—

Obs. III. The power of Christ in his word is irresistible, as to whatever effects he doth design it, Isa. lv. 10, 11.

The power of Christ in his word is by many exceedingly despised and slighted. Few there are who seem to have any real effects of it produced in them or upon them. Hence it is looked on in the world as a thing of no great efficacy; and those who preach it in sincerity are ready to cry out, "Who hath believed our report?" But all this ariseth from a mistake, as though it had but one end designed unto it. Had the Lord Christ no other end to accomplish by his word but merely that which is the principal, *the conversion of the souls of his elect*, it might be conceived to fail towards the far greater number of them to whom it is preached. But it is with him in his word as it was in his own person. He was "set for the fall" as well as "the rising of many in Israel," and "for a sign that should be spoken against," Luke ii. 34. As he was to be unto some "for a sanctuary," so "for a stone of stumbling and a rock of offence to both the houses of Israel; for a gin and for a snare to the inhabitants of Jerusalem," among whom "many were to stumble" at him, "and fall, and be broken," Isa. viii. 14, 15. And these things are all of them effectually accomplished towards them to whom he is preached. They are all of them either raised by him unto God out of their state of sin and misery, and do take sanctuary in him from sin and the law; or they stumble at him, through their unbelief, and perish eternally. None can ever have Christ proposed unto them upon indifferent terms, so as to be left in the condition wherein they were before. They must all be saved by his grace, or perish under his wrath. And so is it also with him in his word. The end, whatever it be that he assigns unto it with respect unto any, shall undoubtedly be accomplished. Now these ends are various, 2 Cor. ii. 14, 15. Sometimes he intends by it only the hardening and further blinding of wicked sinners, that they may be the more prepared for deserved destruction: Isa. vi. 9–11, "Go, tell this people, Hear ye indeed, but understand not; and see ye indeed, but per-

ceive not. Make the heart of this people fat, and make their ears
heavy, and shut their eyes; lest they see with their eyes, and hear
with their ears, and understand with their heart, and convert, and
be healed. Then said I, Lord, how long? And he answered, Until the cities be wasted without inhabitant, and the houses without
man, and the land be utterly desolate." The principal accomplishment hereof was in the personal ministry of Christ himself towards
the people of the Jews, Matt. xiii. 14; Mark iv. 12; Luke viii. 10;
John xii. 40. But the same is the condition of things in the preaching of the word to this day. Christ designs in it to harden and
blind wicked sinners unto their destruction. And herein it misseth
not of its effect. They are so until they are utterly destroyed.
Towards some he designs it only for their conviction; and this it
shall through his power unconquerably effect. There is not one
whom he aimeth to convince but he shall be convinced, whatever
he intends by those convictions. "His arrows are sharp in the
heart of his enemies, whereby the people fall under him," Ps. xlv. 5.
Let men be never so much his enemies, yet if he intends their conviction, he will so sharpen his word upon their hearts as that they
shall let go their professed enmity and fall down in the acknowledgment of his power. None whom he will have convinced by his
word shall be able to withstand it. Now, as the first sort of men
may reject and despise the word as to any convictions from it which
it is not designed to give them, but can never avoid its efficacy to
harden them in their sins; so this second sort may resist and reject
the word as to any real saving work of conversion, which is not in
it or by it assigned unto them, but they cannot withstand its convictions, which are its proper work towards them. With respect
unto others, it is designed for their conversion; and the power of
Christ doth in this design so accompany it as that it shall infallibly
accomplish that work. These dead creatures shall "hear the voice
of the Son of God" in it and live. It is, then, certainly of high concernment unto all men unto whom Christ comes in his word, to
consider diligently what is or is like to be the issue and consequence
of it with respect unto themselves. Things are not issued according
to outward appearance. If there were no hidden or secret events
of the dispensation of the power of Christ in the word, all thoughts
of any great matter in it might easily be cast off; for we see that
the most live quietly under a neglect of it, without any visible effect
upon their hearts or lives. And how then is it "sharper than any
two-edged sword?" Things are indeed quite otherwise; the word
hath its work on all; and those who are neither convinced nor converted by it, are hardened,—which is in many evident to a spiritual
eye. And surely we may do well to consider how it fareth with our
own souls in this state of things. It is to no purpose to think to hide

things secretly in our own thoughts, and to please ourselves in our
own darkness; the power of Christ in the word will reach and search
out all; for it "pierceth to the dividing asunder of the soul and
spirit, and of the joints and marrow." So that,—

Obs. IV. Though men may close and hide things from themselves
and others, yet they cannot exclude the power of Christ in his word
from piercing into them.

Men are apt strangely to hide, darken, and confound things between their soul and their spirit,—that is, their affections and their
minds. Herein consists no small part of the deceitfulness of sin,
that it confounds and hides things in the soul, that it is not able to
make a right judgment of itself. So men labour to deceive themselves, Isa. xxviii. 15. Hence, when a man can countenance himself from any thing in his affections, his soul, against the reflections
that are made upon him from the convictions of his mind or spirit,
or when he can rest in the light of his understanding, notwithstanding the perverseness and frowardness of his affections, he is very apt
to be secure in an ill condition. The first deceiveth the more ignorant, the latter the more knowing professors. The true state of
their souls is by this means hid from themselves. But the power of
Christ in his word will pierce into these things, and separate between them. He doth so as to his—1. *Discerning*, his 2. *Discovering* or convincing, and his 3. *Judging* power. 1. Let things be never
so close and hid, he discerneth all clearly and distinctly; they are
not hid from him, Ps. cxxxix. 4; Jer. xxiii. 24. See John ii. 23–25.
And where he designs, 2. The conviction of men, he makes his word
powerful to discover unto them all the secret follies of their minds
and affections, the hidden recesses that sin hath in them, their close
reserves, and spreads them before their eyes, to their own amazement, Ps. l. 21. So our apostle tells us, that by prophesying, or
expounding the word of Christ, the secrets of men's hearts are discovered; that is, to themselves,—they find the word dividing asunder
between their souls and spirits; whereon they fall down and give
glory to God, 1 Cor. xiv. 24, 25. And hereby also, 3. He exerciseth
his judging power in men. Let men arm themselves never so
strongly and closely with love of sin and pleasure, carnal security,
pride, and hatred of the ways of God, until their brows become as
brass, and their neck as a sinew of iron, or let their sins be covered
with the fair pretence of a profession, Christ by his word will pierce
through all into their very hearts; and having discovered, divided,
and scattered all their vain imaginations, he will judge them, and
determine of their state and condition, Ps. xlv. 5, cx. 6. Hereby
doth he break all their strength and peace, and the communication
of supplies in sin and security that have been between the mind
and the affections, and destroys all their hopes. Men are apt to

please themselves in their spiritual condition, though built on very sandy foundations. And although all other considerations fail them, yet they will maintain a life of hopes, though ungrounded and unwarrantable, Isa. lvii. 10. This is the condition of most false professors; but when the word of Christ by his power enters into their souls and consciences, it utterly casts down all their confidences, and destroys their hopes and expectations. Nothing now remains but that such a person betake himself wholly to the life which he can make in sin, with its lusts and pleasures; or else come over sincerely to him in whom is life, and who giveth life unto all that come unto him. So he "slays the wicked with the breath of his lips," Isa. xi. 4. And this is the progress that the Lord Christ makes with the souls of men:—1. He discerneth himself their state and condition, what is good or evil in them. 2. He discovereth this unto themselves, or convinceth them of their sins and dangers; which surpriseth them with fears, and sometimes with amazements. 3. He judgeth them by his word, and condemns them by it in their own consciences. This makes them give over their old security and confidences, and betake themselves unto new hopes that yet things may be better with them. 4. He destroys these hopes also, and shows them how vain they are. And hereon they either betake themselves wholly to their sins, so to free themselves from their convictions and fears, or sincerely give up themselves unto him for relief. To this purpose, again, it is added, that this Word of God is " a discerner of the thoughts and intents of the heart;" that is, one that so discerns them as to put a difference between them, and to pass judgment upon them.

Obs. V. The Lord Christ discerneth all inward and spiritual things, in order to his future judgment of those things, and the persons in whom they are on their own account.

Our discerning, our judging, are things distinct and separate. Discerning every thing weakly, imperfectly, and by parts or pieces, we cannot judge speedily, if we intend at all to judge wisely. For we must "judge after the sight of our eyes, and reprove after the hearing of our ears;" that is, according as we can take in by weak means an understanding of what we are to make a judgment upon. With the Word or Son of God it is not so; for he at once discerning all things perfectly and absolutely, in all their causes, circumstances, tendencies, and ends, in the same instant he approveth or condemneth them. The end of his knowledge of them is comprised in his knowledge itself. Hence to "know," in the Scripture, when ascribed to God, doth sometimes signify to approve, accept, and justify; sometimes to refuse, reject, and condemn. Wherefore Christ's judging of the thoughts and intents of men's hearts is inseparable from his discerning of them, and the end why he fixeth

his eye upon them.   For this cause is he said to be "of quick understanding in the fear of the LORD," so as "not to judge after the
sight of his eyes, nor approve after the hearing of his ears;" that is,
according to the outward appearance and representation of things,
or the profession that men make, which is seen and heard: but "he
judgeth with righteousness, and reproveth with equity," according to
the true nature of things, which lieth hidden from the eyes of men,
Isa. xi. 3, 4.   He knows to judge, and he judgeth in and by his knowledge; and the most secret things are the especial objects of his knowledge and judgment.   Let not men please themselves in their secret
reserves.   There is not a thought in their hearts, though but transient,
never arising to the consistency of a purpose, not a pleasing or seeming desirable imagination in their minds, but it lies continually
under the eye of Christ, and at the same instant that very judgment is by him passed on them which shall be given out concerning
them at the last day.   O that we could always consider with what
awe and reverence, with what care and diligence, we ought continually to walk before this holy, all-seeing One!   In the description
that is given of him when he came to deal with his churches, to
"judge them with righteousness, and reprove them with equity,"
"not according to the sight of his eyes or the hearing of his ears,"—
that is, the outward profession that they made,—it is said that "his
eyes were as a flame of fire," Rev. i. 14; answerable unto that of
Job to God, "Hast thou eyes of flesh? or seest thou as man seeth?"
chap. x. 4.   He doth not look on things through such weak and failing mediums as poor frail creatures do, but sees all things clearly
and perfectly according as they are in themselves, by the light of
his own eyes, which are "as a flame of fire."   And when he comes
actually to deal with his churches, he prefaceth it with this, "I know
thy works," which leads the way; and his judgment on them upon
the account of those works immediately followeth after, Rev. ii., iii.
And it may be observed, that the judgment that he made concerning them was not only wholly independent of their outward profession, and ofttimes quite contrary unto it, but also that he judged
otherwise of them, yea, contrary to that which in the secret of their
hearts they judged of themselves.   See chap. iii. 17.   So when
Judas was in the height of his profession, he judged him a *devil*,
John vi. 70, 71; and when Peter was in the worst of his defection he judged him a *saint*, as having prayed for him that his
faith might not fail.   So doth he know that he may judge, and so
doth he judge together with his knowledge; and this easily and
perfectly, for "all things are naked and opened before him;" so
that,—

Obs. VI. It is no trouble or labour to the Word of God to discern
all creatures, and all that is of them and in them, seeing there is

nothing but is evidently apparent, open, and naked, under his all-seeing eye.

It would be necessary here to open the nature of the knowledge or omniscience of God, but that I have done it at large in another treatise, whereunto I refer the reader.[1] Now, after the consideration of all the particulars, we may subjoin an observation that naturally ariseth from the multiplying of the instances here given by the apostle, and it is that,—

Obs. VII. It is a great and difficult matter re&lly and practically to convince professors of the practical judging omnisciency of Jesus Christ, the Word of God.

On the account hereof, added to the great importance of the thing itself unto our faith and obedience, doth the apostle here so multiply his expressions and instances of it. It is not for nothing that what might have been expressed in *one* single plain assertion is here set out in so *many*, and with such variety of allusions, suited to convey a practical sense of it unto our minds and consciences. All professors are ready enough to close with Peter in the first part of his confession, "Lord, thou knowest all things;" but when they come to the other, "Thou knowest that I love thee,"—that is, to make a practical consideration of it with respect unto their own hearts and ways, as designing in all things to approve themselves unto him as those who are continually under his eye and judgment,—this they fail in and are hardly brought unto. If their minds were fully possessed with the persuasion hereof, were they continually under the power thereof, it would certainly influence them unto that care, diligence, and watchfulness, which are evidently wanting in many, in the most of them. But love of present things, the deceitfulness of sin, the power of temptations, cares, and businesses of life, vain and uncertain hopes, do effectually divert their minds from a due consideration of it. And we find by experience how difficult it is to leave a lasting impression of it on the souls of men. Yet would nothing be of more use unto them in the whole course of their walking before God. And this will further appear, if, after the precedent exposition of the several particular parts of these verses, and brief observations from them, we duly consider the general design of the apostle in the words, and what we are instructed in thereby.

In the foregoing verses, having greatly cautioned the Hebrews against backsliding and declension in their profession, acquainting them with the nature and danger of unbelief and the deceitfulness of sin whereby that cursed effect is produced, the apostle in these verses gives an account of the reason of his earnestness with them in this matter. For although they might pretend that in their profession they gave him no cause to suspect their stability, or

---

[1] See vol. x. p. 23, of the author's works.—ED.

to be jealous of them, yet he lets them know that this is not absolutely satisfactory, seeing that not only others may be deceived in
the profession of men, and give them "a name to live" who are
really "dead," but they also may please themselves in an apprehension of their own stability, when they are under manifold decays and
declensions. The principles and causes of this evil are so close,
subtile, and deceitful, that none is able to discern them but the all-
seeing eye of Jesus Christ. On the account whereof he minds them
fully and largely of his power and omniscience, whereunto they
ought to have a continual regard, in their faith, obedience, and profession. Hence we are instructed,—

First, That the beginnings or entrances into declensions in profession, or backslidings from Christ and the ways of the gospel, are
secret, deep, and hardly discoverable, being open and naked only to
the all-discerning eye of Christ.

Secondly, That the consideration of the omniscience of Christ, his
all-searching and all-seeing eye, is an effectual means to preserve the
souls of professors from destructive entrances into backslidings from
the gospel.

Thirdly, The same consideration, duly improved, is a great relief
and encouragement unto those who are sincere and upright in their
obedience. For the apostle intends not merely to terrify those who
are under the guilt of the evil cautioned against, but to encourage
the meanest and weakest sincere believer, who desireth to commend
his conscience to the Lord Jesus in his walking before him. And
these things being comprehensive of the design of the apostle in
these weighty words of truth and wisdom, and being greatly our
concernment duly to consider, must be distinctly handled and spoken
unto.

Obs. VIII. For the first of the propositions laid down, it is the design of the apostle to teach it in all those cautions which he gives to
these professing Hebrews against this evil, and concerning the sub-
tilties and surprisals wherewith it is attended. See chapters iii. 13,
xii. 15. Everywhere he requires more than ordinary watchfulness
and diligence in this matter; and plainly intimates unto them, that,
such is the deceitfulness of sin, so various and powerful are the temptations that professors are to be exercised withal, unless they are exceeding heedful, there will be no preventing of a surprisal or seduction into some degrees at least of declension and backsliding from
the gospel. There will be some loss or decay, in faith, or love, or
works, one way or other.

The Asian churches are a sad exemplification of this truth. In a
short time the most of them were greatly fallen off from their first
gospel engagements; yea, so far as that some of them are threatened
with excision and casting off from Christ. And yet no one of those
churches seems to have had the least sense of their own decays;

and those in especial who had made the greatest progress in falling
away were yet justified by others with whom they conversed, having
amongst them " a name to live," and applauded themselves in their
condition, as that which was good and in nothing blamable. In this
state the Lord Christ comes to make a judgment concerning them,
as all things lay open and naked under his eye. In the description
that is given of him upon his entrance into this work, it is said, as
was observed before, that " his eyes were as a flame of fire," Rev. i.
14,—seeing all things, discerning all things, piercing at one view
from the beginning unto the end of all. And he declares that he
will so deal with them that " all the churches shall know that he
searcheth the reins and hearts" of men, chap. ii. 23. And what
work doth he make amongst these secure churches! One is charged
with loss of love and faith; another of works; a third with luke-
warmness and carnal pride; a fourth with spiritual death as to the
generality of them, and most of them with various decays and miscarriages, and those such as themselves took no notice of. But his
eye, which stays not upon the outside of things, be they never so gay
or glorious, but pierceth to the secret embryos and first conceptions
of sin and declensions, found them out, and passed judgment on them
in righteousness and equity.

1. Now, one great reason hereof is taken from the *subtilty* of the
principal causes of backsliding, and of the means or false reasonings whereby it is brought about. That which is wrought subtilely and deceitfully is wrought closely, and is therefore secret and
hidden. And the first impressions that these subtile and deceitful
causes make upon the minds of professors, the first entanglements
which these deceitful reasonings cast upon their affections, if they are
not merely transient, but abide upon their souls, there is in them an
entrance begun into a defection from the gospel. And for these
causes of declensions, they are everywhere expressed in the Scripture,
and everywhere expressly declared to be subtile and deceitful; as,—

(1.) *Indwelling sin* is fixed on as the next cause of declensions and
backslidings. This the apostle in this epistle chargeth (under the
names of a " root of bitterness;" of " the sin that doth so easily beset us," an " evil heart of unbelief," and the like) with the guilt of
this evil. And he himself declares this principle to be deceitful,
subtile; that is, close, secret, hidden in its operation and tendency,
Heb. iii. 13. To this purpose is seducing, enticing, and craft assigned unto it in the Scripture. And it hath among others innumerable this advantage also, that being within us, dwelling in us,
having possessed itself of the principles of our natures, it can insinuate all its corrupt and perverse reasonings, under the specious
pretence of natural self-love, which is allowable. This our apostle
was aware of, and therefore tells us that when he was called to

preach the gospel he "conferred not with flesh and blood," Gal. i. 16. By "flesh and blood" no more is intended but human nature as weak and frail. But in and by them the deceitfulness of sin is so ready to impose upon us its own corrupt reasonings, that the apostle thought not meet to entertain a parley with the very principles of his own nature about self-preservation. But this deceitfulness of sin I have handled at large in another treatise. Here only I observe, that the effects of this deceitful principle are, at least in their beginnings and first entrances, very close and secret, open only to the eye of Christ.

(2.) *Satan* also hath a principal hand in effecting or bringing about the declension of men from and in their profession. It is his main work, business, and employment in the world. This is the end of all his temptations and serpentine insinuations into the minds of professors. Whatever be the particular instance wherein he dealeth with them, his general design is to draw them off from their "first faith," their "first love," their "first works," and to loosen their hearts from Christ and the gospel. And I suppose it is not questioned but that he carrieth on his work subtilely, secretly, craftily. He is not called the "old serpent" for nothing. It is a composition of craft and malice that hath laid him under that denomination. His methods, his depths, his deceits, are we cautioned against. Hereabout treats our apostle with the Corinthians, 2 Epist. xi. 3, "I fear, lest by any means, as the serpent beguiled Eve through his subtilty, so your minds should be corrupted from the simplicity that is in Christ." It is true Eve was so beguiled, but who should now beguile the Corinthians? Even the same old deceiver, as he informs them, verse 14, "For Satan himself is transformed into an angel of light;" namely, in his fair and plausible pretences for the accomplishment of his wicked and abominable ends. He works in this matter by deceit, beguiling the souls of men, and therefore doth his work secretly, closely; for "in vain is the net spread before the eyes of any fowl." But his work also lies under the eye of Christ.

(3.) The *world* also hath its share in this design. The "cares of it," and "the deceitfulness of riches," further this pernicious work on the minds and ways of professors, Matt. xiii. 22. By them is the seed of the gospel choked, when they pretend only to grow up with it, and that there is a fair consistency between them and profession.

Now, though backsliding from Christ and the gospel be thus distinctly assigned to these causes, and severally to one in one place, to another in another, and that as they are especially or eminently predominant in the singular instances mentioned, and so the effect is denominated from them,—this is from indwelling sin, this from Satan, and that from the world; yet indeed there is no apostasy or declension in the minds of any which is not influenced by them all, and they are mutually assistant to each other in their work. Now, where there is a contribution of subtilty and craft from several principles all deeply depraved with that vicious habit, the work itself must needs be close and hidden, which craft and deceit do principally aim at; as that poison must needs be pernicious which is compounded of many poisonous ingredients, all inciting the venom of one another. But the Lord Christ looks through all this hidden and deceitful work, which no eye of man can pierce into.

Again, The *conjunct reasonings* of these deceitful principles, whereby they prevail with professors to backsliding, are plausible, and thereby the malignity of them and their secret influencing of their minds hardly discernible. Many of them may be referred unto these heads, wherein they do consist:—(1.) *Extenuations of duties and sins.* (2.) *Aggravations of difficulties* and troubles. (3.) *Suggestions of false rules* of profession.

Profession is our avowed observation of all evangelical duties, on the account of the authority of Christ commanding them; and abstinence from conformity to the world in all evil, on the same forbidding it. The forementioned principles labour by all ways to extenuate these duties, as to their necessity and importance. Granted it shall be that they are duties, it may be, but not of that consideration but that they may be omitted or neglected. Consider the severals, in that which is comprehensive of them all:—

[1.] This is *constancy in profession* in a time of danger and persecution. The hearts of men are often seduced with vain thoughts of holding their faith and love to Christ, which they hope will save them eternally, whilst they omit that profession of them which would endanger them temporally. A duty that also shall be allowed to be; but not of that necessity or importance as not to be omitted totally, or at least partially and gradually, to save our present concerns, especially whilst the substance of faith and love to Christ is in our hearts entirely preserved. This ruined many of the rich and great among the Jews: John xii. 42, "Among the chief rulers many believed on him; but because of the Pharisees they did not confess him, lest they should be put out of the synagogue." They went a great way in believing. And, considering their places and conditions, who would have required more of them? Would you have men, merely on the account of outward profession, hazard the loss of their places, interests, reputation, and all that is dear unto them? I know not well what men think in this case; the censure of the Holy Ghost in this matter concerning them is, "They loved the praise of men more than the praise of God," verse 43,—than which nothing almost can be spoken with more severity. And these Hebrews were influenced into declensions from the same fallacy of sin. They were fallen into days wherein profession was perilous; and therefore, although they would not renounce the faith whereby they hoped to be saved, yet they would let go their profession, for which they feared they should be troubled. So our apostle intimates, Heb. x. 25. In this and the like instances do the subtile reasonings of sin and Satan secretly corrupt the minds of men, until they are insensibly, and sometimes irrecoverably engaged in a course of withdrawing from Christ and the gospel. The same may be observed as to other duties, and especially as to degrees of constancy and fervency in the performance of them. From these the minds of men are often driven and diverted by the crafty reasonings of sin, whereby they are entered into apostasy. Some of the churches in the Revelation are charged not absolutely with the loss of their love, but of their "first love;" that is, the especial degrees of it in fervency and fruitfulness which they had attained.

[2.] Again, by these reasonings the deceitful principles mentioned do endeavour an *extenuation of the guilt* of such evils as lie in a tendency to alienate the heart from Christ and the gospel. An instance hereof we have in the Galatians. The observation of Judaical ceremonies was by false teachers pressed upon them. They did not once attempt to draw them from Christ and the gospel, nor would they have endured the proposal of any such thing. Only they desired that, together with the profession of the gospel and the grace of Christ, they would also take upon them the observation of the Mosaical rites and institutions. Hereunto they propose unto them a double motive:—1*st.* That they should hereby have *union with the professing Jews,* and so all differences be removed. 2*dly.* That they should escape *persecution,* which was then upon the matter alone stirred up by the envious Jews, Gal. vi. 12. If both these ends may be obtained, and yet faith in Christ and the gospel be retained, what inconvenience or harm would it be if they should engage into these observances? Accordingly many did so, and took upon them the yoke of Judaical rites. And what was the end of this matter? Our apostle lets them know that what they thought not of was befallen them, and yet was the genuine effect of what they did. They had forsaken Christ, fallen from grace, and, beginning in the Spirit, were ending in the flesh; for, under the specious pretences before mentioned, they had done that which was inconsistent with the faith of the gospel. 'Yea, but they thought not in the least of any declension from Christ.' The matter is not what they thought, but what they did. This they did, and this was the effect of it. The corrupt reasonings of their minds, deceived by the pleas and pretences mentioned, had prevailed with them to look on these things as, if not their duties, yet of no ill consequence or importance. So were they deluded by extenuations of the evil proposed unto them, until they justly fell under the censure before mentioned. And the principal mischief in this matter is, that when men are beguiled by false reasonings into unwarrantable practices, their corruptions are variously excited to adhere to and defend what they have been overtaken withal; which confirms them in their apostasies.

[3.] *Aggravations of difficulties* in the way of profession are made use of to introduce a declension from it. For when thoughts and apprehensions of them are admitted, they insensibly weaken and dishearten men, and render them languid and cold in their duties; which tends unto backsliding. The effect of such discouragements our apostle expresseth, Heb. xii. 12, 13: "Wherefore lift up the hands which hang down, and the feeble knees; and make straight paths for your feet, lest that which is lame be turned out of the way." Having laid down the afflictions and persecutions which they were to meet withal, and also declared the end and use of them in the grace and wisdom of God, he shows how ready men are to despond and grow heartless under them; which deprives them of all life and spirit in their profession; which he warns them to avoid, lest all end in apostasy. For if men begin once to think hard and strange of the trials that may befall them on the account of their religion, and cannot find that in it which will outweigh their sufferings, they will not long retain it. Nor is it advisable for any man to entertain a profession that will not keep and maintain him in a dear year, but leave him to sink under those troubles which may befall him on the account thereof; as every thing whose real good doth not outbalance the evil that for it, and upon its single account, we must undergo, is certainly ineligible. Herein, then, lies no small part of the deceitful actings of the subtile principles mentioned. They are ready to fill the mind with dismal apprehensions of the difficulties, dangers, troubles, reproaches, and persecutions that men may undergo on the account of profession. And unless they can make the Lord Christ absolutely to be their end, portion, and measure of all, so as to reckon on all other things not according to their own nature, but according to the respect which they have unto him, and their interest in him, it is impossible but these things will secretly influence them into declensions from their profession. In the meantime aggravating thoughts of trouble please men's minds; it seems reasonable unto them, yea their duty, to be terrifying themselves with the apprehensions of the evils that may befall them. And when they come indeed, if liberty, if goods, if life itself, be required in the confirmation of our testimony to the gospel, there needs no more to seduce us into a relinquishment of its profession, but only prevailing with us to value these things out of their place and more than they deserve, whereby the evils in the loss of them will be thought intolerable. And it is marvellous to think how the minds of men are insensibly and variously affected with these considerations, to the weakening, if not the ruin, of that zeal for God, that delight in his ways, that "rejoicing in tribulation," which are required to the maintaining of a just and due profession. And against the effect of such impressions we are frequently warned in the Scripture.

[4.] Again; these corrupt and fallacious reasonings do cover and conceal the entrances of apostasy, by proposing false rules of walking before God in profession, wherein men are apt to satisfy and deceive themselves. So in particular they make great use of the examples of other men, of other professors; which on very many accounts is apt to deceive them, and draw them into a snare. But this head of the deceit of sin I have spoken to at large in another discourse.[1]

2. The beginnings of declensions from Christ and the gospel are deep and hidden, because ofttimes they are carried on by very secret and imperceptible degrees. Some men are plunged into apostasy by some notorious crimes and wickednesses, or by the power of some great temptations. In these it is easy to discover the beginning of their fall; as it was with Judas when the devil entered into him, and prevailed with him for money to betray his Master. And many such there are in the world, who for money, or the things that end in money, part with their professed interest in Christ and the gospel. And if they get more than Judas did, it is because they meet with better chapmen in the world than were the priests and Pharisees. The fall of such men from their profession is like the dying of a man by a fever. The first incursion of the disease, with its whole progress, is manifest. It is with others in their spiritual sickness and decays as with those who are in a hectical distemper; which at first is hardly known, and in its progress hardly cured. Small negligences and omissions are admitted, and the soul is habituated unto them, and so a progress is made to greater evils; of which also, as I remember, I have treated elsewhere.

3. Revolters and backsliders do their utmost endeavour *to hide the beginnings of their falls from themselves and others.* This makes the discovery and opening of them to be difficult. By the false and corrupt reasonings before mentioned they labour to blind their own eyes, and to hide their own evils from themselves: for in this case men are not deceived, unless they contribute to their own beguiling. Their own hearts seduce them before they feed on ashes. And herewith they willingly attend unto the delusions of Satan and the world; which they do in not watching against them as they ought. So are they deceived themselves. And when they have made such a progress in their declensions as that they begin themselves, it may be, to be sensible of it, then do they endeavour by all means to hide them from others; by which means, at length, they hide them from themselves, and rest satisfied in what they have pleaded and pretended, as if it were really so. They will use pleas, excuses,

---

[1] Treatise on Indwelling Sin, vol. vi. of the author's works.—ED.

and pretences, until they believe them. Was it not so with the church of Sardis? Even when she was almost dead, yet she had outwardly so demeaned herself as to have a "name to live;" that is, a great reputation to be in a good thriving state and condition. And Laodicea, in the height of her apostasy, yet persuaded herself that she was "rich," and increased, and wanted nothing; and knew not, as is expressly testified, that she was "poor," and fallen under the power of manifold decays.

From these and the like causes it is that the beginnings of men's backslidings from the gospel are so secret and hidden, as that they are open only to the all-seeing eye of Jesus Christ; which our apostle here minds these Hebrews of, to beget in them a watchful jealousy over themselves.

And this effect it should have upon all. This the nature of the thing itself, and frequent Scripture admonitions, do direct us unto, —namely, that we should continually be watchful over our own hearts, lest any beginnings of backslidings or declensions from the gospel should have taken place or prevailed in us. Cautions to this purpose the Scripture abounds withal: "Let him that standeth," that is, in the profession of the gospel, "take heed lest he fall;" or, beware that he decay not in his faith, and love, and zeal, and so fall into sin and apostasy. And again, "Take heed that we lose not those things which we have wrought," 2 John 8. That profession which is not working is ever false, and to be despised. "Faith worketh by love." Hath it been so with us, that profession hath been effectual in working? Let us look to it carefully, lest we discontinue that course, or by apostasy forfeit all the benefit and advantage of it. And our apostle in this epistle in an especial manner abounds with admonitions to the same purpose; because the Hebrews, on many accounts, were much exposed to the danger of this sin. And it is the duty of the dispensers of the gospel to apply themselves particularly to the state, condition, and temptations of them with whom in an especial manner they have to do. And let not any man think that the earnest pressing of this duty of constant watchfulness against the first entrances of spiritual declensions is not of so much use and necessity as is pretended. We see what the neglect of it hath produced. Many who once made a zealous profession of the truth, having strong convictions upon their souls, and were thereby in a way of receiving more grace and mercy from the Lord, have, through a neglect of this duty, fallen from the ways of God, and perished eternally, 2 Pet. ii. 20–22. And many more have exceedingly dishonoured God, and provoked his indignation against the whole generation of professors in the world; which hath caused him to fill all his dispensations with tokens of his displeasure. This hath laid all the virgins, even wise and foolish, asleep, whilst the Bridegroom standeth at the door. There is, then, no greater evidence of an unsound heart than to be careless about the beginnings of spiritual decays in any kind. When men once lay up all their spiritual interest in retaining some kind of persuasion that in the end they may come to heaven, and, so they may by any means retain that persuasion, are regardless of exact watchfulness and walking, they are even in a perishing condition. There needs no greater evidence that self is their utmost end, that they have neither care to please God, nor love to Christ, nor delight in the gospel, but, with Balaam, desire only to "die the death of the righteous." Yet thus is it with them who neglect the first entrances of any cold, careless frame or temper of heart in gospel duties. They little consider either the power or deceitfulness of sin who are negligent in this matter, and how backsliding will get and firm its ground in the soul after a while, which might with ease have been at first prevented. Let us, therefore, because of the importance of this duty, consider some directions for the preventing of this evil, and some instructions how to discover it in the ways and means of its prevalency:—

Take heed of *weariness* in and of those ways of God wherein you have been engaged according to his mind. A spontaneous lassitude in the body is esteemed an ill prognostic; some great distemper usually ensues upon it. So is weariness of any of God's ways; its hidden cause and consequent, that will in time appear, is some great spiritual distemper. And this our apostle intimates to be the beginning of most men's apostasy, Heb. x. 36–39. Men, through want of patience to continue in well-doing, grow weary, and ofttimes "draw back unto perdition." And there are three things that men are apt to grow weary of in the ways of God, and thereby to enter into spiritual decays:—

1. Of *duties*. Many duties are burdensome to flesh and blood; that is, nature as weak and frail. All of them are opposite to flesh and blood; that is, nature as corrupt and sinful. In the one sense, nature is ready to faint under them; in the other, to raise up an opposition against them, and that by a secret aversation in the will, with innumerable corrupt reasonings, excuses, and pretences in the mind. If they prevail to an effectual weariness,—that is, such as shall introduce a relinquishment of them, in part or in whole, as to the matter of them or the manner of their performance,—those in whom they do so will have cause to say, " We were almost in all evil in the midst of the congregation and assembly," Prov. v. 14. Hence is the caution of our apostle, 2 Thess. iii. 13, " Brethren, be not weary in well-doing;" and Gal. vi. 9. 'A patient continuance in an even, constant course of well-doing, in a due observance of all gospel duties, will be burdensome and grievous unto you; but faint not, if you intend to come to the blessed end of your course in peace with God.' Now,

weariness in duty discovers itself by impairing it in the intenseness of our spirits, or constancy of its performance. Where there is a decay in either of these, weariness is at the root; and after weariness ensues contempt, Mal. i. 13. And whatever interpretation men may put upon this frame, God calls it a being weary of himself, Isa. xliii. 22; which is the next step to forsaking of him. Wherever, therefore, this begins to discover itself in the soul, nothing can relieve it but a vigorous shaking off all appearances of it, by a warm, constant application of the mind unto those duties whose neglect it would introduce.

2. Of *waiting to receive any particular good or special mercy from God* in his ways. God is a good and gracious master. He entertains none into his service but he gives them in hand that which is an abundant recompense for the duties he will require of them. "In keeping of his commands there is great reward," Ps. xix. 11. Every part of his work carries its own wages along with it. Those who serve him never want enough to make them "rejoice" when they fall into "manifold temptations," and to "glory in tribulations;" which are the worst things that do or can befall them on his account. But, moreover, besides the pledges that he gives them in hand, they have also many "great and precious promises," whereby they are justly raised up to the expectation of other and greater things than at present they do enjoy. Whatever mercy or grace by any or all the promises of God they have been made partakers of, there is still more in them all, nay, in every one of them, than they can here come to the actual enjoyment of. Yet are all these things theirs, and they have a right unto them. This makes waiting on God so excellent a grace, so necessary a duty. Now, sometimes this hath respect unto some mercy that a man may in an especial manner stand in need of. Here he would have his faith expedited, his expectation satisfied, and his waiting have an end put unto it. If he fail herein, it maketh his heart sick. But here lieth the great trial of faith. "He that believeth," that is, truly and sincerely, "he will not make haste;" that is, he will abide in this duty, and not "limit the Holy One" as to times and seasons. If those who are called hereunto wax weary of it, they are in the high road to apostasy. Consolation, light, and joy, do not come in through the administration of the ordinances answerable to the measures they have themselves given unto or taken of things; strength against a temptation or corruption is not yet received upon prayer or supplication; they are weary of waiting, and so give over. This will end in absolute apostasy if not timely prevented. See the cautions of our apostle in this matter, Heb. vi. 11, 12, x. 35, 36.

3. *Weariness of troubles and persecutions* is of the same tendency. It opens a door to apostasy. They are for the most part

the portion of believers in this world.   Nor have they cause to complain of their lot.   They are told of it beforehand.   Had they been allured on unto faith and profession with hopes and expectations of peace and prosperity in this world, and were they afterwards surprised with the cross, they might have some reason to complain.   But the matter is quite otherwise.   Our Saviour hath told us plainly, that if we will not " take up the cross" we must let him alone.   ' If,' saith he, ' you will follow me, you must take up the cross; yea, fathers, mothers, houses, lands, and possessions, if called for (and probably they will be called for), must all go, or be foregone, for my sake and the gospel's.   If you like not these terms, you may let them and me alone.'   So our apostle assures us, that " they who will live godly in Christ Jesus shall suffer persecution," 2 Tim. iii. 12.   There is a kind of profession that may escape well enough in the world, such as men shall have no disadvantage by in this life,—nor advantage in that which is to come.   But that profession which causeth men to " live godly in Christ Jesus," will for the most part be attended with persecution.   And this are we all forewarned of.   But so foolish are we generally, as that when these things befall us, we are apt to be surprised, as if some strange thing, something foreign to our condition, had seized on us; as the apostle Peter intimates, 1 Pet. iv. 12.   And if men by their natural courage, their spirit to sustain infirmities, can hold out the first brunt of them, yet when they begin to return and to be prolonged, to follow one upon another, and no way of deliverance or of ending them be in view, they are apt to be weary, and cast about, like men in a storm, how they may give over their intended voyage and retreat into some harbour, where they may be in peace and safety.   Omission of provoking duties or compliance with pleasing ways, in such a condition, begins to be considered as a means of relief.   And this with many is an entrance into apostasy, Matt. xiii. 21.   And this is confirmed, as by testimonies of the Scripture, so by instances and examples in all ages of the church.   This, therefore, our apostle in an especial manner treats with these Hebrews about, plainly declaring that if they grew weary of their troubles, they would quickly fail in their profession, chap. vi. 11, 12; and he multiplies both reasons and examples to encourage them unto the contrary, chap. x.-xii.   For when men begin to wax weary of troubles and persecutions, and to make their own carnal reasonings, affections, and desires, to be the measure of their suffering, or what it is meet for them to undergo upon the account of the gospel, they will quickly decline from it.   Now, because this is the common way and means whereby men are brought to decays in their profession, and insensibly unto apostasy, it may not be amiss to subjoin some few considerations which may help to relieve our spirits under their troubles, and to preserve them from fainting or being weary; as,—

1. What is it that these troubles do or can deprive us of, whatever their continuance be? Is it of heaven, of everlasting rest, of peace with God, of communion with Christ, of the love and honour of saints and angels? These things are secured utterly out of their reach, and they cannot for one moment interrupt our interest in them. This is Paul's consideration, Rom. viii. 38, 39. And had we a due valuation of these things, what may outwardly befall us in this world on their account would seem very light unto us, and easy to be borne, 2 Cor. iv. 15–18.

2. What is it that they fall upon and can reach unto? It may be they may deprive us of our riches, our liberty, our outward ease and accommodations, our reputation in the world. But what perishing trifles are these, compared to the eternal concerns of our immortal souls! It may be they may reach this flesh, these carcasses that are every day crumbling into dust. But shall we faint or wax weary on their account? Suppose we should, to spare them, turn aside to some crooked paths, wherein we suppose we may find security, God can send diseases after us that shall irrecoverably bring on us all those evils which by our sins we have sought to avoid. He can give a commission to a disease to make the softest bed a severe prison, and fill our loins and bones with such pains as men cannot inflict on us and keep us alive under them. And for death itself, the height, complement, and end of temporary trouble, how many ways hath he to cast us into the jaws of it, and that in a more terrible manner than we need fear from the children of men! and shall we, to preserve a perishing life, which, it may be, within a few days a fever or a feather may deprive us of, startle at the troubles which, on the account of Christ and the gospel, we may undergo, and thereby forfeit all the consolations of God, which are able to sweeten every condition unto us? This consideration is proposed unto us by Jesus Christ himself, Matt. x. 28.

3. Whereunto, in the wisdom and grace of God, do these things tend, if managed aright in us and by us? There is nothing that the Scripture doth more abound in, than in giving us assurance that all the evils which we do or may undergo upon the account of Christ and his gospel, shall work effectually towards our unspeakable spiritual advantage. See Rom. v. 1–5.

4. For whom or whose sake do we or are we to undergo the troubles mentioned? A man of honesty and good nature will endure much for a parent, a child, a friend; yea, the apostle tells us, that " for a good man some would even dare to die," Rom. v. But who is it whom we are to suffer for? Is it not He who is infinitely more than all these in himself and to us? Consider his own excellency, consider his love to us, consider the effects of the one and the fruits of the other, whereof we are and hope to be made partakers,

and it will be granted that he is worthy of our all, and ten thousand times more if it were in our power. Besides, he calls us not to any thing but what he went before us in; and he went before us in many things wherein he calls not us to follow him, for he underwent them that we might escape them. He died that we might live; and was made a curse that the blessing might come upon us. Let us not then be so foolish, so unthankful, so brutish, as to think any trouble too great or too long to be undergone for him. This our apostle at large expresseth, Phil. iii. 7–10.

5. What is the end of these trials and troubles which we are so ready to faint and despond under? Eternal rest and glory do attend them. See 2 Thess. i. 7; 2 Cor. iv. 17; Rev. vii. 13, 14.

These and the like considerations, being pleaded in the mind and soul, may be a means to preserve them from fainting under troubles that do or may befall men on the account of the profession of the gospel, which are apt to dispose them unto backslidings.

There are sundry means that may be improved to prevent the entrances of the decays insisted on; amongst all which none is so proper as that here mentioned by our apostle, and which is comprised in our next proposition. For,—

Obs. IX. A due and holy consideration at all times of the all-seeing eye of Jesus Christ is a great preservation against backslidings or declensions in profession.

This is the end for which the mention of it is here introduced by the apostle. It was not in his way, nor was any part of his design, to treat absolutely about the omniscience of Christ; nothing could be more foreign to his present discourse. But he speaks of it on purpose, as an effectual means to awe and preserve their souls from the evil that he dehorted them from and warned them of. And the consideration of it is so on many accounts; for,—

1. If we retain this in remembrance, that all the most *secret beginnings of spiritual declensions* in us are continually under his eye, it will influence us unto watchful care and diligence. Some, with Sardis, are ready to please themselves whilst they keep up such a profession as others with whom they walk do approve of, or cannot blame. Others, with Laodicea, think all is well whilst they approve themselves, and have no troublesome accusations rising up against their peace in their own consciences, when, it may be, their consciences themselves are debauched, bribed, or secure. For lesser things, which neither others observe to their disreputation, nor themselves are affected with to their disquiet, many men regard them not. And hereby are they insensibly betrayed into apostasy, whilst one neglect follows another, and one evil is added to another, until a breach be made upon them " great like the sea, that cannot be healed." Herein, then, lies a great preservative against this ruining

danger. Let the soul consider constantly that the eye of Christ, with whom principally, and upon the matter solely in these things, he hath to do, and to whom an account of all must be one day given, is upon him; and it cannot but keep him jealous over himself, lest there should any defiling root of bitterness spring up in him. To him ought we in all things to approve ourselves; and this we cannot do without a continual jealousy and constant watchfulness over our hearts, that nothing be found there that may displease him: and whatever is there, it is all "naked and open unto him." And,—

2. The Lord Christ doth not behold or look on the evils that are or may be in the hearts of professors as *one unconcerned* in them, by a mere intuition of them; but as one that is deeply concerned in them, and as it were troubled at them: for by these things is his good Spirit grieved and vexed, and great reproach is cast upon his name. When the miscarriages of professors break out so far as that the world takes notice of them, it rejoiceth in them, and triumpheth over that truth and those ways which by them are professed. And when other believers or professors observe them, they are grieved and deeply afflicted in their minds. And who knows not that even the consideration of these things is of great use to prevail with sincere professors unto watchfulness over their ways and walkings; namely, lest the name of God should be evil spoken of by reason of them, or the spirits of the servants of Christ be grieved by them. How often doth David declare that he would take heed to his ways, because of his enemies or observers, those that watched for his halting, and would improve their observation of it to the dishonour of his profession! And, on the other side, he prays that none which feared God might be ashamed on his account, or troubled at his failings. And therefore did he labour in all things to preserve his integrity, and keep himself from sin. Nor have they any respect unto the glory of God who have not the same sense and affections in such cases. Now, if these things are, or ought to be, of such weight with us, as to what comes under the cognizance of men, that is open and naked unto men, according to their capacity of discerning, what ought our thoughts to be of all things of the same nature that fall fully and solely under the cognizance of Christ, considering his concernment in them, and how he is affected with them? And so it is with respect unto the first, most secret, and imperceptible spiritual decays that may befall us; yea, he lays most weight on the things that are known to himself alone, and would have all the churches know and consider that he "searcheth the hearts and trieth the reins" of men. Neither can we have in any thing greater evidence given unto our sincerity, than when we have an especial watchful regard unto those things which lie under the eye of Christ alone, wherein we have to do with him only. This

testifieth a pure, unmixed, uncorrupted faith and love towards him. Where, therefore, there is any thing of sincerity, there will be a continual care about these things upon the account of the concernment of Christ in them.   And,—

3. We may do well to remember that he so sees all our neglects and decays, as in an especial manner to *take notice of their sinfulness and demerit.*   Many of the churches in the Revelation pleased themselves in their state and condition, when yet, because of their decays, the Lord Christ saw that guilt in them and upon them as that for it he threatened them with utter rejection, if they prevented it not by repentance; which accordingly befell some of them.   We are apt to take a very undue measure of our failings, and so esteem this or that folly, neglect, or decay, to have no great guilt attending it; so that we may well enough spare it and ourselves in it.   And the reason hereof is, because we are apt to consider only acts or omissions themselves, and not the spring from whence they do proceed, nor the circumstances wherewith they are attended, nor the ends whereunto they tend.   But saith our apostle, 'All things are open and naked before him, neither is there any thing that is hid from his eyes.'   There is no omission of duty, no neglect of the acting or stirring up of any grace, no sinful miscarriage or worldly compliance, wherein the beginnings of our decays do or may consist, but that, together with all their causes and occasions, their aggravating circumstances, their end and tendency, they are all under the eye of Christ; and so their whole guilt is spread before him.   And oftentimes there is a more provoking guilt in some circumstances of things than in the things themselves.   He sees all the unkindness and unthankfulness from whence our decays proceed; all the contempt of him, his love and grace, wherewith they are attended; the advantage of Satan and the world in them; and the great end of final apostasy whereunto they tend, if not by grace prevented.   All these things greatly aggravate the guilt of our inward, spiritual decays; and the whole provocation that is in them lies continually under his eye.   Hence his thoughts of these things are not as our thoughts commonly are; but it is our wisdom to make his the rule and measure of ours.

4. He so sees all things of this kind as that he will *pass judgment* on us and them accordingly; it may be in this world, by sore afflictions and chastisements, but assuredly at the last day.   Alas! it is not the world that we are to be judged by,—if it were, men might hide their sins from it; nor is it the saints nor angels, who discover not the secret frames of our hearts; but it is he who is " greater than our hearts, and knoweth all things."   This our apostle directs us to the consideration of; for after he hath given the description of the Word of God insisted on, he adds, that it is he to whom

we must give up our account. And how shall backsliders in heart escape his righteous judgment? Secrecy is the relief of most in this world,—darkness is their refuge; but before him these things have their aggravation of guilt, and will yield no relief.

5. Again; He so discerns all declensions in the hearts and spirits of professors, as withal to be ready to give them supplies of help and strength against all the causes of them, if sought unto in a due manner. And there can be no greater encouragement to them that are sincere, unto the use of their utmost endeavours, to preserve their faith and profession entire for him. And this will be further improved in our consideration of the last observation which we drew from the words of the apostle and the exposition of them, which is that,—

Obs. X. A due, holy consideration of the omniscience of Christ is a great encouragement unto the meanest and weakest believers, who are upright and sincere in their faith and obedience.

To this purpose are all these properties of Christ proposed unto us, and to be improved by us. They all are suited to give encouragement unto us in our way and course of obedience.

Hence is he able to take care of and to encourage the least beginnings of grace in the hearts of his disciples. It is his office to take care of the whole seed of God, of all the work of the Spirit of grace. This he could not do without that all-discerning ability which is here ascribed unto him. By this he takes notice of the beginning, increase, growth, and decays of it, from first to last. Hence he says of himself, that he " will not break the bruised reed, nor quench the smoking flax," Matt. xii. 20. Be our spiritual strength but like that which is naturally in a bruised reed, which is the next degree to none at all, he will not break it; that is, he will take care that it be not bruised, despised, or discouraged, but will cherish it, and add strength unto it. The smoking of flax also expresseth the least degree imaginable of grace;[1] yet neither under his eye and care shall this be quenched. It is easy with him to discover and blast the hypocrisy of false pretenders. He did so by one word to him who boasted of keeping all the commandments from his youth, Matt. xix. 18–22. So by the breath of his lips he slays the wicked, Isa. xi. 4. Be their profession never so specious or glorious, do they please themselves in it, and deceive others by it, he can come to their consciences under all pretences, and by his word and Spirit slay all their false hopes, discover their hypocrisy, and strip them naked of their profession, to the contempt of all. And so doth he know and take care of the least dram of sincerity in the weakest soul that belongs unto him. So he did in the poor woman, when she owned herself

---

[1] In the original edition the word is " sin,"—an evident misprint for " grace," or some similar word.—ED.

to be no better than a dog, Matt. xv, 27, 28. He doth not only bear his lambs in his arms, the weakest of the flock who have an appearance of life, and of following him in it; but also " gently leads those that are with young," Isa. xl. 11, who as yet have but newly conceived his grace in their hearts.

And this gives us a stable ground whereon to answer that great objection, which many souls make against their own peace and consolation. They are convinced of the excellency of Christ, and of the suitableness of his grace and righteousness unto their wants. They are also satisfied in the faithfulness of gospel promises, and the stability of the covenant of grace, with all other principles and grounds of evangelical consolation. But they look on themselves as unconcerned in all these things. As far as they know, they have no grace in them; and therefore have no interest in or right unto what is proposed to them. And hereon ensue various entanglements in their minds, keeping them off from sharing in that " strong consolation" which God is abundantly willing that all " the heirs of promise" should receive. The consideration of the properties of the Lord Christ insisted on is exceedingly suited to the removal of this objection out of the way. To confirm this, I shall consider the whole case a little more largely. We may then observe,—

1. That the *beginnings of most things are imperceptible.* Things at first are rather known by their causes and effects than from any thing discernible in their own beings. As they are gradually increased, they give evidence of themselves; as a little fire is known by the smoke it causeth, when itself cannot be seen.

2. That the beginnings of spiritual things in the souls of men are, moreover, *very secret and hidden,* upon many especial accounts and reasons. Grace in its first communication is a thing new to the soul, which it knows not how to try, examine, or measure. The soul is possibly put by it under some surprise; as was Rebekah when she had conceived twins in her womb. Until such persons seriously consult with God by his word, they will be at a great loss about their own state and condition. Again, Satan useth all means possible to darken the mind, that it may not aright apprehend the work of God in it and upon it. His first design is to keep us from grace; if he be cast therein, his reserve is to keep us from consolation. His sleights and methods herein are not now to be insisted on. Hence most of the objections we meet with, from persons under darkness as to gospel comforts and refreshment, may be easily manifested to be his suggestions. Moreover, indwelling corruption doth exceedingly endeavour to cloud and darken the work of God's grace in the soul. And it doth so two ways especially:—(1.) By a more open discovery of itself in all its evil than it did before. Grace is come upon it as its enemy, and that which fights against it, designing its

ruin. The very first actings of it lie in a direct opposition to the
former rule of sin in the heart. This inbred corruption meeting
withal, sometimes it is excited unto rage, and presseth for its own
satisfaction with more earnestness than formerly, when it was as it
were in the full and quiet possession of the soul. This causeth darkness and trouble in the mind, and keeps it off from discerning any
thing of the work of God in it. (2.) By a sensible opposition to
gospel duties. This it will raise against that spiritual manner of
their performance which a gracious soul now aims at, though it was
more quiet when only the outward bodily exercise was attended
unto. These things surprise beginners in grace, and leave them in
the dark as to what is their interest in it.

3. Believers in this state and condition have in themselves many
just grounds of fears and jealousies concerning themselves, which
they know not how to disentangle themselves from. The many self-
deceivings which they either see the example of in others or read
of in the Scripture, make them jealous, and that justly, over their
own hearts. And whereas they find much hypocrisy in their hearts
in other things, they are jealous lest in this also they should deceive
themselves. And many other reasonings there are of the same nature whereby they are entangled.

Against all these perplexities much relief may be administered
from this consideration, that the Lord Christ, " with whom we have
to do," sees, knows, and approves of the least spark of heavenly fire
that is kindled in us by his Spirit; the least seed of faith and grace
that is planted in us is under his eye and care, to preserve, water,
and cherish it. And this may be pressed in particular instances;
as,—

1. He sees and takes notice of the least *endeavours of grace* in
the heart against the power of sin. This the soul wherein it is may
not be acquainted with, by reason of that pressing sense which it
hath from the assaults that sin makes upon it. These so imbitter
it that it cannot find out unto its satisfaction the secret lustings and
warrings of the Spirit against the flesh; as one that is deeply sensible of the weight of his burden, which is ready to overbear him,
doth not perceive his own strength whereby he standeth under it.
But this lies under the eye of Christ distinctly, and that, so as to give
in suitable help and succour unto it in a time of need, as is declared
in the next verses.

2. He sees and perceives the *principle and actings of grace* in
that very sorrow and trouble wherewith the soul is even over-
whelmed in an apprehension of the want of it. He knows that
much of many a soul's trouble for want of grace is from grace.
There is in it the search of grace after an increase and supply. He
sees the love that works in trouble for want of faith; and the faith

that works in trouble for want of holiness. And these things he takes care of.

3. He finds *grace in those works and duties* wherein they by whom they are performed, it may be, can find none at all. As he will manifest at the last day that he observed that filth and wickedness, that perverse rebellion in the ways of wicked men, which themselves took no notice of, or at least were not thoroughly convinced about; so he will declare the faith and love which he observed in the duties of his disciples, which they never durst own in themselves. This is fully declared, Matt. xxv., from verse 34 to the end.

4. How small soever that grace be which he discovers in the souls of his, *he accepts of it, approves it*, and takes care for its preservation and increase. The life of it doth not depend on our knowledge, but his. And as these things do really tend to the relief and consolation of believers, so they do justly deserve to be more largely insisted on and more fully improved, but that the nature of our present design will not admit of it in this place.

VERSES 14–16.

In the close of this chapter the apostle gives us a summary improvement of all the foregoing discourses and arguings contained in it. Especially he insists on a double inference unto the practice of those duties which, by his former reasonings, he had evinced to be incumbent on all professors of the gospel. And these are two; the one more general, with respect unto that great end which he aims at in the whole epistle; the other containing an especial means conducing unto that end. The first is expressed in the 14th verse, the other in those two that do ensue. The first is, that we should "hold fast our profession;" which is now the third time mentioned, chap. iii. 6, 14, and here, besides sundry other times in terms equivalent. The latter consists in our application of ourselves to the Lord Jesus Christ, our "high priest," for help and assistance, to enable us so to do; for this is a great and difficult duty, which, without especial supplies of grace, we are not able to discharge.

Unto this twofold duty there is likewise proposed a double encouragement. And in these, various motives, reasons, and directions are included respectively. The first of these encouragements is expressed verse 14, consisting in sundry particulars, all tending unto our furtherance under the great duty of holding fast our profession unto the end. The other in verse 15, wherein on many grounds we are assured of the assistance which we do stand in need of; unto the use and due improvement whereof we are exhorted, verse 16.

Moreover, in these words the apostle makes a transition from what in general he had discoursed on unto the handling of that wherein his great design lay, which he had now fully made way for. And this was destructive to the life and soul of Judaism. Having, there-fore, chap. iii. 1, affirmed that Jesus Christ was "the apostle and high priest of our profession," he first undertakes the former. There-in he positively declares that he was the apostle, legate, and am-bassador of God, to reveal and declare his will unto the church. And because this was the office of Moses of old with respect unto the church of the Jews, in the giving of the law, he makes a com-parison between them; which, as it was necessary in his dealing with the Hebrews, who adhered unto, and extolled, yea, almost deified Moses, so it gave him occasion to express much of the excellency of Christ in that office, as also to declare the true nature of the missive or apostolical office of Moses, that undue apprehensions thereof might not keep them off from believing the gospel, or cause them to backslide after they had professed it. From his discourse to that purpose he educeth all his arguings, reasonings, and exhortations unto faith, obedience, and permanency in profession, which ensue in that and this chapter unto these verses. Having therefore dis-charged that work, and confirmed the first part of his proposition, namely, that the Lord Christ was the "apostle of our profession," and applied that truth to his present purpose, he returns to the other part of it, namely, his being our "high priest" also. And this was the principal thing which he aimed at in the didactical part of the whole epistle. This, therefore, he pursues from hence unto the end of the 10th chapter. The nature of the priesthood of Christ; his excellency and preference above Aaron, as vested with that office; the nature of the sacrifice that he offered, with the end, use, and efficacy of it; and, on occasion hereof, the nature of the typical priesthood, sacrifices, and law of old, are the subject of his glorious discourses. And this ocean of spiritual truth and heavenly mysteries are we now launching into. And therefore do we most humbly implore the guidance and conduct of that good and holy Spirit, who is promised unto us to lead us into all truth; for who is suffi-cient for these things?

In these verses, then, the apostle makes a transition unto, and an entrance upon his great design. But whereas his direct scope and aim was to prevail with the Hebrews, and all others in the like con-dition with them,—that is, all professors of the gospel,—unto per-manency and stability in faith and obedience, he doth here, as elsewhere, fill up his transition with insinuations of duties, attended with exhortations and encouragements unto the performance of them. And this is the only useful way of teaching in all practical sciences. The principles of them are to be accompanied with instances, ex-amples, and exhortations unto practice, wherein their end consisteth. And in so doing, the apostle plainly declares what we ought to be intent upon in our learning and consideration of the truths of the gospel. The end of them all is to teach us to live unto God, and to bring us to the enjoyment of him; therefore to the further-ance of our faith and obedience are they continually to be ap-plied.

VERSE 14.

Ἔχοντες οὖν ἀρχιερέα μέγαν διεληλυθότα τοὺς οὐρανούς, Ἰησοῦν τὸν Υἱὸν τοῦ Θεοῦ, κρατῶμεν τῆς ὁμολογίας.

Seeing then that we have a great high priest, that is passed into [*through*] the heavens, Jesus the Son of God, let us hold fast our profession.

There being no difficulty in the words in the original, nor much diversity in translations, we shall cast what is worth observation on their account into the exposition of the words itself.

Ἔχοντες οὖν, "habentes igitur," "having therefore;" or, as ours, "seeing then that we have." And so the Syriac, "whereas, therefore, we have." The illative οὖν declares ᾿Ἔχοντες οὖν. the relation of what is under assertion unto that which went before. That which the apostle is now instructing us in, directing us unto, is educed from what he had before laid down. It is not a conse-quence in way of argument that is here inferred, but the consequent in way of duty: "Seeing we have."

Ἀρχιερέα μέγαν, "pontificem magnum." Some translations, as the Arabic and Syriac, in this place transpose the words, and place the person of Christ as the immediate object ᾿Ἀρχιερέα μέ-γαν. of our "having," or that which the word ἔχοντες doth firstly and formally respect: "Having Jesus the Son of God to be a high priest." And in this way the person of Jesus Christ should be proposed unto us firstly, and that described by the ad-junct of his office, and his acting therein, "he passed into heaven." But in the original it is a "high priest," as formally considered, which is the object proposed unto us. And he is described,—1. By his quality and condition; he is "passed through the heavens." 2. By the particular nomination of his person; he is "Jesus the Son of God." In the condition wherein we are, we stand in need of the help and assistance of a high priest. Such a one we have. We have a high priest, as they had of old; and this such a one as "is passed through the heavens, even Jesus the Son of God." This is the order of the words.

Ἀρχιερέα μέγαν. Arab., "the chief prince of the priests;" rightly as to sense, because of the twofold use of the word ἀρχιερεύς, for it is applied to denote two sorts of persons. First, it signifies him who was eminently and signally so called, the high priest,—that is Aaron, and the chief of his family, who succeeded him in the office of the high priesthood. In the Old Testament he is called הַכֹּהֵן הַגָּדוֹל, ὁ ἱερεὺς ὁ μέγας, "the great priest." This is frequently expressed by ἀρ-χιερεύς, as the Latins do it by "pontifex," and "pontifex maximus." Again, the word is often used to denote them who were the princi-pal heads, rulers, or leaders of any one of the twenty-four orders which the priests were cast into for the service of the temple, 1 Chron. xxiv. These are those which are intended in those places where some are expressed by name, and it is added, "They and their brethren;" that is, those who being of the same order with them, were yet in dignity not so conspicuous as themselves. And these in the gospel are frequently called ἀρχιερεῖς, as Matt. ii. 4, xvi. 21, xx. 18, xxi. 15, and in the other evangelists frequently. And when the word is so applied we render it by "chief priests," to distinguish them intended from the "high priest" properly so called, who was one set over them all, the peculiar successor of Aaron.

If the word ἀρχιερεύς be here taken in the latter sense, as it may denote a "pontifex minorum gentium," a high priest of the second rank and order, one of the chief priests, then the adjunct of μέγας, "great," is discriminative; showing that it is not they who were merely so, but he only who was הַכֹּהֵן הַגָּדוֹל, "the great priest," "pon-tifex maximus," that is alluded unto. But if ἀρχιερεύς do of itself denote the single high priest, Aaron, or his successor, as most fre-quently it doth, then μέγας, "great," is added κατ᾽ ἐξαίρετον, by way of eminency, and is accumulative with respect unto Aaron. He is a great high priest in comparison of him, exalted above him, more excellent, glorious, powerful, and able than he. And this is that which is intended in the words; for the especial design of the apostle is to compare him with Aaron, and not with any inferior priests, as we shall see in his ensuing discourses. Therefore "a great high priest," is one eminently, excellently, gloriously so, and that on the accounts mentioned in his subjoined description.

Διεληλυθότα τοὺς οὐρανούς, "that is passed into the heavens." So our translation; in which expression the thing intended Διεληλυθότα τοὺς οὐρανούς. is plain, but the difficulty that is in the words is as plainly concealed, and somewhat of their proper sense and meaning. Syr., "who is ascended into heaven;" laying the emphasis upon and directing our thoughts unto his ascension, and not to his present abode in heaven, which ours seem to point unto, "who is passed into the heavens." Ethiop., "who came from heaven into the world;" which kind of mistakes are not infrequent with that interpreter. Διέρχομαι is "pertranseo," "to pass through;" that is, any one place into another. 1 Cor. xvi. 5: Ὅταν Μακεδονίαν διέλθω· Μακεδονίαν γὰρ διέρχομαι·—"When I shall pass through Macedonia; for I pass through Macedonia." So Acts xv. 41, John iv. 4. And no other signification can it have in this place: "Is passed through τοὺς οὐρανούς," " the heavens." Διέρχεσθαι τοὺς οὐρανούς, is plainly to "pass through the heavens," and not to " pass into them." Neither the sense nor construction of the words will allow any such interpretation; nor will any thing else but his passing through the heavens answer the apostle's design.

The " heavens," therefore, are taken two ways:—First, and most frequently, to denote the place of God's glorious residence, the holy habitation of God, the resting-place of blessed souls, and palace of the great King, where is his throne, and thousands of his holy ones stand ministering before him. This heaven the Lord Christ did not pass through, but into, when ἀνελήφθη ἐν δόξῃ, he was "taken up into glory," 1 Tim. iii. 16. There he sits, " on the right hand of the Majesty on high;" and these heavens "must receive him until the times of restitution" shall come, Acts iii. 21. Secondly, The " heavens" are taken for the air, as when mention is made of the " fowls of heaven;" that is, which "fly above the earth in the open firmament of heaven," Gen. i. 20: as also for the ethereal regions, the orbs of the sun, moon, and stars, which are set " for lights in the firmament of heaven," Gen. i. 15,—the aspectable heavens above us, which " declare the glory of God," and " shew his handywork," Ps. xix. 1; which he " garnished by his Spirit" for that end, Job xxvi. 13. These are the heavens here intended. And concerning them our apostle says again of our high priest, ὑψηλότερος τῶν οὐρανῶν γενόμενος, Heb. vii. 26, " made higher than the heavens;" he passed through them, and was exalted above them. These ethereal regions the disciples looked towards when he was " taken up into glory," Acts i. 9, 10. So Eph. iv. 10, " He ascended up, far above all heavens." He passed through them, and ascended above them, into that which is called "the third heaven," or the "heaven of heavens," where is his blessed residence.

This being the sense of the words, we may nextly inquire into what the apostle peculiarly designs to instruct us in by them. And this will appear from the consideration of what it is that in this expression he alludes unto. Now, it is the high priest peculiarly so called that he hath respect unto; and he designs an explanation of what was, in and by him, typically represented unto the church of old. Known it is, that he was the principal officer of the church in things immediately pertaining unto the worship of God. And the chief or most signal part of his duty in the discharge of his office, consisted in his annual entrance into the most holy place, on the day of expiation, with the services thereunto belonging. This is at large described, Lev. xvi. And herein three things were eminent:—

1. That he departed out of the *sight of the people,* yea, and of all the ministering priests also. The people were without in the court; and the priests that ministered in the tabernacle, when he was to

open the veil to enter into the holy place, left the tabernacle, that they might not look in after him: Lev. xvi. 17, "There shall be no man in the tabernacle of the congregation when he goeth in to make an atonement in the holy place, until he come out, and have made an atonement." 2. In this entrance he *passed through the second veil* of the tabernacle, which received him and hid him by the closing of the curtains from the sight of all. 3. In the place whither he thus went were the *especial pledges* of the presence and tokens of the covenant of God, Lev. xvi. 2. How all these things were really and in a glorious manner accomplished in and by our high priest, the apostle declares in these words. For,—1. He had a holy place to pass into. He entered into the holy place not made with hands, even "heaven itself, to appear in the presence of God for us," Heb. ix. 24; that is, the heaven of heavens, the place of the glorious residence of the majesty of God. 2. Hereinto he passed through these aspectable heavens; which the apostle compareth unto the second veil of the temple, because they interpose between us and the holy sanctuary whereinto he entered. Hence, when in his great trial and testimony he miraculously enabled Stephen to see into the heavenly place, where he is in glory on the right hand of God, these heavens were opened, Acts vii. 55, 56. The curtains of this veil were turned aside, that he might have a view of the glory behind them. 3. By these heavens was he taken and hid out of the sight of all men in his entrance, Acts i. 9, 10. Thus, in answer to the type of old, he passed through the veil of these heavens, into the glorious presence of God, to appear there as our intercessor.

Ἰησοῦν τὸν Υἱὸν τοῦ Θεοῦ, "Jesus the Son of God."

Ἰησοῦν τὸν Υἱὸν τοῦ Θεοῦ. Translations do not well express the emphasis of these words, through the interposition of the article, Ἰησοῦν τὸν Υἱὸν,—the Son eminently, peculiarly, *that* Son of God; that is, the natural, only-begotten Son of the Father. And there is in the words a double designation of the person of our high priest; first by his name, and then by his relation unto God.

1. By his name; that is, "Jesus,"—a name given him from the work he had to do. He was to "save his people."

Ἰησοῦν. Jesus, a saviour. Matt. i. 21, Καλέσεις τὸ ὄνομα αὐτοῦ Ἰησοῦν, saith the angel; "Thou shalt call his name Jesus." For what cause? Saith he, Αὐτὸς γὰρ σώσει τὸν λαὸν αὐτοῦ ἀπὸ τῶν ἁμαρτιῶν αὐτῶν,—"For" (or "because") "he shall save his people from their sins." So our apostle calls him Ἰησοῦν τὸν ῥυόμενον,—"Jesus the de-liverer," 1 Thess. i. 10. Our high priest is our saviour; and he is so [that is, the latter] in a great measure by his being so [that is, the former]. And this name was given him as born of a virgin: "She shall bring forth a son, and thou shalt call his name Jesus." It doth not, therefore, in this place *only*—nay, *not so much*—denote him by his work of saving, according to the signification of his name, "Jesus;" but declares his human nature, whereof he was made partaker " that he might be a merciful high priest," wherein he was called by that name.

2. He describes him by his relation unto God: Τὸν Υἱὸν τοῦ Θεοῦ,—"that Son of God;" the eternal Son of God. The reason and nature of this sonship of our high priest hath been elsewhere declared. At present it may suffice *Τὸν Υἱὸν τοῦ Θεοῦ.* to observe, that his divine nature is included in this appellation; for in his one person, as comprising both these natures, is he our high priest, as he is Θεάνθρωπος, God and man in one. And we are here minded of it as a great encouragement unto our duty, expressed in the next words.

Κρατῶμεν τῆς ὁμολογίας, " let us hold fast our profession." Vulg. Lat., in some copies, " spei et fidei nostræ," "of our hope and faith;" words taken from chap. iii. 6, which here *Κρατῶμεν τῆς ὁμολογίας.* have no place. " Hold fast the profession,"—that is, which we make, or have made; and so " our profession," as we supply the words.

Two things are to be inquired into for the opening of these words: —1. What is meant by ὁμολογία, or " profession;" 2. What is included in κρατῶμεν, " let us hold fast."

1. For the word ὁμολογία, it hath been opened, and the thing itself intended somewhat spoken unto, on chap. iii. 1, where the Lord Christ is called " the apostle and high priest of our profession." I shall therefore here only so far treat of it as it contains the duty which the apostle exhorts us unto, and wherein all the lines of his discourse do meet and centre. This makes it assuredly a matter of singular consideration, as being that about which he doth so greatly labour.

Our ὁμολογία is our "*professed subjection to the gospel of Christ,*" 2 Cor. ix. 13; or the subjection of our souls in the acknowledgment of the power and authority of Jesus Christ in the gospel: ʹΥποταγή ὁμολογίας. It contains both our *secret subjection* unto the gospel, and our *solemn declaration* of it. The former, which respects the matter of our profession, is συνειδήσεως ἀγαθῆς ἐπερώτημα εἰς Θεὸν δι' ἀναστάσεως ʹΙησοῦ Χριστοῦ, 1 Pet. iii. 21;—' "the answer" (or "reply") " of a good conscience," by virtue of the resurrection of Christ, unto the demands of God in the precepts and promises of the gospel.' And it hath two parts:—(1.) Faith in Christ. (2.) Obedience unto him; the "obedience of faith," Rom. i. 5.

(1.) Faith is the root, and obedience the fruit of our profession. And that faith which constitutes evangelical profession is distinctly acted on Christ, the Son of God, the mediator of the covenant, the king, priest, and prophet of his church. This he calls for, John

xiv. 1, " Ye believe in God, believe also in me," expressly. See John iii. 18, 36; chap. vii. 38. This, I say, makes our profession formally evangelical, distinguishing it from that of believers under the old testament. Their faith was directly in God as one, Deut. vi. 4; consequentially in the Messiah, as promised. Ours is express in Christ also, John xvii. 3; and in the Father by him, 1 Pet. i. 21.

(2.) Unto faith is added *obedience*, which is indeed inseparable from it. See a full description of it, Rom. vi. 22. It may be considered two ways:—[1.] As it is internal and absolutely spiritual, or the constant acting of all the graces of the Spirit of God, unto purification and holiness, 2 Cor. vii. 1; 1 Thess. v. 23; Acts xv. 9. This belongs unto our profession, not absolutely as profession, but as sincere and saving; on which account we ought to hold it fast. [2.] As it is external also, in the diligent observation of all gospel commands in our course and practice. And these are of two sorts:—1*st*. The *moral duties* of a holy conversation, Phil. i. 27; Tit. ii. 10–13. By a failure herein our whole profession is overthrown, Phil. iii. 17, 18; Tit. i. 16; 2 Tim. ii. 19. 2*dly*. The *instituted duties* of holy gospel worship, Matt. xxviii. 20. And herein consists that part of our profession which the apostle in this epistle doth principally intend, as hath been declared. This is the matter of our profession; herein consists our subjection to the gospel.

To complete our profession, yea, to constitute our ὁμολογία, there is required that we make a solemn declaration of our subjection unto the gospel in these things. And this is made two ways. (1.) By works. (2.) By words.

(1.) Our profession by works, is our constant and solemn observation of all Christ's commands in and concerning gospel-worship, Matt. xxviii. 20; John xiv. 15, xv. 14. And the discharge of our duty herein is to be attended, [1.] With prudence; and that, 1*st*. Not to provoke the world causelessly, by any irregularities of misguided zeal, or other disorders, Matt. x. 16, 1 Cor. x. 32, 2 Cor. vi. 3; 2*dly*. Not to cast ourselves into dangers or troubles without just cause, call, or warrant, Matt. x. 23. [2.] With constancy and confidence; so as, 1*st*. Not to be terrified with any persecutions or troubles which may befall us on the account of the gospel, 1 Pet. iii. 14, Phil. i. 28; 2*dly*. Not on any account to decline the constant observance of the duties of worship required of us, Heb. x. 25.

(2.) By words; for " with the mouth confession is made unto salvation," Rom. x. 10. And this also is twofold:—[1.] With respect unto all times in general, 1 Pet. iii. 15. We are on all occasions to declare whose servants we are, and whom we own as our Lord and Master. [2.] Unto especial seasons. 1*st*. Of *temptation*. Such arise from company, which may be so circumstanced as to awe us or corrupt us, that we shall not own the gospel as we ought. So

it befell Peter in the highest instance, Matt. xxvi. 70. And so are
others in lesser degrees foiled every day. 2dly. Of *persecution.*
Then is our profession to be turned into confession, or we lose it.
The oral, open avowing of the Lord Christ, his ways and worship,
in and under persecution, is the touchstone of all profession, Matt.
x. 32, 33; 1 Cor. iii. 13. This is the profession we are to hold fast.

2. Κρατῶμεν, "let us hold it fast." So have we rendered κατάσχωμεν, chap. iii. 6. But this word is more emphatical than
that, and intimates another frame of mind, and a more   Κρατῶμεν.
severe endeavour: κρατεῖν is to hold a thing "strongly," "firmly,"
"totis viribus," "with all our strength," by all lawful means, with resolution and intension of mind. For the word is from κράτος,—that
is, "power," "strength," "efficacy;" which are to be exercised in
the holding fast intended: Rev. ii. 25, "That which ye have κρα-
τήσατε ἄχρις οὗ ἂν ἥξω," "hold fast," 'with all care, against all opposition,' "till I come." So chap. iii. 11, Κράτει ὃ ἔχεις, ἵνα μηδεὶς λάβῃ
τὸν στέφανόν σου: "Hold fast,"—that is, with all thy might, with
all diligence and intension of mind, "what thou hast," as a man
would hold fast his crown, if any should attempt to take it from
him or deprive him of it. And this word is used concerning the
Pharisees, with respect unto their traditions; which they adhered so
firmly and resolutely unto, that nothing could move them or prevail with them to the contrary, Mark vii. 3, Κρατοῦντες τὴν παρά-
δοσιν τῶν πρεσβυτέρων,—"Holding fast" (or "tenaciously") "the tradition of the elders." So also of them who, having entertained false
and noxious opinions, are obstinate in their adherence to them:
Rev. ii. 15, Οὕτως ἔχεις καὶ σὺ κρατοῦντας τὴν διδαχὴν τῶν Νικολαϊ-
τῶν,—"So hast thou them who," against light and persuasions,
"retain the doctrine of the Nicolaitanes." Wherefore the sense of
the command here given is, that we should with our utmost ability
and diligence hold fast against all oppositions, and take care that
we lose not our profession after we are once engaged in it.

So, then, this verse containeth the prescription of a duty, with a
motive and encouragement unto the due performance of it. The
duty is expressed in these last words, "Let us hold fast our profession." And the reason for it, with an encouragement unto it, in
those which go before, "Seeing then we have a great high priest,
that is passed into the heavens, Jesus the Son of God." And this
is further amplified by the declaration of his qualifications, verse 15,
and an exhortation to make use of and improve his assistance in
this matter, verse 16, as we shall see afterwards. At present we
may take some observations from this verse, according to the exposition of the words already given, which will further direct us to
answer in our practice the mind of the Holy Ghost in this matter.
Now, there is included in the words,—

Obs. I. First, that great opposition is, and always will be, made
unto the permanency of believers in their profession.

This the word of exhortation unto it plainly intimates. It is
" injectâ manu fortiter retinere,"—to " lay hold of a thing, and to
retain it with all our might," as if it were ready every moment to
be taken from us with a violent and strong hand; it is to keep a
thing as a man keeps his treasure when it is ready to be seized on
by thieves and robbers. This argues great opposition, and no small
hazard thereon ensuing. So our blessed Saviour informs us, Matt.
vii. 25. When men hear the word, they build a house by profession. This all who make profession do, whether they build upon
the rock or upon the sand. And when this house is built, " the
rain will descend, and the floods will come, and the winds will
blow and beat upon it." Profession will be assaulted and pressed
by all manner of hazardous and dangerous oppositions. And if the
house be not well secured, it will fall,—if our profession be not well
guarded, it will be lost. What our Lord Jesus told Peter with
respect unto this very matter, is even so concerning all professors.
When he was led to speak with much confidence,—which his present
convictions of duty and resolutions for its performance prompted
him unto,—that he would abide in his profession, and never forsake
him, whatever other men might do; he answers, " Simon, Simon,
Satan hath sought to winnow thee," Luke xxii. 31, 32. He minds
him, that although he had called him Peter, for the unmovableness of
that Rock which his faith was fixed on, yet he would appear in
himself to be but Simon still,—a man, exposed to danger, and easy
to be prevailed against; and therefore he might do well, in the midst
of his confidence, to consider his dangers and the surprisals that he
might be overtaken withal. And the same is the condition of all
professors, the best and meanest, the strongest and weakest.

From this opposition, our continuance in profession is called
" enduring," Matt. xxiv. 13, 'O δὲ ὑπομείνας εἰς τέλος, οὗτος σωθήσεται,
—" He that patiently tolerateth" (beareth opposition) " unto the
end shall be saved." So we render ὑπομονή, Rom. ii. 7, " patient
continuance." And to the same purpose are the words προσκαρτερέω,
Acts ii. 42, and προσκαρτέρησις, Eph. vi. 18, used, and of the same
signification,—" constantly to abide and endure against oppositions."
So is the word commonly applied. Men endure hunger, cold, bonds,
imprisonment, the pains of death. They are hard things that men
endure. "Durate" is the word of encouragement in difficulties:
" Durate et vosmet rebus servate secundis. Durare, est verbum
quod perferendis malis convenit," Donat in Virg. Æn. i. 211. There
is, then, a supposition of a conflict with all sorts of evil, where we
are enjoined to " endure;" that is, to continue in our course with
patience, courage, and constancy. Hence are the multiplied cau-

tions that are given us, especially in this epistle, to take heed that we be not prevailed against and cast down from our stability by these oppositions. See 2 John 8; Rev. ii. 24–26, iii. 2.

We are exceedingly apt to deceive ourselves in this matter. Desires, false hopes, appearing helps, do insinuate themselves into our minds, and prevail to ingenerate a persuasion that we shall not meet with any great difficulties in our profession. And these self-deceivings do exceedingly unprepare the mind for what we have to encounter, which the apostle warns us against, 1 Pet. iv. 12, 13.

The principles, causes, reasons, and means, of the opposition that is made to the profession of believers, are commonly handled. Could we take but one view of that constant preparation which there is amongst "principalities and powers," those "spiritual wickednesses in high places," in the world and all its fulness, and in the deceitfulness of sin which dwelleth in us, for an opposition unto our profession, we would either constantly stand upon our guard to defend it, or presently give it up as that which is not tenable. See Eph. vi. 10-13.

Obs. II. It is our duty, in the midst of all oppositions, to hold our profession firm and steadfast unto the end. This is the substance of what we are here exhorted and pressed unto, and the great design of the apostle in this whole epistle; which also we have occasionally insisted on in sundry precedent passages.

What this profession is hath been declared. The principle of it is "faith in God" by Christ Jesus. The fruits of it are the whole "obedience of faith," or "a conversation in all things becoming the gospel," "adorning the doctrine of our Saviour" in all holiness and godliness. And it is expressed by a constant observation of all the ordinances and institutions of worship appointed by Christ or his authority, with an open confession of him at all times. For by such institutions did God in all ages try and exercise the faith and obedience of the church, whence they were the means of giving glory to himself in the world. And from this expression of them do our faith and obedience take the denomination of "profession." And thereby are they proved in this world, and must be tried at the last day.

This profession we are to hold in the manner expressed in the opening of the words; that is, with watchfulness, diligence, constancy, and our utmost endeavour in all of them. And this duty hath respect unto the contrary sins, which the apostle dehorts us from. Now these fall under two heads:—1. *Apostasy,* or a total desertion of our profession. 2. *Declension,* or going back gradually from our diligence, progress, and attainments in it; which make way for the former evil.

1. Some totally fall off from their profession. These the apostle describes and reflects upon, chap. vi., x. In which places we must take their sin and punishment under consideration. And against

this evil it is our duty to "hold fast our profession." None doubt of it until they are under the power of the contrary evil, and are blinded or hardened thereby. And this total desertion from the gospel is twofold:—(1.) *Express*, by an open abrenunciation of it. This we hear not of much amongst us, because none is tempted thereunto. The prodigious eruptions of some men's atheism we consider not. (2.) *Interpretative*, when men really cast off all inward regard unto the authority of Christ in the gospel, and their outward compliance with any thing required in it is on motives foreign to the gospel itself; and this too much abounds in the world.

Our apostle supplies us with considerations of the greatest and highest nature that can be conceived. In brief,—(1.) The *glory of God* in Christ is in the highest manner concerned in it. Every sin tends to the dishonour of God, all sinners dishonour him; but all is nothing, as it were, to the despite that is done to him by this sin. So it is described, Heb. x. 29. It is a "treading under foot the Son of God,"—an act of the highest despite, malice, and contempt that a creature can be capable of. (2.) *Assured destruction attends it*, and that in a peculiar, terrible, and dreadful manner, Heb. x. 29–31; 2 Pet. ii. 1. It is, therefore, undoubtedly our duty and our wisdom to "hold fast our profession," so as neither by the blindness of our minds nor sensuality of life to lose and forego it.

2. It is so as to the degrees of it. All the parts of our profession have their degrees whereby they are varied. Faith is strong or weak, stable or infirm. Obedience may be more or less exact, precise, and fruitful in good works. Our observation of instituted ordinances of worship may be exact and circumspect, or loose and negligent. In holding fast our profession, an endeavour to keep up to the degrees that we have attained, and a pressing forward in them all toward perfection, are required of us. That which our Lord Jesus Christ blames in his churches, Rev. ii., iii., is the decay in their profession as to these degrees. Their faith, their love, their diligence, were decayed; and they performed not the works they had some time been fruitful in. And in all these things are men liable to let go their profession. Again, growth and progress in all these is required of professors. The kingdom 'of God is a growing thing, and ought to be so in all them in whom it is by its grace, and who are in it by the observation of its laws. Where growth is not, profession is not held firm. This is, in general, the nature of the duty we are charged with. The principal intendment of this verse, and those following, is to declare the encouragement and assistance which we have in Christ for its discharge, as he is our high priest; which must further be insisted on, and therein a fuller explication of the things contained in this verse will be given. And the whole of what is aimed at may be comprised in this observation,—

Obs. III. Believers have great encouragement unto and assistance in the constancy of their profession, by and from the priesthood of Jesus Christ.

So it is expressly laid down in the text, and to that end is it by us to be improved. And to this purpose is,—1. The priesthood of Christ in itself, and our relation thereunto, proposed and asserted; " we have an high priest." 2. Described,—(1.) By the qualification of our high priest; he is " a great high priest:" (2.) By his action, and his exaltation therein; he is " passed through the heavens:" (3.) By his name and nature; he is " Jesus the Son of God." And from every one of these considerations we have both encouragement and assistance in the great duty of holding fast our profession.

1. The Lord Christ is a " high priest;" and we have in our obedience and profession a relation unto him,—he is our high priest, the " high priest of our profession." He is the " high priest over the house of God," not only to direct us in our profession, but also to assist us in it. The difficulty of this duty lies in the opposition that is made unto it by sin, Satan, and the world, as we have showed: he that hath not found it never yet knew what it was to profess the gospel. And the effects of it lie under our view every day; they have done so in all ages. And we can never be jealous enough of our own hearts and ways, lest we should be made an example unto others, as others have been unto us. But herein lies our help and relief; for,—

(1.) Whilst we are in this condition our high priest *pitieth* us and hath compassion on us, Heb. ii. 17, 18. This is part of his duty and office, chap. v. 2. And there is some help in pity, some relief in compassion. Want hereof our Saviour complained of as a great aggravation of his distresses, Ps. lxix. 20: " I am," saith he, " full of heaviness: I looked for some to take pity," (or " lament with me,") " but there was none; and for comforters, but I found none." Compassion, indeed, doth not communicate new strength; yet it greatly refresheth the spirits of them that suffer, especially if it be from those whom they greatly value. And this we are assured of in and from our high priest, in all the oppositions and sufferings that we meet withal in the course of our profession. See chap. ii. 17, and the two verses following in this place. He is himself on his throne of glory, on the right hand of the Majesty on high, in eternal rest and blessedness, as having finished his personal works and labour, as hath been showed; but from the habitation of his holiness he looks on his labouring, suffering, tempted disciples, and is " afflicted in all their afflictions," and is full of compassion towards them. ' So,' saith he, ' was I tempted, so was I opposed. And what thus befalls them is for my sake, and not for their own;' and his bowels are moved to-

wards them.   Whose heart will not the consideration hereof refresh?
whose spirit will it not revive?

(2.) As our high priest, he gives us *actual help* and assistance in
this case.   The ways whereby he doth this have been partly declared on chap. ii. 18; and must yet be spoken unto, verse 16 of this
chapter.   At present I shall only show in general that the aid which
he gives us is sufficient to secure our profession, and conquer the
opposition that is made against it; for, as hath been observed, there
are three parts of it,—our *faith*, our *obedience* in general, and our
especial *observance of instituted worship*.   And there are three especial principles of the opposition made to them:—

[1.] Our faith is opposed by Satan and his temptations in chief,
with a contribution of aid from the world and our own corruptions.
Faith's overthrow is his principal design, Luke xxii. 31, 32.   No such
irreconcilable enemies as faith and the devil.   And this adversary
is prevailed against by our high priest.   He hath contended with
him, bruised his head, conquered him, bound him, spoiled him,
triumphed over him, and destroyed him, Gen. iii. 15; Col. ii. 15;
Heb. ii. 14, 15.   And shall we suffer ourselves to be deprived of
our profession by one thus dealt withal in our behalf?   He shall
not prevail in his attempt.   [2.] Our obedience is opposed principally by our own corruptions, aided by Satan and the world.   These
"war against our souls," 1 Pet. ii. 11; and tend unto death, James i.
14, 15.   Whence our apostle warns us to take heed that these prove
not the cause of our apostasy, Heb. iii. 13.   And against these also
there is relief for us in and by our high priest; for as "he was manifested to destroy the works of the devil," 1 John iii. 8, or all the effects
of his first temptation in our hearts; so whatever evil it intends towards us, there is a remedy provided for it and against it in his
grace, his blood, and by his Spirit.   [3.] Our profession, as formally
such, consisting in the diligent observance of the laws and ways of
Christ, is continually opposed by the world, not without assistance
from Satan and the treacheries of indwelling sin.   But he also hath
" overcome the world," John xvi. 33.   He hath overcome it *for* us,
and he will overcome it *in* us.   And who, on this account, would not
be encouraged to contend earnestly for the preservation of that profession wherein they are sure they shall be assisted?

Professors have an *aim* and an end in their profession.   They do
not " run in vain," nor " fight uncertainly," nor " beat the air," in
what they do.   Now their great design is to have their profession,
and their persons therein, "accepted with God."   Without this they
must acknowledge themselves to be " of all men most miserable."
For what would it avail them to spend their time in fears, hazards,
conflicts, sorrows and troubles in this world, and when they have
done all, be rejected of God, and have their everlasting portion

amongst them who take the full of their sins and satisfactions in this world? And if it be so, why do they yet suffer persecution? And yet there are two things that do vehemently assault their faith and hope in this matter:—[1.] The sinfulness and unworthiness of their own persons. Whatever be the duties that they perform, yet they find their persons on many accounts so vile, as that both they and their duties may be justly rejected of God. Hence they suppose themselves to defile whatever they touch. The guilt and defilement of their consciences by sin perplex their thoughts when they consider what it is to appear before the great and holy God. [2.] They find that even the duties themselves wherein their profession doth consist are so weak, so mixed and imperfect, as it is hard for them to conceive how they should obtain acceptance with God. Their endeavours are weak and faint, their strivings against sin uneven and uncertain, their prayers ofttimes languid, and a fading is on all their duties. And say they often in themselves, 'What ground of hope is there that a profession so made up will be accepted with God, and rewarded by him?'

But against all these considerations believers have relief in their relation to this high priest; for in this matter lies the principal part of his office. As such he hath undertaken to render our persons and duties accepted with God. This he respects both in his oblation and intercession; by which two ways he dischargeth the duties of this office :—

[1.] By them he gives acceptance with God unto our persons. For as he hath "made reconciliation for our sins," Heb. ii. 17, so he hath "brought in everlasting righteousness," Dan. ix. 24. Yea, he himself is "our righteousness," Jer. xxiii. 6. "In him have we righteousness and strength," Isa. xlv. 24; he being "made of God unto us righteousness," 1 Cor. i. 30; having been "made a curse for us," that the blessing of faithful Abraham might be ours, Gal. iii. 13, 14; who "believed God, and it was imputed unto him for righteousness," Gal. iii. 6. So that although we have no such righteousness of our own as on the account whereof our persons may be accepted with God, yet upon the account of him and his who is ours, we shall not fail thereof.

[2.] He dealeth so likewise in reference unto our duties: for, as he "bears the iniquity of our holy things," Exod. xxviii. 38, that they should not be rejected because of any sinful imperfections cleaving to them; so he adds unto them the sweet incense and perfume of his own righteousness, Rev. viii. 3, 4, which causeth them to come up with a grateful and acceptable savour before the Lord.

And these few things have I mentioned as instances of the encouragements that we have to abide in our profession in the midst of all hazards and against all oppositions, from the consideration of this one thing, that we have a high priest;—the end aimed at in this place by our apostle.

2. There is weight added hereunto from the *qualification* of the person vested with that office, here expressed. He is "a great high priest." He is so both comparatively and absolutely. He is so in comparison of others so called; and not only so,—for he may be great in comparison of another who is but little in himself,—but he is so absolutely also, as we shall see afterwards.

(1.) He is great *comparatively* with respect unto Aaron; which the apostle, as was showed, hath in this assertion regard unto: for he is now entering upon his great design, or showing his answering unto Aaron, and his pre-eminence above him. The high priest, in his office, sacred garments, and administrations, was the principal glory of the Judaical church. If that office ceased, all their solemn worship was to cease. And so excellent was his office, so beautiful were his garments, so glorious was his work and ministry, that these Hebrews, though now in some measure instructed in the doctrine and worship of the gospel, could not be persuaded utterly to relinquish that sacred service which he had the conduct of. And here lay the principal occasion of their obstinate adherence to Mosaical institutions. They had a high priest whose order and service they were exceedingly pleased withal. The prevalency of these thoughts on their minds our apostle obviates, by letting them know that they should undergo no loss or disadvantage by the relinquishment of him; inasmuch as in that profession which they were called unto by the gospel they had in like manner a high priest, and that " a great high priest,"—that is, one incomparably exalted and preferred above Aaron and his successors; which he afterwards invincibly demonstrates. And hereby he presseth them to constancy in profession, the duty at present proposed to them. For if God had appointed destruction unto him who forsook the worship and service of the law under the guidance of Aaron and his sons, what must and will their lot and portion be who shall forsake and desert the worship of the new testament, when we have a high priest far more excellent and glorious than they?

(2.) He is *absolutely* great: and this the apostle proves by a double instance, wherein he gives a further description of him;—[1.] By his exaltation; [2.] By his name and person.

[1.] He is "a great high priest," because he is "passed through the heavens." The triumphant passage of the Lord Christ into glory is that which is expressed in these words.

But for the right understanding hereof some things must be premised. As,—1*st*, That the person of the Lord Christ, in all that he did, was still clothed with *all his offices.* Yet, 2*dly*, In sundry things he exerciseth the power and faculty of *one office,* and not of another immediately. Some things he did as a king, and some things as a priest, but he is still both king and priest who doth them all. *3dly*, In some things he puts forth the power of *both these offices* at the same time and in the same manner, though with different respects. Thus, in his passing through the heavens as king, it was his triumph over all his enemies, and his glorious ascension into his throne, or " sitting down on the right hand of the Majesty on high;" as priest, it was his entrance through the veil into the holy place not made with hands, " to appear in the presence of God for us." This is that which is here principally intended, but I shall explain the whole; because even his acting as king, though it belongs not unto him as a priest, yet it doth to his glory as he is " a great high priest." And there are three things which herein set out his greatness and glory.

1*st*. His *passage itself;* concerning which sundry things are observable, as, (1*st*.) His *entrance* into it, or the time and place when and where he began his triumphant entry into heaven. These are recorded Acts i. 9–12. Forty days after his resurrection, assembling his disciples he spake unto them of the kingdom of God. " And when he had spoken these things, while they beheld, he was taken up; and a cloud received him out of their sight. And while they looked steadfastly toward heaven as he went up, behold, two men stood by them in white apparel; which also said, Ye men of Galilee, why stand ye gazing up into heaven? this same Jesus, which is taken from you into heaven, shall so come in like manner as ye have seen him go into heaven. Then returned they unto Jerusalem from the mount called Olivet, which is from Jerusalem a sabbath-day's journey." The time is expressed verse 3. It was forty days after he was alive, " after his passion." As he went forty days in the wilderness to be tempted of the devil before he entered on his ministry, so he continued forty days in the world triumphing over him after he had finished his ministry. But the chief reason hereof was, that whereas his apostles, who were to be the eye-witnesses of his resurrection, could not bear his continual presence with them, he might have opportunity to show himself unto them by " many infallible signs and tokens," Acts i. 3. The place was mount Olivet, " a sabbath-day's journey from Jerusalem," verse 12. This place was near unto Bethany, for Luke affirms that " he led his disciples as far as to Bethany," chap. xxiv. 50; which was a village near that mount, " about fifteen furlongs from Jerusalem," John xi. 18. The Jews constantly affirm that a sabbath-day's journey was the space of two thousand cubits, which amount not to above seven furlongs of our measure; so that John had respect unto some other measure among the Jews, or Bethany was directly on the east of the mount, which took up the other space. This mount Olivet, therefore, near Bethany, was about a mile from Jerusalem. It was on the east side of the city, whither our Lord Jesus did often retreat for prayer and rest. It was a hill so high, that from the top of it a man might look into all the streets of Jerusalem, and into the temple. This was the last of his bodily presence on the earth, and the last that shall be " until the times of the restitution of all things.'.' Fabulous superstition hath feigned that on a stone he left here the impression of his feet. This was the mountain unto which " the glory of the LORD went up," when it left the temple and city of Jerusalem, Ezek. xi. 23. And so did He now who was " the brightness of his glory, and the express image of his person." With him the glory of God utterly departed from the temple and city, or the worship and people. Here he was taken up; and his disciples were ἀτενίζοντες, earnestly, carefully, with love, diligence, and delight, looking on whilst these things were doing. Those who had not long before seen him hanging on the cross between two thieves, bleeding and dying, now saw him gloriously and triumphantly taken up into heaven. From their eyes a cloud received him. Elijah was taken up, before, alive into heaven, 2 Kings ii. 11; but it was with fire and in a whirlwind, with dread and terror, insomuch that the young prophets much questioned what was become of him. But here, when his disciples were fully instructed, and were now no longer to live by sense, but by faith, whilst they earnestly and steadily looked on him as he ascended, a cloud draws the curtain, placidly interposing between him and their sight, who were not able as yet to look on what was doing within that veil.

(2dly.) This was the time and day of *heaven's triumph*. Ever since the apostasy of angels and men by sin, there had been an enmity and war between heaven and earth, pleaded by the interest of heaven in the earth here below. God had sent forth his champion, the Captain of salvation, typed out of old by Joshua, and David, and all those worthies which were employed to vanquish the enemies of the church in their especial stations. He had now finished his work, having fully conquered the first apostate, the great enemy of God, and spoiled him of his power. And he was now entering into that glory which he had left for a season to engage in the difficult and perilous service of subduing all the adversaries of God. And now was all heaven prepared for his triumphant reception. As when a great conqueror of old returned from a far country, where he had subdued the enemies of his people and brought home the leaders of them captives, all the citizens went forth with applauses and shouts of joy to meet him,—to which custom our apostle alludeth in this matter, Col. ii. 15 ; so was it with the glorious inhabitants of heaven upon the return of this victorious Captain of salvation. So the prophet describeth the fall of the oppressing tyrant of Assyria,

Isa. xiv. 9, " Hell from beneath is moved for thee to meet thee at thy coming; it stirreth up the dead for thee, even all the chief ones of the earth; it hath raised up from their thrones all the kings of the nations." He was theirs, they had looked for him, and he was to have a principal share in their condition. How much more was heaven stirred up, when the " everlasting gates were opened, and this King of glory entered in!" The psalmist expresseth it, Ps. xlvii. 5, 6, " God is gone up with a shout, the LORD with the sound of a trumpet. Sing praises to God, sing praises: sing praises unto our King, sing praises." It is the glorious ascension of the Lord Christ into his kingdom and throne which is described in that psalm; and this all are exhorted to rejoice in.

(3dly.) His *attendants* in this his passage through the heavens are also described unto us, Ps. lxviii. 17, 18: " The chariots of God are twenty thousand, even thousands of angels: the LORD is among them, as in Sinai, in the holy place. Thou hast ascended on high." And this place our apostle applies to the ascension of Christ, Eph. iv. 8. As when he descended of old upon the earth at the giving of the law on mount Sinai, he was attended with the heavenly host, who ministerially wrought all those glorious and dreadful effects which were wrought on the mount, Exod. xix.; so now in his ascension he was attended with the angels of God, who were as the chariots in his triumph, that carried and bore up the human nature, and waited on him, ready to do his will and to manifest his glory. They had received command from God to " worship him," Heb. i. 6, and now they appeared eminently in the discharge of their duty. They compassed him about with joyful acclamations, doing their obeisance unto him as to their head and king. With them, then, and by their ministry, he "passed through the heavens;"—a sight too glorious for mortal eyes to behold.

(4thly.) The *disposal of his enemies* is also declared, Ps. lxviii. 18: " He ascended on high, he led captivity captive;" that is, the authors of all bondage, of all captivity in sin and misery. See the phrase explained, Judges v. 12. And this our apostle expresseth, Col. ii. 15, " He spoiled principalities and powers,"—all the fallen, apostate angels; " making a show of them openly" in his triumph. He took them along with him in chains, tied, as it were, to his chariot wheels; making a show of them to the citizens of heaven. So dealt the old Roman conquerors with their enemies: they led them in chains, bound to their triumphal chariots, making them a spectacle to the people, and then returned them to prison, unto the time appointed for their execution. So dealt he with these implacable enemies of the glory of God and the salvation of the souls of the elect: he showed them openly, as judged, conquered, and fully subdued, remanding them to their prisons, until the time of their final doom should come. Thus did he pass through the heavens; and all the glory of God was laid open for his reception, all his saints and angels coming forth to meet him, to congratulate that success the fruits whereof they had before enjoyed.

2*dly.* His actual reception into the especial presence of God, as the end of his passage, adds to the manifestation of his greatness and glory. This our apostle declares, 1 Tim. iii. 16, 'Aνελήφθη ἐν δόξῃ,—He was "received up into glory." This himself calls his "entering into his glory," Luke xxiv. 26. See Heb. xii. 22–24. He was received gloriously into the highest heaven, the habitation of the blessed. Then and there had he his entertainment and refreshment, after all the travail of his soul. Then was the time of the espousals of his church, "the day of the gladness of his heart." There is joy in heaven upon the returning and repentance of one sinner; and what was there when He that causes them to return, and saves all that do so, was received into his glory? No heart can conceive, much less can any tongue express, the glorious reception of the human nature of Christ in heaven.

3*dly.* His exaltation, which ensued upon his reception. And this respects first God himself, and then the creation.

In respect of God the Father two things are spoken of him:— (1*st.*) That he sat down in his throne. He "overcame, and sat down with his Father in his throne," Rev. iii. 21. The throne is the place and ensign of rule and judgment. And the Father did not forego his throne, but he sits down with him in it, inasmuch as the actual administration of all rule and judgment is committed unto him, John v. 22. (2*dly.*) As he sat down in the throne, so it was "on the right hand of God," or "at the right hand of the Majesty on high." This God promised him of old, and now gave him the actual possession of it. Of these things, see our exposition on chap. i. 2–4.

In respect of others; so he had power over the whole creation given into his hand,—"all power in heaven and in earth;" concerning which, see also the digression about his kingdom and power, on chap. i. 3.

These things, as they were openly glorious, belonged unto his passing through the heavens as the king of his church and the captain of our salvation; but there was in the thing itself a respect unto his priestly office and the exercise thereof. So in his dying, the principal thing intended was the offering up of himself, through the eternal Spirit, an offering for sin and a sacrifice of atonement as a priest; but yet withal he died as a prophet also, "to bear witness unto the truth," for which cause he came into the world, John xviii. 37. So, although he thus passed through the heavens triumphantly as a king, he at the same time, and by the same action, passed through as our high priest, as they were the veil through which he entered into the holy place: which shall, God willing, be explained on chap. ix. 23, 24.

And these things belong to the greatness of our high priest upon the account of his exaltation, or his passing through the heavens; and,—

[2.] The second consideration of our high priest evincing his greatness, is taken from his name and person, or who he is. He is "Jesus the Son of God." Sundry things must be observed to manifest the necessity and usefulness hereof, namely, that our high priest is and was to be "Jesus the Son of God;"—first, absolutely "the Son of God," and then "Jesus the Son of God." But the things of the priesthood of the Son of God being handled at large in our Exercitations, I shall only here give a brief summary of them:—

1st. *Before the entrance of sin, there was no need of the office of priesthood between God and man.* Every one in his own name was to go to God with his worship; which would have been accepted according unto the law of the creation. If man, therefore, had continued in that state wherein he was made, there would have been no such office in the church of God; for it is the office of a priest to represent them acceptably unto God who in their own persons might not appear before him. This was manifest in the after solemn institution of that office, wherein the nature and work of it were declared. On all occasions that interdiction is severely repeated and inculcated, 'None shall come near but he who is of the seed of Aaron; and if any one do so, he shall be cut off.' And this God afterwards confirmed in sundry instances, especially that of Uzziah the king, who was smitten with leprosy for attempting to approach unto the altar of incense, 2 Chron. xxvi. 16–21. And, by the way, God will much more sorely revenge the sin of them who take the priestly office of the Lord Christ out of his hand; as by their false, pretended sacrifices and oblations the Papists attempt to do. Now this was needless before the entrance of sin, and therefore so was the office also; for every one had acceptance with God upon the account of his own personal interest in the covenant, as hath been showed elsewhere.

Whatever other rule, dignity, or pre-eminence there would or might have been in that state amongst men, the office of priesthood would have been needless, and would not therefore have been appointed; for it is not natural, but a mere institution. So are things among the angels. There is dignity and pre-eminence in their order. Hence some of them are called שָׂרִים רִאשֹׁנִים, "the first," or "chief princes." And this they seem to retain in their apostasy, one being everywhere represented as the head of the rest: "The devil and his angels." But every one of them was immediately to perform his service and worship unto God in his own person, without the interposition of any other on their behalf. And so would it have been with Adam and his posterity in a state of integrity and holiness.

2dly. Sin being entered into the world, there was no more worship to be performed immediately unto God. Two cannot walk together unless they be agreed, Amos iii. 3. All our obedience unto God and worship of him is our "walking before him," Gen. xvii. 1. This we cannot do, unless there be a covenant agreement between him and us. But this now by sin was utterly broken, and rendered useless as unto any such end. The agreement failing, the walking together also ceaseth. None could now obtain acceptance with God in any of their duties, on their own account, inasmuch as "all had sinned, and come short of his glory."

3dly. That the worship of God might be restored again in the world, *it was indispensably necessary that some one must interpose between sinners and the holy God.* Should they approach unto him immediately in their own names, he would be unto them a consuming fire, Isa. xxvii. 4, 5. And here, because God would not lose the glory of his grace, and other holy excellencies of his nature, but would have a revenue of glory continued unto him from the worship of his creatures here on earth; and because in his love he would not have all sinners to perish under the curse of the old covenant that they had broken; he found out and appointed, in the counsel of his will, the office of priesthood,—namely, that there should be one to transact the whole worship of sinners in the presence of God for them, and render what they should do themselves in their own persons acceptable unto him. This is the rise, reason, and foundation of that office which was undertaken by the Son of God; for,—

4thly. In this condition *no creature could undertake the office of being a priest for the church of God, which now consisted all of sinners.* This both the nature of the office itself, and the work which he was to perform that should undertake it, do declare:—

(*1st.*) For the *office* itself, it was to be a gracious interposition between God and sinners. The priest must approach unto God, even to his throne, representing the persons and worship of the church unto him, rendering them and it acceptable upon his account. Who was meet to be intrusted with this honour? who amongst the creatures could undertake this office? The best of them stand in need of goodness and condescension, to obtain and continue their own acceptance with him; for in the strictness of his justice, and infinite purity of his holiness, "the heavens," that is, the inhabitants of them, "are not pure in his sight," and "he charged his angels with folly," Job iv. 18, xv. 15. How, then, should any of them, upon his own account, and in his own name, undertake to appear for others, for sinners, in the presence of God? They were doubtless utterly unmeet to interpose in this matter.

(2*dly*.) The *general work* of such a priest is utterly exclusive of the whole creation from engaging herein; for the first thing that he undertakes must be to make atonement for sin and sinners. This is his first work, and the only foundation of what else he has to do, —namely, to make reconciliation for the sins of the people in whose stead he appeareth before God. That this could not be performed by any creature I have manifested on the second chapter. Failing in this, no other thing that can be done is of any value. Wherefore,—

5*thly*. The Son of God undertakes to be this priest for sinners: " We have a great high priest, Jesus the Son of God." The whole enunciation is expressive of his person jointly, and each nature therein is also distinctly signified. "The Son of God,"—which in the first place we intend and consider,—denotes his divine person and nature. How the second person in the Trinity did undertake to be a mediator and priest for all the elect of God, hath been opened in our exposition of the second chapter of the epistle, and it shall not here be again in particular insisted on. This counsel was of old between the Father and the Son, namely, that he, the Son, should become the " seed of the woman,"—that is, should be " made of a woman," and be thereby " made under the law;" that he should come to do the will of God in making atonement by the offering up or sacrifice of himself for sin; that he should undertake the cause of sinners, pay their debts, and satisfy for their offences,—that is, by his appearance and acting for them, he should procure acceptance for them and their services at " the throne of grace." All this the Son of God undertook, and therein both became the high priest of his people and discharged that office for them. And herein is the mystery of God, his truth and his grace, made conspicuous, as hath been at large declared in our Exercitations; for,—

(1*st*.) Here the sacred truth of the *trinity of persons* in the divine nature or essence openeth itself unto the creatures. The nature, the essence, or being of God, is absolutely and numerically one. All the natural and essential properties of that being are absolutely and essentially the same; and all the operations of this divine essence or being, according to its properties, are undivided, as being the effects of one principle, one power, one wisdom. Hence it could not by any such acts be manifested that there was more than one person in that one nature or being. But now, in these actings of the persons of the Trinity in such ways as firstly respect themselves, or their operations "ad intra," where one person is as it were the object of the other persons' acting, the sacred truth of the plurality of persons in the same single, undivided essence is gloriously manifested.

The Son undertaking to the Father to become a high priest for sinners, openly declares the distinction of the Son, or eternal Word, from the person of the Father. And in these distinct and mutual actings of the persons of it is the doctrine and truth of the holy Trinity most safely contemplated. See concerning this our Exercitations at large.

(*2dly.*) It opens the mystery of the *fountain of divine grace*, the springs of life and salvation which are with God. These things flow from the counsel that was between the Father and the Son, when he undertook to be a high priest for us. Grace and mercy are the way suited to the pursuit and accomplishment of those counsels. Hereon also depend all that religion and all those institutions of worship which were of old in the church. Upon the entrance of sin there was an end put unto all the religion that was in the world, as to any glory of God or advantage to the souls of men. How came it, then, to be restored, revived, accepted? Wherefore did God appoint anew a priesthood, sacrifices, and worship? What was aimed at, attained, or effected hereby? Men were sinners still, obnoxious to the law and the curse thereof, and what could their service do or signify? Here lay the invisible foundations of this new order of things. The Son of God had made an interposition for sinners, undertaken to be their high priest, to reconcile them unto God, and thereon to make their worship acceptable unto him. God was not pleased at first to bring this forth unto light, *but hid the mystery of it in himself* from the beginning of the world until the fulness of time came. In the meantime he appointed the worship mentioned to be a shadow and obscure representation of what was secretly transacted between the Father and Son within the veil. This did the office of the priesthood among the people of God of old, and all their sacrifices, teach. This gave them life and efficacy; without a respect whereunto they were of no worth nor use. Thus is our high priest "the Son of God," and thus ought he so to be.

Again; this Son of God is Jesus: "Jesus the Son of God." Jesus is the name of a man: "She shall bring forth a son, and thou shalt call his name Jesus," Matt. i. 21. And this our high priest also was to be. "Every high priest," saith our apostle, "is ordained to offer gifts and sacrifices unto God." And "therefore of necessity" he who would be our high priest "must have somewhat to offer," and that somewhat of his own. And what had the Son of God, absolutely considered, of his own to offer? His divine nature or person is not to be offered. All things necessarily required in the matter and form of an offering are eternally incompatible with the infinite excellencies of the divine nature. God cannot be a sacrifice, though he who is God was so to be. Shall he, then, take an offering out of the works of the creation? Shall he take the blood of bulls and goats for this purpose, as did Aaron? The offering, indeed, of these things might represent the sacrifice that should take away sin, but take away sin itself it could not do. For what wisdom, righteousness, or equity, is in this, that whereas man had sinned, other brute creatures, that were none of his own (for whatever right he had to any creatures of God, belonging to his original dominion over them, after his sin he had none at all), should be accepted a sacrifice in his stead? Besides, what proportion did the blood of bulls and goats bear to the justice of God, that satisfaction for sin should be made unto it thereby? Should, then, the Son of God have taken and appointed any one man to be a sacrifice for himself and others? Every man being a sinner, the sacrifice of any one would have been a provocation unto God. In the typical sacrifices, he would not admit of a lamb or a kid that had the least blemish in it to be offered unto him. And shall we suppose that he would allow of a real expiatory sacrifice by that which was leprous all over? It would have been so far from yielding " a sweet savour to God," from being an atonement for all men, for any one man, for the man himself that should have been offered, that it would have been the highest provocation unto the eyes of his glory. Wherefore the Son of God himself became " Jesus;" that is, he took human nature, "the seed of Abraham," into union with himself, that he might have of his own to offer unto God. This by its oneness with our nature, the nature that had sinned, being itself not touched with sin, was meet to be offered for us; and by its union with his person was meet and able to make atonement with God for us; and so " God redeemed his church with his own blood," Acts xx. 28. Thus our high priest is " Jesus, the Son of God." And in these things consists his greatness, which the apostle proposeth for our encouragement unto steadfastness in profession. And it may do so on sundry accounts, which have been partly before insisted on, and deserve here to be enlarged, but that we must not draw out these discourses unto too great a length.

VERSE 15.

But this precedent description of our high priest may be thought to include a discouragement in it in reference unto us, which may take off from all the encouragements which might be apprehended to lie in his office. For if he be in himself so great and glorious, if so exalted above the heavens, how can we apprehend that he hath any concernment in us, in our weak, frail, tempted, sinning condition? and how shall we use either boldness or confidence in our approach unto him for help or assistance? If the apostle Peter, upon a discovery of his divine power in working of one miracle, thought himself altogether unmeet to be in his presence, whilst he was on the earth, in the days of his flesh, and therefore cried out unto him, "Depart from me, for I am a sinful man, O Lord," Luke v. 8,—how much more may we be terrified by his present glory from attempting an access unto him! And how shall we conceive that, in all this glory, he will entertain compassionate thoughts concerning such poor, sinful worms as we are? 'Yea,' saith the apostle, 'we may, on the consideration of him and his office, "come boldly to the throne of grace;"' the especial reason whereof, removing this objection, and adding a new sort of encouragement, he gives us, verse 15.

Ver. 15.—Οὐ γὰρ ἔχομεν ἀρχιερέα μὴ δυνάμενον συμπαθῆσαι ταῖς ἀσθενείαις ἡμῶν, πεπειρασμένον δὲ κατὰ πάντα καθ' ὁμοιότητα, χωρὶς ἁμαρτίας.

Οὐ γὰρ ἔχομεν. Syr., לָא גֵּיר אִית לַן, "for there is not to us;" an Hebraism, "we have not."

Μὴ δυνάμενον συμπαθῆσαι. Syr., דְּלָא מֵצֵא דְּנֶחַשׁ, "qui non possit compati," "qui non possit, ut patiatur;" "who cannot suffer." Vulg. Lat., "qui non possit compati;" "that cannot have compassion," "that cannot suffer with." Beza, "qui non possit affici sensu;" "who cannot be affected with a sense." Arab., "qui non possit deflere," "that cannot mourn."

Ταῖς ἀσθενείαις ἡμῶν. Syr., "with our infirmity," in the singular number. We follow Beza, "touched with the feeling of our infirmities;" which well expresseth the sense of the words, as we shall see.

Πεπειραμένον[1] δέ, "sed tentatum." Syr., דְּמִנַסַּי, "who was tempted;" one copy reads πεπειρασμένον; of which word we have spoken before.

Κατὰ πάντα. Vulg. Lat., "per omnia." Rhem., "in all things." So Erasm. and Beza, "in omnibus," "in all things." Syr., בְּכָל מֵדֶם, "in omni re," "in every thing."

Καθ' ὁμοιότητα. Bez., "similiter." Vulg. Lat., Erasm., "pro similitudine." Rhem., "by similitude." Syr., אָכְוָתַן, "even as we." Ours, "like as we are," supplying the verb substantive; "secundum similitudinem."

Χωρὶς ἁμαρτίας. Bez., "absque tamen peccato;" whom we follow in the supply of "tamen,"—"yet without sin." Vulg. Lat., "absque peccato," "without sin." Syr., סְטַר מִן חֲטִיתָא, "excepto peccato," "sin being excepted." Some use we shall find in these varieties.[1]

Ver. 15.—For we have not an high priest who cannot be touched with the feeling [*affected with a sense*] of our infirmities; but was every way tempted in like manner [*with us*], without sin.

The words contain a further description of our high priest, by such a qualification as may encourage us to make use of him and improve his office unto our advantage. For whereas those things which may induce us to put our trust and confidence in any, or to expect benefit or advantage thereby, may be reduced unto two heads,— 1. Greatness and power; 2. Goodness and love,—he manifests both sorts of them to be eminently in our high priest. The former he

---

[1] Πεπειραμένον is the reading of Knapp and Tischendorf, on the authority of C J K, and most other MSS.—ED.

declares, verse 14; for he is "Jesus the Son of God, who is passed through" and exalted above "the heavens." The latter sort are ascribed unto him in these words.

The causal connection, γάρ, "for," doth not so much regard the connection of the words, or express an inference of one thing from another, as it is introductive of a new reason, enforcing the purpose and design of the apostle in the whole. He had exhorted them to "hold fast their profession" upon the account of their high priest, verse 14; and directs them to make addresses unto him for grace and strength enabling them so to do, verse 16. With regard unto both these duties, to show the reasonableness of them, to give encouragement unto them, he declares the qualifications of this high priest, expressed in this verse. These things we may, these things we ought to do,— *Γάρ.*

" For we have not an high priest that cannot." The manner of the expression is known and usual. A double negation doth strongly and vehemently affirm. It is so with our high priest, even the contrary to what is thus denied. He is such a one as can be affected. *Οὐκ ἔχομεν ἀρχιερία μὴ δυνάμενον.*

" We have an high priest." The apostle introduceth this for another purpose. Yet withal he lets the Hebrews know that in the gospel state there is no loss of privilege in any thing as to what the church enjoyed under the law of Moses. *Ἔχομεν ἀρχιερία.* They had then a high priest who, and his office, were the life and glory of their profession and worship. 'We also,' saith he, 'have a high priest;' who how much, in his person, and office, and usefulness unto the church, he excelleth the high priest under the law he hath partly showed already, and doth more fully declare in the ensuing chapters. The mention of it is introduced for another end, but this also is included in it. The people of God under the gospel are not left without a high priest; who is in like manner the life and glory of their profession, worship, and obedience. For our apostle takes a diverse course in dealing with the Gentiles and the Jews in this matter. Treating with the Gentiles, he minds them of their miserable condition before they were called to the knowledge of Christ by the gospel, as Eph. ii. 11–13; but treating with the Jews, he satisfies them that they lost no advantage thereby, but had all their former privileges unspeakably heightened and increased. And our relation to him and interest in him are expressed in this word ἔχομεν, "we have him;" or, as the Syriac, "there is to us." God hath appointed him, and given him unto us; and he is ours, as to all the ends of his office, and by us to be made use of for all spiritual advantages relating unto God. The church never lost any privilege once granted unto it, by any change or alteration that God made in his ordinances of worship, or dispensations towards it; but, still keeping what it had before, it was carried on towards that completeness and perfection which it is capable of in this world, and which it hath received by Jesus Christ. Presently upon the giving of the first promise, God instituted some kind of worship, as *sacrifices*, to be a means of intercourse between him and sinners, in and by the grace and truth of that promise. This was the privilege of them that did believe. After this he made sundry additional ordinances of worship, all of them instructive in the nature of that promise, and directive towards the accomplishment of it. And still there was an increase of grace and privilege in them all. They were "the mountains of myrrh and hills of frankincense" on which the church "waited until the day brake, and the shadows fled away," Cant. iv. 6. All along the church was still a gainer. But when the time came of the actual accomplishment of the promise, then were all former privileges realized unto believers, new ones added, and nothing lost. We have lost neither sacrifice nor high priest, but have them all in a more eminent and excellent manner. And this is enough to secure the application of the initial seal of the covenant unto the infant seed of believers. For whereas it was granted to the church under the old testament as a signal favour and spiritual privilege, it is derogatory to the glory of Christ and honour of the gospel to suppose that the church is now deprived of it; for in the whole system and frame of worship God had ordained "the better things for us, that they without us should not be made perfect." And he says not, 'There is an high priest,' but, "We have an high priest;" because all our concernment in spiritual things depends absolutely on our personal interest in them. They may do well to consider this, who, 1. Either know not the nature of this priesthood, or do not at all endeavour to improve this office of Christ as that which they have an interest in. Some call themselves Christians, and exercise themselves in the outward worship of God, who are ready to despise, yea, and deride, all spiritual improvement and use of this great privilege, that we have a high priest, and scarce take it any more into any real consideration in the worship of God than if there were no such thing at all. 2. Those who, not contented with it, have invented and appointed unto themselves a priesthood and sacrifice, to the contempt of this of Christ. Had our apostle dealt with these Hebrews on the principles of the present church of Rome, he would have told them, 'You had under the law an *high priest*, but we have now a *pope*, a pontifex maximus, a great high priest; far richer, braver, and more potent, than yours was. You had many *bloody sacrifices*, but we have *one in the host*, of more use and profit than were all yours whatever.' But dealing with the principles of the gospel, he declares and proposeth to them "Jesus the Son of

God," as our only priest, sacrifice, and altar,—expressly intimating that others we have none.

"That cannot be touched with a feeling," "who cannot be affected with a sense," "who cannot suffer with." The negative expression, μὴ δυνάμενον, "who cannot," as it includes and asserts a power and ability for the work or acts mentioned, so it doth it in opposition unto and to the exclusion of some other considerations, that infer a disability to this purpose. Now, the ability here intended is either moral only, or moral and natural also. If it be moral only, and intend a constant goodness, kindness, tenderness, and benignity, attended with care and watchfulness, unto the end proposed, it may be asserted in opposition to the high priests among the Jews. For as they were the best of them but men, and sinful men, who did ofttimes indulge to their private and carnal affections, to the disadvantage of the people of God,—as did Eli, to the ruin of the church's worship, 1 Sam. ii. 17, 22–25, 28–30, etc.,—and were none of them able at any time to have a due comprehension of all the temptations and infirmities of the people; so many of them were evil men, proud, haughty, wrathful, and such as despised their brethren and relieved them not at all. In opposition hereunto, it is affirmed of our high priest that he is able to do quite otherwise,—that is, with a moral ability of heart, will, and affections. He can and doth, always and constantly, concern himself in all the sins, sufferings, sorrows, temptations, and infirmities of his people.

Again; there may not only be a moral but also a natural ability included in the word. And in this sense there is respect had unto the human nature of Christ, and something moreover ascribed unto him [more] than could have been in him if he had been God only, —which is a great encouragement unto us to make our addresses to him for help and assistance. And this seems to be designed from the following words, wherein mention is made of his being "tempted like unto us." To understand this ability, we must inquire into the meaning of the next word, expressing that which it is applied unto or exercised about.

Συμπαθῆσαι. I have showed how variously this word is translated, —"to suffer," "to suffer with," "to have compassion," "to be touched with a feeling," "to be affected with a sense," "to condole" or "bewail." The word is once more used by our apostle in this epistle, and nowhere else in the New Testament, chap. x. 34, Τοῖς δεσμοῖς μου συνεπαθήσατε, where we render it by "having compassion:" "Ye had compassion of me in my bonds;" though I should rather say, "Ye suffered with me in my bonds." 1 Pet. iii. 8, the noun συμπαθής occurs, where we render it again "having compassion." And, indeed, the origination of that word "compassion" is comprehensive

of its whole sense; but its common use for "pity" is not. Συμπα-
θεῖς is more fully rendered in that place by Beza, "mutuo moles-
tiarum sensu affecti,"—"affected with a mutual sense of the troubles
of each other."

First, Συμπαθέω includes a *concern in the troubles*, or sufferings, or evils of others, upon the account of concernment in any
common interest wherein persons are united, as it is in the natural
body.   Sometimes some part is affected with a disease, which hath
seized on it.   Another part of the body is affected with it, although
nothing of the disease hath really seized on it.   That part thereof
cannot be said to be absolutely sick or ill-affected, for no part of
the disease is in it; but it may be said συμπάσχειν,—that is, not to be
free from being affected, though not upon its own account, Galen,
de Locis Affectis, lib. i.   This suffering is by the consent or harmony that is in the same nature branched into its individuals.   So
we have a sense of the suffering of humanity or of human nature,
wherein we are interested, in other men, in any man whatever.

Secondly, It includes a *propensity* to relieve them in whose
troubles or sufferings we are concerned, and that whether we have
power to effect that relief or no.   So David, in the deep sense that
he had of the death of Absalom, wished that he had died for him,
or relieved him from suffering by dying in his stead.   And where this
is not in some measure, there is no sympathy.   We may not be able,
in some cases where we are concerned, to relieve; it may not be lawful for us, in some cases, to give that help and succour which our
compassion would incline us unto; but if there be no such inclination there is no sympathy.

Thirdly, Properly it contains in it a *commotion of affections*, which
we express by " condolentia;" whence the Arabic renders the word
" who can mourn with us."   So is the Hebrew נוּד used, Ps. lxix.
21: אָקַוֶּה לָנוּד; LXX., 'Υπέμεινα συλλυπούμενον·—" I looked for any to
be grieved with me;" "to be affected with sorrow on my behalf;"
" to take pity," say we; "to lament with me," by a motion or agita-
tion of their affections, as the word signifies.   And those intended
are joined with מְנַחֲמִים, " comforters."   This belongs to this sympathy, to have a moving of affection in ourselves upon the sufferings
of others.

And these things are here ascribed unto our high priest on the
account of his union with us, both in the participation of our nature
and the communication of a new nature unto us, whereby we become " members of his body," one with him.   He is deeply concerned in all our infirmities, sorrows, and sufferings.   This is attended
with an inclination and propensity to relieve us, according to the
rule, measure, and tenor of the covenant; and herewithal, during
the time of our trials, he hath a real motion of affections in his holy

nature, which he received or took on him for that very end and purpose, chap. ii. 16–18.

In this sense of the word, συμπαθῆσαι, " to be affected with a sense,"
ascribes this ability in a moral and natural sense unto the Lord
Christ, our high priest, as he is man, in contradistinction unto God
absolutely, whose nature is incapable of the compassion intended.
There are, indeed, in the Scripture assignations of such kind of
affections unto God; as Isa. lxiii. 9, בְּכָל צָרָתָם לֹא צָר. For לֹא, " not,"
the reading is לֹו, " to him;" and accordingly we translate it, " In all
their afflictions he was afflicted;" or, " there was straitening, affliction unto him,"—he was afflicted with their straits and afflictions.
But there is an anthropopathy allowed in these expressions. These
things are assigned unto God after the manner of men. And the
true reason of such ascriptions, is not merely to assist our weakness
and help our understandings in the things themselves, but to show
really what God doth and will do in the human nature which he
hath assumed, and intended to do so from of old ; on which purpose
the superstructure of his dealing with us in the Scripture is founded
and built. And thus it is said of our high priest that " he is able
to be affected with a sense of our infirmities," because in his human
nature he is capable of such affections, and, as he is our high priest,
is graciously inclined to act according to them.

Ταῖς ἀσθενείαις ἡμῶν, " our infirmities." Ἀσθενεία, " imbecillitas,"
" debilitas," " infirmitas," is used, both in the Scripture
and all Greek authors, for any debility, weakness, or in-   Ταῖς ἀσθε-
firmity, of body or mind. Frequently bodily diseases are   νείαις ἡμῶν.
expressed by it, as by the adjective ἀσθενής, and the verb ἀσθενέω, " to be
sick," " to be diseased," with respect unto the weakness or infirmity
that is introduced thereby, Matt. x. 8, xxv. 43; Luke iv. 40; John
v. 3, 5. And sometimes it expresseth the weakness of the mind
or spirit, not able, or scarcely able, to bear the difficulties and troubles
that it is pressed withal, 1 Cor. ii. 3; weakness of judgment, Rom.
xiv. 2; spiritual weakness, as to life, grace, and power, Rom. v. 6,
viii. 26. So that this word is used to express every kind of imbecility or weakness that doth or may befall our natures with respect
unto any difficulties, troubles, or perplexities that we have to conflict withal. And whereas it is here mentioned generally, without a
restriction to any special kind of infirmities, it may justly be extended to all weaknesses of all sorts that we are, or upon any pressures may be, sensible of; but whereas, in the following words, the
reason of the ability of Christ, our high priest, to be affected with a
sense of our infirmities, is placed in his being tempted, it is manifest that the weaknesses here chiefly intended are such as respect
afflictions and temptations, with persecution for the gospel. Our
infirmities and weaknesses under these things, to wrestle with them

or remove them, and consequently our trouble, sorrow, suffering, and danger, by them and from them, our high priest is intimately affected withal. He takes himself to be concerned in our troubles, as we are members of his mystical body, one with him; he is inclined from his own heart and affections to give in unto us help and relief, as our condition doth require; and he is inwardly moved during our sufferings and trials with a sense and fellow-feeling of them.

Obs. The church of God hath a standing, perpetual advantage, in the union of our nature to the person of the Son of God, as he is our high priest.

We all acknowledge that so it is with us, upon the account of the sacrifice that he was to offer for us. He had thereby somewhat of his own to offer. Thence it was that " God redeemed his church with his own blood," Acts xx. 28; and that " he laid down his life for us," 1 John iii. 16. But we are apt to think that this work being well over, we have now no more concernment in that nature nor advantage by it, but that what yet remains to be done for us may be as well discharged by him who is only God, and absolutely so in every respect. For since he " dieth no more," what profit is there in his flesh? It is true, the flesh of Christ, carnally and sensually considered, " profiteth nothing," as he told the Capernaites of old, John vi. And they will find his words true, who, in their own imagination, turn bread into his flesh every day. Yea, and our apostle tells us, " though he had known Christ after the flesh, yet now henceforth he knew him so no more," 2 Cor. v. 16; that is, though he had known Christ in the days of his flesh here in the world, whilst as a mortal man he conversed with mortal men, yet all the privilege thereof and advantage thereby, which some in those days boasted of, were past, and of use no longer; he was now to be known after another manner, and under another consideration,—as exalted at the right hand of God. Yet doth not all this in the least impeach our assertion of the greatness of our concernment in the continuation of his human nature in the union of his person. If, when he had finished his sacrifice, and the atonement which he made for sin, by the offering up of himself, he had then left off his human nature, which he had for that end taken on him, notwithstanding that offering we could not have been delivered nor saved. For besides that he himself had not been sufficiently manifested to be the Son of God for us to have believed on him, seeing he was " declared to be the Son of God with power by the resurrection from the dead," Rom. i. 4; so our apostle declares that without his resurrection from the dead we could neither be delivered from our sins nor have been ever raised again unto glory, 1 Cor. xv. 12–21.

It is therefore confessed that many and great are the advantages of the resurrection of the body of Christ, and therein of his human nature; for this was the way and means of his entrance into glory: He "revived, that he might be Lord both of the dead and living," Rom. xiv. 9. And this was the testimony that he was acquitted and discharged from the penalty of the law, and the whole debt he had undertaken to make satisfaction of unto God for sinners, Acts ii. 24, Rom. viii. 33, 34; without which we could have said of him only as the disciples did when they knew not of his resurrection, "We trusted that it had been he who should have redeemed Israel," Luke xxiv. 21. And hereby had he an illustrious and uncontrollable testimony given to his being the Son of God, Rom. i. 4; as also, he laid the foundation and gave an infallible pledge of the future blessed resurrection, which all that believe in him shall by him obtain. But this being also past and over, what further concernment hath the church in the continuation of the union of his natures? I might mention many, and those of the greatest importance. For there yet remained some parts of his mediatory work to be discharged, which could not be accomplished without this nature; for he had not yet appeared in the holy place with his own blood, whereby he had made atonement, that the whole sacrifice might be completed. And the exaltation of our nature in glory was needful for the supportment and consolation of the church. But I shall mention that alone which is here proposed by our apostle, namely, his ability from thence to be affected with a sense of our infirmities and sufferings. This, as I have showed, is appropriate unto him on the account of his human nature. And on this account we may consider his compassion four ways:—

1. As it is an eminent *virtue in human nature* as absolutely innocent. So was the nature of Christ from the beginning; for therein was he "holy, harmless, undefiled, and separate from sinners." Now, though in that blessed estate wherein we were created there was no actual object for us to exercise compassion upon or towards, seeing every thing was at rest in its proper place and order, yet was there no virtue more inlaid in our rational constitution, as being absolutely inseparable from goodness and benignity, upon a supposition of a suitable object. Hence they are justly esteemed to be fallen into the utmost of degeneracy from our first make, frame, and state, and to be most estranged from our common original, who have cast off this virtue where it may and ought to have its actual exercise. Nor are any more severely in the Scripture reflected on than those who are unmerciful and without compassion, fierce, cruel, and implacable. No men more evidently deface the image of God than such persons. Now, our nature in Christ was and is absolutely pure and holy, free from the least influence by that depravedness which befell the whole mass in Adam. And herein are the natural virtues of goodness, benignity, mercy, and compassion, pure, perfect, and

untainted. And he hath objects to exercise these virtues on which Adam could not have, and those such as are one with himself, by their participation in the same common principles of nature and grace.

2. This compassion is in him as a *grace of the Spirit.* For besides the spotless innocency and purity of our nature in him, there was a superaddition of all grace unto it, by virtue of its union with the person of the Son of God and the unction it had from the Spirit of God. Hence there was an all-fulness of created grace communicated unto him; for he received not the Spirit and his graces by measure, John iii. 34. Of this fulness compassion is a part, and that no mean part neither; for of this rank and kind are all the principal fruits of the Spirit, Gal. v. 22, 23. And in and by these did he make a representation of God's nature unto us, which he hath described as full of pity, compassion, and tender affections; whence he compares himself unto those creatures and in those relations which have the most intense and merciful affections. And hereby doth the compassion of Christ, our high priest in our human nature, receive an eminent exaltation.

3. He had a peculiar furnishment with graces, virtues, habits of mind, and *inclinations,* suited to the good and useful discharge of his office in our behalf. The Spirit of the Lord was upon him, and peculiarly anointed him to that end, Isa. xi. 2–4, lxi. 1–3. Now unto the office of a high priest it is in especial required that he should be able to have compassion, Heb. v. 2; the reasons whereof we shall see afterwards. He had, therefore, in his human nature, an especial provision of compassion inlaid by the Holy Ghost, by whom he was anointed, for the due discharge of this office. Thus was he every way framed in his nature unto mercy and compassion. And whereas there seems nothing now wanting but an outward object of weakness, infirmities, and temptations, to excite and occasion the exercise of this virtue and grace, that this might be the more effectual to that purpose,—

4. He took an *experience of such sufferings in himself* as are the proper objects of compassion when they are in others. This the next words declare, which we shall afterwards consider.

By these means is the nature of our high priest filled with *tenderness,* compassion, or *sympathy,* the foundation of whose exercise towards us lies in the oneness of his nature and ours. And these things belonging to the pure constitution of his nature, and receiving their improvement by the unction of the Spirit, are not lessened or impaired by his present glorification; for they all belonging unto him on the account of his office, continuing still in the *exercise of the same office,* their continuation also is necessary. And hence it is, namely, because of our concernment therein, that he gave so many particular instances of his retaining the same human nature wherein he suffered. For he did not only "shew himself alive to his disciples after his passion by many infallible proofs, being seen of them forty days, and speaking of the things pertaining to the kingdom of God," Acts i. 3, providing particularly that they should not think or take him now to be a mere spirit, and so to have lost his *natural human constitution*, saying unto them, "Behold my hands and my feet, that it is I myself: handle me and see; for a spirit hath not flesh and bones, as ye see me have," Luke xxiv. 39;—but when he left the world with that body of flesh and bones, the angels witnessed that he should "come again in like manner" as he then went away, Acts i. 11. For "the heaven must" in that nature "receive him until the times of the restitution of all things," Acts iii. 21. And to confirm our faith in this matter, he appeared afterwards in the same nature to Stephen, Acts vii. 56; and to our apostle, telling him that he was "Jesus whom he persecuted," chap. ix. 5. All this to assure us that he is such a high priest as is able to be "affected with a sense of our infirmities." And those who by the monstrous figment of transubstantiation, and those others who feign the Lord Christ to have an ubiquitarian body, both of them by just consequence destroying the verity of his human nature, do evert what lies in them a main pillar of the church's consolation. Much more do they do so who deny him to retain the same individual body wherein he suffered, in any sense. Herein lies a great advantage of the church, a great encouragement and supportment unto believers under their infirmities, in their trials and temptations. For,—

1. It is some relief *to be pitied in distress*. The want hereof Job complained of, and cried out pathetically about it: chap. xix. 21, "Have pity upon me, have pity upon me, O ye my friends; for the hand of God hath touched me." It went unto his heart, to find that his friends were not affected with a sense of his sufferings; and it added exceedingly to the weight of them. And such was the complaint of David, as a type of Christ: Ps. lxix. 20, "Reproach hath broken my heart, and I am full of heaviness; and I looked for some to take pity, but there was none; and for comforters, but I found none." It is a representation of the state of our Saviour when all his disciples fled and left him, and he was encompassed with fierce and reproaching enemies. This is a high aggravation of the sorrows and sufferings of any that are in distress. And there is relief in compassion. Some going to the stake have been much refreshed with a compassionate word whispered unto them. And it cannot but be a cause of great refreshment unto believers, in all the hardships that befall them, and their weakness under them, that they have the compassion of their high priest accompanying of them. He is in himself exceedingly great and glorious, nearly allied unto us, able to relieve us, being far

above all those persons and things that occasion our troubles, for they are all under his feet; all which considerations render his compassion, as before described, refreshing and relieving.

2. Herein lies a great encouragement to make our addresses unto him in all our straits and weaknesses. For if he be so concerned in us and our troubles, if he be so affected in himself with a sense of them, and have in his holy nature, and upon the account of his office, such a propensity to relieve us, which also he is so able for, as hath been declared,—what should hinder us from making our addresses unto him continually for help and supplies of his assisting grace, according as our necessities do require? But this being the peculiar use that the apostle makes of this doctrine in the next verse, it must be there considered.

3. There lies no small warning herein, how heedfully we should take care that we miscarry not, that we faint not in our trials. He looks on us with a great concernment, and his glory and honour are engaged in our acquitting of ourselves. If we have a due regard to him and his love, it will excite us unto all care and diligence in the discharge of every duty we are called unto, notwithstanding the difficulties that it may be attended withal.

In the next words an especial reason is assigned of this merciful ability of our high priest to be "affected with a sense of our infirmities:" "But was in all things tempted as we are, yet without sin." The assertion which is the ground of the reason assigned, is that he was "tempted;"—expressed with the extent of it; it was κατὰ πάντα, "in all things;" and an appropriation unto our concernment, "like as we are;" with a limitation of the extent and appropriation, "yet without sin."

The whole substance of what is here intended hath been largely treated on, chap. ii. 17, whither I refer the reader, that we may not repeat the same things again. Some very few words may be added, in the explication of what is peculiar to this place.

Πεπειραμένον δέ. The particle δέ, "but," is contradictory to what was before denied: 'He is not such a one as cannot be affected, but one who was himself tempted.' And this plainly shows that what is now introduced is the principal proof of the former assertion: 'It is evident that he can be "affected with a sense of our infirmities," because he was "tempted."'

Δί.

Πεπειραμένον, "tempted;" that is, "tried," "exercised," for no more doth the word originally import. Whatever is the moral evil in temptation, it is from the depraved intention of the tempter, or from the weakness and sin of the tempted. In itself, and materially considered, it is but a trial, which may have a good or a bad effect. How, whereby, or wherein our high priest was thus tried and tempted, see the place before mentioned.

Πιστιραμίνον.

Κατὰ πάντα, "every way," "in all things;" that is, from all means and instruments of temptation, by all ways of it, and in all things, wherein as a man, or as our high priest, he was concerned.

Κατὰ πάντα.

Καθ᾽ ὁμοιότητα, "secundum similitudinem," "in like manner." There is a plain allusion or relation unto the temptation of others. For whatever is "like," is of necessity like to somewhat else; and what is done in "like manner," or "according to similitude," hath something that answers unto it. Now this is the trials and temptations of them that do believe, the things that press on them by reason of their weakness. See as above.

Καθ᾽ ὁμοιότητα.

Χωρὶς ἁμαρτίας, "without sin." Sin with respect unto temptation may be considered two ways;—1. As the *principle* of it; 2. As its *effect.* 1. Sin sometimes is the principle of temptation. Men are tempted to sin by sin, to actual sin by habitual sin, to outward sin by indwelling sin, James i. 14, 15. And this is the greatest spring and source of temptations in us who are sinners. 2. It respects temptation as the effect of it, that which it tends and leads unto, which it designs, which it bringeth forth or produceth. And it may be inquired with respect unto which of these considerations it is that the exception is here put in on the behalf of our high priest, that he was "tempted without sin." If the former, then the meaning is, that he was tried and tempted by all ways and means, from all principles and causes, in like manner even as we are, excepting only that he was not tempted by sin, which had no place in him, no part, no interest, so that it had no ground to make suggestions unto him upon. And hereby the apostle preserves in us due apprehensions of the purity and holiness of Christ, that we may not imagine that he was liable unto any such temptations unto sin from within as we find ourselves liable unto, and which are never free from guilt and defilement. If the latter be intended, then all success of temptation upon our high priest is denied. We are tried and tempted by Satan, and the world, and by our own lusts. The aim of all these temptations is sin, to bring us more or less, in one degree or other, to contract the guilt of it. Ofttimes in this condition sin actually ensues, temptation hath its effect in us and upon us; yea, when any temptation is vigorous and pressing, it is seldom but that more or less we are sinfully affected with it. It was quite otherwise with our high priest. Whatever temptation he was exposed unto or exercised withal, as he was with all of all sorts that can come from without, they had none of them in the least degree any effect in him or upon him; he was still in all things absolutely "without sin." Now, the exception being absolute, I see no reason why it should not be applied unto sin with both the re-

Χωρὶς ἁμαρτίας.

spects unto temptation mentioned. He neither was tempted by
sin, such was the holiness of his nature; nor did his temptation produce any sin, such was the perfection of his obedience. And concerning all these things the reader may consult the place before
mentioned.

VERSE 16.

The last verse of this chapter contains an inference from what
was discoursed in the two foregoing, as the contexture of the words
declares. The exhortation is insisted on, verse 14, that we would
"hold fast our profession" unto the end. The motive and encouragement hereunto is taken from the consideration of the priesthood
of Christ, with the several concerns thereof before explained. Here
a further improvement of them in particular is directed unto, for the
same end; for it is supposed that we may meet with many difficulties, oppositions, and temptations, in the discharge of that duty,
which in and of ourselves we are not able to conflict withal and to
overcome. Wherefore we are guided and encouraged to seek for
help and assistance against them on the account of what hath been
declared concerning the priesthood of the Son of God.

Ver. 16.—Προσερχώμεθα οὖν μετὰ παρρησίας τῷ θρόνῳ τῆς χάριτος, ἵνα
λάβωμεν ἔλεον, καὶ χάριν εὕρωμεν εἰς εὔκαιρον βοήθειαν.

Οὖν, "therefore;"—' seeing we have an high priest, and him such
a one as we have described.' The consideration hereof is to encourage, guide, and influence us unto the ensuing duty, and in all
the concerns of it. Without this we have no might unto it, no
ability for it.

Προσερχώμεθα, "let us come;" so we. But that is only ἐρχώμεθα.
Προσερχώμεθα. There is some addition of sense from the composition.
Nor is it by any translators rendered "veniamus"
singly, "let us come;" but "adeamus," or "accedamus," or "appro-
pinquemus,"—"let us come to," "draw near," or "approach."
Syr., נֶתְקָרַב, "let us draw near," in a sacred manner, or to sacred
purposes. So have we rendered the same word, chap. x. 22; and
it is used absolutely for to come unto God in his worship, chap. vii.
25, x. 1, xi. 6. It answers קָרַב in the Hebrew, which, as it is used
for "to approach" or "draw nigh" in general, so it is peculiarly
used to signify the solemn approach that was to be made unto God
in his worship or service. Hence, also, it signifies "to offer sacrifices and offerings," which are thence called קָרְבָּנִים. The word,
therefore, hath respect unto the access either of the people of old
with their sacrifices to the altar in the temple, or the priests' approach
unto the holy place, as the next words will more fully declare.

Having asserted the Lord Jesus Christ, the Son of God, to be our
high priest, as typed out by the high priest among the Jews, he expresseth our addresses unto God by him, in answer to the way and
manner whereby the priests or people of old made their approaches
unto God, as that which agreeth therewith in its general nature,
though on other accounts variously exalted above it: ' " Let us draw
near," in a holy, sacred manner, according to his appointment;'
that is, with our prayers and supplications.

Μετὰ παῤῥησίας, "with boldness." This word hath been spoken
unto on chap. iii. 6. Here it is variously rendered.
Syr. עין אֱלִבָּה, "with an open" or "revealed eye," Vulg.
Lat. "cum fiducia," "with confidence." So the Ara- Μετὰ παῤ-
ῥησίας.
bic. By the Ethiopic it is wholly omitted. Beza, "cum loquendi
libertate," "with liberty of speech" or "speaking." It is a principal
adjunct of the worship of God which our apostle expresseth in this
word, both here and chap. x. 19; and this somewhat that is peculiar to the worship of the new testament in opposition unto that of
the old. This he elsewhere calls ἐλευθερίαν, "liberty," 2 Cor. iii. 17;
the liberty that is given by the Holy Spirit under the new testament unto believers, which those who were kept under bondage by
the letter of the old had no interest in: " For where the Spirit of
the Lord is, there is liberty." And he calls it πρόσωπον ἀνακεκαλυ-
μένον, verse 18, "open face;" whence is the "oculus revelatus" of
the Syriac in this place. This, as it hath an especial opposition to
the veil that was on the Jews, and is to this day, filling them with
darkness and fear, so it denotes boldness and confidence of mind,
in a freedom from fear, shame, and discouragements.

There are, therefore, two things that the apostle intends to remove, and to have us free or delivered from, in our drawing near to
the throne of grace with our prayers and supplications, on the account
of the interposition of our high priest:—

First, A *bondage frame of spirit*, or a "spirit of bondage unto
fear," which was upon the people under the old testament in the
worship of God. This he elsewhere frequently both ascribes unto
them and removes from us, Rom. viii. 14, 15; 2 Cor. iii. 12–18.
God, in the giving of the law and the institution of the ordinances
of worship, wherein he taught the people how he would be reve-
renced by them, had so encompassed himself with fire and terror,
that it ingenerated a great and awful horror in their minds. This
made them remove and stand afar off, desiring that God would not
approach to them, nor that they might approach unto God, but that
all things between them might be transacted at a distance, by an
internuncius, Exod. xx. 18, 19. This legal diffidence and distrust
in our approaches unto God, which shuts up the heart, straitens the
spirit, and takes away the liberty of treating with him as a father,

is now by Christ removed and taken away, Gal. iv. 4–6. Christ was "made under the law," to deliver us from the dread and bondage of it; whereby, also, we receive the adoption of children, and therewithal the Spirit of Christ, to treat with God with the liberty, boldness, and ingenuity of children, crying " Abba, Father," with the genuine actings of faith and love.

Secondly, A *disbelief of acceptation*, arising from a sense of our own unworthiness. From an apprehension of God's greatness and terror there arises a dread in persons under the law; and from the consideration of their own vileness there arises a distrust in sinners, accompanied with fear and despondency, as though there were no hope for them in him or with them. This also the apostle would remove, upon the account of the priesthood of Christ. The manner assigned unto us for our approach to God includes all this. We are to do it μετὰ παῤῥησίας, " with boldness;" which word imports,—

1. " Orationis," or " orandi libertatem." Παῤῥησία is παυρησία, " a freedom and liberty in speaking;" rendered here by Beza, "loquendi libertas." This liberty is internal and spiritual, and is opposed unto the legal diffidence and bondage before described. This παῤῥησία, therefore, in the first place, is our spiritual liberty and freedom, attended with a holy confidence, in our access unto God, to make our requests known unto him, expressing our condition, our wants, our desires, freely and with confidence.

2. " Exauditionis fiduciam," or a spiritual confidence of acceptance with God through the interposition of Jesus Christ. In another place our apostle seems to make this to be a thing distinct from the παῤῥησία here mentioned: Eph. iii. 12, Ἐν ᾧ ἔχομεν τὴν παῤῥησίαν, καὶ τὴν προσαγωγὴν ἐν πεποιθήσει, διὰ τῆς πίστεως αὐτοῦ·—" In whom we have boldness, and an access with confidence, through the faith that is in him." Our " access with confidence" includes a persuasion of acceptance, and is distinguished from the "boldness" that it is accompanied withal ; but yet as this παῤῥησία and προσαγωγὴ ἐν πεποιθήσει, this " boldness" and " access with confidence," are inseparable in and from the same duty, so they may be mentioned the one for both in other places, as here they seem to be. And we thus " draw near,"—

Τῷ Θρόνῳ τῆς χάριτος, " to the throne of grace." The proper and immediate object of our access or approach is and must be a person. Who that is, is not here expressed, but is left to be understood from the manner of his being represented unto us. A throne is a seat of majesty, and is ascribed to God and men; to God frequently, as he is גָּדוֹל מֶלֶךְ, the "great king" over all. Isaiah saw him " on a throne, high and exalted," chap. vi. 1; and Ezekiel, as on " the likeness of a throne," chap. i. 26. So "justice and judgment" are said to be "the habitation of his throne," Ps. lxxxix. 14. There they abide and dwell, when other thrones have but some partial visits from them.   In general, heaven is said to be God's throne, Matt. v. 34, as the place where principally he manifests his glory and majesty.   But the expression being metaphorical, is not to be restrained to any one thing in particular.   The Hebrews say that God hath a double throne; כסא הדין, "a throne of judgment;" and כסא רחמים, "a throne of compassion" and tender mercy,—that is, θρόνος τῆς χάριτος, a "throne of grace."   A throne, then, is the place where and from whence judgment is exercised and mercy administered; and therefore our coming unto God in his worship for mercy and grace, is said to be a coming unto his throne. Or there may be an allusion unto the mercy-seat in the tabernacle, which being laid on the ark with a coronet of gold round about it, and shadowed with the cherubim, it was as the throne or seat of God in that most solemn representation of his presence amongst that people; for that which the apostle here calls our "coming to the throne of grace," in chap. x. 19 he expresseth by "drawing nigh with boldness into the holiest," the place where the ark and mercy-seat were placed.   And it is the love and grace of God in Christ which was thereby represented, as hath been manifested elsewhere.

Our next inquiry is after the person whom we are distinctly to consider as on this throne in our addresses thereunto.   Some say ' it is the Lord Christ as our mediator and high priest who is intended: for concerning him directly is the discourse immediately preceding; he is also in particular here described as our merciful, faithful, and careful high priest,—all which are encouragements to come unto him, which accordingly we are exhorted unto, and that with boldness ; and a throne is peculiarly ascribed unto him in this epistle, chap. i. 8; and he sits in the throne of God, Rev. iii. 21; and at his throne of grace we may be sure of acceptance.'

But yet this seems not to be the especial intention of this place. For,—1. A throne, rule, and government, are ascribed unto the Lord Christ with respect unto his kingly and not his priestly office, of which the apostle here discourseth.   It is said indeed of him that he should be "a priest upon his throne," Zech. vi. 13; but that is to intimate the concomitancy of his kingly power as inseparable from his person,—he shall be a priest, though sitting, or whilst he sits as a king on his throne.   2. Wherever the Lord Christ is spoken of as on his throne, exalted in the glory and majesty of his kingdom, it is always with reference to his power and authority over his church for to give laws and rules unto it for his worship, or over his enemies for their ruin and destruction.   3. The context requires another sense; for the Lord Christ, in his office and interposition on our behalf, is not proposed as the object of our coming, but as the means of it, and a great encouragement unto it; for "through him we have an access by one Spirit unto the Father," Eph. ii. 18.   On

the account of his undertaking for us, his appearance before God on
our behalf, the atonement he hath made, we may come in his name
with confidence of acceptance unto the throne of God. See Rev. iv.
2, 3, v. 6, 7; Heb. vii. 25.

I cannot omit one argument that is used by Primasius, Haymo,
and Ludovicus de Tena, on this place, to prove that it is the throne
of Christ that is here intended. And this is because it is called a
" throne of grace;" ' that is,' say they, 'of Christ, for so is he called by
our apostle, chap. ii. 9.' For, following the Vulgar translation, and
reading the words, " ut gratia Dei gustaret mortem pro omnibus,"
they say " gratia" is of the nominative and not of the ablative case,
—that " the Grace of God should taste of death for all." And herein
Tena urgeth the consent of Thomas and the ordinary gloss. Such
woful mistakes do men, otherwise wise and learned, fall into, who
undertake to expound the Scriptures without consulting the original, or an ability so to do. The "throne of grace," therefore, is unto
us, God as gracious in Christ, as exalted in a way of exercising grace
and mercy towards them that through the Lord Jesus believe in
him and come unto him.

This is the duty exhorted unto. The end hereof is twofold:—1.
General and immediate; 2. *Particular,* as an effect and product
thereof. The general end hath two parts:—(1.) " That we may
obtain mercy;" (2.) "That we may find grace." The particular and
determinate end of all is,—" seasonable help," " help in a time of
need."

The first thing designed, as a part of the end to be aimed at in
the discharge or performance of this duty, is, *ἵνα λάβωμεν*
ἔλεον, " that we may receive mercy," " that we may
obtain mercy." *Λαμβάνω* doth sometimes signify " to
obtain," " to acquire;" and so by most interpreters it is here rendered, " ut obtineamus," " ut consequamur," as by ours, " that we
may obtain;" but the first and most usual signification of the word
is only " to receive," or " to take," " that we may receive." And I
see no reason why that sense of it may not be most proper unto this
place; for the apostle seems to intimate that mercy is prepared for
us, only our access unto God by Christ with boldness is required to
our being made actual partakers thereof. And this answers his prescription of " boldness," or spiritual confidence in our approaches to
the throne of grace for the receiving that mercy which in and
through Christ is prepared for us.

" That we may receive *ἔλεος.*" This word is often used to signify
that " mercy" in God from whence we obtain and receive the pardon of our sins,—mercy in pardoning, הַפְלִיחָה.
So most expound this place, that we may obtain mercy for our
sins, that we may be pardoned. But this doth not seem to answer the

"Ἵνα λάβωμεν
ἔλεον.

"Ἔλεος.

present purpose of the apostle; for he is not discoursing about *sin* in the guilt of it, but about *temptations*, afflictions, and persecutions. Wherefore the ἔλεος, or "mercy," here intended, must be that which is the principle or cause of our supportment, assistance, and deliverance,—namely, in the effects of it. This is חֶסֶד in the Hebrew, which the LXX. frequently render by ἔλεος, and we by "mercy," though it rather signifies "kindness and benignity," than pardoning grace. Moreover, it is not about the first approach of sinners unto God by Christ for mercy and pardon, whereof he treats, but about the daily access of believers unto him for grace and assistance. To "receive mercy," therefore, is to be made partakers of gracious help and supportment from the kindness and benignity of God in Christ, when we are in straits and distresses; which springs, indeed, from the same root with pardoning grace, and is therefore called "mercy."

Καὶ χάριν εὕρωμεν, "and that we may find grace." This is the next general end of our access unto the throne of grace. Εὕρωμεν, "that we may find," or rather *Καὶ χάριν εὕρωμεν.* "obtain;" for so is this word often used. And there may be a twofold sense of these words:—

1. "To find" or "obtain favour," or *favourable acceptance* with God. When God is pleased χαριτῶσαι, to make us acceptable unto himself in Christ, as he is said to do, Eph. i. 6, then we find χάριν, "grace," or "favour" with him. *Χάριν.* And this is the foundation of all grace that is communicated unto us. The phrase of speech occurs frequently in the Old Testament. "Let me find grace in thine eyes," or "favour in thy sight;" that is, "be accepted with thee,"—מָצָא חֵן. And to this doth εὑρεῖν χάριν exactly answer; and that is, "to be accepted." See Gen. vi. 8, xviii. 3, xxxix. 4, Eph. i. 6. So is the Greek phrase, Acts vii. 46, "Ος εὗρε χάριν ἐνώπιον τοῦ Θεοῦ,—"Who found favour in the sight of God;" and Luke i. 30, Εὗρες γὰρ χάριν παρὰ τῷ Θεῷ,—"Thou hast found favour with God." So we, instead of "grace;" and thence, verse 28, she is said to be κεχαριτωμένη, "graciously accepted," or "highly favoured."

This sense is pious, and agreeable to the analogy of faith; for our free, gracious acceptance with God is the foundation and cause of all that grace or assistance that we are made partakers of. But,—

2. The apostle is not treating of the personal acceptance of sinners or believers in or by Christ in this place, but of that *especial assistance* which, upon particular addresses unto him, we do obtain. Now this may be considered two ways:—(1.) In respect of the fountain of it, and so it is "beneficentia," the will of God to assist us; or, (2.) Of the effect itself, the "beneficium," the actual assistance and help we do receive. So when our apostle, in his strait upon his temptation, made his address to God for relief, he received that answer, "My grace is sufficient for thee; for my strength is

made perfect in weakness," 2 Cor. xii. 9.   Wherein he had an intimation both of God's gracious care and good-will towards him, as also
of the actual powerful assistance which he should be supplied with
against his temptation. And this sense is determined by the next words.

Εἰς εὔκαιρον βοήθειαν.   What kind of help βοήθεια is hath been de-

Εἰς βοήθειαν.   clared on chap. ii. 18.   It is a "succour;" that is, aid
yielded unto any upon their *cry*.   Θεῖν εἰς βοήν, "to run
in to assist upon the cry of any," is the original of the word's signification.   And this help is,—

Εὔκαιρος, "seasonable;" that is, help בְּעִתּוֹ, "in its time," its proper

Εὔκαιρος.   time or season.   Prov. xv. 23, דָּבָר בְּעִתּוֹ מַה־טּוֹב;—"A word
in its time" (or "its season"),"how good is it!"   Help
that is fit, suitable, seasonable,—that is, on the part of God that gives
it, of the persons that receive it, of the time wherein it is afforded,
of the end for which it is bestowed,—is εὔκαιρος.   This kind of help it
becometh the greatness and wisdom of God to give.   And it is an
impression on the minds of men by nature that such kind of help is
from God.   Hence the proverb, Θεὸς ἀπὸ μηχανῆς, for unexpected aid
when all things otherwise would be lost.   This the psalmist excellently expresseth, Ps. xlvi. 2, עֶזְרָה בְצָרוֹת נִמְצָא מְאֹד;—"God is a help
wonderfully found in straits."   And so the Syriac version adds in this
place, "help in time of affliction" or "persecution."   Grace, therefore, effectual for our assistance in every time of need, upon our cry to
God in Christ, is that which is here intended.   I know not whether
I may add an allusion that may be found in the Hebrew words, if
respect may be had to that language here.   For as כִּפֵּא is a "throne,"
the throne whereunto we approach for help; so כֶּפֶא is as much as
זְמָן an "appointed time" or "season."   We come לַכִּפֵּא for help בַכְּפֵא.

We have opened the words in their order as they lie in the text.
Our observations from the resolution of the sense will arise from the
last clause and ascend unto the first; and in them the meaning of the
words themselves will be yet more fully explained; as,—

Obs. I.   There is, there will be a season, many a season in the
course of our profession and walking before God, wherein we do or
shall stand in need of especial aid and assistance.

This is included in the last words, "help in a time of need,"—
help that is suitable and seasonable for and unto such a condition,
wherein we are found earnestly to cry out for it.   This I shall a little
enlarge upon.   Our condition all along and in all things is wanting
and indigent.   We do live, we must live, if we intend to live, always
in a constant dependence on God in Christ for supplies.   There is a
continual ἐπιχορηγία τοῦ Πνεύματος, Phil. i. 19, or "additional supply
of the Spirit" unto what we have received, without which we cannot
well spiritually subsist one moment.   And "God supplies all our
wants according to his riches in glory" (that is, his glorious riches in

grace) " by Christ Jesus," Phil. iv. 19. But besides that want which always attends our condition in this world, and which God constantly supplies according to the tenor of the covenant of grace, there are especial straits and difficulties, which in especial seasons we are exposed unto. I need not prove this to them that read; they have found it, they have felt it, and so have I also. I shall therefore only call over a few instances of such seasons, some whereof we have already been exercised in, some whereof we cannot escape for the future, and the rest may probably befall us, if they have not done so already.

1. A time of *affliction* is such a season. God is a help בְּצָרוֹת, Ps. xlvi. 2, in all sorts of straits and afflictions. And the Scripture abounds in instances of believers making their especial application unto God for especial assistance in such a season, and directions for them so to do. And the rule of the covenant in sending relief, is upon the coming up of the cry of the afflicted unto God, Ps. l. 15, Exod. ii. 23–25. And let men's stock of wisdom, grace, experience, and resolution, be what it will, or what they can fancy, they are not able to go through with the least new affliction to the glory of God without new especial aid and assistance from him.

2. A time of *persecution* is such a season, yea, it may be the principal season here intended; for hence arose the great danger of these Hebrews in the course of their profession, as our apostle declares at large, Heb. x. And this is the greatest trial that in general God exerciseth his church withal. In such a season some seed quite decayeth, some stars fall from heaven, some prove fearful and unbelieving to their eternal ruin. And few there are but that, where persecution is urgent, it hath some impression upon them to their disadvantage. Carnal fears, with carnal wisdom and counsels, are apt to be at work in such a season; and all the fruit that comes from these evil roots is bitter. Hence many make it their only design, in such a season, to creep through it and live; to be " strong in the Lord, and in the power of his might," unto the performance of all the duties which the gospel requireth, and as it requires them, they have no design. But by this means, as God hath no revenue of glory from them, nor the church of advantage, so they will scarce find inward peace when outward trouble is over. This, then, is a season wherein, if ever, an especial address is needful for especial aid.

3. A time of *temptation* is such a season. Our apostle found it so when he had the " messenger of Satan sent to buffet him." Thrice did he pray and cry out for especial assistance against it, or deliverance from it; and he got assurance of them both. This, added to the former, completed the condition of these Hebrews. With their persecutions they had manifold temptations. These made it a time of need unto them. In reference to this season and the power of it doth our apostle give that great caution, " Let him that thinketh he

standeth take heed lest he fall," 1 Cor. x. 12. And wherein doth this heedfulness principally consist? In an application to him who is "faithful, who will not suffer us to be tempted above what we are able, but will with the temptation also make a way to escape, that we may be able to bear it," verse 13; that is, who will give out seasonable help, "help in a time of need."

4. A time of *spiritual desertion* is such a season. When God in any way withdraws himself from us, we shall stand in need of special assistance. "Thou didst hide thy face," saith David, "and I was troubled." Trouble will ensue on God's hiding himself from us. But this is of the mystery of his grace, that when he withdraws himself from any soul as to sense and experience, whereby it is troubled, he can secretly communicate of himself unto it in a way of strength whereby it shall be sustained.

5. A time wherein we are called unto *the performance of any great and signal duty* is such a season also. So was it with Abraham when he was called first to leave his country, and afterwards to sacrifice his son. Such was the call of Joshua to enter into Canaan, proposed to our example, Heb. xiii. 5; and of the apostles to preach the gospel, when they were sent out "as sheep in the midst of wolves." Now, although we may not perhaps be called in particular to such duties as these, yet we may be so to them which have an equal greatness in them with respect unto us and our condition. Something that is new, that we are yet unexperienced in, something that there is great opposition against, somewhat that may cost us dear, somewhat that as to the state of the inward and outward man we may seem to be every way unfit for, somewhat that the glory of God is in an especial manner concerned in, we may be called unto. And there is nothing of this nature which doth not render the time of it a season wherein we stand in need of especial aid and assistance.

6. Times of *changes, and the difficulties wherewith they are attended*, introduce such a season. "Changes and war," saith Job, are against me," chap. x. 17. There is in all changes a war against us, wherein we may be foiled if we are not the more watchful, and have not the better assistance. And freedom from changes is in most the ground of carnal security: Ps. lv. 19, "Because they have no changes, therefore they fear not God." Changes will beget fear; they are trials to all that are subject unto them. And these we are in all instances of life continually obnoxious unto. No man can enumerate the vicissitudes of our course; yet no one of them can we pass through in a due manner without renewed especial assistances of grace.

7. The time of *death* is such a season. To let go all hold of present things and present hopes, to give up a departing soul entering into the invisible world, and an unchangeable eternity therein, into

the hands of a sovereign Lord, is a thing which requires a strength above our own for the right and comfortable performance of.

Now it is easy to apprehend how great an influence these things have into our whole course of walking before God, and how much of our lives and ways is taken up with them,—either afflictions, or persecutions, or temptations, or defections from God, or signal difficult duties, or changes, are continually before us, and the last of them, death, lies still at the door,—and there is none of these but render their seasons times of need. It may, indeed, then be said, ' Wherein doth the specialty of the grace and aid mentioned consist, seeing it is that which we always stand in need of, and always receive ?' I answer, that indeed all grace is special grace. It proceeds not from any common principle, but from the especial love of God in Christ; and is given out in an especial, distinguishing manner; and that for especial ends and purposes; so that no supply of it hath a peculiar specialty in its own nature. But it is here so called because it is suited unto especial occasions, to be " seasonable help in a time of need." And although we may stand in need of it always, yet we do not so always on the same account, which gives it its specialty. Sometimes one thing, sometimes another, makes it needful and suitable. That which presently presseth upon us, be it affliction or persecution, be it duty or change, it makes the grace we seek for " help in a time of need." And God is pleased so to dispose of things that we shall have occasion at all times to make our applications unto him for especial assistance. If things should be left unto an ordinary course, without some peculiar concernment to excite us, to awaken us, it is inconceivable how formal and secure we should quickly grow. Wherefore we have, in the wisdom of God, always somewhat that in particular presseth upon us, to make us intent, earnest, and vigilant in our addresses to him for help. And the especial supplies which we obtain on any particular occasion afford a contribution of new spiritual strength to the soul for all its duties. The remaining observations may be briefly presented; for hence it appears,—

Obs. II. That there is with God in Christ, God on his throne of grace, a spring of suitable and seasonable help for all times and occasions of difficulty. He is " the God of all grace," and a fountain of living waters is with him for the refreshment of every weary and thirsty soul.

Obs. III. All help, succour, or spiritual assistance in our straits and difficulties, proceeds from mere mercy and grace, or the goodness, kindness, and benignity of God in Christ: " That we may receive mercy, and obtain grace to help." Our help is from grace and mercy; and thence must it be, or we must be for ever helpless. And, not to exclude that sense of the words,—

Obs. IV. When we have, through Christ, obtained mercy and grace for our persons, we need not fear but that we shall have suitable and seasonable help for our duties. If we "obtain mercy" and "find grace," we shall have "help."

Obs. V. The way to obtain help from God is by a due gospel application of our souls for it to the throne of grace: "Let us come" for it "to the throne of grace." How this application is to be made by faith and supplications, and how indispensable it is for the procuring of the aid aimed at, shall be elsewhere declared.

Obs. VI. Great discouragements are used to interpose themselves in our minds and against our faith, when we stand in need of especial help from God, and would make our application unto him for relief. It is included in the exhortation to "come with boldness;" that is, to cast off and conquer all those discouragements, and to use confidence of acceptance and liberty of speech before him.

Obs. VII. Faith's consideration of the interposition of Christ in our behalf, as our high priest, is the only way to remove discouragements, and to give us boldness in our access unto God: "Let us come therefore with boldness;" that is, on the account of the care, love, and faithfulness of Christ as our high priest, before discoursed on. And we may add,—

Obs. VIII. That in all our approaches unto God, we are to consider him as on a throne. Though it be a "throne of grace," yet it is still a throne; the consideration whereof should influence our minds with "reverence and godly fear" in all things wherein we have to do with him.

These observations are, as included in the text, so of importance in themselves, as concerning the principal parts of the life of faith, and our daily spiritual exercise in our walking before God; yet I shall forbear any enlargements upon them, that these discourses be not drawn forth unto too great a length.

Μόνῳ τῷ Θεῷ δόξα.

CHAPTER V.

THERE are three general parts of this chapter;—First, A description of the office and duties of *a* high priest, verses 1–4. Secondly, The application of this general description unto the person and priesthood of *Jesus Christ* in particular, verses 5–10. Thirdly, An occasional diversion into a reproof of and expostulation with the Hebrews, for and about their backwardness in learning the mysteries of the gospel, begun in this, and carried on in the beginning of the next chapter, verses 11-14.

In the first part, the general description of a high priest is given: 1. From his original; he is "taken from among men." 2. From the nature of his office; he is "ordained for men in things pertaining to God." 3. From the especial end of it; to "offer both gifts and sacrifices for sins," verse 1. 4. From the qualification of his person for the discharge of his office; for he must be one that "can have compassion on the ignorant, and on them that are out of the way:" whereunto is subjoined the ground of that qualification; for "he himself also is compassed with infirmity," verse 2. 5. From the continual duty arising from his office and personal qualification for it, in respect of others and himself; for "by reason hereof he ought, as for the people, so also for himself, to offer for sins," verse 3. 6. From his call to his office: which is,—(1.) Asserted to be from God, "And no man taketh this honour to himself, but he that is called of God;" (2.) Exemplified in the instance of Aaron's, "As was Aaron," verse 4.

Secondly, The ἀπόδοσις, or "application" of this description unto the person of Jesus Christ (which is the second part of the chapter), is not to show an exact conformity thereunto, as though all things should be the same, and even or equal, in the high priest which he had described and him whom he would now represent unto them. This would have been contrary to the design of the apostle. For the description he hath given us of a high priest is of him, or such a one as the Hebrews had under the law ; and his purpose was to show them how much more excellent a priest he was of whom he treated. There must, therefore, of necessity be sundry differences between them. Wherefore, in the application of this description of a legal high priest unto the person and office of Christ, three things (as we shall show afterwards in particular) the apostle aimeth at :— 1. To demonstrate that there was nothing *essentially* requisite unto the constituting of any one to be a high priest, or in the discharge of that office, but it was found in and agrees unto the Lord Jesus Christ ; 2. Whatever was of weakness or infirmity in the high priest of old, on the account of his infirm and frail condition, *that* Jesus Christ was free from ; 3. That he had in this office several preeminences and advantages which the old high priest was not partaker of or sharer in: which things will in our progress be explained. Hence the application made by the apostle of the precedent description is not to be expected such as should exactly correspond with it in all particulars. Wherefore,—

1. By a ὕστερον πρότερον, he insisteth first, in the application, on the last instance of his description, namely, the *call* of a high priest. And this as to the person of Christ is expressed,—(1.) Negatively, "He glorified not himself to be made a priest:" (2.) Positively, it

was of God; which he proves by a double testimony, one from Ps. ii. 7, the other from Ps. cx. 4–6.

2. On the *discharge* of his office whereunto he was so called of God: which he describes,—(1.) From the season of it; " it was in the days of his flesh:" (2.) The manner of its performance; " he offered up prayers and supplications, with strong crying and tears: (3.) The general issue of it; he " was heard in that he feared," verse 7.

3. He proceeds by the anticipation of an *objection*, and therein the declaration of a singular pre-eminence that he had above all other priests, with the love and condescension with which the discharge of his office was accompanied; together with the great benefit which ensued thereon: " Though he were a Son, yet learned he obedience by the things which he suffered." verse 8.

4. The glorious *end* of his priesthood, manifesting the incomparable excellency of it above that of Aaron, is expressed verse 9. All issuing,—

5. In a summary description of his call and office, as he intends afterwards to enlarge upon them, verse 10.

The third part of the chapter contains a diversion unto a *reproof* of and expostulation with the Hebrews, about the things concerning which he intended to treat with them: wherein is expressed,— 1. The occasion; and that,—(1.) On the part of the things which he treated about, not absolutely, but with respect unto them, " Of whom we have many things to say, and hard to be uttered;" (2.) On their part, " Seeing that ye are dull of hearing," verse 11.   2. This fault of theirs, occasioning their reproof, is aggravated,—(1.) From the means and advantages to the contrary which they had enjoyed, verse 12; (2.) By a particular elegant description of the nature of that weakness, evil, and defect which he blamed in them, verses 12, 13; (3.) By a declaration of the contrary virtue, the want whereof in them he complains of, verse 14.

This is the substance of the discourses of this chapter, considered apart by themselves. We must also inquire into their relation unto those foregoing, and the design of the apostle in them, which is twofold; for,—

First, They have respect unto his general purpose and aim. And herein they contain an entrance into a full and particular description of the sacerdotal office of Christ, with the excellency of it, and the benefits which thereby redound unto the church. This was the principal intention of the apostle in the writing of this epistle; for besides the excellency of the doctrine hereof in itself, and the inestimable benefits which the whole church receiveth thereby, it was peculiarly for many reasons necessary for the Hebrews, as hath been showed. Wherefore in the first chapter he lays down a description of the person of Christ, which, under the new testament, is vested with all those sacred offices in and over the church of God which were typically exercised by others under the old. Of these, in the following chapters he more particularly treats of his kingly and prophetical; comparing him therein with Moses and Joshua, showing in sundry instances his pre-eminence above them. He had also by the way interserted several things concerning his sacerdotal office, with a general description whereof, and declaration of the advantage of the church thereby, he closeth the foregoing chapter.

In all these things it was the purpose of the apostle not to handle them absolutely, but with respect unto that exercise of them which, by God's appointment, was in use in the church of the Hebrews under the old testament; for that the nature of his treaty with them did require. And herein he effected two things, both apposite unto his principal end; for,—1. He declares what it was in all those institutions which God intended to instruct them in, seeing they were all " shadows of good things to come." So he lets them know that whatever esteem they had of them, and however they rested in them, they were not appointed for their own sakes, but only for a time, to foresignify what was now, in the person and mediation of Christ, actually and really exhibited unto them. 2. He makes it evident how exceedingly the way and worship of God which they were now called unto, and made partakers of under the gospel, did excel those which before they were intrusted with; whence the conclusion was easy and unavoidable, unto the necessity of their steadfastness in the profession of the gospel,—the principal thing aimed at in the whole.

On these grounds, the apostle undertaketh a comparison between the priesthood of Aaron and his successors and that of Jesus Christ, which was prefigured thereby. And this he doth with respect unto both the ends mentioned; for, first, he shows them how they were of old instructed in the nature and use of that priesthood which, according to the promise of God, was to be introduced and erected in the church in the person of his Son. Hence he lays down sundry things which they knew to belong unto the priesthood of old, whence they might learn somewhat, yea much, of the nature of this now exhibited, seeing they were instituted on purpose to declare it, although they did it but obscurely. And then also he makes known the excellency of this priesthood of Christ above that of old, as the substance excels the shadow, and the permanent thing represented, the obscure and fading representations of it. Unto the handling of these things an entrance is here made, which, with sundry occasional diversions, is pursued to the end of the 10th chapter.

Secondly, In particular, the present discourse of this chapter hath relation unto what immediately precedes in the close of the foregoing; for having therein proposed to their consideration the priestly

office of Christ, and given a glorious description of it in general,
with respect unto his person and exaltation, he shows how greatly
this conduces to the advantage and consolation of the church, as
may be seen in the text, and our exposition of it. To confirm what
he had so proposed, and to strengthen our faith in expectation of
the benefits expressed, he enters upon a particular description of
that office as exercised by Christ; and in this respect the ensuing
discourse renders the reasons and gives the grounds of what he had
immediately before laid down and declared.

VERSE 1.

Πᾶς γὰρ ἀρχιερεὺς ἐξ ἀνθρώπων λαμβανόμενος, ὑπὲρ ἀνθρώπων καθίσταται
τὰ πρὸς τὸν Θεόν, ἵνα προσφέρῃ δῶρά τε καὶ θυσίας ὑπὲρ ἁμαρτιῶν.

Ἐξ ἀνθρώπων. Syr., דְּמִן בְּנֵי נָשָׁא, "who is of" (or "from amongst") "the sons
of men." Ὑπὲρ ἀνθρώπων καθίσταται. Syr., חְלָף בְּנֵי נָשָׁא קָאֵם, "stands for men;"
that is, in their stead. Τὰ πρὸς τὸν Θεόν. Syr., אִילֵין דְּאַלְהָא אֵנֵין, "over the things
which are of God," or which belong to him; not so properly, as we shall see.
The Arabic renders τὰ πρὸς τὸν Θεόν, "in the things that are offered unto God;" a
good sense of the words. And the Ethiopic is, "appointed for men with" (or
"before") "God;" that is, to do for them what is to be done with God. Vulg.
Lat., "in iis quæ sunt ad Deum," "in the things appertaining unto God," or
which are to be done with him. So Arias, "ea quæ ad Deum," to the same purpose. Beza, "in iis quæ sunt apud Deum peragenda," "in the things that are to
be performed towards God;" more properly than ours and the Rhemists, "in
things pertaining to God," for so do things innumerable, on one account or other,
that are not here intended. Δῶρα. Syr., קוּרְבָּנָא, "oblations," "offerings;" a
general name for all sacrifices.

Πᾶς γὰρ ἀρχιερεύς,—that is, כָּל כֹּהֵן הַגָּדוֹל, "every chief" or "great
priest." Or as the Syriac, כָּל רַב כּוּמְרָא, "prince" or
"chief of the priests." The first mention of a high
priest is Lev. xxi. 10, הַכֹּהֵן הַגָּדוֹל מֵאֶחָיו, "the priest that is great among
his brethren." LXX., ὁ ἱερεὺς ὁ μέγας ἀπὸ τῶν ἀδελφῶν αὐτοῦ. Jun., "sacerdos qui maximus est fratrum suorum." All the *males* of the family
of Aaron were equal, and brethren, as to the priesthood; but there
was *one* who was the head and prince of the rest, whose office was
not distinct from theirs, but in the discharge of it, and preparation
for it there were many things peculiarly appropriated unto him.
And these things are distinctly appointed and enumerated in several
places. The whole office was firstly vested in him, the remainder
of the priests being as it were his present assistants, and a nursery
for a future succession. The whole nature of the type was preserved
in him alone. But as in one case our apostle tells us of these high
priests themselves, that by the law they "were many,"—that is, in
succession one after another, "because they were not suffered to
continue by reason of death," Heb. vii. 23, (one single high priest
had been sufficient to have represented the priesthood of Christ,

but because God would have that done constantly during the continuance of that church-state, and every individual person of them
died in his season, they were to be multiplied by succession;) so
because of their weakness, and the multiplied carnal services which
they had to attend unto, no one man was able to discharge the whole
office, there were others therefore added unto the high priest for the
time being, as his assistants, which were so far also types of Christ as
they were partakers of his office. But because the office was principally collated on and vested in the high priest, and because many
important parts of the duty of it were appropriated unto him; as
also, because the glorious vestments peculiar to the office, made "for
glory and for beauty," to represent the excellency and holiness of
the person of Christ, were to be worn by none but him; he alone
is singled out as the principal representative of the Lord Christ in
this office.

And the high priest was a single person, there was but one at one
time, the better to type out the office of Christ. It is true in the
gospel there is mention τῶν ἀρχιερέων, of the "high priests" that
then were, Matt. ii. 4, xvi. 21, which we render "chief priests." So
Sceva, the father of the vagabond exorcists, is said to be ἀρχιερεύς,
Acts xix. 14. But these were only such as were ἐκ γένους ἀρχιε-
ρατικοῦ, Acts iv. 6, of the stock and near kindred of him who was
at present high priest, or of that family wherein at present the
high priesthood was; for out of them in an ordinary course a successor was to be taken. It may be, also, that those who were the
heads or chiefs of the several orders or courses of the priests were
then so called. But absolutely by the law the high priest was but
one at one time.

And it is of the high priest according to the law of Moses that
the apostle speaks. Grotius thinks otherwise: " Non tantum legem
hîc respicit; sed et morem ante legem, cum aut primogeniti famili-
arum, aut à populis electi reges, inirent sacerdotium;"—"He respects
not only the law, but the manner before the law, when the first-
born of the families, or kings chosen by the people, took and exercised the priesthood." But it is of a high priest distinctly concerning
whom the apostle speaks; and that there were any such among the
people of God, either by natural descent or the consent of many,
before the law, is not true. And this supposition is contrary to the
design of the apostle, who treats with the Hebrews about the privileges and priesthood which they enjoyed by virtue of the law of
Moses. So he says expressly, chap. vii. 11, "If perfection were by
the Levitical priesthood." That is it whereof he speaks. And verse
28, "The law maketh men high priests." He discourseth of the
priests appointed by the law, that is, of Moses, and of them only.

Some expositors of the Roman church, as our Rhemists, take

occasion to assert the necessity of a Christian priesthood to offer
sacrifices to God, as also to dispose of all things wherein the worship
of God is concerned, and to reprove kings and princes if they interpose aught therein, it being a matter wherewith they have not any
thing to do. But they cannot really imagine that the apostle had
the least intention to teach any such thing in this place; and therefore the most sober interpreters amongst them do confine their discourses unto the Levitical priesthood. Yea, indeed, the purpose of
the apostle is to prove that all priesthood properly so called, and all
proper sacrifices to be offered up by virtue of that office, were issued
in the priesthood and sacrifice of Christ, seeing the sole use and end
of them were to represent and prefigure these in the church. And
to deny them now to be passed away, or to plead the continuance
of any other proper priesthood and sacrifice, is to deny that Jesus
is come in the flesh; which is "that spirit of antichrist," 1 John
iv. 3.

Ἐξ ἀνθρώπων λαμβανόμενος, "taken from among men." This expression is not part of the subject of the proposition, or
descriptive merely of that which is spoken of, as if the
whole should be, "every high priest taken from among
men;" in which way and sense they are restrictive of the subject
spoken of, as containing a limitation in them, and so intimate that
it is thus with every high priest who is taken from amongst men,
though it may be otherwise with others who are not so. But this is
one of the things which is attributed unto every high priest, every
one that is so absolutely; he who is so is to be "taken from among
men." And "ex hominibus assumptus" is as much as "ex hominibus assumitur," is taken from amongst men; and the whole sense
may be supplied by a copulative interposed before the next words,
" is taken from amongst men, and is ordained." This is, then, the
first thing that belongs unto a high priest, and which here is ascribed unto him, "he is taken from amongst men."

And two things are here considerable:—1. That he is from amongst
men; and, 2. That he is taken from amongst them.

1. He is ἐξ ἀνθρώπων, and herein two things are included:—(1.)
That he is "naturæ humanæ particeps." He is, and
must be, partaker in common of human nature with the
rest of mankind, or he is not, on many reasons, meet for the discharge of this office. Neither the divine nature nor angelical is
capable of the exercise of it for men; and this is principally intended. (2.) That antecedently unto his assumption unto this office
he was among the number of common men, as having nothing in
his nature to prefer him above them. So was it with Aaron; he was
a common man amongst his brethren, yea, a mean man in bondage,
before his call to office. The first of these declares what every high

priest is and ought to be; the latter, what the first legal high priest actually was.

I showed before that in this description of the office of a high priest, and the application of it unto Jesus Christ, those things which are essential thereunto, and without which it could not be duly executed, are found in him, and that in a far more perfect and excellent manner than in the priests of the law; but those things which, although they were found necessarily in all that were vested with this office, yet belonged not to the office itself, nor the execution of it, but arose from the persons themselves and their imperfections, they had no place in him at all. So is it here. It was essential to the office itself that he should be partaker of human nature; and that it was so with the Lord Christ our apostle signally declares, with the reason of it, chap. ii. 14: but it was not so that he should be absolutely in the common state of all other men, antecedently to his call to office; for so the apostle declares that he was not, but he was the Son, the Son of God, chap. v. 8. So "the Son was consecrated," that is, a priest, "for evermore," chap. vii. 28. For he was born into this world king, priest, and prophet unto his church.

2. Λαμβανόμενος, "assumptus," or "is taken," is separated from them. Being made a high priest, he is no more of the same rank and quality with them.

'Υπὲρ ἀνθρώπων καθίσταται, τὰ πρὸς τὸν Θεόν, "is ordained for men." 'Υπέρ is sometimes "vice," or "loco," "in the stead," John x. 11, 15, xiii. 38; sometimes "pro," only as it denotes the final cause, as to do a thing for the good of men, 2 Tim. ii. 10. And both these senses may have place here; for where the first intention is, the latter is always included. He that doth any thing *in the stead* of another, doth it always *for his good*. And the high priest might be so far said to stand and act in the stead of other men, as he appeared in their behalf, represented their persons, pleaded their cause, and confessed their sins, Lev. xvi. 21. But 'in their behalf,' or 'for their good and advantage, to perform what on their part is with God to be performed,' is evidently intended in this place.

Καθίσταται τὰ πρὸς τὸν Θεόν. Some suppose that because καθίσταται is, as they say, "verbum medium," it may in this place have an active signification; and then the sense of it would be, that he might "appoint," "ordain," or "order the things of God." But as it is used most frequently in a neuter or a passive sense, so in this place it can be no otherwise. So the apostle explains himself, chap. viii. 3, Πᾶς ἀρχιερεὺς εἰς τὸ προσφέρειν δῶρά τε καὶ θυσίας καθίσταται,—"Every high priest is ordained to offer gifts and sacrifices;" which place expoundeth this. And two things are intended in the word:—1. God's *designation and appointment;*

2. Actual *consecration* according to the order of the law. For so it was in the case of Aaron.

1. God gave command that he should be set apart to the office of the priesthood. "Take Aaron thy brother," saith God to Moses, "מִתּוֹךְ בְּנֵי יִשְׂרָאֵל," "from amongst the children of Israel" (that is, ἐξ ἀνθρώπων, "from among men") "that he may minister unto me in the priest's office," Exod. xxviii. 1. This was the foundation of his call, separation, and function.

2. He was actually *consecrated* unto his office by sundry sacrifices, described at large, Exod. xxix. So was he ordained τὰ πρὸς τὸν Θεόν. Now this latter part of his ordination belonged unto the weakness and imperfection of that priesthood, that he could not be consecrated without the sacrifice of other things. But the Lord Christ, being both priest and sacrifice himself, he needed no such ordination, nor was capable thereof. His ordination, therefore, consisted merely in divine designation and appointment, as we shall see. And this difference there was to be between them who were made high priests by the law, and which had infirmity, and him who was made by the word of the oath of God, who is the Son, Heb. vii. 28.

Τὰ πρὸς τὸν Θεόν. The expression is elliptical and sacred; but what
Τὰ πρὸς τὸν is intended in it is sufficiently manifest, namely, the
Θεόν. things that were to be done with God, or towards God, in his worship, to answer the duties and ends of the office of the priesthood,—that is, to do the things whereby God might be appeased, atoned, reconciled, pacified, and his anger turned away. See Heb. ii. 17.

Ἵνα προσφέρη δῶρά τε καὶ θυσίας ὑπὲρ ἁμαρτιῶν,—"that he may offer,"
Ἵνα προσφέρη. וַיִּקְרַב; the word compriseth the whole sacerdotal performance from first to last, in bringing, slaying, and burning the sacrifice, according to the law; of which see Leviticus, chap. i.–v., and our former Exercitations concerning the sacrifices of the Jews. The object of this sacerdotal action is δῶρα καὶ θυσίαι.

Δῶρα καὶ θυσίας. Interpreters are much divided about the application of these words unto the ancient sacrifices. Some think they answer מִנְחוֹת and עוֹלוֹת, any "offering" in common, and "whole burnt-offerings;" some שְׁלָמִים and עוֹלֹת, "peace-offerings" and "burnt-offerings;" some חַטָּאת and אָשֵׁם, the "sin" and "trespass-offering." The most general opinion is, that by "gifts" all offerings of things inanimate are intended,—as meats, drinks, oils, first-fruits, meal, and the like; and by "sacrifices," the offerings of all creatures that were slain,—as lambs, goats, doves, whose blood was poured on the altar. And this difference the words would lead us unto, the latter signifying directly the offering of things killed or slain. But our Saviour seems to comprise all offerings whatever under the name of "gifts," Matt. v. 23. And if a distinction be here to be supposed, I should think that by "gifts" all "free-will offerings" might be intended; and by "sacrifices," those that were determined, as to occasions, times, and seasons, by the law. But I rather judge that the apostle useth these two words in general to express all sorts of sacrifices for sin whatever; and therefore that expression, ὑπὲρ ἁμαρτιῶν, "for sins," may refer to δῶρα, "gifts," as well as to θυσίας, "sacrifices."

Ver. 1.—For every high priest, taken from amongst men, is ordained for men in things pertaining to God, that he may offer both gifts and sacrifices for sins.

What is the relation of these words unto the discourse of the apostle, both in general and particular, hath been declared before. I shall pursue that only which is particular and immediate. Having therefore proposed the priesthood of Christ as a matter of great advantage and comfort unto believers, he engageth into the confirmation thereof, by declaring the nature of that office, making application of what he observes therein unto the Lord Christ, as our high priest. In this verse we have, as was said, a general description of a high priest, as his office was constituted and consummated by the law. For,—

1. he is described from his *original.* He is one "taken from among men," from amongst those for whom he is to be a priest, that so he may be one partaker of the same nature with them, Exod. xxviii. 1. He was not to be an angel, whose nature was incapable of those compassionate impressions which are required unto a due discharge of this office. Besides, the administrations of an angel amongst sinners would have been attended with dread and terror, and have taken away that spiritual boldness and confidence which a high priest is to encourage men unto. Moreover, there would not have been hereby any representation of that union between the Lord Christ and us which was indispensably necessary unto our high priest, who was to be himself both priest and sacrifice. Wherefore a high priest was to be "taken from among men," and so was our Lord Christ, as hath been at large declared on chap. ii. 10–16. And we are taught that,—

Obs. I. Christ's participation of our nature, as necessary unto him for the bearing and discharge of the office of a high priest on our behalf, is a great ground of consolation unto believers, a manifest evidence that he is and will be tender and compassionate towards them. The reader may consult what hath been discoursed to this purpose on chap. ii. 10, 11, etc.

2. He is described from the *nature of his office* in general. He is "ordained for men in things pertaining to God." There are things to be done with God on the behalf of men as sinners, and with re-

spect unto sin, as is declared in the close of the verse. Hence arose
the necessity of priests, as we have showed elsewhere. Had there
been no sin, no atonement to be made with God for sin, every one
in his own person should have done that which appertained unto
God, or what he had to do with God. For God required nothing of
any man but what he might do for himself. But now, all men being
sinners, God will not immediately be treated withal by them; and
besides, there is that now to be done for them which in their own
persons they cannot perform. It was therefore upon the account of
the interposition of Jesus Christ, with respect unto his future priesthood, that any one was ever admitted to treat with God about an
atonement for sin; and this was the ground of the typical priesthood
of old. Those priests were " ordained for men in things pertaining
to God."

Obs. II. It was the entrance of sin that made the office of the
priesthood necessary. This hath been abundantly confirmed elsewhere.

Obs. III. It was of infinite grace that such an appointment was
made. Without it all holy intercourse between God and man must
have ceased; for neither, 1. were *the persons of sinners meet* to approach unto God, nor, 2. was any service which they could perform, or
were instructed how to perform, *suited* unto the great end which
man was now to look after,—namely, peace with God. For the
persons of all men being defiled, and obnoxious unto the curse of the
law, how should they appear in the presence of the righteous and
holy God? Isa. xxxiii. 14; Mic. vi. 6, 7. It may be it will be said,
' That these priests themselves, of whom the apostle treateth in the
first place, were also sinners, and yet they were appointed for men
in things appertaining unto God; so that sinners may appear in such
matters before the Lord.' I answer, It is true, they were so. And
therefore our apostle says that they were to offer for their own sins
as well as for the sins of the people, verse 3; but then they did none
of them officiate in that office merely in their own names and on
their own account, but as they were types and representatives of him
who had no sin, and whose office gave virtue and efficacy unto theirs.
Again, men in their own persons had nothing to offer unto God but
their moral duties, which the law of their creation and the covenant
of works required of them. Now these, as is known, for many reasons were no way meet or able to make atonement for sin, the
great work now to be done with God, and without which every thing
else that can be done by sinners is of no consideration. God therefore appointing a new service for this end, namely, that of sacrifices,
appointed also a new way, with performance by a priest in the name
and behalf of others. And a most gracious appointment it was, as
that on which all blessed intercourse with God and all hopes of ac-

ceptance with him do solely depend.   Though the occasion was grievous, the relief is glorious.

Obs. IV. The priest is described by the especial discharge of his duty or exercise of his office; which is his "offering both gifts and sacrifices for sins." This is the proper and principal work of a priest, as we have at large declared in our Exercitations. Priests and sacrifices are so related as that they cannot be separated. Take away the one, and you destroy the other. And these sacrifices here are "for sin;" that is, offered unto God to make atonement, propitiation, and reconciliation for sin.

Obs. V. Where there is no proper propitiatory sacrifice there is no proper priest. Every priest is to "offer sacrifices for sin;" that is, to make atonement. And therefore,—

Obs. VI. Jesus Christ alone is the high priest of his people; for he alone could offer a sacrifice for our sins to make atonement. This our apostle designs to prove, and doth it accordingly, in this and the ensuing chapters.

Obs. VII. It was a great privilege which the church enjoyed of old, in the representation which they had, by God's appointment, of the priesthood and sacrifice of Christ in their own typical priests and sacrifices. In themselves they were things low and carnal, such as could by no means expiate their sins: that is a work not to be done by the blood of bulls and goats. An expectation of that issue and effect by the mere virtue of such sacrifices, is the highest affront to the nature, rule, holiness, and righteousness of God. But this was their glory and excellency, that they typed out and represented that which should really accomplish the great and mighty work of taking up the controversy between God and man about sin.

Obs. VIII. Much more glorious is our privilege under the gospel, since our Lord Jesus hath taken upon him, and actually discharged, this part of his office, in offering an absolutely perfect and complete sacrifice for sin. Here is the foundation laid of all our peace and happiness. And this is now plainly proposed unto us, and not taught by types or spoken in parables. Their teachings of old were obscure, and therefore many missed of the mind of God in them. Hence some thought that they must trust to their sacrifices for their righteousness and pardon. Of these, some took up with them, and rested in them to their ruin. Others, more galled with their convictions, thought of other ways, and how they might outdo what God required, seeing they could not trust unto what he did so require, Mic. vi. 6, 7. But now all things are clearly revealed and proposed unto us; for Jesus Christ in the gospel is "evidently crucified before our eyes," Gal. iii. 1. Our way is made plain, so that "wayfaring men, though fools, shall not err therein," Isa. xxxv. 8. The veil being removed, "we all with open face behold as in a glass the glory of the Lord," 2 Cor. iii. 18. The sum of all is,—

Obs. IX. What is to be done with God on the account of sin, that it may be expiated and pardoned, and that the people of God who have sinned may be accepted with him and blessed, is all actually done for them by Jesus Christ, their high priest, in the sacrifice for sin which he offered on their behalf. He was ordained τὰ πρὸς τὸν Θεόν,—to do all things with God that were to be done for us; namely, that we might be pardoned, sanctified, and saved. This he undertook when he took his office upon him. His wisdom, faithfulness, and mercy, will not allow us to suppose that he hath left any thing undone that belonged thereunto. If any thing be omitted, as good all were so: for none besides himself in heaven or earth could do aught in this matter. He hath therefore faithfully, mercifully, fully done all that was to be done with God on our behalf. Particularly, he hath offered that great sacrifice which was promised, expected, represented, from the foundation of the world, as the only means of reconciliation and peace between God and man. So saith the text he was to do: he was to offer sacrifice for sin. How he did it, and what he effected thereby, must be declared in our progress. For the present it may suffice, that there is no more to be done with God about sin, as to atonement, propitiation, and pardon. There needs no more sacrifice for it,—no masses, no merits, no works of our own.

VERSE 2.

Two things the apostle hath proposed unto himself, which in this and the ensuing verses he doth yet further pursue. 1. *A description of a high priest* according to the law. 2. The evincing, (1.) That whatever was useful or excellent in such a high priest was to *be found in a more eminent manner in Jesus Christ,* the only real and proper high priest of the church; as also, (2.) That whatever was *weak* and *infirm* in such a priest, necessarily attending his frail and sinful condition, which either eclipsed the glory or weakened the efficacy of the office as by him discharged, *had no place in him at all.* For whereas the affections and infirmities of our human nature are of two sorts,—(1.) Such as arise from the essence and constitution of it, and so are naturally and absolutely necessary unto all that are partakers thereof as created; (2.) Such as came occasionally on it by the entrance of sin, which adhere to all that are partakers of our nature as corrupted;—the former sort were necessary unto him that should be a high priest, and that not only unto his being so, as is the participation of our nature in general, but also as to such a qualification of him as is useful and encouraging unto them for whose good he doth exercise and discharge his office; but the latter sort are such as that although they did not evacuate the office in

their discharge of it who were obnoxious unto them, as to the proportion of their interest therein, yet was it an impeachment of its
perfection, and absolutely hindered it from being able to attain the
utmost end of the priesthood.   Wherefore the first sort of these
affections, such as are compassion, love, condescension, care, pity,
were not only in Christ, our high priest, but also, as graciously prepared, did belong unto his holy qualification for the effectual and
encouraging discharge of his office.   The latter sort, as death natural,
sickness, distempers of mind, producing personal sins inevitably, with
other frailties, as they were found in the high priest according to the
law, and belonged unto the imperfection of that priesthood; so being
either sinful or penal, with respect unto the individual person in
whom they were, they had no place in Jesus Christ, the Son of God.
To understand, therefore, aright the comparison here made between
the high priest under the law and Jesus Christ, or the application
of it as spoken concerning a high priest by the law, unto him, we
must observe that the apostle designs the two things mentioned in
the second particular before laid down:—

1. That all real, necessary, useful conditions and qualifications of
a high priest, as required in him by the law, were all of them
found in Jesus Christ as our high priest, whereby he did answer
and fulfil the representation and prefigurations that were made of
him under the old testament.

2. That whatever did adhere necessarily unto the persons of the
high priests of old as they were sinful men, partakers of our nature as depraved or corrupted, was not to be sought for nor to be
found in him.   And unto these there is added, as a necessary exur-
gency of both,—

3. That sundry things, wherein the peculiar eminency, advancement, and perfection of this office doth consist, were so peculiar
unto him, as that they neither were nor could be represented by
the high priest made so by the law.

Wherefore it is not an exact parallel or complete resemblance
between the legal high priest and Christ, the Son of God, which
the apostle designeth, but such a comparison as wherein, there
being an agreement in things substantial with respect unto a certain end, yet the differences are great and many; which only can
take place where one of the comparates is indeed on many accounts
incomparably more excellent than the other.   To this purpose is
the observation of Chrysostom on the place: Τέως οὖν ἃ κοινά ἐστι
τίθησι πρῶτα· καὶ τότε δείκνυσιν ὅτι ὑπερέχει· ἡ γὰρ κατὰ σύγκρισιν ὑπε-
ροχὴ οὕτω . . . . . ὅταν ἐν μὲν τοῖς κοινωνῇ, ἐν δὲ τοῖς ὑπερέχῃ· εἰ δὲ μὴ οὐκ
ἔτι κατὰ σύγκρισιν.—"First, he sets down the things that are common
to both, then declares wherein he" (that is, Christ) "excelleth; for
so an excellency is set out by comparison, when in some things

there is an equality, in others an excellency on one side; and if it
be otherwise there can be no comparison." The words of the second
verse are,—

Ver. 2.—Μετριοπαθεῖν δυνάμενος τοῖς ἀγνοοῦσι καὶ πλανωμένοις, ἐπεὶ καὶ
αὐτὸς περίκειται ἀσθένειαν.

Μετριοπαθεῖν δυνάμενος. Vulg. Lat., "qui condolere possit," "that can grieve
with." Rhem., "that can have compassion." Arias, "mensuratè pati potens,"
"that is able to bear moderately." Syr., וְאַיְנָא מְשְׁכַּה דְּמַךְ נַפְשֵׁה תְּנַחֵשׁ עַט, "and
who can let down" (or "humble himself") "his soul, and suffer with," or condescend to suffer with. Arab., "who can spare and forgive." The Ethiopic
translation, referring this wholly to the high priest under the law, by way of opposition, not comparison, reads it, "who cannot relieve them who err under their
hands," or by their conduct. Eras., "qui compati possit," "who can suffer
together with," or have compassion on. Beza, "qui quantum satis est possit
miserari vicem ignorantium;" that is, "who can sufficiently pity and have compassion on the condition," etc. There is not only a variety of expression used, but
various senses also are intended by these interpreters, as we shall see in the examination of them. Ours, "who can have compassion on;" and in the margin,
"reasonably bear with."

Τοῖς ἀγνοοῦσι καὶ πλανωμένοις, "ignorantibus et errantibus." Bez., "aber-
rantibus;" whence is ours, "out of the way." One "out of the way" is properly
"aberrans." Rhem., "and do err." Arab., "who deal foolishly and err."

Περίκειται ἀσθένειαν. Syr., לבִישׁ, is "clothed," compassed with infirmity, as a
man is with his clothing that is about him and always cleaving to him.

Ver. 2.—Who can have compassion on [*is able mercifully
to bear with*] the ignorant, and those that wander from
the way, seeing that he himself also is compassed with
infirmity.

The discourse begun in the preceding verse is here continued,
and all things spoken in it are regulated by the first words of it,
"Every high priest;"—' Every high priest is one who can have
compassion.' And the same construction and sense is carried on in
the next verse.

There are three things in the words:—1. A great and necessary
qualification or endowment of a high priest; he is, he was to be,
one who is "able to have compassion." 2. The peculiar object of
his *office acts*, proceeding from and suited unto that qualification;
which is, "those who are ignorant, and do wander from the way."
3. A special *reason*, rendering this qualification necessary unto him,
or the means whereby it is ingenerated in him; "he himself is
compassed with infirmity:" which things must be particularly inquired into.

1. Μετριοπαθεῖν δυνάμενος. Δύναμαι doth first and properly signify
natural ability, a power for the effecting of any thing.
And it is used concerning God and man, according to
their distinct powers and abilities;—the one original and absolutely

Δυνάμενος.

infinite; the other derived, dependent, and variously limited. This is the first and proper signification of the word, which is so known as that it needs no confirmation by instances. Secondly, It signifies a *moral power*, with respect unto the bounds and limits of our duty. So, " Illud possumus quod jure possumus,"—" That we can do which we can do lawfully." Men can do many things naturally that they cannot do morally,—that is, justly; and they do so every day. 1 Cor. x. 21, Οὐ δύνασθε ποτήριον Κυρίου πίνειν καὶ ποτήριον δαιμονίων,—" Ye cannot drink the cup of the Lord and the cup of devils;" ' ye cannot do it righteously, ye ought not to do it.' 2 Cor. xiii. 8, Οὐ γὰρ δυνάμεθά τι κατὰ τῆς ἀληθείας,—" We can do nothing against the truth, but for it." So, then, it expresseth a power commensurate unto our duty, and exerted in the discharge of it, Gen. xxxix. 9. Thirdly, Δυνάμενος, "potens," is as much as ἱκανός, "idoneus," one that is meetly qualified with dispositions and inclinations suited unto his work, or that which is affirmed of him. This sense of the word we have opened on chap. ii. 17, 18, iv. 15. And this sense, which is here intended, may be conceived two ways, or it includes two things:—(1.) The *denial of an incapacity* for what is affirmed: He is not of such a nature, of such a condition, or so qualified, as that he should be unable—that is, unmeet and unfit—for this work. (2.) An assertion of a *positive inclination*, meetness, readiness, and ability for it: Who is able, hath nothing in nature or state to hinder him, is disposed unto it, and ready for it.

Μετριοπαθεῖν. This word is nowhere used in the New Testament but in this place only; and, as most suppose, it is here   *Μετριοπαθεῖν.* used in a sense new and peculiar. Hence have interpreters so variously rendered this word, as we before observed. Nor are expositors less divided about its sense, though the differences about it are not great nor of importance, seeing all ascribe a sound and useful meaning unto it. In other writers it signifies constantly to "moderate affections." Μετριοπαθής is "modicè," or "moderatè affectus; qui modum tenet in animi perturbationibus;"—"one who is moderate in his affections; who exceeds not due measure in perturbations of mind." And μετριοπάθεια is rendered by Cicero, "Modus naturalis in omni perturbatione;" that is, in the consideration of such things as are apt to disturb the mind and affections, especially anger, to observe a mean, not to be moved above or beyond due measure. So μετριοπαθέω is "moderatè ferre," to "bear any thing," especially provocations unto anger, "moderately," without any great commotion of affections, so as to be stirred up to wrath, severity, and displeasure. So Arias, "mensuratè" (better "moderatè") "pati potens." An example hereof we may take in Moses. He was μετριοπαθής in a high and excellent manner; whence is that character given of him by the Holy Ghost, Num. xii. 3, "Now the man Moses was עָנָו מְאֹד " (πραὺς σφόδρα), "very meek above all men." It is spoken of him with respect unto his quiet and patient bearing of exasperating provocations, when he was opposed and reproached by Miriam and Aaron. He was μετριοπαθής; but as the best in the best of men is but weak and imperfect, so God in his wisdom hath ordered things that the failings of the best should be in their best, or that wherein they did most excel; that no man should glory in himself, but that "he that glorieth should glory in the Lord." Thus Abraham and Peter failed in their faith, wherein they were so eminent. And the failure afterwards of Moses was in this meekness or moderate bearing with provocations. He was not able in all things μετριοπαθεῖν, but, upon the provocation of the people, "spoke unadvisedly" and in wrath, saying, "Hear now, ye rebels; must we fetch you water out of this rock?" Num. xx. 10. This privilege is reserved in every case for Christ alone; he can always bear "quantum satis est," so much as shall assuredly prevent any evil consequent whatever.

If the word be used in this sense, then respect is had to what is of provocation and exasperation in those who are "ignorant and out of the way." 'The high priest is one who is fit and able to bear moderately and quietly with the failings, miscarriages, and sins of those for whom he executes his office; not breaking out into any anger or excess of indignation against them by reason of their infirmities.' And this, as applied unto Jesus Christ, is a matter of the highest encouragement and consolation unto believers. Were there not an absolute sufficiency of this disposition in him, and that as unto all occurrences, he must needs cast us all off in displeasure.

Erasmus expresseth it by "qui placabilis esse possit," one "who may be appeased," who is ready to be pleased again when he is angry or provoked. But the apostle doth not teach us herein how the high priest may be appeased when he is angry, but how remote he is, or ought to be, from being so on any occasion.

The Vulg. Lat., as we saw, reads, "qui condolere possit;" which is the same with δυνάμενος συμπαθῆσαι, chap. iv. 15, "can be touched with a feeling." And it is not improbable but that μετριοπαθεῖν may be used here in the same sense with συμπαθῆσαι, chap. iv. 15. But then it may be questioned whether "condoleo," "to grieve with," be as extensive and significant as "compatior;" which also it may, seeing the proper signification of "doleo" is to have a sense of pain. And thus no more should be intended than what we have already opened on those other places. What is said belongs to the description of the nature of a high priest as he is merciful, and of his disposition unto pity and compassion, with his readiness thereon to relieve and succour them that are tempted.

But I cannot judge that the apostle useth this word merely as it were for change, without a design to intimate something further and peculiar therein. Hence is that translation of Beza, "qui quantum satis est miserari possit vicem,"—"who can meetly and sufficiently pity the condition of the ignorant." By μέτριος, in this composition, the apostle intends the just and due measure of a disposition unto compassion. Not that he sets bounds unto it with respect unto any excess, as if he had said, 'He hath no more compassion or condolency than becomes him,—he shall observe a measure therein, and not exceed it;' which, although it be true, yet is not the intimation of it in this place unto his purpose. But he is one that doth not come short herein, who will not fail in any instance, who hath a sufficient measure of it to answer the condition and necessities of all with whom he hath to do. And this doth not infer a new sense, distinct from that last before mentioned, but only further explains it, according to the intention of the apostle in the peculiar use of this word.

I see no reason to confine myself unto either of these senses precisely, but do rather think that the apostle on purpose made use of this word to include them both. For,—

Suppose the object of this qualification of the high priest, in them that are ignorant and do wander out of the way, be their *ignorance* and *wanderings,* that is, their sins, and those considered as containing a provocation of himself, as every sin is attended with provocation; then δυνάμενος μετριοπαθεῖν is "qui potest moderate ferre," "who is able to bear with them with that due moderation of mind and affections," as not to have any vehement commotion of the one or the other against them: for if he should be liable unto such impressions he would be provoked to call them "rebels," as did Moses; and to say, as in the prophet, "I will feed you no more; let that that dieth die," Zech. xi. 9. But he is able to bear with them patiently and meekly, so as to continue the faithful discharge of his office towards them and for them. This, as we observed, Moses was not able always to do, as he also complains, Numb. xi. 12, "Have I conceived all this people? have I begotten them, that thou shouldest say unto me, Carry them in thy bosom, as a nursing father beareth the sucking child?" Yet this is required in a high priest, and that he should no more cast off poor sinners for their ignorance and wanderings than a nursing father should cast away a sucking child for its crying or frowardness; which whoso is ready to do is very unfit for that duty. So our apostle, in his imitation of Jesus Christ, affirms that in the church he was "gentle among them, even as a nurse cherisheth her children," 1 Thess. ii. 7;—not easy to be provoked, not ready to take offence or cast off the care of him. So it is said of God, Acts xiii. 18, that for forty years ἐτροποφόρησε, "he bare with the manners of the people in the wilderness;" or as some read it, ἐτροφοφόρησε, "he bare" or "fed them, as a nurse feedeth her child." Thus ought it to be with a high priest, and thus is it with Jesus Christ. He is able, with all meekness and gentleness, with patience and moderation, to bear with the infirmities, sins, and provocations of his people, even as a nurse or a nursing father beareth with the weakness and frowardness of a poor infant.

Again; suppose the immediate object of this qualification of the high priest to be the *sins, temptations,* and *infirmities* of his people, as they are grievous, troublesome, and dangerous unto themselves; then this δυνάμενος μετριοπαθεῖν signifies his nature and disposition as meet, prepared, and inclined, so to pity and commiserate, and consequently relieve in the way of his office, as shall be sufficient on all occasions. He is one that wants no part nor degree of a compassionate frame of heart towards them.

Both these the word signifies as diversely applied; and both of them, if I mistake not, are intended by the apostle; and for this end, that they might be both included, did he make use of this singular word. At least, I am not able to embrace either of these senses unto the exclusion of the other. A high priest, therefore, is one who can quietly bear with the weaknesses and sinful provocations of them that are ignorant and wander out of the way, as also commiserate or pity them unto such a measure and degree as never to be wanting unto their help and assistance; such a person as is מַשְׂכִּיל אֶל־דָּל, Ps. xli. 2,—one that is so " wise and understanding " in the state and condition of the poor as duly to relieve them.

2. The compassion described, accompanied with meek and patient bearing, is exercised towards the "ignorant and them that are out of the way." These words may be taken two ways;—first, as *distinctive;* secondly, as *descriptive* of the object of this compassion. In the first way the sense of them is, ' Whereas there are amongst the people of God some, or many, that are ignorant and out of the way, the compassion of the high priest is to be extended unto them; yea, this qualification doth respect them chiefly: so that they need not be discouraged, but boldly make use of his help and assistance in every time of distress.' " The ignorant and them that are out of the way;" that is, those among the people who are so. In the latter way, all the people of God are intended. There are, indeed, degrees in these things, some being more affected with them than others; for there are degrees in the infirmities and sins of believers. And those who are most obnoxious unto them are hereby encouraged to expect relief by the high priest. Yet in general this is the condition of all the people of God, they fall more or less under these qualifications. And because they are so, so obnoxious unto ignorance and wanderings; because actually in sundry things they are ignorant and do err from the right way; and because they know this in some measure of themselves, and are therefore apt to be cast

down and discouraged, the Holy Ghost here proposeth this qualification of a high priest for their relief, as that which is required in
him, and necessary unto him for that end. And as such, he had
peculiarly to do with the people in his dealing with God on their
behalf, both in his oblations and intercessions. So it is said of our
Saviour, the great high priest, that he "made reconciliation for the
sins of the people," and "intercession for the transgressors." And
this is the proper sense of the words. It is the whole people of God
who are thus described, as they lie under the eye and care of their
high priest. But because, also, it is their duty to make application
unto him for relief, which they will not do without a sense of their
want, it is required, moreover, in this description, that they be burdened with an apprehension of the guilt and danger that are in these
things,—those who are sensible of their ignorance and wanderings.

Τοῖς ἀγνοοῦσι, " to them that are ignorant." Not the mere affection
of the mind or ignorance itself, but the consequences and
effects of it in actual sins, are principally intended : ' To   Τοῖς ἀγνοοῦσι.
such as are obnoxious to sinning, to such as sin, through the ignorance and darkness of their minds.' There was under the law a sacrifice provided for them who sinned בִּשְׁגָגָה, through "ignorance" or
"error," Lev. iv. For whereas, in the first three chapters, Moses had
declared the institution and nature of all those sacrifices in general
whereby the justification and sanctification of the church was typically wrought and represented, with the obligation that thence was
upon them to walk in new obedience and holiness; he supposeth
yet, notwithstanding what was done, that there would be sins yet
remaining among the people, which, if they had no relief for or
against, would prove their ruin. As our apostle, in answer thereunto, having declared the free justification of sinners through the
obedience and blood of Christ, Rom. iv., v., with their sanctification
flowing from the efficacy of his life and death, chap. vi., yet adds
that there will be a remaining principle of sin in them, bringing
forth fruits and effects answerable unto its nature, chap. vii., which
he declares how we are relieved against by Jesus Christ, chap. viii.;
so was it in the institution of these sacrifices, whose order and nature
is in this chapter [Lev. iv.] unfolded. For, as was said, after the declaration of the sacrifices which concerned the justification and sanctification of the church in general, Moses distributes the following
sins of the people into two sorts; into those which were committed
בִּשְׁגָגָה, by "ignorance," unadvisedly, or in error; and those which
were committed בְּיָד רָמָה, with a " high hand," or " presumptuously."
For those of the first sort there were sacrifices allowed; but those
who were guilty of the latter were to be cut off: Num. xv. 27, 28,
30, " If any soul sin through ignorance, then he shall bring a she
goat of the first year for a sin-offering. And the priest shall make

an atonement for the soul that sinneth ignorantly, when he sinneth by ignorance before the LORD, to make an atonement for him; and it shall be forgiven him. But the soul that doeth ought presumptuously" (with an high hand),......" the same reproacheth the LORD; and that soul shall be cut off from among his people." And it is so also under the gospel. For after we profess an interest in the sacrifice of Christ unto our justification and sanctification, there are sins that men may fall into "presumptuously," and "with an high hand," for which there is no relief: "For if we sin wilfully after we have received the knowledge of the truth, there remaineth no more sacrifice for sins, but a certain fearful looking for of judgment and fiery indignation, which shall devour the adversaries," Heb. x. 26, 27. All other sins whatever come within the rank and order of them which are committed בִּשְׁגָגָה, by "ignorance" or error of mind. Of these there is no man that liveth and is not guilty, Eccles. vii. 20; 1 Sam. ii. 2. Yea, they are so multiplied in us or upon us as no man living can know or understand them, Ps. xix. 12. By sins of ignorance, then, are not understood only those which were "ex ignorantia juris," or when men sinned against the law because they knew it not; doing what it forbade, as not knowing that it was forbidden; and omitting what was commanded, as not knowing that it was commanded. This kind of ignorance Abimelech pleaded in the case of his taking Sarah, the wife of Abraham, in that he knew her not to be a married woman; which plea, as to some part of his guilt, God admits of, Gen. xx. 4–6. And this ignorance was that which preserved the case of our apostle, in his blasphemy and persecution, from being remediless, and his sin from being a sin of presumption, or with a high hand, 1 Tim. i. 12, 13. But this sort of sins only is not intended, although we see by these instances how great and heinous provocations may be of this kind. But those are in this case, and in opposition unto presumptuous sins, reckoned unto sins of ignorance, when the mind or practical understanding, being corrupted or entangled by the power of sin and its advantageous circumstances, doth not attend unto its duty, or the rule of all its actions; whence actual sin doth ensue. And this is the principal cause and spring of all the sins of our lives, as I have elsewhere declared, treating of the power of indwelling sin.[1] Those, therefore, who are "ignorant" in this place, are such as who, through the inadvertency of their minds, or want of a due and diligent attendance unto the rule of all their actions, do fall into sin as well as those who do so through a mere ignorance of their duty.

He adds, καὶ πλανωμένοις, "to them that wander out of the way." The reader may see what we have spoken concerning this word on

---

[1] See vol. vi. p. 153 of the author's works.—ED.

chap. iii. 10. Our sinning is often thus expressed, Ps. cxix. 176, " I
have gone astray like a perishing sheep." Isa. liii. 6, " We like sheep
have gone astray; we have turned every one to his own way." We
have erred, or wandered astray from the way of God, and turned
unto our own ways. " Ye were as sheep going astray," 1 Pet. ii. 25.
But we must observe, that there is a twofold erring or wandering expressed by this word in this epistle. The one is *in heart:*
'Αεὶ πλανῶνται τῇ καρδίᾳ,—" They always err in their heart." The
other is *in our ways,* going out of them; which is here intended.
The former is the heart's dislike of the ways of God, and voluntary
relinquishment of them thereon. This answers to the presumptuous
sinning before mentioned, and is no object of compassion either in
God or our High Priest; for concerning them who did so, " God
sware in his wrath that they should not enter into his rest." But
there may be a wandering in men's ways, when yet their hearts are
upright with God. So it is said of Asa, that " his heart was perfect
all his days," 2 Chron. xv. 17; yet his great wanderings from the
ways of God are recorded, chap. xvi. 7–10, 12. There is therefore
included in this word a seduction by temptation into some course of
wandering for a season from the ways of God. Who then are these οἱ
πλανώμενοι? Even those who by the power of their temptations have
been seduced and turned from the straight paths of holy obedience,
and have wandered in some crooked paths of their own.

And in these two words doth the apostle comprise all sorts of
sinners whatever, with all sorts of sins, and not merely those which
are commonly esteemed of infirmity or ignorance; for he intends all
those sins which the high priest was to confess, sacrifice, and inter-
cede for, on the behalf of the people. And this was, " all the iniquities of the children of Israel, and all their transgressions in all
their sins," Lev. xvi. 21. It is true, as the law was the instrument
of the Jewish polity, there was no sacrifice appointed for some sins, if
precisely known and legally proved by witnesses; because the sinners
were to be punished capitally, for the preservation of public order
and peace. And God would not allow an instance of accepting a
sacrifice where the offender was to suffer; which would have overthrown the principal notion of sacrifices, wherein the guilt of the
offerer was, as to punishment, transferred unto the beast to be offered.
But otherwise, without respect unto civil rule and legal proof, all
sorts of sins were to be expiated by sacrifices. And they are here
by our apostle reduced unto two heads, whence two sorts of sinners
are denominated:—(1.) Such as men fall into by *the neglect and
failure of their minds* in attending unto their duty; which is their
sinful ignorance. (2.) Such as men are *seduced unto some continuance in* through the power of their temptation, and that against
their light and knowledge. Such are ignorant or wanderers out of

the way.   All sorts, therefore, of sins and sinners are comprised in
these expressions.   And with respect unto them it is required of a
high priest,—(1.) That he should not take the provocation of them
so high or immoderately as to neglect them or cast them off on their
account.   (2.) That he should have such pity and compassion towards them as is needful to move him to act for their relief and
deliverance.   And this the high priest of old was prompted unto,—

3. 'Επεὶ καὶ αὐτὸς περίκειται ἀσθένειαν.   'Επεί, "quoniam," "seeing it
is so;" καὶ αὐτός, "that even he himself."   His own state
and condition will mind him of his duty in this matter.

'Επεὶ καὶ αὐ-
τός.

Περίκειται. Περίκειται ἀσθένειαν.   This is more than if he had said
that he was ἀσθενής, "weak and infirm:" 'He is beset
and compassed about on every hand with infirmity.'   Περικειμένην
ἔχων ἀσθένειαν, as is the meaning of the phrase, 'having infirmity round about him,' attended with it in all that
he sets himself unto.   Now this ἀσθένεια is twofold:—(1.) Natural.
(2.) Moral.   (1.) There is an infirmity which is inseparable from our
human nature.   Such are the weaknesses of its condition, with all
the dolorous and afflictive affections in doing or suffering that attend
it.   And this our Lord Jesus Christ himself was compassed withal;
whence he was "a man of sorrow, and acquainted with grief," as
hath been declared.   Had it been otherwise he could not have
been such a merciful high priest as we stood in need of; nor, indeed, any priest at all, for he would not have had any thing of his
own to offer, if he had not had that nature from which in this life
that sort of infirmity is inseparable, Matt. xxvi. 41.   (2.) There is a
moral infirmity, consisting in an inclination unto sin and weakness
as to obedience.   "Οντων ἡμῶν ἀσθενῶν, Rom. v. 6, "When we were
yet infirm (without strength)," is the same with "Οντων ἡμῶν ἁμαρ-
τωλῶν, verse 8, "while we were yet sinners;" for our weakness was
such as was the cause of our sin.   See 1 Cor. viii. 7.   And the words,
both substantive, adjective, and verb, are frequently used in the
New Testament to express bodily weakness by sickness and infirmities of every kind.   Nothing hinders but that we may take it
here in its most comprehensive signification, for infirmities of all
sorts, natural, moral, and occasional.   For the first sort do necessarily attend the condition of our human nature, and are requisite
unto him that would discharge aright the whole office of a priest.
And the following verse, affirming that "for this cause" it was
necessary for him "to offer sacrifice for himself," declares directly
that his moral or sinful infirmities are also included.   He himself
was subject to sin, as the rest of the people.   Whence there were
peculiar sacrifices appointed for the anointed priest to offer for himself and his own sin.   And for the last, or infirmities in bodily distempers unto sickness and death, it is a necessary consequent of the

former. Wherefore, as these words have respect unto them that go
before, or yield a reason why the high priest is such a one as " can
have compassion on the ignorant," they express the infirmity of
nature which inclined him thereunto from a sense of his own weakness and suffering. As they respect what ensues, verse 3, they intend his moral infirmities, or sinful infirmities, with their consequences; from whence it was necessary that he should offer sacrifice
for himself. And in the latter sense the things intended belong
peculiarly to the high priest according to the law, and not to
Christ.

And this obviateth an objection that may be raised from the words.
For it may be said, ' If this be so, why is it mentioned in this
place as an advantage for the inducing of the high priest unto a
due measure of compassion, or to equanimity and forbearance? For
if this were not in Christ, he may be thought to come short in his
compassion of the legal high priest, as not having this motive unto
it and incentive of it.' *Ans.* (1.) That natural infirmity whereof our
Lord Christ had full experience, is every way sufficient unto this
purpose; and this alone was that which qualified the legal high
priest with due compassion. His moral infirmity was not any advantage unto him, so as to help his compassion towards the people;
which was, as all other graces, weakened thereby. It is therefore
mentioned by the apostle only as the reason why he was appointed
to offer sacrifice for himself, which Christ was not to do. And what
advantage soever may be made of a sense of moral weakness and
proneness unto sin, yet is it in itself an evil, which weakens the
duty that it leads unto; nor where this is can we expect any other
discharge of duty but what proceeds from him who is liable to sin
and miscarriage therein. Now, the Lord Christ being absolutely
free from this kind of infirmity, yet made sensible of the one by the
other, doth in a most perfect manner perform all that is needful to
be done on our behalf. (2.) The apostle treats not of the nature of
the priesthood of Christ absolutely, but with respect unto the legal
high priests, whom he exalts him above. It was necessary, therefore, that their state should be represented, that it might appear as
well wherein he excelled them as wherein there was an agreement
between them. And this he did, among other things, in that he
was not obnoxious unto any moral infirmity, as they were. From
the whole we may observe,—

Obs. I. Compassion and forbearance, with meekness, in those from
whom we expect help and relief, are the great motive and encouragement unto faith, affiance, and expectation of them.

It is unto this end that the apostle makes mention of this qualification or endowment of a high priest, with respect unto its application to Jesus Christ. He would thereby encourage us to come

unto him, and to expect all that assistance which is necessary to relieve us in all our spiritual distresses, and to give us acceptance with God. No man will expect any good or kindness from one whom he looks upon as severe, incompassionate, and ready to lay hold on occasions of anger or wrath. When God himself saw it necessary to exercise severity, and give frequent instances of his displeasure, for the preservation of his worship in holiness and order among that stubborn generation in the wilderness, they spake unto Moses, saying, "Behold, we die, we perish, we all perish. Whosoever cometh any thing near unto the tabernacle of the Lord shall die: shall we be consumed with dying?" Num. xvii. 12, 13. "Behold, the sword hath killed some of us; and behold, the earth hath swallowed some of us; and behold, some of us are dead with the pestilence," as the Chaldee Targum expresseth it. Most apprehend this to be a sinful repining against the righteous judgments of God, wherewith they were consumed for their sins. I rather judge it an expression of that bondage, legal apprehension of the terror of the Lord and his holiness, which they were then kept under, finding "the commandment which was ordained to life" to become unto them, by reason of sin, "unto death," Rom. vii. 9, 10. And therefore that last expostulation, "Shall we be consumed with dying?" is a deprecation of wrath: as Ps. lxxxv. 5, "Wilt thou be angry with us for ever?" and Lam. v. 22, "Wilt thou utterly reject us?" But evident it is, that want of a clear insight into God's compassion and forbearance is full of terror and discouragement. And he who framed unto himself a false notion of Christ was thereby utterly discouraged from diligence in his service: " I knew thee, that thou art an hard man," or an austere, severe man; "and I was afraid, and went and hid thy talent in the earth," Matt. xxv. 24, 25; Luke xix. 22. His undue apprehensions of Christ (the proper effect of unbelief) ruined him for ever. Wherefore God himself doth not, in his dealings with us, more properly or more fully set out any property of his nature than he doth his compassion, long-suffering, and forbearance. And as he proposeth them unto us for our encouragement, so he declares his approbation of our faith in them. He delighteth in them that "hope in his mercy," Ps. xxxiii. 18. Hence, when he solemnly declared his nature by his name to the full, that we might know and fear him, he doth it by an enumeration of those properties which may convince us of his compassionateness and forbearance, and not till the close of all makes any mention of his severity, as that which he will not exercise towards any but such as by whom his compassion is despised, Exod. xxxiv. 6, 7. So he affirms that "fury is not in him," Isa. xxvii. 4. Although we may apprehend that he is angry and furious, ready to lay hold of all occasions to punish and destroy, yet is it not so towards them who desire sincerely to "lay hold of him strongly," and to "make peace with him" by Jesus Christ, verse 5.   Elihu supposed that Job had such apprehensions of God: "Thou hast said, Behold, he findeth occasions against me, he counteth me for his enemy.   He putteth my feet in the stocks, he marketh all my paths," Job xxxiii. 10, 11. And, indeed, in his agony he had said little less, chap. xiv. 16, 17. But it is not so; for if God should so mark iniquities, who could stand? Ps. cxxx. 3.   Wherefore the great recompense that God gives to sinners from first to last is from his compassion and for-bearance.   And as for our Lord Jesus Christ, as mediator, we have evinced that all things were so ordered about him as that he might be filled with tenderness, compassion, and forbearance towards sin-ners.   And as this we stand in need of, so it is the greatest encou-ragement that we can be made partakers of.   Consider us either as to our sins or sufferings, and it will appear that we cannot maintain a *life of faith* without a due apprehension of it.

Obs. II.   Wherefore, secondly, we live, the life of our souls is principally maintained, upon this compassionateness of our high priest; namely, that he is able to bear with us in our provocations, and to pity us in our weaknesses and distresses.   To this purpose is the promise concerning him, Isa. xl. 11.   There are three things that are apt to give great provocations unto them that are concerned in us:—1. *Frequency in offending;* 2. *Greatness of offences;* 3. *Instability in promises and engagements.*   These are things apt to give provocations beyond what ordinary moderation and meekness can bear withal, especially where they are accompanied with a disregard of the greatest love and kindness.   And all these are found in be-lievers,—some in one, and some in another, and in some all.   For, 1. There is in us all a *frequency of provocation*, as Ps. xix. 12.   They are beyond our numbering or understanding.   What believer is there that doth not constantly admire how the Lord Christ hath patiently borne with him in the frequency of his daily failings? that he hath carried it towards him without such provocations unto anger as to lay him out of his care?   2. Some of them are over-taken with *great offences*, as was the case of Peter; and there is not one of them but, on one account or other, hath reason to make use of the prayer of the psalmist, "Be merciful unto my sin, for it is great."   And great sins are attended with great provocations. That our souls have not died under them, that we have not been rejected of God utterly for them, it is from this holy qualification of our high priest, that he is able sufficiently to bear with all things that are required in the discharge of his office.   Were it not so, he would, on one occasion or another wherein now we admire his lenity and forbearance, have "sworn in his wrath that we should not enter into his rest."   3. *Instability* in promises and engagements, especially as breaking forth into frequent instances, is a matter of great provocation. This is that which God complains of in Israel, as wherewith he was almost wearied, Hos. vi. 4. And herein also do we try, and exercise the forbearance of our high priest. There is not a day wherein we answer and make good the engagements of our own hearts, either in matter or manner, as to our walking before him in the constant exercise of faith and love. And that we are yet accepted with him, it is that δύναται μετριο- παθεῖν, he can bear with us in all patience and moderation.

Again; our ignorances and wanderings are our sufferings, as well as our sins. Sin is the principal affliction, the principal suffer- ing of believers; yea, all other things are light unto them in com- parison hereof. This is that which they continually groan under, and cry out to be delivered from. Herein our high priest is able so to pity us as undoubtedly to relieve us; but this hath been already insisted on.

Obs. III. Though every sin hath in it the whole nature of sin, rendering the sinner obnoxious unto the curse of the law, yet as there are several kinds of sins, so there are several degrees of sin, some being accompanied with a greater guilt than others.

The Papists have a distinction of sins into mortal and venial, which is the foundation of one moiety of their superstition. Some sins, they say, are such as in their own nature deserve death eternal; so that there is no deliverance from the guilt of them without actual contrition and repentance. But some are so slight and small as that they are easily expiated by an observance of some outward rites of the church; however, they endanger no man's eternal salvation, whe- ther they repent of them or no. The worst is but a turn in purga- tory, or the charge of a pardon. Because this distinction is rejected by Protestants, they accuse them of teaching that all sins are equal. But this they do untruly. That distinction, I confess, might be allowed with respect unto offences against the law of old, as it was the rule of the Jewish polity. For some of them, as murder and adultery, were to be punished capitally without mercy; which therefore were mortal unto the offenders. Others were civilly as well as typically expiated by sacrifice, and so were venial in the constitution of the law; that is, such as were pardoned of course, by attending to some instituted observances. But with respect unto God, every sin is a transgression of the law; and the "wages" or re- ward "of it is death," Rom. vi. 23. And the curse of the whole law was directed against every one who did not every thing required in it, or failed in any one point of obedience, Deut. xxvii. 26, Gal. iii. 10. And "whosoever shall keep the whole law, and yet offend in one point, he is guilty of all," James ii. 10. But there are degrees of sin, and degrees of guilt in sinning; as,—1. There is a distinction of sins with respect unto the *persons* that commit them. But this distinction ariseth from the event, and not from the nature of the sin itself intended. As suppose the same sin committed by an unregenerate person, and by one that is regenerate: unto the latter it shall be pardoned; unto the former, continuing so, it shall never be pardoned. But whence is this difference? Is it that the sin is less in the one than in the other? Nay, being supposed of the same kind, commonly it hath more aggravating circumstances in the regenerate than in the unregenerate. Is it because God is less displeased with sin in some than in others? Nay, God is equally displeased with equal sins, in whomsoever they are found; if there be any difference, he is more displeased with them in believers than in others. But the difference ariseth merely from the event. Regenerate persons will, through the grace of God, certainly use the means of faith and repentance for the obtaining of pardon, which the other will not; and if they are assisted also so to do, even they in like manner shall obtain forgiveness. No man, therefore, can take a relief against the guilt of sin from his state and condition, which may be an aggravation, but can be no alleviation of it. 2. There are degrees of sin amongst men *unregenerate*, who live in a course of sin all their days. We see it is so, and it ever was so in the world. And sometimes here, but certainly hereafter, God deals with them, not only according to their state of sin, and their course of sin, but according to the degrees and aggravations of sin in great variety. All do not sin equally; nor shall all be equally punished. 3. In the sins of believers there are different degrees, both in divers and in the same persons. And although they shall be all pardoned, yet have they different effects; with respect, (1.) Unto peace of conscience; (2.) Sense of the love of God; (3.) Growth in grace and holiness; (4.) Usefulness or scandal in the church or the world; (5.) Temporal afflictions; and, (6.) A quiet or troublesome departure out of this world;—but in all a reserve is still to be made for the sovereignty of God and his grace.

Obs. IV. Our ignorance is both our calamity, our sin, and an occasion of many sins unto us.

Having declared that the high priest was first to offer sacrifices for the sins of men, and then that he was to be compassionate towards them, both in their sins and sorrows, the first instance which the apostle gives of those who are concerned herein is of "them that are ignorant." They stand in need both of sacrifice and compassion. And ignorance in spiritual things is twofold:—1. *Original*, subjective, and universal. This is that whereby men have " their understandings darkened," and are "alienated from the life of God," Eph. iv. 18; the ignorance that is in men unregenerate, not savingly enlightened, consisting in the want or defect of a principle of heavenly or spiritual light in their minds; which I have elsewhere at large described. But it is not this sort of persons nor this sort of ignorance which is here intended. 2. There is an ignorance which is *objective* and *partial*, when the light and knowledge that is in us is but weak and infirm, extending itself unto some objects, and affecting the mind with darkness and disorder in the apprehension of them also. And this also may be considered two ways:— (1.) *Absolutely;* and so the best, and the most wise, and the most knowing are ignorant, and to be esteemed among them that are so; for the best "know but in part, and prophesy but in part," and "see darkly, as in a glass," 1 Cor. xiii. 9, 12. Yea, "how little a portion is it that we know of God!" We "cannot by searching find out the Almighty to perfection;" "such knowledge is too wonderful for us." Yea, we "know nothing perfectly," neither concerning God nor ourselves. If we know him so as to believe him, fear him, and obey him, it is all that is promised us in this life, all that we can attain unto. Wherefore let the best of us,—[1.] Take care that we be not puffed up, or fall into any vain elation of mind upon the conceit of our knowledge. Alas! how many things are there to be seen, to be known in God, that we know nothing of; and nothing do we know as we ought or as it shall be known. [2.] Endeavour, in the constant use of all means, to grow in the knowledge of God and our Lord and Saviour Jesus Christ. The more we learn here, the more we shall see there is to be learned. [3.] Long for the time, or rather that eternity, wherein all these shades shall flee away, all darkness be removed from our minds, all veils and clouds taken away from about the divine being and glory; when "we shall see him as he is," with "open face," and "know even as we are known:" which is the eternal life and blessedness of our souls. [4.] Know that on the account of the ignorance that is yet in the best, yea, that was in the most holy saint that ever was on the earth, they all stand in need of the compassion of our high priest, to bear with them, pity and relieve them. (2.) This second sort of ignorance may be considered *comparatively.* So among believers some are more chargeable with this evil than others, and are more obnoxious unto trouble from it. And these we may distinguish into four sorts:—[1.] Such as are *young* and *tender*, either in years or in the work of grace upon their souls. These the apostle calls "babes," and "children," that have need to be nourished with milk, and not to have their minds overcharged with things too high and hard for them. And concerning this sort many things are spoken graciously and tenderly in the Scripture. [2.] Such as, through the weakness of their *natural capacities*, are slow in learning, and are never able to attain unto any great measure of sound knowledge and judgment; although we often see many notable natural

defects in the minds of them that are sincere to be abundantly
compensated by the "light of the knowledge of the glory of God in
the face of Jesus Christ" shining plentifully upon them and in them.
[3.] Such as are so disposed of by the providence of God, in their
outward concerns in this world, as that they enjoy not the means
of knowledge and growth therein, at least in so full and effectual a
manner as others do.   Hereby are they kept low in their light and
spiritual apprehensions of things, and are thereby obnoxious to manifold errors and mistakes.   And of these, partly through the blindness of them who in many places take upon themselves to be the
only teachers and guides of the disciples of Christ, partly through
some sloth of their own in not providing as they ought for their
own edification, there is a great number in the world.   [4.] Such
as by reason of some *corrupt affections*, spiritual sloth, and worldly
occasions, perpetually diverting their minds, are dull and slow in
learning the mysteries of the gospel, and thrive but little in light
or knowledge under an enjoyment of the most effectual means of
them.   These our apostle complains of, and reproves in particular,
verses 11–13.   And this sort of comparative ignorance is attended
with the greatest guilt of any; the reasons whereof are obvious.   But
yet unto all these sorts doth our high priest extend his compassion,
and they are all of them here intended.   And he is compassionate toward us under our ignorance,—1. As it is our calamity or
trouble; for so it is, and as such he pities us in it and under it.
Who is not sensible of the inconveniencies and perplexities that he
is continually cast into by the remainders of darkness and ignorance
in him? who is not sensible how much his love and his obedience are
weakened by them? who doth not pant after fuller discoveries and
more clear and stable conceptions of the glorious mystery of God in
Christ?   Yea, there is nothing on the account whereof believers do
more groan for deliverance from their present state, than that they
may be freed from all remainders of darkness and ignorance, and
so be brought into a clear and intimate acquaintance with the in-
created glories of God, and all the holy emanations of light and
truth from them.   Herein, then, our merciful high priest exerciseth
compassion towards us, and leads us on, if we are not slothfully
wanting unto ourselves, with fresh discoveries of divine light and
truth; which, although they are not absolutely satisfactory to the
soul, nor do utterly take away its thirst after the all-fulness of the
eternal Fountain of them, yet do they hold our souls in life, and
give a constant increase unto our light towards the perfect day.
2. That this ignorance also is our sin, as being our gradual falling
short of the knowledge of the glory of God required in us, and the
occasion of manifold failings and sins in our course,—most of our
wanderings being from some kind of defect in the conducting light

of our minds,—are things known and confessed. And with respect hereunto, namely, that efficacious influence which our ignorance hath into our frequent surprisals into sin, it is principally that we have relief from the compassion of our high priest.

Obs. V. Sin is a wandering from the way. See on chap. iii. 10.

Obs. VI. No sort of sinners is excluded from an interest in the care and love of our compassionate high priest, but only those who exclude themselves by their unbelief. Our apostle useth these two expressions to comprise all sorts of sinners, as they did under the law, unless they were such presumptuous sinners as had no relief provided for them in the institutions thereof. Of this nature is final unbelief alone under the gospel; therefore on all others our high priest is able to have compassion, and will especially exercise it towards poor, dark, ignorant wanderers. And I would not forbear to manage from hence some encouragements unto believing, as also to declare the aggravations of unbelief, but that these discourses must not be drawn out unto a greater length. Wherefore I shall only add on this verse,—

Obs. VII. It is well for us, and enough for us, that the Lord Christ was encompassed with the sinless infirmities of our nature.

Obs. VIII. God can teach a sanctified use of sinful infirmities, as he did in and unto the priests under the law.

VERSE 3.

In the third verse the apostle illustrates what he had asserted concerning the high priest, as to his being "compassed with infirmity," from a necessary consequent thereof: he was to offer sacrifices for his own sins. Before, he had declared in general that the end of his office was to "offer gifts and sacrifices to God,"—that is, for the sins of the people; but proceeding in his description of him, he mentions his own frailty, infirmity, and obnoxiousness unto sin. And this he did, that he might give an account of those known institutions of the law wherein he was appointed to offer sacrifices for his own sins also.

Ver. 3.—Καὶ διὰ ταύτην ὀφείλει, καθὼς περὶ τοῦ λαοῦ, οὕτω καὶ περὶ ἑαυτοῦ, προσφέρειν ὑπὲρ ἁμαρτιῶν.

For διὰ ταύτην one manuscript has δἰ αὐτήν,—that is, ἀσθένειαν, "because of which infirmity." Vulg. Lat., "propterea debet;" "wherefore," or "for which cause he ought." Or, as we, "and by reason hereof." Syr., "so also for himself to offer for his own sins."

Ver. 3.—And by reason hereof he ought, as for the people, so also for himself, to offer for sins.

Καὶ διὰ ταύτην: that is, say some, for διὰ τοῦτο, the feminine
put for the neuter, by a Hebraism. Hence it is rendered by some "propterea." But ταύτην plainly and Διὰ ταύτην.
immediately refers unto ἀσθένειαν, "propter hanc," or "istam infirmita-
tem." Had the high priest under the law been ἀναμάρτητος, without
any sin, or sinful infirmity, as the Lord Christ was, he should have
had nothing to do but to offer sacrifice for the sins of the people.
But it was otherwise with him, seeing he himself also, as well as
they, was encompassed with sinful infirmities.

Ὀφείλει, "he ought." He ought to offer for his own sins, and
that on a double account, whereinto this duty or necessity is resolved:—1. The nature of the things them- Ὀφείλει.
selves, or the condition wherein he was. For seeing he was infirm
and obnoxious unto sin, and seeing he did, as other men, sin actually
in many things, he must have been ruined by his office if he might
not have offered sacrifice for himself. It was indispensably necessary that sacrifices should be offered for him and his sin, and yet
this no other could do for him; he ought therefore to do it himself.
2. The command of God. He ought so to do, because God had so
appointed and ordained that he should. To this purpose there are
sundry express legal institutions, as we shall see immediately.

Καθὼς περὶ τοῦ λαοῦ, "in like manner as for the people;" that is,
either the whole people collectively, or all the people
distributively, as their occasions did require. In the Περὶ τοῦ λαοῦ.
first way the great anniversary sacrifice which he celebrated in his
own person for the whole body of the people is principally intended,
Lev. xvi. 16, 24. Add hereunto the daily sacrifice belonging unto
the constant service of the temple,—which is therefore used synecdochically for the whole worship thereof, Dan. viii. 11, 12,—for
herein also was the whole church equally concerned. In the latter
way, it respects all those occasional sacrifices, whether for sin or
trespasses, or in free-will offerings, which were continually to be
offered, and that by the priests alone.

Οὕτω καὶ περὶ ἑαυτοῦ, "so for himself;" in like manner, on the same
grounds and for the same reasons that he offered for
the people. He had a common interest with them Οὕτω καὶ περὶ
in the daily sacrifice, which was the public worship of ἑαυτοῦ.
the whole church; and therein he offered sacrifice for himself also,
together and with the people. But besides this there were three
sorts of offerings that were peculiar unto him, wherein he offered
for himself distinctly or separately:—

1. The solemn offering that ensued immediately on his inauguration: Lev. ix. 2, "And he said unto Aaron, Take thee a young calf
for a sin-offering, and a ram for a burnt-offering, without blemish,
and offer them before the LORD." This was for himself, as it is

expressed, verse 8, " Aaron therefore went unto the altar, and slew the calf, which was the sin-offering for himself." After this he offered distinctly for the people " a kid of the goats for a sin-offering," verses 3, 15. And this was for an expiation of former sins, expressing the sanctification and holiness that ought to be in them that draw nigh unto God.

2. There was an occasional offering or sacrifice which he was to offer distinctly for himself, upon the breach of any of God's commandments by ignorance, or any actual sin: Lev. iv. 3, "If the priest that is anointed do sin according to the sin of the people" (that is, in like manner as any of the people do sin), "then let him bring, for his sin which he hath sinned, a young bullock without blemish unto the LORD for a sin-offering." After which there is a sacrifice appointed of the like nature, and in like manner to be observed,— (1.) For the sin of the whole people, verse 13; and then (2.) For the sin of any individual person, verse 27. And hereby the constant application that we are, on all actual sins, to make unto the blood of Christ for pardon and purification was prefigured.

3. There was enjoined him another solemn offering, on the annual feast, or day of expiation, which he was to begin the solemn service of that great day withal: Lev. xvi. 3, " Aaron shall thus come into the holy place: with a young bullock for a sin-offering, and a ram for a burnt-offering." Verse 11, "And Aaron shall bring the bullock of the sin-offering, which is for himself, and shall make an atonement for himself, and for his house, and shall kill the bullock of the sin-offering which is for himself." After this, he offers also on the same day, for the sins of the people, verse 15 ;—a bullock for himself, and a goat for the people. And this solemn sacrifice respecting all sins and sorts of them, known and unknown, great and small, in general and particular, represents our solemn application unto Christ for pardon and sanctification; which as to the sense of them may be frequently renewed. The Jews affirm that the high priest used at his offering this sacrifice the ensuing prayer:—אנה השם עויתי פשעתי חטאתי לפניך אני וביתי ובני אהרן עם קדושך אנא השם כפר נא לעונות ולפשעי ולחטאי שעויתי ושפשעתי ושחטאתי לפניך אני וביתי ובני אהרן עם קדושך ככתב בתורת משה עבדך כי ביום הזה יכפר עליכם לטהר אתכם מכל חטאתיכם לפניה;—that is, " I beseech thee, O Lord, I have done perversely, I have transgressed, I have sinned before thee; I and my house, and the children of Aaron, and thy holy people. I beseech thee, O Lord, be propitious unto, or pardon, I beseech thee, the iniquities, transgressions, and sins, wherein I have done amiss, transgressed, and sinned before thee, I and my house, and the sons of Aaron, and thy holy people; according as it is written in the law of Moses thy servant, that in this day thou wouldst pardon and purify us from all our sins."—Mishnaioth, Tract. Jom. Perek. iv. And all these several

sorts of sacrifices for himself were, all of them, as our apostle here speaks, ὑπὲρ ἁμαρτιῶν, "for sins." And this was necessary, because he was encompassed with infirmities and obnoxious unto sin, and so stood in no less need of expiation and atonement than the people.

Ὑπὲρ ἁμαρτιῶν.

Expositors generally agree that this is peculiar unto the high priest according to the law, the Lord Christ being neither intended nor included in this expression; for we have showed that, in this comparison, the things compared being on some accounts infinitely distant, there may be that in the one which nothing in the other answers unto. And that the Lord Christ is not intended in this expression appears,—

1. The necessity of this offering for himself by the high priest arose from two causes, as was declared:—(1.) From *his moral infirmity* and weakness; that is, unto obedience, and obnoxiousness to sin. (2.) From *God's command* and appointment; he had commanded and appointed that he should offer sacrifice for himself. But in neither of these had our Lord Christ any concern; for neither had he any such infirmities, nor did God ordain or require that he should offer sacrifice for himself.

2. Actually Christ had *no sin of his own* to offer for, nor was it possible that he should; for he was made like unto us, "yet without sin." And the offering of the priest here intended was of the same kind with that which was for the people. Both were for actual sins of the same kind; one for his own, the other for the people's.

3. It is expressly said, that the Lord Christ " *needed not, as they, to offer first for his own sins, and then for the people's;*" and that because he was in himself " holy, harmless, undefiled, separate from sinners," Heb. vii. 26, 27. This, therefore, belonged unto the weakness and imperfection of the legal high priest.

Two expositors of late have been otherwise minded. The first is Crellius or Schlichtingius, who says that the infirmities and evils that Christ was obnoxious unto, are here, by a catachresis, called " sins;" and for them he offered for himself. The other is Grotius, who speaks to the same purpose: " Cum hoc generaliter de omni sacerdote dicitur, sequitur Christum quoque obtulisse pro se ὑπὲρ ἁμαρτιῶν, *i. e.*, ut a doloribus illis qui peccatorum poenae esse solent, et occasione peccatorum nostrorum ipsi infligebantur, posset liberari;" —" Whereas this is spoken generally of every priest, it follows that Christ also offered for himself for sins; that is, that he might be freed from those pains which are wont to be punishments of sins, and which, on the occasion of our sins, were inflicted on him." It is well enough known what dogma or opinion is intimated in these expressions. But I answer,—

1. This assertion is not universal and absolute concerning every

high priest, but every high priest that was "under the law," who was appointed to be a type of Christ, so far as was possible by reason of his infirmities.

2. It is not without danger, to say that "Christ offered for himself ὑπὲρ ἁμαρτιῶν." He "knew no sin," he "did no sin," and therefore could not offer a sin-offering for himself. His "offering himself to God for us,"—"making his soul an offering for sin," our sins,—his being "made sin for us," to make "atonement" or "reconciliation" for our sins, is fully declared; but this offering for himself, especially for sin, is nowhere taught nor intimated.

3. If he be intended here, then must he offer for himself, as the high priest did of old; this the letter of the text enforceth. But the high priest of old was to offer distinctly and separately, "first for himself, and then for the people." So the words require it in this place, by the notes of comparison and distinction, κάθως and οὕτω, "as for the people, so" (or "in like manner") "for himself." Therefore if the Lord Christ be intended, he must offer two distinct sacrifices, one for himself, another for us. Now, whereas this he needed not to do, nor did, nor could do, it is undeniably manifest that he hath no concern in this expression.

There remaineth one difficulty only to be removed, which may arise from the consideration of this discourse. For if the high priest of old, notwithstanding his own sins, could first offer for himself and then for the people, and so make expiation for all sin, what necessity was there that our high priest should be absolutely free from all sin, as our apostle declares that he was, and that it was necessary he should be, chap. vii. 26, 27; for it seems he might first have offered for his own sin, and then for ours?

Ans. 1. It is one thing to expiate sin *typically*, another to do it really; one thing to do it in representation, by virtue of somewhat else, another to do it effectually by itself. The first might be done by them that were sinners, the latter could not.

2. On that supposal it would have been indispensably necessary that our high priest must have offered *many sacrifices*. Once he must have offered for himself, wherein we should have had no concern; and then he must again have offered himself for us. Hence, whereas he had nothing to offer but himself, he must have died and been offered more than once; which lay under all manner of impossibilities.

3. That a real atonement might be made for sin, it was required that our nature, which was to suffer and to be offered, should be *united* unto the divine nature in the person of the Son of God; but this it could not be had it not been absolutely sinless and holy. Some observations ensue.

The order of God's institution, with respect unto the sacrificing of the high priest for himself and the people, is observable; and this was, that he should first offer for himself, and then for them. This order was constant, and is especially observable in the great anniversary sacrifice for atonement on the day of expiation, Lev. xvi. Now the reason of this was,—1. Typical, that having first received pardon and purification for himself, he might the better prefigure and represent the spotless holiness of our high priest in his offering of himself for us. 2. Moral, to declare how careful they ought to be of their own sins who deal about the sins of others. And we may observe that,—

Obs. I. The absolute holiness and spotless innocency of the Lord Christ in his offering of himself had a signal influence into the efficacy of his sacrifice, and is a great encouragement unto our faith and consolation.

This our apostle informs us to have been necessary, chap. vii. 26, Τοιοῦτος γὰρ ἡμῖν ἔπρεπεν ἀρχιερεύς,—" It was meet" (convenient, necessary for and unto us) " that we should have such an high priest as was holy, harmless, undefiled, separate from sinners." No other sort of high priest could have done what was to be done for us. Had he had any sin of his own he could never have taken all sin from us. From hence it was that what he did was so acceptable with God, and that what he suffered was justly imputed unto us, seeing there was no cause in himself why he should suffer at all. This, therefore, is frequently mentioned and insisted on where his sacrifice is declared: 2 Cor. v. 21, "He made him to be sin for us, who knew no sin; that we might be made the righteousness of God in him." He was " made sin for us" when he was made a " sacrifice for sin," when " his soul was made an offering for sin." Hereon depends our being " made the righteousness of God in him," or righteous before God through him; but not on this as absolutely considered, but as " he was made sin who knew no sin," who was absolutely innocent and holy. So the apostle Peter, mentioning the redemption which we have by his blood, which was in the sacrifice of himself, says it was " as of a lamb without blemish and without spot," 1 Pet. i. 19. And treating again of the same matter, he adds, " Who did no sin, neither was guile found in his mouth," chap. ii. 22. So Rom. viii. 3. And we may see herein,—1. Pure, unmixed love and grace. He had not the least concern in what he did or suffered herein for himself. This was " the grace of our Lord Jesus Christ," that being " rich, for our sakes he became poor." All that he did was from sovereign love and grace. And will he not pursue the same love unto the end ? 2. The efficacy and merit of his oblation, that was animated by the life and quintessence of obedience. There were in it the highest sufferings and the most absolute innocency, knit together by an act of most inexpressible obedience. 3. The perfection

of the example that is set before us, 1 Pet. ii. 21, 22. And from
hence we may also observe, that,—

Obs. II. Whosoever dealeth with God or man about the sins of
others, should look well, in the first place, unto his own. The high
priest was to take care about, and " first to offer for his own sins,
and then for the sins of the people." And they who follow not this
method will miscarry in their work. It is the greatest evidence of
hypocrisy, for men to be severe toward the sins of others and careless about their own. There are four ways whereby some may act
with respect unto the sins of others, and not one of them wherein
they can discharge their duty aright, if in the same kind they take
not care of themselves in the first place.

1. It is the duty of some to endeavour the *conversion of others*
from a state of sin. As this belongs to parents and governors in
their place, so is it the chief work of ministers, and principal end of
the ministry. So the Lord Christ determines it in his mission of
Paul: "I send thee to the Gentiles, to open their eyes, to turn them
from darkness to light, and from the power of Satan unto God, that
they may receive forgiveness of sins, and an inheritance among them
which are sanctified by faith that is in me," Acts xxvi. 17, 18. How
shall he apply himself hereunto, how shall he be useful herein, who
was never made partaker of this mercy himself? How can they
press that on others which they neither know what it is, nor whether
it be or no, any otherwise than as blind men know there are colours?
By such persons are the souls of men ruined, who undertake the
dispensation of the gospel unto them for their conversion unto God,
knowing nothing of it themselves.

2. It is our duty to *keep* those in whom we are concerned as much
as in us lieth *from sinning*, or from actual sin. " These things I
write unto you," saith the apostle, " that ye sin not." 1 John ii. 1.
With what confidence, with what conscience, can we endeavour this
toward others, if we do not first take the highest care herein of ourselves? Some that should watch over others are open and profligate
sinners themselves. The preaching, exhortations, and reproofs of
such persons do but render them the more contemptible; and on
many accounts tend to the hardening of those whom they pretend
to instruct. And where men " regard iniquity in their hearts," although there be no notoriety in their transgressions, yet they will
grow languid and careless in their watch over others; and if they
keep up the outward form of it, it will be a great means of hardening themselves in their own sin.

3. To direct and assist others in the *obtaining pardon for sin* is
also the duty of some. And this they may do two ways:—(1.) By
directing them in their *application* unto God by Jesus Christ for
grace and mercy; (2.) By earnest *supplications* with them and for
them. And what will they do, what can they do in these things

sincerely for others, who make not use of them for themselves? I look on this as one of the greatest blessings of the ministry, that we have that enjoined us to do with respect unto others which may sanctify and save their souls; and God hath so ordered things that we neither can nor will diligently attend unto any thing of that kind towards others concerning which we do not first endeavour to have its effect upon ourselves.

4. To administer *consolation* under sinning, or surprisals with sin, unto such as God would have to be comforted, is another duty of the like kind. And how shall this be done by such as were never cast down for sin themselves, nor ever spiritually comforted of God?

It behoves us, therefore, in all things wherein we may deal with others about sin, to take care of ourselves in the first place, that "our consciences be purged from dead works," that in all we do we may " serve the living God."

Obs. III. No dignity of person or place, no duty, no merit, can deliver sinners from standing in need of a sacrifice for sin. The high priest, being a sinner, was to " offer for himself."

Obs. IV. It was a part of the darkness and bondage of the church under the old testament, that their high priests had need to offer sacrifices for themselves and their own sins. This they did in the view of the people; who might fear lest he could not fully expiate their sins who had many of his own, and was therefore necessitated in the first place to take care of himself. It is a relief to sinners, that the word of reconciliation is administered unto them, and the sacrifice of Christ proposed, by men subject unto the like infirmities with themselves; for there is a testimony therein, how that they also may find acceptance with God, seeing he deals with them by those who are sinners also. But these are not the persons who procure the remission, or have made the atonement which they declare. Were it so, who could with any confidence acquiesce therein? But this is the holy way of God: Those who are sinners declare the atonement which was made by him who had no sin.

VERSE 4.

The foregoing verses declare the *personal qualifications* of a high priest. But these alone are not sufficient actually to invest any one with that office; it is required, moreover, that he be lawfully called thereunto. The former make him meet for it, and this gives him his right unto it. And in the application of the whole unto Jesus Christ, this is first insisted on, verse 5.

Ver. 4.—Καὶ οὐχ ἑαυτῷ τις λαμβάνει τὴν τιμὴν, ἀλλὰ ὁ καλούμενος ὑπὸ τοῦ Θεοῦ, καθάπερ καὶ ὁ Ἀαρών.[1]

---

[1] The article before καλούμενος is omitted by Griesbach, Scholz, Lachmann, Tischendorf, and most other modern critics.—ED.

Ver. 4.—And no man taketh this honour unto himself, but he that is called of God, as was Aaron.

There is no difficulty in the rendering of these words, and consequently very little difference among translators. The Syr. and Vulg. Lat. read "honour" absolutely, without taking notice of the article τήν, which is here emphatical, "*this* honour;" the honour of the priesthood. And for "himself," the Syriac reads, "to his own soul;" by an idiom of speech peculiar to the eastern languages.

The words may be taken as a negative universal proposition, with a particular exception subjoined. "No man taketh this honour to himself but" only "he who is called." He that is called taketh this honour to himself, or he that hath right so to do,—namely, to possess and exercise the office of a high priest. Or they may be resolved into two disjunctive propositions: the one universally negative, without exception or limitation, "No man taketh this honour unto himself;" the other particularly affirmative, "He that is called of God," he doth so, or he receiveth this honour. Thus there is an opposition expressed between a man's taking this honour unto himself and his receiving of it on the call of God. Or we may yet more plainly express the meaning of the apostle. Having laid down the qualifications necessary unto him who was to be a high priest, he declares what is required for his actual investiture with this office. And this he expresseth,—1. *Negatively*, he is not to assume this honour to himself: 2. *Positively*, he is to be called of God; which he exemplifies in the instance of Aaron, "as was Aaron."

Οὐχ ἑαυτῷ τις λαμβάνει, "any one doth not take;" that is, no man doth. And λαμβάνω is not here simply "sumo," "to take;" but "assumo," "to take upon," "to take to him:" or as it sometimes signifies, "prehendo, corripio," "unduly to take," by laying hold of any thing. "No man taketh," that is, according to the law, according to divine institution. It was not the law that men should so do. Men might do otherwise, and did do otherwise, both as to the office and exercise of the priesthood. So did king Uzziah as to the exercise of it, 2 Chron. xxvi. 16. And at the time of the writing of this epistle, as also for many years before, there had been no lawful order or call observed in those who possessed the office of the high priesthood among the Jews. Some invaded it themselves, and some were intruded into it by foreign power. And both Chrysostom and Œcumenius suppose that our apostle in this place doth reflect on that disorder. His principal intention is plainly to declare how things ought to be, by the law and constitution of God. "No man doth;" that is, no man ought so to do, for it is contrary to the law and the order appointed of God in his church. See Num. xviii. God's institution in the Scripture is so far the sacred rule of all things to be done in his worship, that whatever is not done by virtue thereof, and in conformity thereunto, is esteemed as not done, or not at all done to him. But,—

Τὴν τιμήν. This is the object of the act prohibited: "The honour;" 'this honour whereof we treat.' Τιμή here intends either the *office* itself or the *dignity* of it. The office   Τὴν τιμήν. itself may be called "honour," because it is honourable. So also is the word used, chap. iii. 3. 'No man taketh this honourable office upon him of his own head, of himself, without warrant, call, and authority from God.' If only the dignity of the office be intended, then it is, 'No man arrogateth so much to himself, so sets up or advanceth himself, as to set himself out for an high priest.' I judge the office itself is first intended, yet not absolutely, but as it was honourable, such as men would naturally desire and intrude themselves into, had not God set bounds to their ambition by his law. So did Korah; for which he was first rebuked and afterwards destroyed, Num. xvi. 9, 10, etc. And this office was exceeding honourable, on a twofold account:—

1. From the *nature* of it: wherein there was, (1.) An especial separation unto God, Exod. xxviii.; (2.) An especial appropinquation or drawing nigh unto him, Lev. xvi.; (3.) The discharge of all peculiar divine services. These things made the office honourable,— a high honour unto them that were duly vested with it. For what greater honour can a mortal creature be made partaker of, than to be peculiarly nigh unto God?

2. Because God required that honour should be given both unto the office and person vested with it. For this end partly was he to be adorned with garments made "for beauty and for glory," and had power given him to rule in the house of God, 1 Sam. ii. 30. But even in general, it is a great honour, on any account, to be made nigh unto God.

Ἀλλὰ ὁ καλούμενος, "but he that is called of God." The called one of God, he hath, he receiveth, he is made partaker   ῾Ο καλούμενος. of the honour of this office. He is the high priest whom God calls. And this call of God is the designation of a man unto an office or employment. He doth, as it were, look on a person among others, and calls him out to himself, as Exod. xxviii. 1. It compriseth also the end of the call, in the collation of right, power, and trust, whatever is necessary unto the due exercise of that whereunto any one is called; for God's will and pleasure is the supreme rule of all order and duty. And this call is here exemplified in the instance of Aaron: "even as was Aaron."

Καθάπερ καὶ ὁ Ἀαρών, "even as Aaron," "in like manner as Aaron." And the note of similitude is regulated either by the word "called," or by the subject of the instance, "Aaron."   Καθάπερ καὶ ὁ Ἀαρών. If by the former, no more is intended but that he must have a call of God, as Aaron had. The comparison proceeds no farther but unto the *general nature* of a call. A call he must have, but the especial nature of that call is not declared. But if the note of comparison be regulated by the instance of Aaron, then the especial manner and nature of the call intended is limited and determined: ' He must be called of God as was Aaron;' that is, immediately and in an extraordinary way. And this is the sense of the words and place.

It may be objected, ' If this be so, then all the high priests who succeeded Aaron in the Judaical church are here excluded from a right entrance into their office; for they were not immediately called of God unto their office, as Aaron was, but succeeded one another by virtue of the law or constitution, which was only an ordinary call.' *Ans.* It doth not exclude them from a right entrance into their office, but it doth from being considered in this place. They had that call to their office which God had appointed, and which was a sufficient warranty unto them in the discharge of it. But our apostle disputes here about the erection of a new priesthood, such as was that of Christ. Herein no ordinary call, no law-constitution, no succession, could take place, or contribute any thing thereunto. The nature of such a work excludes all these considerations. And he who first enters on such a priesthood, not before erected nor constituted, he must have such a call of God thereunto. So had Aaron at the first erection of a typical priesthood in the church of Israel. He had his call by an immediate word of command from God, singling him out from among his brethren to be set apart unto that office, Exod. xxviii. 1. And although in other things which belonged unto the administration of their office, the Lord Christ is compared to the high priests in general, executing their office according to the law, wherein they were types of him, yet as unto his entrance into his office upon the call of God, he is compared with Aaron only.

This being the proper design of the words, the things disputed by expositors and others from this place, about the necessity of an ordinary outward call to the office of the priesthood, and, by analogy, unto the ministry of the gospel, though true in themselves, are foreign unto the intention of this place; for the apostle treats only of the first erection of a priesthood in the persons of Aaron and Christ, whereunto an extraordinary call was necessary. And if none might take on him the office of the ministry but he that is called of God as was Aaron, no man alive could do so at this day.

Again, the note of similitude expresseth an agreement in an extraordinary call, but not in the manner of it and its special kind. This is asserted, that the one and the other had an immediate call from God, but no more. But as unto the especial kind and nature of this immediate call, that of Christ was incomparably more excellent and glorious than that of Aaron.   This will be manifest in the next verses, where it is expressed and declared.   In the meantime we shall consider the call of Aaron, as our apostle doth the ministry of Moses, chap. iii., declaring wherein indeed it was excellent, that so the real honour of the call of Christ above it may appear:—

1. He was " called of God," by a *word of command* for his separation unto the office of the priesthood: Exod. xxviii. 1, " Take thou unto thee Aaron thy brother, and his sons with him, ... that he may minister unto me in the priest's office."   His sons were also mentioned, because provision was herein made for succession.   This made his call extraordinary,—he was "called of God."   But, (1.) This command was not given by a word from God immediately unto himself.   God doth not say unto him, ' Thou art my priest; this day have I called thee.'   But it is Moses to whom the command is given, and with whom the execution of it is intrusted.   So that, (2.) He is in his call put as it were in the power of another; that is, of Moses.   To him God says, " Take unto thee Aaron thy brother;"— ' Be thou unto him in the room of God, and act towards him in my name.'

2. This command or call of God was expressed in his *actual separation* unto his office, which consisted in two things:—

(1.) His being arrayed by God's appointment with glorious garments, Exod. xxviii. 2.   And they are affirmed to be contrived on purpose "for beauty and for glory."   But herein also a double weakness is included or supposed:—[1.] That he stood in need of an outward robe to adorn him, because of his own weakness and infirmities, which God would as it were hide and cover, in his worship, under those garments.   [2.] That indeed they were all of them but typical of things far more glorious in our high priest, namely, that abundant fulness of the graces of the Spirit, which being poured on him rendered him " fairer than the children of men."   It was therefore a part of the glory of Christ, that in the discharge of his office he stood in no need of outward ornaments, all things being supplied by the absolute perfection of his own personal dignity and holiness.

(2.) His actual consecration ensued hereon; which consisted in two things:—[1.] His unction with the holy consecrated oil.   [2.] In the solemn sacrifice which was offered in his name and for him, Exod. xxix.   And there was much order and glory in the solemnity of his consecration.

But yet still these things had their weakness and imperfection. For, (1.) He had nothing of his own to offer at his consecration, but he was consecrated with the blood of a bullock and a ram.   (2.) Another offered for him, and that for his sins.   And this was the call of Aaron, his call of God; and that which God vindicated, setting a notable mark upon it, when it was seditiously questioned by Korah, Num. xvi. 3, xvii. 10. And all these things were necessary unto Aaron, because God in his person erected a new order of priesthood, wherein he was to be confirmed by an extraordinary call thereunto. And this is that, and not an ordinary call, which the call of Christ is compared unto and preferred above. After this all the successors of Aaron had a sufficient call to their office, but not of the same kind with that of Aaron himself. For the office itself was established to continue by virtue of God's institution. And there was a law of succession established, by which they were admitted into it, whereof I have treated elsewhere. But it is the personal call of Aaron which is here intended.

Obs. I. It is an act of sovereignty in God to call whom he pleaseth unto his work and especial service, and eminently so when it is unto any place of honour and dignity in his house.

The office of the priesthood among the Jews was the highest and most honourable that was among them, at the first plantation of the church. And an eminent privilege it was, not only unto the person of him who was first called, but with respect also unto his whole posterity; for they, and they only, were to be priests unto God. Who would not think, now, but that God would call Moses to this dignity, and so secure also the honour of his posterity after him? But he takes another course, and calls Aaron and his family, leaving Moses and his children after him in the ordinary rank and employment of Levites. And the sovereignty of God is evident herein,—
1. Because every call is accompanied with *choice and distinction.* Some one is called out from among others. So was it in the call of Aaron, Exod. xxviii. 1, " Take unto thee Aaron, from among the children of Israel." By a mere act of sovereign pleasure God chose him out from among the many thousands of his brethren. And this sovereign choice God insisteth on to express the favour and kindness that is in any call of his, 1 Sam. ii. 27, 28. And herewith he reproacheth the sins and ingratitude of men, upbraiding them with his sovereign kindness, Num. xvi. 9, 10. 2. Because antecedent unto their call there is *nothing of merit* in any to be so called, nor of ability in the most for the work whereunto they are called. Under the new testament none was ever called to greater dignity, higher honour, or more eminent employment, than the apostle Paul. And what antecedaneous merit was there in him unto his vocation? Christ takes him in the midst of his madness, rage, persecution, and blasphemy, turns his heart unto himself, and calls him to be his apostle, witness, and great instrument for the conversion of the souls of men, bearing forth his name to the ends of the earth. And this we know that himself mentions on all occasions as an effect of sovereign grace, wisdom, and mercy. What merit was there, what pre-

vious disposition unto their work, in a few fishermen about the lake of Tiberias or sea of Galilee, that our Lord Jesus Christ should call them to be his apostles, disposing them into that state and condition wherein they "sit on twelve thrones, judging the twelve tribes of Israel?" So was it ever with all that God called in an extraordinary manner. See Exod. iv. 10, 11; Jer. i. 6; Amos vii. 14, 15. In his ordinary calls there is the same sovereignty, though somewhat otherwise exercised. For in such a call there are three things:—1. A *providential designation of a person* to such an office, work, or employment. When any office in the house of God, suppose that of the ministry, is fixed and established, the first thing that God doth in the call of any one thereunto, is the providential disposition of the circumstances of his life, directing his thoughts and designs toward such an end. And were not the office of the ministry in some places accompanied with many secular advantages, yea, provisions for the lusts and luxuries of men that are foreign unto it, this entrance into a call from God thereunto, by a mere disposal of men's concerns and circumstances, so as to design the ministry in the course of their lives, would be eminent and perspicuous. But whilst multitudes of persons, out of various corrupt ends, crowd themselves into the entrances of this office, the secret workings of the providence of God towards the disposal of them whom he really designs unto his work herein are greatly clouded and obscured. 2. It is part of this call of God, when he blesseth, succeedeth, and *prospereth the endeavours of men* to prepare themselves with those previous dispositions and qualifications which are necessary unto the actual call and susception of this office. And hereof also there are three parts:—(1.) An *inclination of their hearts*, in compliance with his designation of them unto their office. Where this is not effected, but men proceed according as they are stimulated by outward impressions or considerations, God is not as yet at all in this work. (2.) An *especial blessing* of their endeavours for the due improvement of their natural faculties and abilities in study and learning, for the necessary aids and instruments of knowledge and wisdom. (3.) The *communication of peculiar gifts* unto them, rendering them meet and able unto the discharge of the duty of their office; which, in an ordinary call, is indispensably required as previous to an actual separation unto the office itself. 3. *He ordereth things so, as that a person whom he will employ in the service of his house shall have an outward call*, according unto rule, for his admission thereinto. And in all these things God acts according to his own sovereign will and pleasure. And many things might hence be educed and insisted on. As,—1. That we should have an awful reverence of, and a holy readiness to comply with the call of God; not to *run away* from it, or the work called unto, as did

Jonah, chap. i.; nor to be weary of it, because of difficulty and opposition which we meet withal in the discharge of our duty, as it sundry times was ready to befall Jeremiah, chap. xv. 10, xx. 7–9; much less desert or give it over on any earthly account whatever, seeing that he who sets his hand to this plough, and takes it back again, is unworthy of the kingdom of heaven,—and it is certain that he who deserts his calling on worldly accounts, first took it up on no other. 2. That we should not *envy nor repine* at one another, whatever God is pleased to call any unto. 3. That we engage into no work wherein the name of God is concerned without his call; which gives a second observation, namely, that,—

Obs. II. The highest excellency and utmost necessity of any work to be done for God in this world, will not warrant our undertaking of it or engaging in it, unless we are called thereunto. Yea,—

Obs. III. The more excellent any work of God is, the more express ought our call unto it to be.

Both these observations will be so fixed and confirmed in the consideration of the instance given us in the next verse, as that there is no occasion here to insist upon them.

Obs. IV. It is a great dignity and honour, to be duly called unto any work, service, or office, in the house of God.

Verse 5.

The description of a high priest according to the law, with respect, —1. Unto his *nature;* 2. His *employment*, verse 1; 3. His *qualification*, verse 2; 4. His especial *duty*, with regard (1.) to himself, (2.) to others, verse 3; 5. His *call*, in the instance of him who was the first of the order, verse 4,—being completed, an application of the whole is in this verse entered upon unto our Lord Jesus Christ. And this is done in all the particulars wherein there was or could be an agreement or correspondency between them and him with respect unto this office. And it was necessary to be thus declared by the apostle, unto the end designed by him, for two reasons:—1. Because the original institution of those priests and their office was to teach and represent the Lord Christ and his; which was his main intention to manifest and prove. Now this they could not do unless there were some analogy and likeness between them; neither could it be apprehended or understood for what end and purpose they were designed, and did so long continue in the church. 2. That the Hebrews might be satisfied that their ministry and service in the house of God was now come to an end, and the whole use whereunto they were designed accomplished. For by this respect and relation that was between them, it was evident that he was now actually exhibited, and had done the whole work which they were appointed to prefigure and represent. It was therefore impossible that there should be any further use of them in the service of God; yea, their continuance therein would contradict and utterly overthrow the end of their institution. For it would declare that they had a use and efficacy unto spiritual ends of their own, without respect unto him and his work whom they did represent; which is to overthrow the faith of both churches, that under the old testament and that under the new. Wherefore a full discovery of the proportion between them, and relation of the one unto the other, was necessary, to evince that their continuance was useless, yea, pernicious. But on the other side, it could not be but that those high priests had many imperfections and weaknesses inseparable from their persons in the administration of their office, which could represent nothing nor receive any accomplishment in our Lord Jesus Christ. For if any thing in him had answered thereunto, he could not have been such a high priest as did become us, or as we stood in need of. Such was it that they were subject to death, and therefore were necessarily many, succeeding one another in a long series, according to a certain genealogy: "They truly were many priests, because they were not suffered to continue by reason of death: but this man, because he continueth ever, hath an unchangeable priesthood," or a priesthood that passeth not from one to another, chap. vii. 23, 24. Herein, therefore, there was a dissimilitude between them, because of their being obnoxious unto death; whence it was inevitable that they must be many, one succeeding to another. But Jesus Christ was to be one high priest only, and that always the same.

Again, they were all of them personally sinners, and that both as men and as high priests; whence they might and did miscarry and sin, even in the administration of their office. Wherefore it was needful that they should offer sacrifice for their own sins also, as hath been declared. Now, as nothing could be represented hereby in Jesus Christ, " who knew no sin," " did no sin, neither was guile found in his mouth," nor could he therefore offer sacrifice for himself; so these things do cast some darkness and obscurity on those instances wherein they did represent him. Wherefore our apostle steers a straight course between all these difficulties: for, First, He manifests and proves that the legal high priests were indeed types of Jesus Christ in his office, and did bear forth a resemblance of him therein; as also, that they were appointed of God for that very end and purpose. Secondly, He shows what were their qualifications and properties; which he distinguisheth into two sorts:—1. Such as belonged essentially, or were required necessarily, unto the office itself, and its regular discharge. 2. Such as were unavoidable consequents or concomitants of their personal weakness or infirmity. This latter sort, in this application of their description unto Christ and his office, as prefigured thereby, he discards and lays aside, as things

which, though necessary unto them from their frail and sinful condition, yet had no respect unto Christ, nor accomplishment in him.
And as for the former, he declares in the discourse immediately ensuing how they were found in Christ, as exercising this office, in a
far more eminent manner than in them. This is the design of the
discourse in the second part of the chapter, which we are now entering on. Only, whereas in the description of a high priest in general,
he begins with his nature, qualifications, work, and duty, closing and
issuing it in his call; in his application of the whole unto the Lord
Christ, he taketh up that first which he had lastly mentioned, namely,
the call of a high priest, and proceedeth unto the others in an order
absolutely retrograde.

Ver. 5.—Οὕτω καὶ ὁ Χριστὸς οὐχ ἑαυτὸν ἐδόξασε γενηθῆναι ἀρχιερέα,
ἀλλ' ὁ λαλήσας πρὸς αὐτόν· Υἱός μου εἶ σύ, ἐγὼ σήμερον γεγέννηκά σε.

Ver. 5.—So also Christ glorified not himself to be made
an high priest; but he that said unto him, Thou art my
Son, to-day have I begotten thee.

Οὕτω καί, " so also," " and so," or " in like manner;" a note τῆς
ἀποδόσεως, of the application of things before spoken
unto the subject principally intended. A respect may
be herein unto all the instances in the preceding discourse: ' As it
was with the legal high priest in all the things necessary unto that
office, so in like manner was it with Christ;' which he now designeth
to manifest. Or the intention of this expression may be restrained
to the last expressed instance, of a call to office: 'As they were called
of God, so, or in like manner, was Christ also;' which he immediately
declares. And this is first regarded, though respect may be had unto
it in all the particular instances of analogy and similitude which
ensue.

On this note of inference there ensueth a double proposition on
the same supposition. The supposition that they both are resolved
into is, that " Christ is an high priest." Hereon the first proposition, with respect unto his call and entrance on that office, is negative, " He glorified not himself to be made an high priest." The
other is positive or affirmative, " But he that said unto him, Thou
art my Son;" that is, he glorified him so to be, or he made him so.

Ὁ Χριστός, " Christ," the subject spoken of; that is, the promised
Messiah, the anointed one. The apostle in this epistle
calls him occasionally by all signal names, as " the
Son," chap. i. 2, 8; the " Son of God," chap. iv. 14; the " Word of
God," chap. iv. 12; "Jesus," chap. ii. 9; "Christ," chap. iii. 6; "Christ
Jesus," chap. iii. 1. Here he useth the name of Christ as peculiarly
suited unto his present occasion; for he had designed to prove that

the promised Messiah, the hope and expectation of the fathers, was to be the high priest for ever over the house of God.   Therefore he calls him by that name whereby he was known from the beginning, and which signified his unction unto his office,—the anointed one. He was to be כֹּהֵן הַמָּשִׁיחַ, the "anointed priest;" that is, "Christ."

The subject spoken of being stated or described by his name, the supposition of his being a high priest takes place.   This the apostle had before taught and proved, chap. ii. 17, iii. 1, iv. 14.   But yet, considering the constitution of the law, and the way of any one's entering on that office, a difficult inquiry yet remained, namely, how he came so to be.   Had he been of the tribe of Levi, and of the family of Aaron, he might have been a priest, he would have been so, and have been so acknowledged by all.   But how he should become so, who was a stranger to that family, who "sprang of the tribe of Judah, concerning which Moses spake nothing of the priesthood," might be highly questioned.   Fully and satisfactorily to resolve this doubt, and therein to take in the whole difficulty whence it arose, the apostle in the preceding verse lays down a concession in a universal maxim, that none who had not a right thereunto, by virtue of an antecedent law or constitution,—which Christ had not, as not being of the tribe of Levi,—could be a priest, without an immediate call from God, such as Aaron had.   By and on this rule he offers the right of the Lord Christ unto this office to trial; and therein acknowledgeth that if he were not extraordinarily called of God thereunto he could be no high priest.   To this purpose he declares,—

First, *Negatively*, that "he glorified not himself to be made an high priest."   Outward call by men, or a constitution by virtue of any ordinance of the law, he had none.   Οὐχ ἑαυτὸν ἰδόξασι. Seeing therefore he is a priest, or if so he be, he must be made so by God, or by himself.   But as for himself, neither did he take this honour to himself, nor was it possible that so he should do; for the whole office, and the benefit of his discharge of it, depended on a covenant or compact between him and his Father. Upon the undertaking of it, also, he was to receive many promises from the Father, and was to do his will and work; as we have elsewhere declared and fully proved.   It was therefore impossible that he should make himself a high priest.

The Socinians do but vainly raise a cavil against the deity of Christ from this place.   They say, 'If he were God, why did another glorify him in any kind, why did he not glorify himself?'   And the Jews on all occasions make the same exception.   There were, indeed, some force in the objection against us, if we believed or professed that the Lord Christ were God *only;* but our doctrine concerning his person is that which is declared by our apostle, Phil. ii. 6, 7, "Being in the form of God, he thought it not robbery to be equal with God; but he made himself of no reputation, and took upon him the form of a servant, and was made in the likeness of men." Wherefore there is no more weight in this cavil than there would be in another, namely, if one, unto those testimonies, that "all things were made by him," and that he " in the beginning laid the foundation of the earth," should ask, 'How could this be, seeing he was a man, born in the fulness of time?' But this objection, for the substance of it, was raised by the Jews of old, and fully answered by himself. For whereas they objected unto him that he, being not fifty years old, could not have seen Abraham, as he pretended, who was dead near two thousand years before, he replied, "Before Abraham was, I am," John viii. 58. If he had no other nature than that wherein they thought he was not fifty years old (being indeed little more than thirty), he could not have known Abraham, nor Abraham him. As, therefore, if he had been *man only*, he could not have been before Abraham, so had he been God only, another could not have glorified him to be a priest. But he was man also; and these words are spoken not with respect unto his divine nature, but his human.

Again; as it was impossible he should, so it is plain that he did not glorify himself to be a high priest, or take this dignity and honour to himself by his own will and authority. And this may be evidenced by a brief rehearsal of the divine acts necessary to the making of him a high priest; all which I have handled at large in the previous Exercitations. And they were of two sorts:—1. *Authoritative*, and wholly without him; 2. *Perfective*, whereunto his own concurrence was required. Of the first sort were,—(1.) His eternal *designation* unto this office. (2.) His *mission* unto the discharge of it. (3.) His *unction* with the Spirit for its due discharge. (4.) The *constitution of the law* of his priesthood, which consisted of two parts; the first prescribing what he should do, what he should undergo, what he should offer, or what should be the duties of his office; the other declaring, appointing, promising what should be attained, effected, and accomplished thereby. (5.) The committing and giving a *people* unto him, for whose sake and on whose account he was to bear, execute, and discharge this holy office. And all these, whereby he was authoritatively vested with his office, were sovereign acts of the will and wisdom of the Father, as I have elsewhere proved. By these was he called and glorified to be a high priest. Again, there were some acts perfective of his call, or such as gave it its complement; and these were wrought in him and by him, neither could they be otherwise: but yet by them did he not make himself a high priest, but only complied with the will and authority of the Father. Thus, when Aaron was called of God to his office, the law for its constitution being made and given, the person designed and called out by name, his pontifical garments put on, and the anoint-

ing holy oil poured on him, a sacrifice was to be offered, to complete
and perfect his consecration. But because of his imperfection, whence
it was necessary that he should come to his office by degrees and the
actings of others about him, he could not himself offer the sacrifice
for himself. He only laid his hand on the head of it, to manifest his
concernment therein, but it was Moses that offered it unto God,
Exod. xxix. 10–12. Thus it could not be with respect unto Jesus
Christ, nor did he need any other sacrifice than his own for his consecration, seeing it was necessary unto the legal high priests on the
account of their personal sins and infirmities. But although he was
perfectly and completely constituted a high priest, by those acts of
God the Father before mentioned, yet his solemn consecration and
dedication, not to his office, but to the actual discharge of it, were
effected by acts of his own, in his preparation for and actual offering
up of himself a sacrifice, once for all. And so he was perfected and
consecrated in and by his own blood. Wherefore he did not glorify
himself to be made a high priest, but that was an act and effect of
the will and authority of God.

It remains only, as unto this first clause, that we inquire how it is
said that " Christ glorified not himself," as unto the end mentioned.
Was there an addition of glory or honour made unto him thereby ?
Especially may this be reasonably inquired, if we consider what befell
him, what he did, and what he suffered, in the discharge of this
office; nay, doth not the Scripture everywhere declare this as an act
of the highest condescension in him, as Phil. ii. 6–9, Heb. ii. 9?
How, therefore, can he be said not to glorify himself herein? Let
those answer this inquiry who deny his divine nature and being.
They will find themselves in the same condition as the Pharisees
were when our Saviour posed them with a question to the same
purpose; namely, how David came to call Christ his Lord, who was
to be his son so long after. Unto us these things are clear and
evident. For although, if we consider the divine nature and person
of Christ, it was an infinite condescension in him to take our nature,
and therein to execute the office of a priest for us; yet with respect
unto the nature assumed, the office itself was an honour and dignity
unto him, on the accounts to be afterwards insisted on.

Secondly, In the *affirmative* proposition the way whereby Christ
came unto his office is declared, or by what authority he was appointed a high priest: 'Αλλ' ὁ λαλήσας πρὸς αὐτόν,—   'Αλλ' ὁ λα-
" But he that said unto him." There is an ellipsis in the   λήσας πρὸς
words, which must be supplied to complete the anti-   αὐτόν.
thesis: " But he glorified him," or " he made him to be an high
priest, who said unto him, Υἱός μου εἶ σύ, ἐγὼ σήμερον
γεγέννηκά σε." It is not easily apprehended how the   Υἱός μου εἶ σύ.
apostle confirmeth the priesthood of Christ, or his call to office, by

these words (they are twice used elsewhere by himself to other ends, Heb. i. 5, Acts xiii. 33); for these words do originally signify the eternal relation that is between the Father and the Son, with their mutual love therein. To this purpose are they applied, Heb. i. 5. And because this was manifested in and by the resurrection of Christ from the dead, when and wherein he was " declared to be the Son of God with power," Rom. i. 4, this testimony is applied thereunto, Acts xiii. 33. For the direct intention and the full meaning of the words, the reader may consult our exposition on chap. i. 5, where they are handled at large. But how they are produced by our apostle here, as a confirmation of the priesthood of Christ, is an inquiry that is not without its difficulties; and seeing expositors are variously divided about it, their apprehensions must necessarily be inquired into and examined.

First, Those of the Socinian way, as Crellius and Schlichtingius, affirm that these words are constitutive of the priesthood of Christ; and that they were spoken to him after his resurrection. Hence they suppose two things will ensue:—1. That the Lord Christ was not a priest, at least no complete priest, until after his resurrection; for not until then was it said unto him, "Thou art my Son." 2. That his priestly and kingly offices are the same; for his exaltation in his kingly power is principally intended in these words. But these things are fond and impious. For if the Lord Christ were not a priest until after his resurrection, then he was not so in the offering of himself to God, in his death and blood-shedding; which to say is to offer violence to the common sense of all Christians, the whole institution of the types of old, the analogy of faith, and express tesmonies of Scripture in particular, as hath been evinced in our Exercitations. It expressly contradicts the apostle in this very place, or would make him contradict himself; for after this he affirms that as a priest he offered unto God "in the days of his flesh," verse 7. They say, therefore, that he had some kind of initiation into his office by death, but he was not completely a priest until after his resurrection. The meaning whereof is, that he was not a complete priest until he had completely finished and discharged the principal work which belonged unto that office! I say, therefore,—1. That this distinction, of the Lord Christ being first an incomplete priest, and then afterwards made so completely, is foreign to the Scripture, a vain imagination of bold men, and inconsistent with his holy perfection, who was at once made so by the oath of God. 2. It is destructive of all the instructive parts of the type; for Aaron neither did nor could offer any sacrifice to God until he was completely consecrated unto his office. Nor is any thing in the law more severely prohibited, than that any one should draw nigh to God in offering sacrifice that was not completely a priest. 3. Thus to interpret the testimony urged by the apostle, is completely to disappoint his purpose and intention in it. For he designs by it to prove that Christ, in the offering which he made in the days of his flesh, did not glorify himself to be made a priest, but was made so by him who said unto him, "Thou art my Son, this day have I begotten thee." And if this was not said unto him until after his resurrection, then in his offering of himself before, he glorified himself to be a priest, for he was not yet made so of God the Father. 4. The vanity of confounding the kingly and priestly offices of Christ hath been sufficiently detected in our Exercitations.

Secondly, Others say that the confirmation of the priesthood of Christ in these words, is taken from the ancient usage before the law, whereby the priesthood was annexed unto the primogeniture. Wherefore God declaring the Lord Christ to be his only-begotten Son, the first-born, lord and heir of the whole creation, did thereby also declare him to be the high priest. And this exposition is embraced by sundry learned men, whose conjecture herein I cannot comply withal. For,—1. The foundation of it is very questionable, if not unquestionably false; namely, concerning the priesthood of the first-born before the law. This, indeed, is the opinion of the Jews, and is so reported by Jerome, Epist. ad Evagr.; but the matter is not clear in the Scripture. Abel was not the first-born, nor Abraham either; yet they both offered sacrifice to God. 2. This would include an express contradiction unto the scope of the apostle. For his design is to prove that Christ was a priest after the order of Melchisedec, called of God, and raised up extraordinarily, in a way peculiar and not common to any other. But on this supposition, he should be a priest after the order of the first-born. For what belonged unto Christ as the first-born, see our exposition on chap. i. 3.

Thirdly, Some judge that although the apostle recites expressly only these words, "Thou art my Son, this day have I begotten thee," yet he directs us thereby to the whole passage in the psalm whereof these words are a part, verses 7, 8, "I will declare the decree: the LORD hath said unto me, Thou art my Son; this day have I begotten thee. Ask of me, and I shall give thee the heathen for thine inheritance, and the uttermost parts of the earth for thy possession." Here seems to be an express constitution, such as the apostle refers unto. For if we would know when or how God the Father glorified Christ to be a high priest, it was in that decree of his which is declared, Ps. ii. 7. It was before established in heaven, and then declared in prophecy. And moreover, there is added an especial mention of the discharge of one part of his office as a priest, in these words, "Ask of me;" wherein authority is given him to make intercession with God. And this exposition, whereof, as far as I can find, Junius was the author, I shall not oppose; only for two reasons I cannot readily assent unto it. For,—1. It seems not probable that the apostle, in the quotation of a testimony, should omit that which was directly to his purpose, and produce those words only which alone were not so.   2. The asking here enjoined, is not his sacerdotal intercession, but only an expression denoting the dependence of Christ, as king, on God the Father for the subduing of his enemies.

Fourthly, Some conceive that the apostle intends not a testimony of the constitution of Christ in his office of priesthood, but only to give an account of the person by whom he was called thereunto: ' He made not himself a high priest; but was made so by him from whom he had all his honour and glory as mediator, and that because he was his Son, and in his word declared so to be.'   But the testimony given unto his priesthood is brought in in the next verse. Nor do I see any more than one exception which this exposition is liable unto, but which those that follow it have taken no notice of. And this is, that the manner of the introduction of the next testimony, " As he also saith in another place," doth evidence that they are both produced and urged to the same purpose, for the confirmation of the same assertion.   But withal I answer thereunto by concession, that indeed they are both here of the same importance, and used to the same purpose.   For these words in this place, "Thou art a priest for ever after the order of Melchisedec," are considered as spoken to him by God the Father, even as the former were.   This, therefore, is the design of the apostle in the introduction of this testimony; for the clearing whereof we may observe :—1. That it is not the priesthood of Christ, but his call thereunto, which in this place the apostle asserts, as was before declared.   2. As to this, he intends to show only that it was God the Father from whom he had all his mediatory power, as king, priest, and prophet to his church. 3. This is evidently proved by this testimony, in that therein God declares him to be his Son, and his acceptance thereby of him in the discharge of the work committed unto him.   For this solemn declaration of his relation unto God the Father in his eternal sonship, and his approbation of him, doth prove that he undertook nothing, performed nothing, but what he had appointed, designed, and authorized him unto.   And that he had so designed him unto this office is more particularly declared in the ensuing testimony.

Obs. I. The office of the high priesthood over the church of God was an honour and glory to Jesus Christ.

It was so unto his *human nature*, even as it was united unto the divine; for it was capable of glory, of degrees of glory, and an augmentation in glory, John xvii. 1, 1 Pet. i. 21.   And the Lord Christ had a twofold glory upon him in the bearing and discharging of this office:—1. The glory that was upon him, or of the work itself; 2. The glory that was proposed unto him, in the effects of it.

1. There was a glory upon him in his work, from the nature of the work itself. So it was prophesied of him, Zech. vi. 13, " He shall build the temple of the LORD, and he shall bear the glory." All the glory of the house of God shall be on him, Isa. xxii. 24. And it was a glory unto him, because the work itself was great and glorious. It was no less than the healing of the breach made between God and the whole creation by the first apostasy. Sin had put variance between God and all his creatures, Gen. iii., Rom. viii. 20. No way was left, but that God must be perpetually dishonoured, or all creatures everlastingly cursed. And hereby there seemed to be a kind of defeatment of God's first design, to glorify himself in the making of all things; for to this purpose he made them all " exceeding good," Gen. i. 31. And his glory depended not so much upon their being, as their being good; that is, their beauty, and order, and subjection to himself. But this was now lost as to all the creation, but only a part and portion of the angels, who sinned not. But yet the apostasy of those who were partakers of the same nature, privileges, and advantages with them, made it manifest what they also in their natural state and condition were obnoxious unto. How great, how glorious a work must it needs be, to put a stop unto this entrance of confusion; to lay hold on the perishing creation, running headlong into eternal ruin, and to preserve it, or some portion of it, some first-fruits of it, unto God from destruction! Must not this be a work equal unto, if not exceeding, the first forming of all things? Certainly it is a glorious and honourable thing unto him that shall undertake and accomplish this great and glorious work. What is said with respect unto one particular in it, may be applied unto the whole. When the sealed book containing the state of the church and the world was represented unto John, it is said that there was " no man in heaven, nor in earth, neither under the earth, that was able to open the book, neither to look thereon," Rev. v. 3. Whereon the apostle wept that none was found worthy to engage in that work. But when the Lord Christ, "the lion of the tribe of Judah," appeared to do it, and prevailed therein, verse 5, all the host of heaven, all the saints of God, joined together in ascribing glory and honour unto him, verses 6–14. The work was great and honourable, and therefore on the account of it doth that harmonious ascription of glory and honour unto him ensue. How much more must the whole work be esteemed such, whereof that book contained only a small portion! Herein, then, was the Lord Jesus Christ exceedingly glorious in his priestly office, because in the discharge of it he was the only means and way of the recovery and advancement of the glory of God; the greatness of which work no heart can conceive nor tongue express. 2. It appears from the effects and consequents of the discharge of his office, or the glory proposed unto him. And that,—

(1.) On *the part of them for whom he did discharge it.* And these
were all the elect of God. He himself looked on this as a part of the
glory set before him, that he should be a captain of salvation unto
them, and bring them unto the eternal enjoyment of God in immortal glory. And a double honour ariseth hence unto Jesus Christ:
—[1.] Initial, the love, thankfulness, and worship of the church in
all ages, in this world. See Rev. i. 5, 6. This is a glory wherein
he is delighted, that all his saints, in all parts of the world, do severally, and in their assemblies, with all humility, love, and thankfulness, worship, adore, bless, praise, and glorify him, as the author and
finisher of their recovery unto God, and eternal salvation. Every
day do they come about his throne, cleave unto him, and live in the
admiration of his love and power. [2.] This glory will be full at
the latter day, and so hold unto all eternity, when all his saints, from
the beginning of the world unto the end thereof, shall be gathered
unto him, and abide with him, adoring him as their head, and shout-
ing for joy when they behold his glory. (2.) On *his own part.* There
is a peculiar honour and glory given him of God, as a consequent of
his discharge of this office, and on the account thereof, 1 Pet. i. 21;
Phil. ii. 9, 10; Eph. i. 20–23: whereof see our exposition on chap.
i. 2. (3.) That glory wherein *God will be exalted* unto all eternity
in the praise of his grace,—the end of all his holy purposes towards
his church, Eph. i. 6,—doth ensue and depend hereon. For these
and the like reasons it was that our blessed Saviour, knowing how
unable we are in this world to comprehend his glory, as also how great
a part of our blessedness doth consist in the knowledge of it, makes
that great request for us, that, after we are preserved in, delivered
from, and carried through our course in this world, as a principal
part of our rest and reward, we may be with him where he is, to
behold his glory which is given him of his Father, John xvii. 24.
And our present delight in this glory and honour of Christ, is a
great evidence of our love of him and faith in him.

Obs. II. Relation and love are the fountain and cause of God's
committing all authority in and over the church to Jesus Christ.

By this expression of relation and love, " Thou art my Son, this
day have I begotten thee," doth the apostle prove that God called
him to be the high priest of the church. To the same purpose himself [1] speaketh, John iii. 35, " The Father loveth the Son, and hath
given all things into his hand." In his constitution and declaration
to be the great and only prophet of the church, God did it by an
expression of his relation and love to him: "This is my beloved
Son, in whom I am well pleased; hear ye him," Matt. xvii. 5. And
this also was the foundation of his kingly office. Heb. i. 2, " He
hath spoken unto us by his Son, whom he hath appointed heir of

---

[1] Or rather, John the Baptist.—ED.

all things;"—he who was his Son, and because he was his Son. God would give this glory and honour unto none but unto his only Son; which to prove is the design of our apostle in the first chapter of this epistle. And this his relation unto God manifested itself in all that he did in the discharge of his office; for saith the evangelist, " We beheld his glory, the glory as of the only-begotten of the Father, full of grace and truth," John i. 14. Now, first, the *relation* intended is that one single eternal relation of his being the "Son of God," the " only-begotten of the Father," through the divine ineffable communication of his nature with him, or unto him. And hence the faith hereof is the foundation of the church; for when Peter made that confession of it, in opposition unto all false conceptions of others concerning his person, "Thou art the Christ, the Son of the living God," he answers, " Upon this rock I will build my church," Matt. xvi. 16, 18. And why doth the Lord Christ build his church on the profession of this article of our faith concerning his person? It is because we declare our faith therein that God would not commit all power in and over the church, and the work of mediation in its behalf, unto any but him who stood in that relation to him, of his only-begotten Son. And hereby, as God declares the greatness of this work, which none could effect but his Son, he who is God with himself, and that none other should partake with him in this glory; so he directs us to the worship and honour of him as his Son: for it is the will of God that " all men should honour the Son, even as they honour the Father," John v. 23. And those who put in themselves, their wills and authorities, as the pope; or bring in others into the honour of this work, as saints and angels; do rise up in direct opposition to the design of the will and wisdom of God. They must first give some one the relation of an only Son to God, before they ought to ascribe any thing of this great work or the honour of it unto him. Secondly, The *love* intended is twofold:—1. The natural and eternal love of the Father unto the Son, and his delight in him, as participant of the same nature with himself. This is expressed, Prov. viii. 30, 31; which place hath been explained and vindicated before. 2. His actual love towards him on the account of his infinite condescension and grace in undertaking this work, wherein his glory was so deeply concerned. See Phil. ii. 6–11. And this love hath a peculiar influence into the collation of that glory and honour on Christ which God bestowed on him. And in these things, which must not be here enlarged on, doth lie the blessed, sure, stable foundation of the church, and of our salvation, by the mediation of Christ.

VERSE 6.

The next verse gives us a further confirmation of the call of Christ unto his office, by another testimony, taken from Ps. cx. 4. And much time, with diligence, would be needful to the explanation hereof, but that this is not its proper place. For that the whole psalm was prophetical of Jesus Christ I have proved before, and vindicated it from the exceptions of the Jews, both in our Exercitations and expositions on the first chapter. The subject-matter also spoken of, or the priesthood of Melchisedec, with the order thereof, the apostle expressly resumes and handles at large, chap. vii., where it must be considered. There is, therefore, only one concernment of these words here to be inquired into; and this is, how far or wherein they do give testimony unto the assertion of the apostle, that Christ did not glorify himself to be made a high priest, but that he was designed thereunto of God, even the Father.

Ver. 6.—Καθὼς καὶ ἐν ἑτέρῳ λέγει· Σὺ ἱερεὺς εἰς τὸν αἰῶνα κατὰ τὴν τάξιν Μελχισεδέκ.

Ver. 6.—As he saith in another [*psalm*], Thou [*art*] a priest for ever after the order of Melchisedec.

There are two things in these words:—First, The *manner* of the introduction of a new testimony; Secondly, The *testimony* itself.

The first, "As he saith in another." And therein we may consider,—1. The connection unto and compliance with that foregoing: Καθὼς καί, ' In the same manner as he had said in Ps. ii., "Thou art my Son, this day have I begotten thee," so he speaks "in another place" to the same purpose.' So great and important a truth had need of solid confirmation. 2. The author of the testimony, or he that spake the words of it: Λέγει, "He saith." And this may be taken two ways;—(1.) With respect unto the *delivery* of the words; (2.) With respect unto the *subject-matter* of them, or the thing signified in them. (1.) In the first way, he that speaks may be [1.] David. He who was the penman of the second psalm was so also of this hundred and tenth. As, therefore, the words foregoing, as to the declaration of them, were his, so were these also. As he said in that place, so he saith in this. Or, [2.] The Holy Spirit himself, who in both places spake in and by David: "Saying in David," chap. iv. 7. (2.) But the thing spoken and signified is principally here intended. And λέγει, "he saith," referreth immediately to God the Father himself. That which the apostle designed to prove, is that Christ was called and constituted a high priest by the authority of God the Father. And this was done by his immediate speaking unto him. The Holy Ghost, by the mouth of David, speaks these things to us. But he doth only therein declare what the Father said unto the Son; and that was it whereby the apostle's intention was proved and confirmed.

"He saith." This was that which God said unto him. And this is recorded ἐν ἑτέρῳ, "in another;" that is, τόπῳ, "place," or rather ψαλμῷ, "in another psalm," that is, Ps. cx. 4.   *'Εν ἑτέρῳ.*

Secondly, The *testimony* itself is expressed, or the words of the Father unto the Son, whereby the apostle's assertion is confirmed: "Thou art a priest for ever after the order of Melchisedec." It was sufficient for the apostle at present to produce these words only; but he will elsewhere make use of the manner how they were uttered, namely, by and with the oath of God, as it is declared in the psalm, "The LORD hath sworn, and will not repent, thou art a priest," etc. And these words of verse 4 do indissolubly depend on the first verse: "The LORD said unto my Lord;" that is, God the Father said unto the Son, with respect unto his incarnation and mediation, as I have proved elsewhere. And this word, "Thou art," is "verbum constitutivum," a "constituting word," wherein the priesthood of Christ was founded. And it may be considered,—1. As *declarative* of God's eternal decree, with the covenant between the Father and Son, whereby he was designed unto this office; whereof we have treated expressly and at large in the previous Exercitations. 2. As *demonstrative* of his mission, or his actual sending to the discharge of his office. These words are the symbol and solemn sign of God's conferring that honour upon him, which gave him his instalment. 3. There is included in them a supposition that God would prepare a body for him, wherein he might exercise his priesthood, and which he might offer up unto him. On the whole, it is undeniable from this testimony, that God called and appointed him to be a priest; which was to be proved.

Thus Christ was "called of God, as was Aaron;"—that is, immediately, and in an extraordinary manner; which was necessary in the first erection of that office in his person. But yet, as to the especial manner of his call, it was every way more excellent and glorious than that of Aaron. What his call was, and what were the weaknesses and imperfections of it, were before declared. But the call of Christ,—1. Had no need of any *outward ceremony* to express it, yea, it had a glory in it which no ceremony could express. 2. It consisted in the words of God spoken immediately *to himself*, and not to any others concerning him; only they are reported unto the church in the two psalms mentioned. 3. The words spoken are present, *effective*, constituting, authoritative words, and not merely *declarative* of what God would have done. By these words was he called and made a priest. 4. They are expressive of infinite love to and acquiescency in the person of Christ as a high priest. "THOU art my Son; THOU art a priest for ever." 5. They were spoken and pronounced with the solemnity of an *oath*,—"The LORD hath sworn;" whereof elsewhere. He was not, therefore, only called of God, as

was Aaron, but also in a peculiar way, far more eminently and gloriously. We may hence observe,—

Obs. That in all things wherein God hath to do with mankind
Jesus Christ should have an absolute pre-eminence.

It was necessary that of old some things should be made use of to
represent and prefigure him. And it is necessary now that some
things should be made use of to reveal and exhibit him unto us.
And these things must, as they are appointments of God, effects of
his wisdom, and out of their respect unto him, be precious and excellent. But yet in and through them all it is his own person, and
what he doth therein, that hath the pre-eminence. And this is so
on a twofold account:—1. Because in the representation which they
made of him there was an imperfection, by reason of their own nature,
so that they could not perfectly represent him. So Aaron was called
in an extraordinary manner, to prefigure his call unto his priesthood;
but that call of his was accompanied with much weakness and imperfection, as hath been declared. It belonged unto the pre-eminence of Christ, that there should be something, yea, very much, in
his call absolutely peculiar. 2. The principal dignity of all these
things depended on their respect and relation unto him; which exalts
him infinitely above them. And so also is it with all the means of
grace, whereby at present he is exhibited, and the benefits of his mediation communicated unto us.

VERSE 7.

In this verse two instances of the qualifications of a high priest
are accommodated unto our Lord Jesus Christ, and that in the retrograde order before proposed. For the last thing expressed concerning a high priest according to the law was, that he was " compassed
with infirmity," verse 3. And this, in the first place, is applied
unto Christ; for it was so with him when he entered upon the discharge of his office. And therein the apostle gives a double demonstration:—1. From the *time* and season wherein he did execute his
office; it was " in the days of his flesh." So openly do they contradict the Scripture who contend that he entered not directly on
his priestly office until these days of his flesh were finished and
ended. Now, in the days of his flesh he was compassed with infirmities, and that because he was in the flesh. 2. From the *manner*
of his deportment in this discharge of his office, he did it with
" cries and tears." And these also are from the infirmity of our
nature.

Secondly, The *acting* of the high priest, as so qualified, in the discharge of his office, is accommodated unto him. For a high priest
was appointed ἵνα προσφέρῃ δῶρά τε καὶ θυσίας ὑπὲρ ἁμαρτιῶν, verse 1;—
" that he might offer gifts and sacrifices for sins." So it is here

affirmed of our Saviour that he also "offered" to God; which is expressive of a sacerdotal act, as shall be declared. And this is further described,—1. By an *especial adjunct* of the sacrifice he offered, namely, "prayers and tears;" 2. By the *immediate object* of them, and his sacrifice which they accompanied, "Him that was able to save him from death;" 3. By *the effect and issue* of the whole, "He was heard in that which he feared."

Ver. 7.—Ὃς ἐν ταῖς ἡμέραις τῆς σαρκὸς αὐτοῦ δεήσεις τε καὶ ἱκετηρίας πρὸς τὸν δυνάμενον σώζειν αὐτὸν ἐκ θανάτου, μετὰ κραυγῆς ἰσχυρᾶς καὶ δακρύων προσενέγκας, καὶ εἰσακουσθεὶς ἀπὸ τῆς εὐλαβείας.

Ἐν ταῖς ἡμέραις τῆς σαρκὸς αὐτοῦ. Syr., "also when he was clothed with flesh." Arab., "in the days of his humanity." Μετὰ κραυγῆς ἰσχυρᾶς. Syr., "with a vehement outcry." Ἀπὸ τῆς εὐλαβείας. This is wholly omitted in the Syriac; only in the next verse mention of it is introduced, as דֶחְלְתָא, "fear," or "dread:" which is evidently transferred from this place, the interpreter, it seems, not understanding the meaning of it in its present construction.[1]

Ver. 7.—Who in the days of his flesh offered up prayers and supplications, with a strong cry [or *vehement outcry*] and tears, unto him that was able to save him from death, and was heard [or *delivered*] from [*his*] fear.

The person here spoken of is expressed by the relative ὅς, "who;" that is, ὁ Χριστός, mentioned verse 5, to whose priest- hood thenceforward testimony is given. "Who," that   Ὅς.
is Christ, not absolutely, but as a high priest.

The first thing mentioned of him is an intimation of the infirmity wherewith he was attended in the discharge of his office, by a de- scription of the time and season wherein he was exer-   Ἐν ταῖς ἡμί-
cised in it; it was ἐν ταῖς ἡμέραις τῆς σαρκὸς αὐτοῦ,—"in   ραις τῆς σαρκὸς
the days of his flesh." That these infirmities were in   αὐτοῦ.
themselves perfectly sinless, and absolutely necessary unto him in this office, was before declared. And we may here inquire,— 1. What is meant by the "flesh" of Christ? 2. What were "the days of his flesh?"

1. The "flesh" of Christ, or wherein he was, is in the Scripture taken two ways:—

(1.) Naturally, by a synecdoche, for his whole *human nature:*

---

[1] EXPOSITION.—Chrys., Phot., Theophyl., Vulg., Luther, Calov, Olshausen, Bleek, and some others, understand εὐλαβ. in the sense of "fear of God;"—Jesus was heard on account of his piety. The Peschito, Itala, Ambrose, Calvin, Beza, Grotius, Gerhard, Cappellus, Limborch, Carpzov, Bengel, Morus, Storr, Kuinoel, Paulus, De Wette, Tholuck, and a whole host of critics besides, render εὐλαβ. by *fear, anxiety;* which signification has been vindicated on philological grounds by Casaubon, Wetstein, and Krebs. Ebrard proceeds to argue, that though the prayer of Christ was to be saved from *death*, it was *not* unheard, inasmuch as he was divested of *the fear of death*. Others understand the fear to be simply that horror of soul under which he was "exceeding sorrowful."—ED.

John i. 14, "The Word was made flesh." 1 Tim. iii. 16, "God
was manifest in the flesh." Rom. ix. 5, "Of whom was Christ
according to the flesh." Heb. ii. 14, "He partook of flesh and
blood." 1 Pet. iii. 18; Rom. i. 3. See our exposition of chap. ii.
9–14. In this flesh, or in the flesh in this sense, as to the substance of it, Christ still continues. The body wherein he suffered
and rose from the dead was altered, upon his resurrection and ascension, as to its qualities, but not as to its substance; it consisted still of
"flesh and bones," Luke xxiv. 39. And the same spirit which, when
he died, he resigned into the hands of God, was returned unto him
again when he was "quickened by the Spirit," 1 Pet. iii. 18; when
God showed him again "the path of life," according to his promise,
Ps. xvi. 11. This flesh he carried entire with him into heaven,
where it still continueth, though inwardly and outwardly exalted
and glorified beyond our apprehension, Acts i. 11; and in this flesh
shall he come again unto judgment, chap. i. 11, iii. 21, xvii. 31; Rev.
i. 7: for the union of this flesh with the divine nature in the person
of the Son of God, is eternally indissoluble. And they overthrow
the foundation of faith, who fancy the Lord Christ to have any
other body in heaven than what he had on the earth; as they also
do who make him to have such flesh as they can eat every day. It
is not, therefore, the flesh of Christ in this sense, as absolutely considered, which is here intended; for the days of this flesh abide
always, they shall never expire to eternity.

(2.) "Flesh," as applied unto Christ, signifies the *frailties, weaknesses, and infirmities of our nature;* or our nature as it is weak
and infirm during this mortal life. So is the word often used: Ps.
lxxviii. 39, "He remembereth בְּי־בָשָׂר הֵמָּה,"—"that they are but
flesh;" that is, poor, weak, mortal, frail creatures. Ps. lxv. 2, "Unto
thee shall all flesh come;" poor, helpless, creatures standing in need
of aid and assistance. So "flesh and blood" is taken for that principle of corruption, which must be done away before we enter into
heaven, 1 Cor. xv. 50. And this is that which is meant by the
flesh of Christ in this place,—human nature not yet glorified, with
all its infirmities, wherein he was exposed unto hunger, thirst,
weariness, labour, sorrow, grief, fear, pain, wounding, death itself.
Hereby doth the apostle express what he had before laid down in
the person of the high priest according to the law,—he was "compassed with infirmity."

2. What were "the days of his flesh" intended? It is evident that in general his whole course and walk in this world may
be comprised herein. From his cradle to the grave he bare all the
infirmities of our nature, with all the dolorous and grievous effects
of them. Hence all his days he was אִישׁ מַכְאֹבוֹת וִידוּעַ חֹלִי, Isa. liii. 3;
—"a man of sorrows," filled with them, never free from them; and

familiarly "acquainted with grief," as a companion that never departed from him. But yet respect is not had here unto this whole space of time, only the subject-matter treated of is limited unto that season; it fell out neither before nor after, but in and during the days of his flesh. But the season peculiarly intended is the close of those days, in his last suffering, when all his sorrows, trials, and temptations came unto a head. The sole design of the expression is to show that when he offered up his sacrifice he was encompassed with infirmities; which hath an especial influence into our faith and consolation.

Secondly, An account is given of what he did in those days of his flesh, as a high priest, being called of God unto that office. And this in general was his acting as a priest, wherein many things are to be considered:—

1. The *act* of his oblation, in that word προσενέγκας. Προσφέρω is "accedo," "appropinquo," or "accedere facio," when applied unto things in common use, or unto persons in Προσενέγκας. the common occasions of life. So doth קָרַב signify in the Hebrew. But when it doth so, the LXX. constantly render it by ἐγγίζω and προσεγγίζω; that is, "to draw near." But when it is applied to things sacred, they render it by προσφέρω; that is, "offero," or "to offer." And although this word is sometimes used in the New Testament in the common sense before mentioned, yet it alone, and no other, is made use of to express an access with gifts and sacrifices, or offerings, to the altar. See Matt. ii. 11, v. 23, 24, viii. 4; Mark i. 44; Luke v. 14. כִּי־יַקְרִיב קָרְבָּן, Lev. i. 2;—that is, προσφέρῃ δῶρον, "offer a gift;" that is, at the altar. And in this epistle it constantly expresseth a sacerdotal act, chap. v. 1, 3, viii. 3, 4, ix. 7, 9, 14, 25, 28, x. 1, 2, 8, 11, 12, xi. 4, 17. And προσφορά is a "sacred oblation," or a "sacrifice," chap. x. 5, 8, 10, 14, 18. Nor is the word otherwise used in this epistle. And the end why we observe it, is to manifest that it is a priestly, sacerdotal offering that is here intended. He offered as a priest.

2. The *matter of his offering* is expressed by δεήσεις καὶ ἱκετηρίας, "prayers and supplications." Both these words have the same general signification. And they also agree in Δεήσεις καὶ ἱκετηρίας. this, that they respect an especial kind of prayer, which is for the averting or turning away of impendent evils, or such as are deserved and justly feared. For whereas all sorts of prayers may be referred unto two heads,—(1.) Such as are petitory, for the impetration of that which is good; (2.) Such as are deprecatory, for the keeping off or turning away that which is evil; the latter sort only are here intended. Δεήσεις are everywhere "preces deprecatoriæ;" and we render it "supplications," 1 Tim. ii. 1. And "supplicationes" are the same with "supplicia," which signifies both "punish-

ments," and "prayers" for the averting of them; as in the Hebrew, חַטָּאת is both "sin" and a "sacrifice" for the expiation of it.

Ἱκετηρία is nowhere used in the Scripture but in this place only. In other authors it originally signifies "a bough, or olive-branch, wrapped about with wool or bays," or something of the like nature; which they carried in their hands, and lifted up, who were supplicants unto others for the obtaining of peace from them, or to avert their displeasure. Hence is the phrase of "velamenta pretendere," to hold forth such covered branches. So Liv. de Bell. Punic. lib. xxiv. cap. xxx.: "Ramos oleæ ac velamenta alia supplicum porrigentes, orare, ut reciperent sese;"—"Holding forth olive branches, and other covered tokens used by supplicants, they prayed that they might be received into grace and favour." And Virgil, of his Æneas, to Evander, Æn. lib. viii. 127:—

> "Optime Grajugenûm, cui me fortuna precari,
> Et vittâ comptos voluit pretendere ramos."

And Herodian calls them ἱκετηρίας θαλλούς,—"branches of supplication." Hence the word came to denote a supplicatory prayer; the same with ἱκέτευμα. And it is in this sense usually joined with δεήσεις, as here by our apostle. So Isoc. de Pace, cap. xlvi.: Πολλὰς ἱκετηρίας καὶ δεήσεις ποιούμενοι,—"Using many deprecatory entreaties and supplications." So constantly the heathen called those prayers which they made solemnly to their gods, for the averting of impendent evils, "supplicia," and "supplicationes." Liv. lib. x. cap. xxiii.: "Eo anno prodigia multa fuerunt: quorum averruncandorum causâ supplicationes in biduum senatus decrevit;" that is, "Iræ deûm averruncandæ," as he speaks lib. viii. cap. vi.—to turn away the wrath of their gods. And such a kind of prayer is that whose form is given in Cato de re Rustic. cap. xiv.: "Mars pater, te precor, quæsoque, ut calamitates intemperiasque prohibessis, defendas, averrunces." Hesychius explains ἱκετηρία by παράκλησις, a word of a much larger signification; but ἱκετώσυνα, a word of the same original and force, by καθαρτήρια, λυτήρια,—"expiations and purgations," from guilt deserving punishment. Ἱκετηρία, Gloss. Vet., "Oratio, precatio supplicum;"—"the prayer of suppliants." The word being used only in this place in the Scripture, it was not unnecessary to inquire after the signification of it in other authors. It is a humble supplication for peace, or deprecation of evil, with the turning away of anger. And this sense singularly suits the scope of the place; for respect is had in it to the sufferings of Christ, and the fear which befell him in the apprehension of them as they were penal, as we shall see afterwards.

But it must also be here further observed, that however this word might be used to express the naked supplication of some men in distress unto others, yet whenever it is used in heathen authors, with respect unto their gods, it is always accompanied with expiatory sacrifices, or was the peculiar name of those prayers and supplications which they made with those sacrifices. And I have showed before that the solemn expiatory sacrifice of the high priest among the Jews was accompanied with deprecatory supplications; a form whereof, according to the apprehensions of their masters, I gave out of the Mishna. And so he was appointed, in the great sacrifice of expiation, to confess over the head of the scape-goat " all the iniquities of the children of Israel, and all their transgressions in all their sins," Lev. xvi. 21; which he did not without prayers for the expiation of them, and deliverance from the curse of the law due to them. And they are not the mere supplications of our blessed Saviour that are here intended, but as they accompanied and were a necessary adjunct of the offering up of himself, his soul and body, a real propitiatory sacrifice to God. And therefore, wherever our apostle elsewhere speaks of the "offering" of Christ, he calls it the "offering of himself," or of his "body," Eph. v. 2, Heb. ix. 14, 25, 28, x. 10. Here, therefore, he expresseth the whole sacrifice of Christ by the "prayers and supplications" wherewith it was accompanied; and therefore makes use of that word which peculiarly denotes such supplications. And he describes the sacrifice or offering of Christ by this adjunct for the reasons ensuing:—

1. To evince what he before declared, that in the days of his flesh, when he offered up himself unto God, he was encompassed with the weakness of our nature, which made prayers and supplications needful for him, as at all seasons, so especially in straits and distresses, when he cried from " the lion's mouth," and " the horns of the unicorns," Ps. xxii. 21. He was in earnest, and pressed to the utmost in the work that was before him. And this expression is used,—

2. That we might seriously consider how *great* a work it was to expiate sin. As it was not to be done without suffering, so a mere and bare suffering would not effect it. Not only death, and that a bloody death, was required thereunto, but such as was to be accompanied with "prayers and supplications," that it might be effectual unto the end designed, and that he who suffered it might not be overborne in his undertaking. The " redemption of souls was precious," and must have ceased for ever, had not every thing been set on work which is acceptable and prevalent with God. And,—

3. To show that the Lord Christ had now made this business his own. He had taken the whole work and the whole *debt of sin* upon himself. He was now, therefore, to manage it, as if he alone were the person concerned. And this rendered his prayers and supplications necessary in and unto his sacrifice. And,—

4. That we might be instructed how to make use of and plead his sacrifice in our stead. If it was not, if it could not be, offered by

him but with prayers and supplications, and those for the averting of divine wrath, and making peace with God, we may not think to be interested therein whilst under the power of lazy and slothful unbelief. Let him that would go to Christ, consider well how Christ went to God for him; which is yet further declared,—

Thirdly, In the *manner* of his offering these prayers and supplications unto God, whereby he offered up himself also unto him. He did it μετὰ κραυγῆς ἰσχυρᾶς καὶ δακρύων, "with strong crying" (or "a strong cry") "and tears." Chrysostom on the place observes, that the story makes no mention of these things. And, indeed, of his tears in particular it doth not; which from this place alone we know to have accompanied his sacerdotal prayers. But his "strong crying" is expressly related. To acquaint ourselves fully with what is intended herein, we may consider,—1. How it was expressed in prophecy; 2. How it is related in the story; 3. How reported here by our apostle:—

1. In prophecy the supplications here intended are called his "roaring:" Ps. xxii. 1–3, "My God, my God, why hast thou forsaken me? why art thou so far from helping me, and from דִּבְרֵי שַׁאֲגָתִי," "the words of my roaring?" "Rugitus," the proper cry of a lion, is κραυγὴ ἰσχυρά, "clamor validus," "a strong and vehement outcry." And it is used to express such a vehemency in supplications as cannot be compressed or confined, but will ordinarily break out into a loud expression of itself; at least such an intension of mind and affection as cannot be outwardly expressed without fervent outcries. Ps. xxxii. 3, "When I kept silence,"—that is, whilst he was under his perplexities from the guilt of sin, before he came off to a full and clear acknowledgment of it, as verse 5,—"my bones waxed old through my roaring all the day long." The vehemency of his complainings consumed his natural strength. So Job iii. 24, "My sighing cometh before I eat, וַיִּתְּכוּ כַמַּיִם שַׁאֲגֹתָי,"—"and my roarings are poured out like waters," namely, that break out of any place with great noise and abundance. So is a sense of extreme pressures and distresses signified: "I have roared by reason of the disquietness of my heart," Ps. xxxviii. 8. This is κραυγὴ ἰσχυρά, "a strong cry." And if we well consider his prayer, as recorded Ps. xxii., especially from verse 9 to verse 21, we shall find that every word almost, and sentence, hath in it the spirit of roaring and a strong cry, however it were uttered. For it is not merely the outward noise, but the inward earnest intension and engagement of heart and soul, with the greatness and depth of the occasion of them, that is principally intended.

2. We may consider the same matter as related in story by the evangelists. The prayers intended are those which he offered to God during his passion, both in the garden and on the cross. The

first are declared Luke xxii. 44, "And being in an agony, he prayed more earnestly, and his sweat was as drops of blood falling on the earth." The inward frame is here declared, which our apostle shadows out by the external expressions and signs of it, in "strong cries and tears." 'Εν ἀγωνίᾳ γενόμενος,—"constitutus in agonia." He was in, under the power of, wholly pressed by "an agony;" that is, a strong and vehement conflict of mind, in and about things dreadful and terrible. 'Αγωνία is φόβος διαπτώσεως, saith Nemes. de Natur. Hom.;—"a dread of utter ruin." "Timor extrinsecus advenientis mali," Aquin.;—"a dread of evil to come upon us from without." It signifies, "ita vehementi discriminis objecti metu angi ut quodammodo exanimis et attonitus sis," saith Maldonat. on Matt. xxvi. 37. He prayed ἐκτενέστερον, "with more vehement intension of mind, spirit, and body." For the word denotes not a degree of the acting of grace in Christ, as some have imagined, but the highest degree of earnestness in the actings of his mind, soul, and body;—another token of that wonderful conflict wherein he was engaged, which no heart can conceive nor tongue express. This produced that preternatural sweat wherein θρόμβοι αἵματος, "thick drops of blood" ran from him to the ground. Concerning this he says, כַּמַּיִם נִשְׁפַּכְתִּי, Ps. xxii. 15,—"I am poured out like water;" that is, 'my blood is so, by an emanation from all parts of my body, descending to the ground.' And they consult not the honour of Jesus Christ, but the maintenance of their own false suppositions, who assign any ordinary cause of this agony, with these consequents of it, or such as other men may have experience of. And this way go many of the expositors of the Roman church. So à Lapid. in loc.: "Nota secundo hunc Christi angorem lacrymas et sudorem sanguineum, testem infirmitatis a Christo assumptæ, provenisse ex vivaci imaginatione, flagellationis, coronationis, mortis dolorumque omnium quos mox subiturus erat; inde enim naturaliter manabat eorundem horror et angor." He would place the whole cause of this agony in those previous fancies, imaginations, or apprehensions, which he had of those corporeal sufferings which were to come upon him. Where, then, is the glory of his spiritual strength and fortitude? where the beauty of the example which herein he set before us? His outward sufferings were indeed grievous; but yet, considered merely as such, they were, as to mere sense of pain, beneath what sundry of his martyrs have been called to undergo for his name's sake. And yet we know that many, yea, through the power of his grace in them, the most of them who have so suffered for him in all ages, have cheerfully, joyfully, and without the least consternation of spirit, undergone the exquisite tortures whereby they have given up themselves unto death for him. And shall we imagine that the Son of God, who had advantages for his supportment and consolation in-

finitely above what they had any interest in, should be given up to
this dreadful, trembling conflict, wherein his whole nature was almost
dissolved, out of a mere apprehension of those corporeal sufferings
which were coming on him? Was it the forethought of them only,
and that as such, which dispelled the present sense of divine love and
satisfaction from the indissoluble union of his person, that they should
not influence his mind with refreshments and consolation? God forbid we should have such mean thoughts of what he was, of what he
did, of what he suffered. There were other causes of these things,
as we shall see immediately.

Again; on the cross itself it is said, Ἀνεβόησε φωνῇ μεγάλῃ, Matt.
xxvii. 46; that is plainly, "He prayed μετὰ κραυγῆς ἰσχυρᾶς,"—"He
cried with a great outcry," or "loud voice," with a "strong cry." This
was the manner of the sacerdotal prayers of Christ which concerned
his oblation, or the offering himself as a sacrifice, as is reported in
the evangelist. The other part of his sacerdotal prayer, which expressed his intercession on a supposition of his oblation, he performed
and offered with all calmness, quietness, and sedateness of mind,
with all assurance and joyful glory, as if he were actually already in
heaven; as we may see, John xvii. But it was otherwise with him
when he was to offer himself a sin-offering in our stead. If, therefore, we do compare the 22d psalm, as applied and explained by the
evangelists and our apostle, with the 17th of John, we shall find a
double mediatory or sacerdotal prayer of our Saviour in behalf of
the whole church. The first was that which accompanied his oblation, or the offering of himself an expiatory sacrifice for sin. And
this having respect unto the justice of God, the curse of the law, and
the punishment due to sin, was made in an agony, distress, and conflict, with wrestlings, expressed by cries, tears, and most vehement
intensions of soul. The other,—which though in order of time antecedent, yet in order of nature was built on the former, and a supposition of the work perfected therein, as is evident, John xvii. 11,
—represents his intercession in heaven. The first was μετὰ κραυγῆς
ἰσχυρᾶς καὶ δακρύων, the other μετὰ πεποιθήσεως καὶ πληροφορίας.

3. These are the things which are thus expressed by our apostle,
"He offered up prayers and supplications, with strong cries and tears."
Such was the frame of his soul, such was his prayer and deportment
in his sacrifice of himself. His tears, indeed, are not expressly mentioned in the story, but weeping was one of those infirmities of our
nature which he was subject unto: John xi. 35, "Jesus wept." He
expressed his sorrow thereby. And being now in the greatest distress, conflict, and sorrow, which reached unto the soul, until that was
"sorrowful unto death," as we may well judge that in his dealing with
God he poured out tears with his prayers, so it is here directly mentioned. So did he here "offer up himself through the eternal Spirit."

Fourthly, The *object* of this offering of Christ, he to whom he offered up prayers and supplications, is expressed and described. And this was ὁ δυνάμενος σώζειν αὐτὸν ἐκ θανάτου,—"he that was able to save him from death," that had power so to do. It is God who is intended, whom the apostle Πρὸς δυνάμενον σώζειν αὐτὸν ἐκ θανάτου. describes by this periphrasis, for the reasons that shall be mentioned. He calls him neither God, nor the Father of Christ, although the Lord Jesus, in the prayers intended, calls upon him by both these names. So in the garden he calls him Father: "O my Father, if it be possible, let this cup pass from me," Matt. xxvi. 39. And on the cross he called him God: "My God, my God, why hast thou forsaken me," Matt. xxvii. 46; and "Father" again, in the resignation of his life and soul into his hands, Luke xxiii. 46. But in the reporting of these things our apostle waiveth these expressions, and only describeth God as "Him who was able to save him from death." Now this he doth to manifest the consideration that the Lord Christ at that time had of God, of death, and of the causes, consequents, and effects of it. For his design is, to declare what was the reason of the frame of the soul of Christ in his suffering and offering before described, and what were the causes thereof.

In general, God is proposed as the object of the actings of Christ's soul in this offering of himself, as he who had all power in his hand to order all his present concernments: "To him who was able." Ability or power is either natural or moral. Natural power is strength and active efficiency; in God omnipotency. Moral power is right and authority; in God absolute sovereignty. And the Lord Christ had respect unto the ability or power of God in both these senses: in the first, as that which he relied upon for deliverance; in the latter, as that which he submitted himself unto. The former was the object of his faith, namely, that God, by the greatness of his power, could support and deliver him in and under his trial. The latter was the object of his fear, as to the dreadful work which he had undertaken. Now, because our apostle is upon the description of that frame of heart, and those actings of soul, wherewith our high priest offered himself for us unto God, which was with "prayers and supplications," accompanied with "strong cries and tears," I shall consider from these words three things, considering the power or ability of God principally in the latter way:—1. What were the general causes of the state and condition wherein the Lord Christ is here described by our apostle, and of the actings ascribed unto him therein. 2. What were the immediate effects of the sufferings of the Lord Christ in and upon his own soul. 3. What limitations are to be assigned unto them. From all which it will appear why and wherefore he offered up his prayers and supplications unto him who was able to save him from death; wherein a fear of it is included, on the account of the righteous authority of God, as well as a faith of deliverance from it, on the account of his omnipotent power.

1. The general causes of his state and condition, with his actings therein, were included in that consideration and prospect which he then had of God, death, and himself, or the effects of death upon him.

(1.) He considered God at that instant as the supreme rector and judge of all, the author of the law and the avenger of it, who had power of life and death, as the one was to be destroyed and the other inflicted, according to the curse and sentence of the law. Under this notion he now considered God, and that as actually putting the law in execution, having power and authority to give up unto the sting of it, or to save from it. God represented himself unto him first as armed and attended with infinite holiness, righteousness, and severity,—as one that would not pass by sin nor acquit the guilty; and then as accompanied with supreme or sovereign authority over him, the law, life, and death. And it is of great importance under what notion we consider God when we make our approaches unto him. The whole frame of our souls, as to fear or confidence, will be regulated thereby.

(2.) He considered death not naturally, as a separation of soul and body; nor yet merely as a painful separation of them, such as was that death which in particular he was to undergo; but he looked on it as the curse of the law due to sin, inflicted by God as a just and righteous judge. Hence, in and under it, he himself is said to be "made a curse," Gal. iii. 13. This curse was now coming on him, as the sponsor or surety of the new covenant. For although he considered himself, and the effects of things upon himself, yet he offered up these prayers as our sponsor, that the work of mediation which he had undertaken might have a good and blessed issue.

From hence may we take a view of that frame of soul which our Lord Jesus Christ was in when he offered up prayers and supplications, with strong cries and tears, considering God as him who had authority over the law, and the sentence of it that was to be inflicted on him. Some have thought, that upon the confidence of the indissolubleness of his person, and the actual assurance which they suppose he had always of the love of God, his sufferings could have no effect of fear, sorrow, trouble, or perplexity on his soul, but only what respected the natural enduring of pain and shame, which he was exposed unto. But the Scripture gives us another account of these things. It informs us, that "he began to be afraid, and sore amazed;" that "his soul was heavy, and sorrowful unto death;" that he was "in an agony," and afterwards cried out, "My God, my God, why hast thou forsaken me?" under a sense of divine dereliction.

There was, indeed, a mighty acting of love in God toward us, in the giving of his Son to death for us, as to his gracious ends and purposes thereby to be accomplished; and his so doing is constantly in the Scripture reckoned on the score of love. And there was always in him a great love to the person of his Son, and an ineffable complacency in the obedience of Christ, especially that which he exercised in his suffering; but yet the curse and punishment which he underwent was an effect of vindictive justice, and as such did he look upon it and conflict with it. I shall not enter into the debates of those expressions which have been controverted about the sufferings of Christ, as whether he underwent the death of the soul, the second death, the pains of hell. For it would cause a prolix digression to show distinctly what is essential unto these things, or purely penal in them, which alone he was subject unto; and what necessarily follows a state and condition of personal sin and guilt in them who undergo them, which he was absolutely free from. But this alone I shall say, which I have proved elsewhere, whatever was due to us from the justice of God and sentence of the law, that he underwent and suffered. This, then, was the cause in general of the state and condition of Christ here described, and of his actings therein, here expressed.

2. In the second place, the effects of his sufferings in himself, or his sufferings themselves, on this account, may be reduced in general unto these two heads:—

(1.) His dereliction. He was under a suspension of the comforting influences of his relation unto God. His relation unto God, as his God and Father, was the fountain of all his comforts and joys. The sense hereof was now suspended. Hence was that part of his cry, "My God, my God, why hast thou forsaken me?" The supporting influences of this relation were continued, but the comforting influences of it were suspended. See Ps. xxii. 1–3, etc. And from hence he was filled with heaviness and sorrow. This the evangelists fully express. He says of himself, that "his soul was exceeding sorrowful, even unto death," Matt. xxvi. 38; which expressions are emphatical, and declare a sorrow that is absolutely inexpressible. And this sorrow was the effect of his penal desertion; for sorrow is that which was the life of the curse of the law. So when God declared the nature of that curse unto Adam and Eve, he tells them that he will give them "sorrow," and "multiply their sorrow," Gen. iii. 16, 17. With this sorrow was Christ now filled, which put him on those strong cries and tears for relief. And this dereliction was possible, and proceeded from hence, in that all communications from the divine nature unto the human, beyond subsistence, were voluntary.

(2.) He had an intimate sense of the wrath and displeasure of

God against the sin that was then imputed unto him. All our sins were then caused, by an act of divine and supreme authority, "to meet on him," or "the LORD laid on him the iniquity of us all," Isa. liii. 6. Even all our guilt was imputed unto him, or none of the punishment due unto our sins could have been justly inflicted on him. In this state of things, in that great hour, and wonderful transaction of divine wisdom, grace, and righteousness, whereon the glory of God, the recovery of fallen man, with the utter condemnation of Satan, depended, God was pleased for a while, as it were, to hold the scales of justice in æquilibrio, that the turning of them might be more conspicuous, eminent, and glorious. In the one scale, as it were, there was the weight of the first sin and apostasy from God, with all the consequents of it, covered with the sentence and curse of the law, with the exigence of vindictive justice,—a weight that all the angels of heaven could not stand under one moment. In the other were the obedience, holiness, righteousness, and penal sufferings, of the Son of God,—all having weight and worth given unto them by the dignity and worth of his divine person. Infinite justice kept these things for a season, as it were, at a poise, until the Son of God, by his prayers, tears, and supplications, prevailed unto a glorious success, in the delivery of himself and us.

3. Wherefore, as to the limitation of the effects of Christ's sufferings in and upon himself, we may conclude, in general,—(1.) That they were such only as are consistent with absolute purity, holiness, and freedom from the least appearance of sin; (2.) Not such as did in the least impeach the glorious union of his natures in the same person; (3.) Nor such as took off from the dignity of his obedience and merit of his suffering, but were all necessary thereunto: but then, (4.) As he underwent whatever is or can be grievous, dolorous, afflictive, and penal, in the wrath of God, and sentence of the law executed; so these things really wrought in him sorrow, amazement, anguish, fear, dread, with the like penal effects of the pains of hell; from whence it was that he "offered up prayers and supplications, with strong cries and tears, unto him that was able to save him from death,"—the event whereof is described in the last clause of the verse.

Καὶ εἰσακουσθεὶς ἀπὸ τῆς εὐλαβείας, "and was heard in that which he feared." To be *heard* in Scripture signifies two things: —1. To be accepted in our request, though the thing requested be not granted unto us. "God will hear me," is as much as, 'God will accept of me, is pleased with my supplication,' Ps. lv. 17, xxii. 21. 2. To be answered in our request. To be heard, is to be delivered. So is this expressed, Ps. xxii. 24. In the first way there is no doubt but that the Father always heard the Son, John xi. 42,—always in all things accepted him, and was well pleased in him; but our inquiry is here, how far the Lord Christ was heard in the latter way, so heard as to be delivered from what he prayed against. Concerning this observe, that the prayers of Christ in this matter were of two sorts:—

1. Hypothetical or conditional; such was that prayer for the passing of the cup from him, Luke xxii. 42, "Father, if thou wilt, remove this cup from me." And this prayer was nothing but what was absolutely necessary unto the verity of human nature in that state and condition. Christ could not have been a man and not have had an extreme aversation to the things that were coming upon him. Nor had it been otherwise with him, could he properly have been said to suffer; for nothing is suffering, nor can be penal unto us, but what is grievous unto our nature, and what it is abhorrent of. This acting of the inclination of nature, both in his mind, will, and affections, which in him were purely holy, our Saviour expresseth in that conditional prayer. And in this prayer he was thus answered,—his mind was fortified against the dread and terror of nature, so as to come unto a perfect composure in the will of God: "Nevertheless, not my will, but thine, be done." He was heard herein so far as he desired to be heard; for although he could not but desire deliverance from the whole, as he was a man, yet he desired it not absolutely, as he was wholly subjected to the will of God.

2. Absolute. The chief and principal supplications which he offered up to him who was able to save him from death were absolute; and in them he was absolutely heard and delivered. For upon the presentation of death unto him, as attended with the wrath and curse of God, he had deep and dreadful apprehensions of it; and how unable the human nature was to undergo it, and prevail against it, if not mightily supported and carried through by the power of God. In this condition it was part of his obedience, it was his duty, to pray that he might be delivered from the absolute prevalency of it, that he might not be cast in his trial, that he might not be confounded nor condemned. This he hoped, trusted, and believed; and therefore prayed absolutely for it, Isa. l. 7, 8. And herein he was heard absolutely; for so it is said, "He was heard ἀπὸ τῆς εὐλαβείας."

The word here used is in a singular construction of speech, and is itself of various significations. Sometimes it is used for a *religious reverence*, but such as hath fear joined with it; that is, the fear of evil. Frequently it signifies *fear* itself, but such a fear as is accompanied with a reverential care and holy circumspection. The word itself is but once more used in the New Testament, and that by our apostle, Heb. xii. 28, where we well render it " godly fear." Εὐλαβής, the adjective, is used

'Aπὸ τῆς εὐλαβείας.

three times, Luke ii. 25, Acts ii. 5, viii. 2; everywhere denoting a religious fear. Heb. xi. 7, we render the verb, εὐλαβηθείς, by "moved with fear;" that is, a reverence of God mixed with a dreadful apprehension of an approaching judgment. And the use of the preposition ἀπό added to εἰσακουσθείς is also singular,—"auditus ex metu," "heard from his fear." Therefore is this passage variously interpreted by all sorts of expositors. Some read it, " He was heard because of his reverence." And in the exposition hereof they are again divided. Some take "reverence" actively, for the reverence he had of God; that is, his reverential obedience: " He was heard because of his reverence," or reverential obedience unto God. Some would have the reverence intended to relate to God, the reverential respect that God had unto him; God heard him, from that holy respect and regard which he had of him. But these things are fond, and suit not the design of the place; neither the coherence of the words, nor their construction, nor their signification, nor the scope of the apostle, will bear this sense. Others render it, " pro metu;" " from fear," or "out of fear." And this also is two ways interpreted:—1. Because "heard from fear" is somewhat a harsh expression, they explain " auditus " by "liberatus,"—"delivered from fear;" and this is not improper. So Grotius: "Cum mortem vehementer perhorresceret,......in hoc exauditus fuit ut ab isto metu liberaretur." In this sense fear internal and subjective is intended. God relieved him against his fear, removing it and taking it away, by strengthening and comforting of him. Others by "fear" intend the thing feared; which sense our translators follow, and are therefore plentifully reviled and railed at by the Rhemists: " He was heard;" that is, delivered from the things which he feared as coming upon him. And for the vindication of this sense and exposition, there is so much already offered by many learned expositors as that I see not what can be added thereunto, and I shall not unnecessarily enlarge myself. And the opposition that is made hereunto is managed rather with clamours and outcries, than Scripture reasons or testimonies. Suppose the object of the fear of Christ here to have been what he was delivered from, and then it must be his fainting, sinking, and perishing under the wrath of God, in the work he had undertaken; yet,—1. The same thing is expressed elsewhere unto a higher degree and more emphatically; as where in this state he is said λυπεῖσθαι καὶ ἀδημονεῖν, and ἐκθαμβεῖσθαι, Matt. xxvi. 37, Mark xiv. 33,—to be " sorrowful," " perplexed," and " amazed." 2. All this argues no more but that the Lord Christ underwent an exercise in the opposition that was made unto his faith, and the mighty conflict he had with that opposition. That his faith and trust in God were either overthrown or weakened by them, they prove not, nor do any plead them unto that purpose. And to deny that the soul of Christ was engaged in an ineffable conflict with the wrath of God in the curse of the law,—that his faith and trust in God were pressed and tried to the utmost by the opposition made unto them, by fear, dread, and a terrible apprehension of divine displeasure due to our sins,—is to renounce the benefit of his passion and turn the whole of it into a show, fit to be represented by pictures and images, or acted over in ludicrous scenes, as it is by the Papists.

It remains that we consider the observations which these words afford us for our instruction, wherein also their sense and importance will be further explained. And the first thing that offers itself unto us is, that,—

Obs. I. The Lord Jesus Christ himself had a time of infirmity in this world.

A season he had wherein he was beset and "compassed with infirmities." So it was with him "in the days of his flesh." It is true, his infirmities were all *sinless*, but all troublesome and *grievous*. By them was he exposed unto all sorts of temptations and sufferings; which are the two springs of all that is evil and dolorous unto our nature. And thus it was with him, not for a few days, or a short season only, but during his whole course in this world. This the story of the gospel gives us an account of, and the instance of his "offering up prayers with strong cries and tears," puts out of all question. These things were real, and not acted to make an appearance or representation of them. And hereof himself expresseth his sense: Ps. xxii. 6, 7, "I am a worm, and no man; a reproach of men, and despised of the people. All that see me, laugh me to scorn." So verses 14, 15. How can the infirmities of our nature, and a sense of them, be more emphatically expressed? So Ps. lxix. 20, "Reproach hath broken my heart; and I am full of heaviness: and I looked for some to take pity, but there was none; and for comforters, but I found none." And Ps. xl. 12, "Innumerable evils have compassed me about." He had not only our infirmities, but he felt them, and was deeply sensible both of them and of the evils and troubles which through them he was exposed unto. Hence is that description of him, Isa. liii. 3.

Two things are herein by us duly to be considered:—First, That it was out of infinite condescension and love unto our souls that the Lord Christ took on himself this condition, Phil. ii. 6–8. This state was neither natural nor necessary unto him upon his own account. In himself he was "in the form of God, and thought it not robbery to be equal with God;" but this mind was in him, that for our sakes he would take on himself all these infirmities of our nature, and through them expose himself unto evils innumerable. It was voluntary love, and not defect or necessity of nature, which brought him into this condition. Secondly, As he had other ends herein,—

for these things were indispensably required unto the discharge of his sacerdotal office,—so he designed to set us an example, that we should not faint under our infirmities and sufferings on their account, Heb. xii. 2, 3, 1 Pet. iv. 1. And God knows such an example we stood in need of, both as a pattern to conform ourselves unto under our infirmities, and to encourage us in the expectation of a good issue unto our present deplorable condition.

Let us not, then, think strange, if we have our season of weakness and infirmity in this world, whereby we are exposed unto temptation and suffering. Apt we are, indeed, to complain hereof; the whole nation of professors is full of complaints; one is in want, straits, and poverty; another in pain, under sickness, and variety of troubles; some are in distress *for* their relations, some *from* and by them; some are persecuted, some are tempted, some pressed with private, some with public concerns; some are sick, and some are weak, and some are "fallen asleep." And these things are apt to make us faint, to despond, and be weary. I know not how others bear up their hearts and spirits. For my part, I have much ado to keep from continual longing after the embraces of the dust and shades of the grave, as a curtain drawn over the rest in another world. In the meantime, every momentary gourd that interposeth between the vehemency of wind and sun, or our frail, fainting natures and spirits, is too much valued by us.

But what would we have? Do we consider who, and what, and where we are, when we think strange of these things? These are the days of our flesh, wherein these things are due to us, and unavoidable. "Man is born unto trouble, as the sparks fly upward," Job v. 7,—necessarily and abundantly. All complaints, and all contrivances whereby we endeavour to extricate ourselves from those innumerable evils which attend our weak, frail, infirm condition, will be altogether vain. And if any, through the flatteries of youth, and health, and strength, and wealth, with other satisfactions of their affections, are not sensible of these things, they are but in a pleasant dream, which will quickly pass away.

Our only relief in this condition is a due regard unto our great example, and what he did, how he behaved himself in the days of his flesh, when he had more difficulties and miseries to conflict with than we all. And in him we may do well to consider three things:—.

1. His *patience*, unconquerable and unmovable in all things that befell him in the days of his flesh. "He did not cry, nor lift up, nor cause his voice to be heard in the street," Isa. xlii. 2. Whatever befell him, he bore it quietly and patiently. Being buffeted, he threatened not; being reviled, he reviled not again. "As a sheep before her shearers is dumb, so he opened not his mouth." 2. His

trust in God. By this testimony, that it is said of him, " I will put my trust in God," doth our apostle prove that he had the same nature with us, subject to the same weakness and infirmities, Heb. ii. 13. And this we are taught thereby, that there is no management of our human nature, as now beset with infirmities, but by a constant trust in God. The whole life of Christ therein was a life of submission, trust, and dependence on God; so that when he came to his last suffering, his enemies fixed on that to reproach him withal, as knowing how constant he was in the profession thereof, Ps. xxii. 8, Matt. xxvii. 43. 3. His *earnest, fervent prayers and supplications,* which are here expressed by our apostle, and accommodated unto the days of his flesh. Other instances of his holy, gracious deportment of himself, in that condition wherein he set us an example, might be insisted on, but these may give us an entrance into the whole of our duty. Patience, faith, and prayer, will carry us comfortably and safely through the whole course of our frail and infirm lives in this world.

Obs. II. A life of glory may ensue after a life of infirmity.

" If," saith our apostle, "in this life only we have hope, we are of all men most miserable." For besides that we are obnoxious to the same common infirmities within and calamities without with all other men, there is, and ever will be, a peculiar sort of distress that they are exposed unto who " will live godly in Christ Jesus." But there is nothing can befall us but what may issue in eternal glory. We see that it hath done so with Jesus Christ. His season of infirmity is issued in eternal glory; and nothing but unbelief and sin can hinder ours from doing so also.

Obs. III. The Lord Christ is no more now in a state of weakness and temptation; the days of his flesh are past and gone.

As such the apostle here makes mention of them, and the Scripture signally in sundry places takes notice of it. This account he gives of himself, Rev. i. 18, " I am he that liveth, and was dead; and, behold, I am alive for evermore." The state of infirmity and weakness, wherein he was obnoxious unto death, is now past; he now lives for evermore. " Henceforth he dieth no more, death hath no more power over him;" nor any thing else that can reach the least trouble unto him. With his death ended the days of his flesh. His revival, or return unto life, was into absolute, eternal, unchangeable glory. And this advancement is expressed by his " sitting at the right hand of the Majesty on high;" which we have before declared. He is therefore now no more, on any account, obnoxious, —1. Unto the *law,* the sentence, or curse of it. As he was " made of a woman," he was " made under the law;" and so he continued all the days of his flesh. Therein did he fulfil all the righteousness it required, and answered the whole penalty for sin that it exacted.

But with the days of his flesh ended the right of the law towards him, either as to require obedience of him or exact suffering from him: hence, a little before his expiration on the cross, he said concerning it, " It is finished." And hereon doth our freedom from the curse of the law depend. The law can claim no more dominion over a believer than it can over Christ himself. He lives now out of the reach of all the power of the law, to plead his own obedience unto it, satisfaction of it, and triumph over it, in the behalf of them that believe on him. Nor, 2. Unto *temptations.* These were his constant attendants and companions during the days of his flesh. What they were, and of what sorts, we have in part before discoursed. He is now freed from them and above them; yet not so but that they have left a compassionate sense upon his holy soul of the straits and distresses which his disciples and servants are daily brought into by them,—which is the spring and foundation of the relief he communicates unto them. Nor, 3. Unto *troubles,* persecutions, or sufferings of any kind. He is not so in his own person. He is far above, out of the reach of all his enemies;—above them in power, in glory, in authority and rule. There is none of them but he can crush at his pleasure, and " dash them in pieces like a potter's vessel." He is, indeed, still hated as much as ever, maligned as much as in the days of his flesh, and exposed unto the utmost power of hell and the world in all his concerns on the earth. But he laughs all his enemies to scorn, he hath them in derision; and, in the midst of their wise counsels and mighty designs, disposes of them and all their undertakings unto his ends and purposes, not their own. He is pleased, indeed, as yet, to suffer and to be persecuted in his saints and servants; but that is from a gracious condescension, by virtue of a spiritual union, not from any necessity of state or condition. And some may hence learn how to fear him, as others may and do to put their trust in him.

Obs. IV. The Lord Christ filled up every season with duty, with the proper duty of it.

The days of his flesh were the only season wherein he could "offer" to God; and he missed it not, he did so accordingly. Some would not have Christ offer himself until he came to heaven. But then the season of offering was past. Christ was to use no strong cries and tears in heaven, which yet were necessary concomitants of his oblation. It is true, in his glorified state, he continually represents in heaven the offering that he made of himself on the earth, in an effectual application of it unto the advantage of the elect; but the offering itself was in the days of his flesh. This was the only season for that duty; for therein only was he meet unto this work, and had provision for it. Then was his body capable of pain, his soul of sorrow, his nature of dissolution; all which were necessary unto this duty. Then was he in a condition wherein faith, and trust, and prayers, and tears, were as necessary unto himself as unto his offering. This was his season, and he missed it not. Neither did he so on any other occasion during the days of his flesh, especially those of his public ministry; wherein we ought to make him our example.

Obs. V. The Lord Christ, in his offering up himself for us, laboured and travailed in soul to bring the work unto a good and holy issue.

A hard labour it was, and as such it is here expressed. He went through it with fears, sorrows, tears, outcries, prayers, and humble supplications. This is called נַפְשׁוֹ עֲמַל,—the pressing, wearying, laborious " travail of his soul," Isa. liii. 11. He laboured, was straitened and pained, to bring forth this glorious birth. And we may take a little prospect of this travail of the soul of Christ as it is represented unto us. 1. All the holy, *natural affections* of his soul were filled, taken up, and extended to the utmost capacity, in acting and suffering. The travail of our souls lies much in the engagement and actings of our affections. Who is there who hath been acquainted with great fears, great sorrows, great desires, great and ardent love, who knows it not? All and every one of these had now their sails filled in Christ, and that about the highest, noblest, and most glorious objects that they are capable of. The sorrows of his holy mother, Luke ii. 35; the danger of his disciples, Zech. xiii. 7; the scandal of the cross, the shame of his suffering, Heb. xii. 2; the ruin of his people according to the flesh for their sin, Luke xxiii. 28–30; with sundry other the like objects and considerations, filled and exercised all his natural affections. This put his soul into travail, and had an influence into the conflict wherein he was engaged. 2. All his graces, the gracious qualifications of his mind and affections, were in a like manner in the height of their exercise. Both those whose immediate object was God himself, and those which respected the church, were all of them excited, drawn forth, and engaged: as,—(1.) *Faith and trust in God.* These himself expresseth in his greatest trial, as those which he betook himself unto, Isa. l. 7, 8; Ps. xxii. 9, 10; Heb. ii. 13. These graces in him were now tried to the utmost. All their strength, all their efficacy, was exercised and proved; for he was to give in them an instance of an excellency in faith, rising up above the instance of the provocation that was in the unbelief of our first parents, whereby they fell off from God. There is no object about which faith can be exercised, no duty which it worketh in and by, but what it was now applied unto, and in, by Jesus Christ. (2.) *Love to mankind.* As this in his divine nature was the peculiar spring of that infinite condescension whereby he took our nature on him, for the work of mediation, Phil. ii. 6–8; so it wrought mightily and effectually in his human nature, in the whole course of his obedience, but especially in the offering of himself unto God for us.

Hence where there is mention made of his "giving himself for us," which was in the sacrifice of himself, commonly the cause of it is expressed to have been his love: 'The Son of God "loved me, and gave himself for me,"' Gal. ii. 20; "Christ loved the church, and gave himself for it," Eph. v. 25, 26; "He loved us, and washed us from our sins in his own blood," Rev. i. 5. With this love his soul now travailed, and laboured to bring forth the blessed fruits of it. The workings of this love in the heart of Christ, during the trial insisted on, whereby he balanced the sorrow and distress of his sufferings, no heart can conceive nor tongue express. (3.) *Zeal* for the glory of God. Zeal is the height of careful, solicitous love. The love of Christ was great to the souls of men; but the life of it lay in his love to God, and zeal for his glory. This he now laboured in, namely, that God might be glorified in the salvation of the elect. This was committed unto him, and concerning this he took care that it might not miscarry. (4.) He was now in the highest exercise of *obedience* unto God, and that in such a peculiar manner as before he had no occasion for. It is observed as the height of his condescension, that he was "obedient unto death, the death of the cross," Phil. ii. 8. This was the highest instance of obedience that God ever had from a creature, because performed by him who was God also. And if the obedience of Abraham was so acceptable to God, and was so celebrated, when he was ready to offer up his son, how glorious was that of the Son of God, who actually offered up himself, and that in such a way and manner as Isaac was not capable of being offered! And there was an eminent specialty in this part of his obedience; hence, Heb. v. 8, it is said that "he learned obedience by the things which he suffered;" which we shall speak to afterwards. And in the exercise of this obedience, that it might be full, acceptable, meritorious, every way answering the terms of the covenant between God and him about the redemption of mankind, he laboured and travailed in soul. And by this his obedience was a compensation made for the disobedience of Adam, Rom. v. 19. So did he travail in the exercise of grace. 3. He did so also with respect unto that confluence of calamities, distresses, pains, and miseries, which was upon his whole nature. And that in these consisted no small part of his trials, wherein he underwent and suffered the utmost which human nature is capable to undergo, is evident from the description given of his dolorous sufferings both in prophecy, Ps. xxii., Isa. liii., and in the story of what befell him in the evangelists. In that death of the body which he underwent, in the means and manner of it, much of the curse of the law was executed. Hence our apostle proves that he was "made a curse for us," from that of Moses, "Cursed is every one that hangeth on a tree," Gal. iii. 13, Deut. xxi. 22, 23. For that ignominy of being hanged on a tree was peculiarly appointed to represent the execution of the curse of the law on Jesus Christ, "who his own self bare our sins on the tree," 1 Pet. ii. 24. And herein lies no small mystery of the wisdom of God. He would have a resemblance, among them who suffered under the sentence of the law, of the suffering of Christ; but in the whole law there was no appointment that any one should be put to death by being hanged; but whereas God foreknew that at the time of the suffering of Christ the nation would be under the power of the Romans, and that the sentence of death would be inflicted after their manner,—which was by being nailed unto and hanged on a cross,—he ordered, for a prefiguration thereof, that some great transgressors, as blasphemers and open idolaters, after they were stoned, should be hanged upon a tree, to make a declaration of the curse of the law inflicted on them. Hence it is peculiarly said of such a one, "He that is hanged on the tree is the curse of God;" because God did therein represent the suffering of Him who underwent the whole curse of the law for us. And in this manner of his death there were sundry things concurring:—(1.) A *natural sign* of his readiness to embrace all sinners that should come unto him, his arms being, as it were, stretched out to receive them, Isa. xlv. 22, lxv. 1. (2.) A *moral token* of his condition, being left as one rejected of all between heaven and earth for a season; but in himself interposing between heaven and earth, the justice of God and sins of men, to make reconciliation and peace, Eph. ii. 16, 17. (3.) The accomplishment of *sundry types;* as,—[1.] Of that of him who was hanged on a tree, as cursed of the Lord, Deut. xxi. 22. [2.] Of the brazen serpent which was lifted up in the wilderness, John iii. 14; with respect whereunto he says, that when he is "lifted up" he would "draw all men unto him," John. xii. 32. [3.] Of the waveoffering, which was moved, shaken, and turned several ways; to declare that the Lord Christ, in his offering of himself, should have respect unto all parts of the world, and all sorts of men, Exod. xxix. 26. And in all the concerns of this death, all the means of it, especially as it was an effect of the curse of the law, or penal, immediately from God himself, (for "he that is hanged" on a tree "is accursed of God,") did he labour and travail in the work that lay before him. 4. The conflict he had with Satan and all the powers of darkness was another part of his travail. This was the hour of men, and power of darkness, Luke xxii. 53,—the time when the prince of this world came, John xiv., to try the utmost of his skill, interest, horror, rage, and power, for his destruction. Then were all infernal principalities and powers engaged in a conflict with him, Col. ii. 14, 15. Whatever malice, poison, darkness, dread, may be infused into diabolical suggestions, or be mixed with external representations of things to the sight, or imagination, he was now contending with. And herein he laboured for that victory and success which, in the

issue, he did obtain, Col. ii. 13–15; Heb. ii. 14; 1 John iii. 8. 5. His
inward conflict, in the "making his soul an offering for sin," in his
apprehensions, and undergoing of the wrath of God due unto sin,
hath been already spoken unto, so far as is necessary unto our present purpose. 6. In and during all these things there was in his eye
continually that unspeakable glory that was set before him, of being
the repairer of the breaches of the creation, the recoverer of mankind, the captain of salvation unto all that obey him, the destruction of Satan, with his kingdom of sin and darkness; and in all, the
great restorer of divine glory, to the eternal praise of God. Whilst
all these things were in the height of their transaction, is it any wonder if the Lord Christ laboured and travailed in soul, according to the
description here given of him?

Obs. VI. The Lord Christ, in the time of his offering and suffering, considering God, with whom he had to do, as the sovereign
Lord of life and death, as the supreme Rector and Judge of all, casts
himself before him, with most fervent prayers for deliverance from
the sentence of death and the curse of the law.

This gives the true account of the deportment of our Saviour in
his trial, here described. There are two great mistakes about the sufferings of Christ and the condition of his soul therein. Some place
him in that security, in that sense and enjoyment of divine love, that
they leave neither room nor reason for the fears, cries, and wrestlings here mentioned; indeed, so as that there should be nothing
real in all this transaction, but rather that all things were done for
ostentation and show. For if the Lord Christ was always in a full
comprehension of divine love, and that in the light of the beatific
vision, what can these conflicts and complaints signify? Others grant
that he was in real distress and anguish; but they say it was merely
on the account of those outward sufferings which were coming on
him; which, as we observed before, is an intolerable impeachment of
his holy fortitude and constancy of mind. For the like outward
things have been undergone by others without any tokens of such
consternation of spirit. Wherefore, to discern aright the true frame
of the spirit of Christ, with the intension of his cries and supplications (the things before insisted on), are duly to be considered,—

1. How great a matter it was to *make peace with God for sinners, to make atonement and reconciliation for sin.* This is the
life and spirit of our religion, the centre wherein all the lines of it
do meet, Phil. iii. 8–10; 1 Cor. ii. 2; Gal. vi. 14. And those by
whom a due and constant consideration of it is neglected, are
strangers unto the animating spirit of that religion which they outwardly profess; and therefore Satan doth employ all his artifices to
divert the minds of men from a due meditation hereon, and the
exercise of faith about it. Much of the devotion of the Romanists

is taken up in dumb shows and painted representations of the sufferings of Christ. But as many of their scenical fancies are childishly ridiculous, and unworthy of men who have the least apprehension of the greatness and holiness of God, or that he is a spirit, and will be worshipped in spirit and in truth; so they are none of them of any other use but to draw off the mind, not only from a spiritual contemplation of the excellency of the offering of Christ, and the glorious effects thereof, but also from the rational comprehension of the truth of the doctrine concerning what he did and suffered. For he that is instructed in and by the taking, shutting up, and setting forth of a crucifix, with painted thorns, and nails, and blood, with Jews, and thieves, and I know not what other company, about it, is obliged to believe that he hath, if not all, yet the principal part at least, of the obedience of Christ in his suffering represented unto him. And by this means is his mind taken off from inquiring into the great transactions between God and the soul of Christ, about the finishing of sin, and the bringing in of everlasting righteousness; without which those other things, which by carnal means they represent unto the carnal minds and imaginations of men, are of no value or use. On the other hand, the Socinians please themselves, and deceive others, with a vain imagination that there was no such work to be done now with God as we have declared. If we may believe them, there was no atonement to be made for sin, no expiatory sacrifice to be offered, no peace thereby to be made with God, no compensation to his justice, by answering the sentence and curse of the law due to sin. But certainly if this sort of men had not an unparalleled mixture of confidence and dexterity, they could not find out evasions unto so many express divine testimonies as lie directly opposite to their fond imagination, unto any tolerable satisfaction in their own minds; or suppose that any men can with patience bear the account they must give of the agony, prayers, cries, tears, fears, wrestlings, and travail, of the soul of Christ, on this supposition. But we may pass them over at present, as express " enemies of the cross of Christ;" that is, of that cross whereby he made peace with God for sinners, as Eph. ii. 14-16. Others there are who by no means approve of any diligent inquiry into these mysteries. The whole business and duty of ministers and others is, in their mind, to be conversant in and about morality. As for this fountain and spring of grace, this basis of eternal glory; this evidence and demonstration of divine wisdom, holiness, righteousness, and love; this great discovery of the purity of the law and vileness of sin; this first, great, principal subject of the gospel, and motive of faith and obedience; this root and cause of all peace with God, all sincere and incorrupted love towards him, of all joy and consolation from him,—they think it scarcely deserves a place in the objects of their contemplation, and are ready to guess that what men write and talk about it is but phrases, canting, and fanatical. But such as are admitted into the fellowship of the sufferings of Christ will not so easily part with their immortal interest and concern herein. Yea, I fear not to say, that he is likely to be the best, the most humble, the most holy and fruitful Christian, who is most sedulous and diligent in spiritual inquiries into this great mystery of the reconciliation of God unto sinners by the blood of the cross, and in the exercise of faith about it. Nor is there any such powerful means of preserving the soul in a constant abhorrency of sin, and watchfulness against it, as a due apprehension of what it cost to make atonement for it. And we may also learn hence,—

2. That a sight and sense of the wrath of God due unto sin will be full of dread and terror for the souls of men, and will put them to a great conflict, with wrestling, for deliverance.

We find how it was with the Lord Christ in that condition; and such a view of the wrath of God all men will be brought unto sooner or later. There is a view to be had of it in the curse of the law for the present; there will be a more terrible expression of it in the execution of that curse at the last day; and no way is there to obtain a deliverance from the distress and misery wherewith this prospect of wrath due to sin is attended, but by obtaining a spiritual view of it in the cross of Christ, and acquiescing by faith in that atonement.

Obs. VII. In all the pressures that were on the Lord Jesus Christ, in all the distresses he had to conflict withal in his suffering, his faith for deliverance and success was firm and unconquerable. This was the ground he stood upon in all his prayers and supplications.

Obs. VIII. The success of our Lord Jesus Christ, in his trials, as our head and surety, is a pledge and assurance of success unto us in all our spiritual conflicts.

VERSE 8.

The things discoursed in the foregoing verse seem to have an inconsistency with the account given us concerning the person of Jesus Christ at the entrance of this epistle. For he is therein declared to be the Son of God, and that in such a glorious manner as to be deservedly exalted above all the angels in heaven. He is so said to be the Son of God, as to be " the brightness of the Father's glory, and the express image of his person," even partaker of the same nature with him; God, by whom the heavens were made, and the foundations of the earth were laid, chap. i. 8–10. Here he is represented in a low, distressed condition, humbly, as it were, begging for his life, and pleading with " strong cries and tears" before him who was able to deliver him. These things might seem unto the Hebrews to have some kind of repugnancy unto one another. And, indeed, they are a "stone of stumbling, and a rock of offence," unto many at this day; they are not able to reconcile them in their carnal minds and reasonings. Wherefore, since it is by all acknowledged that he was truly and really in the low, distressed condition here described, they will not allow that he was the Son of God in the way declared by the apostle, but invent other reasons of their own for which he should be so termed. Their pleas and pretences we have discussed elsewhere. The aim of the apostle in this place is, not to repel the objections of unbelievers, but to instruct the faith of them who do believe in the truth and reason of these things. For he doth not only manifest that they were all possible, upon the account of his participation of flesh and blood, who was in himself the eternal Son of God; but also that the whole of the humiliation and distress thereon ascribed unto him was necessary, with respect unto the office which he had undertaken to discharge, and the work which was committed unto him. And this he doth in the next ensuing and following verses.

Ver. 8.—Καίπερ ὢν Υἱός, ἔμαθεν ἀφ' ὧν ἔπαθε τὴν ὑπακοήν.

I observed before that the Syriac translation hath transposed some words in these two verses, and thus reads this latter of them, "And although he were a Son, from the fear and sufferings which he underwent he learned obedience." That concerning "fear" is traduced out of the foregoing verse, where it is omitted. Some copies of the Vulgar read, "et quidem cum esset Filius Dei," as do our old English translations, restoring it before its connection, as also in other places. The Rhemists only, "and truly, whereas he was the Son;" no other translation acknowledgeth the addition of "God." Arias, "existens Filius:" which some other translations add some epithet unto, to express the emphasis;—"a faithful Son," Ethiop.; "a Son always," Arab.[1]

Ver. 8.—Although he were a Son, yet learned he obedience by [or *from*] the things which he suffered.

Καίπερ, "quamvis," "tametsi," "although;" an adversative, with a concession. An exception may be supposed unto what   Καίπερ. was before delivered, namely, 'If he were "a Son," how came he so to pray and cry, so to stand in need of help and relief?' This is here tacitly inserted. Saith the apostle, 'Although he were so, yet these other things were necessary.' And this gives us a connection of the words unto those foregoing. But according to the apostle's usual way of reasoning in this epistle, there is also a prospect in this word towards the necessity and advantage of his being brought into the condition described; which in our translation is supplied by the addition of "yet."

---

[1] TRANSLATION.—Υἱός. The word becomes definite from its connection and well-known application; as in Matt. xii. 41, 42, "men of Nineveh," and "a queen of the South," necessarily recall to the minds of the hearers the generation and royal personage referred to. Here our English idiom allows the most literal translation, and thereby gives the precise meaning: "Though he were Son."— *Turner.*—ED.

Υἱὸς ὤν, " he were a Son," "and yet being a Son;" that is, ' such
Υἱὸς ὤν.   a Son as we have described, or " that Son of God."' It
was no great nor singular thing for a son or child of God
by adoption to be chastised, to suffer, and thereby to be instructed
unto obedience.   He therefore speaks not of him as a son on any
common account, or such as any mere creature can claim interest in.
But he was "God's own Son," Rom. viii. 3; the "only begotten of the
Father," John i. 14; who was himself also " in the form of God,"
Phil. ii. 6.   That *he* should do the thing here spoken of, is great and
marvellous.   Therefore is it said that he did thus, " although he
were a Son."   Two things are included herein, namely, in the introduction of Christ in this place under the title of the " Son:"—1. The
necessity of doing what is here ascribed unto him, with respect unto
the end aimed at.   And this is more fully declared in the next verse.
The things that were in themselves necessary unto the great end of
the glory of God in the salvation of the elect, were not to be waived
by Christ, " although he were the Son."   2. His *love*, that he would
submit to this condition for our sake.   On his own account no such
thing was required of him, or any way needful unto him; but for our
sakes (such was his love) he would do it, " although he were a Son."
   Besides, whereas the apostle is comparing the Lord Christ, as a
high priest, with Aaron and those of his order, he intimates a double
advantage which he had above them:—1. That he was a *Son*, whereas
they were *servants* only; as he had before expressed the same difference in comparing him with Moses, chap. iii. 4–6.   2. That he
learned obedience by what he suffered; which few of them did,
none of them in the same way and manner with him.
   Ἔμαθεν ἀφ᾽ ὧν ἔπαθε, τὴν ὑπακοήν.   As to the manner of the expression or phraseology, ἀφ᾽ ὧν seems to be put for ἐξ ὧν, " by," " out of,"
" from," the things.   And, moreover, there is an ellipsis, or a meta-
ptosis in the words, being put for ἔμαθεν ἀπ᾽ ἐκείνων ἃ ἔπαθε: and so we
express the sense in our translation.   Also, the paranomasia which
is in them, ἔμαθεν ἀφ᾽ ὧν ἔπαθε, is observed by all.   And there is some
correspondence in the whole unto that common ancient saying, Τὰ
παθήματα μαθήματα.[1]
   Three things we are to inquire into:—1. What is the *obedience*
which is here intended.   2. How Christ is said to *learn* it.   3. By
what *means* he did so.
   1. Ὑπακοή is " an *obediential attendance* unto the commands of
Τὴν ὑπακοήν.   another;" "a due consideration of, a ready compliance
with authoritative commands:" for the word cometh
from that which signifieth "to hearken," or " hear."   Hence, to
" hearken" or " hear," is frequently in the Scripture used for to
obey; and to "refuse to hear," is to be stubborn and disobedient:

---

[1] See the speech of Crœsus, Herodot. i. 207.—Ed.

because obedience respects the commands of another, which we receive and become acquainted withal by hearing; and a readiness with diligence therein, is the great means to bring us unto obedience. 'Υπακοή, therefore, is " an obediential compliance with the commands of another," when we hear, and thereby know them.

This obedience in Christ was twofold:—(1.) *General*, in the whole course of his holy life in this world; every thing he did was not only *materially holy*, but *formally obediential*. He did all things because it was the will and law of God that so he should do. And this obedience to God was the life and beauty of the holiness of Christ himself; yea, obedience unto God in any creature is the formal reason constituting any act or duty to be good or holy. Where that consideration is excluded, whatever the matter of any work or duty may be, it is neither holy nor accepted with God. Wherefore the whole course of the life of Christ was a course of obedience unto God; whereon he so often professed that he kept the commands and did the will of him that sent him, thereby "fulfilling all righteousness." But yet this is not the obedience here peculiarly intended, although no part of it can be absolutely excluded from the present consideration; for whereas this obedience hath respect unto suffering, he "learned it from the things which he suffered," his whole life was a life of suffering. One way or other he suffered in all that he did, at least when and whilst he did it. His state in this world was a state of humiliation and exinanition; which things have suffering in their nature. His outward condition in the world was mean, low, and contemptible; from which sufferings are inseparable. And he was in all things continually exposed unto temptations, and all sorts of oppositions, from Satan and the world; this also added to his sufferings. (2.) But yet, moreover, there was a *peculiar obedience* of Christ, which is intended here in an especial manner. This was his obedience in dying, and in all things that tended immediately thereunto. "He became obedient unto death, even the death of the cross;" for this commandment had he of his Father, that he should lay down his life, and therefore he did it in a way of obedience. And this especial obedience to the command of God for suffering and dying the apostle here respects. With regard hereunto he said of old, " Lo, I come: in the volume of thy book it is written of me, I delight to do thy will, O my God," Ps. xl. 7, 8; which was in the offering up of himself a sacrifice for us, as our apostle declares, Heb. x. 9, 10. And concerning the things which befell him herein, he says, " he was not rebellious," but " gave his back to the smiters, and his cheeks to them that plucked off the hair," Isa. l. 5, 6.

2. Concerning this obedience, it is said that ἔμαθε, he " learned" it. Μανθάνω is to learn as a disciple, with a humble, willing subjection unto, and a ready reception of the instructions given. But of the Lord Christ it is said here, " he learned *Ἔμαθε.*

obedience," not that he learned to obey; which will give us light into the meaning of the whole. For, to learn obedience may have a threefold sense:—(1.) To learn it *materially*, by coming to know that to be our duty, to be required of us, which before we knew not, or at least did not consider as we ought. So speaks the psalmist, "Before I was afflicted I went astray; but now have I learned thy commandments." God by his chastisements, and under them, taught him the duties he required of him, and what diligent attendance unto them was necessary for him. But thus our Lord Jesus learned not obedience, nor could so do; for he knew beforehand all that he was to do, or undergo,—what was proposed unto him, what was to come upon him, in the discharge of his office and performance of the work he had undertaken. And the law of the whole of it was in his heart; no command of God was new to him, nor ever forgotten by him. (2.) To learn it *formally;* that is, to be guided, instructed, directed, helped, in the acts and acting of the obedience required of him. This is properly to learn to obey; so is it with us, who are rude and unskilful in holy obedience, and are by supplies of light and grace gradually instructed in the knowledge and practice of it. This wisdom do we learn, partly by the word, partly by afflictions, as God is pleased to make them effectual. But thus the Lord Christ neither did nor could learn obedience. He had a fulness of grace always in him and with him, inclining, directing, guiding, and enabling him unto all acts of obedience that were required of him. Being full of grace, truth, and wisdom, he was never at a loss for what he had to do, nor wanted any thing of a perfect readiness of will or mind for its performance. Wherefore, (3.) He can be said to learn obedience only on the account of having an *experience* of it in its exercise. So a man knoweth the taste and savour of meat by eating it; as our Saviour is said to "taste of death," or to experience what was in it, by undergoing of it. And it was one especial kind of obedience that is here intended, as was declared before, namely, a submission to undergo great, hard, and terrible things, accompanied with patience and quiet endurance under them, and faith for deliverance from them. This he could have no experience of, but by suffering the things he was to undergo, and the exercise of the graces mentioned therein. Thus learned he obedience, or experienced in himself what difficulty it is attended withal, especially in cases like his own. And this way of his learning obedience it is that is so useful unto us, and so full of consolation. For if he had only known obedience, though never so perfectly, in the notion of it, what relief could have accrued unto us thereby? how could it have been a spring of pity or compassion towards us? But now, whereas he himself took in his own person a full experience of the nature of that especial obedience which is yielded to God in a suffering condition, what difficulty it is attended withal, what opposition is made unto it, how great an exercise of grace is required in it, he is constantly ready to give us relief, as the matter doth require.

3. The way or means of his learning obedience is lastly expressed: 'Ἀφ' ὧν ἔπαθε,—"From the things which he suffered." It is a usual saying, Παθήματα, μαθήματα,—" Sufferings" 'Ἀφ' ὧν ἔπαθι. (or "corrections") are instructions." And we cannot exclude from hence any thing that Christ suffered, from first to last, in the days of his flesh. He suffered in his whole course, and that in great variety, as hath been showed elsewhere. And he had experience of obedience from them all, in the sense declared. But seeing the apostle treats concerning him as a high priest, and with especial respect to the offering himself unto God, the suffering of death, and those things which immediately led thereunto, are principally intended: "He became obedient unto death, even the death of the cross," Phil. ii. 8. Now we may be said to learn from sufferings objectively and occasionally. In their own nature and formally they are not instructive. All things that outwardly come upon us are ἐκ τῶν μέσων, and may be abused, or improved unto a good end. But in them that believe, they give a necessity and especial occasion unto the exercise of those graces wherein our obedience in that season doth consist. So from them, or by them, did the Lord Christ himself learn obedience; for by reason of them he had occasion to exercise those graces of humility, self-denial, meekness, patience, faith, which were habitually resident in his holy nature, but were not capable of the peculiar exercise intended but by reason of his sufferings. But, moreover, there was still somewhat peculiar in that obedience which the Son of God is said to learn from his own sufferings, namely, what it is for a *sinless person* to suffer for sinners, "the just for the unjust." The obedience herein was peculiar unto him, nor do we know, nor can we have an experience of the ways and paths of it.

The Lord Christ, undertaking the work of our redemption, was not on the account of the dignity of his person to be spared in any thing that was necessary thereunto. He was enabled *by* it to undertake and perform his work; but he was not *for* it spared any part of it. It is all one for that; "although he were a Son," he must now "learn obedience." And this we have sufficiently cleared on the former verse. And we may hence observe, that,—

Obs. I. Infinite love prevailed with the Son of God to lay aside the privilege of his infinite dignity, that he might suffer for us and our redemption.

"Although he were a Son, yet he learned," etc. 1. The name of "Son" carrieth with it infinite dignity, as our apostle proves at large, chap. i. 3, 4, etc. The Son;—that is, "the Son of the living

God," Matt. xvi. 16; "the only-begotten of the Father," John i. 14; he who "in the beginning was with God, and was God," John i. 1, 2. For as he was "God's own Son," Rom. viii. 3; he was "in the form of God, equal with him," Phil. ii. 5, 6; one with him, John x. 30. So that infinite glory and dignity were inseparable from him. And so long as he would make use of this privilege, it was impossible he should be exposed to the least suffering, nor could the whole creation divest him of the least appurtenance of it. But, 2. He voluntarily laid aside the consideration, advantage, and exercise of it, that he might suffer for us. This our apostle fully expresseth, Phil. ii. 5–8, "Let this mind be in you, which was also in Christ Jesus: who, being in the form of God, thought it not robbery to be equal with God: but made himself of no reputation, and took upon him the form of a servant, and was made in the likeness of men : and being found in fashion as a man, he humbled himself, and became obedient unto death, even the death of the cross." Concerning which we must observe,—That the Son of God could not absolutely and really part with his *eternal glory*. Whatever he did, he was the Son of God, and God still. Neither by any thing he did, nor any thing he suffered, nor any condition he underwent, did he really forego, nor was it possible he should so do, any thing of his divine glory. He was no less God when he died than when he was "declared to be the Son of God with power, by the resurrection from the dead." But he is said to "empty himself" of his divine glory,—1. With respect unto the *infinite condescension* of his person; 2. With respect unto the *manifestations* of it in this world:—

1. Of his *condescension*, when he forewent the privilege of his eternal glory, the apostle observes sundry degrees. (1.) In his taking of *our nature* on him. He "took on him the form of a servant;" and therein "made himself of no reputation,"—that is, comparatively unto the glory which he had "in the form of God," wherein he was "equal with God," that is, the Father. Hence "the Word was made flesh," John i. 14; or, "God was manifest in the flesh," 1 Tim. iii. 16. This was an infinite, unspeakable, unconceivable condescension of the Son of God, namely, to take our nature into union with himself; whereby he who was God, like unto the Father in all things, "the brightness of his glory, and the express image of his person," became a man like unto us in all things, sin only excepted. (2.) In his *so becoming a man* as to take on him "the *form of a servant.*" He did not immediately take the nature he had assumed into glory ; but he first became a "servant" in it,—a servant to God, to do his will, and that in the most difficult service that ever God had to do in this world. (3.) In that in this service he "made himself of *no reputation.*" The work, indeed, he undertook, was great and honourable, as we have before declared ;

but the way and manner whereby he did accomplish it was such as exposed him unto scorn, reproach, and contempt in the world, Isa. liii. 1, 2; Ps. xxii. 6, 7. (4.) In that in this *work he " became obedient unto death."* Had he staid at the former degrees, his condescension had been for ever to be admired and adored; this only remains to be added, that he should die, and that penally and painfully. And this also he submitted unto. The Prince, the Author, the God of life, became obedient unto death! which also, (5.) Hath an aggravation added to it,—it was " the *death of the cross,"* a shameful, ignominious, cursed death. In all these things did he lay aside the privilege of his infinite dignity; all this he did "although he were a Son."

2. As to *manifestation.* He did, as it were, hide and eclipse unto the world all the glory of his divine person, under the veil of flesh which he had taken on him. Hence at the close of this dispensation, when he was finishing the work committed to him, he prays, John xvii. 5, " O Father, glorify thou me with that glory which I had with thee before the world was ;"—'Let that glory which was necessarily hid and eclipsed in my debasement, wherein I have been made low for the suffering of death, now shine forth again conspicuously.' Now the reason why the Son of God did thus forego the privilege and dignity of his glory, was his *infinite love.* "Forasmuch as the children are partakers of flesh and blood, he also himself likewise took part of the same," Heb. ii. 14. The reason why he condescended unto this condition, was, that he might redeem and save the children which God gave unto him; and this out of his own unspeakable love towards them, Gal. ii. 20; Rev. i. 5; Phil. ii. 5. This was that which engaged him into, and carried him through his great undertakings.

And here we may, as it were, 1. *Lose ourselves* in a holy admiration of this infinite love of Christ. Our apostle prays for the Ephesians, that they " might be able to comprehend with all saints, what is the breadth, and length, and depth, and height; and to know the love of Christ, which passeth knowledge," Eph. iii. 18, 19. This, it seems, is the work, the design, the endeavour of "all saints,"— namely, to come to an acquaintance with, or to live in the contemplation of the love of Christ. The dimensions here assigned unto it are only to let us know, that, which way soever we exercise our thoughts about it, there is still a suitable object for them. It wants nothing that may be a proper object for that prospect which a soul may take of it in the way of believing ; and he so prays for the knowledge of it, as that he lets us know that absolutely it is incomprehensible, it " passeth knowledge." Then do we in our measure know the love of Christ, when we know that it passeth knowledge,— when we comprehend so much of it, as to find we cannot comprehend it ; and thereby we have the benefit and consolation of what

we do not conceive, as well as of what we do. For as contemplation
is an act of faith with respect unto our measure of comprehension,
so is admiration with respect unto what exceeds it. And what way
soever faith acts itself on Christ, it will bring in advantage and refreshment to the soul. And we are never nearer Christ than when
we find ourselves lost in a holy amazement at his unspeakable love.
And, indeed, his love herein, that "although he were a Son," the
eternal Son of God, yet he would condescend unto the condition
before described for our deliverance and salvation, is that which
fills the souls of believers with admiration, not only in this world,
but unto eternity. And, 2. Here we may, as it were, *find ourselves.*
The due consideration of this love of Christ is that alone which will
satisfy our souls and consciences with the grounds of the acceptance
of such poor unworthy sinners as we are in the presence of the
holy God. For what will not this love and the effects of it prevail
for? what can stand in the way of it? or what can hinder it from
accomplishing whatever it is designed unto?

Obs. II. In his sufferings, and notwithstanding them all, the
Lord Christ was the " Son " still, the Son of God.

He was so both as to real relation and as to suitable affection.
He had in them all the state of a Son and the love of a Son. It is
true, during the time of his suffering, a common eye, an eye of sense
and reason, could see no appearance of this sonship of Christ. His
outward circumstances were all of them such as rather eclipsed than
manifested his glory, Isa. liii. 2, 3. This was that which the world
being offended at, stumbled and fell; for he was unto them " a
stone of stumbling, and rock of offence," Rom. ix. 33. The mean-
ness of his condition, the poverty of his life, and shame of his death,
proved an offence both to Jews and Gentiles. How could such a
one be thought to be the Son of God? Besides, God himself so
dealt with him, as flesh and blood would not conceive him to deal
with his only Son. For he laid his curse upon him, as it is written,
" Cursed is he that is hanged on a tree." And in all this state of
things, he speaks of himself as one made so much beneath the condition of glory which was due to the Son of God, as that he was
lower than any sort of men ; whence he complains, " I am a worm,
and no man ; a reproach of men, and despised of the people," Ps.
xxii. 6. Yet, during all this, he was still the Son of God, and suffered as the Son of God. Hence it is said, that " God spared not
his own Son, but delivered him up for us all,"—that is, to suffering
and death, Rom. viii. 32. He " sent his own Son in the likeness of
sinful flesh," and " condemned sin in the flesh," verse 3. It is true,
he suffered only in his human nature, which alone was capable thereof;
but HE suffered who *was the Son of God,* and as he was the Son of
God, or God could not have "redeemed the church with his own

blood," Acts xx. 28. In all that he underwent neither was the union of his natures dissolved, nor the love of the Father unto him as his own Son in the least impeached.

Obs. III. A practical experience of obedience to God in some cases will cost us dear.

We cannot learn it but through the suffering of those things which will assuredly befall us on' the account thereof. So was it with the Lord Christ. I intend not here the difficulties we meet withal in mortifying the internal lusts and corruptions of nature; for these had no place in the example here proposed unto us. Those only are respected which do, or will, or may, come upon us from without. And it is an especial kind of obedience also, namely, that which holds some conformity to the obedience of Christ, that is intended. Wherefore, 1. it must be *singular ;* it must have somewhat in it that may, in a special manner, turn the eyes of others towards it. A common course of obedience, clothed with a common passant profession, may escape at an easy rate in the world. There seems to be somewhat singular denoted in that expression, "He that will live godly in Christ Jesus," 2 Tim. iii. 12. To live in Christ Jesus, is to live and walk in the profession of the gospel, to be a professing branch in Christ, John xv. 2. But of these there are two sorts; some that "live godly in him," some branches that bring forth fruit,—that is, in an eminent and singular manner. Every branch in the true vine hath that whereby he is distinguished from brambles and thorns; and every one that lives in the profession of the gospel hath somewhat that differenceth him from the world, and the ways of it; but there is a peculiar, a singular fruit-bearing in Christ, an especial "living godly in him," which will turn an observation upon itself. So our apostle says, that they "were made a spectacle unto the world, and to angels, and to men," by the especial ministry which was committed unto them, 1 Cor. iv. 9. 2. It is required that this obedience be *universal.* If there be an allowance in any one instance where there is a compliance with the world, or other enemies of our obedience, the trouble of it will be much abated. For men, by indulging any crooked steps to themselves, do compound for outward peace, and ofttimes thus obtain their aims, though greatly to their spiritual disadvantage. But the gospel obedience which we inquire into, is such as universally agrees in conformity with Christ in all things. And this will cost us dear. Sufferings will attend it. "They that live godly in Christ Jesus shall suffer persecution." For this kind of obedience will be observed in the world. It cannot escape observation, because it is *singular ;* and it provokes the world, because it is *universal,* and will admit of no compliance with it. And where the world is first awaked, and then enraged, trouble and suffering of one kind or another will ensue. If it do not bite and tear, it will bark and rage. And Satan will see enough to make such his especial mark, as to all the opposition and actings of enmity which he puts forth against any in this world. Yea, and God himself ofttimes delighteth to give a trial unto eminent graces, where he endows any with them. For he gives them not for the peculiar advantage of them on whom they are bestowed only, but that he himself may have a revenue of glory from their ex-ercise.

Obs. IV. Sufferings undergone according to the will of God are highly instructive.

Even Christ himself learned by the things which he suffered; and much more may we do so, who have so much more to learn. God designs our sufferings to this end, and to this end he blesseth them. And this hath frequently been the issue of God's dealing with men; those who have suffered most, who have been most afflicted, most chastised, have been the most humble, most holy, fruitful, and wise among them; and he that learneth such things, profiteth well under his instruction.

Obs. V. In all these things, both as to suffering, and learning or profiting thereby, we have a great example in our Lord Jesus Christ.

As such is he proposed unto us in all his course of obedience, especially in his sufferings, 1 Pet. ii. 21; for he would leave nothing undone which was any way needful, that his great work of sanctify-ing and saving his church to the utmost might be perfect.

Obs. VI. The love of God towards any, the relation of any unto God, hinders not but that they may undergo great sufferings and trials.

The Lord Christ did so, " although he were a Son." And this instance irrefragably confirms our position. For the love of God to Jesus Christ was singular and supereminent; he doth not love any with a love so much as of the same kind. The relation also of Christ unto God was singular; none ever standing in the same relation unto him, he being his only-begotten Son. And yet his sufferings and trials were singular also. No sorrows, no pains, no distresses of soul and body, no sufferings like his. And in the whole course of the Scripture we may observe, that the nearer any have been unto God, the greater have been their trials. For,—1. There is not in such trials and exercises any thing that is absolutely *evil*, but they are all such as may be rendered good, useful, yea, honourable and glorious, to the sufferers, from God's conduct in them and the end of them. 2. The love of God, and the gracious emanations of it, can and do abundantly *compensate* the temporary evils which any do undergo according to his will. 3. The glory of God, which is the end designed unto, and which shall infallibly ensue upon all the sufferings of the people of God,—and that so much the greater as any of them, on any account, are *nearer* than others unto him,—is such a good unto them which suffer, as that their sufferings neither are, nor are esteemed by them to be evil.

VERSE 9.

The words and design of this verse have so great a coincidence with those of chap. ii. 10, that we shall the less need to insist upon them. Something only must be spoken to clear the context. The apostle having declared the sufferings of Christ as our high priest, in his offering of himself, with the necessity thereof, proceeded to declare both what was effected thereby, and what was the especial design of God therein. And this in general was, that the Lord Christ, considering our lost condition, might be every way fitted to be a "perfect cause of eternal salvation unto all them that obey him." There are, therefore, two things in the words, both which God aimed at and accomplished in the sufferings of Christ:—1. On his own part, that he might be "made perfect;" not absolutely, but with respect unto the administration of his office in the behalf of sinners. 2. With respect unto believers, that he might be unto them an "author of eternal salvation." Unto both these ends the sufferings of Christ were necessary, and designed of God.

Ver. 9.—Καὶ τελειωθεὶς ἐγένετο τοῖς ὑπακούουσιν αὐτῷ πᾶσιν αἴτιος σωτηρίας αἰωνίου.

Τελειωθείς, "perfectus," "consummatus," "consecratus;" "perfect," "consummated," "fully consecrated." Syriac, וְהַכְנָא אֶתְנְמַר, "and so being made perfect;" "perfectus redditus," as Erasmus. Ἐγένετο, "factus est," "fuit;" "he became." Τοῖς ὑπακούουσιν αὐτῷ. Vulg., "sibi obtemperantibus." So Arias, Eras., Syr. And Beza, "qui ipsi auscultans," keeping to the word; which in all the three languages, Hebrew, Greek, and Latin, signifies originally "to hearken," "to hear, to attend unto, with a design to learn and obey." Αἴτιος. Syr., עֶלְתָא, "causa;" so most. Beza, "auctor;" whom we follow, "the author." Σωτηρίας αἰωνίου, "salutis æternæ." Syr., דְּחַיֵּא דְּלָעֲלַם, "of life," or lives which are eternal." One learned grammarian hath translated αἴτιος, by "causa efficiens et exhibens." Ethiop., "the rewarder with life eternal, and the redeemer of the world."

Τελειωθείς, "being perfected," "consummated," "fully consecrated;" for the word is sacred, and expresseth sacred consecration. As to the sense of it in this place, with respect unto the verses foregoing, it answers directly unto its use, chap. ii. 10, διὰ παθημάτων τελειῶσαι, "to perfect by sufferings;" only that it is used actively, with respect unto God the Father, "It became him to make perfect the Captain of our salvation." Here it is used passively, with respect unto the effect of that act of God on the person of Christ, who by his suffering was "perfected." The signification of this word, and the constant use of it in this epistle, the

Τελιωθείς.

reader may find at large in our exposition on chap. ii. 10. The
sum is, that it signifies to dedicate, to consecrate, to sanctify and
set apart, and that by some kind of suffering or other. So the
legal high priests were consecrated by the suffering and death of the
beasts that were offered in sacrifice at their consecration, Exod. xxix.
But it belonged unto the perfection of the priesthood of Christ to
be consecrated in and by his own sufferings. I shall therefore only
remove out of the way the corrupt exposition given us of this word
by Schlichtingius:—

Τελείωσις, " Ista, seu consummatio Christi opponitur diebus carnis
ejus: tum enim cum Christus infirmus esset, et ipse alieno auxilio
indigeret, non potuerat aliis perfectum in omnibus auxilium ferre.
Sed postquam consummatus est, id est, postquam immortalitatem,
seü naturam incorruptibilem, supremamque in cœlo et terra potes-
tatem est adeptus, sicut nihil illi desit amplius; seu postquam est
adeo penitus consecratus, et plenè in sacerdotem inauguratus (quemadmodum aliqui hanc vocem explicandam putant), factus est causa
salutis æternæ; nempe causa perfectissima. Nam et in diebus carnis
suæ erat causa salutis æternæ; sed consummatus, factus est causa
perfectissima. Tunc causa erat nostræ salutis tanquam Dei maximus
legatus et apostolus; nunc tanquam summus pontifex et rex noster
cœlestis a Deo constitutus." There is also another expositor, who,
although he grants that the τελείωσις here mentioned hath respect
unto the מִלֻּאִים, or " sacrifices" at the consecration of priests, which
was antecedent unto their right of offering any thing in their own
persons, yet so far complies with this interpretation as to understand,
I know not what, " inauguration into a Melchisedecian priesthood,
which consisted in a power of blessing after his resurrection;" and
so, in the application of the word unto Christ, falls into a contradiction unto his own exposition of it, making it consist in his exaltation
and endowment with power. But there is nothing sound in these
discourses. For,—1. There is no opposition between this *consecration
of Christ* and the *days of his flesh;* for it was effected in and by his
sufferings, which were only in the days of his flesh. And we have
given the reason before, and that taken from the perfection of his
person and his office, why he was himself consecrated for ever in
and by that sacrifice which he offered for us; for neither could he
often offer himself, and it was destructive of his whole office to have
been consecrated by the offering of any other. 2. There is too much
boldness in that expression, that Christ could not *perfectly help*
others in the days of his flesh. For, set aside the consideration of his
divine nature, wherein he wrought whatever the Father wrought
(which this sort of men will not admit), he had declared openly that
" all power," " all things," were given into his hand, Matt. xi., xxviii.;
" power over all flesh," John xvii.,—which surely extended unto an

ability of relieving all them that were committed to him of God. It is true, he had not as yet absolutely perfected all the means of our salvation; but he was furnished with a fulness of power in their accomplishment, according to the method and order appointed of God unto them. 3. It is not said, that after he was *consecrated*, or *perfected*, or made *immortal*, as though these things were of the same importance; for he was consecrated in and by his sufferings, as is expressly affirmed, chap. ii. 10, which were antecedent unto and issued in his death. 4. That the Lord Christ was not constituted and consecrated a high priest before his *entrance into heaven*, is a direct contradiction unto the whole design of the apostle in this place. His purpose is, as hath been evidenced, and is acknowledged by all, to compare the Lord Christ as a high priest with the priests according to the law; and therein he shows his pre-eminence above them. Among the things which to this purpose he makes mention of, are his *sufferings*, verses 7, 8. Now if he suffered not when he was a priest, and as he was so, nothing could be less to his purpose. But whereas he principally designed to magnify the priestly office of Christ, or his person in the exercise of it, on the account of mercy and compassion, verse 2, he proves his excellency unto that end from his sufferings as he was a priest; whence in the future discharge of his office he is inclined to give out merciful assistance unto them that suffer. 5. The pretended distinction, that Christ in the days of his flesh was indeed the *cause of salvation*, but afterwards a *most perfect cause of salvation*, is unscriptural. The Lord Christ, in every condition, was the most perfect cause of salvation, although he performed some acts and works belonging thereunto in one estate, and some in another, according as the nature of the works themselves to be performed unto that end did require: for some things that were necessary unto our perfect salvation could not be accomplished but in a state of humiliation; and some, on the other hand, depended on his exaltation. 6. What is affirmed concerning Christ's being the *prophet* of the church, and *apostle* of God, in the days of his flesh, but of his being a king and priest afterwards, is another invention of this sort of men. He was always equally the king, priest, and prophet of the church, though he exercises these offices and the several acts or duties of them variously, according as the nature of them doth require.

Τελειωθείς, then, is, "consecrated," "dedicated," "consummated" sacredly. And it was necessary that Christ should be so, both from the nature of his office and work, which he was sacredly and solemnly to be set apart unto; and to answer the types of the Aaronical priesthood, which were so consecrated and set apart. And in this consecration of the Lord Christ unto his office of the priesthood, and his offering of sacrifice by virtue thereof, we may consider,—1. The sovereign *disposing cause;* 2. The *formal cause* constitutive of it; 3. The *external means.* 1. For the first, it was God, even *the Father.* He by his sovereign authority disposed, designed, called, and separated the Lord Christ unto his office; which we have spoken unto once, and must again consider it on the verse following. 2. The formal cause of it was his *own will,* obedientially giving up himself unto the authority and will of the Father, and that out of love unto and delight in the work itself, Ps. xl. 6–8. And in especial did he thereby dedicate, separate, and consecrate himself unto the principal work and duty of his office, or the offering of a sacrifice, John xvii. 19. 3. The external means were his *own sufferings,* especially in the offering of himself. This alone hath any difficulty attending it, how the Lord Christ can be said to be consecrated by his own sufferings in his offering, when his offering was an act of that office which he was consecrated unto. But I answer, that seeing an external means of the consecration of Christ was necessary, it could be no other but only his own sufferings in the offering of himself. For,— (1.) It was impossible for him, unworthy of him, and beneath both the dignity of his person and excellency of his office, with the very nature of it, that he should be consecrated by any other sacrifice, as of beasts and the like, as were the priests of old. To suppose the suffering and offering of beasts to be useful to this purpose, is repugnant to the whole design of God, and destructive of the office of Christ itself, as is manifest. (2.) He could not consecrate himself by an antecedent offering of himself; for he could not die often, nor suffer often, nor indeed had any need, or could righteously on the part of God have so done. It was therefore indispensably necessary that he should be consecrated, dedicated, and perfected himself, in and by the sacrifice that he offered for us, and the suffering wherewith it was accompanied. But withal, this was only the external means of his consecration; concerning which we may observe two things:—(1.) That as to the main or substance of his office, he was consecrated by his sufferings only in a way of evidence and manifestation. Really he was so by the acts of God his Father and himself before mentioned; only hereby he was openly declared to be the high priest of the church. (2.) There were some acts and duties of his sacerdotal office yet remaining to be performed, which he could not orderly engage into until he had suffered, because they supposed and depended on the efficacy of his suffering. These he was now made meet and fit for, and consequently unto the complete discharge of the whole course of his office.

Being thus consecrated, ἐγίνετο, " he was made," " he became," or "he was" only. Nothing was now wanting unto the great end aimed at in all these things, which is expressed in the next place.

'Εγίνετο.

Αἴτιος σωτηρίας αἰωνίου. Where his consecration is before mentioned, chap. ii. 10, he is said to become ἀρχηγὸς σωτηρίας,
a "captain of salvation." And it is affirmed of him   *Αἴτιος.*
with respect unto his actual conduct of believers unto salvation, by
the plentiful and powerful administration of his word and Spirit,
supplying them with all fruits of grace and truth needful unto that
end. Somewhat more is here intended. Αἴτιος is both "a cause in
general," and "he who is in any kind the cause of another thing."
And sometimes an "efficient cause," and sometimes a "meritorious
cause" is expressed thereby. In the first sense it is used by Isocrates
ad. Phileb.: Θεοὺς τῶν ἀγαθῶν ἡμῖν αἰτίους ὄντας,—"The gods are the authors" (or "causes") "of good things unto us;" that is, they bestow
them on or work them in us. And Aristotle, de Mundo, useth a phrase
of speech not unlike this: Ἡ ἐν οὐρανῷ δύναμις σύμπασιν αἴτιος γίνεται
σωτηρίας,—"The power that is in heaven is the cause of safety to all
things." And sometimes it is taken for a meritorious or procuring
cause, or him by whom any thing is procured; though most frequently in other authors he who is guilty or deserves evil is intended
thereby. So he: Οὐκ ἐγὼ αἴτιος εἶμι ἀλλὰ ζεὺς καὶ μοῖρα. So αἴτιος
is expounded by Eustathius, ὑπεύθυνος καὶ κολάσεως ἄξιος; but it is of
the same importance with respect unto what is good. The apostle,
therefore, hath in this word respect unto all the ways and means
whereby the Lord Christ either procured salvation for us or doth
actually bestow it upon us.

And here also it will be necessary, for the further clearing of the
importance of this word, to examine the endeavour of the forementioned expositor to corrupt the sense of it: " Est vero," saith he, "perfectissima salutis causa, quia perfectissima ratione salutem affert; nihil
illi deest, nec ad vires, ac facultatem, nec ad studium et voluntatem
salutis nostræ perficiendæ. Nam et pœnas peccatorum omnes a nobis
potentia suâ arcet, et vitam æternam largitur; spiritus nostros in
manus suas suscipit; succurrit nobis in afflictionibus et opem promptè
fert ne in fide succumbamus, inque pœnas peccatis debitas ea ratione
incidamus."

This, indeed, is "the voice of Jacob," but "the hands" of this
doctrine "are the hands of Esau." For whilst by these words, for
the most part true, we have a description given us how and on what
account the Lord Jesus Christ, as our high priest, is the author and
cause of our salvation, that which is indeed the principal reason
hereof, and without which the other consideration would not be effectual, is omitted and excluded. For in the room of his satisfaction
and expiation of sin by the propitiatory sacrifice of himself, we are
supplied with a keeping off, or driving from us, the punishment due
unto our sins. But this kind of delivery from the punishment of sin
by Christ is unscriptural, both name and thing. The true way was

that whereby he delivereth us from the curse and penalty of the law, so saving us from "the wrath to come." And this was by his "bearing our sins in his own body on the tree;" by being "made sin for us, that we might become the righteousness of God in him." See 2 Cor. v. 21, Rom. viii. 3, Gal. iii. 13, 1 Pet. ii. 24, Isa. liii. 6–8. The other things mentioned by this author Christ doth indeed, in carrying on the work of our salvation, and many other things of the like nature which he mentioneth not; all which are here included, but all with respect unto that foundation which was laid in his satisfactory oblation,—which is by him here excluded.

We may therefore consider the Lord Christ as the "author of eternal salvation," either with respect unto his *own acts* and works, whereby he wrought it or procured it; or with respect unto the *effects* of them, whereby it is actually communicated unto us: or we may consider him as the *meritorious*, procuring, purchasing, or as the *efficient* cause of our salvation. And in both respects the Lord Christ is said to be the author of our salvation, as the word doth signify him who is the cause of any thing in either kind. And where he is said to be the author of our salvation, nothing is to be excluded whereby he is so. In the *first* way, as the *meritorious cause* of our salvation, he is the author of it two ways:—1. By his *oblation;* 2. By his *intercession.* Both these belong unto the means whereby he procures our salvation. And these, in the first place, are respected, because the apostle treats immediately of our salvation as arising from the priestly office of Christ. And, 1. In his oblation, which was the offering of himself as an expiatory sacrifice for our sins, accompanied with the highest acts of obedience, and the supplications mentioned, verse 7, two things may be considered unto this end: —(1.) The satisfaction he made therein for sins, with the expiation of our guilt; which is the foundation of our salvation, without which it was impossible we should be partakers of it. (2.) The merit of his obedience therein, by which, according to the tenor of the covenant between God and him, he purchased and procured this salvation for us, Heb. ix. 14. On these two accounts was he in his oblation the author or cause of our salvation. 2. He is so also on the account of his intercession; for this is the name of that way whereby, with respect unto God, he makes effectual unto us what in his oblation he had purchased and procured, Heb. vii. 25–27. And this he doth as the meritorious cause thereof. But *secondly*, he is also the *efficient cause* of our salvation; inasmuch as he doth by his Spirit, his grace, and his glorious power, actually communicate it unto us and collate it upon us. And this he doth in sundry instances, the principal whereof may be named:—1. He teacheth us the way of salvation, and leads us into it; which Socinus fondly imagined to be the only reason why he is called our Saviour. 2. He makes us meet for it, and saves us from the power of sin, quickening, enlightening, and sanctifying of us, through the administration of his Spirit and grace. 3. He preserves and secures it unto us, in the assistance, deliverance, and victory he gives us against all oppositions, temptations, dangers, and troubles. 4. He both gives an entrance into it and assurance of it, in our justification and peace with God. 5. He will actually, by his glorious power, bestow upon us immortal life and glory, or give us the full possession of this salvation. In all these respects, with those many other streams of grace which flow from them, is the Lord Christ said to be the "author of our salvation."

This salvation is said to be "eternal;" whereof see our exposition on chap. ii. 3. So the redemption purchased by this offering of Christ is said to be "eternal," chap. ix. 12. *Αἰωνίου.* And it is called so absolutely, comparatively, and emphatically. 1. Absolutely; it is eternal, endless, unchangeable, and permanent. We are made for an eternal duration. By sin we had made ourselves obnoxious to eternal damnation. If the salvation procured for us were not eternal, it would not be perfect, nor suited unto our condition. 2. It is also said to be eternal in comparison with and in opposition unto that or those temporal deliverances, or salvations, which the people under the law were made partakers of by the interposition of their legal priests and their sacrifices. For there were temporary punishments, and excisions by death, threatened unto divers transgressions of the law, as it was the administration of a temporal covenant unto that people. From these they might be freed by the ministry of their priests and carnal atonements. But those who were delivered from those penalties, and saved from the sentence of the law, were not thereby absolutely secured of deliverance from the curse annexed unto the moral law as a covenant of works. Their salvation, therefore, was not eternal. And perhaps, also, respect may be had unto the deliverance of the people of old out of bondage, with their introduction into the land of Canaan, which was a temporary salvation only. But this is so absolutely; and, 3. Emphatically. It takes off indeed all temporal punishments as effects of the curse of the law. It gives temporal deliverance from fear and bondage by reason thereof. It supplies us with mercy, grace, and peace with God in this world. But all these things issuing in eternal blessedness, that being the end of them, being all bestowed on us in a tendency thereunto, the whole is emphatically called "eternal."

Lastly, There is a limitation of the subject of this salvation, unto whom the Lord Christ is the cause and author of it; it is to "all them that obey him,"—τοῖς ὑπακούουσιν αὐτῷ πᾶσιν. The expression is emphatical. To all and every one of them that obey him; not any one of them shall be excepted *Τοῖς ὑπακού-ουσιν αὐτῷ πᾶσιν.* from a share and interest in this salvation; nor shall any one of any other sort be admitted thereunto. He is "the author of eternal salvation" only unto "them that obey him;" whether there be any other author of salvation to those who neither know him nor obey him, they may do well to inquire who suppose that such may be saved. A certain number, then, they are, and not all men universally, unto whom he is the author of salvation. And as these elsewhere are described by the antecedent cause hereof, namely, their election, and being given unto Christ by the Father; so here they are so by the effects of it in themselves,—they are such as "obey him." Ὑπακούω is "to obey upon hearing," "dicto obedire;" originally it signifies only "to hearken" or "hear," but with a readiness, or subjection of mind unto what is heard, to do accordingly. Hence it is faith in the first place that is intended in this obedience. For it is that which, in order unto our participation of Christ, first "cometh by hearing," Rom. x. 17; and that partly because the object of it, which is the promise, is proposed outwardly unto it in the word, where we hear of it and hear it; and partly because the preaching of the word, which we receive by hearing, is the only ordinary means of ingene-rating faith in our souls. Hence to believe is expressed by ὑπακούειν, "to hear" so as to answer the ends of what is proposed unto us. The ensuing subjecting our souls unto Christ, in the keeping of his com-mands, is "the obedience of faith." We may now draw some ob-servations from the words, for our further instruction: as,—

Obs. I. All that befell the Lord Christ, all that he did and suffered, was necessary to this end, that he might be the cause of eternal sal-vation to believers.

Being "consecrated," or "perfected," he became so; and what be-longed unto that consecration we have declared. This was that which he was of God designed unto. And the disposal of all things concern-ing him to this end was the fruit of infinite wisdom, goodness, and righteousness. No more was required of him, that he might be the author of eternal salvation unto believers, but what was absolutely necessary thereunto; nor was there an abatement made of any thing that was so necessary. Some have said, that "one drop of the blood of Christ was sufficient for the salvation of the whole world." And some have made use of that saying, pretending that the overplus of his satisfaction and merit is committed to their disposal; which they manage to their advantage. But the truth is, every drop of his blood,—that is, all he did and all he suffered, for matter and man-ner, in substance and circumstance,—was indispensably necessary unto this end. For God did not afflict his only Son willingly, or without cause in any thing, and his whole obedience was afflictive. He did not die nor suffer δωρεάν, Gal. ii. 21, without an antecedent cause and reason. And nothing was wanting that was requisite hereunto. Some suppose that Christ was and is the author of salvation unto us only by showing, teaching, declaring the will of God, and the way of faith and obedience, whereby we may be saved. But why, then, was he consecrated in the way before described ? why did it " become God to make him perfect through sufferings?" why was he " bruised and put to grief ?" for what cause was he reduced unto the state and condition described in the verse foregoing ? Certainly such men have low thoughts of sin and its guilt, of the law and its curse, of the holiness and righteousness of God, of his love to Jesus Christ, yea, and of his wisdom, who suppose that the salvation of sinners could be attained without the price and merit of all that he did and suffered, or that God would have so dealt with his only Son, might it any otherwise have been attained. I might show in particular from the Scripture, how every thing that Christ did and suffered was not only useful, but necessary also, to this purpose, allowing the wisdom and righteousness of God to give the standard and measure of what is so; but I must not too far digress. And hence it is evident,—1. How great a matter it is to have sinners made partakers of eternal redemption; 2. How great, how infinite was that wisdom, that love and grace, which contrived it and brought it about; 3. How great and terrible will be the ruin of them by whom this salvation is despised, when tendered according to the gospel, etc.

Obs. II. The Lord Christ was consecrated himself in and by the sacrifice that he offered for us, and what he suffered in so doing. This belonged to the perfection both of his office and his offering. He had none to offer for him but himself, and he had nothing to offer but himself.

Obs. III. The Lord Christ alone is the only principal cause of our eternal salvation, and that in every kind. There are many instrumental causes of it in sundry kinds. So is faith; so are the word and all the ordinances of the gospel; they are instrumental, helping, furthering causes of salvation,—but all in subordination unto Christ, who is the principal, and who alone gives use and efficacy unto all others. How he is so, by his oblation and intercession, by his Spirit and grace, in his ruling and teaching, offices and power, is the chief work of the ministry to declare. God hath appointed that in all things he should have the pre-eminence. There are both internal and external means of salvation that he hath appointed, whereby he communicates unto us the virtue and benefit of his mediation. These it is our duty to make use of according to his appointment; so that we expect no relief or help from them, but only by them. So much as they have of Christ in them, so much as they convey of Christ unto us, of so much use they are, and no more. Not only, therefore, to set up any thing in competition against him, as the works of the law, or in conjunction with him, as the Papists do their penances, and pilgrimages, and pardons, and purgatory, is pernicious and

ruinous unto the souls of men; but also, to expect any assistance by,
or acceptance in, such acts of religion or worship as he hath not
appointed, and therefore doth not fill up with his grace, nor communicate from his own fulness by it, is the highest folly imaginable.
This, therefore, is the great wisdom of faith, to esteem of Christ
and to rest upon him as that which he is indeed, namely, the only
author of salvation unto them that believe. For,—

Obs. IV. Salvation is confined to believers; and those who look
for salvation by Christ, must secure it unto themselves by faith and
obedience. It is Christ alone who is the cause of our salvation; but
he will save none but those that obey him. He came to save sinners, but not such as choose to continue in their sins; though the
gospel be full of love, of grace, of mercy, and pardon, yet herein the
sentence of it is peremptory and decretory: " He that believeth
not shall be damned."

<h2 style="text-align:center">VERSE 10.</h2>

In the 10th verse the apostle returns unto the improvement of
the testimony given unto the priesthood of Christ taken from Ps.
cx. And hereby he makes way unto another necessary digression,
without which he could not profitably pursue the instruction which
he intended [for] the Hebrews from that testimony, as we shall see in
the following verses. He had drawn forth nothing out of that testimony of the psalmist, but only that the Lord Christ was a priest; and
when he had done this in general, which was necessary for him to do,
he declares his sacerdotal actings which he was enabled unto by
virtue of that office: for a priest he must be who so " offered" unto
God as he did. But he had yet a further and peculiar intention in
the production of that testimony. And this was, not only to prove
him to be a priest in general, and so to have right to perform all
sacerdotal offices and duties in behalf of the people, which he did
accordingly, verses 7–9, but withal to declare the especial nature and
pre-eminence of his priesthood, as typed or shadowed out by the
priesthood of Melchisedec. The demonstration and declaration
whereof is that which he now designs. But so soon as he hath laid
down his general assertion, in this verse, considering the greatness of
the matter he had in hand, as also the difficulty of understanding it
aright which he should find among the Hebrews, he diverts unto a
preparatory digression, wherein he continues the remainder of this
and the whole ensuing chapter, resuming his purpose here proposed in the beginning of the seventh chapter.

Ver. 10.—Προσαγορευθεὶς ὑπὸ τοῦ Θεοῦ ἀρχιερεὺς κατὰ τὴν τάξιν Μελχισεδέκ.[1]

---

[1] TRANSLATIONS.—Προσαγ. Declared of God.—*Craik.* Having been named

Ver. 10.—Called of God an high priest after the order of Melchisedec.

Προσαγορευθείς, "called." He refers unto the testimony produced, verse 6. And it is here manifest who it is that is intended in those words, "As he saith in another place, Thou art a priest." That is, God said so; for he was   *Προσαγορευ-θείς.* προσαγορευθείς ὑπὸ τοῦ Θεοῦ,—*dictus, cognominatus,* נִקְרָא; "called," "pronounced." "Salutatus," as "salutare aliquem regem," is to pronounce him so. And we may inquire into the reason of this peculiar expression. He had before declared that the Lord Christ, the Son of God, was "a priest after the order of Melchisedec." Now there may be more supposed herein than is indeed intended. When we say that Phinehas, and Eli, and Zadok, were high priests of the order of Aaron, we intend that they had the very same priesthood that Aaron had. But that is not the meaning of the expression in this place and matter. The priesthood of Christ and of Melchisedec were not the same; for that of Christ is such as no mere man could possibly sustain or exercise: only these two priesthoods, as expressed in the Scripture, had an especial agreement in sundry things, the particulars whereof the apostle enumerates and explains, chap vii. For on the account of sundry things that were singular in the person of Melchisedec (either absolutely, or as his story is related in the Scripture, which is the rule of our comprehension of sacred things), and suited to prefigure or shadow out the Lord Christ in his priesthood, above what was in Aaron or his office, he is said to be made "a priest after the order of Melchisedec," or according to the things spoken of Melchisedec. He is not said to be a priest of the order, but עַל־דִּבְרָתִי, κατὰ τάξιν, according to the things spoken of Melchisedec, as he was a priest; after the manner of what is related concerning him. And this, in my judgment, is the reason of the use of this word προσαγορευθείς in this place; for it doth not signify a call to office,—that is κλητός constantly,—but it is the denomination of him who is so called, for some certain reason. 'Because,' saith the apostle, 'of the especial resemblance that was between what Melchisedec was and what Christ was to be, God called his priesthood Melchisedecian; whereon I must necessarily declare wherein that resemblance did consist:' which he doth afterwards. So was his priesthood surnamed from his type, and not Aaronical.

"Called of God ἀρχιερεύς." Verse 6, he renders the Hebrew כֹּהֵן by ἱερεύς only, "a priest." And it signifies no more. For where the high priest in a note of distinction is intended, they call him כֹּהֵן הַגָּדוֹל, the "great" or "high priest;"   *Ἀρχιερεύς.*

of God.—*Conybeare and Howson.* Genannt.—*De Wette.* Craik justly remarks, "The term ought to be distinguished from καλούμενος, verse 4. It literally signifies 'addressed,' and refers to the form of the declaration in Ps. cx."—ED.

" sacerdos magnus," " summus;" " pontifex," "pontifex summus."
But the whole nature, right, and privilege of the office, belonged
unto any one as a priest. Every high priest was a priest absolutely;
but every priest was not a high priest also. Aaron and his
sons were together separated unto the same office of the priesthood,
Exod. xxviii. 1; but some duties in the execution of the office were
peculiarly reserved unto him who was chief and singular. And
because he who was singular had thus sundry pre-eminences above
other priests, and also that the discharge of some duties, and offering
of some sacrifices, as that of the great atonement, were committed
unto him alone, which were peculiarly typical of the sacerdotal
actions of Christ; as he is called ἱερεύς, a "priest" absolutely, as being
invested in the real office of the priesthood, so is he termed ἀρχιερεύς
by our apostle, the " chief" or "high priest," not because there were
any other in or of the same order with himself, but because all the
pre-eminences of the priesthood were in him alone, and he really
answered what was typed out by the singular actings of the Aaronical high priest.

He was thus " called an high priest κατὰ τὴν τάξιν Μελχισεδέκ,"—
"according to the order of Melchisedec." This is not a
limitation of his priesthood to a certain order, but a reference unto that priesthood whereby his was most eminently prefigured. And there are two things intended herein by the
apostle. First, A concession that he was not a high priest according
unto the constitution, law, and order of the Aaronical priesthood. And
this he doth not only grant here, but elsewhere positively asserts, chap.
viii. 4; yea, and proves at large that it was impossible he should be so,
and that if he had been so, his priesthood would not have been of
advantage unto the church, chap. vii. 11-14, etc. He was neither
called as they were, nor came to his office as they did, nor was confirmed in it by the same means, nor had right unto it by the law, nor
was his work the same with theirs. Secondly, That there was a priesthood antecedent unto and diverse from that of Aaron, appointed of God
to represent the way and manner how he would call the Lord Christ
unto his office, as also the nature of his person in the discharge thereof,
in what is affirmed and what is concealed concerning him who singly
and alone was vested with that office; that is, Melchisedec. Look in
what manner and by what means he became a priest; by the same,
with other peculiar excellencies and pre-eminencies added thereunto,
was Christ also called, so as that he may be said, and is termed of
God, a priest after his order or manner of appointment. For as he,
without ceremony, without sacrifice, without visible consecration,
without "the law of a carnal commandment," was constituted a
high priest, so was Christ also, by the immediate word of the Father,
saying unto him, " Thou art my Son, a priest for ever," or " after

the power of an endless life." And in this sense is he called "a priest after the order of Melchisedec."

I have elsewhere evinced the corruption of the Targum on Ps. cx. 4, whence these words are taken; also the malice of some of the late Jewish masters, who would have Melchisedec to be there called כֹהֵן, a "priest" improperly, as David's sons were said to be כֹּהֲנִים,—that is, "princes." So the Targum, "Thou art a great prince." But the expression here used by the psalmist is taken directly from Gen. xiv. 18, וְהוּא כֹהֵן לְאֵל עֶלְיוֹן,—"And he was a priest of" (or "unto") "the most high God." Here none of the Jews themselves are so profligate as to pretend that a prince is intended,—a prince to the most high God! It is nothing, therefore, but that obstinacy which is the effect of their unbelief, which casts them on the shift of this evasion. Some observations do ensue:—

Obs. I. God was pleased to put a signal honour upon the person and office of Melchisedec, that in them there should be an early and excellent representation made of the person and priesthood of Jesus Christ.

I am not here to inquire who this Melchisedec was, nor wherein the nature of his priesthood did consist. I shall do it elsewhere. Here he is reflected on as an eminent type of Christ in his office. And in how many particulars the resemblance between them did consist, our apostle doth afterwards declare. In the meantime we may observe, in general, 1. That all the real honour which God did unto any persons under the old testament, it was in order unto the prefiguring of Christ, "that in all things he might have the pre-eminence." Other reason of the great exaltation of Melchisedec in the church, even above Abraham, the father of the faithful, there was none. 2. He was the only type of the person of Christ that ever was in the world. Others were types of the Lord Christ in the execution of his office, but none but he were ever types of his person. For being introduced "without father, without mother, having neither beginning of days nor end of life," he was "made like unto the Son of God," and represented his person, which none other did. 3. He was the first personal type of Christ in the world. After him there were others; as Isaac and Aaron, Joshua, David, and Solomon; but he was the first, and therefore the most eminent. 4. He was a type of Christ in these two great offices of a king and a priest; which none but he ever was. 5. The circumstances of his name, and the place of his reign, whence he was a "king of righteousness and peace," do most gloriously represent the whole effect of the mediation of Christ; all which may be spoken to afterwards. Now the exaltation of any one in the like kind is a mere act of sovereign grace in God. He might so honour whom he pleased. Hence is Melchisedec introduced without the consideration of any circumstances of prerogative on his own part whatever, that all his dignity might be owned to be of God's sovereign pleasure. God, therefore, having referred all to Christ, it is our wisdom to do likewise.

Obs. II. As the Lord Christ received all his honour, as mediator, from God the Father, so the ground and measure of our giving glory and honour unto him as such depend on the revelation and declaration of it unto us. He was termed, called, and declared of God "an high priest after the order of Melchisedec." He made him so, which was his honour; he declared him to be so: whence we ought to give all honour unto him. But this hath been spoken unto elsewhere.

And from the respect that these words have unto the precedent verse, we may observe, that,—

Obs. III. It is an evidence and testimony that the Lord Christ was able to be, and is "the author of eternal salvation unto all them that obey him," because he is "a priest after the order of Melchisedec;" that is, his priesthood is eternal.

VERSE 11.

In the 11th verse the apostle enters upon his designed digression. And first he expresseth the occasion and reason of it, taken from the subject or matter which in this place it was necessary for him to insist upon, and the condition, with the former carriage, or rather miscarriage, of them unto whom he spake. Hence he evidenceth the necessity of his digression, which consists in such awakening admonitions as they then and we now stand in need of, when we are to be excited unto a due attendance unto spiritual and mysterious truths.

Ver. 11.—Περὶ οὗ πολὺς ἡμῖν ὁ λόγος καὶ δυσερμήνευτος λέγειν, ἐπεὶ νωθροὶ γεγόνατε ταῖς ἀκοαῖς.

Περὶ οὗ, "de quo," "of whom." The Syriac, עֲלוֹהִי דֵין עַל הָנָא מַלְכִּיזֶדֶק; "of whom, even of the same Melchisedec:" which no other translation followeth. Πολὺς ἡμῖν ὁ λόγος. Vulg., "grandis nobis sermo." Rhem., "of whom we have great speech;" improperly, and unintelligibly. Arias, "multus nobis sermo," "we have much to say." Eras., "multa nobis forent dicenda," "many things should be spoken by us:" intimating as if they were pretermitted; namely, what might have been spoken. Beza, "multa nobis sunt dicenda," "we have many things to say." Syriac, סַגִּיאָא הִי לַן מֶלְתָא לְמֵאמְרָהּ, "multa forent verba facienda." Translat. Polyglot., "we might use many words." Tremel., "multus est nobis sermo quem eloquamur;" "we have much discourse that we may utter" or "speak:" properly, "we have many words to be spoken." Καὶ δυσερμήνευτος λέγειν. Vulg. Lat., "et interpretabilis ad dicendum." Valla corrected this translation. Erasmus first suspected that it was originally in the translation, "ininterpretabilis;" which, although a barbarous word, yet evidently intends the sense of the original. Hence it is rendered by the Rhemists, "inexplicable to utter;" which expresseth neither the Latin nor the original. The expositors who follow that translation contend, (whilst the word doth signify negatively, "that cannot be interpreted;" or affirmatively, "that needs interpretation;") with wonderful vanity, as Erasmus

manifests, if the word have any signification, it is, "that which is easy to be interpreted," contrary to the original. Arias, "difficilis interpretatio dicere." Eras.,
"difficilia explicatu," "things hard to be explained." So Beza. Ours, "hard to
be uttered;" difficult to be expounded in speaking. Syr., וְעֻסְקָא לִמְפַשָּׁקוּתָהּ, "et
labor ad exponendum;" or, as Tremel., "et occupatio ad exponendum illud;"—
"and it is hard labour to expound it,"—a laborious work. "Of whom we have
many things to say, and those difficult to be expounded." Ἐπεὶ νωθροὶ γεγόνατε.
Vulg., "quoniam imbecilli facti estis;" "because ye are become weak," improperly. Arias, "segnes," "slothful." So Erasmus and Beza. "Dull." Syr,
כְּרִיהָא, "infirm," "weak." Ταῖς ἀκοαῖς. Vulg. Lat., "ad audiendum," "weak
to hear." Arias, "auribus." So Erasmus and Beza. But ἀκοή signifies the
faculty of hearing and the act of hearing, as well as the instrument of it. "Dull
of hearing."[1]

Ver. 11.—Concerning whom we have many things to
speak, and difficult to be explained, seeing you are become slothful in hearing [or *dull of hearing*].

There are four things combined in this verse in the way of a summary of the discourse that is to ensue:—1. The subject whereof he
would treat; "concerning whom." 2. The manner how he would
treat concerning it; he had "many things to say." 3. The nature of
those things, not so much absolutely in themselves as out of respect
unto the Hebrews; they were "difficult to be explained" and understood. 4. The reason hereof, namely, because "they were become
dull in hearing."

"Concerning whom;"—that is, Melchisedec, not Christ; and so the
"Syriac" translation expresseth it. But he intends not
to treat of him absolutely, neither of his person nor his
office. These were things now past, and to search curiously into
them was not for the edification of the church. And the apostle
had no design to trouble the minds of believers with things unnecessary or curious. And it had not been amiss if this had been
well considered by them who have laden us with so many needless
speculations about his person and office; and some of them directly
opposite to the scope and design of the apostle. But the purpose
of the apostle is, to treat of him so far and wherein he was a type of
Christ, and as such is represented in the story concerning him.
Hence some render περὶ οὗ, by "de qua re," "of which matter;" that
is, the similitude and conformity between Melchisedec and Christ,
which was a great, necessary, and instructive truth.

Πολὺς ἡμῖν ὁ λόγος, "we have much to say;" many things to speak
or treat of. But not the multitude of the things only
which he had to speak, but the weight and importance
also of them is intended in this expression. So the

Περὶ οὗ.

Πολὺς ἡμῖν
ὁ λόγος.

[1] TRANSLATION.—Γεγόν. implies a course of declension, which our author sufficiently brings out by his translation. Conybeare and Howson render it more
emphatically, "since ye have grown dull in understanding."—ED.

"grandis sermo" of the Vulgar, intends not loftiness of speech, but the weight of the things spoken of. And when the apostle comes to insist particularly on the things here intended, they appear rather to be mysterious and important than many. However, I deny not but that the apostle intimates that there were sundry, yea many things of that importance to be declared and insisted on, on this occasion.

Some translations, as we have seen, supply the words by "forent," some by "sunt." The former seems to have apprehended that the apostle intended wholly to forbear treating on this subject, and that because it was so deep and mysterious, that, considering their condition, it would not be profitable unto them, nor for their edification. Wherefore he lets them know, that although he could treat of many things concerning Melchisedec, and such as were necessary to be declared, yet, because of their incapacity to receive them, he would forbear. And sundry interpreters do so apprehend his mind. But this is no way consistent with his express undertaking to declare all those things unto them, chap. vii. Wherefore he only declares in general, that he hath many weighty mysteries to instruct them in, but would not *immediately* engage in that work, until he had spoken that unto them which was needful to prepare them unto a due attention. And his ensuing discourses, before he returns unto this subject again, are not reasons why he will totally intermit the handling of them, but a due admonition unto them for precedent negligences, whereby they might be excited to prepare themselves in a due manner for the receiving of what he had to declare.

The nature of the things treated of, with respect unto the capacity of the Hebrews, is nextly declared: Λόγος δυσερμή-νευτος λέγειν. How variously these words are rendered we have seen before. It may be the things which Paul himself here calls δυσερμήνευτα, are those which Peter intends in his epistle, calling them δυσνόητα, 2 Pet. iii. 16, "things hard to be understood;" which is the same with what our apostle here intends. The phrase, δυσερμήνευτος λέγειν, is somewhat unusual, and the sense of it not easy to be expressed to the full in our language. Λέγειν seems to be for ἐν τῷ λέγειν, "in dicendo," "in the speaking" or uttering of it: or, when it is spoken and uttered, it is "hard to be interpreted," that is, to be understood. For the interpretation intended is not that of the apostle in speaking, but that which is made in the understanding of them that hear it. For he that hears a thing uttered, and considers it, makes the interpretation of it unto himself, as Jerome observes, Epist. ad Evagr. The apostle doth not, therefore, intimate,—1. That it would be any *hard or difficult matter unto him to declare* all things concerning the conformity between Melchisedec and Christ, which were necessary to be known unto the edification of the church; for what he had by revelation and inspiration (as he had all that he wrote as a part of the church's canon, or rule of faith and obedience) was no matter of difficulty in him to find out and express. It is true, that being called to be an apostle in an especial manner, not having conversed with the Lord Christ in the flesh, he was in vision taken up into heaven, and there heard immediately from him ἄρρητα ῥήματα ἃ οὐκ ἐξὸν ἀνθρώπῳ λαλῆσαι, 2 Cor. xii. 4,—"unspeakable words, that were not possible" (or "lawful") "for a man to utter." The things and manner of Christ's speech unto him were accompanied with such a glory as human nature unperfected cannot bear. But these things belonged unto his own particular confirmation in his office and work, and not to the edification of the church in general. For what he received by revelation unto that end he freely and fully declared, Acts xx. 20, 27. Nor, 2. That his *manner* of the declaration of it would be obscure and hard to be understood; as some have blasphemously accused his writings of obscurity and intricacy. Nor can any pretence be taken hence against the clearness and perspicuity of the Scriptures in the declaration of divine truths and revelations. For it is of *things themselves*, and not of the manner of their declaration, that he speaks, as also doth Peter in the place before mentioned. Two things, therefore, are intended by the apostle in this expression:—1. That, in what he had to speak on this subject, there were some things *in their own nature sublime and mysterious.* In divine revelations there are great differences in the matter of them. For the manner of their declaration in the Scripture, they thus far agree, that every thing is declared absolutely as it ought to be, with respect unto the end of the Scripture; that is, the glory of God and the edification of the church. But among the things themselves revealed there is great difference. Some of them are nearer and more exposed unto our understandings and capacities; others of them are more sublime and mysterious, and more exceed our comprehension. And such are the things intended by the apostle. Wherefore, 2. He doth not speak of these things only with respect unto *their own nature*, but unto *our understandings*, which are weak and imperfect. It is a difficult matter for us in any tolerable measure to comprehend divine mysteries, when plainly propounded unto us. But yet neither are these things spoken positively in this place with respect merely unto the understanding of them to whom they are delivered, but with respect unto a peculiar indisposition in the minds of some, hindering them in the discharge of their duty. This the apostle chargeth in particular upon these Hebrews in this verse; and then aggravates their fault, from its causes, nature, circumstances, and consequences, in those that follow to the end of this chapter and the midst of the next.

And when he hath hereby prepared them to a more diligent attention, he returns to declare the things themselves which he here intends. And the Romanists do very weakly shield themselves from the force of an argument which ariseth up of its own accord against the great foundation of their superstition, from the nature of the apostle's discourse in this epistle. For whereas he professedly treateth of the priesthood and sacrifice of Christ in all their concerns, and in their whole use in the church of God, whence is it that he makes no mention in the least, nor gives the least intimation of their priesthood, mass, and sacrifice of it; by which alone, if you will believe them, the other things are communicated and made effectual to the church? I do not mention now what (God assisting) I shall prove afterwards, namely, that he declares those things which are utterly inconsistent with them, and destructive of them; but we only inquire at present whence it should come to pass that in this discourse,—which, if the things they pretend are true, is neither complete, nor useful, nor scarcely intelligible without them, —he should make no mention of them at all? 'This,' say our Rhemists on this place, 'was because the mass was too great a mystery for St Paul to acquaint these Hebrews withal; and therefore he here intimates that he would not acquaint them with it, or impart the doctrine of it unto them.' It seems, therefore, that the mass is a greater mystery than the sacrifice of Christ on the cross, or any thing that concerned his own personal priesthood! This seems to be a supposition of a competent boldness, wherein it is much if they should believe themselves. Besides, whereas the mass is one of the sacraments of the church, continually to be celebrated among the faithful, whence is it that the apostle should dread to speak of the nature of that unto them which they were made partakers of, and which they were exercised in every day, if it were then known, or in use in the church? They would make Christianity a very strange religion, wherein it should be a thing dangerous and unlawful to instruct men in their duty. But, as we have proved before, the things here intended by the apostle are all of them resumed and handled by him in the ensuing chapters; which makes it sufficiently evident that their mass and priesthood were none of them.

Lastly, The reason of the foregoing assertion is added, "Seeing ye are slothful," "slow," or "dull in hearing." Νωθροί.
Νωθροὶ ταῖς ἀκοαῖς. This word is nowhere used in the New Testament but here and chap. vi. 12, where we render it "slothful." Νωθρός est, "qui non facilè potest ὠθεῖσθαι;" "one that is not easily stirred or moved, heavy, slothful, inactive, dull," opposed to him that is diligent in his business; as Prov. xxii. 29. Ταῖς ἀκοαῖς. Ἀκοή is used both for the "ear," the "faculty of hearing," the "act

of hearing," and "things heard." Wherefore "slothful in hearing," whereby the apostle declares the fault of these Hebrews, is a metaphorical expression. 'You are,' saith he, 'in hearing of the word, like slothful persons, who do no work, accomplish no endeavours, attain no good end, because of their earthly, dull, inactive constitutions and inclinations.' The conditions and qualities of such persons Solomon paints to the life, Prov. xii. 27, xv. 19, xviii. 9, xix. 24, xxi. 25, xxii. 13, xxiv. 30–34, xxvi. 13–15. He abounds in the reproof of it, as being one of the most pernicious vices that our nature is subject unto. And in the reproach that Christ will cast upon unfaithful ministers at the last day, there is nothing greater than that they were "slothful," Matt. xxv. 26. Unto such persons, therefore, the apostle compares these Hebrews, not absolutely, but as to this one duty of hearing. The gospel, as preached, he calls λόγον τῆς ἀκοῆς, "the word of hearing," Heb. iv. 2 ;—the word that is communicated unto men by hearing, which they so receive, Rom. x. 17; which ought to be heard and diligently attended unto. This duty the Scripture expresseth by προσέχειν, Acts xvi. 14; which is "diligently to hearken and attend, so as to cleave unto the things heard." A neglect hereof the apostle chargeth the Hebrews withal. 'You stir not up,' saith he, 'the faculties of your souls, your minds and understandings, to conceive aright and comprehend the things that are spoken unto you ; you attend not unto them according to their importance and your concernment in them ; you treasure not them up in your hearts, consciences, and memories, but let them slip out, and forget them:' for the apostle intends all faults and negligences that concur unto unprofitable hearing. It is not a natural imbecility of mind that he blames in them ; nor such a weakness of understanding as they might be obnoxious unto for want of improvement by education; nor a want of learning and subtilty to search into things deep and difficult: for these, although they are all defects and hinderances in hearing, yet are they not crimes. But it is a moral negligence and inadvertency, a want of the discharge of their duty according to their ability in attending unto the means of their instruction, that he chargeth them withal. The natural dulness of our minds in receiving spiritual things is, it may be, included ; but it is our depraved affections, casting us on a neglect of our duty, that is condemned. And there are sundry things wherein we are hereby instructed ; as,—

Obs. I. There are revealed in the Scripture sundry deep and mysterious truths, which require a peculiar diligence in our attendance unto their declaration, that we may rightly understand them or receive them in a due manner. To evince this proposition, I shall lay down and confirm the ensuing observations :—

1. There are some things or truths revealed in the Scripture which

have a *peculiar remark* put upon them, as those which are deep
and mysterious. See 1 Tim. iii. 16; Eph. v. 32; 1 Cor. ii. 6–8, xv.
51; Eph. iii. 4, 5.

2. The *doctrines* concerning these things are not dark and obscure, but clear, evident, and perspicuous. We may safely grant
that what is not clearly delivered in the Scripture is of no indispensable necessity to be known and believed. And there are reasons
innumerable why God would not leave any important truth under
an obscure revelation. And none pretend they are so but those
who first reject the things revealed; then all things spoken of them
seem dark and obscure unto them. There are two practices about
these things that are equally pernicious:—(1.) A pretence of things
mysterious, that are not clearly revealed. This the apostle calls a
curious prying or "intruding into things which we have not seen;"
which who so do are "vainly puffed up by their fleshly mind," Col.
ii. 18; and which he cautioneth us against, Rom. xii. 3. The mysteries that are clearly revealed in the Scripture, as to the doctrine
of them, are sufficient to exercise the utmost of our sober inquiries
and humble speculations. To create heavenly mysteries, like the
pretended Areopagite, in our own imaginations,—to squeeze them
out of single letters, words, or expressions, like the cabbalistical
Jews,—to vent our own fancies for mysteries,—or to cover plain
and sober truths with raw and uncouth terms, that they may put
on the vizard of being mysterious,—is to forsake the word, and to
give up ourselves to the conduct of our own imaginations. (2.) A
neglect and contempt of clear, open revelations, because the things
revealed are mysterious. And as this is the foundation of the most
outrageous errors that at this day infest Christian religion, as in the
Socinians and others, so it is that poison which secretly influenceth
many amongst ourselves to an open contempt of the most important
truths of the gospel. They will not, indeed, declare them to be
false; but they judge it meet that they should be let alone where
they are, as things not by us to be understood.

3. The depths and mystery of the things intended lie in *them-*
selves and their own nature. They are effects of divine wisdom,
yea, the greatest which ever God will either work or declare. Hence
the doctrine of them is called his "wisdom," 1 Cor. ii. 7; his "manifold wisdom," Eph. iii. 10; as having put the most eminent cha-
racters of infinite wisdom upon them. We can see other things by
the light of the sun better than we can see the sun itself; not because the sun is less visible and discernible in itself, but because
our visive faculty is too weak to bear its resplendent light. So is
it with these mysterious things: they are great, glorious, true, evident in themselves; but our understandings are weak, and unable
fully to comprehend them.

4. The principal of these mysteries concern the *person, offices,* and *grace* of our Lord Jesus Christ. So as to his person, it is declared by our apostle, 1 Tim. iii. 16; as to his work and office, Phil. ii. 7–11; and as to his grace, Eph. iii. 8–11. And therefore,—

5. Of all things which we are to learn in the dispensation of the word, these are we with most diligence to attend unto, Phil. iii. 8–10, as those wherein the glory of God and our own obedience are most concerned. Some suppose that we should wholly content ourselves with the plain lessons of morality, without any further diligent inquiry into these mysteries; which is at once to reject, if not the whole, yet the principal part of the gospel, and that without which what remains will not be available. Sad indeed would be the condition of the church of God, if preachers and hearers should agree in the neglect and contempt of the mysteries of the gospel. These, I say, are the things which our utmost diligence, in reading, hearing, and meditating on the word, in prayer and holy supplications for light and wisdom, that we may know them, and grow in the knowledge of them, is indispensably required of us.

Obs. II. It is necessary for the ministers of the gospel sometimes to insist on the most abstruse and difficult truths, that are revealed for our edification.

The apostle doth not only insist upon the sacerdotal office of Christ, the nature and exercise of it in his own person, but he judgeth it necessary to explain the mystical prefiguration of it in the priesthood of Melchisedec. Why might not that have been omitted, seeing he expressly acknowledgeth that the things concerning it were hard and difficult in the sense before explained, and the doctrine which he proposed in general might be declared and taught without it? Is not this a needless curiosity, and such as tended rather to the amusing and perplexing of his disciples than their edification? 'No,' saith he; 'there may be curiosity in the manner, but there can be none in the matter, when we declare and expound only what is revealed in the Scripture. It was not in vain that the Holy Ghost recorded these things concerning the person and office of Melchisedec. The faith and obedience of the church are concerned in the due understanding of them; and therefore this explanation is not to be neglected.' Wherefore, to clear and direct our duty in this matter, we may consider,—1. That it ought to be the design of every faithful minister, in the course of his ministry, *to withhold nothing* from those committed unto his charge that belongs unto their edification, as do all things that are written in the Scripture, but to declare unto them "the whole counsel of God," so far as he himself hath attained, Acts xx. 20, 27. To give times and seasons unto especial truths, doctrines, expositions, is committed unto his own prudence by Him by whom he is

made an "overseer, to feed the church of God;" but his design in
general is, to "keep back nothing that is profitable,"—as is the sense
of all the Scripture, even in its most abstruse and difficult passages,
2 Tim. iii. 16.   2. That his duty is, as much as in him lieth, to carry
on his hearers unto *perfection*, Heb. vi. 1 : for the ministry itself
being given to the church "for the perfecting of the saints," Eph.
iv. 12, 13, or the bringing of them all "unto a perfect man" in Christ
Jesus, every one who is faithful in that office ought to make it his
design and work.   And hereunto doth their growth in light and
knowledge, and that of the most mysterious truths, in an especial
manner belong.   And whereas some, through the blessing of God
on their holy diligence and endeavours, do thrive and grow in light
and knowledge above others, they are not to be clogged in their
progress, by being bound up always unto their lines and measures
who, it may be, are retarded through their own sloth and negligence.   This we shall have afterwards occasion to speak unto.   But,
3. Whereas the greatest part of our congregations, it may be, frequently are such as stand in need of milk, and are not skilful as yet
in the word of righteousness, it is our duty also to insist on those
plainer truths which are suited unto their edification.   4. Those
who are called by the state of their flocks to engage sometimes in
the exposition of *abstruse and mysterious* passages of Scripture,
may do well to observe the ensuing rules, all which may be evidently gathered from the way and manner of our apostle's treating
concerning Melchisedec and his office:—(1.) That their interpretations be openly and evidently conformable to the *analogy of faith*.
To search after new opinions in, or to found new or peculiar doctrines on, abstruse and mystical passages of Scripture, is a pestilent
curiosity.   (2.) That the exposition of them be *necessary* from present circumstances, which are principally two:—[1.] That the things
contained in them do belong unto some important truth, which is
plainly declared for the substance of it in other places, although
from them it may receive light and illustration.   Thus our apostle
doth not designedly, and on set purpose for its own sake, choose
out that abstruse and mysterious passage about Melchisedec; but
whereas he was engaged in the declaration of the priesthood of
Christ, he taketh in the consideration thereof, as that which did
belong thereunto, and which would add light and argument to the
truth he had in hand.   And herein consists the greatest wisdom in
the treating of such places, namely, when we can reduce them to
that proper head and seat of doctrine in other places whereunto
they do belong, which is our sure guide in their interpretation.   To
choose out such places for our subjects to speak on separately, and
to make them the sole basis of our discourse, may have somewhat
of an unwarrantable curiosity.   [2.] When they offer themselves in

the course of our work or ministry, where God gives light into the sense of the Holy Ghost in them, they are not to be *waived*, as we would be esteemed faithful in our work   (3.) Always to remember that what is so abstrusely expressed is so on purpose, *for the exercise*, as of our faith, humility, and subjection of mind unto the authority of the Holy Ghost speaking in the Scripture, so of our diligence and dependence on him for instruction; which calls for an especial frame of spirit in the work we undertake.   (4.) That the difficulty and necessity of treating concerning such things be intimated unto them who are to be instructed, that so they may be prepared to attend with diligence, and judge with sobriety of what is delivered.   So deals our apostle with the Hebrews on this occasion in this place.   Under a due observation of these rules, it will be necessary sometimes for ministers of the gospel to insist on the most abstruse and difficult truths that are revealed in the Scripture, and that because their doing so is necessary unto the edification of the church.

Obs. III. There is a glorious light and evidence in all divine truths, but by reason of our darkness and weakness, we are not always able to comprehend them.   Our want of that acquaintance with them which it is our duty to have, and which is needful unto our edification, is from ourselves alone, and for the most part from our sinful neglect of what is required thereunto.

Obs. IV. Many who receive the word at first with some readiness, do yet afterwards make but slow progress either in knowledge or grace.   This the apostle here chargeth on the Hebrews; which we must further afterwards consider.

Obs. V. It is men's slothfulness in hearing that is the sole cause of their not improving the means of grace, or not thriving under the dispensation of the word; or, all our miscarriages, with respect unto the gospel, are to be resolved into our own sloth, negligence, and depraved affections.   For it is not any one particular vice, fault, or miscarriage in hearing, that the apostle intendeth and reproveth; but the want in general of such an attendance to the word as to be edified thereby, proceeding from corrupt affections and neglect of duty.   And whereas this is a sin of so perilous a nature as to deprive us of all benefit by the gospel, it will be necessary to give a summary account of the duty of *hearing the word in a due manner*, so as to discover those defects and faults which constitute this sloth that we are thus warned of.   Unto hearing, therefore, as intended and enjoined in the gospel, belong all things required on our part to make the word useful, and to give it its proper effect upon our souls: "Faith cometh by hearing," Rom. x. 17.   Whatever is required of us that we may believe and obey the word, it belongs in general to this duty of hearing; and from a neglect of any thing material thereunto we are denominated *νωθροὶ ταῖς ἀκοαῖς*, and do contract the guilt of the vice here reproved. Three things in this sense do concur to the duty intended:—1. What is *preparatory* thereunto; 2. *Actual* hearing, or attendance on the word preached; 3. What is *afterwards* required to render our hearing useful and effectual. Which I shall speak unto in one or two instances under each head:—

1 We may consider what is necessary hereunto in way of *preparation*, that we be not slothful hearers. There is a preparation due unto the right sanctification of the name of God in any obedience in general, which I do not now intend, and I have spoken unto it elsewhere. Prayer, meditation, and a due reverence and regard to the authority and especial presence of God, with faith exercised on his promises, are necessary hereunto. These things, therefore, I here suppose, and shall only give one or two instances of what peculiarly respects the duty of hearing, peculiarly in way of preparation:—

(1.) Scarce any sort of persons fall under such fatal miscarriages in this great concernment of souls, as those whose hearts are inordinately influenced by the love, business, and cares of this world; for besides that the matter of them,—which, being earthly, is diametrically opposite unto that of the word, which is heavenly,—doth alienate and keep the mind at a distance from the proposals and reasonings of it, there are so many secret colourable pretences whereby these things will insinuate themselves into the thoughts and affections so disposed, as that there is no contending against them where they are habitually fixed. Wherefore the Scripture doth not draw up so heavy a charge against any one cause or occasion of unprofitable hearing as it doth against these cares and love of the world. Where men are over diligent in and about these things, they do but certainly deceive themselves, if on any supposition they judge that they are not slothful in hearing. Either before, or under, or after this duty, they will discover themselves to have been predominant. "Covetousness," the apostle tells us, "is idolatry," Col. iii. 5. And the covetous hearts of men do never worship the idol of this world with so much solemnity and devotion as when they set it up in the ordinances of God, as under the preaching of the word; for then they actually erect it in the room of God himself. Nay, they do it with a contempt of God, as flattering him with their outward appearance, which he despiseth, and giving up their inward affections to their endeared idol. And this is done not only when the thoughts and affections of men are actually engaged and exercised about earthly things during the dispensation of the word, but when their minds, through a love unto them and fulness of them, are previously indisposed unto that frame and temper which the nature of this duty doth require. Unless, therefore, these cares and businesses of the world are effectually cast out, and our hearts are duly exonerated of

them, we shall be *νωθροὶ ταῖς ἀκοαῖς*, and fall under the guilt of the
sin here reproved.

(2.) Antecedent unto hearing, and in way of preparation for it,
there is required in us *a desire after the word* " that we may grow
thereby," 1 Pet. ii. 2.   The end which we propose unto ourselves in
hearing hath a great influence into the regulation of the whole duty.
Some hear to satisfy their convictions; some, their curiosity and inquiry after notions; some, to please themselves; some, out of custom;
some, for company; and many know not why, or for no end at all.
It is no wonder if such persons be slothful in and unprofitable under
hearing.   Wherefore, in order unto a right discharge of this duty, it
is required of us that we consider what is our condition or stature in
Christ; how short we come of that measure in faith, knowledge,
light, and love, which we ought and hope to attain unto.   To supply
us with this growth and increase, the preaching of the word is appointed of God as food for our souls; and we shall never receive it
aright unless we desire it and long for it to this end and purpose.
When we know our weakness, imbecility, and manifold defects, and
come to the word to obtain supplies of strength suited unto our condition, we are in the way of thriving under it.   And as for them who
have not this desire and appetite, who understand not a suitableness
between the word and their spiritual condition, answerable to that
of food to his natural state who is hungry and desires growth and
strength, they will be " dull in hearing," as to all the blessed and
beneficial ends of it.

(3.) It is required of us to free our minds, what lies in us, from
being prepossessed with such corrupt affections as are apt to repel
the word, and deny it an entrance into our hearts.   " Intus existens
prohibet alienum ;"—when the mind is filled with things of another
nature, there is no room whereinto the seed of the word may have
admission.   And these things are of two sorts:—

[1.] Corrupt *lusts* or *sins indulged*.   The ejection of these is enjoined us, James i. 21, " Lay apart all filthiness, and superfluity of
naughtiness, and receive with meekness the ingrafted word."   If the
one be not done, the other will not.   If "filthiness and superfluity
of naughtiness" be not cast away and thrust from us, the word will
not be "received," at least not with "meekness."   We must put away
πᾶσαν ῥυπαρίαν, "all filthiness."   'Ρυπαρία, "sordes," belongs first to the
body, as *ῥύπος* doth, 1 Pet. iii. 21.   And from the *ἀπόθεσις ῥύπου* there
mentioned, the " doing away the filth of the body" by the washing
of water, is this *ἀποθέμενοι πᾶσαν ῥυπαρίαν*: which, as applied unto the
mind, answers unto the spiritual part of baptism, in the cleansing of
the soul from spiritual filth and corruption.   See Isa. iv. 4.   *Καὶ περισ-
σείαν κακίας*, " and the superfluity of naughtiness."   ' It should seem
that some " naughtiness" may remain, only the " superfluity" of it

must be cast away.' No; but "all naughtiness" in the mind is as a superfluous humour in the body, which corrupts and destroys it. It is the corrupting, depraving power and efficacy of prevailing lusts in the mind which is intended; and this is to be "laid apart," if we intend to receive τὸν ἔμφυτον λόγον, "the ingrafted (implanted) word;" that is, the word of the gospel, which was not designed of God to be "written in tables of stone, but in the fleshy tables of our hearts," 2 Cor. iii. 3. Hence is that great promise of taking away the heart of stone, figured by the tables of stone wherein the law was written, and giving a heart of flesh, wherein the word of the gospel should be written and ingrafted. See this text further interpreted, 1 Pet. ii. 1, 2. He, therefore, that comes with his mind filled and prepossessed with noisome lusts, as they are all, will be dull and slothful in hearing, seeing his heart will be sure to wander after its idols. For men's minds, filled with their lusts, are like Ezekiel's chambers of imagery, which were full of all manner of representations, "pourtrayed upon the wall;"—which way soever they turned their eyes they had idolatrous objects to entertain them, chap. viii. 10, 12. Such pictures do the corrupt imaginations of sensual, earthly persons fill their minds withal, that every thought has an object ready for its entertainment, effectually diverting the soul from the entertainment of the ingrafted word. Without this we may receive it as a notional word, as a truth in our understandings, but we cannot receive it as an implanted word in our hearts to save our souls.

[2.] *Cares and businesses* of the world having prepossessed the mind, produce in it the same indisposition in hearing. God himself giveth this reason why a professing people profited not by the dispensation of the word, namely, because "their hearts went after their covetousness," Ezek. xxxiii. 31. The prophet preached, and the people sat diligently before him as his hearers; but their minds being prepossessed with the love of the world, the word was unto them as wind, and of no use. Partly it was kept out by the exercise of their minds about other things; and what was received was quickly choked,— which is the proper effect of the cares of the world, Matt. xiii. 22.

2. In the *act* or duty *of hearing* itself, there are sundry things required of them who would not incur the guilt of the crime reproved; as,—

(1.) A due *reverence of the word* for its own sake. Spiritual reverence is our humble, religious respect of any thing upon the account of its authority and holiness. So is it due unto every thing that God hath put his name upon, and to nothing else. Whereas, therefore, God hath "magnified his word above all his name," Ps. cxxxviii. 2, or every other ordinance whereby he reveals himself unto us, it is thereunto due in an especial manner. So is this duty expressed in the instance of the Thessalonians, 1 Epist. ii. 13: "When ye received the word of God, which ye heard of us, ye received it not as the word of men, but (as it is in truth) the word of God, which effectually worketh in you that believe." The apostle commendeth their receiving of the word when preached unto them, from the *manner* of their attention unto it, with that respect and reverence which was due unto its relation to God; which also had a great influence unto its efficacy on them. ' Ye have received λόγον ἀκοῆς παρ' ἡμῶν τοῦ Θεοῦ,—" verbum auditus;" דְּבַר־שְׁמַע, "the word of hearing." ' Because preaching and hearing were the constant way that God had appointed for the communication and receiving of the gospel, the word itself was so denominated. To despise them, therefore, is formally to despise the gospel. And this word they are said to receive παρ' ἡμῶν, "of us;" that is, as instruments of its promulgation and declaration. On this account he sometimes calls it " our word," and "our gospel;"—'that word and gospel of God which we have preached;' as it is added, Θεοῦ, " of God;" not concerning God, but whereof God is the author, and which he hath appointed to be so preached and dispensed in his own name, 2 Cor. v. 18, 19. This, therefore, they attended unto, " not as the word of men," but, according to the truth, "as the word of God." The opposition may be either to the *original* of the word, or unto the *dispensation* of it. If unto the original, then the sense is, ' Not as unto a word that was devised or invented by men;' as Peter declares that in the preaching of the gospel "they did not follow cunningly-devised fables," 2 Pet. i. 16. Yet this seems not here to be intended, though it may be included. But the opposition is unto the administrators or preachers of it; as if he had said, ' In your attention to the word, you did not consider it merely as dispensed by us, but ascended in your minds to Him whose word originally it is, by whom it was appointed, and in whose name it was preached unto you.' And this gives us the just nature of that reverence which is required of us in hearing, namely, a humble respect unto the authority and holiness of the word, impressed upon it by Him whose word it is.

It may be objected, ' That this reverence is due only to the word as written, which is purely and wholly the word of God; but not unto it as preached by men, wherein there is, and must needs be, a mixture of human infirmities.' Hence some have been charged with arrogancy for expressing those words of the apostle's in their prayers, ' That the word preached by them might be received, " not as the word of men, but, as it is in truth, the word of God."' *Ans.* [1.] It is true, " we have this treasure in earthen vessels, that the excellency of the power may be of God, and not of men," 2 Cor. iv. 7. The ministry whereby the word is conveyed unto us is but a " vessel;" and ministers are but " earthen vessels,"—frail, weak, brittle, and it may be sometimes defiled. But still, in and by them the word of God is a "treasure," a heavenly treasure, enriching our souls. [2.] We may consider how far the word, as preached, is the pure word of God; and so, having his name upon it, is the object of our reverence. And, 1*st.* It is his *originally;* it proceeds from him, and not from the invention of men, as was showed before. 2*dly.* It is his word *materially.* The same things are preached that are declared in the Scripture, only they are explained and accommodated unto our understanding and use; which is needful for us. 3*dly.* The preaching of it is the *ordinance* of God, which his name is upon, in the same kind as on his word; and therein an especial reverence and respect unto the name and authority of God is due thereunto. 4*thly.* By virtue of this institution of God, the word preached, which is in itself only *materially* the word of God, becomes *formally* so; for it is the application of the word of God unto our souls, by virtue of his command and appointment. Wherefore there is the same reverence due to God in the word as preached, as in the word as written; and a peculiar advantage attends it beyond reading of the word, because God hath himself ordained it for our benefit.

It may be further objected, 'That we find by experience that the preachers of it will sometimes immix their own infirmities, and it may be mistakes in judgment, with their preaching of the word; and this must needs abate of the regard which is proposed as our duty.' *Ans.* [1.] God hath been pleased to ordain that the word should be dispensed unto us by *weak, sinful* men like ourselves; whence it unavoidably follows that they may, and probably sometimes will, mix some of their infirmities with their work. To except, therefore, against this disposition of things, is to except against the wisdom of God, and that especial order which he hath designed unto his own glory, 2 Cor. iv. 7. [2.] In a pipe which conveys water into a house there may be such a *flaw* as will sometimes give an entrance unto some dust or earth to immix itself with the water; will you therefore reject the water itself, and say, that if you may not have it just as it riseth in the fountain you will not regard it, when you live far from the fountain itself, and can have no water but such as is conveyed in pipes liable to such flaws and defects? Your business is to separate the defilement and use the water, unless you intend to perish with thirst. [3.] That such a thing may fall out, and that it doth ever so, gives us an opportunity of exercising *sundry graces*, and for the performance of *sundry duties*, whereby it turns to our advantage. For,— 1*st.* Here lies the proper exercise of our *spiritual understanding* in the gospel, whereby we are enabled to " try all things, and hold fast that which is good." To this end our apostle requires that we should " have senses exercised to try" (or " discern") "both good and evil." Hereby, according to our duty, we separate the chaff from the wheat; and no small exercise of grace and spiritual light, to the great improvement of them, doth consist herein. *2dly. Tenderness* towards men in the infirmities which we discern in their work, proceeding either from weakness or temptation. *3dly.* The consideration hereof ought to keep us in a constant dependence on and *prayer* unto the Lord Christ for the *communication of his Spirit unto us,* to "lead us," according to his promise, "into all truth;" which is the great reserve he hath given us in this matter. And hence follows,—

(2.) An immediate *subjection of soul and conscience* unto whatever is delivered in the dispensation of the word. A readiness hereunto Cornelius declared when he was to hear Peter preach: Acts x. 33, " Now are we all here present,......to hear all things that are commanded thee of God;" that is, so to hear as to give up our souls in obedience unto the word, because of the authority of God, whose word it is. And when we are not in this frame we shall be unprofitable hearers; for the immediate end of our hearing is practice. And the Scripture doth so fully testify hereunto, that in sundry places it positively declares that no kind of hearing, whatever appearance of zeal or diligence it may be accompanied withal, which doth not issue in practical obedience, is in the least to be esteemed of. But I intend not at present this practice, which is in order of nature consequential unto the hearing of the word, but that practical subjection of the soul and conscience to the word which alone will make way for it. For even that practice or obedience which proceeds not from hence is faulty and corrupt, as having certainly a false foundation or a wrong end. Herein, then, lies the great wisdom of faith in hearing, namely, in delivering up the soul and conscience unto the commanding authority of God in the word, Rom. vi. 17. And hereunto, among other things, it is required,—

[1.] That the heart hath no *approved reserve* for any lust or corruption, whose life it would save from the sword of the word ; [2.] That it be *afraid of no duty* on the account of the difficulties and dangers with which it may be attended: for where these things are, the heart will close itself against the influences of God's authority in his word. [3.] A diligent watchfulness against *distractions and diversions*, especially such as are growing to be habitual from temptations and sloth. This is much spoken unto by others, and therefore is here dismissed without further consideration. And where we are negligent in these things, or any of them, we shall be found " dull in hearing."

3. There are duties also belonging hereunto which are *consequential* unto actual hearing; whose discharge is required to free us from the guilt of the evil reproved; as,—

(1.) A due *examination of what is new or doubtful* in the things delivered unto us. When the gospel itself was first preached, and so was new unto them to whom it was delivered, the Bereans are commended for examining what was delivered unto them by the Scriptures which they had before received, Acts xvii. 11. And in case of things doubtful is the command given us, to "try all things, and to hold fast that which is good," 1 Thess. v. 21; as also to "try the spirits," 1 John iv. 1, or what is taught under pretence of any spiritual gift whatever. Not that any thing is spoken to encourage that cavilling humour which so abounds in some as that they will be excepting and disputing against every thing that is delivered in the dispensation of the word, if not absolutely suited to their sentiments and conceptions, or because they think they could otherwise, and it may be better, have expressed what they have heard; which kind of persons well may be reckoned amongst the worst sort of unprofitable hearers, and such as are most remote from subjecting their consciences unto the authority of God in his word, as they ought. We may therefore give some rules in this matter; as,— [1.] Some things there are which are such *fundamental principles* of our profession, that they ought to be so far from being exposed unto a doubting examination, that they are part of that rule whereby all other doctrines are to be tried and examined, as those also by whom they are taught, 2 John 9–11. And, [2.] Other doctrines also there are, so evidently deduced from the Scripture, and so manifest in their own light, carrying the open conviction of their truth along with them, as that they ought not at any time to be made the matter of a *doubtful trial.* Only what is delivered concerning them may be compared with the Scriptures, to their further illustration and confirmation. [3.] Neither ought what is delivered by any faithful, approved minister of the gospel, whose way, and course, and doctrine, and zeal for the truth, have been known, be lightly called into question; nor, without *manifest evidence* of some failing or mistake, be made the matter of "doubtful disputations." For whereas every man is obnoxious unto error, and some we have found, after a long course of their profession of the truth, to fall actually into such as are perilous to the souls of men, if not pernicious, it is not meet that any thing which they teach should, on just occasion, be exempt from a sober trial and examination; so whereas such ministers of the gospel as those mentioned have the word of truth committed unto them by Christ himself, and his promise of direction in the discharge of their duty, whilst they behave themselves as his stewards and dispensers of the mysteries of God, what they declare in his name is not lightly to be solicited with every needless scruple. Wherefore this duty, which in some cases and seasons is of so great importance, may in other cases and at other seasons be less necessary; yea, a pretence of it may be greatly abused to the ruin of all profitable hearing. When errors and false teachers abound, and when, by our best attendance unto the rule, we cannot avoid the hearing of them sometimes; or when things new, uncouth, or carrying an appearance of an opposition to the analogy of faith, or those doctrines of the gospel wherein we have been instructed and settled, are imposed on us; it is necessary we should stand upon our guard, and bring what is taught unto a due examination. But where there is a settled approved ministry, and the things delivered evidence in a good manner their own consonancy unto the Scripture and analogy of faith, a disposition and inclination, under pretence of trying and examining what is delivered, to except against it and dispute about it, is the bane of all profitable hearing.

(2.) Let us be sure to learn what we are learning. The apostle complains of some who are " ever learning, and never able to come to the knowledge of the truth," 2 Tim. iii. 7. Of this sort are many still amongst us. And hence it is that, after they have been long under the means of instruction in sound truth and knowledge, they are ready to hearken after and greedily embrace any fancy that is contrary thereunto. The reason hereof is, because they did not learn what they were so long in learning. To learn any truth as we ought, is to learn it in its proper principles, true nature, and peculiar use; to learn it in the respect it hath unto, and the place it holds in the system of gospel truths; so to learn it as to get an experience of its usefulness and necessity unto a life of holy obedience. Unless we thus learn what we hear, in its compass and circumstances, it will not prove an " ingrafted word" unto us, and we shall lose, the things which we seem to have wrought. Our duty herein may be reduced unto heads : [1.] That we learn doctrinally what respect every truth hath unto Christ, the centre of them all. [2.] Practically what influence they have into our obedience and holiness. [3.] A diligent heedfulness to retain the things which we have heard is also required hereunto. But this hath been sufficiently spoken unto, chap. ii. 1, where it is expressly enjoined us. The like also may be said concerning meditation and holy conference; whereof see chap. iii. 12. [4.] A diligent care to avoid partiality in obedience unto what we hear. All men, it is hoped, design to obey in some things, most in most things, but few in all. God blamed the priests of old that they were " partial in the law," Mal. ii. 9. Either they taught not men the whole law, and therein the whole of their duty, but reserved such things from them as, if known and practised, might turn to their own disadvantage; for they had learned in those days to " eat up," and so to live on, " the sin of the people," Hos. iv. 8: or they taught them according as they knew they would be pleased to hear, therein accepting their persons, as the words seem to import. And for this God says he would make them " contemptible and base before all the people." It shall be no

otherwise with them who are partial in their obedience. Such are
persons who will do as much as consists in their own judgment with
their interests, societies, inclinations, and the liberty they have
fancied unto themselves. For we are fallen into such days wherein
some professors do judge it a great freedom and liberty to be
exempted from obedience unto sundry commands of Christ, and
those such as they cannot but know to be so. Alas for the pride
and folly of the heart of man!—to serve sin, to serve vanity and
unbelief, which are the things alone that keep us off from a
universal compliance with all the commands of the gospel, and
submission unto all the institutions of Christ, shall be accounted
liberty and freedom, when it is a part of the vilest bondage in the
world. What are such persons afraid of? Is it that they shall
engage themselves too far in a way towards heaven, so as that they
cannot retreat when they would? Is it that they shall have too
many helps against their corruptions and temptations, and for the
furtherance of their faith and obedience? Or is it lest they should
give over themselves wholly to Christ, and not be at liberty, when
a better master comes, to lay a claim to a share in him? How
great is the misery of such poor souls! This is the generation of
perishing professors in our days. Out of them proceed Quakers,
worldlings, and at last scoffers. This is the field wherein all apostasy
visibly grows. Those that are openly profane cannot apostatize or
fall away. What should they fall from? Christ is pleased to secure
his churches in some good measure, so as that we have not frequent
instances in them of this fatal miscarriage; but from among the
number of professors who will walk at large, and are partial in their
obedience, we have multitudes of examples continually. Let not
such persons think they shall profit under the dispensation of the
word; for they will at last be found to have been "slothful in hearing," and that in one of the worst instances of that sin.

Where there is a neglect of these things,—which are all necessary
and required unto profitable hearing,—it cannot be but that men will
be νωθροὶ ταῖς ἀκοαῖς, and fall deservedly under the rebuke here given
by the apostle unto the Hebrews, as we see multitudes to do every
day. And whereas all this proceedeth from the sinful and wilful
carelessness of men about their own eternal concernments, it is evident that all want of a due progress and improvement under the
means of grace must be resolved into their own sloth and depraved
affections.

Obs. VI. It is a grievous matter to the dispensers of the gospel, to
find their hearers unapt to learn and thrive under their ministry,
through their negligence and sloth. The apostle complaineth of it
here as that which was a cause of sorrow and trouble unto him.
And so is it unto all faithful ministers whose lot it is to have such

hearers. As for others, who are themselves negligent or slothful in
their own work, it cannot be but that they will be regardless of the
state of their flock.

VERSES 12–14.

The three ensuing verses, as they all treat of the same matter with
that foregoing, so they have all the same design in themselves, and
cannot be severed in their exposition. The reasons of the reproof
entered on in the 11th verse are here expressed, and the crime reproved is laden with sundry aggravations. And these aggravations
are taken from such circumstances of the persons, and such consequents and effects of their fault, as make it evident that the reproof
given was both just and necessary.

Ver. 12–14.—Καὶ γὰρ ὀφείλοντες εἶναι διδάσκαλοι διὰ τὸν χρόνον, πάλιν
χρείαν ἔχετε τοῦ διδάσκειν ὑμᾶς, τίνα τὰ στοιχεῖα τῆς ἀρχῆς τῶν λογίων τοῦ
Θεοῦ, καὶ γεγόνατε χρείαν ἔχοντες γάλακτος, καὶ οὐ στερεᾶς τροφῆς. Πᾶς
γὰρ ὁ μετέχων γάλακτος, ἄπειρος λόγου δικαιοσύνης· νήπιος γάρ ἐστι. Τελείων δέ ἐστιν ἡ στερεὰ τροφή, τῶν διὰ τὴν ἕξιν τὰ αἰσθητήρια γεγυμνασμένα
ἐχόντων πρὸς διάκρισιν καλοῦ τε καὶ κακοῦ.

Καὶ γὰρ ὀφείλοντες εἶναι, "etenim debentes esse," Arias ; "etenim cum debe-
retis esse," Vulg.; "etenim cum debeatis," Eras.; "vos enim quos oportuit,"
Beza. All to the same purpose. "For when you ought," or rather, "for when
as you ought to be." חַיָּבִין דֵּין אַתּוּן גֵּיר, Syr., "debitores estis enim." The word
denotes a debt of any kind, in things real or moral ; whatever is due from us, or
justly required of us, is so expressed. Διδάσκαλοι. Vulg. Lat., Rhem., "ma-
gistri," "masters." Eras., Bez., "doctores." Syr., מַלְפָנָא, "teachers," instructors of others.

Διὰ τὸν χρόνον. Vulg. Lat., "propter tempus." Rhem., "for your time;"
supplying "your" needlessly. "Pro temporis ratione," Bez., Eras.; "considering the time." "For the time," is proper in our language. The Syriac para-
phraseth this expression, מֶטוּל דְּזַבְנָא לְכוֹן בְּיוּלְפָנָא, "seeing you have had time in," or
"under institution," discipline, instruction, doctrine ;—'for the time wherein you
have been taught and instructed.' Arab., "for the length of the time;" which
is intended, but not expressed. One of late, "jamdudam," "now long ago;"—
'you have been so long since taught, that you might have been teachers long ago.'

Πάλιν, "rursum." Syr., הָשָׁא דֵּין תּוּב, "but now again." "Contra," "on the
other side;"—'whereas you ought to have been teachers, on the other side.'

Χρείαν ἔχετε, "indigetis," Vulg.; "you need," Rhem.; "opus habetis," "opus
est ut;" "you have need," "you stand in need," it is necessary.

Τοῦ διδάσκειν ὑμᾶς, "ut vos doceamini," "that you should be taught ;" in the
passive voice. Syr., דְּתֵאלְפוּן, "that you should learn." Properly, "to teach
you;"—'that I should, that we should, that one should teach you.'

Τίνα τὰ στοιχεῖα τῆς ἀρχῆς τῶν λογίων τοῦ Θεοῦ. Vulg. Lat., "quæ sint elementa
exordii sermonum Dei." Rhem., "what be the elements of the beginning of the
words of God;" improperly and obscurely. Syr., אִילֵין אֶנִין כְּתִיבָתָא קַדְמָיָתָא דְּרִיש
מֶלוֹהִי דַאלָהָא, "the very first writings of the beginning of the words of God;" supposing στοιχεῖα to intend the letters of the alphabet. "Quæ sint elementa initii
eloquiorum Dei," Eras., Beza ; that is, "oraculorum." Λόγια, Θέσφατα. Ours,
"which be the first principles of the oracles of God;"—'which are the fundamental principles of divine revelation.'

Πᾶς γὰρ ὁ μετέχων γάλακτος. "Qui lactis est particeps," Vulg. Lat. Rhem., "that is partaker of milk." "Cui cum lacte res est," Bez. Which we render, "that useth milk;" that is, for his food : as Syr., דְּמֵאכוּלָתֵח דַלְבָּא הוּ, "whose food is milk;" who, as we speak, liveth on milk.

Ἄπειρος λόγου δικαιοσύνης. "Expers est sermonis justitiæ," Vulg. Rhem., "is unskilful of the word of justice." "Rudis est;" is "unskilful in," or rather, "hath no experience of the word of righteousness." The Syriac somewhat otherwise, לָא מְפַס בְּמֶלְתָא דְכָאנוּתָא; "is not taught," persuaded, instructed, "in the word of righteousness."

Νήπιος γάρ ἐστι. "Parvulus enim est," Vulg.; "for he is a little one." Rhem., "a child." "Infans enim est." Syr., דְשַׁבְרָא הוּ, "he is unskilful," "unexperienced." "For he is a babe."

Τελείων. "Perfectorum," Vulg.; "the perfect." "Adultorum," Eras., Beza. "Those of full age." Syr., דִגְמִירָא, "perfectorum;" so ad verbum.

Ἡ στερεὰ τροφή, "cibus solidus," "solida alimonia;" "strong meat," "strong nourishment."

Τῶν διὰ τὴν ἕξιν. "Eorum qui pro ipsa consuetudine," Vulg. Lat.; "them that by custom." "Propter habitum," Bez.; "by reason of a habit," properly. "Of use," say ours; which is the way whereby a habit is obtained. Syr., דִמְדַרְשִׁין, "who have much inquired;" who are ready in inquiries.

Τὰ αἰσθητήρια γεγυμνασμένα ἐχόντων. "Exercitatos habent sensus;" "sensuum organa;" "the organs or instruments of their senses;"—who have their senses ready and expedite.

Ver. 12–14.—For whereas for the time ye ought to be teachers, ye have need that one should teach you again which be the first principles of the oracles of God; and are become such as have need of milk, and not of strong meat. For every one that useth milk is unskilful in the word of righteousness; for he is a babe. But strong meat belongeth unto them that are of full age, even those who, by reason of use, have their senses exercised to discern both good and evil.

The charge of a crime or fault intimated in the preceding verse is, as was said, improved and managed for a fuller and more unavoidable conviction. These two things, therefore, doth the apostle design in these words:—1. To give the reason of the general charge he had burdened them withal, and to prove the equity of it in particular instances. This he declareth in that causal conjunction, καὶ γάρ, "for whereas." 2. To enlarge and further declare the nature of the fault charged on them, from its effects and consequents, with other circumstances. And this is done,—(1.) From an aggravating circumstance of time, or the duration of the season of instruction and growing in knowledge which they had enjoyed: "Whereas for the time." (2.) From the consideration of a duty which might justly be expected from them, with respect unto that time and season: "Ye ought to have been teachers." (3.) From a contrary event, or how things were indeed fallen out with them on the other side:

" They had need to be taught what were the first principles of the oracles of God." And, (4.) The whole is enforced by an antithesis between two sorts of hearers of the word, expressed in an elegant similitude or metaphor. The instructive nature of this similitude consists, [1.] In that likeness or conformity which is between bodily food and the word of the gospel as preached. [2.] In the variety of natural food, as suited unto the various states and conditions of them that feed thereon; answered by the doctrines of truth in the gospel, which are of various kinds. And in the exemplification hereof natural food is reduced unto two kinds,—[1.] " Milk;" [2.] " Strong meat:" and those that feed thereon unto two sorts,—children, and men of ripe age; both which are applied unto the hearers of the word. Wherefore the apostle, in the application of this similitude, represents unto us two sorts of professors of the gospel, or hearers of the word, and gives a description of them by their several qualities. For, [1.] Some there are who are νήπιοι, "babes," and continue so; and some are τέλειοι, such as are " of full age," or " perfect." [2.] These νήπιοι, or "babes," are described by a double property: for, 1st. They are νωθροὶ ταῖς ἀκοαῖς, verse 11, " dull in hearing;" 2dly. They are ἄπειροι λόγου δικαιοσύνης, "unskilful in the word of righteousness." In opposition hereunto, τέλειοι, those who are spiritually adult, are, 1st. Supposed to be ἔχοντες νοῦν, such as have understandings, so as to be capable of instruction; 2dly. Are said to have αἰσθητήρια γεγυμνασμένα, senses exercised to discern good and evil. The different means to be applied unto these different sorts for their good, according to their respective conditions, are expressed in the terms of the metaphor: to the first, γάλα, " milk;" to the other, στερεὰ τροφή, "strong food," or nourishment; all comprised in the ensuing scheme:—

AUDITORES EVANGELII.

1. Νήπιοι. Suntque	2. Τέλειοι. Suntque
(1.) Νωθροὶ ταῖς ἀκοαῖς.	(1.) Φρόνιμοι.
(2.) Ἄπειροι λόγου δικαιοσύνης. Opus habent Γάλακτος.	(2.) Τὰ αἰσθητήρια γεγυμνασμένα ἔχοντες. Opus habent Στεριᾶς τροφῆς.

And the intention of the apostle is to represent unto the Hebrews herein their state and condition, arising from their being " dull in hearing." And this he doth both absolutely and comparatively, with respect unto what others were, and what they themselves might and ought to have been. For he shows that they were yet " babes, unskilful in the word of righteousness," and such as had need "to be fed with milk."

FIRST, The first thing considerable in these words, is an aggravation of the fault reproved in the Hebrews, from a circumstance of time : Διὰ τὸν χρόνον, "pro ratione temporis." 'Considering the time and season you Hebrews have had, you might

Διὰ τὸν χρόνον.

have been otherwise long ago;'—"jamdudum," as one renders the words. Or διὰ τὸν χρόνον may not intend the *space of time*, but the *nature of the season* which they were under. 'The season is such, whether you consider the opportunities of it, or the dangers of it, or the shortness of its continuance, as that you ought so diligently to have improved it, that yourselves might have been at work in the teaching of others, had you been zealous for the gospel, as you ought to be, or careful about your own duty.' Such times as were then come on and passing over the Hebrews, as to their profession of the gospel, called for more than ordinary diligence in their improvement. There is no inconvenience in this sense, and it hath good instruction in it ; but I shall rather adhere unto that which is more commonly received. Διὰ τὸν χρόνον, "for the time," is as much as ' with respect unto the time past and gone since their first calling unto and profession of the gospel.' But men may have time enough, and yet have no advantage by it, for want of other necessary helps and assistances. A tree may have been planted a long time in a dry and barren wilderness, and yet it would be a vanity to expect any great growth or thriving from thence, as having the benefit neither of rain nor a fruitful soil. And when God expects fruit from his vineyard, he gives it not time only, but all other things necessary to its improvement, Isa. v. 1-4. Wherefore it is supposed, that during the time intended, these Hebrews wanted no necessary means of instruction. This the apostle had before declared, chap. ii. 1, 3. The word of the gospel was both "preached" and "confirmed" unto them. And as they had for a season the ministry of all the apostles, and of sundry of them for a longer continuance, so it is justly supposed they had yet one of them surviving and abiding among them. Moreover, they had in common use the scriptures of the Old Testament, which testified unto all that they had been taught concerning Jesus Christ; and most of the writings of the New Testament were before this time communicated unto them. Wherefore, during the season intended, they enjoyed sufficient means of "growing in grace, and in the knowledge of our Lord and Saviour Jesus Christ." Without a supposition hereof they could not have been justly reproved for a want of proficiency. Yea, in every expression of their crime this is supposed. They were "dull in hearing;" which they could not have been had not the word been constantly preached unto them, for without preaching there can be no hearing. And all this the apostle makes evident, chap. vi. 7, where he compares them unto the earth, which hath frequent showers of rain falling upon it, because of the abundant waterings which they had received by the constant preaching of the word unto them.

As for the duration of this season in particular, it was not equal unto them all. Every one had only the time since his own conversion to account for. If we shall take the words with respect unto the whole church at Jerusalem, then the date of this time is to be fixed on the day of Pentecost, when, upon the effusion of the Holy Ghost on the apostles, testified and evidenced by the miracle of tongues, with the sermon of Peter unto them that ensued thereon, so many thousands of them were converted to the faith, Acts ii. And if this be allowed, the space of time intended was about thirty years. But, not to bind up the expression unto any especial epocha, it is enough that they had, all and every one of them whom the apostle intends, more time than they had well used or improved. And we ought to observe, that,—

Obs. I. The time wherein we enjoy the great mercy and privilege of the dispensation of the gospel unto us, is a matter which must in particular be accounted for.

This time is variously dispensed, its measure being given by the sovereign will and wisdom of God. All who have time given them to this purpose, have not the same time. The day of the gospel is not of the same length unto all nations, churches, persons, unto whom it is granted. But all have time and light enough to do the work that is required of them. And it is a talent to be accounted for. Neither must we account for it only in general, but as to our improvement of it in particular duties. These Hebrews had such a time. And it was not enough, it did not answer the design of God in it, that they professed the gospel, and did not renounce Jesus Christ, as some among them did ; it was moreover expected from them, that they should grow and thrive in knowledge and holiness proportionable to their time and means : and not doing so, it is charged on them as a great aggravation of their guilt. An evil it was that they had not profited under the dispensation of the gospel, but especially it was so, in that they had not answered the time that God had graciously intrusted them withal. And we may all do well to consider it, who have the like day of grace, mercy, and patience, with what they enjoyed. See our exposition of chap. iii. 13, 15.

Secondly, A duty is expressed, the want of whose performance is charged also as an aggravation of the sin insisted on. Ὀφείλοντες εἶναι—διδάσκαλοι, "you ought to have been teachers." Διδάσκαλος is the word whereby the writers of the New Testament express "Rabbi," which was the usual name of the public teachers of the law among the Jews. He is such a one, not only that is fit and meet to teach and instruct others occasionally, but also hath disciples committed to him, depending on him, and learning from him. So is our Saviour himself called in the Gospel; and so he termed himself with respect unto his disciples, Mark iv. 38, John

Διδάσκαλοι.

xiii. 13. And John tells us that it is the same name with the Hebrew "Rabbi," and the Syriac "Rabboni," chap. i. 38, xx. 16. And it
is the name of the teaching officer given by Christ unto the church,
1 Cor. xii. 28, Eph. iv. 11. Nor is it anywhere used but for a
public teacher, preacher, or instructor of disciples in the knowledge
of God.

'Οφείλοντες εἶναι, "you ought to be." He doth not only say that
they had enjoyed such a time and season of instruction
as that they might have been able to teach and instruct
others; but this he declares was expected from them as
their duty. And the right understanding hereof depends on the
consideration of the state and condition of the churches in those
days. For this reproof would now seem uncouth and unreasonable.
Our hearers do not look upon it as their duty to learn to be teachers;
at least not in the church, and by means of the knowledge to be
attained therein. They think it enough for them, if at best they can
hear with some profit to themselves. But this was not the state of
things in primitive times. Every church was then a seminary, wherein provision and preparation was made, not only for the continuation
of the preaching of the gospel in itself, but for the calling, gathering,
and teaching of other churches also. When, therefore, a church was
first planted by the ministry of the apostles, it was for a while continued under their own immediate care and inspection, and then
usually committed by them unto the ministry of some evangelists.
By them were they instructed more and more in the mysteries of
religion, and directed in the use of all means whereby they might
grow in grace and knowledge. And in this state were they continued, until some were found meet among themselves to be made
overseers and instructors of the rest, 2 Tim. ii. 2; Acts xiv. 23; Tit.
i. 5. Upon their decease, others were to be called and chosen from
among themselves to the same work by the church. And thus were
the preservation and successive propagation of the churches provided
for; it being suited to the nature and law of all societies, as also to
the institution and love of Christ unto his churches, that, in compliance with his appointment, they should be able to continue and preserve their being and order. And this course, namely, that teachers
of the church should be educated thereunto in the church, continued
inviolate until the public school at Alexandria, which became a precedent unto other places for a mixed learning of philosophy and religion; which after a while corrupted both, and at length the whole
church itself.

And this also was the manner before in the synagogues of the Jews.
They had in them public teachers of the law, who were their rabbis,
or διδάσκαλοι. By these, others, their disciples, sitting at their feet
whilst they taught and preached, were instructed in the knowledge

thereof; as Paul giveth an instance in himself and his teacher Gamaliel, Acts xxii. 3. And among these disciples, those who profited above others in an especial manner, as Paul affirmeth he did "above his equals" (that is, those who had enjoyed the same time and means with him), Gal. i. 14, were afterwards themselves designed and called to be διδάσκαλοι, or teachers.

And men in those days did not only learn in the church that they might be able afterwards to teach in the same, but also that they might be instrumental in the work of the gospel in other places: for out of the churches went those who were made use of in the propagation of the gospel ordinarily; which cannot now well be imitated, unless the whole ancient order were restored, which we are not yet to expect. Wherefore hearers in the church were not only taught those things which might be sufficient unto their own edification, but every thing also that was necessary to the edification of others; an ability for whose instruction it was their duty to aim at.

I do not say that this was the duty of *all* hearers. Every one was not to labour to profit by the word that he might himself be a teacher. Many things might invincibly incapacitate sundry persons from any such work or office. But yet in those days it might be the duty of many, especially in that church of the Hebrews; for this was the great seminary of preachers for the whole world all that time wherein the law was to go forth from Zion, and healing waters from Jerusalem. And there were two reasons why the ministry of the Jews was so necessary and useful to the world, whereby the Gentiles were made debtors unto them, by a participation of their spiritual things; not only which were theirs originally, and possessed by them before the Gentiles had any interest in them, but also because by their ministry they were communicated unto them, Rom. xv. 27:—1. Because, upon their conversion to Christ, they immediately made a great progress in knowledge. For they had before received the seeds and foundations of all evangelical truths in the scriptures of the Old Testament; and so soon as the light of the gospel shined into their hearts, all things were cleared up unto them, from the true sense of those principles wherein they had before been instructed which was now made manifest unto them. And our apostle immediately blames these Hebrews for the want of an acquaintance with those principles. But hence were those who did really profit by the word quickly ready for this work. On the other side the Gentile converts,—setting aside the consideration of extraordinary illumination, revelation, and inspiration by the Spirit of God, which many in those days were made partakers of,—must needs require a longer time to be perfectly instructed in the mysteries of the gospel, whereunto they had been such utter strangers. 2. It was in the Jews' synagogues, throughout their dispersions in the world, that the preachers of the gospel began to divulge their message. For God had so ordained, that in all places *the accomplishment of the promise* made unto their fathers should first be declared unto them, Acts xiii. 32, 33, 46. Now this could not be done but by those that were Jews; for the Gentile converts, being uncircumcised, could neither have access unto their synagogues nor acceptance with them. On this account it was greatly incumbent on these Hebrews to thrive in knowledge, that they might be able to teach others, when God in his providence should call them thereunto. And hence it was, that when this church, not long after its first planting, was scattered by persecution, all the members of it went up and down preaching the gospel with great success, first to the Jews, and then to the Grecians also, Acts viii. 4, xi. 19, 20. After this those that succeeded, as it seems, were remiss and negligent in learning, and so unfit for this work; which the apostle blames in them.

This I take to be the meaning of the place. But if you will suppose that the apostle useth the word διδάσκαλοι in a larger sense, for any that are able to instruct others, as their neighbours, families, or relations, as occasion should require, then it was the duty of all these Hebrews to have been such teachers, and their sin it was wherein they were not able so to be.

Obs. II. Churches are the schools of Christ, wherein his disciples are trained up unto perfection, every one according to the measure appointed for him, and his usefulness in the body.

We may consider the church in general, and with respect unto some particular members of it. *First,* In general, every one that belongs unto it ought to have a double aim; first his own *edification,* and then his *usefulness* in respect of others. The first is the principal end, both of the ministry and the administration of all ordinances in the church, Eph. iv. 11–13. This, therefore, in the first place, is that which every one ought to attend diligently unto; which also they are continually exhorted, encouraged, and persuaded unto in the Scripture, as that which is indispensably required of them, 2 Pet. iii. 18. And those who are negligent herein do frustrate all the ends of Christ's love and care towards them in his church; which they must answer for. And the want of it, in some good measure, is a dreadful symptom of approaching eternal ruin, as our apostle declares, Heb. vi. 7, 8. The church is the garden of Christ, enclosed and watered; and every plant which continueth in a withering, unthrifty condition will at length be plucked up and cast out. Herein, therefore, ought all to be trying and examining themselves who have any care of their own souls, and who intend not to make use of the ordinances of the gospel only to countenance them in their security, and so to hasten and aggravate their destruction. And there is nothing more lamentable, in the present profession of Christian religion, than the woful negligence of most herein. They hear the word, for the most part, as company, or custom, or their lusts, or ease, direct them. And they content themselves in hearing of it, without any endeavours for its improvement. So do many souls under the best of means come to the worst of ends. But this is not all. We are so to learn in the church as that we may be useful to others; a matter which few think of or trouble themselves about. But this Christ expects of all the members of his churches in an especial manner. For every church is " the body of Christ, and members in particular," 1 Cor. xii. 27; that is, of the whole body, and unto one another. And the apostle there shows what a monstrous thing it is for a member to be useless in the body. Every one is to contribute to the growth of the whole, Eph. iv. 16; Col. ii. 19. He that doth not so is dead. One way or other every one may contribute to this building, cast into this sanctuary, some their talents, some their mites. Times, seasons, opportunities, advantages for usefulness, are in the hand of God; but our duty it is to be prepared for them, and then to lay hold upon them. It is not every one's lot or call to be public teachers of others; and the undertaking of that work without a due ability and an orderly call is forbidden, James iii. 1: but every one may have occasion to make use of the utmost of that light and knowledge which is communicated unto them in the dispensation of the word. They who have not flocks to watch over may yet have families, relations, children, servants, masters, whom, by their light and knowledge, they may benefit; and it is required of them that so they should do. It may not be the duty of every one, at all times, to " convince gainsayers," and to stop the mouths of them that oppose the truth; but it is so to be "always ready to give an answer unto every man that asketh a reason of the hope that is in them, with meekness and fear," 1 Pet. iii. 15; and it will be so, to plead for and defend the truth, if they are called to suffer for it, like the martyrs in former days. In these and such like things lies that usefulness in the body of Christ which every member of it ought to aim at under the means of instruction which he affords in his church. And those who do not will have their portion with the unprofitable. See Phil. ii. 15, 16. It is a sad condition, when a person can return no tolerable answer unto that inquiry, ' Of what use are you in the church of Christ?' *Secondly,* In particular, it were doubtless well if some persons in every church might be trained up under instruction with this very design, of being made meet to be teachers of others. The Lord Christ will indeed provide labourers for his harvest, but in his own way, and not in a compliance with our negligence.

Obs. III. It is the duty of ministers of the gospel to endeavour their hearers' increase in knowledge, until they also are able to instruct others, according to their calls and opportunities.

So did those who taught these Hebrews, whence they are reproved for failing their expectation. Some, it may be, are apt to fear lest their hearers should know too much. Many corrupt lusts and affections may prompt them hereunto; which are all resolved into self, with respect unto profit or reputation. And this hath proceeded so far in the degeneracy of the church of Rome, as to produce the commendation of blind obedience and ignorance, as the mother of devotion; than which nothing could be invented more contrary to the whole course and design of the gospel. And it is well if no others are tainted with the same disease. Even good men had need to watch against discomposures of mind, when they find on trial, it may be, some of their hearers to be like David, "wiser" in the things of God "than their teachers." And Joshua himself was earnest with Moses to forbid Eldad and Medad from prophesying; out of no good frame, as appeareth by the reply of Moses, "Enviest thou for my sake?" Num. xi. 29. But this occasioned the prayer of that holy man, which is unto us a rule of duty, "Would God that all the LORD'S people were prophets, and that the LORD would put his Spirit upon them!" And to a faithful minister, there is no greater crown nor cause of rejoicing, than when he can be instrumental so to carry on any of his hearers towards perfection, as that their gifts and abilities may outshine his own, especially if they are accompanied with humility and holiness. And for those who are either negligent in this work, or, taking upon them the place and duty of teachers, are unable for it, they betray the souls of men, and shall bear their own judgment.

The SECOND branch of the apostolical reproof consists in a declaration of the consequent or effect of the negligence reproved: "You have need that one should teach you again which be the first principles of the oracles of God."

Χρείαν ἔχετε, "you have need;"—'There is need of it on your account; if you are not thus taught again, you will not know the "principles of the oracles of God."' We are said χρείαν ἔχειν, to need those things naturally without which we cannot well live, as Matt. vi. 8; and morally without which we cannot perform our duty.

Τοῦ διδάσκειν ὑμᾶς. There is an antithesis herein, between their duty and the event, or unto what was before mentioned as expected from them. It was expected justly, that they should be διδάσκαλοι, "teachers;" but they had need τοῦ διδάσκειν αὐτοῦς, "that one should teach them." And so πάλιν, which we render "again," may be well rendered, "on the contrary," or "on the other side:" 'It is thus fallen out, by your negligence, that instead of being "teachers of others," of being masters of the assemblies, you, "on the other hand," had need to be

placed on the lowest form of those who learn;—the highest evidence
of your dulness and want of proficiency.' Τοῦ διδάσκειν,—that is, say
we, "that one should teach you;" τίνα, that "some one or other
should do it." Or μὲ may be supplied; "that I should teach you."
So he useth the same kind of expression, Οὐ χρείαν ἔχετε γράφειν
ὑμῖν,—" Ye have no need to write unto you;" that is, ' that I should
write untó you,' 1 Thess. iv. 9. As he expressly speaks, 1 Thess. i.
8, "Ὥστε μὴ χρείαν ἡμᾶς ἔχειν λαλεῖν τι,—"That we should not need to
speak any thing." But yet whereas the apostle treats not about his
own personal ministry towards them, but of their continued instruction by the constant means they enjoyed, it may be left indefinitely,
that " one," or " some," should do that work,—' That you should be
taught.'

Τίνα τὰ στοιχεῖα, " which be the first principles;" not only which
they are, but what they are, is intended. The words, as
they lie in our translation, seem to intimate that this   Τίνα   τὰ
alone is aimed at, namely, that they should be taught   στοιχεῖα.
to distinguish between the first principles of Christian religion and
the superstructions on them, or necessary deductions from them;
but the very nature of the things themselves is intended. They were to be instructed in the principles   Τίνα.
of Christian religion in the sense to be explained.

Στοιχεῖον is used by our apostle indifferently, so as that it may be
taken in a good or bad sense, according as its adjuncts
require. Frequently he applies it to the principles and   Στοιχεῖον.
rudiments of the Jewish religion, or Mosaical institutions: Gal. iv. 3,
Στοιχεῖα τοῦ κόσμου,—" The rudiments of the world;" earthly, carnal,
worldly, as opposed to the spiritual, heavenly principles of the gospel: verse 9,'Ασθενῆ καὶ πτωχὰ στοιχεῖα,"Weak and beggarly elements,"
which could not enrich the souls of men with grace. See Col. ii. 8,
20. Nor doth he at any time make use of this word but when he
treateth with the Jews, or those that did Judaize. By Peter the
word is used in another sense; either properly or metaphorically,
2 Pet. iii. 10, 12.

Στοιχεῖα are the " first principles" of any thing, natural or artificial, or the first ground of any science; as the letters of the alphabet
are the στοιχεῖα of reading,—the principles, rudiments, elements.

Στοιχεῖα τῆς ἀρχῆς,—that is, τὰ στοχεῖα τὰ πρῶτα, the
" first principles," as in our translation; " the principles   Τῆς ἀρχῆς.
of the beginning."

Τῶν λογίων τοῦ Θεοῦ, " of the oracles of God," " eloquiorum Dei."
Λόγια Θεοῦ are the Scriptures; usually in the New
applied unto those of the Old Testament: Acts vii. 38,   Τῶν λογίων
"Ος ἐδέξατο λόγια ζῶντα δοῦναι ἡμῖν,—" Who received the   τοῦ Θεοῦ.
living oracles to give unto us;" that is, the law, " which if a man

do, he shall live therein." The Jews ἐπιστεύθησαν τὰ λόγια τοῦ Θεοῦ,
—" were intrusted with the oracles of God," Rom. iii. 2; that is,
all the scriptures of the Old Testament: so that what was not
committed unto them in the same way is not to be reckoned
among the "oracles of God" belonging unto the Old Testament.
1 Pet. iv. 11, Εἴ τις λαλεῖ, ὡς λόγια Θεοῦ,—" If any man speak,
as the oracles of God;" that is, let them that teach, speak with
gravity and authority, and every way conformably to the Scriptures. And the Scriptures are thus called, because as oracles
they were given out from God by inspiration, 2 Tim. iii. 16, 2 Pet.
i. 21.

We may now, therefore, inquire what it is that the apostle intends
by these "first rudiments" or "principles of the oracles of God."
It is generally apprehended that he designs the *catechetical principles* of Christian religion,—which also, as it is supposed, he reckons
up in the beginning of the next chapter; such principles as converts, or young children, are usually instructed and catechised in.
And it may be he calls them "principles," as the Jews call the
principal heads of their religion "fundamenta legis," the "foundations of the law;" as he also calls these principles θεμέλιον, the
"foundation," Heb. vi. 1. But yet, upon the consideration of the
words, and his use of them in other places, before declared, I judge
that he hath another design. Στοιχεῖα he elsewhere declares to be
the institutions of the law; and λόγια τοῦ Θεοῦ peculiarly denote the
scriptures of the Old Testament. The use and end of these institutions, as appointed and declared in the oracles of God, was to type
out Jesus Christ, as our apostle will more fully afterwards prove and
confirm. This was the first thing that the Jews were to learn in
them, by them, and from them; namely, that unto the Lord Christ,
his person, his office, his death and sacrifice, testimony was given by
Moses and the prophets; as also that these things alone were represented in the institutions of the law. These were "the rudiments of
the oracles of God" committed unto the Jews; and these,—that is, the
meaning, sense, end and use of them,—they had not learned, but had
need to be taught them again. This made them incline to their old
Judaism, make little progress in the perception of the mysteries of
the gospel, and desire to mix the ceremonies of the law with the
ordinances thereof. But as this was peculiar unto them, so I deny
not but that, by just analogy, it may be extended unto the first
necessary principles of Christian religion. And from the whole of
this discourse we may observe,—

Obs. IV. That the holy Scriptures are to be looked on, consulted,
and submitted unto, as "the oracles of God."

The consideration of their being so adds to our duty, and directs
us in its discharge. For we are called by it to weigh aright what is

ascribed unto them and what belongs to them as such. And this will influence us with that due regard and reverence which is required towards them. Thus we may consider,—1. Their *efficacy and power*. Stephen calls them τὰ λόγια ζῶντα, the "living oracles" of God, Acts vii. 38. They are so in respect of their Author,—they are the oracles of "the living God;" whereas the oracles wherewith Satan infatuated the world were most of them at the shrines and graves of dead men; whence, in their idolatries, the Israelites were charged to have "ate the sacrifices of the dead," Ps. cvi. 28. And they are so in respect of their use and efficacy; they are "living," because life-giving oracles unto them that obey them. "Keep this word," saith Moses, "for it is your life," Deut. xxxii. 47. And God says that he gave the people precepts, "which if a man do, he shall live in them," Ezek. xx. 11. And it hinders not that Stephen speaks of the law given by Moses, concerning which our apostle says that it was "the ministry of death," 2 Cor. iii. 7; for it was not so in itself, but by reason of the sin and inability of men to keep it. So the law could not give life, in that it was weak through sin, Rom. viii. 3. Besides, Paul speaks only of the *preceptive part* of the law, with the curse annexed unto its transgression. Stephen treats of the whole, as it had respect unto Jesus Christ. They are words accompanied with divine power and efficacy, to quicken and give life unto them that obey them; which proceeds from their Author, and his power in them, as Heb. iv. 12. The Scriptures are not a "dead letter," as some have blasphemed, but the "living oracles of God," —that is, life-giving, quickening; or they are accompanied with a living power, which they will put forth and exert toward the souls of men. For God still speaks in them unto us. So saith Stephen: "Moses received the living oracles of God to give unto us;"—'not to our fathers only, who lived in those days, but unto us also, now so many generations after.' And in the same manner doth God, by his prophets and apostles, continue to speak to us; which gives power and efficacy unto their word. 2. *Authority*. They are the "oracles of God," who hath supreme authority over the souls and consciences of us all. So the Thessalonians are commended, that "when they received the word, they received it not as the word of men, but as it is in truth, the word of God," 1 Epist. ii. 13; that is, absolutely submitting their souls and consciences unto the authority of God, speaking therein and thereby. And without this respect we can never read nor hear the Scripture in a due manner. 3. *Infallible truth* and absolute certainty. They are the "oracles of God," who is the first truth, whose being is truth, and who cannot lie. Every thing that may be false hath an inconsistency with his being. To suppose that any thing which is not absolutely true can proceed from him, is to deny him to be God. Peter gives no other proof

that in the preaching of the gospel they "followed not cunningly-
devised fables," but that they were confirmed by the oracle of God,
2 Pet. i. 16–21. God is "a God of truth," Deut. xxxii. 4; and all
his words are "words of truth," Eccles. xii. 10. Herein then, alone,
the souls of men can find assured rest and peace. Whatever else
they may lean upon, whatever appearance of truth it may have, yet
falsehood and a lie may be in it. Before God gave his oracles unto
men,—that is, before he sent out his light and truth to lead and
guide them,—they did nothing but perpetually wander in ignorance,
error, and darkness, unto destruction. And so far as any yet take
any thing else but the oracles of truth for their guide, they must
continually fluctuate; and though they are not always actually deceived, they are never certain but that they are so. "I will show
thee what is noted in the scripture of truth," Dan. x. 21, is the only
guide we have for our souls. 4. *Mysteries.* "Oracles" have
mysteries in them, and under this covert Satan endeavoured to hide
his delusions. For whereas the oracles of God were mysterious
from the matter contained in them, which is sacred, holy, sublime,
and incomprehensible, he delivered himself in dark, enigmatical,
dubious expressions, that, making an appearance of something mysterious, he might draw a cloud of darkness over his lies and false-
hoods. And it is in opposition unto all the pretended mysteries of
Gentile worship, that our apostle, summing up the principal doctrines concerning the person and mediation of Christ Jesus, says,
"Without controversy great is the mystery of godliness," 1 Tim.
iii. 16. The oracles of God are mysterious from the depths and excellency of the things revealed, delivered in words of truth and sober-
ness. And this will teach us how we ought to behave ourselves
with respect unto the word, these oracles of God. It is generally
owned to be our duty to read it, to study it, to meditate upon it,
and to attend unto its dispensation in preaching; and those by
whom these things are neglected shall bear their own judgment:
but as to the manner of the discharge of these duties, there may be
a great failure among the best. That diligence, that reverence, that
submission of mind and conscience, that dependence on God for the
revelation of his mind and will, which ought constantly to accompany all them who consider and attend unto the oracles of God, we
are too often at a loss in.

Obs. V. God hath, in infinite love and wisdom, so disposed of his
word as that there are first principles, plain and necessary, laid down
in it, to facilitate the instruction he intends thereby.

Men have learned this wisdom in teaching of all arts and sciences.
They first lay down general principles and theorems, which they
make the basis and foundation of all their following instructive deductions. And so there are "first principles of the oracles of God."

And,—1. They are *plain*, and easy to be learned. The things themselves contained in them, as hath been showed, are deep and mysterious; but they are all of them so plainly declared, as that he who runs may read them. It is an unquestionable truth, that what is not clearly and plainly revealed in the word, though it be true, and the knowledge of it very useful, yea, necessary to some persons in some circumstances, yet it doth not belong unto those "principles of the oracles of God," which it is the duty of all men expressly to know and believe. I could go over all the principles that are of this nature, and evince that they are all of them so plainly, so fully, so clearly revealed, taught, and expressed, and that in words and terms so suited unto the reason and understandings of men, that none unto whom the word of God comes can be ignorant of them without the guilt of supine negligence and horrible sloth; nor will any err about them, unless their minds are prepossessed with invincible prejudices, or carnal, corrupt, and earthly affections. And this is necessarily required unto the nature of first principles. They must be maxims plainly and evidently declared and asserted, or they are very unmeet to be the first principles of knowledge in any kind.

2. They are such as being learned, received, believed in a due manner, the way is plain for men towards *perfection;* they have such an influence into all other sacred truths,—which, indeed, are but deductions from them, or lesser streams from that blessed fountain which is contained in them,—and do so suit and prepare the mind for them,— that they have an easy access unto it. The minds of men being duly inlaid with these "first principles of the oracles of God," it is unconceivable how they may thrive in the knowledge of the deepest mysteries, and that in a due manner. If, indeed, when men have been instructed in these principles, they grow careless and negligent, as though they had obtained enough, and need seek no farther, as is the manner of many, they will be of no advantage unto them. He that lays the foundation of a house, and neglects the carrying on of the building, will find it but a sorry shelter in a storm. And whereas God hath designed the knowledge of these principles as a means unto a further growth and improvement, from whence they are so termed, where that end is neglected, he will blast the other attainment, that it shall be utterly useless. But where this foundation is well laid, where these principles are duly learned, and improved as they ought to be, they make the way smooth and easy unto greater degrees of knowledge; I mean, unto such as are industrious in the use of means. And this, as it makes evident what is our duty concerning them, so it gives great encouragement unto the discharge thereof. We ought to learn them, because they are principles; and we are encouraged to learn them, because they open the way to further improvement.

3. They are such, as that if they are not *duly learned*, rightly understood, and if the mind be not possessed with them, all endeavours after higher attainments in light and knowledge are preposterous, and will prove fruitless. Yea, some are *reaching;* and among others, sundry consequents, all of them dangerous, and some of them pernicious, do ensue on this neglect. For, (1.) Some are apt to be reaching after *abstruse speculations*, both in themselves and in the manner of their revelation, before they have any acquaintance with those "first principles of the oracles of God." And constantly one of these events doth ensue; for either they are "always learning, and never come to the knowledge of the truth," wearying themselves in the search of such things as they cannot comprehend nor be led into a right understanding of; or else are "vainly puffed up in their fleshly minds," upon a presumption that they know some marvellous thing beyond the common rate of other men, when they know nothing as they ought, nothing with respect unto its proper principles. (2.) This is the cause whence so many persons, using industry and diligence in the hearing of the word, do yet learn, thrive, and profit so little as they do. All preaching, at least for the most part, supposeth a knowledge of these first principles; without which not one word that is spoken therein can well be understood. Many, therefore, being unacquainted with them, must of necessity lose that advantage by the preaching of the word which otherwise they might attain. And this was the very case in hand between our apostle and the Hebrews, which put him to such a strait. He knew that it was his duty to declare to the church "the whole counsel of God," and that in the deepest and most mysterious truths of the gospel, so carrying them on to perfection; but he also found that these things would prove unprofitable to many, because their minds were not as yet well inlaid with the "first principles of the oracles of God." This put him to the strait he expresseth in the beginning of the sixth chapter. And so it falls out among ourselves. It is ofttimes a grief unto us, to consider how many of our hearers seem to have little advantage by the best of our endeavours, because of their ignorance in the supposed principles and foundations of what we deliver. Hence they hear, and go away altogether unconcerned in what they have heard; and, it may be, complain of the sermon or preacher, when the fault was solely in their own understandings. But as we ought, for the sake of some who are real beginners, to divert unto their instruction in those fundamental principles of religion; so we ought not, in a compliance with their sloth and negligence who have carelessly omitted the acquainting of themselves with them, cease our endeavour to carry on more diligent and thriving souls toward perfection,—nor would Paul do so in this place. In the meantime, parents, masters, ministers, all in

their several stations and capacities, ought to consider of how great importance it is to have all those committed to their care, or under their inspection, well instructed in those "first principles of the oracles of God." (3.) Hence it is that multitudes are so easily seduced unto foolish and sottish errors, and such as overthrow the foundation of truth and faith in them who do entertain them. Things are proposed unto them under specious pretences, which at first seem to have somewhat excellent and peculiar in them, and, as far as they can discern, are of no evil tendency; but after they have embraced them, and are brought under their power, it is found, when it is too late, that they have virtually renounced the foundation of the gospel, and are now taken in the snare that cannot be broken, for it is for their life.

4. These principles are such, as that if they alone are known, received, believed, obeyed, provided their progress in knowledge be not obstructed by men's own negligence, prejudices, or lusts, they may attain the *end of faith* and obedience, in the salvation of their souls. They are such, as without the express knowledge whereof in those that are adult, the Scripture speaks nothing of any possibility of attaining unto life and immortality. And as was declared before, the knowledge of them, where they are not duly improved unto an increase of light, according to the means we do enjoy, is no way available; but upon a supposition that a man is brought unto an acquaintance with these principles of the oracles of God, in the want of means and advantages to carry him on towards perfection in the knowledge of other principles of truth, useful and necessary in their places and circumstances, though he should be ignorant of them, or fall into errors about them, not inconsistent with or destructive of the principles he hath received, they are sufficient in their own kind to lead and conduct him unto rest with God. And as this consideration will not give the least countenance unto the sloth or negligence of any who do or may enjoy the advantage of growing in the knowledge of God, and of our Lord Jesus Christ; so it is a relief with respect unto their condition who, by reason of the blindness of their pretended guides, or on any other occasion, are not supplied with the means of a further improvement.

And from what hath been discoursed it appears, both of what great importance it is unto our faith and obedience, to be well instructed in the chief principles of religion, as also what an inexcusable fault it is, in those who for any season have enjoyed the means of instruction, to be found defective herein.

Obs. VI. Those who live under the preaching of the gospel are obnoxious to great and provoking sins, if they diligently watch not against them. Such was that of these Hebrews here mentioned. But hereof, as also of the danger of such sins, we must treat more afterwards.

THIRDLY, It follows, as an illustration of what was before charged on the Hebrews, and to the same purpose, "And are become such as have need of milk, and not of strong meat." This allusion the apostle chose, to represent unto them the state or condition whereinto they were brought by their sinful negligence, as also to give life and strength unto his reproof; and therefore pursues it to the end of the chapter.

Γεγόνατε. Γεγόνατε, "ye are become." The word may be taken in a twofold sense; for,—

1. It may signify, 'It appears what you are, and what you stand in need of. It may be some have had other thoughts of you, by reason of your profession, and the time of instruction you have enjoyed. You have had "a name to live," and possibly to be in a very flourishing condition, as being the first church in the world, the mother in some sort of all other churches, and such as have had privileges which no other church ever had, or ever shall enjoy. But, upon trial, it is made manifest how dull and slothful you have been, how ignorant you are, and how little you have improved your season.' And it will in like manner be one day evident, that many churches and persons who make a goodly appearance, on the account of their outward privileges and enjoyments, will be found, when they are brought into the balance of the sanctuary, to be light, empty, dead, and every way insufficient. But things are changed in the world. Churches are now esteemed of, or pretend unto an esteem, by their pleas of antiquity, outward order, solemnity of forms, and a seemingly sacred grandeur, without the least respect unto the light, knowledge, and holiness of their members. In the days of the apostles it was not so. Unless churches in their members did thrive in grace, knowledge, and holiness, they had no respect unto outward things, though never so good in their place and order, but as aggravations of the sin and judgment of unprofitable professors. And this may be the sense of that expression, γεγόνατε, "ye are become;" for so are many things in the Scripture said then to be, when they are made manifest, or appear so to be.

2. It may be the apostle by this expression denotes a decay and declension in them. 'You are become,' that is now, 'what formerly you were not.' So Chrysostom on the place: Οὐκ εἶπε χρείαν ἔχετε, ἀλλὰ γεγόνατε χρείαν ἔχοντες· τουτεστι ὑμεῖς ἠθελήσατε, ὑμεῖς ἑαυτοὺς εἰς τοῦτο κατεστήσατε,—"This is that which you have now brought yourselves unto." They had been taught, and they had learned the things of the gospel; but now, through their carelessness, forgetfulness, and want of industry to grow in grace and knowledge, they were decayed into great darkness, ignorance, and confusion. And it is known that this is no unusual thing among professors. Through their inadvertency, sinful negligence, worldly-mindedness, they lose

the knowledge which they had attained; and, on a perverse continuance in such an evil course, through the righteous judgment of God, even all that they seemed to have is taken from them. Knowledge may be lost as well as holiness, at least as unto the degrees of it. And it is most probable, from the nature and tenor of his whole discourse, that this is the evil which the apostle chargeth them withal; which sufficiently manifests the greatness of their sin and the danger of their condition. For it is worse with them who have, through their own default, lost what they had attained in the ways of God, than with those who never attained what was their duty so to do; for the loss of light and knowledge proceeds from causes of a more enormous guilt than a mere ignorance of them ordinarily doth, or indeed can do.

What they were thus become, as to their state and condition, the apostle in the same similitude expresses. 1. *Positively;* they were such as had need γάλακτος, of "milk." 2. *Negatively; καὶ οὐ στερεᾶς τροφῆς,* "and not of strong meat." Χρείαν ἔχοντες, in the same sense as χρείαν ἔχετε before; only, as joined with γεγόνατε, it may intend their decay and declension into a worse estate than what they were in formerly: 'You are come to stand in need.' In the similitude proposed, the word of God is compared to food, and the several sorts of it, both as to their nature and use; for it is the food of our souls. And natural food is distinguished by the apostle in this place into "milk" and "strong meat;" which gives us a distribution of the oracles of God into two general heads also, answering in respect of use unto these two sorts of food. *(Χρείαν ἔχοντις.)*

1. Positively, "*You have need of milk.*" The whole word of God is, it may be, sometimes compared absolutely unto milk, because of its purity and freedom from corrupt mixtures, *(Γάλακτος.)* whence it is fit for nourishment: 1 Pet. ii. 2, "As new-born babes, desire the sincere milk of the word, that ye may grow thereby." Nothing is of a more natural nourishment than milk; and it is never hurtful but where the body is prepossessed with obstructions. These in the mind, with respect to the word, the apostle in that place warns us to cast out. Verse 1, "Wherefore, laying aside all malice, and all guile, and hypocrisies, and envies, and evil speakings, as new-born babes." So James doth in like manner, chap. i. 21. In this place, I say, it is supposed that the whole gospel, the whole word of God, which is the food of our souls, is compared unto milk. But I rather judge that even here some especial parts or doctrines of the word, suited to the condition of them to whom the apostle speaks, are intended. He calls them "new-born babes;" that is, persons newly converted to Christ, and it may be but weak in the faith. These he adviseth to seek after suitable food in the word, for the nourishment of their souls, or the strengthening of them in faith and obedience; and that is those

plain doctrines of truth which were meet for them who as yet were
not capable of higher mysteries. It is therefore some parts of the
word only, and some things taught therein, which are compared to
milk, both with respect unto the nature and common use of it. It
is a kind of food that is easy of digestion, needs no great strength
of nature to turn it into nutriment; and is therefore the common
nourishment of babes, and children, and sick persons, not sufficing to
maintain the health and strength of persons of full age and a
healthy constitution. So our apostle useth the same similitude,
1 Cor. iii. 1, 2, "And I, brethren, could not speak unto you as unto
spiritual, but as unto carnal, even as unto babes in Christ. I have
fed you with milk, and not with meat; for hitherto ye were not able
to bear it, neither yet now are ye able." The same similitude, the
same distribution of the parts of it, is used as in this place. The
reason why babes are fed with milk is because they want strength
of nature to digest stronger meat; so he says they were able to bear
milk, but not strong meat spiritually. It is evident, therefore, what
the apostle here understandeth by "milk," namely, such doctrines of
truth as he calls "the first principles of the oracles of God,"—plain
and fundamental truths; such in some measure they might be capable of, but not of the great and deep mysteries of the gospel. And
he declares whom he intends by these "babes," even such as are
"carnal;" that is, such as, by reason of their indulgence unto their
carnal affections, had kept their souls in a weak and distempered
condition as unto spiritual things.

This condition of theirs, as it was a consequent of their own sin,
so it was a grief and discouragement unto him who designed and
earnestly desired to carry them on unto perfection, "unto a perfect
man, unto the measure of the stature of the fulness of Christ." And
this being the great end of the ministry towards the church, Eph.
iv. 12, 13, it is no small trouble unto all that are faithful in the discharge of their office, when they find their hearers not so to thrive
as to be capable of receiving the highest mysteries of truth. It is
grievous unto them, either always to dwell on the first rudiments of
religion, or to treat of things which they fear to be above the capacity of their auditors. Their delight and satisfaction is to be dis-
persing the mysteries of the gospel and of the kingdom of God.
Hereof we have a most eminent instance in our apostle. His writing and his preaching to the churches were of the same kind, as in
sundry places he doth declare. And we see that the greatest part
of his epistles is taken up with the declaration of the deepest mysteries of the will, wisdom, and counsel of God. And for this cause
he is now by some reflected on, as a person whose writings are obscure, and hard to be understood; for men begin not to fear to
cast the shame and guilt of their own ignorance on a pretended obscurity in his writings. Thus these Hebrews had need of milk, and

that not through the tenderness of their constitution, but by having contracted an ill habit of mind.

2. Negatively, he says they had *not need of "strong meat;"* that is, it was not expedient, in their present condition, to set it before them, unless they were first sufficiently excited out of their stupid negligence. Στερεὰ τροφή is "meat yielding solid nourish-   Στερεᾶς τροφῆς.
ment." Now, as in general all the principal mysteries of the gospel, that whole wisdom which he preached ἐν τοῖς τελείοις, 1 Cor. ii. 6,—"unto" (or "among") "them that were perfect" or adult, and grown up unto some good measure in the stature of Christ,—are intended hereby; so in especial he hath respect unto the things which belong unto the priesthood and sacrifice of Christ. These are solid meat unto the souls of sound believers. And hereby Christians may take a due measure of their spiritual health, strength, and growth. If the solid doctrines concerning the offices of Christ, especially his priesthood and sacrifice, are suited to their minds and affections, if they find food and spiritual nourishment in them, it is a good evidence of their progress in the knowledge of Christ and the gospel. But if such things have neither taste nor relish in them unto their spiritual appetite; if they do not readily digest them, nor find benefit by them, it is manifest they are but weak and feeble, as the apostle further proves in the following verses.

And we may observe from the first sense of that expression, "You are become,"—

Obs. VII. There will be a time when false and unprofitable professors will be made manifest and discovered, either to their present conviction or their eternal confusion.

And from the second sense of it, it may be observed,—

Obs. VIII. That men do oftentimes secretly wax worse and worse under profession and means of grace. Of the causes and ways hereof see our exposition on chap. iv. 13.

Obs. IX. There are provisions of truth in the Scripture, suitable to the spiritual instruction and edification of all sorts of persons that belong to Jesus Christ. There is in it both "milk" and "strong meat."

The disciples of Christ ever were, and ever will be, in this world, of several sorts, sizes, and capacities. In the house of God there are all sorts of vessels, of lesser and greater quantity, cups and flagons, Isa. xxii. 24. There are in the church babes, young men, and fathers, 1 John ii. There are among the hearers of the gospel persons sound, healthy, thriving; and those that are weak, sickly, and feeble. Their different ages and capacities, with their distinct measures of opportunities and diligence, their temptations and occasions of life, make this diversity necessary and unavoidable;—as in the same flock of sheep there are lambs, and strong sheep, and ewes great with young. Now, in a house where there dwell together old men, and strong men, and children or babes, those that are healthy and those

that are sick, if they should be all of them bound up unto the same
diet or food, some of them must necessarily perish. But a wise
householder will provide for them differently, according to their
several states and capacities, that which shall be wholesome and convenient for them all; and the principal wisdom of the steward of the
house is to give out to every one a portion proper for him. So is it in
the church of Christ, which is the family of God; and therefore the
great Householder hath prepared his heavenly manna according to
the spiritual appetite and digestion of them all. As upon the receiving of manna every one gathered לְפִי־אָכְלוֹ, Exod. xvi. 18,—according to his appetite and need,—so is the heavenly manna of the word
disposed, that every one may have what suits him. There are in
the word, as was said of old, fords where the lamb may wade, and
depths where the elephant may swim. There are in it plain doctrines and first principles, necessary unto all; and there are truths of
a deeper search, that are profitable to some. And concerning these
things we may observe,—1. That the Lord Christ hath an *especial
care of the weak, the young, the sick,* and *the diseased* of his flock.
There is, indeed, a difference to be put between them who are so invincibly by their natural infirmities, temptations, and tenderness in
the ways of religion, and those who are so through their own neglect
and sloth, as it was with these Hebrews. The latter sort are severely
to be admonished and rebuked; but to the former Christ showeth
singular tenderness and compassion. So in the first place he com-
mitteth unto Peter the care and charge of his lambs, John xxi. 15.
And the like affection he declareth in his own person, as he is the
great Shepherd of the sheep, Isa. xl. 11. He will take care of the
whole flock, according to the office and duty of a shepherd, but his
especial care is concerning his lambs, and those that are with young;
and in the severity which he threateneth against false and idle
shepherds, he regards principally their neglect of the diseased, the
sick, the broken, and that which is driven away, Ezek. xxxiv. 4.
These, therefore, in the dispensation of the gospel, must be carefully
attended unto, and food convenient, or nourishment suitable to their
state and condition, is carefully to be provided for them. And not
only so, but they are in all things to be dealt withal with the same
gentleness, tenderness, and meekness, that Christ exerciseth towards
them. He will one day call some to an account for rough and
brutish usage of his lambs. Whether they have hindered them from
being fed according to their necessity, or have driven them from their
pasture, or have further exercised severity against them, it must be
all accounted for unto the love and care of Christ. But, 2. The *delight* of Christ is in them that thrive, and are strong in the faith, as
those from whom he receives most of honour and glory. We, therefore, ought to aim that they may all be such, such as may take in

and thrive upon solid food, the deeper mysteries of the gospel. To pretend, from Christ's care of the weak, that those other more deep and mysterious truths, which the apostle compareth unto "strong meat," are needless to be inquired into, is highly blasphemous. This some are come unto; they think we have no need to search into the principal mysteries of the gospel, but to take up with the plain lessons of morality which are given us therein, and in other good books besides. But a higher reflection on the wisdom of God men can scarcely contract the guilt of. To what end hath he revealed these things unto us? Why hath he recorded that revelation in his word? Why doth he appoint his whole counsel, so revealed, to be declared and preached? Certainly never was any thing more unwisely contrived than the giving the Scripture to the church, if it be not our duty to endeavour an acquaintance with the principal things contained in it. But these men seem not to know the design of God towards his church. They may learn it if they please from our apostle, Eph. iv. 7-14. It is not merely that men may have so much light and knowledge, faith and obedience, as will, as it were, serve their turn, to bring them at last unto heaven, though no pretended measures of these things are sufficient for that end, where men rest in them to the neglect of further attainments. But God aimeth to bring men unto clearer discoveries of his wisdom, grace, and love, than they have yet attained; into nearer communion with himself; to a fuller growth in light, knowledge, faith, and experience; that even in this world he may more eminently communicate of himself unto them: which he doth in and by the truths which they despise. These truths and doctrines, therefore, also, which the apostle calls "strong meat" for "them that are of full age," are to be searched, inquired into, and preached. Wherefore, hence it will follow in general,—1. That it is the wisdom of the dispensers of the gospel to consider what doctrines are most suitable unto the capacity and condition of their hearers. And in particular, 2. That it is a preposterous and unprofitable course, to instruct them in the greater mysteries of the gospel who have not as yet well laid the foundation, in understanding the more common and obvious principles of it; which the apostle confirms and illustrates:—Verses 13, 14, "For every one that useth milk is unskilful in the word of righteousness; for he is a babe. But strong meat belongeth unto them that are of full age, even those who, by reason of use, have their senses exercised to discern both good and evil."

These verses contain a further illustration and confirmation of what was before asserted; and a reason is added with respect unto the Hebrews, why they stood in need of milk, and not of strong meat. To this end the apostle gives a description of the two sorts of hearers before mentioned. First, Of those that use *milk*, verse

13; that is, who ought so to do. Secondly, Of those unto whom
strong meat doth more properly appertain, verse 14. Of the first
he says, "Every one that useth milk is unskilful in the word of
righteousness." It may be the reasoning of the apostle would have
seemed more perspicuous if the subject and predicate of this proposition had been changed; as if he had said, 'Those who are unskilful in the word of righteousness had need of milk.' And so he
speaks in the next verse, where those who are of "full age," and
"have their senses exercised to discern good and evil," are said to
have need or use of "strong meat." But all comes to the same
purpose. Having told them in the verse foregoing that they were
"such as had need of milk," he describes in this what sort of persons they are who are in that condition, even such as are "unskilful
in the word of righteousness;" such are "babes."

Πᾶς ὁ μετέχων γάλακτος, "quisquis lacte participatur." This is
the subject spoken of: every one who is of the number
Πᾶς ὁ μετέ- of them who, by reason of their infirm, weak state and
χων γάλακτος. condition, ought to be fed and nourished with milk.
What is this milk, what is intended by it, and what it is to be fed
with it, have been already declared. It is mentioned here only to
repeat the subject spoken of, and which is further to be described.
For he is,—

Ἄπειρος λόγου δικαιοσύνης. "Unskilful," say we. "Rudis," "in-
Ἄπειρος. expertus." Properly, "one that hath no experience,"
as in the margin of our translation. So any one is
said to be "inexpertus armorum," "unexpert in arms." So David
put off Saul's armour, no doubt excellent in itself, because he had
not been so exercised in such arms as to be ready and expert in
them. Ἄπειρος is, he who is "unacquainted" with any thing, either
as to its nature or its use. And when this is referred unto the understanding, it is not amiss rendered by "want of skill," "unskilful."
And this is spoken, not of him who is utterly ignorant of any matter,
but who, having some general knowledge of it, is not able wisely
to manage and improve it unto its proper end. And it is spoken
with respect unto "the word of righteousness."

Λόγου δικαιοσύνης. One thinks that by δικαιοσύνη here, τελειότης is
intended,—λόγος τελειότητος: and this is put for τέλειος:
Λόγου δικαιο- and λόγος τέλειος is the same with that σοφία, 1 Cor. ii. 6,
σύνης. and γνῶσις, Eph. iii. 10. But whatever we please or
fancy may be thus collected out of any word or text, by hopping
from one thing to another without any reason or consequence. This
"word of righteousness" is no other but the word or doctrine of the
gospel. It is λόγος σταυροῦ, the "word of the cross," from its principal subject, 1 Cor. i. 18; and it is λόγος δικαιοσύνης, from its nature,
use, and end. Therein is the righteousness of God revealed unto

us, Rom. i. 17; and the righteousness of Christ, or Christ as he is "the end of the law for righteousness to every one that believeth," Rom. x. 4, and so alone declares the way of righteousness,—what that is which God approves and accepts, and how we come to be interested therein; as we shall see afterwards more at large.

Now, the Hebrews are not said to be ignorant, that is utterly, of this "word of righteousness," for they owned and made profession of the gospel; but only to be "unskilful" in it, especially in the great mysteries of it, such as he was now communicating unto them. They had not attained unto a distinct and clear understanding of the truths of the gospel, so as to be able to improve them to their proper ends; or, they had not experience in themselves of their power, efficacy, and reality.

Lastly, The apostle gives the general reason of this whole state and condition, whence it is thus with any one: Νήπιος γάρ ἐστι. 'It can be no otherwise with such a one, see- Νήπιος. ing he is but a babe.' He intends, therefore, in the former words, not such as use milk occasionally, but such as feed on milk only. Such are νήπιοι. The word is used to signify either the least sort of children, such as we call babes, or such as are weak and foolish like them. The allusion is unto the first sort,—such as live on milk alone. There are sundry qualities that are proper unto children, as simplicity, innocency, submission, weakness, and ignorance. And because these are different, believers are sometimes, with respect unto some of these qualities, compared unto them; and sometimes are forbidden to be like them, with respect unto others of them. David says of himself that he was as a "weaned child," because of his submission, and the resignation of his will unto the will of God, Ps. cxxxi. 2. And our Saviour requires us to receive the kingdom of God as little children, casting out those perverse and distem-pered affections and passions which are apt to retard us in our duty, Matt. xviii. 3, Luke xviii. 17; and, on the other side, with respect unto that weakness, ignorance, and inconstancy, which they are under the power of, we are forbidden to be like them, 1 Cor. xiv. 20, Eph. iv. 14. Here the respect unto a babe is upon the account of these latter qualities. "Such," saith Chrysostom, "as must be fed with milk; for being left unto themselves, they will put dirt and straw into their mouths." And it is plain what sort of persons the apostle intendeth in this description: they are such as, enjoying the dispensation of the word, or who have done so for some season, yet, through their own sloth and negligence, have made little or no proficiency in spiritual knowledge. Such persons are babes, and have need of milk, and are not capable of instruction in the more heavenly mysteries of the gospel. And we may observe, that,—

Obs. I. The gospel is the only "word of righteousness," in itself and unto us.

Utterly in vain will it be to seek for any material concernment of righteousness elsewhere. The law was originally a word of righteousness both in itself and unto us. As it was in our hearts, it was that effect of the righteousness of God in us, whereby we were made conformable and like unto him; which was our righteousness, Eph. iv. 24, Col. iii. 10, Eccles. vii. 29. As written in tables of stone, it was a transcript of what was created in our hearts, representing the righteousness of God *objectively* in the way of doctrine, as the other did *subjectively* by the way of principle. The sum of its precepts and promises was, "Do this, and live;" or, "The man that doeth those things shall live by them," Rom. x. 5, from Lev. xviii. 5; Ezek. xx. 11; Deut. xxx. 14. Hence it was every way a complete word of righteousness. And on all occasions it is in the Scripture pleaded as just or righteous, holy, equal, good; such as God was glorified in, and man had no reason to complain of. But now, upon the entrance of sin, this law, although it continues eternally righteous *in itself*, yet it is no longer a word of righteousness *unto us*. Nay, it is become an occasion of more sin and more wrath, and on both accounts, of a greater distance between God and us; which are contrary to that righteousness which it was originally the word of, Rom. iv. 15, vii. 10–13. We were dead, and it could not give life; and after we were once sinners, it could do nothing at all towards the making of us righteous, Rom. viii. 3, 4. Wherefore the gospel is now the only "word of righteousness," both in itself and unto us. It is so declaratively, as the only means of its revelation; and it is so efficiently, as the only means of its communication unto us.

1. It is so *declaratively*, because "therein is revealed the *righteousness of God*," Rom. i. 17. This at first was revealed by the law; but now, as to our interest in it and benefit by it, it is so only by the gospel. For that declaration of the righteousness of God which remains in the law, however it be pure and holy in itself, tends not to beget righteousness in us, nor to give us peace with God. This, therefore, is done only by the gospel, and that on several accounts. For,—

(1.) Therein the *righteousness* and *severity* of God against sin are more fully revealed than ever they were or could be by the law, in its sanction or most severe execution. It is true, our apostle tells us that "by the law is the knowledge of sin,"—that is, of what it is, or what is so; but the knowledge of what it deserves in the righteousness of God is made more openly manifest by the gospel. Had God executed the sentence of the law on all offenders, he had thereby declared that he *would not* pardon sin; but in the gospel he declares that he *could not* do so, with the honour of his holiness, without an equivalent price and satisfaction. His righteousness and severity against sin are more fully manifested in the suffering and sacrifice of Christ to make atonement for sin,—which are the foundations of the gospel,—than ever they could have been in or by the law, Rom. iii. 25, viii. 2, 3.

(2.) The *faithfulness* of God in the accomplishment of his promises is frequently in the Scripture called his " righteousness;" and it is so. And the first express promise that God ever gave unto his creatures was concerning Christ and his coming in the flesh, Gen. iii. 15. From this did all other promises of God arise, as from their spring and fountain; and upon the accomplishment thereof do all their accomplishments depend. For if this be not fulfilled, whatever appearance there may be of any such thing, yet indeed no one promise of God was yet ever fulfilled from the foundation of the world. Hereon, then, alone depended the declaration of the righteousness of God, as it consists in his faithfulness. And this is done in and by the gospel, which is a declaration of God's fidelity in the accomplishment of that ancient, that original promise, Rom. xv. 8; Luke i. 70; Acts iii. 18, 24–26.

(3.) The righteousness *which God requireth,* approveth, accepteth, is therein alone declared and revealed. And this is frequently also called " the righteousness of God," 2 Cor. v. 21, Rom. x. 3; or " the righteousness which is of God by faith," Phil. iii. 9. It is not now the righteousness revealed in the law that God doth require of us, as knowing it impossible unto us; but it is that righteousness only wherein "Christ is the end of the law for righteousness to every one that believeth," Rom. viii. 3, 4, x. 3, 4. Hence,—

2. The gospel is the word of righteousness declaratively, because it alone reveals unto us *our own righteousness;* that is, what God requireth in us and will accept from us. This is the great inquiry of mankind not utterly hardened in sin,—that is, who are not one half in hell already,—namely, what they shall do for a righteousness wherewith to appear before God, to answer his justice, and to be accepted with him; for these are the ends of our righteousness, this it must do, or it will not avail us. Here mankind, left unto themselves and unto the law, would wander everlastingly, until they were swallowed up in eternal ruin; and a thousand paths have they been tracing to this purpose. And after everything within them, without them, about them, above them, hath said unto them, 'This is not the way,' they must all, after they have walked a little while in the light of the fire and the sparks they have kindled, receive this from the hand of God, that they shall lie down in sorrow, Isa. l. 11. See the loss they are brought unto expressed, Mic. vi. 6, 7. But here the gospel ariseth like the sun in its brightness, dispelling all darkness and mists, and evidently declaring a righteousness

satisfactory unto all the wants and whole design of the soul,—a righteousness suited to the holiness of God, answering his justice, becoming ours in a way expressing the goodness, grace, and love of God, whereby all the holy properties of his nature are glorified, and our souls secured. And this is the righteousness of Christ, both in what he did and suffered for us or in our stead, imputed unto us, or reckoned unto us for our righteousness, through faith in him. This is declared in the gospel alone; and indeed the whole gospel is nothing but the declaration of it, in its nature, causes, effects and consequents. Hence principally is the gospel called a "word of righteousness," as being that blessed mystery of truth wherein the righteousness of God, of Christ, and of man, do meet and centre, to the eternal glory of God, the honour of Christ, and our salvation.

3. It is a word of righteousness declaratively, because the doctrine thereof doth clearly and eminently teach and instruct us to be righteous with that righteousness which consisteth in universal holiness and fruitfulness in good works; that is, in the discharge of all duties towards God and man. This also is called our righteousness, and therein are we commanded to be righteous, 1 John iii. 7. And although all duties of righteousness and holiness are taught and enjoined by the law, yet are they more perfectly, fully, and clearly so by the gospel. For therein the nature of them is more fully explained, directions instructive for their due performance are more full of light, plain, and evident, and enforcements of them are administered far more effectual than under the law. The doctrine of the gospel is universally a doctrine of holiness and righteousness, allowing not the least countenance, indulgence, or dispensation, on any pretence, to the least sin, but condemning the inmost disorders of the heart with the same severity that it doth the outward perpetration of actual sin, nor allowing a discharge from any duty whatever. See Tit. ii. 11, 12. And there is no more required of us in this world but that our conversation be such as becometh the gospel. And those who, upon any pretence, do make it the ministry of sin and unrighteousness, shall bear their own judgment.

Again; It is "the word of righteousness" *efficiently*, as it is the instrument of communicating righteousness unto us, or of making us righteous. For,—1. Take our righteousness for that wherewith we are righteous before God, the righteousness of God in Christ, and it is tendered unto or communicated unto us by the promises of the gospel alone, Acts ii. 38, 39. 2. Faith, whereby we receive those promises, and Christ in them, with righteousness unto life, is wrought in us by the preaching of the gospel, Rom. x. 17. And, 3. Our sanctification and holiness is wrought in us thereby, John xvii. 17. Which things ought to be more largely explained, but that I must now contract my discourse; wherefore, on all these accounts, and with respect unto all other real concernments of it, the gospel is in itself and unto us the word of righteousness. Therefore,—

Obs. II. It is a great aggravation of the negligence of persons under the dispensation of the gospel, that it is a "word of righteousness."

To evince this, it is here so called by the apostle, that such persons may know what it is that they neglect and despise. To be regardless of any message from God, not to attend unto it diligently, not to use and pursue it unto its proper end, is a high affront to the divine Majesty; but whereas this message from God is such a word of righteousness, wherein all the concerns of God's righteousness and our own are inwrapped, this is the highest aggravation that our disobedience is capable of. Consider also,—

Obs. III. That God requires, of all those who live under the dispensation of the gospel, that they should be " skilful in the word of righteousness."

Those are blamed here who, after the time they had enjoyed in hearing, were yet "unskilful" in it; and this is part of that great and severe charge which the apostle in this place manageth against some of the Hebrews. Now, this skill in the gospel which is required of us respecteth either doctrines or things. As the doctrine of the gospel is respected, so it is practical knowledge that is intended. As it respects things, so it is experience. And this the word in the original casts a regard upon; whence we place in the margin, as the true signification of it, " hath no experience." I shall not absolutely exclude either sense. And as to the first, or skill as it is a practical knowledge, it is an ability, readiness, or dexterity to use things unto their proper ends. It supposeth a notional knowledge of their nature, use, and end, and asserteth an ability and dexterity to employ them accordingly; as he who is skilful in a trade or mystery is able to manage the rules, tools, and instruments of it unto their proper end. Wherefore in the duty proposed, it is supposed that a man have the knowledge of the doctrines of the gospel; and it is required that he be able readily to manage them to their proper ends. To know the nature of this duty, we must consider what are those ends of the gospel with respect whereunto it is required of us that we be able skilfully to use and improve the truths of it. I shall name only three of them:—

1. The *increase and establishment of our faith.* There is nothing to us of greater concernment, nor is it otherwise to be done but by the word of the gospel. Thereby is faith first ingenerated; and thereby alone it is nourished, strengthened, and increased. It is the seed, it is the food, it is the life of faith. Wherein, then, consists the dexterity and ability of using the doctrine of the gospel

unto the strengthening and preserving of our faith, which is required of us? It may be reduced unto these three heads:—

(1.) The *clearing* and due application of its proper object unto it. Christ is the peculiar, immediate, and proper object of faith, and through him do we believe in God, 1 Pet. i. Now he is every way as such, in his person, offices, work, righteousness, revealed, declared, and proposed unto us, in the doctrine and promises of the gospel. Herein, therefore, consists our skill in the word of righteousness, in having in a readiness, and duly applying by faith, the doctrine and promises concerning Christ and his mediation. These are the nourishment of faith, whereby it grows and gets strength by the genuine and proper exercise of it, 2 Cor. iii. 18. And where this skill is wanting, where persons are not able out of their own stores to present their faith daily with suitable objects, as tendered in the doctrine and promises of the gospel, it will decay, and all the fruits of it will wither.

(2.) This *skill* in the word of righteousness is exercised in the preservation of faith, by a resistance unto the temptations that rise up against it. The great way of preserving faith in the assaults of Satan, is to have in a readiness some suitable and seasonable word out of the gospel whereby it may be assisted and excited. Then will faith be able to hold up its shield, whereby the fiery darts of Satan will be quenched. So dealt our Lord Jesus Christ himself in his temptation. No sooner did Satan make any assault upon him, but immediately he repelled his weapons, and secured his faith, by a suitable word out of the Scripture, all whose stores lay open to him, who was of " quick understanding in the fear of the LORD." He, therefore, who is skilful in the gospel will have in a readiness, and be able dexterously to manage, seasonable precepts, promises, warnings, instructions, and to oppose them unto all the suggestions of Satan, unto the preservation and security of his faith. Others will be at a loss, and not know what to do when temptations do befall them, yea, they are commonly bewildered in their own darkness and by their own reasonings, until they are taken in the snares of the evil one. There is a peculiar antidote in the Scripture against the poison of every temptation or suggestion of Satan. If we have them in a readiness, and are skilful in the application of them, it will be our safety or our healing.

(3.) Hereby alone is faith secured against " the cunning crafts of men that lie in wait to deceive." It is known how variously and continually faith is assaulted by the crafts, violences, and sophisms of seducers; as, for instance, by those who " have erred concerning the truth, saying that the resurrection is past already." And what is the issue of it? " They overthrow the faith of some," as 2 Tim. ii. 18. The like may be said of all other important doctrines of evangelical truth. And we see what havoc hath been made among professors by this means; how not only the faith of some, but of multitudes in our days, hath been overthrown hereby. And the reason is, because they have not been skilful in the word of righteousness, nor have known how to draw out from that magazine of sacred truths that which was necessary for the defence of their faith. The Scripture was the " tower of David, built for an armoury, wherein there hang a thousand bucklers, all shields of mighty men." There are weapons prepared in abundance for the defence of faith, if we are but ready and dexterous in their management.

It may be spoken with a confidence which the truth will warrant, that the reasons why so many do fall from the faith of the gospel unto Popery, Quakerism, or the like, may be reduced unto these two heads:—[1.] The satisfaction of some *special lust,* perverse humour or inclination; and, [2.] *Want of skill in the word of righteousness,* as it is such: all other pretences are but shades and coverings of these two reasons of apostasy.

And so there are two sorts of persons that fall from the faith:—

[1.] Such as principally seduce themselves by their own lusts and several interests. Ἄνθρωποι κατεφθαρμένοι τὸν νοῦν, ἀδόκιμοι περὶ τὴν πίστιν, 2 Tim. iii. 8; 1 Tim. vi. 5;—men of corrupt minds, that refuse and reject the truth for the love of their lusts and sins. And,—

[2.] Such as are deceived and seduced; and they are ἄκακοι, not perversely evil, Rom. xvi. 18, but unstable, because unskilful in the word.

There are two ways whereby, or two cases wherein, we have need to secure our faith against the oppositions of men, and both of them depend on our skilfulness in the word:—

[1.] When we are to prove and confirm the truth against them. So it is said of Apollos, that " he mightily convinced the Jews, showing by the Scriptures that Jesus was Christ," Acts xviii. 28. But how was he able so to do? Because he himself was " mighty in the Scriptures," verse 24; that is, he was ready and skilful in the word of righteousness,—and this whilst he was only a private disciple.

[2.] When we are to defend it against the opposition of gainsayers, and their mouths can no otherwise be stopped. If men be but skilful and ready in the Scriptures, though destitute of all advantages of learning, it is inexpressible how able they will be, and such persons have been, in confounding all the sophistry of the most subtile adversaries of the truth. When without this ability, men lie to be seized on as a prey by the next seducer. Wherefore, without the duty here enjoined, we may easily see what, on all accounts, our condition is with respect unto our faith.

2. The next end of the doctrines of the gospel, which we need

this skill to manage them unto, is the *guidance of us in the whole course of our duty*, that we be not out of our way, nor at a loss about it. The word is our rule, our guide, our light, in all our walking before God; but if we have not an acquaintance with it, if we are not ready to use and apply it, we shall never walk steadily nor uprightly.

(1.) This is our guide in the whole course of our lives. "Thy statutes," saith David, "are the men of my counsel,"—those with whom he advised on all occasions. Those who are skilful in the word, in the precepts, directions, and instructions of it, have their rule in a readiness for all occasions of duty, and in the whole course of their affairs. The way wherein they should walk will still be represented unto them; whilst others wander in the dark, and at best walk at "peradventure," or hazard, with God; which we render "walking contrary" unto him, Lev. xxvi. 21.

(2.) In particular difficult cases, which often befall us in the course of our conversation in this world. Such as these, where men are unskilful in the word, do either entangle them and fill them with perplexities, so as that they are at their wit's end, and know not what to do, or else they violently and presumptuously break through them, to the wounding of their consciences, and the hardening of their spirits against a sense of sin. But he who is thoroughly acquainted with the word, and is able dexterously to apply it unto all occasions of duty, will extricate himself from these straits in a due manner; for there is no case of this nature can befall us, but there are rules and directions in the Scripture that will guide us safely through it, if we are skilful in their application.

(3.) The right discharge of all duties towards others depends hereon, and without it we fail more or less in them all. Hence are we enabled to admonish, exhort, instruct, comfort, and reprove, those in whom we are concerned, and that with such authority as may have an influence upon their minds and consciences. Without this, we know neither the true nature, grounds, nor reasons, of any one duty we perform towards others, nor can make use of those things which only will make what we say or do effectual. As therefore it is so with respect unto the increase and preservation of our faith, so also with regard unto all our duties, the whole course of our obedience,—it is necessary that we should be skilful in the word of righteousness.

3. *Consolation* in distress depends hereon. This the Scripture is the only storehouse of. Whatever is taken from any other stores and applied unto that purpose, is but vanity and froth. Here all the springs, principles, causes, reasons, arguments, for true consolation of mind in distress, are treasured up. And on what various occasions, and how frequently, these cases occur wherein we stand

in need of especial consolation, we all know by experience. And in them all, it is unavoidable that we must either be left unto darkness and sorrow, or betake ourselves unto reliefs that are worse than our troubles, if we have not in a readiness those grounds of solid consolation which the Scripture is stored withal. But whatever are our sorrows or troubles, however aggravated or heightened, whatever be their circumstances, from what cause soever they rise, of sins or sufferings, our own or others in whom we are concerned, if we are skilful in the word of righteousness, we may at all times and places, in prisons, dungeons, exiles, have in readiness wherewith to support and refresh our souls. And this I thought meet to add for the discovery of the importance of that duty, a defect whereof is here blamed in the Hebrews by our apostle.

Again; the word signifies "want of experience," and so it respects the things of the gospel. With respect unto them it is said, ' They have not experience of the word of righteousness;' that is, of the things contained in it, and their power. And in this sense also it deserves our consideration; for the want of this experience, where we have had time and means for it, is both our great fault and our great disadvantage. Now, by this experience I intend a *spiritual sense*, taste, or relish, of the goodness, sweetness, useful excellency, of the truths of the gospel, endearing our hearts to God, and causing us to adhere unto him with delight and constancy. And this experience, which is of so great use and advantage, consists in three things:—

1. A thorough *mixture of the promises with faith.* This I shall not enlarge upon, because I have spoken unto it expressly in the second verse of the fourth chapter. In brief, it is that lively acting of faith which the Scripture expresseth by "tasting," "eating," "drinking;" which gives a real incorporation of the things we are made partakers of. When faith is assiduously acted upon the promises of God, so as that the mind or soul is filled with the matters of them, and virtue goes forth from them in all its actings, as they will be influenced by every object that it is filled withal, then the foundation is laid of their experience. This the apostle intends, Eph. iii. 17, " That Christ may dwell in your hearts by faith." Faith, by its frequent lively actings on Christ, brings him, as it were, to make a constant residence in the heart, where he always puts forth his power, and the efficacy of his grace.

2. In a *spiritual sense* of the excellency of the things believed, wherewith the affections are touched and filled. This is our taste, how that the Lord is gracious. And hence are we said to be " filled with joy in believing," as also to have the " love of God shed abroad in our hearts;" which, with sundry things of the same nature, belong unto this experience. And no tongue can express that satisfaction

which the soul receives in the gracious communication of a sense of divine goodness, grace, and love unto it in Christ, whence it "rejoiceth with joy unspeakable and full of glory." And this is different from the evanid joys of hypocrites. They are all from without, occasional, depending merely on something peculiar in the dispensation of the word, and on some circumstances of their own condition which they are commensurate unto; not engaging the heart unto greater love and more firm adherence unto God, but issuing absolutely in the present satisfaction of the affections. But that love, delight, and joy, which are a part or effect of spiritual experience, have their root within,—namely, in those actings of faith we before described. They are the fruits and flowers of it, which may be excited by external occasions, but proceed not from them; and therefore are they abiding, though liable to depressions and interruptions. But to be sure they always increase our love of, and strengthen our adherence unto God.

3. In *experiments* of the power of the word, on all occasions, especially as it is a word of righteousness. Sundry useful instances might here be insisted on; I shall mention two only:—

(1.) There is in it a sense of the power of the word in giving peace with God. This is the difficultest thing in the world to be impressed on the mind of a man really and seriously convinced of the guilt of sin. Many ways such an one cannot but try, to find some rest and satisfaction; but all, after some vain promises, do issue in disappointments. But when the soul doth really close with that way which it is directed unto by the gospel,—that is, when it mixeth it with faith as a word of righteousness,—the authority of the word in the conscience doth secure it that its peace is firm and stable. This it is to have an experiment of the word, when we find our souls satisfied and fortified by the authority of it, against all oppositions, that through Christ we are accepted of God, and are at peace with him.

(2.) In satisfying the heart to choose and prefer spiritual, invisible, and eternal things, before those that are present, and offer us the security of their immediate enjoyment. When we are satisfied that it is good for us, that it is best for us, to forego present earthly things, which we see and handle, and know full well the comfort, benefit, and advantage of, for those things which eye hath not seen, nor ear heard, nor can they by any reasonings of our own take place in the conceptions of our hearts, merely on the authority of the word, testifying to the excellency and certainty of these invisible things, then have we an experiment of the power of the word. Now, as the experience intended consists in these things, so it is easy to discern of how great importance it is, and how much it is our duty to endeavour it.

In the 14th verse, which completes the antithesis proposed, and wherein the apostle issues his discourse on this matter, four things are expressed:—1. The *subject* concerning whom he speaks, in opposition unto them whom he called *νήπιοι*, or "babes;" and these are *οἱ τέλειοι*, "those that are of full age." 2. The *food* that is proper for them, in opposition to the milk of babes; and that is *στερεὰ τροφή*, —"strong meat," or sound, solid nourishment. 3. A description of them, giving an account of what is said concerning the meetness of strong meat unto them; and that is, because they are such as have *αἰσθητήρια γεγυμνασμένα*,—"their senses exercised to discern good and evil:" which belongs unto the description of the subject of the proposition, "those of full age." 4. The *means* whereby they came into this condition; it was *διὰ τὴν ἕξιν*,—"by reason of a habit," "use," or "practice," they had got. And these things must be explained.

1. *Τέλειοι*, as opposed to *νήπιοι*, naturally, are persons adult, grown up, come to "full age." So our apostle makes the opposition, Eph. iv. 13, 14. He would have us come by the knowledge of God *εἰς ἄνδρα τέλειον*,—"to a perfect man;" that we should be no more *νήπιοι*, "children," tossed up and down: which things in both places are morally to be understood. As *νήπιοι*, therefore, are persons weak, ignorant, and unstable in spiritual things, so *τέλειοι* are those who have their understandings enlarged, and their minds settled in the knowledge of Christ, or the mysteries of the gospel.

Τέλειος, also, without respect to *νήπιος*, taken absolutely, is "perfect and complete," such a one as to whom nothing is wanting. תָּמִים, "integer," "rectus;" "upright," "sincere," "perfect." In that sense were they said to be "perfect" under the old testament, who were upright and sincere in their obedience. But this in general is not the perfection here intended; for it only respects an especial qualification of the mind with regard unto the truths of the gospel. This our apostle mentions, 1 Cor. ii. 6, *Σοφίαν λαλοῦμεν ἐν τελείοις*,—"We speak wisdom" (that is, declare the mysteries of the gospel) "among them that are perfect;" that is, such whose minds, being freed from corrupt prejudices, are enlightened by the Spirit of God, and themselves thereby initiated into the mysteries of Christ. And these he afterwards calls "spiritual men," or such as have received the Spirit of Christ, whereby we know the things that are freely given us of God, verses 12, 15.

And there are also degrees in this perfection, seeing it is not absolute. For that which is so the apostle denies to have been in himself, Phil. iii. 12. Much less is it in any of us, or attainable by us. But to "every one of us grace is given, according to the measure of the gift of Christ." An equal measure is not designed unto all, Eph. iv. 13. Every one hath his distinct size, stature, or age, which he is to arrive unto. So every one may grow up to be a

"perfect man," though one be taller and stronger than another.
And to bring every man to perfection, according to his measure, is
the design of the work of the ministry, Col. i. 28. So when any
grace is raised to a constant sincere exercise, it is said to be "perfect,"
1 John iv. 18. Wherefore the τέλειοι here, "the perfect," or "those of
full age," are such as being instructed in the doctrine of the gospel,
and using diligence in attending thereunto, have made a good progress, according to their means and capacities, in the knowledge of
Christ and his will.

2. Unto this sort of hearers "strong meat" doth belong; that is, it is
Στερεὰ τροφή.   to be provided for them and proposed unto them. This is
useful for their state and condition. What is intended by
this strong meat, food, or nourishment, hath been declared already.

3. The reason is subjoined whence it is that strong meat belongs
unto these persons; or rather, a further description is added, whence
it will appear that it doth so. They have "their senses exercised to
discern good and evil." And we must inquire,—(1.) What are the
senses intended. (2.) How they are *exercised*. (3.) What it is to
discern both good and evil.

(1.) For the first, the allusion is still continued between infants
Αἰσθητήρια.   and those that are adult. Infants have all their senses.
For αἰσθητήρια are properly "sensuum organa," the organs
of the external senses. These infants have, even eyes, ears, and the
like. And they have their internal sense in its principle. But they
know not how to use them unto any advantage. They cannot by
their taste distinguish between food which is good and wholesome,
and that which is noxious or pernicious. And the senses intended
are the faculties of understanding and judging spiritual things; the
abilities of the mind to discern, judge, and determine concerning
them. And these, in several degrees, are really in all sorts of
hearers, babes and those of full age. But,—

(2.) In those of full age these senses are γεγυμνασμένα, "exercised."
Γεγυμνασμίνα.   This makes the distinction. They are not so in babes.
Hence they are not ready and expedite in their acts
about their proper objects. They can neither make a right judgment about spiritual truths, nor duly apprehend the mysteries of
the gospel when proposed unto them; and that because the intellec-
tual faculties of their minds are not exercised spiritually about them.
And the word doth not denote an actual exercise, but that readiness,
ability, and fitness for any thing, which is attained by an assiduous
exercise; as a soldier who is trained is ready for his duty, or a
wrestler for prizes (whence the allusion is taken) unto his strivings.
Wherefore, to have our senses exercised in the way intended, is to
have our understandings and minds, through constant, sedulous
study, meditation, prayer, hearing of the word, and the like means

of the increase of grace and knowledge, to become ready, fit, and
able to receive spiritual truths, and to turn them into nourishment
for our souls.   For so it follows, they are thus exercised,—

(3.) Πρὸς διάκρισιν καλοῦ τε καὶ κακοῦ, "to the discerning of good
and evil."   Διάκρισις, is an exact judgment, putting a   Πρὸς διάκρισιν
difference between things proposed to us; a determina-   καλοῦ τε καὶ
tion upon a right discerning of the different natures of   κακοῦ.
things. And that which this judging and determining faculty is here
said to be exercised about, is *good and evil*. But whereas they are
doctrines and propositions of truth that the apostle treats concerning, it might be expected that he should have said, ' to the discerning, or dijudication, of what is *true and false*.' But, [1.] The
allusion to food, which he still carries on, requires that it should
be thus expressed.   Of that which is or may be proposed as food
unto us, some is *wholesome* and nourishing, some *hurtful* and
noxious; the first is *good*, the latter *evil*. [2.] Though the first
consideration of doctrines be, whether they be true or false, yet on
that supposition the principal consideration of them concerns their
subject-matter, whether it be good or evil unto our souls, whether
it tend unto our edification or destruction.   But whereas it is the
oracles of God that are the food proposed, and no evil can be supposed to be in them, what need of this faculty of discerning in this
case between good and evil? [1.] The similitude required a respect
to both, because food of both sorts may be proposed or set before
us. [2.] Though nothing but what is good be prepared for us in
the Scripture, in the oracles of God, yet this ability of judging or
discerning between good and evil is necessary unto us in the dispensation of them.   For, 1*st*, That may, by some, be proposed unto us
as taken from the Scripture, which indeed is not so, which is not
wholesome food, but mere *poison* to the souls of men.   Such are
those hurtful and noisome opinions which men of corrupt minds do
vent, pretending that they are derived from the Scripture, wherein
indeed they are condemned. Or, 2*dly*, Without this spiritual ability
we may ourselves misapprehend or misapply that which is *true* in
its proposal, whereby it may become evil and noxious unto us.   To
avoid these dangers, it is necessary that we have our senses exercised
unto the discerning both of good and evil.

Wherefore these persons of full age, are such as are meet to have
the mysteries of the gospel, and those especially about the priesthood and sacrifice of Christ, preached unto them, seeing their minds
and understandings are so exercised about things evangelical, as that
they are able to judge aright about the things proposed unto them,
discerning their goodness and suitableness unto the nourishment of
their souls, as also to discover what is evil, and to reject it.

4. This ability is attained διὰ τὴν ἕξιν, " by reason of use."   Ἕξις

is a "habit;" and a habit is a firm, rooted disposition, giving readiness unto and facility in acts about its proper object. Now the apostle intends such a habit as is acquired by use and exercise; whence we render it " use." The first principle or spring of spiritual light is infused by the Holy Ghost. The improvement hereof into a fixed habit is by constant and continual exercise. Now this habit or use respects all the ways and means that are appointed for our increase in the knowledge of the mysteries of the gospel. For hereby the mind, being accustomed unto the senses of the word of God, is enabled to make a right judgment of what is proposed unto it. And the observations further clearing the sense of the words, wherewith we shall close our exposition of this chapter, are these that ensue:—

Obs. I. The word of the gospel, in the dispensation of it, is food provided for the souls of men.

A supposition hereof runs through this whole discourse of the apostle, and hath been occasionally spoken unto before; but it being that which leads and determines the sense of this verse also, as to what is instructive in it, it must be touched on again. There is a new spiritual life wrought in all that believe,—the life by virtue whereof they live unto God. The only outward means used by God in the communication of this life unto us, is the word of the gospel, 1 Pet. i. 23; James i. 18. This life God takes care of to preserve. It is the new creature,—that in us which is " born of God," by virtue whereof we are admitted into his family. And God will not bring forth, and then suffer that which is born of him to be starved. Now every thing is increased and maintained by the same means whereby it is ingenerated or begun. Wherefore the provision that God makes for this new creature, the food he prepareth for it, is his word, 1 Pet. ii. 1–3. Hereon the preservation of our spiritual life, our growth, increase, and strength, do absolutely depend. Hence wherever God will have a church, there he will preserve his word. And where he absolutely takes that away, he hath no more family, no more church. So when the woman, through the persecution of the dragon, was driven into the wilderness, into an obscure, distressed condition, yet God took care that there she should be fed, Rev. xii. 6. She was never utterly deprived of the food of the word. It is true, the provision which he makes hereof is sometimes more plentiful, and sometimes more strait; yet will he never suffer it to be so removed from any that are his, but that a diligent hand shall find bread enough. And without further enlargement, we may learn hence sundry things:—

1. No judgment is so to be feared and deprecated as a deprivation of the *dispensation of the word.* No judgment is like famine: " They that are slain with the sword are better than they that be

slain with hunger; for these pine away, stricken through for want of the fruits of the field," Lam. iv. 9. And no famine like that of the word, which God threateneth as the sorest of his judgments, Amos viii. 11. This is as much to be dreaded above the other as the soul is to be preferred before the body, and spiritual life above natural. To be deprived of the food of our souls is of all distresses the most dreadful. And we may do well to consider, that when Egypt was in the midst of its plenty,—which no doubt was sufficiently abused, —it was then that their consuming famine was at the door.

2. No temporal mercy is so liable unto abuse as *fulness of bread*. This, joined with pride and idleness, which usually accompany it in the world, produced the sins of Sodom, Ezek. xvi. 49. So is it with the fulness of this spiritual food,—spiritual pride and spiritual sloth are apt to grow up with it, to corrupt and abuse it. It requires much wisdom and heedfulness to manage ourselves aright under the plentiful dispensation of the word, such as at this time we enjoy. Some apparently are proud and delicate, waxing wanton under their enjoyment, so that wholesome food is despised by them,—nothing will serve them but some poisonous dainties of fond and foolish imaginations. And some are slothful, thinking all pains and charge too much that they take or are at about the word. The curiosity and sloth of these days bode no good. I am almost persuaded that the generality of the Egyptians derided Joseph, when they saw him make such diligent and vast preparations in the years of plenty, when for so long a time together " the earth brought forth by handfuls." If they did not think his labour altogether needless, why did they not do in like manner, why did they make no provision for them-selves?—which afterwards they so smarted for. Learn, therefore, of him as well as you are able, to lay in provision of this spiritual food in a time of plenty, that you may have some stores for your use in an evil day that may be approaching.

3. Those who by any means endeavour to obstruct the dispen-sation of the word, they do their endeavour to famish the souls of men. They keep their food from them, without which they cannot live. Whether this be done by negligence, ignorance, or disability in those who take upon themselves to be God's stewards, but have none of his provision under their disposal, or whether it be done out of a real hatred to the word, the cruelty is dreadful, and the crime will be avenged. The people will curse him who hoardeth corn in a time of dearth; and God will curse them who, at any time, detain from others the bread of life.

4. The word is to be esteemed, valued, and sought after, as our *daily food*. Negligence and carelessness about the food of our souls is too great an evidence that there is no principle of life in us. Think not too much of your pains.

Obs. II. Whereas the word is food, it is evident that it will not profit our souls until it be eaten and digested.

It is called here τροφή, "nourishment;" which food is not as it is prepared, but as it is received. When manna was gathered and laid up, and not eaten, it "stank and bred worms." We see that some take great pains to come and hear the word. This is but the gathering of manna. What do you with it afterwards? If it lie by you, it will be of no use. But what is required unto this eating and digestion, was, as I remember, before declared.

Obs. III. It is an evidence of a thriving and healthy state of soul, to have an appetite unto the deepest mysteries of the gospel, or most solid doctrines of truth, and to be able profitably to digest them.

This is the substance of the character which the apostle here gives of such persons; and he blames these Hebrews that such they were not: and therefore such we ought all to be, who live under circumstances and advantages like to theirs. This is the property of a thriving soul, of a good proficient in the school of Christ. He is naturally inclined to desire the declaration of the most weighty and substantial truths of the gospel; in them is he particularly delighted, and by them is he profited: whereas if you take others beyond milk, or first principles, ordinarily they are at a loss, and very little benefited by any provision you can make for them. But yet sometimes it falls out in these things spiritual as it doth in things natural. Some persons under sickness and distempers, having their appetite corrupted, and their taste vitiated, do greatly desire, and impetuously long after strong food; which is no way meet for them, and which, when they have eaten it, does but increase their indisposition and heighten their distemper. So some, altogether unmeet for the right understanding and due improvement of the deep mysteries of the gospel, yet, out of pride and curiosity, do neglect and despise the things which are suited unto their edification, and desire nothing, delight in nothing but what is above them, and indeed beyond their reach. That we may not be deceived, nor deceive ourselves herein, I shall give some differences between this property of sound, thriving, and healthy souls, desiring, delighting in, and profiting by the strong meat of gospel mysteries, and the inordinate longing of spiritually sick and distempered minds after those things which are not meet for them:—

1. The desires and appetite of the former are kept always within the bounds of what is *written* and plainly revealed in the word; for we have showed that the deepest mysteries have the plainest revelations. Offer them any thing that is not plainly attested by the word, and they turn from it as poison. They have learned in

all things to "think soberly," according to the analogy of faith, Rom. xii. 3. They would be wise, but unto sobriety, and not above what is written. But for the other sort, if any thing be *new, curious,* seemingly *mystical,* removed from the common sense and apprehensions of Christians, without any due consideration whether it be a truth of God or no, that is it which they run greedily after, and catch at the empty cloud of. Their principal business is to "intrude themselves into the things which they have not seen, being vainly puffed up by their fleshly minds," Col. ii. 18.

2. The former sort, upon the declaration and discovery of any deep, important mysteries of the gospel, are greatly taken up with a *holy admiration and reverence of God,* whose these things are. So our apostle, having in the 9th, 10th, and 11th chapters of his Epistle to the Romans, treated of the deep mysteries of electing grace, and the effects of it, he shuts up his whole discourse in an admiration of God, and an ascription of glory unto him, chap. xi. 33–36. So is it with all holy and humble souls, upon their instruction in and view they have of the mysteries of the gospel, in that marvellous light whereinto they are translated. The other sort satisfy themselves in their own speculation, without being much affected with the greatness or glory of God, in the things they imagine themselves to know.

3. The former sort do find *real food* and nourishment in this strong meat, so that their faith is strengthened, their love increased, and holiness promoted in their souls by them. They find by experience that such things do not only sound in their ears or float in their minds in the notion of them, but that really and truly their faith feeds upon them; and their whole souls being affected with them, they are encouraged and directed by them in the course of their obedience. Others, whose desires proceed from the distempers of pride and curiosity, find none of those things ; and so their itching ears are suited, and their inquisitive minds satisfied, they regard them not. Hence it is hard to see one of these notional persons either fruitful or useful ; neither can they bear those parts of the yoke of Christ which would make necessary the constant exercise of faith and love.

4. The former sort are always more and more *humbled,* the latter more and more *puffed up,* by what they attain unto. But I must not further enlarge on these things. There yet remain two observations more, with the naming whereof we shall shut up our discourses on this chapter.

Obs. IV. The assiduous exercise of our minds about spiritual things, in a spiritual manner, is the only means to make us to profit in hearing of the word.

When our spiritual senses are exercised by reason of constant use, they are 'in a readiness to receive, embrace, and improve, what is tendered unto them. Without this we shall be dull and slow in hearing,—the vice here so severely reproved.

Obs. V. The spiritual sense of believers, well exercised in the word, is the best and most undeceiving help in judging of what is good or evil, what is true or false, that is proposed unto them.

END OF VOL. XXI